Male Homosexualities and World Religions

Male Homosexualities and World Religions

Pierre Hurteau

MALE HOMOSEXUALITIES AND WORLD RELIGIONS
Copyright © Editions L'Harmattan, 2010.
English-language translation copyright © 2013 by Pierre Hurteau.

All rights reserved.

First published in French in 2010 as *Homosexualités masculines et religions du monde* by Editions L'Harmattan, Paris, France.

First published in English in 2013 by
PALGRAVE MACMILLAN®
in the United States—a division of St. Martin's Press LLC,
175 Fifth Avenue, New York, NY 10010.

Where this book is distributed in the UK, Europe and the rest of the world, this is by Palgrave Macmillan, a division of Macmillan Publishers Limited, registered in England, company number 785998, of Houndmills, Basingstoke, Hampshire RG21 6XS.

Palgrave Macmillan is the global academic imprint of the above companies and has companies and representatives throughout the world.

Palgrave® and Macmillan® are registered trademarks in the United States, the United Kingdom, Europe and other countries.

ISBN: 978-1-137-36988-8

Library of Congress Cataloging-in-Publication Data

Hurteau, Pierre.
 [Homosexualités masculines et religions du monde. English]
 Male homosexualities and world religions / Pierre Hurteau.
   pages cm
 Includes bibliographical references.
 ISBN 978-1-137-36988-8
   1. Homosexuality—Religious aspects—Comparative studies. 2. Male homosexuality—Religious aspects—Comparative studies. I. Title.
BL65.H64H8713 2013
205'.664—dc23   2013019551

A catalogue record of the book is available from the British Library.

Design by Newgen Knowledge Works (P) Ltd., Chennai, India.

First edition: November 2013
10 9 8 7 6 5 4 3 2 1

Contents

Preface and Acknowledgments vii

Introduction 1
1 Hinduism 7
2 Buddhism 31
3 Judaism 61
4 Christianity 85
5 Islam 125
6 Afro-Caribbean and Afro-Brazilian Religions 157
General Conclusion 177

Notes 185
Bibliography 245

Preface and Acknowledgments

More than a year has passed since the first publication of this book in French. I have taken advantage of this first English version to take into consideration recent material related to my topic and to clarify my thoughts on certain aspects. Some readers suggested that I further clarify certain theoretical questions, especially regarding the use of the words "homosexual" or "homosexuality," which can vary greatly depending on historical or cultural context. They've also proposed that I further affirm my position for a greater recognition of the diversity of experiences of men who have sex with men and for more social justice for them. The concept of globalization, which includes diversity but also universalization of the Western model of gay rights, has been revised to make room for the threats they may pose in a non-Western context.

I want to express my gratitude and thanks to those who allowed me to persevere. The religious sphere encompasses a vast realm of knowledge and human experience, in many cases traditions going back to thousands of years. Research material on homosexuality within the various religious traditions is not always accessible, given the taboo that has long surrounded the issue and that, unfortunately, still persists. First, I want to thank Raynald, my life partner of over 30 years, for his invaluable advice, encouragement, and moral support in difficult times. I also extend my gratitude to friends and former colleagues who have patiently read the manuscript and made valuable suggestions and corrections: Shrinivas Tilak, independent scholar and writer of many books on Hinduism; Frederick B. Bird, Professor Emeritus of religion at Concordia University; Clarise Samuels, Canadian short story writer; and Ross Higgins, anthropologist and lecturer at the Université du Québec à Montréal. My thanks also go to my friends Waldeck Sylvestre and Paul-Emile Pierre who have so kindly introduced me to Kreyòl Ayisyen.

I am also grateful to the following publishers for giving me permission to reproduce some passages of books published by them: Concordia Publishing House (*Luther's Works* Vol. 7), Office of the Law Clerk and Parliamentary Counsel, House of Commons Canada (Standing Committee on Justice and Human Rights, *Evidence Reports*), Wilfrid Laurier University Press (*The Book of Gomorrah*, Pierre J. Payer, translator), University of Texas Press (Pierre Hurteau, "Catholic Moral Discourse on Male Sodomy and Masturbation in the Seventeenth and Eighteenth Centuries," *Journal of the History of Sexuality*, Vol. 4, No. 1 [July 1993]: 1–26), and Stanford University Press (*The Epic of Gilgamesh*, Maureen Gallery Kovacs, translator), the University of Chicago Press (*Mystical Poems of Rumi*, trans. A. J. Arberry and Ehsan Yarshater), and Jaafar Abu Tarab (*Carousing with Gazelles*).

I also wish to thank Burke Gerstenschlager, religion/philosophy academic editor at Palgrave Macmillan, for having confidence in my work, and for his help at every stage of the realization of this project. I also extend my thanks to his assistant, Madeleine Crum, and Deepa John who managed with great professional skill and patience the copyediting and typesetting processes.

INTRODUCTION

> Binary distinctions are an analytic procedure, but their usefulness does not guarantee that existence divides like that. We should look with suspicion on anyone who declared that there are two kinds of people, or two kinds of reality or process.
>
> —Mary Douglas[1]

The idea of writing this book appeared to me several years after reading the collective work *Homosexuality and World Religions*, published in 1993. The thought of putting views of different religious traditions side by side seemed interesting. It permitted me to put certain judgments about homosexual practices in perspective and compare their levels of tolerance for homosexuality.

After spending my first summer as a pensioner luring bass, pike, and sturgeon in the St. Lawrence River, the cold winter of 2006 invited me to exchange the fishing rod for my computer keyboard and begin work on my project. After a short examination of the book that was the source of my motivation, I felt I had to approach the subject differently. *Homosexuality and World Religions* was the result of the collaboration of several specialists from each of the traditions studied. So, I had to ask myself, could I honestly face the challenge alone, without specialized academic training in the religions to be addressed, with the exception of Christianity and Buddhism? Upon reflection, I convinced myself that those others before me, such as David Greenberg (1988) and Louis Crompton (2003), had successfully attempted a similar experiment while researching homosexuality throughout civilization.

Such a project usually must rely on other experts who work from primary sources. Working alone may be perceived as a handicap, insofar as access to primary sources is then possible only through translated material. Involuntary exclusion of certain sources may happen simply due to the absence of translations.

However, several reasons drove me to take on the adventure. A single author could provide more cohesion. Such cohesion was lacking in *Homosexuality and World Religions*. After reading it, I wondered about the effectiveness of its approach with readers with no particular knowledge of these religious traditions and who are abruptly plunged into a complicated and scholarly discussion about homosexuality. For the reader to grasp the doctrinal foundation and the scope of any religious discourse or teaching on homosexuality, it becomes essential to provide a brief overview of the religious traditions and their developments. Also, for the same reasons, any thorough analysis of the discourse on homosexuality is not possible without first taking a close look at the religious views on sex in general. Therefore, each chapter follows the same pattern: (1) the religious tradition itself, (2) the religion's views on sexuality, and finally (3) the religion's views on homosexuality.

Mary Douglas's assertion, quoted in the epigraph, accents the underlying theme of the book. Serious differences lie at the core of diverse experiences of sexuality in the religious traditions of the world. These differences cannot be reconciled by means of a reductive discourse that seeks to understand homosexuality through universalizing binomial concepts, such as the heterosexuality/homosexuality dichotomy. This prospect imposes that I endorse a context-sensitive and historicist methodology, thereby treating information according to specific context, such as historical period, original culture, and social organization.

I chose to focus my attention on the following religious traditions: Hinduism, Buddhism, Judaism, Christianity, Islam, and Afro-Caribbean and Afro-Brazilian religions. I could also have included extinct religions, but there is material in abundance concerning Roman, Greek, or even ancient Near East religions. I may also add that, from the very start, I wished to reach the widest audience possible, including professional educators and social workers in search of a solid understanding of the experiences of men sexually attracted to men. For that reason, I excluded chthonic religions; they may generate great academic interest, but they have a weaker social impact. The general public is not familiar with diacritical marks used to transliterate foreign languages. For this reason, I have decided not to use them, and I write foreign words close to the way they are pronounced. I decided to use Chinese characters in order to avoid any possible confusion, as this language is not alphabetic, and only ideograms can deliver with certainty the meaning of words.

Canada and Western societies as a whole are increasingly faced with cultural diversity, and the solutions that are adopted to integrate marginal sexualities have acquired their own history and social dynamic. Other societies have chosen different paths. The paradigm of sexual orientation projected homosexuality as a fundamental characteristic of the person. It specified a type of personality with rights and distinct legal protections. This emancipation pattern originated from the emergence of human rights philosophy in the West, something that did not necessarily occur in other cultures. Gay youths living in America or Europe, with non-Christian family backgrounds, are sometimes torn between the values and perceptions of their own community of origin and those of the host society. The weight of tradition often reduces them to stay in the closet for fear of displeasing their family and being ostracized by their community. At the same time, we must also recognize that, in the present era of globalization and the Internet, it seems almost impossible to encounter communities unaware of the debates and the successful struggles of gay movements dedicated to the promotion and protection of LGBT (lesbian, gay, bisexual, and transgender) rights across the world. Several groups promoting and protecting the rights of gays and lesbians from the five continents are united in the *International Gay and Lesbian Association*, which organizes international conferences to discuss the situation of gays and lesbians worldwide. Thanks to the Internet, many homosexuals in Africa, Asia, or South America and the Caribbean, where homophobia triumphs and in several cases where homosexuality is totally illegal, can have access to the actual experiences of gays living in countries where homosexuality is legally and socially accepted.

Already the reader may sense that my goal is to write about homosexualities, that is to say, the variety of sexual encounters between men. Some men occasionally have sex with men but marry and have families. Others, for various reasons, have the feeling of living their whole sexual life outside of heteronormativity. Given these different contexts, what is then the true meaning of the word "homosexuality"? The term was first coined in the second half of the nineteenth century by the Austrian journalist Károly Mária Kertbeny, an activist in favor of decriminalizing homosexual relations. The word was quickly adopted by the pioneers of sexology and psychiatry to describe a congenital disease of the sexual instinct, which fails to turn naturally to the opposite sex.[2] If homosexuality is linked to some personal, natural instinct, how then can it be judged as debauchery or sin? The German lawyer Karl Heinrich Ulrichs goes on to define homosexuality (uranism) as a third sex—the soul of a woman being trapped in the body of a man.[3] While these theories found the origin of a pathological inversion of the sexual instinct in some hormonal imbalance appearing during fetal development, Sigmund Freud displaced the origin of homosexuality into the realm of individual psychological development. For him, homosexuality is the result of a poor response to solving the Oedipus complex. The proper solution to the Oedipus complex should normally rest in the boy's identification with masculinity, femininity becoming the natural object of his adult sexual desire. Although, originally, Freudian homosexuality remains intrapsychic, Freud's view of the relationship between a sexual object and sexual identity makes room for the socialization of the individual, so that neither heterosexuality nor homosexuality are the direct result of the natural evolution of the sex drive. With Freud, one slowly departs from the essentialist model of homosexuality, but it is only with the British and American schools of sociology that the constructivist theory of homosexuality becomes fully developed.[4] For this school of thought, eroticism and sexuality are neither determined by biology, nor by the psyche of the person, but are mediated through the symbolic meanings involved in the construction of social reality. Sexuality becomes a cultural and historical category. Social constructivism emphasizes the construction of sex roles and stereotypes, as well as the associated social stigma—all these aspects may be advantageously taken up by gay liberation movements. Foucault's *History of Sexuality*, published in 1976, in a way became the textbook for this stream of thought. This author showed that the medicalization of same-sex activity shifted the focal point from the homogenital act itself to the homosexual subject, who now became a category of person: "The sodomite had been a temporary aberration; the homosexual was now a species."[5] The concept of sexual orientation appeared in the 1960s, but its genealogy goes back to the medical discourse of the late nineteenth century. At the turn of the twentieth century, the state apparatus took over from medicine and tried to control the activities of the homosexual through legislation. Thus, the British politician Henry Labouchere introduced Section 11 in the *Criminal Law Amendment Act* of 1885 (48 & 49 Vict. c. 69). The amendment advocated the concept of gross indecency to punish any form of sexual contact between men in private or in public. In fact, it was used to arrest and try Oscar Wilde in 1895.

The constructivists present homosexuality as an identity construct historically linked to the European culture of the mid-nineteenth century. It cannot and should not be applied or superimposed on other periods of history as it was, for instance, carried out by John Boswell.[6] His temerity generated much debate as he sought to demonstrate the existence of a large gay subculture in full medieval Christianity as well as the existence of a liturgy for celebrating homosexual unions.[7] Among the advocates of the constructivist approach, George Chauncey has shown that male sexuality in 1900 was not structured on the binary opposition—homosexuality/heterosexuality—but rather on the polarity of normal man/effeminate man (fairy, sissy, queen). At least 30 more years had to pass by before the subject's sexual identity would be defined not through gender identity but through choice of the sexual object.[8] David Halperin tried to show that pederasty in Ancient Greece had nothing in common with the concept of homosexuality understood as some sort of identity, something that appeared only later in the nineteenth century.[9]

However, critics of the constructivist school often blame Halperin for losing sight of the subjective, intimate, and emotional aspect of any sexual experience, whether it happened 20 centuries ago or now, in favor of his insistence on discursive practices and social institutions. In the end, should we not all be looking for homosexualities through time and space instead of a single model? Homosexuality is open today to a variety of experiences and the patterns or styles often contrasted in history by constructivism do in fact coexist. One simply has to witness a Gay Pride Parade to realize that sissies, transvestites, transgender, and hypermales are together celebrating sexual diversity, or anything but heteronormativity. This diversity goes beyond borders, as it will be demonstrated in the following chapters. Whether it is in Indian, Chinese, Thai, or Iranian culture, there are several ways to account for the experiences of men who have sex with men. The relevance of Eve Kosofsky Sedgwick's analysis of the homosexual closet leaves no shadow of a doubt: there are, of all times and places, "universalizing" and "minoritizing" views of the homosexual experience.[10] While the first explanation proposes to see homosexuality as a tendency present in every person without any reference to gender, the second seeks instead to identify homosexuals as a distinct group of persons whose gender is either ambiguous or inverted. I will not hesitate to apply Sedgwick's analysis of Western homosexuality to a cross-cultural analysis of homosexuality. For instance, in the case of India, the reader will observe that both views have been present throughout the ages; the separatist or minority view that still exists today has in fact been in existence in the Indian tradition for a long time. The dominant or universalizing view often sees homosexual relations as a kind of natural outburst of male sexuality without any relation to forms of psychological disorder. Accordingly, the person indulging in the act may not acquiesce to any form of subordination—physically, as in anal penetration, or socially, in expressions other than the love of boys (Arab-Persian and Chinese cultures) where the age difference strictly defines the roles in terms of activity and passivity. Universalizing views continue to exist in many cultures, especially when access to female partners is difficult because of taboos surrounding the socialization of women or in situations of scarcity (e.g., in prison). Also, the periodization imposed by the constructivist theory is maybe more a product of an ideological viewpoint than the result of careful observation and confirmation of the presence of homosexual desire as "an essential phenomenon," in various cultures and across different periods.[11] With this affirmation, I am not saying that the modern homosexual model focused on self-conscious orientation and individual rights is trans-historical. I'm just stating that homosexual preference or the desire for sexual intimacy with a member of the same sex cannot be locked in a period of history. We have to look for a model that allows for continuity or similarities, and discontinuity or significant changes.

Inclusiveness should not become synonymous with uniformity. It must give way to the right to express personal difference and dissent. We have found ways to conceive of homosexuality as varying from one religious tradition to another. Even within each of these traditions, divergent viewpoints are represented. The HIV epidemic has led many governments and social actors in non-Western countries to open their eyes to the presence of gays and homosexuals within them, as we encounter in India, Thailand, or even in Haiti. While Joseph Massad argues against a universalizing sexual epistemology imposed by the Gay International, which results in the occultation of same-sex desires that do not espouse gay subjectivity, I do wonder about the fate many Cameroonians, Egyptians, or Indians, for example, would endure without this kind of advocacy. With globalization, recognition and protection of gay rights are spreading rapidly around the world. João Trevisan sees some merit to the rejection by certain Brazilian gay activists of the gay identity model. Defining someone as homosexual and categorizing desire may further encourage normalization in the form of ghettoization and separation instead of a true sexual liberation. While acknowledging the validity of this claim, Trevisan has this to say:

> Yet if these objections to the "construction of a gay identity" are valid, it is also true that desire cannot be denied a name, and certainly note for mere reasons of methodology.

From the simple fact that something resembling homosexual desire exists, it has to be referred to by some kind of designation. Otherwise we will return to the time of suffocating and hypocritical invisibility which only reinforced the mechanisms of repression.[12]

However, constructivism remains a highly useful tool to put things into perspective, and contextualize the concept of homosexuality. Without losing sight of its precious teachings and without attempting to reframe history in favor of the concept of homosexuality as sexual orientation, I will use the word "homosexuality" whenever experiences clearly describe sexual contacts between men, while also being aware of the context, such as gender transgression, active or passive sodomy, pederasty, and so on. Sometimes I will preferably make use of the word "homoeroticism," especially when it comes to describe intense amorous desires and emotions between males without any explicit sexual encounter. My position on the use of the word "homosexual" is quite similar to João Trevisan's. Whatever the form homosexual desire takes, it will always raise doubt. As Trevisan says: "Gay men are exactly that: doubtful—the ones who cause doubt. In other words, they are those who confirm uncertainty, who open a space for difference and who constitute a symbol of contradiction confronting the bounds of normality." While being aware of all the academic debates around the word and the linguistic niceties they may procure, Trevisan thinks there is some valid reason to assume the risk of being imprecise:

When confronted by this same dilemma, Michel Foucault commented, "what is important is *not to be* homosexual but rather to *furiously seek to be* gay (my emphasis). To ask ourselves about our relationship to homosexuality is above all to desire a world where sexual relationships are possible, more than simply to desire a sexual relationship with someone of the same sex." Foucault refers to a state of coming-to-be and being-in-change which seems to me very interesting precisely because it does not claim that homosexuality is a condition in the sanctuary of normality, nor does it refrain from fomenting the nuances of desire which can continue changing indefinitely within the space of a labyrinthine definition.[13]

Trevisan speaks of gay men but his reasoning certainly applies to nonheterosexuality or queer sexuality. Ambiguity calls for complexity and not confusion in the treatment of diversity. Many spaces are present in-between the poles of heterosexuality and homosexuality understood as homosexual orientation. Writing about the politics of difference, Janet Jakobsen has this to say: "The spaces in-between are particularly hard to work with because they are sites of multiple and ambiguous meanings. They lack the clarity of precisely delineated sites of identity and the theoretical purity of the fully open sign."[14]

Some readers will wonder why yet another book on male homosexuality and religion. Why not a book about female homosexuality and religion, to date a seldom treated topic? My area of expertise is clearly male homosexuality, and I would not dare venture into that field alone and without extensive research. There are certainly a multitude of explanations for the dearth of books on the subject. Among them is surely the fact that, typically, only men held knowledge and authority in religious matters. Few writings were produced by women until recently. Another significant reason is that female sexuality is often seen as a threat to masculinity, male power, and even a man's ability to achieve a meaningful spiritual life. Social control and power are key components in the traditional definitions of gender roles, and two women having sex does not threaten the social structure because they both hold subordinate positions in society.[15] Female sexuality is generally viewed in many traditions as a threat to man's ability to control his sexual drive, just like masturbation and homosexual practices. Curiously, only women dressed as men were considered to be a challenge to male domination, the key issue.[16] Socially constructed gender roles tend to preserve a male-advantaged gender hierarchy, and any behavior that interferes with or renders doubtful those gender boundaries must be reprobated.[17] In this context, it is not surprising to find in many societies a stigma on sexual relations between males, especially those that are similar to vaginal penetration, while sexual relations between women are considered harmless.[18]

The book will perhaps raise more questions than answers. My only hope is that it will open doors to all those who wish to bring about a dialogue between the religious traditions in order to break the boundaries of the Eurocentric perspective and celebrate sexual diversity across the planet. Sites of nonheterosexual identity are multiple and give rise to various forms of struggle for more justice and the right to live side by side with heterosexuals.

1

HINDUISM

RELIGION

The population of India stood at 1,028,610,328 people in 2001[1] and is expected to reach 1,263,543,000 in 2016.[2] Here, Hinduism is practiced by 80.5 percent of the population while 13.4 percent are Muslims and 2.3 percent identify themselves as Christians.[3] The census figures for 2001 show clearly that Hinduism holds a majority in the whole country apart from a few regions where significant Buddhist minorities (Maharashtra, Karnataka, and Sikkim), Muslims (Uttar Pradesh, Bihar, West Bengal, Maharashtra, and Kerala), Sikhs (Punjab), and Christians (Kerala and Tamil Nadu) live. Also worth mentioning is the presence of 4,225,053 Jains, mostly concentrated in Maharashtra, Rajasthan, Gujarat, and Madhya Pradesh.

In Nepal, 80 percent of the population (23 million)[4] adhere to Hinduism and in Sri Lanka there are about 1, 329,020 Hindus, mostly of Tamil origin, accounting for 7.88 percent of its total population.[5] Slightly more than 10 million Hindus reside in Bangladesh, 10.5 percent of its inhabitants.[6] In Mauritius, half of the 1 million inhabitants are Hindus,[7] and almost 500,000 adherents live in the United Kingdom[8] and nearly 300,000 in Canada.[9]

The etymology of the word "Hindu" goes back to the Persian "Sindhu"—used, in the past, to describe the people who lived across the river Sind, better known as the Indus River. Its etymology does not refer to any belief system, though it does refer today to an adept of the Hindu religion. Almost all Hindus live on the Indian subcontinent, more specifically in India, and their belief system and practices are intimately linked to the people living in this geographical area. Hinduism, the largest religious mosaic in the world, has evolved tremendously over the ages, but it is constantly growing by incorporating different beliefs and philosophies. Although there is a chronology of its development, from pre-Vedism to Vedism and then Brahmanism at the time of the Puranas, the newest forms do not always supersede the older ones.

Hindus refer to their religious system by the words *sanatana dharma*, meaning the eternal law. This conveys the idea that there is an immanent cosmic order that looks over nature and to which humans must conform to live in cosmic harmony. In this sense, *dharma* rather refers to a lifestyle than to any adhesion to a set of religious beliefs. The origin of this concept is first found in the ancient Vedic concept of *Rta*. The ancient concept of *Rta* expresses the idea of a regulative principle in nature and human society. Thus, *Rta* means that cows give milk, just as the sun rises and sets daily, or that water flows in rivers and streams (*Rig Veda Samhita* IV.23.8–10).[10] Cosmic energies (*Deva*)—Agni the fire, Indra the thunder, and the sun Surya—but also hostile forces (*Asura*)—Vrtra the dragon—and different spirits (*gandharva, apsara*), all are subject to *Rta*.[11] Men's action and those of the gods contribute to maintaining the cosmic order in balance through liturgy, especially with the performance of sacrifices and chanting Vedic hymns. Cosmic order is the manifestation of the ultimate reality (*Brahman*) or truth (*satya*). The *Rig Veda Samhita* X (Ch. 85, 1–2) celebrates the relationship between truth and cosmic law; truth sustains all things and the gods are concrete manifestations of the power of this impersonal cosmic law.[12] From the standpoint of ultimate truth, reality is one. A monistic point of view was further developed in the Upanishads. There, *Brahman* means the vast totality of reality, the One, the reality hidden behind impersonal phenomena. *Tat tvam asi*—you are also this—this great truth (*mahavakya*) marks the presence of the divine in everything.[13] The self, the center of individual personality, the *atman* is also a spark of the divine, *Brahman—ayam atma brahma*.[14]

The Vedic hymns reflect an older religion, corresponding to mass migrations toward the Indo-Aryan Punjab during the second millennium BC. These migrations probably came from the Sintashta-Petrovka culture of the southern Urals and other cultures from the river Amu Darya in central Asia.[15] These pastoral cultures knew the wheeled cart and had domesticated the horse. They mixed with the urban existing civilizations of the Indus Valley.[16] These pre-Aryan civilizations were probably issued from the Neolithic agricultural settlements established from 7000 BC in the Kachi plain at Mehrgarh.[17] This site was abandoned between 2600 and 2000 BC, as the cities of Mohenjo-Daro and Harappa flourished. The archeological study of all these sites shows that there was continuous development from one site to another, as evidenced by the use of amulets and terracotta figurines, anthropomorphic (mostly women, but also men sitting in a yogic position) or zoomorphic representing bulls, elephants, antelopes, and tigers.[18] Several elements of the pre-Aryan civilization were incorporated into the Vedic religion. The Vedic god Rudra lived in the forest and was honored as lord of the animal life, Pashupati, a title that would later be attributed to Shiva,[19] who is often accompanied by Nandi the bull. Several objects in the form of an erect penis (*lingam*) or a receptacle recalling the vagina (*yoni*) were also found in many of these ancient sites. Yet again, the lingam, alone or inserted into the female organ, is traditionally associated to Shiva, the creator, uniting with his consort Parvati.[20] The act of copulation is so fusional that Shiva is sometimes portrayed as a hermaphrodite (*Ardhanarishvara*).[21] Being the creator, Shiva needs the material energy (*shakti*) of the Mother Goddess (Mahadevi). Shiva is also called *Mahayogi*, the great yoga guru wandering naked in the forest. However, he remains a yogi with great sensuality and power of seduction.[22] His erect penis, more importantly, symbolizes not generation but voluptuousness (*bhogavahamidam lingam*) and according to the *Shiva Purana*, people can attain final release (*mukti*) by touching it and meditating on it.[23]

The ancient Vedic religion focuses primarily on ritual sacrifices, accompanied by hymns and incantations (*mantra*) to the forces of nature such as the sun, storm, rain, fire, and so on. Offerings are carried to the devas in the ritual of fire sacrifice, an attempt to coax them to do their job of maintaining cosmic order. The Upanishad literature that developed from 800 BC focuses on final release (*moksha*) of the individual from the cycle of rebirths (*samsara*). Here, the sacrifice ritual becomes internalized through discipline of the body and mind.[24] A new path to the absolute is gradually taking shape, based on renunciation through various techniques of asceticism, including breath control (*pranayama*), meditation (*dhyana*), and mind concentration (*samadhi*).[25] These techniques allow the "self" or *atman*, the inner divine light, to shine in the human body.[26] Consciousness of the unity of *atman* and *Brahman* is the perfect knowledge, for everything—the gods, human creatures, their perceptions, and feelings are guided by the mind, which is nothing but *Brahman* (*pranayama brahma*), the infinite source of life.[27] The ultimate reality, the One, transcends any form or attribute (*nirgunam Brahman*), but may appear in the world in anthropomorphic forms (*Brahman* or *Ishvara sagunam*).[28] Devi (the Goddess),

Shiva, or Vishnu are personal manifestations of *Brahman*, which remains veiled (*maya*) while manifested in the world, thanks to its ability to create the illusion.[29] The material universe unfolds itself as if it were the stage for a puppet theater on which were played (*lila*) the adventures of a multitude of gods who embody the divine by appearing in human or animal shapes (*avatara*). The Upanishadic literature already expresses this idea of a material revelation (*Saguna Brahman*) of the absolute and invisible reality of all things,[30] though it will attain its full growth in Epic and Puranic literature.[31] Besides the yoga of knowledge (*jnana yoga*) practiced by the wise ascetics, the idea of liberating the individual through love or devotion (*bhakti yoga*) to a personal God appeared in the *Bhagavad Gita*, composed in the second century BC as part of Book VI of the great epic the *Mahabharata*. Song 12 of the *Bhagavad Gita* promises release from the cycle of rebirths and unity with the One to the faithful devotee who dedicates his thoughts and actions to his love (*bhakti*) for Lord Krishna. Verse 5 expresses an essential truth in *bhakti* movements emerging from the Middle Ages, particularly in South India (Tamil) and Bengal: "Greater is their trouble whose minds are set on the Unmanifested; for the goal—the Unmanifested—is very difficult for the embodied to reach."[32] *Bhakti* movements will be discussed further ahead.

The Brahmin caste incorporated into Vedic religion non-Aryan cultic elements such as pre-Vedic, proto-Tantric elements in which both eroticism and asceticism found a place. On the outskirts of Aryan society lived beggars who wandered barefoot (*vratyas, ajivikas,* and *yatis*) perpetuating the traditions of the Indus civilization. This eventually led to movements known as Shaivism, Shaktism, and Tantrism.[33]

Around 500 AD, the Brahmins (priests) systematized the ancient Vedic religion by reacting against ascetic currents and the ideal of renunciation through practices of control of the senses and meditation. Brahmanism was somehow a reaction against new spiritual movements such as Buddhism and Jainism. The orthodox Brahmins then proposed an ingenious system that would address the necessities of life as they evolve through a lifetime, in accordance with one's social status and one's duties in society. The idea of dividing society into castes certainly goes back to the Vedic period. The hymn to the sacrifice of the primordial man (*Purusha Sukta*) does mention that the Brahmins or priests were born from his mouth, the *Rajanyas* (*Kshatriyas*) or warriors from his arms, the *Vaishyas* (merchants and farmers) from his thighs, and the *Shudras* from his feet.[34] Overall, the *Rig Veda* did not exhibit a system of social castes (*varnas*[35]) as elaborate as what would come later, after 500 AD, particularly with the *Manu Smriti* and the *Dharma Shastras*. These later texts, written between the first BC and the fourth century AD, specified the roles and duties of each of the four classes or castes, while maintaining a hierarchy between them. The *Shudras* were positioned at the bottom of the scale,[36] with a duty to serve and obey the first three classes whose members were called "twice born" (*djiva*).[37] Shastric literature devised the theory of the four stages of life (*asrhamadharma*), which provided for each male "twice born" a schedule to achieve all four objectives of any human existence (*purusartha*): profit (*artha*), pleasure (*kama*), duty (*dharma*), and release (*moksa*). Thus, after spending a period of training in chastity (*brahmacharya*) with a guru who would introduce him to the sacred texts and grammar,[38] the twice-born bachelor then enters the cycle of social and economic life and enjoys the pleasure of marrying and begetting a son (*grihastha*).[39] After completing his family duties, in his sixties, the "twice born" will retreat to a hermitage (*vanaprastha*)[40] to engage in the reading of sacred texts and various austerities to purify the mind. After the third period, toward the end of his life, the hermit has no need for mortification. Having renounced all material possessions (*sannyasa*), he can finally go, wandering freely, with no permanent dwelling and devote all his time to the practice of yoga and meditation.[41]

The Hindu caste system is inseparable from the law of karma and the successive reincarnations (*samsara*) of the individual soul, until it has reached perfection. Any act or thought produces an effect, either in this life or another. Thus, one's rank in the social hierarchy results from one's conduct in his or her previous life, but it also offers an opportunity to improve one's position in future lives on account of a good conduct in this life. This idea was already expressed in the Upanishads,[42] but finds its fullness in the epic literature, particularly in the *Bhagavad Gita*. Krishna teaches the path of Karma Yoga to Arjuna, one of the Pandava brothers, at war with their cousins the Kauravas for the succession to the throne of Hastinapura. Arjuna is devastated by the idea of attacking his cousins, to the point where he lets his bow slip from his hands. He is bewildered by grief and Krishna comes to his rescue.[43] Lord Krishna teaches him the true path of obtaining release by fulfilling one's duty according to one's status (*svadharma*). Arjuna belongs to the warrior caste (*Kshatriya*)[44] whose duty is to engage in combat without any personal expectation as to the result.[45] Just as the Upanishads offered a reinterpretation of the Vedic sacrifice (*yajna*), accomplishing one's duty without seeking reward or merit also constitutes a reinterpretation of it. This reinterpretation is used to justify the caste system, but it also offers a path to salvation for those who are excluded from Vedic rituals reserved for the "twice born," or those who cannot waive their social duties in the manner of the renunciant engaged in meditation. Whether a *Brahmin* or a *Shudra*, whose sole function is to serve the other castes, the one who performs with detachment the duties of his caste will achieve perfection, true knowledge, and identification with the Absolute (*Brahman*).[46] The fulfillment of duty in total and joyful self-abandonment is true devotion (*bhakti*), the love of God who gives eternal peace.[47]

Jainism and Buddhism are certainly forms of protest against the Vedic tradition, which ensured primacy to the *Brahmins*. Epic and Puranic stories are looked on as a reinterpretation of Brahmanism in favor of the *Shudras* and popular religion. Among these rearrangements, a few words on the *Bhakti* movement, whose origins date back to the beginning of the Christian era, are in order.[48] The *Bhagavad Gita* by its insistence on devotion to Krishna, an avatar of Vishnu, did provide the initial start for the devotional movement that ran through the Middle Ages and modern times, until today. Devotion then revolved around the creator Brahma, Vishnu, and his avatars (especially Rama and Krishna), or Shiva and his wife Mahadevi Kali, the female personification of creative energy (*shakti*). The movement of devotion to Vishnu (*Vaishnava*) developed particularly in Tamil Nadu between the eighth and tenth centuries, thanks to 12 mystics, the Alvars, who sang in temples their dedication to Vishnu, and whose songs were collected in the *Nalaya Prabandham*. Among these poets and mystics, there was the very popular Andal (eighth century) who expressed his devotion to Vishnu by taking the appearance of a fiery female lover in 30 Tamil hymns known as the *Tiruppaavai*. Tradition ascribes the development of devotion to Shiva (Shaivism) to 63 saints from southern India (Tamil Nadu especially) in the seventh and eighth centuries. Devotion to the Goddess (*Shakti*) also took shape during the same period. In all its forms, *bhakti* is always an outpour of feelings from the heart toward the divine. Human love and eroticism are the chosen symbols of the fusion of a human soul with the divine. Among the main *vaishnava* practitioners figured Sri Ramanuja (1031–1137), the holy founder of *srivaishnava*, a devotional movement that preached total abandonment (*prapatti*) in the hands of Narayana (another name for Vishnu), who is an attribute (*vishesha*) of the One, *Brahman*.[49] Vaishnava piety was transported to northern India, starting from the thirteenth century, and often focused on devotion to the avatars of Vishnu, Rama, and Krishna. A native of Uttar Pradesh, Ramananda (d. 1470) spread in Varanasi the devotion to Rama in Hindi, seventh avatar of Vishnu, and welcomed among his followers Muslims, women, and the untouchables. Devotion to Rama was popularized in the north through Goswami Tulsidas's work in dialectical Hindi (1532–1623), the *Ramcaritmanas*. The poem recounts with a personal touch the well-known epic of the *Ramayana*, depicting how Sita, a devoted wife, was abducted from her faithful husband Rama. The poem goes on to relate how the couple was reunited with the help of the monkey Hanuman who helped Rama rescue his beloved Sita, then a prisoner of the demon Ravana. Hanuman symbolizes total abandonment, service for the love of God. A native of Bengal, Shri Chaitanya Mahaprabhu (1486–1533) popularized the devotion to Krishna, metaphorized by Krishna's love for his cowherd girls (*gopis*), particularly Radha, who performed the cosmic dance (*rasa lila*) circling around the young Krishna playing the flute. Considered the founder of a new movement called *Vaishnava Gaudiya Vaishnava*, Shri Chaitanya and his immediate followers (the six Goswamis) believed that devotion to Krishna and his wife Radha is the only way to salvation. They based their teaching on the *Bhagavata Purana*, which summarized all the Vedic literature, and taught that Krishna was the divine reality itself, the source of all incarnations.[50] Chaitanya and his followers were particularly fond of Jayadeva's *Gita Govinda* (twelfth century), which poetically expressed the love of god through the erotic play of Krishna and his mistress[51] Radha and her companion *gopis*, in the secrecy of the Vrindavan forest. Just as in the Western ideal of *amour courtois* where separated lovers are dying to be reunited one day, in Radha and the *gopis*' longing to meet Krishna lies the essence of true love. It stands for the metaphor par excellence of the love that must exist between human beings and the divine. This idea of separation seems to be the feeling that nurtures the *gopis*' love-desire for Krishna while distressed and maddened by his absence.[52] One of Chaitanya's biographies often speaks of his personal despair and anxiety at the thought of being separated from the Lord Krishna.[53] The awakening of the feelings evoked by the recollection of moments of pure bliss (*Madhurya rasa*) in the presence of Krishna opens the heart to the love of God (*bhakti raganuga*) and leads to states of intense emotion (*bhava*) and ecstatic love (*prema*).[54] At the time of Chaitanya, there already existed a Bengali literary tradition,[55] inspired by Tantric Buddhism, that promoted sexual expression of human love as an embodiment of the divine. According to this esoteric doctrine, known as Sahajiya (*sahaja* means natural), enlightenment must be achieved in the microcosm of the human body. Through sexual intercourse the true nature of the self can be achieved with the union of masculine and feminine opposites. Although the Gaudiya Vaishnava movement opposes this doctrine and preaches that love play (*lila*) between Krishna and Radha should strictly be interpreted allegorically, many authors believe that this doctrine has had a positive influence on the works of Jayadeva, the poet Chandidas Bahu (fourteenth century) and his *Shrikrisnakirtan*, and Chaitanya.[56] Today, the International Association for Krishna Consciousness (also known by its acronym ISKCON), founded in New York in the 1960s by A. C. Bhaktivedanta Swami Prabhupada (1896–1977), claims to belong to the movement founded by Chaitanya.

The symbolism of sexual union also holds a singular place in the various Shaiva movements that worship the presence of the absolute in Shiva. The latter is considered as an expression of the absolute undifferentiated consciousness that inhabits all of creation. The world is a reflection of the universal consciousness and its unfolding is made possible by differentiating its energy, its *shakti*. Kashmiri Shaivism (Pratyabhijna), whose most prominent representatives are Vasugupta (ninth century) and Abhinavagupta (tenth century), teaches that the path of realization is completed by recognizing (*pratyabhijna*) the true identity of the universe, the individual soul (*jiva*), and of Shiva. The individual soul, whose self-awareness is limited, needs to be awakened to its pure, transcendental reality, with the help of yogic meditation techniques. Yoga seeks to awaken the practitioner (tantric) to the creative force (*shakti*) that lies at the base of the spine, the *muladhara chakra*, in the form of a coiled snake (Kundalini).[57] From this point, the creative energy travels through the five chakras along the spine to a chakra located above the skull (*saharara chakra*) to be reunited with Shiva. Sexual union is a means of union with the Absolute because it represents the union of masculine and feminine polarities, Shiva-Shakti. Chapter 29 of the *Tantra Loka* of Abhinavagupta is a prime example of the reinterpretation of the Vedic sacrifice in a tantric context.[58]

The Goddess is also seen by some *Bhakta* as the Supreme Being. Thus, for Ramakrishna (1836–1886), an eminent saint and inspiration for a monastic order bearing his name but founded by his disciple Swami Vivekananda, the relationship of the devotee to the divine was expressed at times in the form of the child-mother (*santana bhava*) relationship or at others in the form of the passion that exists between lovers (*vira bhava*).[59] Theologians believe that *Bhakti* and *Tantra* are more appropriate for the present age, the Age of Kali (*Kali Yuga*), one marked by the decline of spirituality in human beings and their turning away from Vedic lessons.[60]

SEXUALITY

We have seen that pleasure and sexuality take up an essential part of the Hindu view of life, the *Dharma*. Before addressing the issue of how homosexuality is viewed by Hinduism, there is a need to further specify the Hindu general discourse on sexuality in itself. As in many religious systems, sexuality appears in several myths about the origins of the world and life. However, there are exceptions; for example, it is absent from the famous hymn *Purusha Shukta* of the *Rig Veda*. It imagines the creation of the universe and social order (*varna dharma*) as the dismemberment or sacrifice of the Primordial Man (*Purusha*).[61] In this myth of origin, what caused the appearance of the world owes nothing to sexuality; creatures are the result of some sort of multiplication by division. Another hymn from the *Rig Veda*, the *Nasadyia Shukta*, features, preexisting any form, the Absolute (*tadekam*), which creates the universe, including the devas, through its own energy (*tapas*), awakening in itself the desire for love (*kama*) and the creative energy symbolized by semen (*retas*).[62] The dyad *tapas/kama* is found in one of the oldest hymns, as is the idea that mindfulness and control of the creative energy by the austerities produces heat (*tapas*), which in turn promotes the desire to procreate. Related to this myth, the hymn *Hiranyagrabha Sukta* tells of Prajapati's birth, the lord of creation or divine order, which will be known later under the name of Brahma, born from a golden embryo.[63] Later texts like the *Shatapatha Brahmana* and the *Manu Smriti* mention the formation of a golden egg floating on the primordial waters, out of which came, after one year, Prajapati.[64] Prajapati creates the world by the heat (*tapas*) he produces, which leads next to his dismemberment and that is why he is considered to be *Purusha*.[65] The concentration necessary to create energy at the macrocosmic level may be transferred to the microcosmic level. Man through ascetic discipline may bring about the concentration of energy.[66] While asceticism concentrates energy, the creative act disperses it and breaks it down. Therefore, Prajapati, exhausted and fearing death, had to regain his strength[67] turning to the god of the sacrificial fire Agni for help.[68] Thus, the Vedic sacrifice is the preferred method for restoring creation and ensuring the continuity of life through the changing seasons and to ensure immortality.[69] The *Brihad-Aranyaka Upanishad* says that originally there was only the Self (*Brahman*) existing as a person (*purusha*) who had to cope with fear and loneliness. Desire (*kama*) to break with this world of loneliness and absence of pleasure grabbed the Self, which split in two, a male a female part and from the union of both were born all sexed beings.[70] The union of male and female symbolizes the fullness of divine creation and sexual intercourse is symbolically raised to a ritual akin to Vedic sacrifice, the semen compared to the liquid produced when the soma plant is pressed for the Vedic sacrifice and the female reproductive organ (*yoni*) described as the altar on which the fire sacrifice is performed.[71] Other myths of origin attributed part of the creation to the incestuous relationship of Prajapati/Brahma with his daughter—a relationship punished by Rudra/Shiva.[72]

Sexual desire and copulation justify the creation of the universe, and the origin myths that I mentioned regard sexuality as sacred and as a gateway to the divine as in *Bhakti* or *Tantra*. Sexuality is not only fun, it allows for the continuity of life.[73] According to the ancient Vedic religion, obtaining a son will help in keeping the relationship with the ancestors (*pitris*) and ultimately with the transmitters of tradition, the first sacrificers and reciters of hymns, the *Rishis*. Through the ritual of the dead (*sraddha*) the ancestors' spirits are honored to facilitate one's journey into the realm of death and to join the world of ancestors. To obtain a male offspring is to ensure that one will someday join the peaceful world of the ancestors. Therefore to beget a son is referred to as paying one's debt to the ancestors.[74] In the Hindu liturgical calendar, the "festival of the dead" (*pitripaksha mela*), two weeks in mid-September, always occupies a prominent place. The human couple itself is valued by the Vedic literature for the rituals are to be accomplished by both the husband and wife together.[75]

However, the sexual economy of the Vedic religion was quickly put in doubt. The sexual drive can be a hindrance to the knowledge of *Brahman* and an obstacle in the way of salvation (*moksha*). The ideal of renunciation (*sannyasa*) and celibacy is ancient in India and dates back at least to the time of the Aranyakas and the Upanishads (from 900 BC), when hermits and sages abandoned the ritual of sacrifice and practiced yoga and meditation instead. The *Taittirya Aranyaka* speaks of the wise (*munis*) that retained their semen (*urdhvaretas*).[76] One of the oldest texts, the *Chandogya Upanishad*, shows that to attain knowledge of the Absolute, the union of the *atman* and *Brahman*, one must be freed from bodily pleasures because they activate the mechanism by which the *atman* remains attached to this world.[77] Abstinence (*brahmacharya*), that is to say, living as a hermit in the forest centered on the practice of meditation and fasting, allows oneself to control desire (*kama*).[78] The translators render the Upanishadic notion of *brahmacharya* by different words that are not, unfortunately, all synonyms: celibacy, abstinence, chastity, study. We saw in the previous section that *brahmacharya* was the first stage (*ashram*) in the life of a "twice born," during which he devoted himself to studying the *Vedas*, meditation, and leading a bachelor's life. The *Dharma Shastra* literature more importantly detailed these stages further. The Upanishads mentioned them without elaborating. Thus, the *Chandogya Upanishad* mentioned *brahmacharya* without telling us much about the rules of sexual conduct.[79] In the *Brihad Aranyaka Upanishad*, the sage Yajnavalkya seemed to indicate that knowledge of the Absolute imposed an ascetic life based on the renunciation of wealth and of the sex drive capable of procuring a son.[80] The *Katha Upanishad* opposed the satisfaction of bodily pleasures to the knowledge of *Brahman*; only the person who controlled his senses could achieve immortality. Thus, renouncing material wealth and sexual pleasures made readily available to him by Yama (god of the realm of the dead), Nachiketa opened his heart to the Absolute and was released from the cycle rebirths.[81]

Very early in the development of the Hindu religious system a pervasive tension between asceticism and eroticism settles in. This paradoxical tension will reveal itself in the person of Shiva, the Mahayogi, and the erotic Shiva who copulated with Parvati for a thousand years! Doniger thinks the tension rises in importance because of the *Vedas*' insistence on having a male offspring.[82] The *Mahabharata* tells the story of Rishi

Mandapala who practiced all kinds of austerities (*tapas*) and retained his semen (*urdhvaretas*) but was denied access to the realm of ancestors because he had no son to pay the debt that could save him from hell.[83] In the *Rig Veda Samhita*, Lopamudra reminded her husband Rishi Agastya of his duty to unite sexually with his wife despite his advanced age.[84] The *Mahabharata* recounts that the same Agastya who practiced asceticism (*tapas*) realized he had to marry and bear a son after seeing his ancestors hung over a precipice, head down.[85] The interest of this story lies in the fact that Lopamudra, daughter of the king of Vidarbha, opposed to such a marriage, still wedded Agastya and at first renounced the opulent life in the royal palace. She instead accompanied her husband into the forest to live by his side a life of true asceticism and renunciation. However, Agastya became sexually aroused (*maithunayajuhava*) at the sight of his wife having a swim totally naked. Lopamudra replied that Agastya's sole desire for a son was insufficient to meet her demands and that he had to prove his genuine love by making love to her in a way suitable for a princess. Agastya begged her in vain not to let him lose all the merits accumulated by a life of asceticism and renunciation and finally the two made love and had a son.[86] This episode is the glorification of domestic life and family and demonstrates the incompleteness of a life based solely on asceticism. In the same category is the story of this female ascetic who led a life of renunciation in the forest and refused to marry. She was convinced that a life of asceticism would earn her a safe passage in the other life, but a sage named Narada said she could not access it without having completed the various duties incumbent upon all human beings during their lifetime.[87] This story not only emphasizes the importance of the age-based system of domestic life, but it is a striking example of the economy of sexual energy during one's lifespan. *Brahmacharya* enables with the practice of austerities (*tapas*) the necessary accumulation of creative energy—as being taught in creation myths. Then comes the time to spend that energy and start a family (*grihastha*), and finally comes the return to the practice of austerities in *vanaprastha* and *sannyasa* before the final release.

The legislator Manu required the husband to have sex only during his wife's fertile period (*ritu*).[88] The *Mahabharata* compared the union of the spouses during this period to abstinence and believed that both have the same moral value. He even predicted an afterlife full of atrocities for the husband who failed in his marital duty.[89] Globalization and urbanization have certainly had an impact on the sexual culture of modern India, but this sexual taboo, like many others, is still part of the landscape for many Hindus.[90] The system of stages of life, therefore, represents a compromise or a sexual economy that allows the reconciliation of two opposites, asceticism and eroticism. While these two poles are spaced in time on the human level, they join in the myths paradoxically, sometimes in violent and outrageous ways, as in the person of Shiva. Doniger has beautifully illustrated how Shiva's uncontrolled eroticism and asceticism constitute a threat to the world of gods and men. Puranic literature, as it were, abounds in narratives where Shiva's chastity threatens the regeneration of the world when it does not directly cause its destruction as in the episode of his castration when the fall of his lingam blazed the earth on coming into contact with it.[91] Puranic stories of the birth of Skanda (also known as Kumara or Karttikeya), son of Shiva and Parvati, also tell of Shiva's extreme chastity, that is, his accumulation of *tapas*. After his semen was spilled on the ground, it was recovered by Agni whose stomach was burnt by it.[92] Shiva's erect penis is the result of his retention of semen through his powers of Maha yogi and has nothing to do with raunchy arousal. He made love to Parvati for a thousand years but only when disturbed and interrupted in his intercourse by the gods who were enraged by the infertility of this union did he spill his seed on the ground.[93] In contrast, Shiva's sexual excesses made him lose his energy and he had to seek solitude to practice austerities and regain his strength to fight the demons that attacked the gods.[94]

The mythological tales, like dreams, often bring together opposite poles without necessarily seeking reconciliation because they are immune to the contingencies imposed by time and space. They can inspire the human quest for meaning, but it is up to another kind of literature to codify social and ethical conduct, the *Dharma Shastra* literature. To understand the importance of these rules of conduct, one must first understand that Hinduism does not see sin in the sense of a rebellion against a god but as a transgression of the moral order (*dharma*). Fault (*papa*) is caused by ignorance (*avidya*), which prevents the individual from being aware of his divine nature. He is drawn prisoner by the fruits of action (law of karma) in the cycle of rebirths (*samsara*) and is incapable of any release. Whoever does not follow rules dictated by the cosmic order commits an offense against oneself. Instead of asking forgiveness from God, one must strive to purify the body and soul so that the pure eternal light of the *atman* may shine. The clean and unclean have a role in the social and religious system of India for they shape social relations, particularly between certain castes, and regulate body functions including food, hygiene, sexuality, birth, and death. Without going into the details of Indian physiology, there is a vital link between food, sexual fluids (semen and blood), and sustaining the vital breath (*prana*), which is a reflection of the divine. Sexual taboos guarantee social order by determining the punishment for violations according to one's place in the caste system, and they cleanse the mind to achieve the ultimate reality by getting rid of desires and emotions.

Adultery (*samgrahana*) is subject to various fines or even corporal punishment, which may include death. The penalties are higher if the act is committed with a married woman, with or without violence, and they vary according to caste: the higher the woman's caste and the lower the man's caste, the more severe the punishment will be.[95] The *Bhagavad Gita* relates the corruption of social order driven by family disorders causing the corruption of women to the mingling of castes.[96] Incest and bestiality are judged severely.[97] Sanctions related to masturbation are still relatively mild, a ritual bath with one's clothes on.[98] He who has broken his vow of celibacy (*brahmacharya*) masturbating will have to beg for food in seven houses, dressed in a donkey skin, and perform ritual baths three times a day.[99] The involuntary discharge of sperm during sleep requires the *brahmacharis* to wash the next morning while invoking the sun three times to recover his strength.[100] In fact, masturbation is never qualified as an act against nature because it is not procreative. In Indian culture, the concern about emission of sperm, even today, focuses on the loss of sexual energy (*virya*) that flows out of the body through ejaculation instead of borrowing the channel to the head and transform itself into spiritual energy (*ojas shakti*).[101] In the *Bhagavad Gita*, Krishna says: "I am...virility in men"[102] (*paurusham nrishu*) and that is the reason why retention of semen is a sign of release and immortality.[103] Epic and puranic literature contain many stories of wise ascetics who ejaculate involuntarily after being sexually aroused at the sight of a celestial nymph (*apsara*). For example, Sarasvat, the son of the sage Gautama, is tempted by the *apsara* Janapadi who was sent by the god Indra who felt his supremacy threatened by the austerities of Gautama and his son. Excited by the presence of the lightly clad *apsara* in the forest, Sarasvat tries to control himself, but he ejaculates unwittingly on a shrub and gives birth to twins.[104] The real concern of the authors of these myths is probably rooted in the defense of the ideal of family life against the ascetic currents developed by the Upanishads, but also promoted by other religious movements that have emerged such as Buddhism or Jainism.

Oral sex and sodomy are more fully discussed in the next section on homosexuality. For now, suffice it to indicate a series of sexual acts categorized by the phrase "*siktva ayoni*," which means any discharge of semen outside the vagina without any consideration for the partner's gender.[105] The penalties for extravaginal sex vary, but may include the loss of caste status when committed with an untouchable,[106] in which case, according to belief, the ancestors may feed on the offender's semen for a month.[107] Chapter IX of the *Kama Sutra*, entitled *Auparishtaka*, deals in considerable detail with oral sex between men, but mentions its execution by women and how it is more popular in certain regions.[108] Its compiler, Vatsyayana,[109] does however suggest that such practice is vulgar (*asabhya*), contrary to the teachings of famous masters and constitutes an act of pollution because the genitalia are in the face.[110] Vatsyayana, however, suggests that the golden rule in this regard is to follow one's inclinations and to take account of local custom.[111] Fellatio and cunnilingus when simultaneously performed (position 69) are called "crows" (*kakila*). According to Vatsyayana, this practice seems inadvisable to Brahmins, even with prostitutes, and according to the commentator Yashodhara this practice should exist between persons of the same caste only.[112] The ingestion of semen is widely condemned by legislators and requires purification rites,[113] although mythical tales have often used it as a method of fertilization.[114] Ayurvedic medicine prescribes ingestion of sperm to counter erectile difficulties.[115] As for heterosexual sodomy (*adhorata*), the *Kama Sutra* classifies it among various modes of copulation (*chitrarata*) such as vaginal penetration from behind or to make love standing up.[116] Vatsyayana notes that heterosexual sodomy is more popular among people from the South. Yashodhara think this copulatory technique is debasing because the penis takes the wrong path (*vimarga*), the anal region (*apana*), which is located under the vagina. Vatsyayana distinguishes very clearly the practice of heterosexual anal intercourse from male sodomy, which he attributed to a reversal of gender roles (*purushayita*), and Yashodhara noted that he would discuss it in his treatment of the third sex (*tritiya prakriti*).[117]

This section would be incomplete without a few lines devoted to the relationship between the masculine and feminine. The psychoanalyst Sudhir Kakar portrays Indian love relationships or marriages as marked by inequality, misunderstanding, and mistrust.[118] He says the relationship between the sexes in Indian culture is strongly influenced by *stridharma*, the code of conduct toward women.[119] Although there is some mutuality between the sexes in marriage relationships, especially regarding the performance of rituals, the relationship between husband and wife are clearly asymmetrical. Women, unlike men, do not receive religious initiation that would familiarize them with the means of salvation (*moksa*). Only men belonging to the first three castes are regarded "twice born." The only way for a woman to achieve salvation is by total dedication (*pativratya*) in marriage to her husband until death.[120] She has no personal identity except through her husband who she must worship faithfully as a true god.[121] In the *Mahabharata*, Draupadi marries the five Pandava brothers to whom she devotes herself entirely as gods, her only refuge.[122] The *Ramayana* also offers women the exemplary conduct of Sita, the *pativrata* or the spouse devoted entirely to her husband Rama whom she accompanies in exile. She continues to serve him despite the unfair treatment he submits her to because of gossip concerning her chastity. Behind this vision of subordination, in which women's salvation depends on men, lies the idea that women's sexuality is naturally unclean.[123] Certainly, they deserve respect as wives and mothers, as begetters of "twice-born" sons, but they are indeed considered as inferior beings because they are more entangled than men in their sexual desires.

According to the *Mahabharata*, women are governed by their sexual appetite and become unfaithful to their husband whenever an opportunity shows.[124] Women's sexuality is considered a threat to men. The ancient narratives are full of stories about ascetics who became sexually aroused by women, spilled their seed, and lost the merit they accumulated through asceticism and celibacy.[125] For example, the ascetic Vibhandaka was seduced by the *apsara* Urvashi bathing in a pool and emitted semen. This was immediately drunk by a doe, which gave him a son named Rishiashringa. The latter was raised by his father in a hermitage in the woods and never had the opportunity of seeing a woman. While drought threatened the kingdom of Anga, King Lopamudra, under the guidance of Brahmins, sent young prostitutes to try and seduce Rishiashringa known to carry the skill to bring rain by his asceticism. He was attracted and disturbed by the beauty of the courtesans he believed to be young students (*brahmacharins*).[126] His father, whom he had informed about this encounter, told him to stay away from those courtesans who were real demons. After a second meeting, the courtesans succeeded in attracting Rishiashringa without too much trouble to the kingdom of Anga, where he tasted the joy of sexual intercourse with them. Rain fell on the kingdom, and King Lopamudra gave him his daughter in marriage.[127] A story with the demon Adi best illustrates in the cultural imagination the dangers posed by female sexuality. Adi, the son of the devil Adhaka, was determined to avenge his father who had been impaled by Shiva, and decided to take the form of Parvati and seduce Shiva. He armed his vagina with sharp teeth (*vagina dentata*); Shiva was drawn to the fake Parvati but then suddenly realized the trick. He immediately attached a sharp object to his penis and killed Adi.[128] The leitmotif of consummation of love unto death, *Liebestsod*, resurfaces periodically, as in the story of King Pandu, condemned to die while making love after having surprised an ascetic transformed into a deer and mating with a doe.[129] Menstrual blood is a source of impurity, and other dangers await the man who approaches or who has sex with a menstruating woman; it will shorten his life.[130]

The relationship between both genders is culturally marked by men's fear of diminishing their spiritual energy due to loss of semen. At the same time, the role played by the spouse as mother of a son carries with it some respect. Just as *Shudras* are marked by the unclean, a woman leads a dependent life under male control in all stages of her life; first under her father, then her husband, and if she is widowed, her son.[131] Ramakrishna's life and thought embody this sheer ambivalence of traditional Indian culture toward female libido: first, she is seen as the source of creative energy, the mother; and second, as the dangerous lover. While, at the same time, he showed a morbid fear of female sexuality, Ramakrishna did worship in each and every woman the mother goddess.[132]

The patriarchal view of Brahmin orthodoxy has certainly exerted a cultural hegemony throughout the Hindu tradition, but other schools of thought also brought a certain temperament. Thus, the *bhakti* movement, which stood opposed to salvation through the study of the Vedas, reserved for the "twice born," proposed salvation by devotion, regardless of caste or gender of the person. By making a wife's devotion to her husband the ideal portrait of the relationship with the divine, *bhakti* has somehow spiritually rehabilitated women. *Bhakta* women have served their God and their husbands with heartbreak as did Bahinabai, a holy Maratha woman of the seventeenth century. Of Brahmin origin, she expressed dismay while committing herself to the Vedic rules that imposed on her absolute devotion to her husband and expressing her boundless love for Krishna as taught by her master Tukaram, the great saint of Maharashtra.[133] Other holy female devotees flatly challenged social stereotypes by abandoning their family life and becoming ascetics like Mirabaï. A hugely popular saint in India, she was born in the aristocracy of Rajasthan and, from childhood, was attracted to Krishna to whom she showed endless devotion, which left her in conflict with the family of the Rajput prince she married. Indeed, she refused to honor Durga, the goddess of the royal family, and instead visited the temples dedicated to Krishna, where she sang his praises among the *Shudras*. When the prince died at a young age, she refused to sacrifice herself on her husband's pyre (*sati*) as required by tradition from a person of her rank. So she left her husband's family and lived as a wandering ascetic in search of salvation, something that was not socially acceptable for a woman.[134] These female role models are, however, in minority, and, for the common people, Brahmin orthodoxy remains the general rule.

Several other aspects deserve to be developed, but this would draw us too far off our topic. Included among them is the role of British colonization, which very early on maintained much of the traditional social norms that had been codified in the *smriti* concerning marriage and inheritance rules. However, it ruled against self-immolation of widows and child marriage for children under 14 years of age and authorized the remarriage of widows.[135] Some authors also like to see in the colonization process an effort to feminize the male Indian subjected to the conqueror's manly authority.[136] The Indian feminist movement and globalization are also factors that gradually transformed the relationship between the masculine and feminine.[137]

Women are deemed to be in need of protection because of their traditional low social status, and their role is usually confined to the domestic sphere. All of this created a situation where homosociality is somehow the norm and socializing with the opposite sex the exception. Even if the wedding ritual of *saptapadi* (seven steps circling the fire) during the traditional ceremony celebrates the friendship between the spouses, the unequal status of the two often proved a difficult obstacle to overcome for a real friendship to develop. As will be discussed in this chapter, homosociality partly explains the ease with which sex between male partners may occur.

Homosexuality

Before examining the relationship between homosexuality and Hinduism, it is worth drawing a social portrait of homosexuality in modern India, while being careful not to bring on to it the Western perspective of sexual orientation and gayness. As in most cultures, religion is not the sole determinant of the social perception of homosexuality. One has also to take into account that there are over one hundred million Muslims in India and Islamic civilization has exercised, especially after the twelfth century, a great impact on culture and Indian society. British colonialism has left its deep impression, first through the East India Company from 1600 until its dissolution on August 2, 1858. An act of government in London, the Government of India Act, terminated that first period and marked the beginning of the Raj that ended with independence in 1947. Globalization of culture, education, and migration outside the subcontinent have certainly brought greater exposure of Indian society to gay lifestyles and struggles for gay rights in other countries, thanks to television, film, literature, and the Internet. The AIDS epidemic has had the effect of introducing homosexuality in the public arena as men having sex with men were clearly included in the populations at risk.

According to some authors, intolerance and homophobia shown by the current Indian law does not originate from Indian civilization, but would have appeared with the adoption by the colonial government of the criminal code (Indian Penal Code or IPC)[138] in 1860.[139] Section 377 of the IPC borrows almost word for word the existing English criminal law and speaks of sexual intercourse against nature: a man with a man, or a woman, or bestiality,[140] meriting a sentence of imprisonment of ten years or life. In our opinion, the Western concept of what is against nature is remarkably different in its theoretical foundation than what the *Dharma Shastras* define as the objective rules of conduct applicable to every caste. In the West, human nature is universal, and the general rules apply to all. As we have already observed, the severity of sentences for sexual offenses in the *Dharma Shastras* often varies according to the social status of individuals. The common denominator or rationale for sanctions is purity rather than failing the purpose of reproductive sex, which is usually the criterion for the morality of sexual conduct in other religious systems.

Ruth Vanita notes that, in India, homosexual acts have never been subject to death penalty. There is no evidence of any organized persecution of homosexuals, she says, before the nineteenth century.[141] Despite the existence of strong penalties provided by section 377 of the criminal code, few cases have found themselves in court until today, about 30 over a period of over 100 years.[142] However, this section of the code has recently been at the forefront in the public space repeatedly, since two NGOs fighting against AIDS, Naz Foundation International and Bharosa Trust, decided in July 2001 to challenge its constitutionality following the arrest and imprisonment for 47 days of four of their employees in Lucknow, Uttar Pradesh.[143] Police searched the premises and seized the material it classified as obscene, claiming that the staff of these organizations operated a gay racket on the Internet and that its members engaged in sodomy and encouraged such behavior.[144] Given the circumstances, the Naz Foundation filed an action for the annulment of section 377 in the High Court of Delhi, which ultimately ruled in 2004 in favor of the government. The High Court accepted the arguments of government lawyers suggesting that homosexuality is a Western importation alien to Indian culture and that the law aims at protecting social order and preventing abuse, namely, toward children.[145] The High Court's decision was appealed by Naz, and the Supreme Court of India decided in February 2006 to return the case to the High Court. In doing so it argued that the appellant Naz had no legal interest necessary to challenge the law because its members had not been found guilty of any illegal acts under section 377. Finally, the Delhi High Court considered the case on its merits and ruled in favor of Naz Foundation, declaring unconstitutional the provisions of section 377, in the case of consenting adults 18 years of age and older.[146] Naz's work and the legal action it undertook have allowed for a more informed picture of homosexual practices in India, traditionally a taboo topic, and have also highlighted some of the police repression against sexual minorities.

Homosexuality in the Indian subcontinent may comprise decidedly different realities of what the West usually includes in the concepts of sexual orientation and an openly gay lifestyle. Indeed, as noted in a document produced by Naz in 1997, some men who have sex with men also have sex with women and are often married. Homosexual practices are also quite common among teenagers.[147] That is why, following the footsteps of the National Aids Control Organization (NACO), India's Ministry of Health has favored over the past 15 years the phrase "Men who have sex with men" (MSM).[148] It reflects a plurality of situations: homosexuals, bisexuals, transvestites, and transsexuals. Among these men or teenagers, some are defined as *kothis*, that is to say, effeminate men who provide sexual services in the form of anal penetration for men called *panthis* or *giriyas* (husbands).[149] The *kothis* come predominantly from poor backgrounds, and have little or no schooling. Several of them are married and have adopted sex work to provide for their family.[150] They are distinct from the *hijras* or transsexuals who have often undergone complete castration (removal of testicles and penis); we will return to this topic later in the chapter. The *kothis* do not usually live as a woman, but go from their role as men with a family to their role as sex workers in the guise of "women," meeting customers in train stations, parks, on beaches or in small tearooms.[151] Neither woman nor man, the *kothi* belongs to a third gender.[152] Unlike his partner or customer, the *panthi* or real man, the effeminate *kothi* allows himself to be penetrated. He thereby becomes the target of oppressive social stigma and marginalization and often encounters verbal and physical harassment by the police, other *kothis* or youth gangs.[153] Violence against *kothis* often takes the form of sexual assault and rape.[154]

Many teens and unmarried young men have sex with each other, often because the girls are not easily accessible. These relationships are made easy by the promiscuity resulting from a lack of living quarters that drive some young men to share the same bed. It is also the fact that male friendships and visible signs of affection between men, holding hands in public, for example, are valued in a society where it is extremely difficult to interact with women, especially when they are unmarried.[155] In this context, the boundary between friendship and sexual intimacy becomes blurred and easy to cross, and this type of sex is often called *dosti*.[156] Unlike what happens with *kothis*, sexual relations with a friend (*dost*) are also marked by reciprocity, mutual masturbation or intercrural sex, or alternation of roles in oral sex or anal intercourse. Most of the time, these homosexual practices are viewed as a normal hormonal burst without too many consequences, a momentary deviation from the rule (*masti*), due to the person's young age.

The first anthology of gay contemporary Indian literature to appear in English was *Yaraana* meaning friendship in Hindi.[157] It gives considerable importance to the phenomenon of *dosti*. Indian cinema (Bollywood) has long praised the unwavering male friendships that are well within the norms of acceptability in Indian society but whose homoerotic taints are now clearly unveiled, the most celebrated being *Sholay* (1975).[158] Since the late 1990s, several Indian movies have had gay themes altogether; the first was probably Riyad Wadia's *Bomgay*, followed by Kaizad Gustad's *Bombay Boys* and Sanjay Sharma's *Dunno Y... Na Jaane Kyon* (English: *Don't Know Why*, 2010). In 1998, the film *Fire* by Deepa Mehta, a Canadian director of Indian origin, stirred a lot of passion and dissent in India. The film presents the abandonment of two women, Radha and Sita, by their husbands, two brothers. One neglects his wife by having adventures with other women while the other takes a chastity vow because his wife cannot conceive. Ignored by their husbands, both women end up making love to each other. Both women are far from representing the traditional values of a spouse's loyalty and devotion to her husband, far away from Sita's model in the *Ramayana*. Indian star Yuvraaj Parasher was disowned by his family for playing a gay man and kissing his partner on screen in *Dunno Y... Na Jaane Kyon*.

Kothi-panthi relationships and male friendships reflect a fluid conception of the manliness in everyday life, in spite of a rigid normative system defining sex roles.[159] This fluidity may explain why the majority of men or boys having homosexual practices do not perceive themselves as having a homosexual identity.[160] There is of course in India today a significant gay movement, which started about 20 years ago and which promotes the rights for respect and dignity of their sexual difference. These movements appeared in certain large cities, in particular Mumbai, Delhi, Kolkata, and Chennai. Their clientele is usually schooled, speaks English, and belongs to more affluent circles.[161] Among the pioneers promoting the right for sexual orientation in the 1980s was the founder of the first gay magazine in India, *Bombay Dost*, Ashok Row Kavi.[162] Without trying to sum up the history of the Indian gay movement, it is worth mentioning that from 1992 homosexuals protested in the streets of Delhi against police repression. Several other demonstrations of the same nature took place since then, in particular since the Lucknow incident.

In summary, homosexuality in India was built in a religious, social, and cultural context of its own and its reality is fundamentally different from the Western concept of homosexuality. Certainly, there is now a variety of homosexual experiences in India, and it would be wholly inappropriate to presume that its existence is the direct consequence of colonization. Although some authors believe that we know little about its reality in ancient India,[163] I will demonstrate that many of these experiences have deep roots in ancient India, contrary to popular myth, which takes it as an evil imported by Muslim invaders[164] or Europeans.[165] History and ancient texts will probably uncover not a rupture but continuity of meaning.

Dharma Shastra literature disapproves of homosexual acts. The *Manu Smriti* mentions the sexual union of a male with a male (*maithunam pumsi*) without clarifying the exact nature of the alleged act.[166] As Professor Sharma noted, the old English translation, dating from the Victorian era, described the act as "against nature," something the Sanskrit text does not show.[167] The ban solely concerns the "twice born," that is to say, a person who must live by higher ethical standards. Sharma also brings a compelling perspective when he draws attention to the preceding verse, which speaks of extravaginal (*ayoni*) emission of semen. A comparison of the severity of penalty applicable to both faults, a ritual bath in the case of copulation with a male and *samtapana kricchra*[168] in other cases, led the author to conclude that the main objective of the codifier was primarily protecting women's virtue.[169] The phrase *maithunam pumsi* is found elsewhere in the *Manu Smriti* and the *Vishnu Smriti*, but this time the alleged act entails the loss of his caste.[170] How can these two positions be reconciled? In fact, I think the two need not be interpreted as opposed, if one examines the context of each of these two statements. Consider first the assertion that sex between men causes a loss of caste. The author of the *Manu Smriti* enumerates various types of fault, the most serious (*mahapataka*) to the lighter (*upupataka*), and those entail the loss of caste.[171] The enumeration is followed by the assertion that all the faults mentioned may be the object of atonement by performing appropriate penances listed thereafter according to their category. Chapter XI, verse 175, imposes a ritual bath to the "twice born" who committed a homosexual act. The reason why the author specifically aimed at the "twice born" could be motivated by the fact that a *Shudra* cannot commit an offense causing loss of caste.[172] The *Vishnu Smriti* differs slightly in that the required penance seems more severe, purification using five different cow products *samtapana kricchra*, with the difference that involuntary acts deserve a less severe penance (*prajapatya*),[173] a distinction also found in *Manu Smriti*.[174] Sharma is probably right in thinking that the position of ancient legislators on penances for homosexual relations remains unclear today.[175] However, it may very well be that the ritual bath may come as an added penance either to the five cow products (*samtapana kricchra*) or to fasting (*prajapatya*) because these latter forms of expiation must be accompanied by a ritual bath three times a day.[176] In short, the loss of caste is not automatic as there are ways to atone otherwise. The *Artha Shastra*, a treatise on political economy from the fourth century BC written by Kautilya, imposes a fine on people who engage in homosexual acts, without specifying their nature. The fines are equivalent to those imposed for extravaginal sex: the first set of fines between 48 and 96 *panas* (metal currency).[177] These two sexual acts must be punished less severely than heterosexual relations involving a female *Brahman*, entailing the highest level of fines (500–1000 *panas*) for a *Kshatriya* man, the seizure of all his property for a *Vaisya* and the stake for a *Shudra*.[178] The man who has sex with a virgin girl must pay 400 *panas*, a second set fine, and has his middle finger cut off.[179] The severity of sentences at first seems to serve the purpose of protecting women and girls and the purity of caste, which would explain the lightness of penalties for homosexual acts. The *Manu Smriti* states very clearly that adultery should be punished severely because it runs the risk of having castes mingled.[180]

Homosexual relations are not clearly defined in the laws and the early legislators may have included a set of practices. They barely mentioned oral sex in general and made no direct mention of homosexual fellatio.[181] Regardless of the sexual partner's gender, the real problem seemed the likely ingestion of semen as we have mentioned. Unlike the legislators, Vatsyayana, in a verse from the *Kama Sutra*, speaks abundantly of homosexual fellatio practiced by people of an independent third gender (*tritiya prakriti*).[182]

Two categories of persons belong to the third gender whether their appearance is male (*purusha rupini*) or feminine (*stri rupini*).[183] The next verse gives an account of the category: they wear dresses and behave like women. Vatsyayana gives no precision on the first category though the commentator Yashodhara seems to indicate that they are male. He calls people of the third gender *napumsaka* and among them are found those who show a manly appearance with beards while others have a breast.[184] The *Sataphata Brahmana* explains the neutral (*napumsaka*) gender in grammar by the image of a castrated bull, neither male nor female.[185] The same text speaks of an individual being neither woman nor man, a defective or impotent (*kliba*) man who cannot inseminate a female partner.[186] Ayurveda recognizes three gender categories: male, female, and neutral (*napumsaka*).[187] The *Mahabharata* states that men who have homosexual sex will reincarnate into beings incapable of having offspring (*kliba*).[188] According to the *Manu Smriti*, the *kliba* cannot inherit but this status is reversible if he weds and has children.[189] This suggests that this condition is not always inherited.[190] Another word is sometimes used, especially in Ayurvedic medicine, to explain this lack of virility and sexual energy, *sandha*.[191] The authors agree to say that these three expressions—*kliba*, *napumsaka*, and *sandha*—are synonymous and usually refer to sexual dysfunction or a deviation from the norm of male heterosexuality whose origin may be physical, congenital, or acquired, in addition to being at times emotional or mental.[192] Besides birth defects such as hermaphroditism, having a curved penis, infertility, some sexual behaviors are also considered to be oddities of nature (*vikriti*) or a lack of virility (*sandha*). The *Sushruta* mentions various cases: the man who performs fellatio (*asekya purusha*),[193] the man who experiences orgasm by smelling genitalia (*saughandhika*), voyeur (*irsyaka*), the man with effeminate behavior (*narasandha* or *naracestita*), the woman with masculine behavior (*narisandha* or *stricestikara*)[194] and the male insertee (*kumbhika*).[195] Impotence (*sandha*) in some cases is a physical phenomenon, while in others it is a lack of heterosexual desire that may transform into homosexual practices. Several translators have rendered the words *napumsaka* and *tritiya prakriti* or others with the word "eunuch" while castration is one outcome in the general outlook of atypical or ambiguous sexuality. Amara Das Wilhelm attributes this usage to the prevalent prudery of the Victorian era that would have prompted the urge to hide something as taboo as homosexuality.[196] Moreover, castration was not widespread in India before the arrival of Muslim invaders in the eleventh century; they imported it to continue to include in their service, especially in harems, castrated slaves.[197] Flattening the meaning of all these expressions by translating them into one word, "eunuch," reveals an agenda that goes far beyond Victorian prudery. It probably demonstrates a deliberate process through which British colonizers attempted to conceal unfamiliar gender ambiguities and limit their public expression.[198] Concealment and ambiguity, on the other hand, allowed some colonizers to experience homosexual encounters without undermining their social status, something inconceivable in England.[199] Ayurvedic medicine attributes to various reproductive pathologies causes related to sperm quality, fertilization, or embryonic development.[200] In this context, it is not surprising to find Vatsyayana using a phrase like *tritiya pakriti* to designate a third gender or sex, together with the male and female categories. The expression is a catch-all category that accounts for both physiological deficits and anatomical abnormalities of the male or female reproductive system, but also any atypical form of sexuality.[201] The *Kama Sutra* appears to limit the category of a third sex or gender to all that defies conformity to gender roles. After having discussed these instances, its author devotes much space to the condition of men who appear to be truly masculine (*purusha rupim*), masseurs and hairdressers, who practice fellatio but hide their attraction to the same sex (*kama purusham*).[202] He also mentions in passing that some women engage in it as well as young servants (*yuvanah paricarakah*) with their masters.[203] Vatsyayana leaves the impression that these men, masseurs or young servants, do not belong to the third sex and are not *napumsaka*,[204] though he is certainly aware that Ayurvedic medicine treats fellatio as a third sex phenomenon.[205] Vatsyayana's approach leans more on the side of an anthropological or sociological account instead of medicine, pathology, and etiology. He observed the sexual mores of the age and sought ways to promote sexual pleasure in all its forms. His effort thus included homosexual men who were socially labeled as belonging to the third sex but also those men who did not. His views join, surprisingly, what we uncovered as the homosexual reality of contemporary India, which is of the *kothi/panthi* pattern, of the *hijra*, but also of those several men who have sex with men without identifying to any group. Thus, he speaks of citizens (*nagarakah*) of the same sex, without any other qualifying epithet, who are so attached to each other that they get married (*parigraha*).[206]

Ayurvedic medicine and the *Kama Sutra*, therefore, provide the description of a multifaceted sexuality, in which ambiguity deserves a prominent place. Religious literature contains many accounts of this ambiguity. Thus, the *Mahabharata* tells the story of the famed warrior hero Arjuna and his brothers who were condemned to remain in exile in the forest for 12 years after losing their kingdom at dice to the Kauravas, and had to spend an extra thirteenth year incognito. Arjuna chose to stay at the court of King Virata as a *sandha* or *kliba*, thus a member of the third sex (*tritiya prakriti*). He arrived dressed as a woman, took the name of Brihanalla and lived in the women's quarters with the palace's women and taught dance to Princess Uttaraa.[207] He was asked to defend the kingdom in battle, but King Virata's son refused to fight alongside Brihanalla, a *sandha*. In the end Brihanalla brought victory over the enemy.[208] Did Arjuna, in fact, become a eunuch or was he only cross-dressing? The *Mahabharata* does not directly answer the question. King Virata had a hard time believing that a person of such strength and stature could have been a *kliba*.[209] The end of the episode seems to favor the interpretation of a cross-dressing when the son revealed to the king Brihanalla's true identity. The king indeed offered to Arjuna his daughter's hand, but he refused only to prove the purity of his intentions toward the princess.[210] He wanted to silence the suspicions and gossip about his past year spent with the king's daughter in the palace's quarters reserved for women. Of greater importance than Arjuna's true anatomical sex is another story from the *Mahabharata* (Book III *Aranyaka Parva*, 36–46) where the hero is presented as a saint, a person in total control of his sexual appetite, in short an ascetic. Indeed, this book recounts the journey undertaken by Arjuna to obtain the necessary weapons that will help the Pandavas win over the Kauravas. He went first to the Himalayas where he practiced asceticism (*tapas*) in order to please Shiva, who then gave him some weapons and then he went to heaven to visit Indra, the king of the gods. Indra, fearing Arjuna might try to become like a god, wanted to put his chastity to test and sent the *apsara* Urvashi to seduce him. Seeing Arjuna's resistance to her advances, she thought that he could not possibly be a man, and, by means of a charm, made him impotent (*sandha*). These stories serve to demonstrate that male sexual transformations into ambiguous or androgynous beings are often used as a subterfuge allowing the hero to collect spiritual energy through ascetic practices (*tapas*).[211] Arjuna undergoes another sexual transformation in the *Padma Purana*.[212] The context is clearly that of the Vaishnava *bhakti* (devotion to Vishnu). Arjuna asks Krishna permission to attend the dance (*rasa lila*) that he secretly executes with the cowherd girls. Krishna sends him with his request to the Goddess-mother who made him take a bath. He then comes out transformed into a beautiful and provocative woman named Arjuniya. He meets the *gopis*, with Radha and Krishna. Lord Krishna finds the intense feeling manifested by Arjuniya toward him and drags her into the forest to engage in love play. Here again Arjuna's transformation is reversible. Krishna asks the Goddess to have his new exhausted love companion take a bath and suddenly Arjuniya becomes Arjuna again. The nature of the transformation undergone by Arjuna is not specified because the author's goal is essentially spiritual, to express the infinite love of God through the metaphor of human love. Given this context, it would be difficult to see any validation of homosexual conduct. However, despite the fact the transformation sets the erotic expression in a perhaps more acceptable heterosexual relationship, none of the actors in the *rasa lila* is taken in by the situation, Arjuna, Krishna, Radha, or the Goddess. In the background there still remains some ambiguity in the expression of Arjuna/Arjuniya's desire for Krishna. The heterosexual nature of the deception normalizes the expression of Arjuna's love and devotion for Krishna.

Arjuna's transformation is not surprising when placed in the context of the friendship (*sakhya*) and intimacy that the two share. In the *Mahabharata*, Krishna says that nothing in the world is dearer to him than his friend Arjuna, more valuable than his wife and children.[213] The expression of this intimacy finds its apotheosis in the *Bhagavad Gita*, especially in Chapter XI when Krishna reveals his divine nature to Arjuna, who apologizes for all the disrespect he had demonstrated through his ignorance of this glorious nature, at times when they were very close during meals, rest, and play.[214] Friendship (*sakhya prema*) is an egalitarian form of devotion in the development of *bhakta* literature, such as in the *Srimad Bhagavatam*,[215] Sri Chaitanya's *Charitamrita*,[216] or Sri Rupa Goswami's *Bhakti Rasamrita Sindhu*.[217] Young male friendships between the *gopa* (shepherd male teens) and Krishna are full of tenderness and sensuality as in song X of the *Srimad Bhagavatam*. These stories serve to highlight this friendship as a metaphor for mystical ecstasy (*sakhya rasa*) experienced by the devout in service of Krishna, joining other forms of mystical ecstasy borrowed from conjugal love or parental care.[218] Krishna's mysticism, particularly within the Gaudhiya Vaishnava movement, has a polysemic structure where homoeroticism can be expressed either in the form of fraternal friendship (*sakhya rasa*) or in the form of conjugal love (*madhurhya rasa*). Chaitanya used to disguise himself as a woman to unite to Krishna in the image of Radha. As so aptly noticed by Wendy Doniger, gender ambiguity mediates the mystical union of a male devotee to a male god. There is, through the use of heterosexual guise or deception, an implicit expression of homosexual eroticism.[219] During his visit to the temple of Jagannath (Krishna) at Puri in Odisha (Orissa), Chaitanya allegedly met Jagannath Das. According to some biographers, the two men never parted one from the other. Jagannath Das lived as Radha, Krishna's servant incarnated in the person of Chaitanya, and he often attributed to himself feminine names.[220] Nowadays, inspired by Krishna, the movement GALVA (Gay and Lesbian Vaishnava Association, Inc.) supports the inclusion of gays, lesbians, transsexuals, and other individuals belonging to the third sex. This movement is international, but its reality is mostly American. GALVA struggles against any form of sex discrimination and preaches that homosexuality is just as natural as heterosexuality. While advocating celibacy and chastity as an ideal, GALVA wants monogamous homosexual relationships to be recognized as legitimate unions, in short the recognition of gay marriage.[221]

In the devotion to the Goddess (*Shakti*) current, but with Tantric overtones, Ramakrishna's life and character have attracted considerable controversy, mainly in 1995 with the publication of Jeffrey Kripal's book, *Kali's Child, the Mystical and the Erotic in the Life and Teachings of Ramakrishna*. According to the author, Ramakrishna's experiences of mystical union with the Goddess Kali arise from repressed homosexual desires. In 1996, the book received the "Best Book of the Year Award" by the prestigious American Academy of Religion, which immediately provoked strong reactions in India, especially in Bengal where the saint enjoys immense popularity. The Indian government considered for a moment a ban on the book on its territory and a formal complaint with US authorities.[222] Several passages in Ramakrishna's biography mention the excitement and attraction he demonstrated in the presence of young male disciples.[223] One can certainly question the psychoanalytic method used by Kripal, but I find it difficult to totally eliminate the libidinous tones in Ramakrishna's reactions, as the Order of Ramakrishna sought to do through Swami Tyagananda's pen.[224] The master's reactions during his first encounters with young Narendra, who would eventually become Swami Vivekananda whose teachings experienced considerable success in the West, speak for themselves. Narendra met Ramakrishna for the first time in Dakshineswar, and the latter seemed subjugated by the young man of 18 to such an extent that he could not help crying after they had parted, shouting that the young man's absence had become unbearable.[225] He admitted to being disturbed by other young men, but not with the same intensity.[226] As Narendra's visits became scarce, Ramakrishna became agitated and sad, his heart broken. He did worry about what people thought of such a bond.[227] Narendra appeared disturbed by the master's bizarre behavior when he hand-fed him while describing him as an incarnation of Narayana (Vishnu).[228] During his third visit to Dakshineswar, Narendra witnessed Ramakrishna having some kind of mystical trance and he himself lost consciousness when touched by the master. When he awakened, he felt Ramakrishna's hand caressing his chest.[229] Narasingha Sil, who, contra Kripal, refuses to see Ramakrishna as a homosexual person, says the master was obviously attracted by the physical appearance of young males, particularly their chests and genitals.[230] Swami Akhandananda tells how the teacher, naked as a worm, removed his clothes and lied with him in a bed on the veranda.[231] The biographer M (Mahendranath Gupta) reports that the young, future Swami Trigunatitananda willingly pandered to the desires of Ramakrishna when the latter asked him to get naked.[232] Narasingha Sil gives several examples of the master's joy and excitement in the presence of young men, which leaves no doubt about their homoerotic nature.[233] Worth mentioning is the incident recounted by Shivanath Shastri while he was traveling in a coach to Calcutta with the master. The latter covered his head in the manner of the married women of Bengal and confided in him the feelings of a woman traveling with her lover.[234] I do not wish to enter into a debate about Ramakrishna's homosexuality, but there is enough evidence to confirm he had homoerotic feelings toward his younger disciples, and that this sort of eroticism was deployed as a path to the divine, as in *Bhakti* and *Tantra*.

Among the fascinating stories of sex changes in the *Yogavashsishta Maharamayana* (eighth century AD) is the story of King Shikidhvaja and his wife Chudala.[235] The story presents Chudala as highly educated and well versed in the techniques of meditation, yoga, and *pranayama*. She tries to teach the king the ways of wisdom, but he gives no credence to the ascetic and intellectual abilities of a woman. Unable to achieve happiness in life, the king decides to renounce the world and retires to the forest without her, probably to accomplish hastily the third stage of life, the *vanaprashta*. Chudala, whom the king has charged to rule the kingdom, one day decides to visit her husband but, through her magical powers, transformed as a young Brahmin with the name Kumbhaka. He teaches the king the chief truths and ways to reach eternal wisdom through renunciation and detachment from any form of desire. The two become friends. However, Chudala/Kumbhaka feels a strong sexual desire for the king and invents a ploy to bring the king to bed without revealing his true identity. He tells the king that the wise Durvasa has cast a spell forcing him to transform each night into a woman named Madanika. The king continues to resist his advances, and Madanika/Kumbhaka asks the reason why. Since he is now in complete control of his desires, how could a single liaison with her make him lose all the energy accumulated by asceticism? The king yields to her sexual advances, and they meet every night and have sex. Finally, Madanika/Kumbhaka reveals her true identity and the king returns to rule the kingdom in the company of Chudala, to whom he expresses his gratitude for showing him the path to liberation. The *Yogavashsishta Maharamayana* teaches the superiority of the path of the householder (*grihastha*) and the prospects for women to attain salvation, contrary to the creed of orthodox Brahmanism. Although Chudala must be transformed into a man to discuss ways of spiritual release with her husband, in the end, all genders become illusory as Kumbhaka/Madanika reveals his true identity. In this story, gender fluidity allows for the expression of a thinly veiled homosexuality since Shikidhvaja knows that the Madanika he meets in the night is no one else but his friend Kumbhaka he associates with during the day. The friendship between these two men simply turns into something else overnight.

The gods also experience sex changes. Thus, Vishnu turns into a woman, the enchantress Mohini, to attract demons and get the elixir of immortality (*amrita*).[236] The demons counterattack and Vishnu takes back his male form to defeat them with his disk of fire. The story of Vishnu's transformation does not stop here. Shiva, who heard about this feat from Narada, asks Vishnu to transform into Mohini. Shiva then becomes sexually aroused at the sight of her, and rapes her before the eyes of his wife Parvati, who looks down in shame. A child is born of this relationship, Mahashata.[237] Pretty much the same story is told in the *Bhagavata Purana* with Shiva being aware of the deception and returning to his senses after the act. He does not seem to experience any discomfort (*avridam*) following his action.[238] Difficult to say whether there is penetration as Mohini struggles, but Shiva grabs her hair and holds her in his arms, like the elephant bull copulating with its mate, says the text. Is it an anal or vaginal intercourse? In all probability, the position is from behind. Whatever the level of alteration undergone by Vishnu, transsexualism or transvestism, we'll never know; the story clearly has some homosexual flavor. The desire to be sexually aroused is certainly not absent from Shiva's intentions when he asked Vishnu to temporarily take the form of the enchantress. It may be that Shiva, blinded by the heat of passion, loses the true identity of the object of his desire; he is nevertheless aware at the very start that the play has a sexual character. Vanita, following Doniger, mentions a Telugu version of the story that shows Vishnu recovering his male identity in the middle of the act while Shiva continues his work.[239]

The legend of Mohini as told by the Puranic literature is the result of a theological attempt at reconciling Vaishnava and Saiva cults. It took a distinct turn in Southern India. At Sabarimala in Kerala, an annual pilgrimage takes place to honor the son born of the union of Shiva and Mohini, Mahashata, who is called Ayappa in the south. According to the *Bhuthanathopakhyanam*, and hymns in Malayalam called *Ayyappan Pattukal*, the child was found near the river Pamba by the king of Pandalam, Rajasekhera, who raised him and named him Ayappa.[240] He became a skilled warrior to defend the kingdom and developed a friendship with Vavar, a Muslim soldier. The king wanted him to become the heir to his kingdom, but Ayappa retired as an ascetic bachelor into the forest. The pilgrimage lasts for 41 days from November to January and yearly attracts millions of men who identify with Ayappa by practicing austerities and abstinence. Some authors notice in this cult homoerotic tones that they explain by the lack of women on the scene and some misogyny associated with Ayappa's rejection of marriage and his fondness for his male friendships, in particular for his companion Vavar.[241] In fact, the pilgrimage to Sabarimala is closely linked to marriage and procreation, despite its appearances. As noticed more than once, eroticism and sexuality never stray from its opposite pole, asceticism. Ayappa's cult allows householders to transform as ascetics briefly and identify with a hypermasculine model throughout their participation in the pilgrimage, which is physically tremendously demanding. This is somehow a form of spiritual renewal for men as well as a celebration of masculinity.[242]

Ayappa's birth without a mother is not uncommon in Hindu literature as the god Kartikeya, also known as Skanda or Murugan in the south, was born from Shiva's sperm that was drunk by Agni.[243] Ruth Vanita opens new perspectives on the fertility of homosexual unions from these myths about childbirth from same-sex parents. She deals primarily with the birth of the hero Bhagirata, king of Kosala, who brought the river Ganga on earth from the celestial regions of Mount Meru. In Bengali versions of the *Padma Purana* and of the *Ramayana* by the fourteenth-century poet Krittivasa, Bhagiratha was born from the loving union of two women and the etymology of his name is related to the fact that he came from the union of two vulvas.[244]

Some of today's gays connect with Ayappa or Skanda, but there are also other legends about Mohini acting mainly as foundational myths for homosexuals, transvestites, and transsexuals in southern India. Several local festivals in Tamil Nadu, as at Melattur or Yervadi, showcase the Aravan Kalabali, the sacrifice of Arjuna's son Aravan, especially with a dance where female parts are held by men. This sacrifice was offered to the goddess Kali to ensure the victory of the Pandavas in the great battle of Kurukshetra. Aravan agreed to sacrifice himself if he was first permitted to marry. As the union would not endure, he found no candidate and then Krishna appeared as the enchantress Mohini to satisfy Aravan's request, and he was beheaded the following morning. This legend is found only in the Tamil versions of the *Mahabharata*.[245] At Kuvakkam, a small village not far from Chennai, is the temple dedicated to Kuttandavar Aravan. At full moon in the month of Chittirai (mid-April to mid-May) in the Tamil calendar, an annual festival is held where thousands of transvestites or transsexuals, or *hijras* called *alis* or *Aravanis* in the south, symbolically recreate Mohini's marriage to Aravan.[246] The *Aravanis* are adorned with bridal ornaments, and then wedded to Krishna by a priest who performs the marriage rites. It is also an opportunity for many men playing Aravan's role to have sex with the "one night Mohinis."[247] A similar event is held annually at Pillaiyarkuppam, near Pondicherry.[248] At Saundatti in Karnataka, devotion to the goddess Yellamma or Renuka leads some men to dress up in feminine garments to perform rituals at temples dedicated to her. These men, called *jogappas*, live dressed as women in memory of the elder son of Yellamma; this son refused to obey the orders of his father Jamadagni, who asked him to behead his mother who he suspected of having succumbed to the charms of a *gandharva* (male spirit).[249] They became eunuchs after a spell cast by their father. The *jogappas* do not undergo ritual castration (*nirvan*), unlike many *hijras* or *aravanis*. It must be underlined that many villagers participating in these festivals may have sex with *alis* only to become widowers, as their ritual marriage enables the completion of Aravan's sacrifice to Kali. Hidden behind transvestism implied in the ritual Krishna/Mohini figure, the villagers vow a genuine cult to *kshatriya* masculinity. The situation is quite different with the *alis* whose transformation is permanent. *Alis* have increased in number since the last 50 years, especially in the Kuvakkam festival, which is an occasion for them to meet and discuss social and political issues related to their condition.[250]

The *hijras*, who may be hermaphrodites, eunuchs, or mere transvestites, worship the goddess Bahuchara Mata, whose main temple is located at Ahmedabad in Gujarat.[251] According to a legend, ritual castration was originally practiced by Bahuchara Mata on the prince she had just married who refused to sleep with her saying he was neither male nor female.[252] Another legend tells of a king who had no son and turned to the goddess to get one. The latter granted his prayer, but he fathered an impotent son named Jetho. One night, the goddess appeared to him in a dream, commanded him to cut off his genitals and dress as a woman. Since then, impotent men experience the same call from the goddess and become *hijras*.[253] They also rely on the *Ramayana* to support their lifestyle. According to their version of the text, when Rama left the kingdom of Ayodhya, his subjects decided to follow him out of solidarity, angry with King Dasaratha's decision to send him into exile with Sita. Rama chose exile because the king had given in to pressure from his wife Kaikeyi who wanted her son Bharata to be crowned instead of Rama. He begged the subjects to return to Ayodhya, which they did, with the exception of those who were neither man nor woman and stayed to await his return on the shores of the river Ganga.[254] Faced with such an expression of solidarity, Rama promised they would become kings in the age of *Kali Yuga*.

Arjuna/Brihanalla, the transvestite dancer and hero of the *Mahabharata*, is an emblematic figure for the *hijras*. As Arjuna/Brihanalla participated as a dancer at weddings and births in the court of King Virata, the *hijras* are called upon to perform rites and ceremonies of blessing, with songs and dances, in homes where a male child is born. They also participate in certain rituals associated with sexuality and fertility in the newlyweds' houses.[255] The ceremonial functions they perform have a direct relationship with their ambiguous sexuality. The fact that they are not procreative beings gives them the ability to accumulate *tapas* like the ascetics or *sannyasin*.[256] Arjuna gives up his marriage to King Virata's daughter but prepares her for her role as bride and mother. Just as Shiva's castration turned out to be creative for the whole universe, Arjuna's renunciation becomes a source of fertility for princess Uttara who married his son Abbhimanyu. She will give him a unique son, Parikshit. Alf Hiltelbeitel persuasively demonstrates the similarities between Arjuna/Brihanalla and Shiva, the ascetic and the erotic, or in his androgynous appearance or body (*Ardhanarisvara*).[257] The *hijras* expect to be a religious community dedicated to celibacy but the truth is quite different since many of them do sell their sexual services to heterosexual men and sometimes live with *panthis*.[258] This does not prevent people from calling for their services in the major stages of life when sexuality and fertility are at the forefront. Precisely because they belong to the third sex, unable to procreate, they transcend the traditional social categories reserved for married people and form a marginal social group, sometimes respected or feared and most of the time despised.

It is difficult to have a clear idea of the number of *hijras* or *aravanis* who live on the Indian territory, even though the census of India 2011 included for the first time the possibility for a person to declare one's gender as "other." It is still too soon to evaluate the impact this will have on the *hijras*' lives. The figures range from 50,000 to 1 million, but the reality is probably somewhere between 500,000 and 1 million.[259] Most authors cannot provide accurate statistics on the percentage of young people taking refuge in their community who undergo complete castration, that is, the removal of the testes and penectomy. Based on interviews with several *hijras* conducted by Zia Jaffrey, the 15- or 16-year-old males enter the "*hijra* family" because they want to become women or in some cases because they are hermaphrodites. After a three-year probation with the master (*guru*), in principle the disciple (*chela*) undergoes ritual emasculation and is officially received in the community. In the *hijra* mentality, a true *hijra* must undergo the surgery, except the hermaphrodite. Those who are not castrated are considered *zenanas* (transvestites) or *kothis*, not *hijras*. However, according to Ashok Row Kavi of the Humsafar Trust in Mumbai, an education and health intervention team for men who have sex with men, 85 percent of the *hijra* population has not undergone the operation. Serena Nanda says that many youngsters join the community after having had homosexual experiences during which they played the passive role in anal intercourse. They usually find in the group a purpose and an environment that facilitates the expression of their sexual preference for men.[260] Belonging to the *hijra* family is based on a multitude of reasons; some more rarely related to their congenital condition (hermaphrodites or intersexuality), but more often to a psychological condition, the feeling of being a woman in a male body, or having a preference for the same sex. Anthropologist Gayatri Reddy has studied *hijras* and *kothis* from the Hyderabad area and has shown how *hijra* identity is a complex phenomenon that goes beyond gender or belonging to the third sex. One remains unable to understand the *hijras*, particularly those identified as *badi hijras*—those who officiate at certain ceremonies—without opposing them to the *kothis*; they are particularly distinguished by their adherence to the ideal of renunciation of sexual pleasure evidenced by castration.[261] There is certainly compelling reason to wonder about the impact in the long run of an emerging Indian gay movement on the social reality of twenty-first-century *hijras*. They surely constitute a complex social and cultural phenomenon that can only be explained by a latent homosexual desire, as Carstairs and Sinha have tried to explain.[262] With the modern gay movement, young male Indians explore other ways to live their sexual orientation without having to socialize as part of the *hijra* family or having to identify as *kothi*. These social groupings have been a kind of shelter or host family for people with a marginalized sexuality for centuries and still retain a particular place in the social ensemble. *Hijra* culture is far from disappearing; since 1998 at least six of them have held public office as mayor or deputy mayor. As Gayatri Reddy explains, this new trend will no doubt help this marginalized group to make gains in society, but she also mentions the dangers represented by an ideology that seeks its legitimacy in asceticism and celibacy seen as a nation-building power.[263]

Conclusion

If I were to choose two words to summarize all of my remarks on Hinduism and homosexuality, I would want these two: diversity and tolerance. The first may appear more markedly than the second. Hinduism, in fact, does not reveal itself as a monolithic doctrine of universal truths equally applicable to all, whatever the personal and social situation of the faithful. Several paths to salvation are actually available to each according to social or personal status. In addition, final release or individual salvation cannot be accomplished at the expense of the individual's purpose on earth, including the satisfaction of material, emotional, and sexual needs. As I hope I have shown, some salvation paths do consider various expressions of eroticism as useful means, including homoerotic expressions. Religious symbolism and mythological stories clearly are fertile ground on which they can reveal themselves significantly.[264] Even in the more moralistic literature of the *Dharma Shastras*, homosexual practices are handled without substantial severity. Can it be said that the Hindu culture appears more tolerant of homosexuality? Though it might be true that social intolerance against homosexuality actually manifested itself with British colonization, it still matters to qualify the traditional tolerance toward it. Speaking of tolerance in the context of caste as a trait often associated with Indians or Hindus, Louis Dumont has this succinct phrase: "They will assign a rank, where the West would approve or exclude."[265] Even if the social system marginalizes small groups, they are never entirely rejected and are still part of the whole. In Hindu culture, the duty to raise a family remains a central reality and all those who do not follow up are outside and are somehow pushed to the margins. Ascetics are certainly among them, but they are not alone. There are also widows and persons of the third sex. The concept of *tritiya prakriti* functions as to include in the social body a variety of people who otherwise, because of their desire for the same sex, would have no place.

This perception of homosexuality was developed in a culture where society overrides the individual. In the West the opposite happened, and it is, therefore, not surprising that homosexuality is now seen as a personal choice and sexual orientation as a fundamental right.

Although the gay movement has recently occupied some portion of the Indian homosexual space, its landscape is still well diversified with local particularities in such a way that no universal global gay identity can be affirmed.[266]

2

BUDDHISM

RELIGION

Buddhism is considered the fourth largest religion in the world, with nearly 350 million adherents. This figure could, in fact, be higher for various reasons. First, in some countries such as China, Japan, Vietnam, and Taiwan, religious syncretism stamps popular culture, so that people alternately practice cults inspired by popular beliefs but also blended with more complex religious systems such as Buddhism, Daoism, or Shinto. Political reasons also, especially in the case of communist regimes, can play a role in governmental data underestimating the reality of religion in favor of its secularist propaganda.

Countries where the concentration of Buddhists in relation to the total population is the highest are Thailand[1] (94 percent), Cambodia (90 percent), Myanmar[2] (89 percent), and Sri Lanka[3] (77 percent). It was in this region that Theravada Buddhism (Doctrine of the Elders) blossomed.[4] Mahayana Buddhism developed in China where there are more than 100 million adherents, Japan[5] (44.5 percent), South Korea[6] (47 percent), Vietnam[7] (9.3 percent), and Taiwan[8] (24 percent). India has almost 8 million Buddhists, most of them belonging to the neo-Buddhist movement founded in 1956 by Bhimrao Ramji Ambedkar, an untouchable who marched to the defense of his brothers, the untouchables of Maharashtra. The United States is home to the greatest number of Western adherents, 2.5 to 4 million or 1.6 percent of its population,[9] whereas in Europe, France and Great Britain have the largest number, 650,000 and 180,000, respectively.[10] Canada had 300,345 Buddhists in 2001, including 45,000 in Quebec.[11]

Buddhism is based on the teachings of the historical Buddha, Gautama Siddhartha, born in Kapilavasthu (somewhere on the border of India and Nepal) in 586 BC. He was born into a family belonging to the *kshatriya* clan of the *Shakyas*, son of King Suddhodana and Queen Mahamaya. Tradition has it that his mother conceived him after a white elephant had entered her womb.[12] The young prince led a life free from the vicissitudes and dangers of life. At the age of 16 he married the princess Yashodara with whom he had a son, Rahula. One day he went to a park outside the royal palace and met an old man, a sick person, a corpse being brought to the pyre, and finally a hermit. These four encounters sparked in his mind thoughts about the sufferings that affect sentient beings and the means to address them. He then decided to leave his family and his princely life to devote himself to the pursuit of truth. Clothed in the yellow robe of the ascetic, he wandered homeless. He met several *sannyasins* who educated him in the art of meditation and concentration, but their teachings were incapable of bringing peace of mind or the complete extinguishing (*nibbana*) of human suffering, since meditative states are only temporary.[13] He also engaged in all kinds of austerities, lack of food and sleep, risking his health, but without obtaining the desired peace. On his arrival at Bodh Gaya, he decided to abandon his ascetic practices, fed himself under the shade of a *pipal*—later named the Bodhi tree

(tree of awakening)—and reflected on the middle path, a middle way between the hedonism of his youth and his current asceticism. Mara, the demon of death, tried to keep him away from his meditative state by tempting him with beautiful young temptresses. Touching the ground with the forefinger of his right hand (*bhumisparsha mudra*), the Buddha then called the earth to witness that he would not allow himself be distracted by temptations until he clearly understood the reality of all things—that is to say, not until he fully became enlightened (Buddha). During his meditation, Gautama became aware of his many past lives and understood that the cycle of rebirths obeyed the rules of karmic causality, that is, that the quality of the actions performed during a lifetime affected the quality of future lives. Above all he saw with absolute clarity that personal liberation from this cycle is only brought through a deep understanding of the four noble truths (*cattari ariyasaccani*) that form the foundation of enlightenment. He became the perfectly awakened, *Sammasambuddha*. Gautama then headed to Varanasi, or specifically to a place called Sarnath Isispatana (better known as the "Deer Park") located 13 miles from the former. There, he shared his findings with the five ascetics who had abandoned him in shock when he broke his fast and gave his first lesson, entitled the "Wheel of Law" or *Dhammachakkapavattana Sutta*,[14] which discussed the four noble truths. He then taught the middle path, one that avoids the extremes of hedonism and asceticism and leads to enlightenment, to blissful peace. This is what he called the "Eightfold Path" (*ariya atthangika magga*).

The first noble truth is based on the observation that life is suffering (*dukkha*). Although *dukkha* means the physical or mental suffering associated with illness and death, it also includes all sorts of mental distress arising from the transitional nature of all things, for instance, separation from a loved one or frustration caused by the end of pleasure. As highlighted by Rahula, *dukkha* has a deeper meaning in connection with the impermanence (*anicca*) of all things that exist, with imperfection related to existence, making it a difficult word to translate.[15] The second noble truth focuses on the origin of suffering (*dukkhasamudaya*), thirst (*tanha*), desire or any type of attachment to the pleasures of the senses, to ideas, goods, beliefs, and so on. Desire or craving may also be directed toward existence in itself—the desire to thrive and become somebody (*bhava-tanha*), and sometimes it may even be focused on the removal or cessation of suffering (*vibhava-tanha*).[16] This insatiable desire causes the cycle of rebirths (*samsara*) or the continuity of existence. However, there is a path to salvation through the cessation of suffering (*dukkhanirodha*), the third noble truth. The release of suffering is *nibbana* (Sanskrit: *nirvana*), that is, the total extinction of all forms of lust, desire, or attachment.[17] As the fourth truth, the Buddha taught the path that eventually leads to this method of salvation—the eightfold path: right view, right thought, right speech, right action, right livelihood, right effort, right mindfulness, and right concentration. Shortly after his enlightenment, the Buddha addressed himself for a second time to his five disciples in the "Deer Park" to further clarify his doctrine of impermanence, by teaching the concept of nonself (*anatta*).[18] Here, the Buddha used the concept of the five aggregates[19] (*panca khandha*) to highlight the impermanence of matter, the fact that there is no ego, no self, and no permanent substrate. Indeed, for Buddhism, a being or an individual "is only a combination of ever-changing physical and mental forces of energies, which may be divided into five groups or aggregates (*pancakkhandha*)."[20] The Buddha taught the five aggregates as a heuristic device so that the subject becomes aware of the profound truth of impermanence. In the *Anattalakhana Sutta*, he analyzes in turn each of the aggregates and always concludes the same: not one represents the self as a permanent substrate, whether matter or body (*rupa*), sensation (*vedana*), perception (*sanna*), mental formation of volitional nature (*samkhara*), or consciousness (*vinnana*).

In other words, these aggregates are constantly changing—they come and go without there being any permanent remaining substrate or actor. This was further explained by Buddhaghosa, the great commentator of the fifth century AD: "For there is suffering, but none who suffers; doing exists although there is no doer."[21] All existence is marked by three characteristics (*ti lakkhana*): suffering, impermanence, and nonself.[22] The impermanence of all things brings suffering, and the sufferer has no permanent self.[23]

By reflecting on the changing character of each of the five aggregates, the monk seizes the three characters of existence and reaches an understanding that leads to the termination of the five aggregates, *nibbana*.[24] There is nothing substantial, permanent, no transcendental subject meaning that all existence is conditioned or relative. In other words, any one thing depends on something other than itself to happen. This is the Buddhist doctrine of conditional or codependent origination (*paticca samuppada*).[25] It expresses a principle of causality (*idappaccayata*) according to which the existence of "this" depends on the appearance of "that" (*sati idam hoti imasmim*) or "this" ceases to appear when "that" stops.[26] The interdependence of all forms of existence follows directly from the impermanence of life. The Buddha gave a complete formulation of the conditional coproduction and explained the existence or cycle of rebirths (*samsara*) by using the metaphor of a wheel. The wheel of dharma is made of 12 links or factors (*nidan*) all dependent on each other: (1) ignorance or delusion (*avijja*), (2) volition or motivation (*sankhara*), (3) consciousness (*vinanna*), (4) the physical and mental phenomena (*nama rupa*), (5) the six powers (the five senses and spirit) (*salayatana*), (6) sensory perception and mental health (*phassa*), (7) sensation (*vedana*), (8) desire (*tanha*), (9) attachment (*upadana*), (10) becoming (*bhava*), (11) birth (*jati*), and ultimately (12) decay and death (*jaramarana*).[27] This sequence of conditions is according to the Buddha the reason for suffering and its causes.[28] Ignorance is the first link in this chain that determines the cycle of rebirths and suffering, just as the removal of ignorance allows the termination of karmic formations[29] until the ultimate cessation of suffering.[30] Coconditioned production serves as an explanation for the four noble truths that form an abridgment of Gautama Siddhartha's core teaching. That is why the Buddha deems that he who has grasped his teaching on conditional coproduction understands all of his teaching (*Dharma*).[31] For the monks who asked him to explain the nature of ignorance, the disciple Sariputta explained that ignorance was a form of blindness of the person who did not understand the suffering of sentient beings, its origin, and its causes. His mind is infected with the poisons (*kilesa*) of envy and pleasure of the senses (*lobha, raga*), hatred (*doha*), and ignorance (*avijja, moha*).[32] In fact, the Buddha describes the mental process by which a human being takes roots into existence, clings to it, and fits into the world. Attachment to pleasure and life is the sheer source of selfishness and various conflicts in society.[33]

To stop the blindness that prevents beings from grasping reality as it is—suffering, impermanence, and nonself—the Buddha proposes a method that consists essentially in polishing the mind, getting rid of the poisons that cause attachment. With *vipassana*, an analytical meditation technique of careful observation, the person entering the path focuses on the experienced physical, emotional, and intellectual processes and dissects them in order to become aware of suffering, impermanence, and nonself.[34] This knowledge or intuitive insight (*panna*) of "reality as-it-is" is accompanied by the observance of a code of ethics (*sila*) and meditation techniques (*jhana, samadhi*). Complementing each other, these are the three components of the salvific path taught by the Buddha, conducive to *nibbana*.[35] For the Buddha, the thoughts behind any action (*kamma*), the intent (*citta*) that leads to action is more salient than the action itself. They leave traces in the mind capable of running the wheel of existence and perpetuating the cycle of rebirths. The Buddha did believe in karmic retribution, but more importantly, the law of karma refers to the individual's ability to act on his future or destiny by cultivating the right intention (volition, *kusala*) and producing a meritorious action. The same person may otherwise entertain an unwholesome intention (*akusala*), thus producing evil actions.[36] The technique taught by the Buddha implies vigilance at all times in regard to mental processes in order to keep the mind pure, free from any form of desire or attachment.[37] Liberation or *nibbana* is primarily a personal issue, that is, a work on the self. The teaching of Buddha is a safe haven, a guide, and whoever enters the path must rely on oneself since there are no absolutes able to save.[38] In this regard, Gautama Siddhartha warns against all forms of dogmatism and servile acceptance of truths based on the authority of sacred writings or respect for reverenced traditions.[39] The discipline imposed by this approach implies a life of monastic renunciation of pleasure, devoted to studying, concentration, and meditation to reach the ultimate goal, arahantship—a state where suffering is eliminated, the cycles of rebirth ended, and *nibbana* attained. That is why the Buddha founded a monastic order and conferred ordination to the first monks (*bhikkhus*): Yasa,[40] Sariputta, Mogallana,[41] Maha Kassapa,[42] and his cousin Ananda who became his secretary.[43] Because of Ananda's insistence, the Buddha admitted, not without hesitation, women (*bhikkhuni*) into the order.[44] The monastic community (*sangha*) of monks and nuns, based on celibacy and renunciation, in the eyes of the Buddha, is the ideal environment to achieve arahantship. He does not, however, neglect the men and women who continue to live in the world. Thus, Yasa's parents became the first lay followers to embrace the three jewels (*tiratana*): the Buddha, his teachings (*dharma*), and the *sangha*.[45] The story of the conversion of the rich merchant Anathapindika[46] during his meeting with the Buddha further defines the role of the laity. Lay persons accumulate merit through generosity (*dana*) to the *sangha* in order to ensure the material life of the monks who devote themselves entirely to the practice of the eightfold path.[47] Like all lay people who submitted their lives to the teachings of the four noble truths, Anathapindika attained the first stage of enlightenment, the *sotapanna*, which guaranteed him a maximum of seven rebirths before attaining *nibbana*.[48] While the monks subject themselves to a comprehensive and strict code of discipline made of 227 rules (311 for nuns), the *Patimokkha*, the laity (*upasaka*) observes the *panca sila*, the five defenses or rules of conduct for monks and laity: (1) do not destroy life, (2) do not steal, (3) proper sexual conduct, (4) no lies, and (5) no alcoholic beverages.[49] The days of full moon, new moon, and days of the first and last quarters are called *uposatha*. They provide an opportunity for the faithful to purify themselves and improve their spirit of detachment by practicing the eight precepts (*sila atthanga*), the five defenses mentioned earlier with additional three: (6) do not eat after noon until the following morning, stay away from entertainment such as music or dance, (7) do not use perfume and jewellery, and (8) sleep on the ground.[50] During *uposatha*, the third precept practiced by a lay person then becomes sexual abstinence (*brhamachariya*) just as for the monks. On the days of new and full moon, the laity comes to the monastery (*vihara*) to hear the monks' sermons or to meditate, to read scriptures, or listen to the monks recite the *Patimokkha*.

What we have just presented is a summary of the Buddha's teaching, as found in the Pali Canon, the *Tripitaka* or the three baskets.[51] These canonical texts were established after Gautama Siddhartha's death, at the first council of Rajagaha. It gathered some 500 *arahants* three months after his death. Theravada Buddhism took shape at this council and at the second council, held at Vaisali nearly a hundred years later. It does not accept any other authority than the writings of the Pali Canon. Many arguments surrounding monastic discipline were the reason for these early councils. During the second council at Vaisali, the first schism led to another school of thought, the *Mahasanghika*, which appeared to be less severe in matters of monastic discipline and more responsive to the needs of the laity. This schism is at the origin of Mahayana Buddhism, which preaches the ideal of the bodhisattva as a method of salvation.

The bodhisattva is that compassionate (*karuna*) being who, unlike the *arahant* fully released from *samsara*, vowed to delay his entry into *nibbana* until all beings have attained enlightenment. The bodhisattva's career is open to lay people as well as monks, provided that they both engage on the path to Buddhahood, going through several stages. These stages are described in particular in the *Ten Stages Sutra* by Vasubandhu.[52] To reach *nirvana*, the Bodhisattva must cultivate certain perfections (*paramitas*) that will guide him through his samsaric existence.[53] The ideal of the Mahayana Bodhisattva conceives the path to perfection pursued by the *arahant* as being too individualistic, too goal-oriented, and too analytical. It proposes a more radical doctrine—the emptiness of all things—including that of *nirvana*, the four noble truths, the five aggregates or any analytical tool used to express the idea of nonsubstantiality. This vision is exposed briefly but clearly by the Bodhisattva Avalokitesvara to Sariputra in the *Heart Sutra*.[54] The *Diamond Sutra*'s message also points in the same direction: words such as "Buddha" and "Bodhisattva" have no substantial reality but are means to guide the practitioner to enlightenment. This sutra explains how emptiness is at the heart of the bodhisattva's compassion. The bodhisattva devotes his life to the salvation of sentient beings without any form of attachment, since everything is empty (*sunya*).[55] As stated by the great teacher Nagarjuna (India, second–third centuries AD), founder of the *Madhyamika* School, the concept of emptiness was preached by the Buddha to liberate the minds from wrong views. It is only a means, and, as such, does not point to any substantial reality.[56] In terms of absolute truth (*paramartha*), nothing is final—everything is changing, without permanence, and all the analytical tools that are used to explain the phenomena on the conventional plan (*samvriti*) only have descriptive value without any ontological status. In fact, the method of "nonresidence" (not dwelling on anything) taught by Nagarjuna, following the literature of the *Prajnaparamita Sutras*,[57] consists in defeating the mind by denying it any kind of support to assert neither existence nor nonexistence.[58] From the standpoint of the absolute, emptiness that constitutes the reality of phenomena has no separate existence; it is the only reality. *Samsara* and *nirvana* may be differentiated epistemologically but, in fact, they are identical as there is nothing beyond the phenomena.[59] The Theravada ideal of the *arahant* attaining full release (*parinibbana*) from rebirths at the time of death supposes duality between *samsara* and *nirvana*. This is transcended in the Mahayana perspective. There is nothing outside the emptiness of phenomena and nirvana consists of exactly understanding this truth; the conditioned and unconditioned are two sides of the same coin. Enlightenment is possible for any being because the *bodhi* principle is dormant in every being, ready to be awakened.[60]

This notion of emptiness gives birth to early forms of even more anti-intellectual practices in the Chinese *Chan* School, better known in the West under its Japanese name *Zen*. Although traditionally attributed to Bodhidharma, an Indian monk who had recently visited China, the real founder of this school was Hongren (弘忍; 601–674 AD) and his disciples, Shenxiu (神秀; 606–706) and Huineng (慧能; 638–713). Bodhidharma and *Chan* patriarchs reject the study of scriptures, rituals, and invocations to the Buddha and develop an intuitive approach to *bodhi* through meditation (*dhyana* becomes *chan* in Chinese) and the master's use of aporia (*gong'an* 公案, Japanese *koan*), in response to questions from his disciples. Bodhidharma favored the practice of contemplating the wall in a sitting position rather than the study of sutras to bring the mind beyond any form of duality and capture the original nature of everything.[61] Legend has it that Bodhidharma meditated in front of a wall at the Shaolin monastery for nine years, and most schools encourage *Chan* sitting in front of a wall (*zuochan*, 坐禅, Japanese *zazen*), which allows the mind to reach a state of thoughtlessness (*wu nian*, 無念). *Gong'an* serves to defeat conceptualization and let the mind grasp the true nature of phenomena. For example, when the meditator Dongshan asked his master what a Buddha is, the latter replied: "Three pounds of flax!"[62]

Chan developed into several schools in China and later migrated to Japan to take different forms. The variations are due to various reasons, but one of the most remarkable difference concerns gradual or sudden enlightenment. Some pretend that enlightenment is sudden. This is the case in China with Huineng and the *Linji Yixuan* School (臨濟義玄; ninth century AD), developed by Eisai in Japan and known as *Rinzai Zen*. Others favor a gradual approach such as Shenxiu, and the *Caodong* School (曹洞宗) founded by Dongshan Liangjie (洞山良价; 807–869) and the *Soto* School in Japan founded by Dogen (1200–1253). Without going into details of the controversy,[63] I will only say that Shenxiu advocates a meditative method based on continuous efforts to purify the mind, to free it from impurities and wrong views so that it becomes like a mirror, reflecting the true nature of things, the emptiness of all things and all thoughts.[64] It is precisely this effort in sitting meditation to attain enlightenment, this assiduous and disciplined pursuit that Huineng questions in *The Platform Sutra*. In a famous passage, he rejects Shenxiu's assertion that mind is intrinsically pure and reflects Buddhahood, as a mirror being constantly polished. The search for spontaneous awakening, which somehow manifests perfect nonduality, gives rise to forms of expression based on an iconoclastic rejection of any doctrine or any discipline or morality, thus opening the door to quietism or laxity. Without doubt, Linji's aphorisms (*gong'an*) illustrate the intentions of this type of Buddhism seeking sudden enlightenment in the ordinary man's concrete, everyday life (*wuwei zhenren*, 無位真人), beyond any duality: "Followers of the Way, as to the Buddha dharma, no effort is necessary. Just be ordinary, with nothing to do—shit, piss, wear clothes, eat food, and lie down when you're tired."[65] The method used by Linji in dialogues with his novices was often a shock treatment because he often answered questions by one shout or a slap.

The bodhisattva's image opened the door to more conventional forms of worship directed at this being of universal compassion, which filled the resolve to save humanity. One of these cults figures in China is the devotion to the Buddha of Infinite Light, *Amitabha, Amituo Fo* (阿彌陀佛), *Amida* in Japan and *Tinh Do* in Vietnam. His story is told in the *Sutra of Infinite Life*.[66] It narrates the story of King Dharmakara who became a monk after his meeting with the Buddha Lokesvaraja. As a bodhisattva, he made 48 vows, and then after a life of compassion, he became the *Buddha Amitabha*, ruling on a paradise located in the West, the Pure Land on which shines his infinite light. The Pure Land School (*Jintu cong* 淨土宗, *Jodoshu* Japanese) took roots in China in the fifth century, and progressed in the sixth century under Tanluan (曇鸞; 476–542) and Huiyuan (慧遠). It appeared later in Japan during the twelfth–thirteenth centuries with Honen and Shinran (1173–1261).[67] This popular form of Buddhism without monasticism has grown significantly in China, Taiwan, Japan, Korea, and Vietnam. For this school, the mere invocation of *Amitabha* (*nianfo*, Japanese *nembutsu*) may itself constitute an effective means for the practitioner to ensure rebirth in the Pure Land.[68] Next to the difficult path to salvation based on personal effort there is an easier path based on faith in *Amitabha*'s power to secure his adepts' rebirth in the Pure Land, and ultimately lead them without difficulty to enlightenment.[69] In Pure Land Buddhism, the bodhisattva Guanshiyin (觀世音) or Guanyin (Avalokitesvara in Sanskrit) is by *Amitabha*'s side, happy to help the practitioner who seeks entry into the Pure Land.[70]

SEXUALITY

The Buddha's diagnosis on human suffering, his analysis of its causes, as well as his philosophy of detachment make the connection to sensual pleasure and sexual desire, to say the least, problematic. The *Makkata Sutta* tells the story about a monkey who had ventured into an area also frequented by men and whose four limbs and muzzle got caught in a hunter's trap. This allegory aims to teach monks about the dangers of the five senses, the gateway through which the subject experiences pleasure. With the experience of sensory satisfaction, the person, at the same time, wishes to replicate it or make it last.[71] According to the Buddha, gratification of the senses is not in itself a problem, but craving for pleasure (*kama-tanha*), desire, and dedication to pleasure (*kama-upadana*) is.[72] Addressing a lay person named Anathapindika, Gautama readily acknowledges the pleasure to own and enjoy property.[73] In his sermon to Sigalaka, he condemns not so much pleasure as he does craving (*tanha*).[74] The only reason the Buddha puts the blame on pleasure is because it is a source of attachment. We want it to last, and then, finally, it becomes a source of frustration or suffering because its sheer nature is transitory.[75] One who avoids sensual pleasures, as dangerous as a snake, will become free from any form of attachment and suffering.[76]

For the monk who pursues the Theravada ideal of the *arahant*, different concentration techniques can help him uncover the true nature of pleasure of the senses, that is to say, fugacity and frustration in the long term.[77] One of these techniques aimed at relinquishing the pleasures of the senses is to meditate on the body by visualizing it as a sore (*ganda*) with nine openings exuding pus and stench,[78] a pile of bones, organs, fluids, and waste.[79] Beauty attracts and nurtures sensuality and desire (*kamacchanda*),[80] and that is why meditation on the most repugnant aspects of the body is used to remove the monk's sexual desires.[81] The Buddha's analysis is quite sharp. He knows that to break away from pleasure, countering physiological satisfaction is simply not enough. Formation of mental impressions (*sankhara*) associated with sensations should also be put to rest because they are the source of the desire to feel pleasure and to see it repeated.[82] The Buddha's discourse to the monk Malunkya highlights the role of imagination and mind in the appearance of desire and sexual appetite. He stresses the importance of mindfulness (*vipassanna*) on the sensations, perceptions, and feelings of pleasure or displeasure, in order to become aware of their impermanence. By this technique, the monk comes to detach himself.[83]

Sexuality, both for male and female, cannot be reduced to its genital components. It uses multiple senses and sensory strategies, such as softness of the voice, singing, perfumes, and sweet talk. Fondling brings about the greatest bond between men and women.[84] Sexual pleasure is probably the most intense pleasure and attraction to physical appearance can make men and women prisoners of their desires.[85] Buddhist detachment requires the practitioner who wants to attain *nibbana* to abandon not only any expression of sensuality and sexual desire, but also all forms of intimate life—love for a dear one as well as family life.[86] Sensual desire (*kamacchanda*), passion (*raga*), love (*pema*), delight in pleasures (*rati*), affection (*sineha*), and friendship (*samsagga*) are a source of thirst (*tanha*) and attachment (*upadana*), and must be eliminated.[87] Lay adepts are faced with marital and family duties and the level of moral perfection required of the monk cannot be expected from them.[88] The *Khaggavisana Sutta*, therefore, proposes as a model of perfection the solitary life of a rhinoceros without wife, children, or companions.[89] In the tradition of Theravada Buddhism, the spiritual path of the celibate monk is of greater value than that of the lay man.[90]

Without doubt, Theravada Buddhism has a different set of rules of conduct in sexual matters for the monk or nun and the lay person. First consider the precepts that should guide the life of the Buddhist laity. Prince Siddhartha was married to Yashodhara and had a son, Rahula. We honestly do not know much about his sex life. His biography, the *Buddhacarita*, refers to an atmosphere of eroticism and lust during his life as a young prince surrounded in the palace by beautiful courtesans. His father made specific arrangements so that everything in the palace was designed to drive him away from the religious vocation that Asita had predicted.[91] One can certainly imagine, as John Stevens[92] does, the prince leading a life of pleasure among courtesans and concubines expert in the art of love before embarking on his spiritual journey. However, one needs to be cautious with this interpretation. Hagiographic accounts tend to embellish and amplify a situation to prove their point, in this case the Buddha's abandonment of sensual pleasures because of their impermanence and the frustration they inevitably bring. Buddhist texts never refer to the couple, Siddhartha and Yashodara, as an example for the married laity.[93] Moreover, marriage itself is not considered a sacrament or a religious institution.

What is the essence of the third precept to which the laity is also subject? Is it meant to prevent sexual misconduct? The Sri Lankan monk Nayanatiloka considers that the Pali words *kamesu micchacara*—which could be translated literally as "misconduct in regard to sensual pleasures"—only refer to adultery or sexual relations with minors or with whom one has custody.[94] Some authors think that the expression *kamesu micchacara* refers to immoderate use of the five senses, whether or not with a person considered a legitimate partner and is not limited to adultery.[95] However, the interpretation given by Nayanatiloka Thera appears to be based on Buddhagosha's commentary on the *Sammaditthi Sutta* where the meaning of the expression is limited to sexual relations with 20 categories of protected or already committed women.[96] This reading matches Gautama's suggestion that fidelity in marriage is a pledge to eternal happiness for the couple, while a person's infidelity leads to self-destruction.[97] For others, the third precept means essentially nonconsensual sexual practices or practices that jeopardize social harmony because they cause harm to a third party: the husband, the spouse, or the family.[98] This precept, therefore, seeks to protect the believer from any unworthy action (*kamma akusala*) whenever it is rooted in envy, the search for multiple pleasures of the senses or in some cases violence or intimidation, with wrong caused to others.

The third precept is putting forward a notion of responsible sexuality, personal responsibility for one's own spiritual growth, and responsible attitude vis-à-vis one's partner. This attitude is built into the general understanding of the moral law, which says that any act (*kamma*) inevitably produces results. It has nothing to do with any concept of defiance against a divine command. The third precept does not itself allude to homosexual or heterosexual acts that would be considered against nature because of their nonprocreative character—acts such as masturbation, sodomy, bestiality, or oral sex. This may be explained by the fact that sexual desire is intimately linked to the cycle of rebirths.[99] The imperative for procreation is not an essential teaching of the Buddha, an approach that has sometimes created tensions in some societies with other systems of thought that value family and generation as a necessary means to maintain the cult of ancestors, for instance, Confucianism in China. Conversely, the Buddhist view, when compared to other religious systems such as Christianity or Islam, encouraged contraception campaigns in some cases as in Sri Lanka or Thailand.[100] The position of some contemporary Buddhist leaders about masturbation, fellatio, sodomy, and homosexuality seems all the more surprising as it appears to be based on a conception of sexuality with procreation as its goal. Thus, the Dalai Lama believes that all sexual practices when the genitals are not used for the purpose for which they were intended by nature constitute sexual misconduct upheld by the third precept, be they homosexual or heterosexual.[101] The Dalai Lama's interpretation raises many questions especially when he admits not being able to support it with authoritative Buddhist texts.[102] He, however, says that some Tibetan lamas, particularly Gampopa (1079–1153), believed that heterosexual sodomy and fellatio, cunnilingus, as well as homosexual relations do violate the third precept.[103] This interpretation pretty much follows the definition of unlawful sexual intercourse established by Vasubandhu in his *Abhidarmakosha*.[104] The Tibetan lama Longchenpa (1308–1364) included masturbation under sexual misconduct in his *Treasury of Natural Perfection*. One of the most celebrated contemporary Thai Buddhists, the monk Buddhadasa, presents a controverting view of sexuality when he tries to impose strict sexual morality to lay adepts, similar to that described in the code of monastic discipline, with the distinction that married people should have sex solely for reproductive purposes.[105]

Celibacy and sexual abstinence (*brahmachariya*) may lead to the cessation of suffering and are, therefore, a necessity for anyone who pursues the ideal of the *arahant*. The code of monastic discipline (*Vinaya Pitaka*) describes rules that monks or nuns must follow to achieve the ideal of purity of body and mind. The first of the 227 rules of the *Patimokkha* forbids the *bhikkhu* to have sex (*methune dhamma*) with a man, woman, or animal.[106] This is a major offense for which the guilty should suffer expulsion (*parajika*) from the monastic community.[107] What kind of sexual misconduct entails such consequence? The expression *methune dhamma* is broad and vague. The *Suttavibhanga*, which contains the *Patimokkha*'s 227 rules, comment, word for word (*padabhajaniya*), each and every rule. Penetration, oral sex, bestiality,[108] and sodomy mean exclusion, whatever the sex of those involved, provided there is penetration into one of three orifices,[109] at least to the equal length of a sesame seed.[110] The penalty seems to apply as much to the monk who plays an active role as to one who plays a passive role. Exclusion may be incurred by the monk who practices autofellatio or who manages to insert his penis into his anus.[111] As always, there are exceptions to the rule, and penetration in other orifices of the body (e.g., an eye or a wound) is not a major but a serious offense (*thullacaya*) that must be confessed by the offender to two or three monks, in a prescribed form (*desana*).[112] If penetration occurs in inanimate objects a smaller penance is required, the *dukkata*.[113]

Any form of hugging or contact with sexual intent with other parts of the body such as breasts or buttocks of a woman does not entail exclusion since no penetration occurs, but the fault is still considered sufficiently serious to require notice to the *sangha*; hence the name of this fault *sanghadisesa*.[114] The *sangha* meets and hears the confession. The offender is then sentenced to a period of six days or more—days that can add up depending on how many days he has hidden his fault—and during this time he is under house arrest in the monastery. He loses during this period all his seniority privileges, including the services he would receive from a novice or a monk of less than five years of service and still subject to a probationary period (*nissaya*) under the wing of an older master (*acariya*).[115] However, masturbation ranks first in the list of the 13 faults worthy of consideration by the *sangha*.[116] The story behind this rule deserves to be told because it contrasts with some ideas circulated in the West in the second half of the nineteenth century. The monk Udayin noticed that his colleague Seyyasaka was exceedingly emaciated and disfigured by a life of celibacy taken painfully. He advised him to eat well, sleep well, and masturbate whenever he had to struggle with thoughts of a sexual nature. Astonished by this counsel, Seyyasaka asked him if this was permitted, and Udayin replied that he indulged in it. Seyyasaka, therefore, followed the monk's advice and quickly looked better, plumper and with a healthy, glowing complexion. His colleagues noticed the change and asked for his recipe. The answer disturbed them and this ultimately led to the enunciation of the rule by the Buddha.[117]

Returning to the comment on the rule itself, which sets out in detail the circumstances that may occur during ejaculation and the 11 types of sexual pleasure, ranging from simple masturbation to ejaculation after gazing at a beautiful woman and so on.[118] In any situation, be it vaginal penetration, masturbation, or other forms of sexual contact, the severity of the rule always gives room for a number of exceptions. They take into account the context in which the act is performed as well as the author's ability to understand and freedom of consent.[119] The *Suttavibangha* excludes all responsibility for forbidden acts committed by a person who has lost his mind.[120] Thus, no fault was attributed to the monk who had fallen asleep in a field and who had sexual intercourse with a woman passing by. Noticing that the monk's tunic was raised, she simply sat on his erect penis![121] Emission of semen (*sukkavvisannhi*) during sleep, or in a dream, or while taking care of one's personal hygiene, or during medical treatment of the genitals does not constitute an offense of the *sanghadisesa* I category, due to their involuntary nature. For the monk to be responsible for an offense of that category, voluntary (*sancetanika*) discharge of semen is required. Thus, the offense committed by the monk who masturbates but does not ejaculate falls under the category of *thullacaya*.[122] The *Suttavibhanga* developed a real casuistry in trying to decipher the true intent of a wrongful act. For example, when a monk ejaculates while looking lustfully at a beautiful woman, or while having with her a conversation containing sexual innuendo, he does not commit a *sanghadisesa* I offense, because he does not masturbate. He is guilty in the first case of a minor fault (*dukkata*) or in the second case of a *sanghadisesa* III offense, that is, sexual innuendo in the presence of a woman.[123]

One can certainly question the basis for all these distinctions made to determine the severity of the incurred misconduct. Nothing suggests that certain sex acts may be more serious than others because they are "against nature," that is to say, they do not follow the procreative purpose of sex. In *Theravada* Buddhism, procreation and family appear as obstacles to spiritual development, which is warranted only by monastic life. The great obstacle to *nibbana* is desire, craving (*tanha*); the continuous search for pleasure. The thwarting of sexual desire may, to some extent, account for the gradation of sins but not entirely. Achieving orgasm and ejaculation are punished more severely by the code of monastic discipline, as the intensity of pleasure may leave traces in the memory and mind of the person compelling him to wish to repeat the experience. However, it is difficult to understand why, in this logic, penetration should be sanctioned more severely than masturbation when orgasm is reached in both cases. Again, I must emphasize that the *Vinaya* forbids any form of vaginal, anal, or oral penetration whether heterosexual or homosexual. This means that the prohibition does not draw the line between procreative vaginal penetration and other forms of penetration. Are these offenses more serious because these sexual practices require a higher degree of physical intimacy or communion with some other person? This sort of intimacy may lead to more clinging (*upadana*) and affection and both belong to the realm of suffering. The entire code of discipline shows a significant distrust vis-à-vis women. The Buddha did regard them as an obstacle to spiritual progress. Several *Patimokkha* rules apply to the monks' behavior in the presence of women, but the most important, aside *parajika* I, is probably *sanghadisesa* II. It prohibits touching a woman, holding her by the hand, or stroking her hair with sexual intent. The penalties are less severe (*dukkata*) when a monk acts with the same intention in respect to a man, but a little more serious (*thullacaya*) without convening the *sangha* in the case of a *pandaka*, that is to say, a man who has sex with men.[124]

Mahayana Buddhism developed a quite different attitude toward sexuality, which was much less severe in nature. The *Teaching of Vimalakirti* features a married layman and father of a son, Vimalakirti, who taught the Buddha's two disciples, Subhuti and Sariputra, a path to enlightenment without monastic discipline. This new path no longer eliminates the passion of love but draws from it the spiritual energy to transform it into a love free from all forms of desire or attachment—a universal compassion for all beings. As Faure so aptly said, the bodhisattva, unlike the *arahant*, does not want his life to come to an end to attain *nibbana*. Awakened, his mind purified, he positions himself in the world, free from any form of dualism, selfishness, and attachment.[125] The same ideas are also taught by a laywoman, the Indian Queen Srimala in the *Sutra on The Lion's Roar of Queen Srimala*.[126] John Stevens (1990) also mentions other lesser-known Mahayana texts in which women bodhisattvas make use of sexual pleasure as a skill (*upaya*) to attract men by first giving them pleasure and then teaching them the true Dharma. Among these texts, the *Da Zhuanyan Famen Jing* (大莊嚴法門經) tells the story of a courtesan nicknamed "woman shining like gold and brilliant by her virtue" (*Shengjinse Guangmingde Nü*, 勝金色光明德女). Speaking with Manjusri, a disciple of Gautama, she stands up for sexuality because, without it, there would be nobody to experience enlightenment.[127] The *Gandavyuha Sutra* portrays Prince Sudhana during a pilgrimage to India to collect lessons from 53 teachers, many of whom are lay persons and women. He meets with Vasumitra, a prostitute who uses the sensory experience of kissing and hugging as a means (*upaya*) to lead people to enlightenment.[128] The legend of the bodhisattva Yulan Guanyin (鱼篮观音) "Guanyin with a fish basket," popularized during the Tang dynasty, makes her a seductress who uses her charms to attract men, and ultimately delivers them forever from desire. The bodhisattva's use of sensuality is also found in homosexual contexts, as indicated by Bernard Faure.[129] Thus, a Japanese tale of the fourteenth century, *Chigo Kannon Engi*, tells the story of the bodhisattva Kannon (Japanese version of Avalokiteshvara) who hears the repeated requests of an old monk who was longing for a young acolyte. Kannon takes the shape of a young acolyte (*chigo*).[130] He then lives with the monk who falls madly in love with him, and mourns his untimely death.[131] Legends often attribute the power of homosexual seduction to the bodhisattva Manjusri.[132]

Experiences of often dreamed or sublimated sexual encounter understood as a way to achieve enlightenment may be described as mild reactions to the austerity of early Buddhism. More vexatious occurrences of sexual transgression are used to indicate the superiority of spontaneous awakening. These occurrences short-circuit the discipline and observance of morality. The *Chan* monk Tengteng puts it thus: "Passions are awakening; the pure lotus grows in mud and manure."[133] In his *Treaty on the Great Virtue of Wisdom*, Nagarjuna tells the story of two bodhisattva monks, Agramati and Prasannendriya. The former was exceedingly observing in discipline and assiduously practiced meditation, but once dead he found himself in hell while his brother, who had preached the attainment of enlightenment (*bodhicitta*) without rejecting sexual pleasure and sensuality, attained Buddhahood.[134] Sex, like consumption of alcohol and meat, often serves as a critique or subversion of the realization method based on effort and discipline in favor of spontaneity in the ordinariness of everyday life. Several accounts of the *Chan* School depict monks engaged in drunkenness and lewdness. Like Faure, one can see in this behavior a certain similarity with that of a trickster[135] figure whose actions often have been ultimately beneficial for humans, even when they violate moral rules. The likeness, however, appears more obvious and natural with the Daoist criticism of Confucian education. While the Confucian model promoted learning and a long apprenticeship, Daoism favored the moral qualities of natural spontaneity (*zi ran* 自然), beyond any form of duality generated by education and the development of the moral subject. In China, during the "Three Kingdoms" period that followed the fall of the Later Han, Daoism inspired several groups and used different ways to criticize the Confucian orthodoxy and its system of values.[136] The "Seven Wise Men of the Bamboo Forest" (*Qixian Zhulin*, 竹林七賢), near the capital Luoyang (洛陽), show a more eccentric and iconoclastic expression of thought than the ideas expressed by Lao Zi and Zhuang Zi. Having taken refuge in the countryside, these musicians, poets, and philosophers pretend to lead a simple and ascetic life capable of leading them to immortality, while, in fact, they often exhibit outrageous behavior and are firm believers in the virtue of wine to achieve natural spontaneity.[137] The two best known are clearly Xi Kang (嵇康) and Ruan Ji (阮籍), often depicted as being drunk and deemed to have been lovers according to the *Shishuo Xinyu* (New Account of Tales of the World, 世說新語).[138] The *Chan* tradition also gives tribute to the eccentricity of "crazy" monks who use transgression of the prohibitions regarding alcohol, meat, and sexual intercourse to teach the emptiness of all phenomena. For them, the monastic rule may even become a source of attachment and thus limit the capture of absolute truth. Thus, the thirteenth-century *Chan* monk from the Lingyin (靈隐) monastery in Hangzhou, Daoji (道濟), also known as Jigong (濟公), slept with prostitutes, ate meat, got drunk, and had fun doing somersaults with a monkey.[139] The *Biographies of Eminent Monks of the Song Dynasty* (*Song Gaoseng Zhuan*, 宋高僧傳) are scattered with details of many eccentricities committed by some of these presumed crazy monks (*kuang*, 狂). For instance, the monk Guangling, who was always drunk, had a strange taste for blood and would unexpectedly kill a dog or a pig.[140] These attitudes show how the bold Mahayanist attitude vis-à-vis the rules of conduct and monastic discipline have changed the rigor of early Buddhism, ill-suited to the cultural context of the Confucian Chinese society. Indeed, Confucianism gives enormous importance to ancestor worship. Family and filial piety is the backbone of its moral edifice. With time, discipline and respect for moral precepts tend to come down to the observance of an internalized rule of conduct, which takes its origin in the Buddha nature residing in every being.[141] The *Brahmajala Sutra* (*Fanwang Jing*, 梵網經) is probably the best example, in the Chinese context, of Mahayanist ease in regard to discipline and adaptation to a Confucian context. This sutra often puts on an equal footing the immense compassion demonstrated by the bodhisattva and filial piety, whereas a monk having sex with a woman, an offense of the *parajika* category, is not anymore excluded from the *sangha*.[142]

A few words about gender and sex roles are needed to conclude this heading on Buddhist attitudes vis-à-vis sexuality. The role and status of women in Buddhism is not straightforward, and perspectives vary according to the school, the times, and especially the sociocultural contexts in which doctrines have evolved—Sri Lanka, Thailand, China, Japan, United States, and so on. Alan Sponberg thinks that early Buddhism showed diverse attitudes toward women. They varied from some form of inclusion at inception that recognized women as spiritual beings capable of attaining *nibbana* to thereafter expressing contempt and women's subordination to men.[143] This hardening could be explained, according to Sponberg, by the development of cenobitic monasticism, which included a women's wing in the monastery and the need to clearly identify the separation between the sexes to maintain the purity of members. Another reason might be added; that is to say, the need to protect the nuns in a society not accustomed to seeing women's groups as being fully autonomous. These factors are somehow the cause of outright misogynist expressions found in the canonical texts, both in the Buddha's speeches and in many *Vinaya* rules meant to keep women from decision-making. Monastic asceticism probably led the *sangha* to incorporate in its misogynist rhetoric harsh words about the impurity or pollution associated with the female body.[144] Gautama approved the ordination of the first woman, his aunt Maha-Pajapati, provided she accepted eight additional rules of conduct (*attha garudhamma*), thus marking the nuns' subordination to monks. For example, a nun must always bow when greeting a monk, even if she is older, a female novice must go through a double-ordination, and her noviciate shall last two years instead of a year as for a monk.[145] The nuns must follow 311 rules while the bhikkhu's *Pattimokkha* has only 227. Although a case could be made that the original intention to include women in the pursuit of high spiritual goals could represent an advance over the Brahmanical social order, the fact remains that the *sangha* backs women's dependence. Early Buddhism somehow endorses the notion of the three patriarchal obligations of women; first to her father, then to her husband, and finally to her son, a concept supported both by the *Manu Smriti* in India and by Confucius's *Classics*.[146] The ordination of women disappeared from Theravada Buddhism around the eleventh century, but survived in Mahayana.

Mahayana might at first sight show greater openness to women because of the universalism of salvation it preaches; its doctrine of Buddha nature, present in every being. Moreover, its doctrine of nonduality seeks to end all forms of difference.[147] In principle, it should abolish distinctions based on gender. Paradoxically, misogyny was not significantly reduced.[148] Thus, the *Nirvana Sutra* presents woman as a demon devouring men, and says that the passions of one single woman are only matched by those of all men put together, which explains their quasi inaccessibility to Buddhahood.[149] Women are seen as an obstacle to the practice of Buddhist precepts and lead people to hell.[150] Just as in the Indian world, where the ascetic male can sublimate his sexual impulses, female libido remains untameable. Women remain biologically impure, especially in regards to menstrual blood and their reproductive functions. In any case, it is the explanation given to a disciple of the Buddha, Mulian (目連, Mogallana in Pali) in the *Sutra of the Bowl of Blood, Xuepen Jing*, from the late twelfth century.[151] Mulian wants to save his mother from the hell formed by a pool of blood. The keeper tells him that the place is reserved for women because they pollute land and waters with menstrual blood or their bleeding during delivery.[152] Despite the theory of the five obstacles, which refuses to see women capable of awakening, some Mahayana texts such as the *Lotus Sutra*, the *Teaching of Vimalakirti*, and the *Sutra on the Lion's Roar of Queen Srimala* are more generous to women in this regard. Chapter 12, *Devadatta*, of the *Lotus Sutra* is the *locus classicus* for the affirmation of women's equality.[153] In this text, the young *naga* or dragon-girl shows Sariputra that she has all the qualities of a bodhisattva, but he keeps on telling her the female body can neither achieve *bodhi* nor complete the career of a high-level bodhisattva, nor attain Buddhahood. She succeeds, however, by instantly turning herself into a man. A woman cannot reach the Pure Land or Amitabha's paradise without turning into a man.[154] The *Teaching of Vimalakirti* seems to take a step forward in affirming the equality of women through the use of the concept of emptiness (*sunyata*) of all phenomena, including gender differences. Here, the goddess objects to Sariputra's suggestion to have her change sex because female gender has no reality in itself. In order to demonstrate the fluidity of genders, she transforms him into a goddess while she takes Sariputra's physical appearance.[155] The Amidist tradition also demonstrates egalitarian claims, especially with Shinran for whom the power of reciting the *nembutsu* produces the same salvific effects in women as in men.[156] Borrowing from the literature of the *Prajna Paramitas* where wisdom is feminine and the mother of all Buddhas, Tibetan Buddhism uses the symbolism of the union of wisdom viewed as female with other male virtues or *paramitas*, such as compassion (*karuna*) or saving skills (*upaya*) to create enlightened beings. However, this rhetoric of the complementary nature of the sexes is far from being a kind of egalitarian symbolism since it leans on the superiority of the male who alone transmits to his progeny the lineage marking his true parentage to Mahayana.[157] Bernard Faure also warns against the urge to take at face value a particular rhetoric of gender equality in Zen (*Chan*) Buddhism or in societies where Confucian patriarchal values have shaped attitudes and institutions.[158] The best example of the *Chan* egalitarian claims is probably found in the *Records of the Transmission of the Lamp* (*Jingde Chuandeng Lu*, 景德傳燈錄) where the nun Maoshan Liaoran (末山了然) tries to convey the doctrine to the *Chan* monk Guanqi (灌溪).¹⁵⁹ The story shows that the nun of the *Linji* tradition is not submissive, and her refusal to become male serves to demonstrate that awakening is sudden, it is a state of mind that has nothing to do with the gender of the follower.

In conclusion, it is not for us now to give a careful analysis of the status of women in Buddhism. Some authors submit a fairly positive outlook on the egalitarian potential of the Buddhism. They consider that the Buddha shows openness to women's becoming *arahant*. This openness is also carried on by the Mahayanist comprehensive view of enlightenment and its doctrine of emptiness. Despite some rhetoric in favor of gender equality, Buddhism has failed to address sexism and the patriarchal ideology that prevailed in the various societies where it took root. Paradoxically, it has allowed some women to escape by ordination from the traditional role of wife and mother, and acquire learning.

Homosexuality

What is the social representation of homosexuality in societies where Buddhism took root? In these countries, the social perception of homosexuality was influenced by Buddhism, but other systems of thought, such as Hinduism, Daoism, and Confucianism, have to be taken into account. Many of these societies have been influenced by one or more of these religious currents, in addition to being marked to varying degrees by the passage of the European settler. The globalization of economies and cultures, through satellite television and the web, has certainly changed the traditional views of homosexuality, and so has the HIV epidemic. Various combinations of these factors contributed to variably modulate social tolerance vis-à-vis homosexuality. I soon realized how difficult it would be to establish here a detailed portrait of the situation, country by country, and that only a general outline was feasible.

In countries with a large Buddhist majority such as Sri Lanka and Myanmar, no law punishing homosexual acts existed before British colonization. The criminal codes of both countries contain, since the late nineteenth century, severe provisions for prison sentences against sexual acts described as "against nature" committed by persons of the same sex, with the opposite sex, or with animals.¹⁶⁰ French colonization had a different approach since the Revolutionary Penal Code of 1791 did not mention sodomy as a crime, so that such legislation was never found in Cambodian, Laotian, or Vietnamese law. Thailand was never colonized but, in the early twentieth century, it made a commitment to its European trading partners to modernize its criminal code. It timidly introduced in its legislation a law against sodomy without actually enforcing it. This provision was even revoked in 1956, so it may be suitable to say that this country has always been tolerant, at least in legal terms, in respect of sexual relations between consenting adults of the same sex.¹⁶¹ Most of these countries have yet adopted laws that protect minors of both sexes against various forms of sexual exploitation. If we look more closely at the case of Vietnam, the criminal codes of the ancient Le (1428–1787) and Nguyen (1802–1945) Dynasties make no mention of homosexual relations.¹⁶² While Vietnamese codes usually follow Chinese law, the Nguyen code did not see fit to follow the Qing law of 1734 and incorporate into its list of offenses consensual homosexual acts of sodomy.

In *Theravada* countries, the code of monastic discipline and its commentaries contain the clearest injunctions on homosexual acts. They are considered on equal footing with other sex offenses involving an orifice in the human body, neither too severe nor too less. As already noted, what determines the severity of a wrongdoing has nothing to do with the anatomical sex or gender of the sexual object. Rather, the seriousness of the fault depends on the presence or absence of penetration or emission of sperm. Thus, a monk being masturbated by another monk commits an offense in the category of *sanghadisesa* I if he ejaculates, but the masturbating monk commits a minor offense (*dukkata*) if he does not himself ejaculate. The gender of the sex object, however, is taken into account when judging the seriousness of a *sanghadisesa* II, that is to say, while touching different parts of a woman's body with a sexual intent. The *Suttavibhanga* then discusses the case of the monk who touches a novice or another monk in a sexual way: he commits a venial sin (*dukkata*), as when he touches in the same way a female animal. If the monk is acting similarly toward a *pandaka*, he is committing a serious fault (*thullacaya*), though without the obligation to convene the *sangha*. The analysis of the monastic code corroborates the Buddha's general injunction against the dangers of women on the path of spiritual growth. The same risk does not occur with respect to men, except perhaps for a group that can be mistaken for women, the *pandakas*. It is this confusion that probably led the ancients to exclude them from ordination.[163] Hermaphrodites (*ubhatovyanjanaka*) also got excluded from ordination.[164] In their own understanding, the authors of the *Vinaya* retrieved the Indian medical theory of a third gender (*tritiya prakriti*), which included men who could not have "normal" sexual relations with women—that is, those who cannot procreate for one reason or another. Brahmanical culture used the word *pandaka* as a synonym for *sandha*, *kliba*, or *napumsaka*, already discussed in the previous chapter. The Buddhist commentators Buddhaghosa and Asanga distinguished between five types of *pandakas*: a man suffering from impotence due to congenital malformation, the voyeur who cannot be sexually satisfied without looking at others copulate, the man who periodically suffers from impotence, the fellator, and whoever gets an orgasm by using some artifice.[165] The list includes fairly broad categories of the third sex described in Indian medicine, and includes in the same fashion men who have sex with men as well as those who are impotent. In the *Mahavagga* of the *Vinaya*, the motive for exclusion from ordination does not seem to lie in physiology. Instead, it insists on the behavior of a morally reprehensible *pandaka* who sought to have sex with novices or other monks.[166] In the case of the hermaphrodite, it is debatable whether exclusion was based on loss of physical integrity.[167] At least, another reason has to be found in the *pandaka*'s case because his physical integrity is not always involved. The logic that prevails throughout the *Vinaya Pitaka* is one of exclusion of women to protect the monks' virtue. The *pandakas* belong to more or less well-defined gender and that ambiguity threatens the purity of the monastic order, which has to be protected by strict rules, especially regarding the exchange between the sexes. The commentator Buddhaghosa labels the *pandakas* as debased beings (*ussanakilesa*), hypersexualized (*avupasanta-parilaha*), with a libido made of loose impulses (*parilahavegabhibhuta*).[168] He does not hesitate to compare them with prostitutes or young sluts. In short, like women, *pandakas* represent a threat to the chastity of monks. Their company should be avoided and they should, therefore, not be admitted into the monastic order. We must also take into consideration in the assessment of these rules of conduct that the *sangha* was the first monastic community of the Indian world, so the monks' conduct had to be above all suspicion in public opinion.[169] The story of the origin of the rule excluding *pandakas* reflects exactly that. A *pandaka* sexually solicited novices and monks but was turned down by them. He finally had his way with the *mahouts* who spread the rumor later: monks are *pandakas*, and those who are not *pandakas* sleep with *pandakas*.[170] The commentator Vasubandhu stigmatized *pandakas* and hermaphrodites by describing them as incapable of becoming spiritual beings, unable to concentrate in meditation because they are fettered by their sexual instincts.[171]

Outside the *Vinaya Pitaka*, which applies only to monks, no further mention of homosexual acts categorized as sexual misconduct appears in the Pali canon or any other texts of Indian Buddhism.[172] The commentator Buddhaghosa seems to go against the tide when he associates in the *Sumangalavilasini* sex between men with the decline of the Buddhist doctrine.[173] The *Sutra of the True Dharma of Clear Recollection* of the ancient Indian *Mulasarvastivada* School interested in the doctrine of retribution refers to various torments suffered by men who have sex with men, in the burning hell of mass destruction (Sanskrit *samghata naraka*).[174] They are consumed by the embrace of a man on fire. Others are torn to pieces in burning hell of tears (Sanskrit *raurava naraka*), while their genitals are devoured by vermin. The same book condemns pedophiles to hell by plunging them into the ocean of sulfur surrounding the three spheres of existence[175] attracted by the cries of boys who are burning in hell and begging for help. In Japan, Genshin (942–1017), a monk of the *Tendai* School, tells a story very similar in *Ojo Yoshu, The Essentials of Rebirth in the Pure Land*.

We know little about the history of the social perception of homosexuality in societies marked by the Theravada tradition. Several accounts of European travelers indicated that homosexual mores were prevalent in certain areas. The Dutch traveler Jan Huyghen van Linschoten (1563–1611) substantiated their existence in Pegu in Burma. Alexander Hamilton, who in 1744 traveled to Burma, referred to a queen of Burma who had imposed on women to wear a sarong to attract the gaze of men, all too busy engaging in sodomy. Ralph Fitch (1552–1611) of the East India Company reported that the men of Pegu and Chiang Mai were so immersed in sodomy and masturbation that the population had declined.[176] Explorers, traders, and European missionaries in Siam seemed more fascinated by the heterosexual manners of its inhabitants, their propensity to polygamy, and reported few cases of vice "against nature," effeminate men or transvestites.[177] Studies and recent archeological research tend to show that Theravada Buddhism migrated from Sri Lanka to Southeast Asian countries in the eleventh century under the aegis of King Anawrahta of Pagan, and considerably influenced the law codes of several countries in the region throughout the premodern period.[178] Therefore, it is not surprising to find in the legal texts named *dhammasat* or *dhammathat*, or in royal ordinances (*rajathat*), defenses and rules of conduct heavily inspired by the Pali canon. Most of these legal texts set forth rules of sexual conduct to guard marriage against adultery. Examples can be found in the *Mangrai Thamassat* from the Lannathai Kingdom of Chiang Mai or the *Kotmai Tra Sat Duang* (*Three Seals Code*) compiled in 1804, the Vientiane Code named *Khamphi Thammasat Buhan Lao* or the Burmese code *Manugye Dhammathat* (*The Laws of Manu*). According to Andrew Huxley, a specialist of the influence of Buddhism on the legal codes of these countries, homosexual practices among the laity are not dealt with by codes or royal decrees. Their rules are almost always limited to sexual misconduct between a man and a woman.[179] In the case of monks, the royal ordinances may sometimes echo the *Vinaya*. King Badon of Burma, in an order of 1810, enacted the exclusion of the monk Shin Tejosara from the *sangha* for allegedly having performed oral sex and sodomy on other monks.[180] This is consistent with the generally restrictive interpretation of the third defense limited to adultery, where it concerns sexual morality applicable to the laity.[181] Peter Jackson has studied the contemporary understanding of the Thai words *pandaka* and *ubhatovyanjanaka* (hermaphrodite), often translated by the word *kathoey* กะเทย. The author cites various sources, Thai dictionaries and books written by monks, to prove that the word somehow draws its meaning from Indian medical theories of a third gender to apply it nowadays to either a transvestite, a hermaphrodite, or a passive homosexual and even a gay person.[182] The origin of the word is uncertain, but according to some authors it would come from the Khmer language. Notice that the Khmer people were strongly Indianized before the introduction of Theravada Buddhism in the fourteenth century, just like the Mon people of Burma. Before the creation of their own kingdoms, during the thirteenth century in Sukhothai and Ayutthaya in the nineteenth century, the Khmers and the Mons ruled over the Thais. In 1991, Anatole Roger Peltier, an expert in Thai-Lao literature, published a translation of a creation myth of the Yuan people of Northern Thailand, the *Pathamamulamuli*,[183] which could explain the origins of the pre-Buddhist *kathoey* in Thailand. In this myth, the primordial couple decides to have children of three sexes, the female (Itthi), male (Pullinga), and neutral (Napumsaka). As adults, Itthi and Pullinga are attracted to each other, and Napumsaka kills his rival Pullinga out of jealousy. A similar myth also exists in the Indianized Mon culture, the *Mula Muh*.[184] It should also be noted that rituals were often the domain of "third gender" shamans in the entire Southeast Asia, prior to the penetration of either Buddhism in the case of Burma, Thailand, Cambodia, and Vietnam, or of Islam in Indonesia and Malaysia.[185] Nevertheless, caution is advised when time comes to consider the Thai myth as the acknowledgment of three genders. Among the things to be aware of, Matzner denotes the negative vocabulary surrounding the word *napumsaka* and the fact that being considered the first murderer in human history does not help in any way social tolerance vis-à-vis the *kathoey*.[186] Whatever the precise origin of the word, many Buddhists use the word *kathoey* to refer to both men who have sex with men and persons with atypical gender identity, the transgender, transvestite, or transsexual. Contemporary authors like Bhikkhu Methangkun Bunmi attempt to explain homosexuality with the theory of *karma*. He argues that sexual misconduct in a previous life predisposes an individual to engage in homosexual practices, in another life.[187] In the *Therigatha*, the nun Isidasi, having achieved enlightenment, tells the story of her successive reincarnations. She first lived as a blacksmith who committed adultery and was reincarnated as various neutered animals, and then as a hermaphrodite or "neither male nor female" each and every time he committed adultery.[188] In the opinion of many psychologists and sexologists, belief in the causality link between being homosexual, or *kathoey*, and sexual misconduct in past lives is deeply rooted in Thai mentality.[189] This etiology has at least the merit, as noted by Jackson, to consider homosexuality or transgenderism as an irreversible congenital condition that demands the practice of an important Buddhist virtue—compassion.[190] Thus Bunmi elaborates this theory to the extent of suggesting that anyone should think twice before ridiculing a *kathoey* because everyone in a past life has probably committed an offense against the third precept, which has had the person reincarnated as a *kathoey*.[191] This suggests some respect toward the *kathoey* or the homosexual in the form of resignation brought about by the Buddhist doctrine of karmic responsibility, but no real acceptance by a society that continues to vilify homosexuality. According to some, the karmic responsibility allows the *kathoey* and a Thai who define themselves as gay to accept their condition without too much psychological distress, just as women embrace their gender, knowing that this may change in another life.[192] Despite the absence of antigay laws or few religious sanctions, at least in the case of lay persons, one should not conclude that Thai society sees homosexual practices in a positive light. Other forms of social control are in place to punish such behavior in the public sphere, because it hurts the social etiquette (*morsom*, *somkuan*) that requires an individual to marry and have offspring.[193] Several testimonies, collected and compiled by Jackson from letters sent to magazines in Bangkok, perfectly illustrate both the resignation of the person having sex with men, its association with karmic causality, and social conformity that forces the individual to keep his sexual activities with men secret.[194] This vision departs substantially from the Western perception of homosexuality seen as sexual orientation and a certain social visibility of homosexuals who were finally guaranteed equal rights after a long historical process. The modernization of Thai society has nothing to do with the model described by Foucault in his *History of Sexuality*, in which the subject manifests the will-to-know and confesses everything about the use of pleasure. The Thai model of social development, particularly with regard to sexuality, does not revolve around the permeability between private and social spheres as found in the Foucauldian model. The pressure from European trading powers on the Kingdom of Siam to adopt a "civilized" lifestyle brought, as of the mid-nineteenth century, King Chulalongkorn (1868–1910) and several others to later adopt public laws inspired by imported social norms, without actually changing deviant private behavior.[195] In fact, to meet European demands Thai authorities simply banned from the public space manifestations European merchants and explorers found to be offensive, especially male and female nude torsos, the difficulty of differentiating male and female appearance, and the exploitation of women in polygamy. The contemporary attitude of concealment or invisibility of the erotic in Thai culture is directly related to this government policy planned to civilize its citizens on the surface but without effective control over private sexual practices.[196] With the same logic, the state began to police the genders by creating a public space where men and women were dressed according to the European standards of decency and genders being now differentiated according to these imported stereotypes. According to Jackson, the will to control specific behaviors in both genders is relatively recent in the history of Thailand, which could certainly account for the increased interest in the *kathoey* in public discourse on sexuality. Before the mid-twentieth century, transvestism attracted little attention in a society where it was sometimes difficult to distinguish the appearance of a man from that of a woman.[197] The insistence of new policies on gender differentiation led to greater feminization of the *kathoey*, becoming increasingly identified with transgenderism or passive homosexuality, the Thai *kween* (queen). Since the 1970s, Thai society, which traditionally mixed up sex with gender, is now learning to distinguish between transgenderism and transsexualism from homosexuality, called *rak-ruamphet*. Increasingly, the epithet *kathoey*, at least in academic circles and among more educated and urbanized population, seems reserved to describe transgender and transsexual persons.[198] The use of the terms "gay" and "gay king" spreads quickly to mean men who have sex with men but who meet the stereotype of the real man, the inserter, as opposed to the "gay queen" or *kathoey*.[199] In summary, the Thai gay world seems to be marked by the ambivalence of social stigma whereas the *kathoey* is reminiscent of the Indian attitude vis-à-vis the *hijra* or the *kothi*, but a kind of resignation and even compassion based on karmic retribution is shown at the same time. Thai people sometimes show a certain respect or fascination with the *kathoey*, some of whom enjoy exceptional popularity such as the "kickboxer" champion Nong Tum, beauty queens, or players from the volleyball team "Iron Ladies" who won the national championship.[200] In 2003, film director Ekachai Uekorngtham showed on screen the life of Nong Tum and the film received numerous national and international awards. The film titled *Beautiful Boxer* narrates the boxer's childhood in a small village in Northern Thailand, his six years as a novice in a Buddhist monastery, his boxing career and his career as a singer, and finally his sex reassignment surgery.

Ambivalence also qualifies the approach of Thai society vis-à-vis gay persons. The absence of antihomosexual legislation should normally promote greater social acceptance of gays, but the importance of family, and duty to conform without losing one's face and keeping up with appearances, prevent complete visibility. For the last 20 years, gay culture has established itself in Bangkok and some tourist resorts such as Phuket and Pattaya. Men, however, who regularly visit restaurants, bars, and saunas, consider their attendance at such drag places as a strictly private matter. They do not wish to identify as gays, outside these places of amusement.[201] These quarters can sometimes be subject to police action. Police are mostly absorbed in controlling drug trafficking and sexual exploitation of minors and raids are not particularly directed against homosexuals.[202] The effect of globalization is also quietly at work in Thailand, and the public body responsible for mental health said in December 2002 that homosexuality was no longer a mental illness, and that a greater openness of families and workplaces could guarantee homosexuals a better and happier life.[203] Thus, social attitudes are changing, and the Thai Buddhist clergy is no exception. In the 1990s, some monks and lay people saw in the AIDS virus nothing less than the karmic retribution for sexual misconduct. Since 2000, compassion took the shape of concrete involvement of monasteries in the fight against AIDS, and replaced the traditional attitude of condemnation.[204]

China had no laws prohibiting consensual homosexual acts before the Qing law of 1679, which remained in force until the end of the dynasty in 1911. Aside from this period, Chinese culture seemed quite tolerant of homosexuality, despite its Confucian ideology based strongly on family. An extensive literature demonstrates the existence of passionate male love affairs in the nobility and ruling class of the literati. Typical examples during the *Spring and Autumn* period (*Chunqiu* 春秋; 722–481 BC) was the love of Duke Ling of Wei (衛靈公) for his favorite Mizi Xia (弥子暇). The legist Han Fei (韓非) reported without any moral judgment that the duke accepted half a peach given to him by Mizi Xia as proof of his sincere love. The gesture earned male love the common reference of "love of the split peach" (*fentao*, 分桃), or "love of the half-eaten peach" (*yutao zhipi*, 餘桃之癖).[205] Still, according to Han Fei, the duke apparently abandoned his lover when he grew older and lost his youthful beauty.[206] Dating from the *Warring States* period (*Zhanguo* 戰國; 453–221 BC), there is also the famous episode of Wang Zhongxian (王仲先) who was seduced by the beauty of his master, the scholar Zhang Pan (潘章). The two studied together, shared a pillow, and died at the same time. People buried them together in one grave on Mount Luofu. A tree grew on the grave with branches intertwined, so it was called the "shared pillow tree" (*gongzhen shu*, 共枕树).[207] Love between men was so popular at the Han court (206 BC–220 AD) that Sima Qian (司馬遷; 145–90 BC), the great historian of the time, devoted in his *Records* (*Shiji*, 史記) an entire chapter to the emperors' male favorites, a phenomenon quite natural according to the Western Han historian Ban Gu (班固; 32–92 AD).[208] In the *Zhangguo Ce*, King Wei was overwhelmed by the beauty of Duke Longyang (龍陽). The duke's name came to mean love between men.[209] The most famous affair between emperor and favorite was that of Emperor Ai (哀) and his lover Dong Xian (董賢) who had fallen asleep on the sleeve of his robe. The emperor decided to cut it instead of waking up his beloved; hence, another expression to describe traditional homosexuality: "passion of the cut sleeve" (*duanxiu zhipi*, 斷袖之癖).[210] Homosexual liaisons are also common among the elite in later periods and even among the military as evidenced by the passion of General Cao Cao (曹操), founder of the Northern Wei Dynasty, for his cavalry commander Kong Gui (孔桂).[211] King Wen of the Kingdom of Chen (陳) made his favorite Han Zigao (韩子高) the army general.[212] Many of these biographies and historical narratives highlighted the emotional ties and the strong connection that bound these partners far beyond mere flirtations. Poetry and prose amply demonstrated the same phenomenon. The poet Ruan Ji celebrated the love of boys in a poem where he referred to famous lovers of the past, such as Long Yang (龍陽), the king of Wei Anli's (安釐) favorite, and An Ling (安陵) favorite of the king of Chu.[213] The Tang writer, Li Yi (李翊), wrote a story about the passionate life of Han Zigao, an account echoed by Feng Menglong (馮夢龍; 1574–1645) in his illustrious *Qingshi* (情史, Love Story). Feng's book assembled different stories on male love under one chapter entitled *Qing Wai* (情外, Other Love).[214] Like in other "petty talk" works (*xiaoshuo* 小小說), that is, romanticized stories in the vernacular language near the end of the Ming Dynasty (明; 1368–1644), Feng Menglong developed a more individualist and romantic approach to love and emotions (*qing*, 情).[215] Several short stories with homoerotic flavor, pornographic in tone, offered various intrigues in which the characters are often involved in violence, male prostitution, theft, and murder. For example, in *Yichun Xiangzhi* (宜春香質), attributed to Zui Xihu Xinyue Zhuren (醉西湖心月主人) is young Niu (鈕), ugly-looking but miraculously transformed by Taoist immortals into a handsome young man. He became the King's lover and "queen" of a land of male pleasures *yinan guo* (宜男國).²¹⁶ However, the book seems to judge love between men severely, describing the brutal death of a young lover gutted by a hook inserted into the anus.²¹⁷ The same Zui also wrote *A Lady's Pin under a Man's Cap*, (*Bian er chai*, 弁而釵), which consisted of four short stories making room for homosexual passions. In the first narrative, *Chronicle of a Loyal Love* (*Qingzhen Ji*, 情貞記), a young scholar named Fengxiang (風翔) fell in love with a fifteen-year-old, Zhao Wangsun (趙王孫), and went back to study at school hoping to seduce him. Zhao was taken by remorse for having acted as a woman, so Fengxiang told him that passion (*qing*) did not stop at the gates of morality (*li*, 理) and left no trace of the distinctions between the masculine and feminine.²¹⁸ The second story, *A Story of Chivalric Love* (*Qingxia ji*, 情俠記) featured two characters who wield both the arts of war (*wu* 武) and literature (*wen*, 文). The pair, Zhangji (張機) and Zhong Tunan (鐘圖南), have sex under the influence of alcohol. Realizing later that he had been sodomized by Zhong Tunan, an angry Zhangji wanted to cut his partner's head, but Zhong dissuaded him with calm and confidence in the expression of his feelings. They both became officers at the imperial court, and they met later on the battlefield in Shaanxi. There, Zhangji rescued his friend Zhong. They decided to make love again, though Zhangji initially refused, because of their high rank. True affection and loyalty bound them unto old age. They united in marriage their sons and daughters, and they finally ended their days together in seclusion, after Zhang had decided to join his friend who had fallen in disgrace.²¹⁹ *Bian er chai* well expressed its author's regard for the ideal of chivalry (*xia*, 俠), which he saw perfectly fulfilled through homoerotic feelings, in which paragons of equality and fairness between soul mates (*zhiji*, 知己) are best exhibited.²²⁰ In both works, Master Zui places romantic male love on equal footing with heterosexual romance, setting it apart from homoerotic relations with boys as a form of entertainment.²²¹

Under the Qing, storybooks continued to offer an honorable place to homosexual liaisons. Li Yu (李 鱼; 1611–1680), author of the famous novel *The Carnal Prayer Mat* (*Rou Putuan* 肉蒲團; 1657), whose heroes have sex with many women but do not discard the opportunity of having sex with male servants, wrote three stories with homosexual adventures.²²² In his collection of stories titled *Silent Operas* (*Wusheng Xi*, 無聲戲), there is a piece called "A Male 'Mother Meng' Thrice Moves Home" (*Nan Meng Mu Jiaohe Sanqian*, 男孟母教合三遷). This story remains significant due to the fact that while a work of fiction, it opens a window on the social reality of homosexuality in Qing Dynasty. The story takes place in Fujian, where the young scholar Xu Jifang (許季芳) married and fathered a son, but rather cold toward women, fell for a beautiful teenager named Ruilang (瑞郎). The youth's father offered his son in marriage to the man who would wage the highest price. According to novelist Li Yu, it was a widespread custom in the south (*nan feng*, 南風) to marry Fujian adolescent boys to men until they reach the nubile age. As he became older, Ruilang decided to cut his genitals to continue to live with Xu Jifang, and changed his name to Rui Niang (娘 *niang* means a woman or a mother). Xu Jifang was accused by a magistrate of having castrated the young man and was beaten to death. Rui brought up Chengxian (承先), the son of his deceased lover, and moved three times to protect the young boy from his masters' sexual advances.²²³

In 1750, Wu Jingzi (吳敬梓) completed his novel *The World of the Literati* (*Rulin Waishi*, 儒林外史). It was a true parody of Confucian scholars and the civil service examination system tainted by favoritism. In chapter 30 Du Shenqing (杜慎卿) told his friend

Li Weixiao (季苇萧) that love between friends (*pengyou*, 朋友) exceeds the love between a man and a woman. When Li asked him if he went to the park to meet opera actors, understood sex workers, Du's response was striking: it would mean satisfying one's sexual needs in a brothel without sharing sincere feelings from the heart. Under the Qing, various scholars and mandarins took transvestite opera actors (*dan*, 旦) for friends, including those of the famous *Kunqu* (崑曲). Author of the novel *Pinhua Baojian* (*Precious Mirror for Appreciating Flowers*, 品花寶鑒) in 70 chapters, Chen Sen (陳森; 1797–1870) focused his story on homosexual relations of Beijing scholars, officials, and wealthy merchants during the reign of Emperor Qianlong (乾隆), with young actors (*dan*). Notice the two couples, the first consisting of young scholar Mei Ziyu (梅子玉) and actor Du Qinyan (杜琴言) and the second consisting of Tian Chunhang (田春航) and actor Su Huifang (蘇惠芳).[224] The two couples exemplify the purity of love (*qing*), which the author contrasts with some vile and grotesque characters such as Xi Shiyi (奚十一)—a man drawn to more adventurous and sordid sexual encounters with actors. In the manner of Ming popular literature, Chen Sen used *qing* aesthetics in homoerotic contexts to express the epitome of romantic love where equality in the sharing of feelings prevail over the duties imposed by gender stereotypes or social status.[225]

Several scholars and officials financially supported the theater and maintained around them social circles where members of the intellectual and political elite (*mingshi*, 名士) of the time exchanged ideas. They also interchanged sexual favors with young actors deemed to be at the lowest of the social scale (*jianmin*, 賤民). Handbooks or catalogs called *Huapu* (花譜), celebrating the charms of young actors, circulated extensively.[226] Thus, the distinguished scholar Mao Xiang (冒襄; 1611–1693) held regular gatherings in his superb Shuihui Garden (水繪園) villa in Rugao where high-society personalities mingled with actors from his company. Among the guests was his friend the poet Chen Weisong (陳維崧; 1625–1682) who fell madly in love with the young actor Xu Ziyun (徐子雲; also known as Yunlang, 雲郎). Under Mao Xiang's patronage, he had with him a relationship that lasted 17 years. This faithful bond inspired several scholars of the time who praised in poems the beauty of the young actor. They actually formed a literary circle in which homoerotic expression triumphed, seeing themselves as Chen Weisong's disciples.[227]

This all-too-brief historical survey may simply demonstrate a strong social acceptance vis-à-vis homosexual relations in preimperial China, right up to the end of the empire. Such a claim calls for some nuances. Nonegalitarianism stamps the majority of sexual encounters between men described in Chinese literature, whether in historical records, poetry, or novels. Indeed, it is almost always kings, dukes, emperors, officials, and scholars who fall in love with younger people, teenagers, whose social status is usually lower, servants at the imperial court or house servants, prostitutes or actors. In almost all cases, the older partner is married and remains so, while the younger usually gets married when he is of age. Tolerance, therefore, manifests itself within a society deeply infused by Confucian moral values. Filial piety here ensures the continuity of patriarchal family values and respect for social hierarchy. Homosexual liaisons are socially accepted insofar as they do not threaten family and patriarchal values. Individuals engaging in homosexual relations are never stigmatized as being perverse or as doing something against the order of nature. However, fear can come from different sides, for example, homosexuality can be seen as an outrage to procreation, gender identity, and social status. The latter concern appears to have pushed Song legislators to punish transvestites (*bu nan*, 不男, nonmale) who became prostitutes and persons of inferior rank (*jian min*, 賤民) by assuming the passive role in sodomy.[228] Remarkably, the inserter was not affected by such legislation. Only with the Qing did the perception of homosexual behavior really change. For the first time in history, until the end of the empire, sodomy was equated with adultery and prostitution, that is to say, illicit sex outside of marriage (姦, *jian*). These acts became punishable, depending on whether they were consensual or not and the victim's age. As shown by Sommer, the Qing strategy of increasing the number of persons with the legal status of honorable person (良人, *liangren*) aimed primarily at protecting the Confucian family values, including safeguarding the honor of young boys coming from respectable families (*liangren*) and thus destined to become real men—that is, able to penetrate their wives when they marry. The rape of boys from respectable families as well as consensual homosexual anal intercourse became criminal acts like adultery. The Qing Code did not punish acts committed against a person of low condition, or a male prostitute.[229] This demonstrates, once again, that homosexual acts are not perceived as evil because of the sexual object, but because they may cause social unrest, threatening the key Confucian value, family. The main purpose of the code of laws is to regulate male sexuality, mainly to regulate the sexual behavior of unmarried men (*guang gun*, 光棍),[230] who may be sexually frustrated and do not always care about the anatomical sex of the person being penetrated.[231] It is this kind of approach that was first favored by the Chinese Communist Party (CCP). Mao Zedong criminalized sodomy by categorizing it as an act akin to vandalism (*liumangzui*, 流氓罪), meaning essentially anything that disrupts the social order.[232] While rejecting the approach based on the hierarchy of social classes and genders found in Qing morality, the CCP promoted traditional views on sexuality in marriage, and conceived of homosexuality (*tongxinglian*, 同性恋) as reactionary.[233] Homosexual acts are selfish because they do not contribute to building a new society.[234] During the Cultural Revolution from 1966 to 1976, intolerance occurred more intensely against men having sex with men. They were persecuted as reactionaries (*fandong fenzi*, 反动分子). The CCP's homophobic campaign often used psychiatry to define homosexuality as a mental illness. Even though persecution ceased after the Cultural Revolution, homosexuals feared to come out in public, as demonstrated by the work of Professors Li Yinhe (李银河) and Wang Xiaobo (王小波) from the Chinese Academy of Social Sciences in the first serious book devoted to homosexuals published in China.[235] At the same time, the book lifted the veil on a homosexual subculture in Beijing, with its clandestine meeting places. The same year, another study among university students in Beijing demonstrated that 7.5 percent of them had one or more homosexual experiences.[236] Beginning in the 1990s, a more liberal attitude toward sexuality, known in Chinese as *xing kaifang* (性开放), made its appearance accompanied by a more romantic view of marriage. The two phenomena were accelerated by a greater openness to the world, economic development, and Internet. All this has led to greater openness vis-à-vis alternative sexualities.[237] The birth control policy introduced in the 1970s has also changed the general perception on sexuality, which became no longer limited to procreation.[238] Obvious signs of this trend are more and more frequent. In 1997, section 160 of the criminal code that allowed for the prosecution of homosexual men was repealed. In April 2001, the Chinese Psychiatric Association stopped classifying homosexuality with mental illnesses whenever the person accepts his condition.[239] The 1990s also saw the emergence of homosexual rights advocacy and support groups. Homosexuals often refer to themselves as *tongzhi* (同志) or comrades. The *tongzhi* culture is thriving today in large cities such as Beijing, Shanghai, or Hong Kong, with bars, saunas, coded language, and a literature specifically developed on the web since 1994 and named *tongzhi wenxue* (同志文学, comrade literature). Cristini (2005) has identified close to 90,000 sites. The genre is sometimes sexually explicit, but usually puts forward romantic liaisons and the difficulties of living openly as homosexual in a Chinese family—always strongly attached to the model of Confucian filial piety. The ancient philosopher Mencius said: "There are three ways of being a bad son. The most serious is to have no heir."[240] This certainly makes any coming out difficult and explains why many homosexuals are still getting married. In short, there is an atmosphere of openness since the 1990s reflected by the growing number of book titles on homosexuality in mainland China, Taiwan, or Hong Kong where the British had decriminalized sodomy before leaving in 1997.[241]

Everything about Chinese culture and history supports the idea of a virtual absence of homophobia through the centuries. This could be explained by evolving standards of male beauty which as early as the Later Han Dynasty gave prominence to more feminine traits, as opposed to the more macho features of military heroes (*yingxiong*, 英雄). This ideal of a feminized male beauty is blatantly obvious in the novelistic tradition of the *caizi jiaren* (才子佳人, talented scholar/young beauty). In this genre, even downright straight heroes such as Jia Baoyu (賈寶玉) from the Qing novel *Dream of the Red Chamber* (*Honglou Meng*, 紅樓夢) by Cao Xueqin (曹雨芹) win the hearts of women, because of their feminine beauty.[242] The same frailty or delicate, feminine traits of a beautiful male also attracted men such as Jia Baoyu. From a very early age, Jia Baoyu seemed to embody feminine qualities, and as a boy, he developed friendship with boys showing these same qualities, notably Qin Zhong and Liu Xianglian.[243] The presence among the literati of that feminine softness was sometimes criticized, particularly early on under Qing administration, when some Confucian philosophers correlated Ming defeat at the hands of the invading Manchus with the feminization of the literati.[244] In general, gender identity does not seem to tear apart or trouble the Chinese for whom masculinity is not defined by the opposition of male to female or heterosexuality to homosexuality. Under the influence of the *yin-yang* philosophy, power relations rather than sex assign gender. The model allows for more gender fluidity because an individual may hold multiple positions, even simultaneously, in the social spectrum. For example, a scholar or a minister may be considered in a *yin* position while serving the emperor, but will fill a *yang* position vis-à-vis his wife.[245]

The Buddhist clergy has often occupied a flimsy position in Chinese society, typically marked by Confucian mentality, particularly when it comes to sexual morality. The rather austere perspective of Buddhism in matters regarding sexuality and sensual pleasure, as well as its monastic ideal, could easily bring its adherents under suspicion, above all because of its lack of interest in familial values. What could be more contrary to filial piety than a celibate life in a secluded monastery? These reasons may partly explain the lack of hostility demonstrated by the *sangha* against homosexual practices in vogue in imperial China. Fear of retaliation is probably the real answer. Nothing, on the Buddhist side, compares with the repeated attacks by the Jesuits who arrived in China in the fifteenth century, particularly those of Matteo Ricci.[246] The missionary fathers were outraged by Chinese sexual mores, a world replete with adultery, prostitution, and sodomy. Their attacks were directed at Buddhist monks, particularly those from the *Chan* School, and altogether at Confucian scholars. In both cases, the agenda appeared quite different. The Jesuits had considerable admiration for Confucian moral values and for Chinese religious beliefs, which they deemed more akin to Christianity than to Buddhism. For instance, the worship of Heaven (*tian*, 天 called the Lord from High, Shangdi 上帝), a spiritual power that ruled the world, and the emperor having the title "son of heaven" (*Tianzi*, 天子) are responsible for executing the mandate of Heaven (*Tianming*, 天命) on earth so that order and harmony in the natural world and among men are maintained. The Jesuits saw in Buddhism idolatry and doctrines without any rational basis as in the belief in successive rebirths and the idea of emptiness that was contrary to the idea of a personal god.[247] In short, the missionaries, in order to be successful with their mission, preferred compromising with Confucianism, as indicated by Father Nicolas Trigault's words about Thacon, a Buddhist monk at the imperial court: "Ricci was of opinion that it would be better to avoid all contact with this man's degraded class."[248] The missionaries obsessed with accommodating the Christian faith to Chinese civilization even wrote treatises, in Chinese, on male friendship in which they base friendship on values of the heart such as loyalty and unselfishness, values in the fashion of the Confucian chivalrous spirit of the day.[249] They did, however, warn their readers against the Chinese excesses of the flesh that could ruin a pure relationship. For these European missionaries, the accusation of "sodomite" had to be the ultimate insult. It is, therefore, not surprising that they extensively used it against their main target, Buddhist monks in the monasteries of China, Japan, and even Thailand.[250]

The Chinese Buddhist clergy did not develop a specific literature on the subject of homosexuality and was not prone to convict adepts for homosexual practices, merely relying on what was found already in the *Vinaya*. One of the great poets of the Tang Dynasty, Bai Xingjian (白行簡; 775–826) mentioned factually and without any moral judgment the existence of homosexual practices in Buddhist monasteries.[251] Tradition in Japan has it that the monk Kukai imported the practice from Buddhist monasteries during his visit to China from 804 to 806.[252] A monk's ability to control his libido seems to be public laughingstock, as suggested by this excerpt from the novel *The Carnal Prayer Mat*:

> Any young man joining the [Buddhist] order has certain problems he must face. However strongly he tries to rein in his lusts, however firmly he tries to extinguish his desires, prayer and scripture will get him through the day enough, but in the wee hours of the morning that erect member of his will start bothering him of his own accord, making a nuisance of itself under the bedclothes, uncontrollable, irrepressible. His only solution is to find some form of appeasement, either by using his fingers for emergency relief or by discovering some young novice with whom to mediate a solution.[253]

It remains difficult to explain what actually occurred in Chinese monasteries, and have a precise idea of the extent of homosexual practices. Canonical literature was of course known to the Chinese monks who widely adopted Dharmagupta's code of discipline (*Dharmaguptaka Vinaya*), translated into Chinese early in the fifth century by Buddhayasha and Zhu Fonian (竺仏念), known as the *Sifenlü* (*The Code of Discipline in Four Parts*, 四分律).[254] This book faithfully followed the *Vinaya* of the *Pali Canon*.[255] It included the usual explanation for penetration of three orifices (*san chu*, 三處)— the anus (*dabian dao*, 大便道), the mouth (口, *kou*), and the vagina (*xiaobian dao*, 小便道)—leading to exclusion from the *sangha* (*parajika, bo luo yi fa*, 波羅夷法). There are also rules relating to masturbation with voluntary emission of semen (*nong shijing*, 弄失精), alone or with another monk, a misconduct leading to an appearance before the *sangha* (*sanghadisesa, sengjia poshisha*, 僧伽婆尸沙). The exclusion of *pandakas* (半擇迦, *banzhaijia*) from ordination found in the Pali *Vinaya* made also its way to China, as well as the five categories of men lacking virility (*wu zhong bu nan*, 五種不男), defined in the various codes of discipline and their commentaries.[256] *Pandakas* were sometimes called "yellow doors" (*huang men*, 黃門), probably referring to the door leading to the women's quarters and guarded by a eunuch, in the Han imperial palace.[257] As already said, among the five categories of *pandakas*, some seemed to suffer from impotence or some form of congenital sexual dysfunction syndrome (*sheng huang men*, 生黃門), while others presented a lack of masculinity of some psychological or behavioral origin, such as the "fifteen days *pandaka*" (*banyue huang men*, 半月黃門) whose impotence bothered him only half of the month.[258] Some clarification is needed on the importation of the concept of *pandaka* derived from Indian medicine into the Chinese culture. Ayurvedic medicine elected to allocate a specific category to certain birth defects and sexual behaviors, which did not conform to anatomical sex, a third gender. Traditional Chinese medicine did not follow the steps of its Indian counterpart. The reason is that the forces of *yin* and *yang* that sustain gender interact in the cosmos in general and more specifically in every individual, regardless of anatomy. Rather than designing the masculine and feminine as opposites, the philosophy of *yin* and *yang* offers a vision of fluid types defined more by social codes and moral imperatives than by physiology.[259]

Monastic discipline did not have the same influence in China as it did in India, or Sri Lanka, and some schools flatly rejected it, for example, the Chan *Linji* School. According to John Kieschnick, Chinese Buddhism was more concerned about the social impacts that could cause the pranks of monks who transgressed the code of discipline than by the act itself or its karmic consequences. The reputation of monasticism was paramount.[260] As already mentioned, rejection of discipline went quite far, as illustrated by the behavior of "mad monks," such as Jigong, transgressing the codified rules. Two crazy monks of the seventh century, Hanshan (寒山) and Shide (拾得), became, at the time of the Song dynasty, legendary characters. A *Chan* monk by the name of Fenggan (豐干) was said to have trained Hanshan at the Guoqing Monastery (國清) on Mount Tientai, where he apparently retired at the age of 30. There, he met Shide, an orphan working at the monastery. Pictorial representations show the pair, Hanshan and Shide, a favorite theme among the monks of the *Chan* Schools during the Song Dynasty (960–1279). Yuan Mei (袁枚; 1716–1798), writer and poet of the Qing Dynasty, echoed this grotesque madness of *Chan* monks in a book entitled *What the Master Would Not Talk About* (*Zi Buyu*, 子不語).[261] The book was blacklisted because of its tone and its iconoclastic, pornographic imagery, which the author used as a way to criticize the rigidity of Confucian morality. Without adopting Buddhism, he showed some interest in *Chan* Buddhism, probably because of its anticonformist and anti-intellectual aspects. Like many scholars of the prestigious Hanlin Academy (翰林), he cherished friendly and amorous relationships with young opera actors, with the most famous of his time, Xu Yunting. In Chapter 17 of *Zi Buyu*, he cleverly joined two ways of demonstrating his opposition to Qing austerity—homosexual relations and Chan Buddhism. The author tells the story of a *Chan* monk named Qingliang Laoren (清凉老人, Old Qingliang) who, after his death, is reincarnated into a young boy in Tibet. The latter proclaimed himself the reincarnation of the old monk, and went to Mount Wutai (五台山) to replace the deceased Qingliang. Li Zhuxi (李竹溪) one day surprised the old man disguised as a woman copulating with a woman while he was simultaneously being sodomized by a man. Shocked by the scene, Li chided his friend for such conduct, unworthy of a living Buddha. Qingliang replied that love for a man or a woman was a natural thing and that sex accounted for life on earth. In Chapter 19 of the same book, a man named Hu Tianbao (胡天保) was killed by a local administrator in Fujian outraged by Hu's declaration of love. Indeed, Hu had been seduced by the administrator's physique and had hidden to see him naked. Upon his arrival in the supernatural world, Hu Tianbao became a supernatural being, taking the shape of a rabbit, Tuershen (兔兒神), a spirit invoked to ensure the success of homosexual relations.

Belonging to the Mahayana tradition, Japanese society before the Meiji era (1868–1912) demonstrated great tolerance vis-à-vis homosexual relations. Meiji Restoration marked the end of Japanese isolation. Its openness to the outside led to the adoption of an antisodomy law, for the first time in its history, in section 226 of the *Kaitei Ritsurei* (*Amendments to the Criminal Code*) in 1873.[262] It was soon abolished in 1881, but the Western medical discourse on the "homosexual pervert" soon invested Japanese scientific and popular discourse.[263] In the Taisho era (1912–1925), homosexual relations were labeled as *seiyoku hentai*, that is, diseases or abnormalities of the sexual desire.[264] The pre-Meiji history of male love (*nanshoku*) presented a decidedly different picture. The traditional discourse on *nanshoku* seemed to emerge mainly during the Muromachi era (1336–1573). The love of boys was of sufficient importance in the daily lives of Japanese monasteries to the point where it gave rise to a particular literary genre called *Chigo Monogatari (Tales of acolytes)*.[265] Among the most famous of these tales was *A Long Tale for an Autumn Night* (*Aki no yo no Nagamonogatari*), a work probably written by a monk of the late fourteenth century. The tale featured an anonymous narrator who recounted a story to older insomniac monks. Keiki, a monk and a *Vinaya* master at the Enryaku-ji Temple atop Mount Hiei, realized that he had not reached a sufficient level of detachment. He went to Ishiyama Temple dedicated to the bodhisattva Kannon, hoping for his assistance to achieve enlightenment. He fell asleep during meditation, and a handsome youth appeared to him in a dream. He returned to the monastery, believing his request had been granted, but the dream he had had still haunted him. He then decided to revisit Ishiyama, but a storm forced him to flee to rival Onjo-ji Temple, later called Miidera, at the foot of Mount Hiei.[266] He fancied seeing in the garden the youth of his dreams. The next day, a child in the service of this youth, identified to him his master Umewaka, the son of the Minister of the Left (*sadaijin*) servicing Emperor Hanazono. Thanks to the servant, Keiki ended up meeting Umewaka with whom he spent the night. Both left in the morning after having exchanged poems. Keiki went back to Hiei to go on with his secluded life. The young Umewaka was in despair because he had not heard back from Keiki. He asked his servant to show him where Keiki lived. On the road, the two boys sought help from a hermit living in the mountains (*yamabuchi*), who then decided to kidnap them. The monks of Miidera thought that the young man's disappearance meant he had been seduced by a monk of the Enryaku-ji, and they decided to retaliate with armed force. Having got wind of the affair, Keiki and 500 monks in arms decided to attack and destroy Miidera. Umewaka eventually escaped from the cave where he had been imprisoned, but he found mere devastation and destruction at his return in Miidera. Feeling responsible for the wreckage, Umewaka decided to kill himself after having put in writing his thoughts for Keiki. The latter, after having read Umewaka's letter, rushed to his side but in vain; the young one had already drowned in a river. Through these unfortunate events, Umewaka's suicide and the destruction of the monastery, Keiki finally became fully aware of the impermanence of all things and continued living in seclusion.[267] The monks of Miidera learned about the appearance of the Bodhisattva Kannon in the form of a beautiful teenager. This story perfectly illustrates the Mahayana doctrine of expedient means (*upaya*), that is, reliance of bodhisattvas and Buddhas on a variety of means—in this case homosexual desire, to guide beings on the path of understanding emptiness and achieving enlightenment. In another tale named *Genmu Monogatari*, the monk Genmu was seduced by the beauty of a young *chigo*, Hanamatsu. Tormented, Genmu could no longer concentrate and meditate. Hanamatsu appeared in one of the monk's dreams, in the guise of a flute player. They spent all night writing poetry together. Genmu felt guilty for being attached to such a passion, which was only a dream. Indeed, Hanamatsu had died two weeks earlier. As in the previous story, we learn that the *chigo* was a bodhisattva, this time Monju (Manjusri), helping the monk on the road to enlightenment.[268] Romantic relationships presented by the *Chigo monogatari* literature always led monks to spiritual achievement, while love affairs with women inevitably led them to spiritual defeat.[269] Pederasty (*wakashu do*, *shudo* for short, the way of beautiful young men), found in Japanese Buddhist monasteries, is inseparable from the history of *nanshoku*. It remains, however, difficult to determine how widespread this practice was, based only on literary sources such as the *Chigo Monogatari*. A well-known picture scroll (*emaki*) kept in the Shingon Daigo-ji Temple near Kyoto, the *Chigo No Zoshi* from the fourteenth century, depicts a young acolyte trying to lubricate his fundament for penetration by the abbot of the monastery.[270] The monk Yoshida Kenko in his famous *Tsurezuregusa* (Essays in Idleness) showed, in a nonjudgmental fashion, how monks were far from following the strict monastic rules on the use of alcohol and women. In Chapter 54, he depicted a group of monks from Omuro excited by the thought of organizing a picnic with a *chigo*.[271] An anonymous work of the late sixteenth century, *Kobo Daishi Ikkan No Sho* (Book of Kobo Daishi) revealed a coded language used by *chigos* to communicate their feelings to the monks and arrange secret meetings. It also contained advise to monks on how to seduce, attract, and train a *chigo*, as well as tips for painless anal penetration.[272] In the seventeenth century, Kitamura Kigin compiled homoerotic poems in a collection entitled *Iwatsutsuji* (Wild Azaleas). The title is taken from a poem attributed to a monk of the tenth century whose memories of past loves with a *chigo* arose in his mind as wild azaleas blooming on the cliffs of Mount Tokiwa. In the preface to his book, Kitamura attributed monks' love for boys to the fact that monastic discipline precluded the natural company of women, thus inducing in the monks the love of adolescents (*wakashu*). Nevertheless, according to Kitamura, what should have been an easy outlet for the monks' passions eventually exceeded the love between a man and a woman. The Tokugawa era (1603–1868) established by the Shogun Ieyasu prompted the development of a new discourse about *nanshoku*. It was no longer confined to monasteries, but reached the world of the Samurais and later the theater. The love of boys did not, however, disappear from the monastic scene and some Zen masters denounced it openly, for instance, the reformer Manzan Dohaku (1636–1715).[273] The poet Ihara Saikaku (1642–1693), born in Osaka in a merchant family, turned to prose at the end of his life, and created a genre consisting of graphic erotic tales, *Ukiyo Zoshi* (Tales of the Floating World).[274] Some of the stories deal in part with *nanshoku*, as in the *Koshoku Gonin Onna* (Five Women Who Loved Love) (1685), which chronicles the love lives of five women. However, Oman, the heroine of the last story, disguised herself as a male teenager in order to entice a Buddhist monk by the name of Gengobei. The monk was living in the mountains, after the death of two teenagers he had passionately loved. Until his encounter with Oman, Gengobei never had any sexual experience with women.[275] He finally fell into Oman's hands and discovered the unfaked sex of Oman. He concluded that the love of a woman is worth that of a young man. Yonosuke, the hero in *Koshoku Ichidai Otoko* (The Life of an Amorous Man) (1682), had his first sexual experience with a male prostitute (*tobiko*) at the age of 14, in the village of Jin-o-do. The prostitute gave him several details about his trade and the different men encountered, from priests to woodcutters. He thereafter frequently visited male and female prostitutes in the brothels of the Shimabara district, Kyoto's red light, and seemed to enjoy the company of young male actors.[276] In 1687, Ihara Saikaku devoted an entire book to male love among Samurais and Kabuki[277] theater actors, the *Nanshoku Okagami* (The Great Mirror of Male Love).[278] The author lingered on descriptions of homosexual liaisons, tinged by loyalty (*nasake*) and a sense of duty (*giri*), which sometimes ended in ritual suicide (*seppuku*). The relations he described happened between young adolescent boys (*wakashu*) of the samurai class and their masters (*nenja*), or between Kabuki transvestite actors (*onnagata*) with merchant class men, samurais, and monks. However, not without some irony, the author liked to portray the hypocrisy of the Buddhist clergy who "rather than waste the offerings of the faithful on things without meaning, use the money to buy the love of young actors," having a marvelous time drinking and organizing sexual orgies in their monasteries, as in the story of the famous young actor Ito Kodayu.[279] Other tales report that the *Rinzai* monks' demand for young male prostitutes was so strong that prices increased seriously. To afford these acquaintances, monks from less fortunate temples had to sell calligraphy or cut down forests and sell timber. The *Great Mirror of Male Love*, unlike other works where bisexuality appeared in vogue, described a subculture where the heroes lived in a world of exclusively homosexual preferences. People showing a preference for *wakashu do* were called *onna girai*.[280] In Tokugawa society, they usually coexisted alongside married men who also displayed a crush for handsome young men (*shojin zuki*), and men who preferred women (*joshoku*).[281] *Nanshoku* or male love described by Ihara Saikaku almost always involved an age difference, the older being the inserter and the younger the insertee. There were exceptions to the rule, like these two men, over 60 years of age, who lived together. One assumed the role of *wakashu* in the tale entitled "Two Old Cherry Trees still in Bloom."[282] In the tale "Bamboo Clappers Strike the Hateful Number," a young monk of 22 years greeted Kabuki actors in his hermitage on Mount Shiroyama, including the famous Tamamura Kichiya. The actors were invited to pick mushrooms in the mountains by Ko-romo-Notan Shiroku, known for his love of boys. The walls of the monk's hut were lined with love letters from young actors, and he admitted he could not help thinking about them. The actors made a fuss about revealing their age, and then the monk snapped the bamboo clapper, which miraculously reported the age of each of them. All were aged over 22 years, and one of them even had 39 years.[283] Even in the *Chigo Monogatari*, where *wakashu do* seemed the norm, the monk Genmu loved and lived peacefully until his last days with the murderer of Hanamatsu, the *chigo* he had loved so much.

In the eighteenth century, Akinari Ueda (1739–1809) upset the interpretation of the love of boys as a spiritual experience of impermanence (*mujo*), where transgression led to enlightenment. In *Ugetsu Monogatari* (Tales of Moonlight and Rain), a tale entitled *Aozukin* (The Blue Hood) told about a monk who could not recover after his *chigo*'s death.[284] To console himself, he had sex with his corpse, eventually eating the remains. Tomita Villagers told Kaian, a Zen monk who was passing by, that every night after the boy's death the monk who lived in the mountains transformed into a demon and would come in search of food and dig up the corpses in the village cemetery. The Zen monk decided to go atop the mountain to meet him. He gave him a *koan* that ultimately would allow the monk, tortured by the demons of lust, to reach enlightenment. Unlike the narratives of enlightenment contained in the *Chigo Monogatari*, this tale shows that sexuality sets in motion a dangerous karmic process that causes more and more torment. The process is not irreversible, as demonstrated by the outcome of the story, with the help of meditation and *koan*. Although one is far from the idealized vision of transgression, yet this story cannot be interpreted as being homophobic. Indeed, the Zen monk told the villagers that a similar event happened when a young woman was changed into a demon after she fell madly in love with a monk in his sleep. Kaian then pointed to the villagers that there are many tales of women transformed into a demon because women are evil by nature, but he had never heard of stories involving men. The author wanted to illustrate that sexual desire, whether heterosexual or homosexual, keeps the person in the dark, conduces to hell, and brings about the cycle of rebirths.

An anonymous text from the Tokugawa era presented a different idea about karmic retribution in relation to the love of boys, much more positive than those offered by Ueda Akinari or Genshin. In *Shin'yuki* (Record of Heartfelt Friends),[285] a master teaches youths that *wakashu do* is nothing but a path of love and compassion taught by the Buddha. Some boys may have an appearance that troubles the mind, but their heart is hard as a rock. They do not reciprocate love, that being the reason why they will be reborn with some physical disability. Those who in their youth answer the love of a man already in their heart, sow the seeds of love and compassion that will have them grow well into adulthood.

Conclusion

At first glance, Buddhism generally has a rather neutral attitude toward homosexuality. It does not assign any stigma to homosexual persons and practices by opposing some sort of heterosexual normality. The Buddha did not say a word about it. The Theravada and Mahayana understanding of the three first defenses do not normally include same-sex relations, at least as far as lay persons are concerned. Even when tradition manifests its opposition in the case of the celibate monk, it never bases its objection on gender confusion that would render it illegitimate. Monastic rule prohibits same-sex relations in the same way it prohibits heterosexual relations. The code of monastic discipline is, however, more uncompromising in its requirements for ordination when dealing with persons whose sexuality does not conform to heterosexual standards, the *pandakas*. They may not conform either anatomically, psychologically, or because they prefer sexual practices such as oral sex or passive sodomy. As I have shown, these standards are still in use today by some Buddhists in an attempt to exclude from ordination persons who identify themselves as homosexual or gay.

One may surmise that the attitude of neutrality stems largely from the fact that sexuality remains for most Buddhists an onset for attachment, while celibacy remains an ideal, effective method of cultivating nonattachment. In light of the goal of *nirvana*, sexuality raises little interest. In such a context, it is difficult to explain this apparent neutrality as a true positive affirmation of homosexuality, contrary to a group of Western Buddhists, the *Friends of the Western Buddhist Order*,[286] who are inclined to do so.[287] I think more skepticism is in order.

European colonization and Western influence in trading posts have been instrumental in the development of homophobia in Asian Buddhist societies. Long before the establishment of Buddhism, homophobia was virtually absent in China and the neutrality of Buddhism on sex between men well suited the Chinese tradition. Reprobation of homosexual behavior may have come from fear of a loss of male dignity or social status but never from religious condemnation.[288] In Southeast Asia, the *kathoey* may well have retained pre-Buddhist origins, which would explain the virtual absence of homophobia in the traditions of the region. One must qualify the claims of an alleged Buddhist tolerance toward homosexuality. It does not always have its source solely in Buddhism.

Finally, there is no doubt that a particular Buddhist discourse, especially in Mahayana but also in the Tibetan *Tantra*, retains a liberating force by transcending the traditional categories through which religious discourse on sexuality and spiritual development is usually shaped. When one moves to the plane of absolute truth, conventional speech no longer holds, including the one on gender, gender identity, or sexual orientation.

The true nature of the person transcends all these distinctions, as expressed by the nun Soma:

Those who think: "I am a woman," "I am a man"
Or those who think: "I'm anything at all"
Is fit for Mara, to address.[289]

3

JUDAISM

RELIGION

Judaism refers to the religion of the Jewish people or the children of Israel, which comprises all those descended from the 12 tribes of Israel, who were descended from the 12 sons of the patriarch Jacob, Abraham's grandson. There are some 13.3 million Jews in the world, with over 8 million living in the Diaspora: 5.7 million in the United States, 519,000 in France, and 364,000 in Canada. A little more than 5 million Jews today live in Israel.[1] A person can be identified as Jewish in three ways: ethnicity (being born to a Jewish mother) together with the practice of Judaism, the practice of Judaism without ethnicity (converts), and finally ethnicity alone. Some people, therefore, see themselves as belonging to Jewish culture without practicing religion on a regular basis. Thus, in Israel, 43 percent of the Jewish population is nonpractising, but 65 percent of Israelis say they observe the *Seder* ritual. The *Seder* is the ritual meal taken the first two nights of the festival of *Pesach* (Passover), and the service includes the reading of the *Haggadah*, the narrative of the exodus of the Jewish people and their liberation from slavery in Egypt. In the United States, 80 percent of Jews say they practice some form of religion, perhaps *Pesach*, *Hanukkah* (Festival of Lights), and *Yom Kippur* (Day of Atonement), but only 46 percent attend the synagogue.[2] Also in the United States, observance of the Sabbath falls to 28 percent and the dietary laws (*kashrut*) to 21 percent.

Judaism has its roots in the ancient monotheistic religion of the Israelites, the faith of a people chosen by a jealous god named YHWH (Yahweh). This God first chose Abraham, who left the city of Ur in Mesopotamia to build a new nation in Canaan, and become the father of his people.[3] To this end, the Lord made an eternal covenant with Abraham, for which male circumcision, on the eighth day after birth, would become the sign.[4] The promise of alliance was actually sealed when the Lord, under the leadership of Moses (Moshe), freed the Israelites, kept as slaves in Egypt by the Pharaohs. Jews had fled to Egypt under the leadership of Joseph, the son of Jacob. Jacob was the son of Isaac, who was Abraham's son. The *Sefer Shemot* (Book of Exodus) relates how Moses miraculously led the Israelites out of Egypt to the Promised Land, the land of Canaan. The journey lasted 40 years through the inhospitable terrain of the Sinai Peninsula. Crossing the Sinai remains a crucial moment, when the alliance was truly sealed under the authority of Moses. Moses then received from the Lord, on Mount Sinai, the Tablets of Law, God's Ten Commandments.[5] When Moses descended the mountain, he saw his people worshipping a golden calf, and overcome with anger, he crushed the Ten Tablets.[6] The Lord recalled Moses on the mountain, and renewed his covenant by engraving on two stone tablets the words written on the original tablets.[7] Moses died on the banks of the River Jordan before entering the Promise Land and appointed Joshua as his successor.

This divine law or teaching is embodied in Judaism's most sacred document, the *Torah*.[8] It consists of five books and is part of the Hebrew Bible (*Tanakh*). It is known by Christians as the *Pentateuch* in the *Old Testament*.[9] The *Torah* stands, therefore, as the primary source of Mosaic Law, which contains 613 *mitzvoth* or commandments of God. The *mitzvoth* govern personal conduct, including details of personal hygiene, diet, clothing, and religious rituals.[10] Yahweh also ordered his people to make a wooden box covered with gold, the Ark of the Covenant (*Aron ha-Berit*), to hold the Tablets of Law (*Luhot ha-Berit*), a symbol for the covenant with his chosen people.[11] It accompanied the Jewish people during their conquest of Canaan. The walls of the Canaanite city of Jericho collapsed after the Ark had been walked in procession seven times around the enclosure.[12] During the conquest of Canaan, the Ark of the Covenant was housed in a tent, the Tabernacle (*Mishkan*), that was eventually integrated in the Temple of Jerusalem, during the time of royalty.[13] At the beginning of the first millennium, David, the second king of Israel, defeated the Philistines and triumphantly brought back the Ark, plundered by the enemy, in his new capital, Jerusalem.[14] King Solomon transferred the Ark from the Tabernacle built by David to the Holy of Holies (*Qodesh ha-Qodashim*) in the newly built Temple.[15]

At Solomon's death (*ca.* 930 BC), a dispute between the tribes caused the Kingdom of Israel to partition—ten tribes under the leadership of Jeroboam in the North formed the Kingdom of Israel, and the tribes of Benjamin and Judah, to the South, formed the Kingdom of Judah, with Jerusalem as its capital.[16] The kingdom of Israel ultimately fell into the hands of the Assyrians around 721 BC.[17] That of Judah was finally crushed in turn, in 586 BC, by Babylonian king Nebuchadnezzar II. He destroyed the First Temple and deported the Jews to Babylon.[18] The *Tanakh* left no doubt about what caused the destruction of the two kingdoms and the misfortunes of the chosen people that followed during exile. It was interpreted as a punishment from Yahweh, who punished His people because of their turning to idolatry, and because their leaders had turned away from His commandments. The Jews had abandoned their commitment to serve Him faithfully and obey His command.[19] The prophets focused on these aberrations as the main component of their oracles, as evidenced by Isaiah in reference to the punishment of Judah and Israel: "Hear, O heavens, and give ear, O earth, for the Lord has spoken; Children I have raised and exalted, yet they have rebelled against Me."[20] With the looting of the Temple, the legends about the lost Ark of the Covenant proliferated. According to an Ethiopian tradition, Menelik 1, an illegitimate son born of the union between Queen Makeda of Sheba (Tigray, Northern Ethiopia) and King Solomon had stolen the Ark during a visit to Jerusalem, and then brought it to Ethiopia.[21] The disappearance of the Ark continues, to this day, to captivate the imagination. Thus, the American filmmaker Spielberg, in his film *Raiders of the Lost Ark*, imagined the location of the ark somewhere in the Nile Delta. According to other legends, the prophet Jeremiah had hidden the Ark of the Covenant in a cave, in the mountain where the Lord had revealed it to Moses, to save it from destruction.[22] The Second Temple of Jerusalem was reconstructed in 515 BC. However, its importance in Jewish life dwindled, particularly because of the disappearance of the symbol par excellence for God's dwelling presence (*Shekinah*), the Ark of the Covenant. The Second Temple was finally destroyed in 70 AD by the Roman legions, under Titus's command. Orthodox Judaism believes that the Temple of Jerusalem will one day be rebuilt, when the dispersed people of Israel finally meet at the coming of the Messiah, who will be the future King issued from David's lineage, announced by the prophets.[23]

Until its destruction, the Temple had been at the center of the religious life of the Jewish people, and many sacrifices (*qorbanot*) were offered by the priests (*kohanim*).[24]

Sacrificial rites were performed daily, as well as during the Sabbath and major holidays that mark the annual liturgical calendar. Thus, on the feast of *Yom Kippur*, the most solemn day of the Jewish liturgy where a 25-hour fast should be observed by the faithful, the High Priest entered the Holy of Holies and sprinkled the blood of a bull he had sacrificed by way of atonement. The day of *Yom Kippur* was immediately followed by the feast of *Sukkot*, a sort of thanksgiving at harvest time.[25] All Jews had to go on pilgrimage to the Temple of Jerusalem for the Passover and offer a lamb sacrificed by the priests. The animal had to be consumed on site, and the meal had to be accompanied by unleavened bread (*matzah*), in memory of the Exodus. Fifty days after Passover, the Jews had to go again to the Temple of Jerusalem for the feast of *Shavuot*, commemorating the gift of the *Torah* to Moses on Mount Sinai, and at the same time offering the first fruits of the season. The prophets openly criticized the practice of religious sacrifices for their inability to transform the human heart in depth:

> So says the Lord of Hosts, the God of Israel; add your burnt offerings upon your sacrifices and eat flesh. For neither did I speak with your forefathers nor did I command them on the day I brought them out of the land of Egypt, concerning a burnt offering or a sacrifice. But this thing did I command them, saying: Obey Me so that I am your God and you are My people, and you walk in all the ways that I command you, so that it may be well with you.[26]

With the exilic period, a new religion favoring righteousness of the heart over religious practices emerged, in which the prophet Jeremiah says that in the new Zion people would not engage in building a new Ark of the Covenant.[27] The interpretation of the *Torah* by a teacher (*Rabbi*) came to occupy a more prominent role in postexilic Judaism, as witnessed by Ezra and Nahemya (Nehemiah), upon their return to Jerusalem, which had been authorized by the Persian king Artaxerxes 1. Upon arrival in Jerusalem, the people gathered around Ezra the scribe, who read them the Book of the Law of Moses, and explained its meaning.[28] The exile and the destruction of the Temple drew religion to new forms of worship, in a new place called the synagogue (*Beit ha-Knesset*, house of assembly), where Scripture reading and prayer replaced the Temple sacrifice.[29] Even with the return of some Jews to Palestine, the country still remained occupied by a foreign power, Persia (539–333 BC) and Greece after the conquest of the Persian Empire by Alexander the Great (333–200 BC). At Alexander's death, his generals willed to divide the empire. Finally, Rome took over Palestine during the capture of Jerusalem by Pompey in 63 BC. During the Hellenistic period, many Jews emigrated from Judea to many flourishing cities in the empire, including Alexandria and Antioch. Until its destruction by Titus in 70 AD, the rebuilt Temple continued to be the center of Jewish worship.[30] The Temple was a celebration of God's presence, which demanded a strict application of rules of purity, in order to protect the sanctity of the site. The altar of sacrifice figured as a locus of reconciliation and communion with the Lord.[31] At the time of the monarchy, the king served as a prominent religious Temple figure but, during the Hellenistic period, the priests (*kohanim*) from the tribe of Levi gained importance. Not only did they preside over religious ceremonies in the Temple, but they became, with the Levites and scribes, the guardians of tradition, by writing, teaching of the law (*halakah*), and exercising adjudicative functions in the person of the High Priest (*Kohen Gadol*) assisted by the Sanhedrin (the supreme court).[32] The Maccabees, a priestly family from the second century BC, organized Jewish resistance against the oppressive Seleucid Antiochus IV Epiphanes. He tried to stop Jews from practicing their religion, and desecrated the Temple. Simon Maccabeus instituted the Hasmonean Dynasty, and presided, as Prince and High Priest, over the religious and political destiny of the Jewish people, until the foundation of the Herodian Dynasty, in the future Roman province of Judea established by Octavian in 30 BC.[33] Sacrifices were accompanied by prayers offered daily in the Temple, as well as during the Sabbath, and during the different events in the liturgical calendar defined by the priests, especially Passover and *Yom* Kippur.[34] Daily prayer (*Amidah* or *Shemoneh Esreh*, the Eighteen Blessings) were still recited by Orthodox Jews three times a day; morning, afternoon, and evening, in private or in a synagogue. It probably first appeared during the exile through the work of the Great Assembly eager to make the religion portable, in the absence of the Temple.[35] This form of prayer probably continued to evolve during the Second Temple period, but no doubt its formalization is explained by the fact that, in the Diaspora, these prayers were not recited anymore in the Temple to accompany the daily sacrifices.[36] Maimonides believed that the mixing of languages during the postexilic period with the use of Aramaic, and Greek as the vernacular colonial language led to the codification of prayers.[37]

Another type of codification of the Jewish religious tradition marked the Second Temple period: the establishment, by the clergy and scribes, of the canon of writings making up the Holy Book, the *Tanakh*. From the exile to the destruction of the Temple by the Romans, Jewish culture was threatened by the dominant culture, sometimes that of Antioch, then that of Alexandria. At the same time, it was exposed to all sorts of new ideas, whether the Greek idea of immortality or the dualism of Persian Zoroastrianism, where the forces of good oppose the forces of evil. These ideas inspired some, while causing defensive reactions in others, but surely generated conflicts among the thinkers and transmitters of Jewish tradition. Among these guardians of tradition, the Pharisees (*Perushim*) exerted a crucial influence in the definition of rabbinic Judaism after the destruction of the Temple in 70 AD.[38] Josephus noted that the Pharisees were carefully attached to the traditions of the elders not documented in the Mosaic Law, and they disputed their viewpoint with the Sadducees (*Tzeduqim*), a group of priestly aristocracy.[39] Their exact name means "separate" (*parush*) and probably originated with their principal concern for purity of the new community formed by Ezra and Nehemiah. It happened during the return from exile when these two reformers were asking the people of Israel, including priests and Levites who had borrowed the customs of surrounding peoples (*Am ha-Aretz*), to abandon those customs. It included a requirement for a divorce of the non-Jewish women they had married.[40]

The Pharisees and the Essenes, another religious group dedicated to monastic asceticism, blasted hereditary priesthood of the Hasmonean High Priests. They considered them dishonest and over-Hellenized, so, at the same time, they relativized the role of the Temple, traditionally played in the expression of piety. The *Book of Jubilees* is a clear example of the Pharisees' desire to separate the religious Jews from any Hellenized social behavior, considered as unclean. This book emphasizes the divine origin of Mosaic Law and some aspects that distinguished Israel from the nations around: circumcision, the Sabbath, and dietary laws regarding the purity of certain foods. The Pharisees made *Torah* study the center of religious practice rather than sacrifices at the Temple. They also placed more emphasis on prayer and blessings. Taking a stand against the exploitation of the poor, particularly by the priestly class, the Pharisees injected a dose of democracy into religious practice, especially with the recitation at home of the daily prayer "*Shema Yisrael*" with the *tefillin*.[41] The Pharisaic idea of "democratization" went even further by substituting for the sanctity of the Temple the sanctification of the practitioner's daily life, who faithfully obeyed the rules of purity, which made the Jews a holy people, chosen by Yahweh.[42] Under Roman occupation, the Pharisees took control of the Sanhedrin, the court of Jewish affairs. The Roman occupants had originally been called to intervene in fratricidal struggles between local leaders, but, during the Hasmonean period of uncertainty, the priestly Hasmonean party lost the people's trust. This meant that the Pharisees, *Torah* scholars par excellence, occupied the office of *Nasi* or president of the Sanhedrin, as, for example, the two great sages—Hillel, just before the Christian era, and later Hillel the Elder's grandson, Gamaliel.[43]

The destruction of the Temple of Jerusalem in 70, somehow, helped spread the Pharisees' vision of a religious life focused on *Torah* study and its application to the practitioner's daily life. It was done through interpretations of the law by teachers (Rabbis) that finally came to be assembled in writing in the *Mishnah* (the first written collection of the laws comprising the oral *Torah*) and the *Gemara*, or rabbinical commentaries, both forming the *Talmud*. After the Temple's destruction, Rabbi Yohanan ben Zakkai, *Nasi* of the Sanhedrin, obtained that the Sanhedrin be moved to Yavne, a town in Central Israel. There, he opened an academy (*yeshiva*) for the study of the *Torah*. It was believed the transmission of oral teaching had been done without interruption from Moses through the prophets and the Great Assembly (*Anshei Knesset ha-Gedolah*), then the School of Hillel, and until Yohanan ben Zakkai, right up to Judas the Prince (*Yehudah ha-Nasi*), editor of the *Mishnah* around 200 AD.[44] He did not edit the *Mishnah* from scratch, but gathered the often conflicting opinions of the learned sages on the applicability of the *Torah*, from the reign of the Hasmonean dynasty under Simon Maccabeus.[45] Hinged mainly on the opinions of the rabbis, the six orders (*sedarim*) of the *Mishnah*, like a true *Holiness Code*, defined the rules (*halachot*) that every fervent Jew must put into daily practice in different spheres of activities, from daily prayers to Shabbat and festivals. These rules of conduct also applied to agriculture, marriages, divorces, kosher food, and the rules of ritual purity (food preparation, personal hygiene, menstrual blood, semen emission, etc.).[46] Other rabbinical schools, including the *Amoraim*, later commented on the often terse sentences of the *Mishnah*, to clarify them. These commentaries were compiled in the *Talmud*.[47] A first version of them (*Gemara*) appeared in Palestine, and in the second half of the fourth century, they became part of the *Jerusalem Talmud*, *Talmud Yerushalmi*. Another version of the *Gemara* was completed in Babylon around 500 AD, and introduced in the *Babylonian Talmud* or *Talmud Bavli*. The *Bavli* is deemed complete and more authoritative, because its compilation was done over a long time by eminent Babylonian rabbinical schools, especially that of Sura.[48] The coexistence of the *Mishnah* and the *Gemara* reads like a real contradiction, since commentaries on the *Torah* transmitted orally came to be written down. Furthermore, a rabbi of the *Tanna* school of Rabbi Ishmael ben Elizah mentioned the prohibition to write the *halachot*, these laws or rules of conduct passed on orally since Moses.[49] As the *Halacha* seeks to codify the practitioner's life in every detail, new questions arose without being necessarily answered by the *Talmud*. These situations were the inspiration behind a new literary genre, the *responsa* (*teshuvot*), answers by rabbis replying to questions in writing. The *Gaonim*, learned rabbis who headed the Sura and Pumbedita *Yeshivot* in Babylonia, were probably the initiators of the genre in the late sixth century—responding in writing to questions contained in letters from their colleagues in Palestine.[50] From the eleventh century, rabbis of the Sephardic community (Iberian Peninsula) also became responsible for drafting *responsa*. They were soon imitated by the Ashkenazi[51] rabbis from Northern France and Germany.[52] Following migrations, associated with the expulsion of Jews from Spain during the Inquisition of 1492, or due to different religious persecutions in France and Germany, *responsa* came then to be written by Eastern European rabbis (Poland, Lithuania, etc.). Rabbis from Greece or Turkey and much later from America became involved in writing *responsa*. Among the rabbis responsible for making decisions, known as *poskim*, Yosef ben Ephraim Caro (1488–1575) played a central role in rabbinic Judaism because of the authority that was granted to his scholarly compilation of Talmudic literature, the *Shulhan Aruch*.

Authority granted to rabbinical opinions defined a form of Judaism, practiced since that time until today. Within rabbinic Judaism several trends emerged over the years and their differences are often related to the degree of authority given to the *Talmud* and *responsa*.

In the eighteenth century, European Jewry, especially in Germany, provided its own contribution to the *Aufklärung* (the Enlightenment) with the *Haskalah* movement.[53] It was an intellectual movement that sought to empower politically the Jewish population from the ghettos to integrate into European society. Thus, the Jewish philosopher Moses Mendelssohn (1729–1786) translated the *Torah* into German and tried, in his writings, to promote freedom of conscience and defend the rationality of the *Torah* against former attacks by Dutch philosopher Baruch Spinoza (1632–1677).[54] The Enlightenment philosophers wanted to clear humanity of superstitions contained in the revealed religions and create a natural religion based on universal spiritual values, accessible by human reason. The core values of Judaism, love of God, charity and justice, providence and eternal life are accessible through reason and as such there is no need for revelation at Mount Sinai, says Mendelssohn. He believed, however, the disclosure of Mosaic Law on Mount Sinai was required because the natural religion of the pre-Sinaitic period had quickly fallen down into idolatry. The *Torah* became a guide that could capture the practitioner's mind to understand eternal truths recorded from the origin in the human heart. The Jewish people had to set an example for nations in search of truth.[55] Although Mendelssohn sought to preserve the value of Mosaic Law, his position nevertheless relativized its importance. Indeed, as necessary as it was at one time, given the circumstances, many of the aspects of Mosaic Law could disappear without posing any difficulty in another context. Some rabbis were able to pick up this kind of relativistic twist, which gave considerable impetus to Reform Judaism. Many reformers then started teaching that the legal and ritual aspects contained in the *Talmud* or the *responsa* were historical expressions of a religion that had to adapt to the times.[56] Rabbi Samuel Holdheim (1806–1860) of Frankfurt an-der-Oder went as far as advocating the observance of Sabbath on Sunday, as Christians do, and declaring himself in favor of mixed marriages. Israel Jacobson (1768–1828) pioneered a revision of the synagogue service by introducing the organ and songs in German in the first Reform Temple in Seesen, Saxony, in 1810. The word "synagogue" was abandoned by the reformists. Other Reform temples soon appeared in Berlin, Brunschweig, Hamburg, and Breslau (Wrocław in Poland). Abraham Geiger (1810–1874), rabbi of Breslau and Berlin's chief rabbi, called circumcision a "barbaric" custom. Reformers often grouped in associations to promote their ideas. The *Verein der Reformfreunde* (Union of Friends of the Reform) in Frankfurt-am-Main, founded in 1842, made a statement of principles by which it rejected the authority of the *Talmud*, refuted the idea that Jews would all be reunited in Israel with the advent of a Messiah. Instead, they promoted a vision whereby the Mosaic religion could grow and adapt to the modern world by ridding it of any ethnic or national characteristic.

It is a disciple and collaborator of Geiger, Kaufmann Kohler (1843–1926), who gave a real boost to the cause of Reform Judaism in America. He became rabbi in New York in 1885, and convened a meeting in Pittsburgh of all Reform rabbis to adopt the principles of Reform Judaism on American soil.[57] Kohler ended his career as president of the first Jewish seminary in America, the Hebrew Union College, founded in 1875, in Cincinnati by Bohemia-born Rabbi Isaac Meyer Wise. All these new stands did not suit the traditionalists, and they organized their response. It settled mainly on two fronts: the orthodox and ultraorthodox response on the one hand, and the conservative on the other.

Rabbi Moses ben Samuel Sofer (1762–1839) crystallized in one sentence the leitmotif of his opponents: "*Hadash asur min ha-Torah*" (the *Torah* does not innovate).

Rabbi Samuel Raphael Hirsch (1808–1888) became the leader of the Orthodox response when he took the leadership in 1851 of a traditionalist group, the *Israelitische Religionsgesellschaft* (Israelite Religious Society) in Frankfurt-am-Main, the Mecca of the reform movement. Annoyed by the assimilationist tendencies of the reformers, Hirsch launched the slogan of the reformist reply: "*Torah im derech eretz*" (*Torah* and openness to the world). Hirsch believed the emancipation of Jews did not require a rejection of *Halacha*. As much as the practitioner involved himself in society through his work, he had to be able to live by the precepts of the Mosaic Law, and at the same time demonstrate openness to secular culture, which included an emphasis on education embracing secular and scientific knowledge (*Torah umadda*). There are several trends in modern Orthodox Judaism, but the centrist majority are now living in Europe, the United States, and Israel. Under the leadership of Rabbi Zacharias Frankel (1801–1875) of Breslau, another traditionalist movement, Conservative Judaism in the United States and Canada, known as the Masorti Movement in Israel and other countries, also rose in response to the reformers. Frankel took a middle-of-the-road position between traditionalism and reformism. He thought that Mosaic Law was revealed by God, and should be retained, but accompanied by a more flexible interpretation that would take into account the historical context.[58] Conservative Judaism became mainstream in the United States during the twentieth century, through the efforts of Rabbi Sabato Morais (1823–1921) who founded the New York Jewish Theological Seminary of America, modeled on the seminary established by Frankel and Rabbi Solomon Schechter (1847–1915), who became its president in 1902.

Finally, others reacted strongly against the concept of religion adapting to modernity. Those were the ultraorthodox or *Haredim*, literally "shakers," that is to say, fearers of God. Members from this group reject modernity, dress in black, apply strict kosher dietary laws, and advocate living in isolated neighborhoods, with their own shops and services. *Haredi* daily life insists on traditional family values, study of the *Torah* and the *Talmud* by men, in a *yeshiva*. The rabbis control social life, marked by the absence of gender interaction, strict separation of gender roles, and a strict sexual moral code, requiring modesty for women, forced to cover their hair. Their rejection of television also comes from the fact that it projects a sexually liberated society, a mere opportunity of temptation against which the practitioner must be protected. There are several streams within the movement whose origins date back to the eighteenth century, in Eastern Europe (Poland, Lithuania, Ukraine, and Russia). With the French Revolution began in Western Europe a strong movement for the emancipation of Jews, who had been historically deprived of civil rights. During the same period, in Eastern Poland, Lithuania, Russia, Belarus and the Ukraine, Jews would be forced to live in small towns (*shtetls*), in designated areas of colonization.

Jews in Poland had enjoyed a system of royal protection granted in the thirteenth century by the duke of Greater Poland (*Wielkopolska*), Bolesław the Pious, who guaranteed them freedom of religion, movement, and the right to be administered and judged according to *Halacha*. A local committee consisting of peers (*Kehila*), chosen among wealthy merchants and rabbis, preformed these duties.[59] Many Jews were getting richer as traders and bankers, which led the Christian majority in some large centers to limit their privileges, and confine them to a specific district, as was done in Lublin, or exclude them from the city like in Kraków (Cracow).[60] Poland became a leading center of Talmudic culture, notably in Kraków, Lublin, Lwów, and Vilnius. Many Jews settled in the Ukraine, which then had passed to Poland, but the Ukrainian revolt led by Bogdan

Chmielnicki in 1648 led to the massacre of Jews, and the dismantling of some *yeshivas*.[61] Over 70 percent of Jews in the Polish-Lithuanian Union[62] lived precisely in that part of Eastern Europe (the Ukraine, Belarus, and Galicia), typically around the market square (*Rynek*), in small towns, where they engaged in commerce.[63] Life in the *shtetl* was not always synonymous with wealth, and many of these communities became impoverished because of the restrictions and persecutions that had escalated from the seventeenth century. The *Kehila* held the power of taxation, and often took advantage of the poor. It became the potting soil for Hasidism, which started to grow in the eighteenth century.[64] Hasidic Judaism appeared as a pietistic movement, close to the suffering of poor people who could not find solace in the cold and harsh legalism of rabbis and experts in the *Talmud*. The great initiator of this movement, Israel ben Eliazar (1698–1760), known by the Hasidim as Baal Shem Tov (Master of the Holy Name), or just Besht (acronym), was born in this region, precisely in Okopy.

Acting as a rabbi about the people, he soon entered into direct conflict with *Talmud* scholars by preaching joyful communion with God (*devekut*), and the primacy of prayer over the study of *Torah* and *Talmud*. He brought down upon him the wrath of a large number of *Talmudists*, including the famous Gaon (means pride, a title given to the president of a Talmudic academy) of Vilnius, Ben Shlomo Zalman Elyahu Kramer (1720–1797). His opponents (*mitnagdim*) accused him, and his successors, among them Dov Ber, of relegating *Halacha* to second place. The opponents also disapproved of the prominent role played by their charismatic spiritual leader, called *Rebbe* or *Tzadik*, who had become something of a guru delivering rulings on all things in life, even the nonreligious. The Besht drew his inspiration from the Jewish mystical tradition, the *Kabbalah*. The *Sefer ha-Zohar* (The Book of Splendour), attributed to Moses de León in the thirteenth century, provided a method of exegesis based on a numerological analysis of Hebrew characters that would reveal the deep meaning of the *Torah* hidden behind the literal text. Hasidism also held its teaching from a sixteenth-century Kabbalist, Rabbi Isaac Luria of Safed, in Israel. One of the most influential branches of contemporary Hasidism, mostly active in Israel and the United States, but also present in France and Canada, the *Chabad Lubavitch* was founded in the eighteenth century by Rabbi Shneur Zalman. Among the *Haredim* who are not of Hasidic tradition, the Lithuanian Jews, known in Yiddish as *Litvish*, exerted an enormous impact on Orthodox Judaism in Israel, the United States, and Canada after World War II.[65] As immigrants, they brought the tradition of the *yeshiva*, especially the *Etz Haim Yeshiva* of Volozhin in Belarus, founded by Reb Chaim Volozhiner (1749–1821), a student of the Vilna Gaon. Despite the historical *Litvish* opposition to Hasidim, in practice their differences are not so well marked today, both showing immense respect and loyalty for the *Torah*, and careful observance of the *mitzvoth*. For the Hasidim, there is no conflict between mysticism in the *Kabbalah* and *Halacha*; the written and oral *Torah* incorporates in a coded language the infinite wisdom of God, hidden in the creation since the beginning. To regulate every aspect of one's life by obeying the *mitzvoth* is, therefore, a privileged way bequeathed by God to attain wisdom. Rebbe Shneur Zalman in his book *Likutei Amarim*, better known as *Tanya*, is a fine example of halachic exegesis by showing that respect for *kashrut* can be a source of elevation to God—as only pure foods defined by the *Torah* hold a spark of the divine.[66]

The concept of Yahweh's Alliance with Israel and the consequences of the latter's failures to remain faithful, which led them to the life of a minority in exile and diaspora, had major importance in defining the rules for marriage and sexual life. A lot of the purity rules were aimed at the protection of the distinctive character of the chosen people. This will be the object of the following section.

Sexuality

The *Tanakh* places a great emphasis on sexuality. The Creation accounts reveal that God created man in His own image, male and female he created them, and commanded them to reproduce.[67] Procreation is part of the *mitzvoth* every loyal Jew must put into practice. The authors of the *Tanakh* used the energy of human love as a metaphor for the love of Yahweh for his people Israel. They did not hesitate to portray God's chosen people as a prostitute and an adulteress, when they became unfaithful to Him.[68] As noted by David Biale, human sexuality plays a vital role in the formation of the national identity of Israel, which gradually defined its monotheistic faith in contradistinction to the polytheism of neighboring nations. Monotheism is presented as standing in opposition to fertility cults, and to all kinds sexual rituals deemed orgiastic.[69] A loving union sanctioned by God's law makes no room for adultery, incest, prostitution, even cultic sex, or bestiality, as evidenced by the *Holiness Code* in the *Vayikra*.[70] In this code is also found the famous injunction to which I shall return later: "You shall not lie down with a male, as with a woman: this is an abomination."[71] Yahweh clearly explained to Moses the context of these sexual taboos:

> And the Lord spoke to Moses, saying: Speak to the children of Israel and say to them: I am the Lord, your God. Like the practice of the land of Egypt, in which you dwelled, you shall not do, and like the practice of the land of Canaan, to which I am bringing you, you shall not do, and you shall not follow their statutes. You shall fulfill My ordinances and observe My statutes, to follow them. I am the Lord, your God.[72]

Man and woman participate in the completion of His creation through the observance of a code of sexual purity; fulfilling their vocation to holiness, becoming the image of God: "Therefore, a man shall leave his father and his mother, and cleave to his wife, and they shall become one flesh."[73] The ban of mixed marriage (with non-Jews), which dated probably from the time of Ezra, only strengthened the relationship between sexuality, fertility, and national identity.[74] This ban had nothing to do with any ritual impurity in other nations, but was probably based on fear of close social relations, and of ties with polytheistic nations, which would have inevitably led Israel into apostasy and idolatry:

> You shall not intermarry with them; you shall not give your daughter to his son, and you shall not take his daughter for your son. For he will turn away your son from following Me, and they will worship the gods of others, and the wrath of the Lord will be kindled against you, and He will quickly destroy you.[75]

To this prohibition was added, probably during the Roman occupation, the rule of matrilineal descent: the mother provides for the transmission of Jewish identity.[76]

Sexual desire and sexual satisfaction were considered positively by ancient and rabbinic Judaism when they spoke in the context of marriage as a means of sanctification.[77] Talmudic literature showed an appreciable openness to pleasure between married partners, in all its forms. Thus, the learned sages of the *Talmud* rejected the opinion of Rabbi Yohanan ben Dahabai, who had claimed that oral sex caused dumbness in the newborn, while sodomy caused lameness. On the contrary, the learned rabbis did not preclude any form of sexual intimacy between husband and wife.[78] Maimonides adopted the same approach, but added a restriction, also found in the *Talmud*: if possible avoid any spillage of semen: "A man's wife is permitted to him. Therefore a man may do whatever he desires with his wife. He may engage in relations whenever he desires, kiss any organ he desires, engage in vaginal or anal intercourse or engage in physical intimacy without relations, provided he does not release seed in vain."[79] The pietistic Ashkenaz Rabbi Eleazar of Worms (1176–1238) considered sexual pleasure and sexual arousal by various caresses as a means to enhance intimacy and love between the couple, and thereby avoid the temptation of adultery.[80] His master, Yehudah the Pious of Regensberg (d. 1217), insisted, in the *Sefer Hasidim*, on how women should dress to stimulate their husband, who may come with the force of an arrow.[81] However, rabbinic Judaism demonstrated much more ambivalence about sexual desire than in biblical times. The sages of the *Babylonian Talmud* offered a perspective that placed pleasure at the very center of sex relations, and refused to make it an accessory necessity brought about by the need to procreate. Thus, the sages criticized the views of a Palestinian rabbi of the third century, Shimon Ben Lakish, who expressed his gratitude to his forefathers whom he thanked for having committed the offense that brought him into existence.[82] That is at least how he legitimized sexual relations between spouses. In the Middle Ages, Maimonides, for whom procreation was the legitimate purpose of sexual activity, showed the same ambivalence vis-à-vis sexual pleasure: "Nevertheless, it is pious conduct for a person not to act frivolously concerning such matters and to sanctify himself at the time of relations, as explained in *Hilchot Deot*. He should not depart from the ordinary pattern of the world. For this act was [given to us] solely for the sake of procreation."[83] He argued that circumcision was meant to mutilate the male sexual organ, so as to reduce the intensity of the pleasure felt.[84] This idea went back to Philo of Alexandria, who also saw in it a form of regulation of pleasure.[85] In fact, several authors agree that Judaism was influenced by Hellenistic Platonic currents marked by body/mind dualism, as well as Aristotelian or Stoic ideas about moderation (Greek: *sophrosune* σωφροσύνη) in the use of body pleasures, or control through discipline (Greek: *enkrateia* ἐγκράτεια) of the body.

At the turn of the Christian era, several texts associated sexual asceticism with success in philosophical or spiritual quests. Many of these texts displayed apocalyptic tones, suggesting that the Jewish ascetic movement originated in the sufferings during the Babylonian Exile, the need to cleanse, to atone for the sins that caused two Temple destructions and prepare the coming of a better world.[86] Among these writings, the *Testament of the Twelve Patriarchs*, the *Book of Jubilees*, the *Wisdom of Ben Sira*, and the *Psalms of Solomon* contained many warnings against the dangers associated with women, hence the need to stay away from them.[87] The idea of self-control, of regulating one's inclinations and one's sexual drives goes back to the practice of sexual abstinence and celibacy among some Jewish and Christians groups.[88] Several church fathers, like Clement of Alexandria, preached to strive for moderation in sexual relations, which had only one acceptable justification, procreation.[89] However, Origen did not hesitate to assert the superiority of celibacy over marriage, in matters of reaching for spiritual goods.[90] Among the most ardent defenders of marriage, St. John Chrysostom believed that the Apostle Paul (1 Cor. 7) made a concession to marriage because of the weakness of the flesh, without detracting from the superiority of celibacy, as exemplified by Jesus's life.[91] St. Augustine said it was better not to seek progeny and not to marry in order to submit to the only spouse, Christ.[92] Celibacy is often interpreted, in particular from the saying of the Pauline Epistle to the Galatians (3:28) as a kind of mental castration, abolishing any difference between the masculine and the feminine in order to enter the Kingdom of God.[93] If we are to believe the historian Eusebius of Caesarea, Origen had even taken the words of the Gospel of Matthew (19:12) literally, which speaks of those who voluntarily became eunuchs for the Kingdom.[94] Voluntary castration does not seem to have had much influence among Jews, even if it seems to have existed.[95]

Greco-Roman culture and customs from the early centuries exerted a certain fascination and influence on Talmudic literature–which is the reason why a commitment to restrain carnal pleasures is present. I will return to this later. However, the sages of the *Talmud*, in no way waived the duty of procreation or even the pleasures that accompany it. Thus, even Rabbi Azzai who seemed to have remained single all his life still endorsed the reproaches made against him by Rabbi Eleazer ben Azariah, who made the accusation of murder against the person who refused to procreate and reproduce the image of God.[96] Ben Azzai tried to defend himself by claiming his tremendous love for *Torah* study, a kind of sublimation of his erotic feelings.[97] The rabbis rejected his opinion, which suggested an unheard of alternative: a celibate clergy, alongside laity, who is left with the burden of child bearing. They all took the opposing side advocating marriage and procreation, and did not hesitate to justify their stance by attacking the hypocritical practice of clerical celibacy, which often opened the door to various licenses.[98] The rabbis' will not to give up the joy of sex may explain the dismissive attitude of some church fathers toward Jews. John Chrysostom began his *De Virginitate* saying that Jews despised the radiance and worth of virginity.[99] Daniel Boyarin uses St. Augustine's charge, who believed that Jews were incapable of contemplating the spiritual reality of Israel, to highlight the rabbinic view of the body and sexuality. The rabbinic stand specifically rejected the mind/body dualism, which, otherwise, persuaded church fathers to bring in opposition spiritual and carnal realities.[100]

Rabbinical anthropology conceived the body and sexuality in a positive way, but not without displaying, at the same time, some suspicion of sexual desire, called *yetser ha-ra*, or the evil inclination. Being all that is both required and good–it is the source of our existence–it can, if not moderated in any way, cause a person to sink into moral decay. The *Babylonian Talmud* tells the story of people who begged the Lord to rid them of evil desires, which had already led Israel to its loss through the practice of idolatrous worship. Yahweh warned against the elimination of sexual desire, which would then cause the end of the world.[101] The prudery and inhibition of one of the great *Tannaim* sages, Rabbi Eleazar, regarding the sexual act is an excellent example of this kind of hesitant anthropology. Thus, Eleazar would make love to his wife in the dark at midnight, the two keeping almost all their clothes on.[102] According to Boyarin, there is no overall discourse policing the couple's sexual practices, but the sages of the *Talmud*, first and foremost, sought with their restrictions or reservations to protect marital intimacy, affection, and reciprocity in love plays. Thus, the learned men accepted all kinds of practices in bed, between husband and wife, even if nonprocreative, but they judged with severity the husband who fantasized about another woman during a sexual relation with his spouse.[103] R. Johanan said: "A man may do whatever he pleases with his wife [at intercourse]: A parable; Meat which comes from the abattoir, may be eaten salted, roasted, cooked or seethed; so with fish from the fishmonger."[104] The rabbis' position may seem akin to the theological stiffening of the church fathers, but it differs slightly in that sexual desire and the act itself have nothing to do with a shameful sin. And nothing to do with Augustine's view, for example, who thought that marital sexual relations should remain hidden because they express a guilty pleasure, the same guilt that led Adam and Eve to cover their nakedness.[105] Contrary to this perception of sexuality linked to an original sin, the rabbis picture Adam and Eve having sex in Eden, before being evicted.[106] Ritual baths (*mikvaot*) after menstruation, or after the emission of semen (*keri*), as well as a ban on having sex for seven days after menstruation (*niddah*) are still practiced today but mostly by traditionalists. Their origin probably goes back to the rules on the pure and the impure, as recorded by the *Priestly Code* of *Leviticus*.[107] These body cleansing rituals, as well as dietary laws, or other practices of hygiene, have nothing to do with a negative view of the body and sexuality, but profess purity requirements to worship Yahweh.[108]

The rabbis of Babylon had fewer reservations toward sexuality than their counterparts in Palestine, and formulated the opinion that if the man forces his wife to have sex with her clothes on, she can apply for a divorce.[109] However, the sages of the *Babylonian Talmud*, like the rabbis of Palestine, believed that men had a stronger libido than women, as is evidenced noticeably during erection and, for that reason, must be controlled.[110] Study of the *Torah* is an effective remedy to fight against the excesses of sexual desire.[111] For the Babylonian sages, sexuality is a basic need that requires satisfaction in marriage. If it is frustrated, it will interfere with studying the *Torah*. For the Palestinian rabbis, marriage can be delayed without question, something that is even advisable since the bonds of marriage may interfere with the study. The Palestinian solution can call to mind the Hindu theory of the stages of life. The call to study the *Torah* was, nonetheless, strong enough so that Babylonian students were allowed to reside, once married, for long periods, outside of their home in order to devote themselves body and soul to study.[112] Among the Hasidim, many also see sexuality competing with the study of the *Torah*. Rabbi Menachem Nachum Twerksy from Chernobyl (1730–1797) and Rabbi Menachem Mendel Morgensztern from Kock (1787–1859) required newly married young men to go immediately to a *yeshiva*, and immerse in study with the *tzadik* to calm their sexual appetite.[113] Despite the more lenient position of the founder of Hasidism, the Baal Shem Tov, his disciples, Rabbi Dov Baer Mezeritch (1704–1772) and Rabbi Nachman of Breslov (1772–1810), preached the superseding of passion and pleasure during intercourse by giving precedence to the love of God.[114] Hasidic thought on sexuality found its inspiration in *Kabbalist* or mystical literature, which imagined human sexuality without desire or pleasure. It was this kind of sexual experience they thought Adam and Eve had enjoyed before eating the forbidden fruit.[115]

The rabbinic discussions on masturbation or involuntary emissions of semen reinforce the idea of distrust against the male sex drive. Thus, the *Mishnah* made no case of women who touched their genitals to see if they were menstruating, but refused the same privilege to the man who wanted to check if there had been emission of semen for fear of a possible erection.[116] The *Torah* itself does not speak directly about masturbation, but tradition linked its prohibition to the story of Onan (*Bereshit* 38: 10) who spilled on the ground the seed of life in coitus interruptus.[117] Opinions differ on the gravity of the offense, and whether it is attributed to unintentional emission of semen or if caused by masturbation. As noted by David Biale, the sanction of a ritual bath is much lighter than the penalties mentioned in the Christian Penitential literature of the Middle Ages.[118] He argues that the Kabbalists and the *Sefer Zohar*, as well as the popular codification of *Halacha*—the *Shulhan Aruch* of Rabbi Yosef Caro (1488–1575)—considered masturbation as a major sin, equivalent to infanticide, while the Ashkenazim, Yehudah Hasid, for example, allow masturbation in some cases, when the sexual drive becomes unmanageable.[119] The judgments of Kabbalists on masturbation, and involuntary nocturnal emissions of sperm, are sometimes extremely harsh. For example, the Kabbalist Rabbi Moshe ben Elijahu Vidas (1518–1592) classified it an unforgivable sin. The Jewish People of Eastern Europe also adopted the *Kabbalist* hard line in the seventeenth and eighteenth centuries.[120] The founder of the *Chabad-Lubavitch* Movement, Rabbi Shneur Zalman, considered it a terrible sin because the seed was left to the forces of evil.[121] The Orthodox Jews of today who rely most often on the *Shulhan Aruch* continue to assess masturbation and nocturnal emissions harshly, and they must necessarily be followed by a ritual bath. Reformers themselves tend to regard masturbation as morally neutral and without consequence for the person.[122]

The openness of rabbinic literature vis-à-vis marital sexuality, the duty of achieving reciprocal sexual pleasure, and the quest for an atmosphere of intimacy in sexual marital encounters, as well as the obligation for the husband to sexually satisfy his wife (*onah*)[123]—all of that might suggest a form of equality between the sexes. In fact, the reality is quite different. Rabbinic literature, an all-male enterprise, presents female libido as an untameable force. Mastering sexual desire requires psychological and moral strength of which only men are capable.[124] Satlow demonstrated, with the help of rabbinic literature, that a Jewish masculinity model developed from men's ability to control their libido, in contrast to women and Gentiles. The control of the libido gains them the exclusive right to devote their time studying the *Torah*. Men must protect themselves against the female libido, which could jeopardize their quest for wisdom and holiness, just like the sages of Hinduism.[125] This threat imposes certain rules of decency in the presence of women.

According to Rabbi Schmuel Ben Unya, a woman has no real existence until she unites with a husband who then transforms the shapeless mass into a usable vase.[126] The feminine world of rabbinic Judaism was essentially confined to domesticity, which allowed men to concentrate fully on prayer and study. The *Babylonian Talmud* reports the story of Rachel, a woman from a wealthy family who married a poor shepherd. She allowed her husband, Akiva, to be absent for 24 years to study the *Torah*. He came back home, one day, with a multitude of followers, and while they tried to prevent Rachel from approaching the master, he shouted at them to let her pass because, without her hard work, he could never have achieved such popularity.[127] As so aptly pointed out by Daniel Boyarin, the masculine model found in rabbinic Judaism goes against the grain of the dominant macho culture, both at the time of the Roman Empire and at the later time of the European Orthodox Jews: the pious Jew, reserved, studious, and nonviolent, quite unlike the prevalent figure of the warrior, or the knight. To illustrate his point of view, Boyarin used a section of the *Babylonian Talmud* narrating Rabbi Yohanan's encounter with Shimon Ben Lakish.[128] The narrator lingered on a description of Yohanan's androgynous physical beauty.[129] The young, beardless rabbi appeared to have seduced Ben Lakish, a man armed with a spear. Expecting to be in the presence of a woman on the bank of the River Jordan, Ben Lakish promptly took off his clothes, and naked, began to chase Yohanan who was swimming. Rabbi Yohanan then invited Ben Lakish to put his physical strength, his manhood, in the service of the *Torah*. He taught him the *Torah* and the *Mishnah*, and offered him his sister in marriage, if he renounced the use of weapons. This vision has shaped Talmudic Jewish European culture in such a manner that Jewish gender roles came to the opposite of what they were in the dominant culture. Here, men retreat into the private sphere of the *yeshiva* to study the *Torah*, while women invest the public space with their work force, often operating some small business to look after the material needs of the family.[130] In Antiquity and European history, anti-Semitic slander has often taken the shape of accusing Jewish men of their unmanly, if not effeminate, manners.[131] Jewish women are in turn attracted to the piety, studious character, patience, and gentleness of men with long side curls in the *yeshiva*.[132] Nineteenth-century emancipation brought along changes to traditional gender normativity, as the European bourgeois model extended its influence over the Jewish communities. Thus, many women, as it was the fashion in the dominant culture, left the labor market to enter the domestic sphere and engage in charitable or philanthropic activities.[133] With their more liberal attitude vis-à-vis the *Halacha*, European and American movements, Reform and Conservative, fought against the idea of pervasive subordination of women in *Halacha*, and its traditional interpretation throughout the ages.[134] In the 1970s, they pushed further the idea of recognizing gender equality, including women's right to the rabbinate.[135] In Orthodox Judaism, despite some claims for equality, women must still show respect and total dedication to their husbands, as stated by Maimonides.[136]

In short, Judaism displays a fairly positive attitude regarding sexual pleasure, which can be lawfully expressed within heterosexual marriage. The duty of procreation is a commandment from God that no Jew can ignore. Therefore, the regulation of sexuality has almost never taken the path of celibacy or virginity.

HOMOSEXUALITY

The sanctity of marriage as an expression for Yahweh's jealous love for Israel, and the duty to procreate to continue God's creation, leave little room for the expression of sexuality outside marriage, and even less room for same-sex practices. Not surprising to find in the *Holiness Code* the prohibition of sex acts such as adultery, bestiality, incest, or homosexuality—associated with fertility cults practiced by the Canaanites or the Egyptians.[137] Compliance with this code preserves Israel from defilement and allows its people to devote entirely to their Lord. Among these prohibitions, one reads: "You shall not lie down with a male, as with a woman: this is an abomination (*toevah*),"[138] and "a man who lies with a male as one would with a woman both of them have committed an abomination; they shall surely be put to death; their blood is upon themselves."[139] Why wonder about the response of the sages of the *Babylonian Talmud* who replied to Rabbi Yehudah (second century), saying there was no danger in two men sharing the same bed since Jews do not engage in homosexual relations?[140] For the drafters of the *Holiness Code*, who sought to establish a code of conduct for the Jewish minority in the land of Canaan, after their exile in Babylon, sex between two men was a matter for the *goyim*, the unclean nations. Curiously, it did not stop the rabbinic tradition to include unlawful sexual relations among the seven Laws of Noah observed by all humanity, while only Jews were required to follow the Mosaic Law in full.[141] In the Middle Ages, Maimonides condemned the two partners, inserter and insertee, engaged in homosexual anal penetration, although little concern was expressed about the possible dangers of homosexual practices within the Jewish community.[142]

The context of the *Holiness Code*, the language in use,[143] the nature of certain taboos, such as prohibiting sex during menstruation or sacrifices of children—everything points to the importance of ritual purity, in the context of worship. Some writers want to see the ban on homosexual relations contained in the code as a reference to cultic prostitution, practiced by other nations of the Ancient Near East.[144] The Deuteronomic Code suggests this connection when it forbids a "[sacred] prostitute (*qedesha*) of the daughters of Israel" or a "[sacred] male prostitute (*qadesh*) among the son of Israel" because "both are abominations to the Lord."[145] It may be that the drafters of the *Holiness Code* had knowledge of the sacred prostitutes (*assinu*)[146] assigned to the worship of the Assyrian-Babylonian goddess Ishtar, the hermaphrodite goddess of love and war. These temple prostitutes revealed an androgynous look to express their affiliation with Ishtar, who embodied both the masculine and feminine. No doubt, these *assinu* were a distinct group, a kind of third sex similar to the *hijras* of India, albeit the exact nature of their sexual transformation remains unknown. Were they eunuchs, transvestites, or hermaphrodites? Whatever the exact nature of their sexual variance, the men in all likelihood had sexual relations with them, by way of anal penetration, in order to get closer to Ishtar herself.[147] The existence of cultic prostitution in Israel involving male homosexual relations cannot be argued with certainty. Indeed, texts revealing the existence of pre-exilic *qedeshim* (plural of *qadesh*) date from a later period, and may have been influenced by the purity standards of the *Holiness Code*. None of these texts do link the *qedeshim* to special sexual behavior.[148] There is no convincing evidence to link the ban on homosexual relations discussed in the *Holiness Code* to the *qedeshim*. A more reasonable explanation lies perhaps in the text of *Leviticus* itself. The words "You shall not lie with a man as one lies with a woman" seems to point to anal penetration, indicating that this sexual act matches vaginal penetration.[149] The first prohibition (*Vayikra* 18: 22) seems to consider the inserter as the unique culprit, while the second (*Vayikra* 20: 13) makes both agents punishable by death. In practice, no evidence exists concerning the use of such punishment for cases of sodomy, even after the destruction of the Temple of Jerusalem, because the Jewish courts had no jurisdiction to impose the death penalty.[150]

The question of the guilt of the inserter or the insertee becomes of less interest when one views the offense as having to do with defiance of gender roles. The inserter forces the passive partner to play the role of a woman, one who is penetrated. It is this "feminine" receptivity, which initially exonerated the insertee, while the inserter was solely responsible for the offense, as he was perceived as the unique agent.[151] In this context, the *Holiness Code* possibly aimed at maintaining a strict code regarding gender identity by banning all forms of ambiguity. This could explain why the code of purity then banned not only homosexual anal penetration but also castration, and transvestism too, because the boundaries between the masculine and the feminine were crossed.[152] It must be said that Israel shared with other peoples of the Ancient Near East a concept of sexuality where the male partner is the active partner, and the female the passive partner. Thus, from the first millennium BC, an Akkadian book of omens, the *Shumma Alu*, spoke of a man who repeatedly allowed a woman to hold his penis in her hand, or had sexual intercourse in a supine position. He was doomed to lose his manhood, and the gods stopped lending an ear to his prayers.[153] In this same collection, as well as in Assyrian-Babylonian laws dating back to approximately the same period, anal penetration of a male by a peer was judged as a transgression of the masculine role. The insertee lost his status within the male population, which did, in fact, hold power in society.[154] In deciding to punish both—insertee and inserter—without any distinction based on social status, the *Holiness Code*, however, differed from Assyrian-Babylonian laws. These did punish but the person who raped a peer, but saw no fault when a man sodomized the enemy. The fact that the *Holiness Code* seems more inclusive probably comes from its authors, who wanted to sever Israel from the neighboring customs considered impure—more distinctly that which consisted in marking one's superiority over the enemy through anal penetration. Nothing in the *Holiness Code* indicates that the ban on homosexual anal penetration was due to its nonprocreative nature, although some authors propose an explanation along these lines.[155] However, this tread of interpretation did not captivate Hellenistic Judaism and Rabbinic Judaism. Only Philo of Alexandria did attack men who wasted their seed by penetrating young males.[156] Flavius Josephus, influenced by the Greco-Roman context of his times, commonly attacked effeminate men who made use of perfume, makeup, and like women, became sexual objects for men to satisfy their sexual urge.[157] In Hellenistic Judaism, the focus was increasingly drawn on the feminization of the insertee, in Greco-Roman pederasty.[158] Also in the *Sifra*, a halachic *Midrash* on *Leviticus* from the third century AD, Rabbi Akiva sought to stigmatize the passive partner along with the active.[159]

In summary, the *Holiness Code* gives rise to different interpretations, but one thing is beyond doubt: the taboo of homosexual sodomy was used to distinguish Israel from the nations that surrounded it, whatever the reason—waste of semen, the humiliation of the passive partner, or the prohibition against gender reversal. It may well be these three reasons that drove the *Torah* codifiers and later the rabbis to prohibit anal sex between men strongly. The inclusive nature of the Jewish prohibition against insertees—a somewhat different viewpoint from that of the Sumerian, Babylonian, and Greco-Roman civilizations, where the inserter is subject to no fault when the insertee's social status is lower—gives full weight to the theory that sees gender ambiguity as the heart of the matter. Be it sodomy, bestiality, or transvestism, all these practices had to be forbidden, as well as other kinds of adulteration. For example, in the case of dietary laws, meat and dairy products must not come into contact, or other unacceptable combinations in agriculture or in clothing should be discarded.[160]

Another passage from the *Torah* has kept alive through the ages the stigma on homosexuality: the story of the destruction of Sodom in *Bereshit* (Gen. 19). Two divine emissaries went to Sodom to verify if the people of this city had sinned, and deserved Yahweh's judgment. They met at the city gate. Lot, Abraham's nephew, took them home to spend the night. Some male citizens came to Lot's door asking him to let the foreigners go, so they could abuse the foreigners sexually.[161] Lot begged them to spare the foreigners, and offered them his daughters in exchange. The men of Sodom refused, and attacked Lot, whom the messengers saved in extremis. They asked Lot to flee the city, which was then destroyed by Yahweh's wrath. At first, the Sodomites' xenophobia, not the sexual nature of the sin, did retain the attention of future generations. Thus, when the prophets Isaiah and Ezekiel mentioned the sin of Sodom, they spoke about the pride of Sodom, the presumptuousness of its people who failed to rescue the unfortunate and poor, without any reference to a sexual sin.[162] Sexual motivation for the sin of Sodom is uncommon in the New Testament, which uses the punishment of Sodom as a leitmotif for the Last Judgment. Thus, the Gospel of Matthew alludes to the story to warn the apostles against persecution and against rejection of Jesus's message.[163]

Sexual misconduct alleged against the inhabitants of Sodom was largely developed and put in the foreground by the extracanonical writings within Hellenistic Judaism. Several books, Hellenistic in spirit, for instance, the *Testament of Levi* or the *Wisdom of Solomon*, linked the destruction of Sodom to all sorts of sexual immorality (Greek: *porneia*), mostly heterosexual, resulting from idolatrous practices.[164] Probably the most interesting text for the topic, the *Testament of Naphtali*, mentioned that the inhabitants of Sodom had changed the order of nature, like the heavenly creatures that copulated with women and caused the flood.[165] According to the author of this text, the sun and the moon followed the course that had been set by the Creator, but the heathens did not recognize the author of all things, and perverted the natural order by worshipping stones and poles, thus resembling the inhabitants of Sodom, or the heavenly creatures that had sex with the daughters of human creatures.[166] Flavius Josephus and Philo of Alexandria further developed the idea that the acts the Sodomites wanted to accomplish were "against nature" (Greek: παρά φύσιν, *para physin*). In doing so, they, at the same time, transposed into the biblical narratives their own knowledge of Hellenistic society by assimilating the inhabitants of Sodom to men having sex with men.[167] Even for these two authors, the sexual aspect of the alleged misconduct by the inhabitants of Sodom is not paramount in that their disordered sexuality is a reflection of a more grievous sin: inhospitality toward a foreigner in need, and an egoistic lifestyle based on material wealth and sensuality.[168]

Rabbinic writings essentially repeat the same idea: the sexual facet of the sin is not the main reason for the destruction of Sodom, but rather the lack of compassion toward others is clearly evidenced by the *Talmud* and the *Bereshit Rabbah*.[169] The sages of the *Talmud* never interpreted the sexual desires of the men of Sodom as same-sex oriented. They saw it as a case of lust for the neighbor's wife.

Despite the harsh judgments on homosexual anal penetration contained in the *Holiness Code* and some interpretations of the destruction of Sodom, homoeroticism is not totally absent from the Hebrew Bible or rabbinic writings. The meeting and friendship between

Shimon Ben Lakish and Rabbi Yohanan in the *Talmud* are an example of the learned rabbis' general ease regarding male friendships. The story of the passionate relationship between David and Jonathan deserves more attention.[170] While King Saul sought to destroy his rival David out of jealousy, the king's son, Jonathan, tried to save his friend to whom he had sworn undying allegiance. King Saul saw this loyal friendship as an affront and a disgrace to the family. The *Tanakh* does not mention any sexual contact between David and Jonathan, but it leaves much room for tenderness in the expression of the bond existing between them. When they had to part—because David had to flee Saul's furor—the two kissed and cried profusely.[171] Ultimately Jonathan's death on the battlefield will have David say: "I am distressed for you, my brother Jonathan, you were very pleasant to me. Your love was more wonderful to me than the love of women!"[172] Some authors have read in the verse homosexual overtones; others see it as only expressing a beautiful and loyal friendship, with no sexual component.[173] Without opting for either reading, the language used by the authors of this story, who probably were contemporary with the *Holiness Code*, showed no restriction about expressing sensuality in this relationship.[174] Several authors highlight the similarities found in the ambiguous poetic expression of their love relationship and that between the mythical heroes of ancient Mesopotamia, Gilgamesh, and Enkidu. In both cases, it is possible that the coded language of loyalty between warriors poetically expressed same-sex attraction.[175] Both pairs were bound by a pact of friendship, and the Sumerian King of Uruk, Gilgamesh, mourned the tragic ending in the death of his friend Enkidu, as would later the future King David for his friend Jonathan. The dream of Gilgamesh is a striking example of homoerotic poetry. He dreams of a "hatchet" that attracts the attention of the people of Uruk. Gilgamesh cajoles it as a wife and places it at his mother's feet who treats it as an equal or brother to her son:

> The mother of Gilgamesh, the wise, all-knowing, said to her son;
> Rimat-Ninsun, the wise, all-knowing, said to Gilgamesh:
> "The axe that you saw (is) a man.
> ...(that) you love him and embrace as a wife,
> but (that) I have compete with you.
> There will come to you a mighty man,
> a comrade who saves his friend—
> he is the mightiest in the land, he is strongest,
> he is as mighty as the meteorite(!) of Anu!"

Gilgamesh spoke to his mother saying: "By the command of Enlil, the Great Counselor, so may it to pass! / May I have a friend and adviser, a friend and adviser may I have! / You have interpreted for me the dreams about him!" After the harlot recounted the dreams of Gilgamesh to Enkidu the two of them made love.[176] In the Middle Ages, many Sephardic poets of Andalusia, such as Ibn Gabirol, Yehuda Halevi, or Moshe Ibn Ezra, composed poems in which they expressed their appreciation for handsome young men they affectionately called "gazelle" (Hebrew *sevi*)—as in Arabo-Andalusian odes of the time, sometimes inspired by the love of David and Jonathan.[177] These poets did not endure any criticism from rabbis and medieval Christian theologians who, like their predecessors, severely judged sexual contacts between two males.[178] Maimonides, the commentator *Rashi*, the *Tosafot* [*Supplements*, medieval Talmudic commentaries], the *Sefer ha-Hinnuk* [*Book on Education*] (thirteenth century), all condemn homosexual relations because they waste seed, affect the stability of family, or pursue egoistic pleasures.[179] It remains difficult to provide a comprehensive answer to this paradox. Similar language, strongly suffused with eroticism, was also used in the nineteenth century to describe male camaraderie in the *yeshivot* run by the *maskilim* of Eastern Europe, or to characterize the affection for the charismatic religious figure of the *tzadik*, in the Hasidic movement.[180] It is reasonable to say that male friendship, even when eroticized, was experienced through these different periods and experiences as a path to spiritual realization. Expressing one's feeling and attraction for a male companion did not pose a problem in itself, provided it did not involve any violation of gender roles, including anal penetration or cross-dressing.

Before addressing the current vision of Judaism on homosexuality let us sum up what has been said so far. In the *Tanakh*, references to sex between male partners are infrequent, and describe exceptional situations, such as gang rape or male prostitution associated with pagan worship. It never showcases persons who have a sexual preference for persons of their sex, and who engage in consensual sex. If these things existed, the *Talmud* and its commentators thought that they belonged to foreigners and non-Jews.

The rabbis and Talmudic literature enforced the ban on homosexual relations contained in the *Holiness Code* to protect family by banning all forms of waste of sperm, and by maintaining strict boundaries between male and female roles. Rabbi Ben Eleazar (1036–1108) summarized his understanding of the offense or abomination (*toeva*) described in the Code: the impossibility of having children.[181] This line of argument also appears at the forefront in contemporary Orthodox Judaism. Thus, Rabbi Baruch Epstein (1860–1941) said that homosexual acts are an abomination because they do not follow what nature dictates by the mere anatomy of the genitalia which were designed for the purpose of generation.[182] Some Orthodox rabbis, Norman Lamm, for example, adopt the following position: *Halacha* condemns homosexual acts in the same way it condemns bestiality and incest because human nature abhors these acts. However, no doubt influenced by scientific research on sexual orientation and the decision of the American Psychiatric Society in 1973 to no longer consider homosexuality as pathological, Lamm said he would condemn the act, and not the person who did not choose to be homosexual.[183] Rabbi Moshe Feinstein (1895–1986), a respected authority in the Orthodox world on the interpretation of *Halacha*, seems to have adopted a less forgiving attitude toward homosexuals. He encouraged them to ponder the seriousness of their misconduct, which goes against the order established by God, and is an act of rebellion against God.[184] For Feinstein, nobody should even question the reasons that make it an abomination, so repugnant this type of violation is to humans.[185] Rabbi Barry Freundel from Washington goes even further by denying any truth to the concept of sexual orientation, and having the male person who has sex with another male responsible for wrongdoing in the eyes of *Halacha*.[186] The discourse of the Orthodox Rabbinical Council of France uses in substance the same language as the one held by American rabbis. Joseph Sitruk, the grand rabbi of France until 2008, describes the sin or abomination (*toeva*) in the following way: "Accepting that couples may be formed otherwise than in the marital bond between a man and a woman goes against the natural equilibrium established by God. Under the guise of democracy, our society tends to legislate according to changing mores. [. . .] When man interferes with nature, he offends God, and destroys himself."[187] Richard Wertenschlag, the grand rabbi of Lyon, ferociously attacked gay civil marriage by comparing homosexuality to pedophilia and bestiality, both being contrary to the codes of conduct established by God.[188] Chief Rabbi Michel Gugenheim, director of the Jewish Seminary of France, conceives of homosexuality as an evil inclination (*yester ha-rah*), which differs from the concept of sexual orientation, and against which the individual must struggle with the support of the community.[189] In Canada, the ultra-Orthodox Agudath Israel Movement in Toronto (partly Hasidim), the Mizrachi Movement of Canada, the Orthodox Union of Canada, the Vaad HaRabbonim of Toronto and Montreal, and the Chief Rabbinate of Quebec have coalesced to oppose the legal recognition of marriages between persons of the same sex.[190] Steven Greenberg, an Orthodox Rabbi, expressed a dissenting voice in 1993 when he published in the magazine *Tikkun* an article entitled "Gayness and God, Wrestling of a Gay Orthodox Rabbi," under the pseudonym of Rabbi Yaakov Levado. The article recounts the sufferings of the author in an Israelite community and his meeting with Rabbi Yosef Sholom Eliashiv, a highly regarded *Haredi* authority on *Halacha*. Levado (Greenberg) reportedly told him to be sexually attracted to both women and men, to which the learned teacher said he thereupon held a dual capacity for love, nothing more. Since 1999, Greenberg has come out of the closet and has argued for a renewed reading of the *Halacha* that would accommodate gays. His latest book, W*restling with God and Men*, published in 2004, makes a daring exegesis of *Leviticus*. He expounds that the abomination resulting from anal sex lies in the fact that one partner is treated as a woman, a transgression of boundaries between the masculine and the feminine. To explain the gender confusion, Greenberg makes a parallel, inspired by the Maharal of Prague (1526–1609) and contemporary ethicist Jeffrey Stout, between cannibalism, bestiality, and homosexuality. All these transgressions are repugnant to the smooth running of relationships between members of society.[191] The author also mentions the Portuguese Rabbi Isaac Abravanel (fourteenth century), who interpreted the prohibition of anal sex found in the *Holiness Code* as a measure to prevent men from dressing as women to try and seduce men.[192]

Is homosexuality forbidden, or is the prohibition an excuse to protect a hierarchical and binary gender system—keeping the masculine and the feminine well separated? Should a true contemporary ethical concern not challenge the community, and bring it to question practices that maintain misogyny, and power based on gender inequality? Greenberg was probably too bold when he suggested that anal homosexual penetration prohibited by the *Holiness Code* only referred to acts done in a context of violence—with an intention to subjugate and humiliate an enemy.[193] The *Holiness Code* does not point in that direction and Greenberg seems the only one in this venture.[194] Greenberg is also trying to initiate a dialogue with those in his community who identify the ban on homosexual practices with nonproductive sexuality, which would indeed go against the divine commandment of *Bereshit*, 1: 28. The *Tanakh* does not endorse this juxtaposition— something that would rather appear as the work of Talmudic commentators, such as Rabbi Yehuda the Pious of Regensberg. According to the learned man, the ban provided protection for the divine command to procreate.[195] Greenberg uses several rabbinical authorities to thwart the use of such an argument to condemn homosexuality. First, procreation is not the only purpose of sexuality, and Talmudic literature make a lot of room for pleasure and intimacy in marital encounters. He also rejects the attempts to ban same-sex relations due to a waste of semen. The prohibition of extravaginal emissions of sperm is not a *mitzvah* originating directly from the *Torah*, but rather a ban of rabbinic origin.[196] The Orthodox, for some time, have recognized elsewhere that he who has no desire for woman and hopelessly feels attracted to men should abstain from marriage and childbearing. Rabbi Joseph Engel of Cracow (1859–1920) already expressed that he who could not fulfill God's command to procreate because of a disability, had to be excused—a position taken over by Chaim Rapoport, a contemporary rabbi in London.[197] Then, according to Greenberg, the true homosexual, the person who clearly has a homosexual orientation, would not violate the *Halacha* by having anal intercourse, or by not marrying, or by pouring sperm outside a vagina, since such a prohibition should apply only to persons under the obligation to procreate.[198] Inspired by the character of Rabbi ben Azzai, the odd single man in Talmudic literature who wanted to leave to others the duty to populate the earth and whose only passion was the *Torah*, Greenberg thinks gays should, however, be subject to the biblical requirement to make the land habitable, as ordered by the prophet Isaiah (45:18), by committing themselves in society in various ways.[199] Greenberg goes beyond the kind of openness to the homosexual person shown by Chaim Rapoport and Norman Lamm, who excuse the person unable to repress his homosexual inclination. He calls for a real change in the interpretation of *Halacha*, which would interpret the rule "*Oness Rahmana Patrei*" (divine mercy forgives any act committed under duress) in favor of a legitimate acceptance of sexual variance rather than seeing homosexuality as a pathological inclination. Even among the Orthodox, the law is not deemed static, and its ability to be interpreted in an evolutionary way was demonstrated in the past, for example, in the case of loans with interest totally prohibited until the thirteenth century.

Liberal or Reform Judaism has spoken far more openly about same sex than Traditionalists. In 1973, Rabbi Samuel Freehof from the Central Conference of American Rabbis (CCAR) answered in a *responsum* a question from a Californian man asking for his advice on the conduct of a rabbi who had formed a congregation of gay men.[200] Freehof believed that the prohibition found in the *Holiness Code* reflected the lifestyle of Jews from Antiquity, who judged these practices widespread among their neighbors as repulsive. Although Freehof does not provide any explanation on the basis for the aversion toward the "abomination," one may easily imagine it as a way of protecting Israel's distinctive purity in the context of idolatry. By the same token, it favored a policy of protection of the Jewish minority by promoting family. The author adds that homosexuals should not be excluded from their natural communities, even if they are to be regarded as sinners. A homosexual union or relationship will never avail itself of the sanctity of marriage. In 1977, the CCAR adopted a resolution supporting the decriminalization of homosexual acts between consenting adults, and the need for civil legislation prohibiting discrimination against homosexuals. In fact, the position of the American Reform Movement has evolved quite dramatically from the 1990s by allowing free access to the rabbinate, regardless of a person's sexual orientation.[201] In 1996, an unexpectedly lengthy *responsum* summed up the divergent positions within the Reform Movement about same-sex marriage, and called for further discussions.[202] A minority group believed that having some form of ritual celebration was necessary, but without naming it a homosexual marriage. The majority pleaded against any sort of official recognition. The position of the minority prevailed finally, in March 2000. Now rabbis who want to bless homosexual unions can do it openly.[203] The ceremonies vary in shape, but many of them do symbolically propose David and Jonathan as a model of faithfulness. At its Annual General Meeting in Toronto, in 2004, the CCAR adopted a resolution opposing any attempt to amend the American Constitution to prevent same-sex marriage.[204] A coalition of liberal rabbis in Canada intervened before the Supreme Court of Canada to argue in favor of the legal recognition of civil marriages between same-sex partners.[205] Efforts by Jewish gay men are also made to reclaim their spiritual belonging to the Jewish tradition. This is the case of Andrew Ramer of the Reform Congregation Sha'ar Zahav in San Francisco, who uses *Midrash* and poetry inspired by Jewish poets of al-Andalus to weave homoerotic love and feelings into Jewish spiritual expression.[206]

The approach of the conservative movement is better characterized by its determination to follow *Halacha*. The Rabbinical Assembly of American Conservative Movement adopted resolutions in March 1992, which had been suggested by the Committee on Jewish Law and Standards (CJLS).[207] The assembly rejected any form of solemnization of homosexual unions and excluded declared homosexuals from tenure as rabbi or *hazzan* (cantor). It did, however, support the need to welcome homosexual persons into the community, synagogue, and schools. It left to each rabbi to determine whether a homosexual could teach or supervise youth activities. Several discussions and *responsa* preceded the adoption of the 1992 resolution. Some minority positions favored a more flexible approach, such as that of Rabbi Bradley Artson, who envisaged no halachic condemnation of homosexuality, understood in the contemporary meaning of sexual orientation. For Artson, prohibitions against homosexuals contained in both the *Tanakh* and the *Talmud*, or in rabbinical commentaries, cover nonconsensual or violent homosexual acts, or acts associated with cultic prostitution. As these ancient prohibitions were not intended against sexual relations between persons with a homosexual orientation wanting to share a life filled with love and mutual respect, the rabbinate should validate some form of sanctification of these unions in a ceremony.[208]

A more traditional Conservative, Rabbi Joel Roth, wrote a lengthy *responsum* providing halachic arguments that would allow the majority to reach a consensus. It kept the condemnation of homosexuals, based on the threat to the traditional structure of a heterosexual family, and because of the nonprocreative aspect of homosexual acts. Roth refused to judge people with a homosexual orientation, but he added that discoveries of modern psychology do not change the legal framework laid down by the *Torah* and the *Talmud*.[209] Roth's argument, opposing his colleague Artson, aimed at demonstrating that from a halachic point of view, the only acceptable standard for sexual conduct remained heterosexual marriage. The ban concerns homosexual acts only to be a serious fault, and not desires or sexual attraction toward persons of the same sex.[210] The Conservative approach puts homosexuals in a difficult personal situation since it does not judge the agent, but condemns homosexual acts as opposed to *Halacha*. Whereas such an attitude undermines the dignity of the homosexual, and pushes him into a form of social isolation—both psychological and sexual—the CJLS decided, in 2006, to reconsider its position.[211] The arguments developed by this *responsum* implemented rabbinic techniques of interpretation to adapt *Halacha* to the concept of sexual orientation, which defines the identity of a person, unlike the traditional view of homosexuality as a sin or an illness to be cured. Because *Halacha* plays a pivotal role in the fate of Jewish Conservatism, adaptation does not mean abandonment. The authors concluded that the only form of homogenital contact repressed by the *Torah*, and interpreted as such thereafter by the sages of the *Talmud*, had to be anal penetration and nothing else.[212]

Rabbinic commentators seem to have understood that any kind of homogenital contact should be punished severely. Thus, Maimonides insisted on refraining from familiarity, proximity, or contact with someone who could solicit the commission of an unlawful sexual act, such as a homosexual act or incest, or having sex with a woman during her menstruation.[213] Rabbi Yosef Caro thought that same-sex partners who take to petting without penetration also had to be punished.[214] These interpretations draw their origin from the strict *Holiness Code* by which the Lord called his people to reject the abominable practices set forth therein—bestiality, incest, homosexual anal penetration, and staying away from people with whom sex was illicit (*aryot*).[215] Ramban (1194–1270) rejected this interpretation—which made any erotic touching or sexual contact without penetration a biblical prohibition—and considered it more like a rabbinical ruling; therefore, with less authority, and the faculty to change it, depending on the context or the times.[216] The CJLS, in 2006, retained this more liberal interpretation, and concluded that the sole homogenital contact rejected by *Halacha* was anal penetration, although within the group several rabbis believed fellatio, masturbation, mutual masturbation, or intercrural sex between two men were also banned.[217] Dorff and his colleagues based their generous understanding on the interpretive rule that imposes the obligation to protect the dignity of the person (*gadol kvod habriot*) at any time, to prevent one from undergoing humiliation by the application of a rule set, not by the *Torah*, but rabbis.[218] Obviously, discussion within the American Conservative Movement is not over. Some reputable rabbis, including Rabbi Joel Roth, resigned following the adoption of the 2006 liberal *responsum*. It is now up to each community to see how far it is ready to welcome homosexuals and gays, who, however, must refrain from anal intercourse. The decision to accept gays in the rabbinate and seminaries, as cantors and teachers in schools, remains for each community to make. Gay marriage is not considered, not even among the most liberals of the movement. Elsewhere in the world, the Conservative Movement is strongly opposed to the liberal positions of 2006 in Europe, Israel, and Latin America as well.[219] Several rabbis in Canada have also protested against the proposed changes because these deviated from halachic tradition and created division within the movement.[220] In France, Ryvon Krygier, a rabbi of the largest Masorti (Conservative) community in Paris, the *Adath Shalom*, followed liberal ideas put forward by Elliott Dorff, Daniel Nevins, and Avram Reisner unlike his other European colleagues who favored views closer to those of the traditionalists.

Several organizations appeared across the world to help gays of Jewish faith and protect their rights. They first appeared in London (The Jewish Gay and Lesbian Group, JGLG) and Los Angeles, in 1972, where the first gay synagogue, the *Beth Chayim Chadashim*, was founded; next the *Beth Simchat Torah* was founded in New York in 1973. The movement quickly spread to other major US cities: Washington, Philadelphia, New York, Miami, Chicago, and San Francisco. In France, the *Beit Haverim* (*House of Friends* in Hebrew) was founded in 1977. In 1975, a first group of gay and lesbian rights was born in Israel, the *Agudah*, and first known as the Society for the Protection of Personal Rights. This group achieved results comparable to those obtained in most liberal societies, since the Knesset decriminalized homosexuality in 1988, and passed a law to end discrimination on the basis of sexual orientation in 1992. With the support of parliamentarian Yael Dayan, daughter of General Moshe Dayan, *Agudah* advanced the rights to equality in many spheres—such as serving in the military, the right to pensions for surviving spouses, without obtaining full legal recognition for homosexual couples. Religious groups strongly opposed the civil recognition of marriage between same-sex partners, but the state recognized certain rights to same-sex common law partners. In 2006, the Israeli Supreme Court ruled that same-sex marriages officiated in countries accepting this type of union were now legal in Israel. In Quebec, in 1974, a discussion group called *Naches* was born, and allowed homosexual Jews to meet and discuss their problems. In 2002, the *Feygelah*[221] association replaced the defunct advocacy and support group *Yakhdav*, and enjoyed the support of the Reform Synagogue *Emanu-El-Beth Sholom*. Toronto also saw groups formed in 1975, *Hamishpacha*, *B'nai Kehilla*, *Chutzpah*, and *Keshet Shalom*, which followed until 2001. The latter two groups received financial assistance from the *Jewish Community Center* in Toronto. *Keshet Shalom* decided to terminate its activities, whereas the situation of gays had improved considerably and there was no necessity in the Reform Movement to maintain a synagogue serving a specifically gay and lesbian community. Though the situation has changed radically within Judaism, the 2001 documentary directed by the American Sandi Simcha DuBowski, *Trembling before G-D*,[222] highlighted the personal suffering endured by gays and lesbians living in Orthodox, *Haredi*, and Hasidim communities. It shows, for example, a Los Angeles Orthodox doctor who tries, in vain, to heal himself by undergoing various therapies; or that other person from New York who, after undergoing electroshock therapy to become heterosexual, decides to abandon his family to live with a partner. Many of the movements mentioned were the organizing force behind several international meetings for gays and lesbians of Jewish origin. The first was held in Washington in 1976. In 1980, the *World Congress* was formed in 2001 to become the *World Congress of Gay, Lesbian, Bisexual, and Transgender Jews*, the *Keshet Ga'avah*, which monitors the rights of gays and lesbians of Jewish heritage worldwide.

Conclusion

Like in Hinduism, human sexuality is sacred. On the one hand, it brings one closer to the divine, since humans are created in the image of God, that is, man and woman, and they received from God the commandment to multiply. On the other hand, sexuality also played an active, historic role in protecting the nation in two ways. It ensured the survival of the exiled nation, conquered by foreigners, and subsequently dispersed throughout Europe and worldwide. However, human sexuality is also part of the *Holiness Code* dictated by God, revealed through Moses to Israel, and setting it apart from other nations through the people's observance of law and its loyalty to its God. Devotion and obedience to this code of life do not have the same importance in all streams of Judaism, some firmly attached to it, while others no longer feel bound by a past historical situation or looking for accommodations to contemporary life.

All seem to agree on the sacredness of sexuality and the importance of the *mitzvah* to reproduce, reprobating any ascetic trend that would advocate the superiority of celibacy, as in other religions. Social pressure to marry and have children is always exercised in the background, even among the most liberal, but it is more strongly felt in the Orthodox community. However, the homosexual ban is not exactly related to this *mitzvah* on procreation because it seems, in the end, to serve to protect and maintain a traditional social division of gender roles, with its goal of keeping a hierarchy of the masculine over feminine. This gender division, including the exclusion of women from study of the *Torah*, resulted in a male world quite removed from the macho Western model. Unlike what happened in that model, the development of Jewish male identity, without eliminating any misogyny, has hardly encouraged the emergence of homophobic panic.[223] The panic is present today among Orthodox Jews in the form of fierce campaigns against a so-called homosexual agenda, educating children to view homosexuality as a legitimate, alternate lifestyle. After Tyler Clementi, an 18-year-old student at Rutgers University in New Jersey, jumped to his death from a bridge in 2010, the New Jersey Legislature passed Bill S2392, "Anti-Bullying Bill of Rights Act." Clementi took his life after seeing his sexual encounter with a man in his dorm room on a video over the Internet, filmed by his roommates, without his knowledge. Rabbi Yehuda Levin, a strong antigay spokesman for the Rabbinical Alliance of America and official spokesman on family values, issued a press release saying that the bill was promoting LGBT values among schoolchildren.[224]

4

CHRISTIANITY

RELIGION

Christianity emerged in the wake of the religious tradition of Israel, but it was actually born two thousand years ago at the instigation of Yeshua, Jesus of Nazareth. Palestine was under Roman occupation at the time of his birth. The life and teachings of Yeshua were recorded many years later in the New Testament, and they formed the basis for the beliefs of this new religion. The Christian community has diversified over the ages due to doctrinal disputes and to schisms, and the Christian faith has spread across the planet. Today there are over 1 billion Catholics, 225 million Orthodox Christians, 83 million Anglicans, 66 million Lutherans, 49 million Pentecostals, 48 million Baptists, 44 million Calvinists and Presbyterians, 23 million Methodists, and 22 million United Church followers worldwide. In addition to these great families, more than 348 million followers grouped into communities whose membership has often been defined by national identity or ethnic and cultural characteristics. In Canada over 75 percent of the population is said to be Christian, including 43 percent Catholics, 32 percent Protestants, and 1.6 percent Orthodox Christians.[1] In Quebec, the Catholic population is said to be 83 percent and Protestants just under 5 percent.[2] The 2011 census did not ask about religious affiliation but the 2011 Home National Survey estimates the total Christian population of Canada at 67 percent, considerably less than 10 years before. This is mainly due to the increase in immigration coming from areas where non-Christian religions predominate and low rates of population growth among Canadian-born.[3] In the United States, Protestant churches nowadays attract a slim majority (51.3 percent) of the adult population distributed as Evangelical Protestant (26.3 percent), mainline Protestant (18.1 percent), and black Protestant churches (6.9 percent). Catholics represent nearly one-quarter (23.9 percent) of the adult population, Mormons 1.7 percent, Jehovah's Witnesses 0.7 percent, and Orthodox Christians 0.6 percent.[4] Within the Protestant churches, Evangelical churches account for 41 percent and Baptist churches for 33.5 percent of all Protestant denominations.

To learn the basics of Christian faith, one must necessarily examine the life of Jesus of Nazareth. The New Testament gives us scarce biographical material, particularly on the period from his birth up to his thirties, when his preaching began. The four Gospels, Matthew, Mark, Luke, and John, slip in a few details, but they happen to be writings of a theological rather than historical nature. Thus, the Annunciation to Mary his mother, the virgin birth of Jesus, and the visit of the Magi in Bethlehem are all theological statements about the Messianic character of Jesus, and they are not historically verified or verifiable facts.[5]

In order to follow Jesus's ministry, beginning with his baptism by John the Baptist on the banks of the River Jordan, it appears necessary to examine the religious culture of the time. Since the destruction of the Temple of Jerusalem, the idea had circulated that a man in the lineage of David, anointed and blessed by God, the Messiah (*Mashiah* in Hebrew and Χριστός, Christos, in Greek), would deliver the Jewish people from its enemies and create a new Israel. The evangelists Matthew and Luke took considerable care to describe the genealogy of Jesus, son of David and Abraham.[6] John the Baptist preached repentance, cleansing of sins, for the Kingdom of God was near. In the Gospel of John, John the Baptist acknowledges Jesus as the Chosen One, a messianic title used by the prophet Isaiah (42:1).[7] Immediately after his baptism, Jesus recruited his first disciples who confessed that he was the Messiah, the Son of Man.[8] The Synoptic Gospels also offer several accounts of miracles and healings performed by Jesus, signs of the coming of the Messiah and the nearness of the Kingdom of God, as professed by Simon Peter: "You are the Messiah, the Son of the living God."[9] After Peter's declaration, Jesus asked his disciples not to tell anyone that he was the Messiah.[10] Indeed, if the rumor of the arrival of a new king of Israel reached the ears of the Roman occupiers, there would inevitably be problems for him and his family. The real reason for this call for caution rests on his preaching. The Kingdom he announced was not of this world, and it had nothing to do with the restoration of David's Kingdom. Jesus introduces a spiritual kingdom based on compassion and relief for the poor or the marginalized, such as prostitutes, the sick, prisoners, and foreigners.[11] Love and not the sole observance of Jewish laws becomes the golden rule by which all actions are judged:

> You have heard that it was said to the people long ago, "You shall not murder, and anyone who murders will be subject to judgment." But I tell you that anyone who is angry with a brother or sister will be subject to judgment. Again, anyone who says to a brother or sister, "Raca," [You good for nothing] is answerable to the court.[12]

His teaching rapidly antagonized Jewish religious authorities, particularly the pious orthodox called the Pharisees. They feared his new interpretation of the law, as when he told his disciples who violated the religious law prohibiting harvesting on a Sabbath day: "The Sabbath was made for man, not man for the Sabbath. So the Son of Man is Lord even of the Sabbath."[13] Jesus's liberal attitude regarding the observance of Jewish law as well as his claims to the title of Messiah were in the eyes of religious authorities in Jerusalem—meeting with the High Priest Caiaphas—a real blasphemy that could encourage riots and have him sentenced to death by crucifixion.[14] As Jesus was in Jerusalem for the Passover celebrations, he was betrayed by his disciple Judas and arrested at Gethsemane by the High Priest's henchmen. He appeared before Caiaphas and the Sanhedrin. Questioned by Caiaphas on whether he was the Messiah, Jesus broke the gag order he had given his disciples, and replied: "You have said so. But I say to all of you: From now on you will see the Son of Man sitting at the right hand of the Mighty One and coming on the clouds of heaven."[15] Then, Caiaphas declared that Jesus had blasphemed; and the Sanhedrin decided to deliver the prisoner to the Roman governor, Pilate, to have him sentenced to death. Jesus was crucified by Roman authorities with this ironic inscription on the cross, "King of the Jews."

More than any other evangelist, John highlights the glorification of Jesus through the tragic event of his death, when he has Jesus declare: "The hour has come for the Son of Man to be glorified. Very truly I tell you, unless a kernel of wheat falls to the ground and dies, it remains only a single seed. But if it dies, it produces many seeds."[16] The true glory of Jesus resides in his death in order to redeem God's people. It is best portrayed by the image of the Suffering Servant, a messianic figure prophesied by Isaiah: "By oppression and judgment he was taken away. Yet who of his generation protested? For he was cut off from the land of the living; for the transgression of my people he was punished."[17] While reporting the Last Supper, the evangelists interpreted the memorial of the Passover as if Jesus had fulfilled the prophecy of the Suffering Servant. During that Last Supper, Jesus foreshadows his death and becomes the paschal sacrificial lamb, his body and his blood shed for the forgiveness of sins of the multitude.

The tragic death of Jesus does not provide a glimpse of the event that would follow, his Resurrection. Jesus certainly lived his passion with a sense of dereliction. A disciple betrayed him; another denied him; and everyone abandoned him. He was left alone in the garden of Gethsemane, and at the foot of the cross, only his mother Mary and his beloved disciple John were present. The experience of the empty tomb and encounters by some witnesses—Mary Magdalene and his disciples—with the risen Jesus, in a glorified body, are not sufficient to establish the Christian hope of salvation through Jesus. An empty tomb and testimonies by certain witnesses to whom they said he appeared do not constitute conclusive evidence of the resurrection. The resurrection of Jesus makes sense only within the messianic and eschatological traditions that developed in Israel, after the Babylonian exile. Jesus seems to understand his ministry and his death in reference to this tradition. The apostles will make sense of the tragic death of Jesus, after the event, when the Spirit of God descends upon them at Pentecost.[18] Peter's first words to the crowd are an excellent example of primitive theology, linking the resurrection to the eschatological tradition of the glorification of God through the coming of the Messiah:

> Fellow Israelites, I can tell you confidently that the patriarch David died and was buried, and his grave is here to this day. But he was a prophet and knew that God had promised him on oath that he would put one of his descendants on his throne. Seeing what was to come, he spoke of the resurrection of the Messiah, that he was not abandoned to the realm of the dead, nor did his body see decay. God has raised this Jesus to life, and we are all witnesses of it. Exalted to the right hand of God, he has received from the Father the promised Holy Spirit, and has poured out what you now see and hear Brothers, he is allowed to tell you confidently of the patriarch David died and was buried and his tomb is still with us today.[19]

The theology of the Apostle Paul strongly emphasizes the eschatological dimension of the Resurrection of Jesus in a glorified body—a sign of God's power and glory, to be manifested at the time of the Second coming of Christ (*Parousia*), when all bodies will resurrect: "But our citizenship is in heaven. And we eagerly await a Savior from there, the Lord Jesus Christ, who, by the power that enables him to bring everything under his control, will transform our lowly bodies so that they will be like his glorious body."[20] In establishing Jesus's Lordship over the world—the *Pantocrator* (Παντοκράτωρ, the Almighty)—God situates in him the beginning and the end of all things, as well as the position of head of the church.[21] The first Christian communities were formed around the preaching of the apostles. They called for repentance and were baptized in the name of Jesus Christ, who died for the forgiveness of sins and rose again for the redemption of all. Breaking the bread and sharing with the needy were the main reasons for the first community meetings.[22] Tensions, however, emerged rapidly in the early Christian communities. The *Acts of the Apostles* show that the apostles' preaching was primarily addressed to Jews in synagogues, either in Damascus, Antioch, or Jerusalem. Some, including James who took care of the Jerusalem community, along with Peter and John, claimed that circumcision and the Jewish dietary laws were required to obtain salvation. Should one apply those precepts of Jewish law to non-Jews who converted to Jesus's message? Paul took a position in favor of more freedom, in a meeting around the year

50 with the apostles in Jerusalem. This meeting is known in the Christian tradition as the Council of Jerusalem.[23] In Antioch, Paul attacked the hypocrisy of Peter, who took his meals with the Gentiles and refused to do so in James's presence. Paul gives the tone to his Gospel: "We who are Jews by birth and not sinful Gentiles know that a person is not justified by the works of the law, but by faith in Jesus Christ."[24] After the meeting in Jerusalem, Paul and his companion Timothy extended their mission in Asia Minor to Macedonia and the Peloponnese. The primitive church progressively distanced itself from Judaism, and it spread around the Mediterranean basin, despite the opposition and oppression it faced from the Roman authorities. The tide changed radically with the conversion of Emperor Constantine, in 313, and the promulgation of the Edict of Milan, which recognized the legitimacy of the Christian religion.

During its expansion within the Roman Empire, Christianity came into close contact with religions and philosophies other than Judaism. The initial message was thus enhanced through confrontation with these new ideas; not without some quarrel, mainly about the person of Jesus and his relationship with the Father or the Holy Spirit. Constantine felt the need to define Christian orthodoxy and ordered in 325 the Council of Nicea to dispute the doctrine spread by an Alexandrian priest named Arius. The priest denied the coeternity of the Son of God; the Son was a creature of the Father. The Nicene Creed adopted by the Council confessed Jesus Christ to be the only Son of God, begotten of the Father before all worlds, God from God, Light from Light, true God of the very God, begotten and not made, of one substance with the Father by whom all things were made. The Nicene Creed also emphatically proclaimed the doctrine of the Incarnation of the Son of God, Jesus made flesh, crucified and risen. The emphasis on the human nature of Jesus was disputed by various Docetist doctrines; they could not believe that the Son of God, eternal as the Father, was incarnated in matter. For them, the Divine Light could not become trapped in a human body; thus, the physical body of Jesus was only a semblance. The Gnostic Gospels of Nag Hammadi pushed this idea unusually far. Thus, the *Second Discourse of the Great Seth* went so far as to reject the doctrine of redemption through the incarnation and death of Jesus.[25] The Christian doctrine of salvation through Christ's death is seen as a sham, preventing human beings from becoming aware that they have within their nature the potential for salvation. If they come to realize that they are themselves a divine emanation of extraterrestrial origin, they will return to the *Pleroma*—their ontological fullness. The gnostic theory of matter and body as prison will have a significant impact on the Christian view of sexuality, but this will be discussed in the second section of this chapter. In the third century, another highly significant shift in the history of Christianity settles in—monasticism—which advocated sexual abstinence as a method of reconciliation with God.

As was noted earlier, Emperor Constantine attempted to rule not only on earthly matters but also on religious affairs. Caesaropapism marked the entire development of the Byzantine Empire, but attempts to enforce it in the West faced resistance from papal authority, which in turn was trying to impose its control on political power. The separation of temporal and spiritual powers finally emerged in the West with the Concordat of Worms in 1122, which put an end to the power exercised by the Carolingian emperors and the Holy Roman emperors on papal elections and appointments of bishops. Nearly 40 years earlier, Pope Gregory VII had coined the doctrine of papal supremacy—the pope having the exclusive authority to appoint bishops—and had begun to reform the clergy by fighting against simony and loose sexual mores within it.

Despite the efforts announced by the Gregorian reform to fight against corruption, intrigues, favoritism, and sexual incontinence of the clergy went on undisturbed and affected the highest levels of authority, including the now all-powerful papacy itself. The papacy of Alexander VI, a Borgia, or that of Julius II illustrates this point. In order to finance the construction of churches and their extravagances, church authorities accepted monetary payment for religious services, the sale of relics, or indulgences that allowed the faithful to expiate more rapidly their future punishment in Purgatory. Martin Luther (1483–1546) and the Protestant Reformation challenged the system that viewed the salvation of souls as a commercial transaction. Luther engaged in a confrontation with the Dominican Johann Tetzel (1465–1519), commissioned by Pope Leo X, for the sale of indulgences in Germany to finance the construction of St. Peter's in Rome. On October 31, 1517, Luther posted *Ninety-Five Theses* on the doors of the Wittenberg church, attacking the practice of indulgences and submitting that only faith in Jesus Christ saved people from their sins. In presenting faith in Jesus Christ as savior and sole instigator of grace, without works, Luther directly contested the traditional view of the church, considered as a mediator of salvation through the sacraments dispensed by clergy. The only reliable guide to salvation became the Word of God—the Bible, translated into the vernacular, which catered to the individual conscience of the believer. Luther rejected the authority of the pope, and loudly proclaimed the royal priesthood of all the baptized without hierarchical distinction between clergy and laity. Rejection of a central government and freedom of conscience encouraged the emergence of a multitude of ecclesial communities, which displayed variations in their interpretation of the Scriptures. He also rejected the idea of celibacy for pastors and decided to marry. This gesture had a tremendous influence on the Protestant understanding of sexual morality and the role of women in the church and society in general.

In response to the attacks of Protestantism and as a way to affirm the orthodoxy of the Catholic Church, Pope Paul III convened a general council, which met three times between 1545 and 1563, in the town of Trento. Several decrees reaffirmed the doctrine of justification by faith and works, the existence of the seven sacraments—Protestants had reduced them to two, baptism and the Eucharist. The council proclaimed the necessity to confess one's sins to a priest who received the authority to absolve. The next section of this chapter will address the importance of this view of the sacrament of penance on sexual morality. The council also reaffirmed the sacramental nature of marriage and its indissolubility. Protestants saw marriage as a natural phenomenon that fell under the total jurisdiction of civil authorities, and they allowed divorce in cases of adultery or heresy.

The Enlightenment openly challenged, on behalf of reason, Christian beliefs, including beliefs in miracles and the resurrection. It instilled in philosophers and theologians a desire to confront the Bible in the open with the culture of the time. In the nineteenth century, Friedrich Schleiermacher, Adolf von Harnack, and Ferdinand Christian Baur, head of the Theological School of Tübingen, questioned the foundations of dogmatic theology, which relied too heavily on the idea of a divine mandate given to the church. Not only did they support the principle of freedom of conscience put forward by Luther, but they advocated a more liberal attitude vis-à-vis the study of the Bible and Christian history by using the method of historical criticism. Scriptures and the development of dogmas had to be subjected to the same methods used in the humanities, which meant that divine inspiration and inerrancy had to be methodically suspended or bracketed. The new liberal theology also spread to Catholic circles, especially through Alfred Loisy, professor at the *Institut Catholique* in Paris. While criticizing the theory of von Harnack, who saw the church as a spiritual community without any material form of government, Loisy still defended the idea that it was impossible, from historical and textual evidence, to demonstrate that Jesus intended to build a church that would withstand the test of time. The church authorities reacted strongly against the liberal current and condemned all theological or philosophical attempts to explain Christianity in terms of a strictly human phenomenon, without resorting to divine Revelation.[26] They called this approach the "modernist errors." To confirm the believers' adherence to solid faith in the teachings of the church and against liberal ideas, Pope Pius IX thought fit to declare the doctrine of papal infallibility in the Apostolic Constitution of Vatican I, *Pastor Aeternus*. He also proclaimed the primacy of the bishop of Rome, to whom all the faithful owe obedience. This doctrine has a significant impact on Catholic sexual morality, as it applies not only to questions of faith but also to morals:

> When the Roman Pontiff speaks EX CATHEDRA, that is, when, in the exercise of his office as shepherd and teacher of all Christians, in honor of his supreme apostolic authority, he defines a doctrine concerning faith or morals to be held by the whole Church, he possesses, by the divine assistance promised to him in blessed Peter, that infallibility which the divine Redeemer willed his Church to enjoy in defining doctrine concerning faith or morals. Therefore, such definitions of the Roman Pontiff are of themselves, and not by the consent of the Church, irreformable.[27]

The lack of narratives on the sexuality of Jesus, the emphasis on the spiritual nature of the Kingdom of God, and the eschatological tension created by the announcement of the coming of Christ in glory, all of these elements certainly contributed to a form of withdrawal from worldly pursuits, something that in turn influenced the Christian views on sexuality. The expansion of Christianity in the Greco-Roman world also left its mark, in particular the influence of the Stoic philosophy of natural law and the control of reason over passions. However, the Reformation's criticism of the clergy and its preaching on the royal priesthood of the baptized have also played an important role in a perception of sexuality that is less angelic and more understanding of the reality experienced by men and women.

Sexuality

The Gospels portray Jesus asking his disciples to imitate him and to abandon their hometown and families to follow him. The request is imbued with radicalism. The Evangelist Matthew illustrated it by giving the example of a disciple who asked Jesus to give him permission to go and bury his deceased father. Jesus replied, "Follow me, and let the dead bury their own dead."[28] Jesus sought to establish a new human family based on the values of a new solidarity, one beyond traditional family blood ties. When informed of the presence of his mother and his brothers, he pointed his finger at his disciples, saying to the crowd: "Who is my mother, and who are my brothers?" Pointing to his disciples, he said, "Here are my mother and my brothers."[29]

Although some would characterize this speech as antifamily, the authors of the Gospels did not praise celibacy or chastity in a special way. They followed the teachings of their fellow Jews in that matter. Matthew condemned sex outside marriage (πορνεία), but he never considered sexuality as intrinsically evil and an enemy of salvation.[30] Matthew sought primarily to protect marital relationships; more so than disavowing sexual pleasure in marriage. He rather espoused for the same reason views from the rabbinical School of Shammai, which limited divorce to cases of adultery, while the School of Hillel dared allow divorce at the slightest departure from the rule—as in the case where the woman had burned her husband's supper! Paul neatly observed the eschatological tension that attracted some Christians to sexual abstinence on account of the imminent second coming of Jesus. At the same time, he acknowledged that those who could not control their libido could enter the path of marriage.[31] Somehow, Paul's ascetic tendencies are reminiscent of those already observed in some rabbis of the first century AD. Marriage and marital duty can become a source of concern and divert the faithful from their spiritual quest.

Michel Despland noted that "our relation to the body and the theming of sexuality seem to be at the heart of a change of culture that occurred during the transition from ancient civilization to Christianity."[32] While the Greeks looked for a sort of balance in the use of pleasures, the Roman approach was tinged with apprehension and increasing anxiety as time progressed. Sexual activity, specifically the emission of semen, is usually treated as an unhealthy waste of energy. Stoic philosophy and medicine created a new relationship with natural body functions that had to be repressed to appease the soul.[33] Already, the attitude changed somewhat in Paul and Luke, as greater distrust against desires of the flesh inhabited their thoughts. Luke presented Jesus as one who could heal the souls lost in sin.[34] In I Thessalonians, Paul wrote: "It is God's will that you should be sanctified: that you should avoid sexual immorality; that each of you should learn to control your own body in a way that is holy and honorable, not in passionate lust like the pagans, who do not know God."[35] We have already seen that around the first century AD the problematization of desire and sexuality was part of the mainstream culture, both in the pagan and Jewish world.[36] When Paul addresses the Romans, the Thessalonians, or even the Corinthians, he always warns them against the perils of fornication or adultery associated with pagan practices.[37] In the fashion of Old Testament writers, the apostle makes of these extramarital practices an indication of devotion to pagan gods, detrimental to the Christian God.[38] Like postexilic literature, Paul urged believers not to marry a partner who worshipped other gods.[39] Peter Brown was perfectly correct in observing that a legitimate interest in the joys of marital sex—a trend clearly present in Rabbinic Judaism—no longer appealed to Paul.[40] He even encouraged people already married to abstain from sexual relations and widows not to remarry.[41] The ascetic tendencies of Pauline literature, somehow, set the table for an interpretation that would soon demonize sexual desire and discredit marriage. In I Corinthians, Paul suggested a different interpretation of the sexual taboos in the Old Testament by labeling them as "evil desires" (ἐπιθυμητὰς κακῶν).[42] For him, violation of the law in itself does not constitute the sin anymore—separating the believer from his god—but the mere intention or desire to act inappropriately is sufficient to cause sin. In Romans, Paul engaged in a pessimistic anthropology of human passions that sought to enslave the body, from which the mind could not free itself without the intervention of grace provided by Jesus Christ:

> We know that the law is spiritual; but I am unspiritual, sold as a slave to sin. I do not understand what I do. For what I want to do I do not do, but what I hate I do. And if I do what I do not want to do, I agree that the law is good. As it is, it is no longer I myself who do it, but it is sin living in me. For I know that good itself does not dwell in me, that is, in my sinful nature. For I have the desire to do what is good, but I cannot carry it out. For I do not do the good I want to do, but the evil I do not want to do—this I keep on doing. Now if I do what I do not want to do, it is no longer I who do it, but it is sin living in me that does it.
>
> So I find this law at work: Although I want to do good, evil is right there with me. For in my inner being I delight in God's law; but I see another law at work in me, waging war against the law of my mind and making me a prisoner of the law of sin at work within me. What a wretched man I am! Who will rescue me from this body that is subject to death? Wretched man that I am! Who shall deliver me from this body devote myself to death?[43]

According to Elizabeth Clark, the ascetic perspective on sexuality developed in the early centuries of Christianity from three geographic poles: Egypt, where Manichean and Gnostic ideas blossomed, then Syria and Palestine.[44] Tatian the Syrian (second century) and his fellow Encratites spread the idea that marriage was equal to fornication; Adam and Eve's sin was sexual in nature and only sexual abstinence could restore the human soul to its pristine purity.[45] While Paul tried to curb the libido through marriage, Tatian took seriously the dangers of the flesh felt by Paul and condemned any form of sexual expression, even between spouses.[46] In the same geographical area, Marcion of Sinope claimed that reproductive organs and sexual fluids were so filthy (*spurcitias genitalium in utero elementorum*) that they could not have contributed to the birth of Christ in any way.[47] It then appeared obvious to Marcion that he had to set aside baptism only for those who had or would renounce marriage and procreation.[48] The solitude of the desert became for some the preferred place to approach God by renouncing sexuality. The founder of monasticism, the hermit Anthony (c. 251–356), quickly discovered that a life of mortification and fasting in the Egyptian desert, as well as the absence of women, failed to delete all sexual urge. The true rival to spiritual progress lodged in the mind. Anthony's biographer portrayed the desperate monk trying through prayer and vigils to expel impure thoughts sent by Satan himself, who appeared before him in the guise of a woman trying to seduce him.[49] With the Desert Fathers, virtue no longer consists of avoiding illegal acts because sex has moved into the "inner theater" of human consciousness.[50] Pachomius, a hermit living in the desert of Scetes (currently Wadi Natrun), described the struggles against temptation on the scene of this inner theater:

> But reckoning that God had spared me, I returned again to the cell. Well, the demon, having restrained himself a few days, then attacked me again more vehemently than at first, so that I very nearly blasphemed. He changed himself into an Ethiopian maiden, whom I had once seen in my youth in the summer-time picking reeds, and sat on my knee. So in a fury I gave her a blow and she disappeared. Well, for two years I could not bear the evil smell of my hand! So I went out into the great desert, wandering up and down discouraged and in despair. And having found a little asp, I picked it up and applied it to my flesh, in order that I might die, even though it were by a bite of this kind. And I rubbed the beast's head on my flesh, as the cause of my temptation, but I was not bitten. Then I heard a voice saying in my thoughts: "Go, Pachon, struggle on. For this is why I have left you to be tyrannized over, that you should not be proud, as if you had any strength, but recognizing your weakness should not trust in your manner of life, but run for the help of God." Thus convinced I returned and dwelt in confidence, and no longer troubling about the war I was in peace the rest of my days. But he, knowing how I despised him, no longer came near me.[51]

Fasting and sleepless nights were part of the hermit's arsenal whenever he attempted to overcome any temptation of the flesh, especially impure thoughts, masturbation, and nocturnal emissions.[52] John Cassian (360–435) exposed the following discipline to achieve true purity of heart:

> One who will withdraw from all frivolous conversation, who will banish anger from his heart, concerns and desires for the world, being content to live on two loaves of bread a day, drinking water with discretion and sleeping three to four hours only, as some people advise it, this person will notice within six months, not that he has attained perfect chastity by his own effort, but that he will one day acquire it by relying on God's mercy rather than the merit of his abstinence.[53]

To achieve optimal control over one's lust, the monk John Cassian suggested a method of self-introspection in six steps. It not only aimed at punishing lewd acts like fornication, but it also tried, by progressing deep into the subject's thoughts (*voluptaria cogitatio*) and desire (*concupiscentia*), to eliminate any motion, even if unintended, in the male body, such as an erection or wet dreams.[54] Spacing out erections or wet dreams, or their absence, became a signal for John Cassian that a monk had reached a high degree of perfection in celibacy: "We may believe that we have arrived at this kind of purity, if no voluptuous sensation disturbs our sleep and if natural accidents happen without our noticing. Eliminating them completely is beyond nature, but we must, by dint of virtue, make them increasingly rare."[55] John Cassian thought that the normal frequency for natural nocturnal emissions should be twice a month. Achieving this level of control implies, of course, work on the self to discard all occasions of impure thoughts. However, fasting is required, "He then will never be able to check the motions of a burning lust, who cannot restrain the desires of the appetite. The chastity of the inner man is shown by the perfection of this virtue."[56] John Cassian attributed the cause of nocturnal emissions to excessive eating, along with the lack of vigilance of the mind, or Satan's intervention.[57] In his *Praktikos*, Evagrius of Pontus (346–399) taught a method of self-control—*apatheia* (ἀπαθεία)—by which the monk voluntarily hunted down thoughts (λογισμός, *logismos*) arising from the demon of obscenity (πορνεία, *porneia*), and replaced them with chaste thoughts.[58] The real enemy does not reside in the body but in erotic dreams, used by the devil to storm the monk's vegetative soul (ἐπιθυμικὸν, *epithumikon*). Erotic dreams associated with nocturnal emissions meant that the soul was sick, but a discharge without erotic dreams was considered a sign of the monk's spiritual well-being.[59] John Cassian went as far as excluding from the Eucharist the monk who had had a wet dream due to fantasies he had while awake.[60] If these nocturnal emissions happen naturally, despite the vigilance of the monk and his fasting, he should not, however, be kept away from the Eucharist, although the author equates those involuntary discharges to some sort of defilement or body impurity denounced by the *Holiness Code*.[61] Dioscorus, another desert monk, adopted the same position.[62] While Mosaic Law prescribed a ritual bath after the discharge of semen, whatever the cause, purity became a matter of the inner man— different from uncleanliness related to physical contact with body fluids. The Syrian hermit Simeon Stylites (380–459) illustrates the excesses displayed by some monks to escape sexual temptations and mortify the flesh. He took refuge atop a tall column of eighteen meters and lived there on a small area of two square meters for 37 years, chasing away women who would gather under his column.[63]

Most likely, Egyptian monasticism had some contact with the texts or ideas conveyed by the Coptic Gnostic writings of Nag Hammadi, where sexuality and reproduction were often associated with the ephemeral nature of existence and ignorance, which prevented human beings from attaining their true incorruptible nature.[64]

High regard for virginity and sexual abstinence may have eventually threatened marriage, especially when certain doctrines, such as those of the Gnostics or Encratites,[65] dared prohibit marriage and procreation. The Christian family then needed defenders. Rehabilitation of marriage, however, took a path decidedly different from the vision of the Old Testament or rabbinic Judaism, since sexual pleasure was being excluded from the benefits of marriage.

Clement of Alexandria claimed that any pursuit of sexual pleasure or discharge of semen, which did not have procreation as its sole purpose, was in itself an act contrary to reason and an insult to nature (παρὰ φύσιν καταισχύνειν).[66] For Clement, nature dictates the way the organs of reproduction should be used, not desire (τὸ γὰρ πάθος οὐ φύσις: desire is not nature). Wherefrom does Clement draw this new moral standard of sexual behavior? Neither the Old Testament nor the New Testament suggests such restrictive a rule. One must look for its origins in Philo of Alexandria when he interprets, influenced by Plato, the Tenth Commandment: "Thou shalt not covet (οὐκ ἐπιθυμήσεις)." In the same fashion, Clement believed that sexual appetite (ἔρως, *eros*) had to be the most voracious of all the passions related to the vegetative soul and the source for various disorders in human beings, as well as evils in society.[67] To control the appetites of the vegetative soul (ἐπιθυμία), as Plato, he appeals to reason, the noblest part of the soul, but also to the benefits of dieting.[68] One is tempted to think that Philo preaches moderation in the use of pleasures, as Plato or the Stoics, but he somewhat moves away from that approach. Philosophers consider the pleasures of sex as positive, when used reasonably. Philo, by contrast, pictures the passions of the flesh, more specifically appetite or desire, as an adversarial force, irrational (ἡ ἄλογος καὶ παρὰ φύσιν κίνησις) and guilt-ridden.[69] Libido has but one purpose, reproduction. Philo did not hesitate to state clearly that the purpose of marriage was not pleasure but procreation (οὐχ ἡδονὴν ἀλλὰ γνησίων παίδων σποράν).[70] Procreation as a justification for all sexual relations became the golden rule, and from it, Philo reinterpreted the purity rules of the *Holiness Code* regarding prohibiting sexual relations with menstruating women. Suddenly, the ban had nothing to do with ritual purity, but it rather strived to ban infertile sex.[71] He used the same kind of argument to condemn homosexual relations. In both situations, man acts stupidly, just like the farmer who sows in a flooded or downright barren field.[72] Clement concurred with Philo's views on the sole purpose of marriage—having legitimate children (ἐπὶ γνησίων τέκνων σπορᾷ).[73] Conjugality and moderate use of pleasures (σωφροσύνη) preached by the Stoics or Platonists philosophers no longer top the list of matrimonial goods. Nature dictates the behavior of spouses: getting together to procreate while dispelling any act contrary to this natural goal (κατὰ φύσιν).[74] Clement is exceedingly clear with respect to control (ἐγκράτεια) of sexual desire: don't try to become moderate, get rid of it.[75] To show his opposition to those who detract marriage, including Tatian, Clement asserts the sanctity of marriage (ἅγιος ὁ γάμος), whereby God's command to multiply is honored.[76] Clement won the honor, if so, to be the first to develop a sexual ethic based solely on reproduction by including in his definition of adultery any nonprocreative act between legitimate spouses.[77] By a curious reversal, Clement eliminates from the act of procreation between spouses any form of instinctual urge to transform it into a reasonable impetus (ὄρεξιν εὔλογον).[78] The Christian doctrine of marriage will undergo little change from the second to the twentieth century, as noted by Jean-Louis Flandrin.[79] There is a natural filiation between *Humanae Vitae* by Pope Paul VI and Clement's teaching.

Clement of Alexandria set on the same footing voluntary celibacy and Christian marriage, two separate but equally compelling ways to serve God.[80] Moreover, the ascetic ideal taught by Paul in 1 Corinthians had its supporters. Thus Tertullian (c. 150–c. 230) wrote:

> I DOUBT not, brother, that after the remission in peace of your wife, you, being wholly bent upon the composing of your mind (to a fight frame), are seriously thinking about the end of your lone life, and of course are standing in need of counsel. Although, in cases of this kind, each individual ought to hold colloquy with his own faith, and consult its strength; still, inasmuch as, in this (particular) species trial), the necessity of the flesh (which generally is faith's antagonist at the bar of the same inner consciousness, to which I have alluded) sets cogitation astir, faith has need of counsel from without, as an advocate, as it were, to oppose the necessities of the flesh: which necessity, indeed, may well easily be circumscribed, if the will rather than the

indulgence of God be considered. No one deserves (favour) by availing himself of the indulgence, but by rendering a prompt obedience to the will, (of his master). The will of God is our sanctification, for He wishes His "image"—us—to become likewise His "likeness"; that we may be "holy" just as Himself is "holy." That good—sanctification, I mean—I distribute into several species, that in some one of those species we may be found. The first species is, virginity from one's birth: the second, virginity from one's birth, that is, from the font; which (second virginity) either in the marriage state keeps (its subject) pure by mutual compact, or else perseveres in widowhood from choice: a third grade remains, monogamy, when, after the interception of a marriage once contracted, there is thereafter a renunciation of sexual connection. The first virginity is (the virginity) of happiness, (and consists in) total ignorance of that from which you will afterward wish to be freed: the second, of virtue, (and consists in) contemning that the power of which you know full well: the remaining species, (that) of marrying no more after the disjunction of matrimony by death, besides being the glory of virtue, is (the glory) of moderation likewise; for moderation is the not regretting a thing which has been taken away, and taken away by the Lord God, without whose will neither does a leaf glide down from a tree, nor a sparrow of one farthing's worth fall to the earth.

One does not become at all agreeable to God by flattering the senses, but by obeying God's will. "But the will of God is that we be holy." In fact, he wants that man, created in his image, become his likeness "so we should be holy as He is holy himself." That good, I mean sanctification, I will split in degrees, so that each of us can be part of it. The first degree is preserved virginity from one's birth. The second is that virginity which, since the second birth, that is to say baptism, cleanses us in marriage by consent of both spouses, as we persevere in celibacy by a voluntary decision. A third level remains, monogamy, when, after the dissolution of a first marriage by death, there is thereafter a renunciation of sexual relations. The first kind of virginity is blessed for ignoring completely what we later regret having known of it. The second heroically disdains what one has known too much. The third, which renounces the marriage after the marriage union is broken, besides the merit of courage, also has the merit of moderation. Is not being moderate than not regret what was kidnapped, abducted by the Lord above, without whose will it is not a leaf falls off the tree, nor the most humble sparrow falling to earth?[81]

Paul claimed that sexual abstinence was not suitable for every Christian, and he advised marriage if abstinence was beyond the strength of an individual. With Origen (185–254), the Pauline ideal of celibacy takes the shape of a universal rule applicable to all human beings, even within marriage.[82] In fighting back Jovian, who claimed that celibacy had no more value than marriage, St. Jerome (340–420) defends the superiority of virginity over marriage. He reaffirms almost the same position as Origen on sexual abstinence in marriage but, like him, he dismissed the idea of repudiating one's wife to live a celibate life:

Having discussed marriage and continence he at length comes to virginity and says (1 Cor. vii. 25, 26), "Now concerning virgins I have no commandment of the Lord: but I give my judgment, as one that hath obtained mercy of the Lord to be faithful. I think therefore that this is good by reason of the present distress, namely, that it is good for a man to be as he is." Here our opponent goes utterly wild with exultation: this is his strongest battering-ram with which he shakes the wall of virginity. "See," says he, "the Apostle confesses that as regards virgins he has no commandment of the Lord, and he who had with authority laid down the law respecting husbands and wives, does not dare to command what the Lord has not enjoined. And rightly too. For what is enjoined is commanded, what is commanded must be done, and that which must be done implies punishment if it be not done. For it is useless to order a thing to be done and yet leave the individual free to do it or not do it. If the Lord had commanded virginity He would have seemed to condemn marriage, and to do away with the seed-plot of mankind, of which virginity itself is a growth. If He had cut off the root, how was He to expect fruit? If the foundations were not first laid, how was He to build the edifice, and put on the roof to cover all!"[83]

Gregory of Nyssa (335–394) calls to mind Paul's thought: the pitfalls of secular life can easily become an obstacle to spiritual progress, which is better enhanced by celibacy. Favoring celibacy, he portrayed married life as not enviable and full of dangers: deceit, adultery, hedonism, greed, selfishness, and power.[84] Several church fathers—John Chrysostom, Jerome, Ambrose—participated, like Gregory, in genuine antimarital diatribes, to equate marriage to a form of bondage.[85]

Augustine took up the reproductive philosophy of marriage:

> The union, then, of male and female for the purpose of procreation is the natural good of marriage. But he makes a bad use of this good who uses it bestially, so that his intention is on the gratification of lust (*in voluptate libidinis*), instead of the desire of offspring (*non in voluntate propaginis*). Nevertheless, in sundry animals unendowed with reason, as, for instance, in most birds, there is both preserved a certain kind of confederation of pairs, and a social combination of skill in nest-building; and their mutual division of the periods for cherishing their eggs and their alternation in the labor of feeding their young, give them the appearance of so acting, when they mate, as to be intent rather on securing the continuance of their kind than on gratifying lust. Of these two, the one is the likeness of man in a brute; the other, the likeness of the brute in man.[86]

He acknowledged, however, that the goods of marriage are threefold: family (*proles*), fidelity (*fides*), and the sacramental bond (*sacramentum*) that makes it indissoluble.[87] For him, the emotional and instinctual dimension attracting a man to a woman in the marital bond transforms the libido in a positive way.[88] Pleasure or sexual desire is not included as such in the marriage goods: "Carnal concupiscence, however, must not be ascribed to marriage: it is only to be tolerated in marriage. It is not a good which comes out of the essence of marriage, but an evil which is the accident of original sin."[89] Sex, a necessary evil!

Augustine of Hippo plainly sorted libido on the side of sin, or even classified it as a defect originally transmitted to every human being at birth:

> Now, this ardour, whether following or preceding the will, does somehow, by a power of its own, move the members which cannot be moved simply by the will, and in this manner it shows itself not to be the servant of a will which commands it, but rather to be the punishment of a will which disobeys it. It shows, moreover, that it must be excited, not by a free choice, but by a certain seductive stimulus, and that on this very account it produces shame. This is the carnal concupiscence, which, while it is no longer accounted sin in the regenerate, yet in no case happens to nature except from sin. It is the daughter of sin, as it were; and whenever it yields assent to the commission of shameful deeds, it becomes also the mother of many sins. Now from this concupiscence whatever comes into being by natural birth is bound by original sin, unless, indeed, it be born again in Him whom the Virgin conceived without this concupiscence.[90]

Any sexual relation intended for the mere sake of pleasure, even that which exists between legitimate spouses in the accomplishment of conjugal duty, is negatively sealed. Sex intended for procreation alone remains sinless:

> This gratification incurs not the imputation of guilt on account of marriage, but receives permission on account of marriage. This, therefore, must be reckoned among the praises of matrimony; that, on its own account, it makes pardonable that which does not essentially appertain to itself. For the nuptial embrace, which subserves the demands of concupiscence, is so effected as not to impede the child-bearing, which is the end and aim of marriage.[91]

The satisfaction of pleasure is a legitimate objective within the scope of conjugal duty, but must always remain open to the rightful purpose of marriage, procreation.[92] Sexual desire is a direct consequence of the sin of Adam and Eve in paradise: "When the first man transgressed the law of God, he began to have another law in his members which was repugnant to the law of his mind, and he felt the evil of his own disobedience when he experienced in the disobedience of his flesh a most righteous retribution recoiling on himself."[93] For Augustine, sexuality is the theater of constant struggles of the will against desire, lust—the human soul trying to recover its paradisaic state before the sin:

> What do you mean by arbitrarily selecting words from my book and pretending I say that, before Adam's sin the institution of marriage was different; that it could have existed without concupiscence, without activity of bodies, and without the need of the two sexes? Subtract from marriage concupiscence by which the flesh lusts against the spirit, subtract the evil you oppose when you engage in glorious combats by means of the virtue of continence, and you need not subtract the rest if you are looking for the kind of marriage which would have existed before the sin of the first men. Has anyone conceived of marriage without activity of bodies and without the need of the two sexes? We say, however, that the war which the chaste, be they celibates or spouses, experience in them would by no means have existed in paradise before sin. Therefore, the very same kind of marriage exists even now, but at that time it would have used nothing evil in generating offspring, while it now uses well the evil of concupiscence.[94]

With Augustine, just as with Paul (e.g., Rom. 6:12–13), fighting the beast of lust calls for an athletic character in the sense that *voluntas* and *voluptas* are locked in a perpetual struggle. Here we are far from *ataraxia* of the Stoic philosophers or *apatheia* (ἀπαθεία) of the Greek fathers. In his *Confessions*, he highlights the triumph of the will over the body, a victory which requires admitting of past personal errors due to a sinful body.[95] His autobiography portrays him at all stages of life struggling with his sexual impulses, as if, he said, "another law in my members rebelled against the law of my mind, and led me captive under the law of sin which was in my members."[96] After his conversion to Christianity, Augustine endorses sexual renunciation without hesitation, putting an end to years of sexual libertinism and living in concubinage. The story of his conversion sheds light on his troubled relationship with sexuality: "But I wretched, most wretched, in the very commencement of my early youth, had begged chastity of Thee, and said, 'Give me chastity and continence, only not yet.'"[97] Finally abstinence triumphed: "For thou convertedst me unto Thyself, so that I sought neither wife, nor any hope of this world."[98]

For Augustine, celibacy does remain a higher state of life on the path of spiritual realization, especially since the inauguration by Jesus of a spiritual kingdom, in place of the ancient kingdom of Israel—a new realm with no need for regeneration.[99] Augustine, therefore, suggested that husbands live as if no women existed, except when they cannot control their libido, in which case some intemperance had to be tolerated:

> But in the married, as these things are desirable and praiseworthy, so the others are to be tolerated, that no lapse occur into damnable sins; that is, into fornications and adulteries. To escape this evil, even such embraces of husband and wife as have not procreation for their object, but serve an overbearing concupiscence, are permitted, so far as to be within the range of forgiveness, though not prescribed by way of commandment: (1 Corinthians 7:6) and the married pair are enjoined not to defraud one the other, lest Satan should tempt them by reason of their incontinence.[100]

The Augustinian pessimism about sexuality exerted considerable influence on Christian sexual morality for centuries. In the Middle Ages, controlling one's libido became an obligation for all and not just monks. The priests and bishops handed out manuals for confessors or Penitentials to regulate lay sexuality, both in and outside marriage. Most of these manuals, for example, the *Summa Confessorum* by Thomas of Chobham or the *Decretum* of Gratian, a Camaldolese monk, imposed a barrier to the sexual drive of spouses by banning carnal knowledge during specific times of the liturgical calendar (Lent, Advent, Sundays, or holidays), or during periods imposed by female physiological changes (pregnancy, menstruation, or childbirth).[101] Any form of copulation opposed to generation was also frowned upon. Ivo of Chartres (1091–1116) seemed to be the first to provide a definition of what was considered against nature (*contra naturam*)—the misuse of the genitals based on an anatomical-physiological notion.[102] Gratian repeated this definition by stating that a sexual act against nature surpassed fornication and adultery in gravity, even incest committed against one's mother.[103] When he attempted to explain Lot's gesture, who had offered his daughters instead of the messengers who were in danger of being abused sexually by the people of Sodom, he turned to the authority of Augustine and Ambrose of Milan to assert that natural copulation was a less serious offense than any sexual act against nature.[104] However, the first Penitentials, for instance, the *Penitential of Cummean Fota*, abbot of Clonfert Abbey in Ireland, provided a list of sins without any systematic distinction between a natural act and an act against nature. The severity of the misconduct rested on the status of the person, whether a bishop, a priest, a lay person, or a teenager.[105] Hincmar of Reims, like most writers, often used the word "sodomy" to represent a variety of acts "against nature," from masturbation to anal penetration of a woman or a man.[106] A detailed analysis of the penitential literature shows adultery as generally considered far more seriously than some acts against nature. Thus the bishop Burchard of Worms punished more severely adultery (*adulterium*) than masturbation or homogenital contacts such as mutual masturbation or intercrural sex, the latter belonging to the category of *fornicatio*.[107] With regard to anal intercourse, Penitentials do not classify it as a separate category but sometimes show more severity toward it. Thus the *Penitential of St. Columbanus* (543–615), Irish missionary to the land of the Franks, imposed a penance of ten years for sodomy committed by a monk and seven years in the case of a layman, while adultery required a sentence of three years in the case of a monk and one in the case of a layman.[108] Some authors did not see the need to deal more severely with sodomites. St. Gildas Rhuys, abbot in Wales in the sixth century, imposed a penance of three years for whoever engaged in natural fornication or sodomy.[109] In the tenth century, Regino of Prüm mentioned that imposed penances could vary considerably and gave the example of sodomy, for which some recommended ten years, others seven or even a year, but if the offense was habitual, more years might be added—five years for a lay person and fourteen years in the case of a bishop.[110]

Penitentials provided pastors with catalogs of sins without giving much justification for the difference in degrees of severity of penances. They also proposed to confessors interrogation techniques to obtain the penitent's full confession. Medieval scholasticism, with its method of *disputatio*, allowed for discussion and confrontation of different ideas or theories in the form of *Quaestiones* or *Summae*. It, therefore, sought to create a comprehensive and systematic knowledge, and claimed to reconcile all that was known within Christian doctrine.

The *Summa Theologica* of Thomas Aquinas tried to approach analytically sexual misconduct in general and define it more accurately than before; so that some sort of *scientia sexualis*[111] was on its way. Pleasures of the senses, which provide satisfaction of the sensitive appetite, such as that of generation or hunger, are deemed "natural"—meaning the subject is experiencing satisfaction in doing something pleasurable. These pleasures, however, can interfere with reason by their vehemence, as is the case with drinking alcohol.[112] As such, sexual pleasures threaten reason, which must lead one toward his personal good:

> As stated above (Q[33], A[3]), it is not the pleasures which result from an act of reason, that hinder the reason or destroy prudence, but extraneous pleasures, such as the pleasures of the body. These indeed hinder the use of reason, as stated above (Q [33], A [3]), either by contrariety of the appetite that rests in something repugnant to reason, which makes the pleasure morally bad; or by fettering the reason: thus in conjugal intercourse, though the pleasure be in accord with reason, yet it hinders the use of reason, on account of the accompanying bodily change. But in this case the pleasure is not morally evil; as neither is sleep, whereby the reason is fettered, morally evil, if it be taken according to reason: for reason itself demands that the use of reason be interrupted at times. We must add, however, that although this fettering of the reason through the pleasure of conjugal intercourse has no moral malice, since it is neither a mortal nor a venial sin; yet it proceeds from a kind of moral malice, namely, from the sin of our first parent; because, as stated in the FP, Q [98], A [2] the case was different in the state of innocence.[113]

As with Augustine, sexual pleasure interferes with our natural capacity for the good, but Thomas acknowledges the necessity of the conjugal act for the conservation of the species.[114] Any sexual act that seeks the enjoyment of sexual pleasure apart from what nature intended as its end—that is, generation—becomes a sin of lust of a particular kind, a vice against nature:

> I answer that as stated above (Q [153], A [3]), the sin of lust consists in seeking venereal pleasure not in accordance with right reason. This may happen in two ways. First, in respect of the matter wherein this pleasure is sought; secondly, when, whereas there is due matter, other due circumstances are not observed. And since a circumstance, as such, does not specify a moral act, whose species is derived from its object which is also its matter, it follows that the species of lust must be assigned with respect to its matter or object.
>
> Now this same matter may be discordant with right reason in two ways. First, because it is inconsistent with the end of the venereal act. In this way, as hindering the begetting of children, there is the "vice against nature," which attaches to every venereal act from which generation cannot follow; and, as hindering the due upbringing and advancement of the child when born, there is "simple fornication," which is the union of an unmarried man with an unmarried woman.[115]

Thomas Aquinas affirms the existence of sexuality in Eden, before the original sin, since propagation of the species requires the sexual union of male and female. But that union of the flesh truly is uncommon in character:

> In the state of innocence nothing of this kind would have happened that was not regulated by reason, not because delight of sense was less, as some say (rather indeed would sensible delight have been the greater in proportion to the greater purity of nature and the greater sensibility of the body), but because the force of concupiscence would not have so inordinately thrown itself into such pleasure, being curbed by reason, whose place it is not to lessen sensual pleasure, but to prevent the force of concupiscence from cleaving to it immoderately.[116]

Thomas views sexual pleasure as a natural consequence of generation and, as such, he calls it a natural passion. However, any pursuit of sexual pleasure for its own sake—pleasure as the object finality of the sexual act rather than procreation—contravenes the natural order established by God because "anyone who copulates for the delight which is in it, not referring to what nature intended for it, acts against nature."[117] Sexual desire remains a source of mental disruption, but this disorder will only cause a venial sin if experienced within the finality of marriage.[118] The use of sexual organs for purposes other than procreation, even in marriage, derives from an inordinate desire and constitutes a serious sin of lust:

> And every such act is evidently disordered of its very self, since we call every that is not properly related to its requisite end a disordered act. For example, eating is disordered if it be not properly related to bodily health, for which as end eating is ordained. And the end of using of genital organs is to beget and educate offspring, and so every use of the aforementioned organs that is not related to begetting and properly educating offspring is as much disordered. And every act of the aforementioned organs outside the sexual union of a man and a woman is obviously unsuitable for begetting offspring.[119]

Thomas Aquinas considers any disordered emission of semen as an attack on human life, based on Aristotelian embryology, which held that sperm contained a human being in potential since the male was seen as the only active partner in generation.[120]

Vice against nature frustrates right reason because man does not fulfill his own good, the propagation of the species.[121] The *Summa Theologica* lists four sexual acts against nature: masturbation (*mollities*), bestiality (*bestialitas*), sodomy (*sodomiticum vitium*), and unnatural manners of copulation (*innaturalis concubendi modus*).[122] The definition of sodomy will be explained in the next section. Remember that it is part of a number of nonprocreative acts, which according to Aquinas are based on a misuse of nature and, as such, are sins more serious than other wrongdoings, which make proper use of genital organs, such as adultery, rape, or incest.[123]

The Protestant reformers rehabilitated sexual pleasure and enhanced marital intimacy. A new appreciation for conjugality was facilitated, inter alia, by the fact that Luther and Calvin abolished the celibacy of priests and the sacramental nature of marriage.[124] In 1563, the Tridentine Decree *Tametsi* reacted to the Reformers' new conception of marriage. It proclaimed the sacramental nature of marriage, and added to it a certain juridical formalism with the requirement of banns and solemnity ensured by the attendance of witnesses. With these measures, marriage sees itself removed from the sphere of private individual contracts, if not often clandestine unions, which had previously favored a multitude of ambiguous situations, among which flourished bigamy. The Council of Trent did not discuss conjugal love as such, but the Protestant approach influenced the vision of Catholic moral theology, which now sought to make room for it in a more prominent way than in the medieval period. Thus, the *Catechism of the Council of Trent* defines natural attraction between the sexes as the first good of marriage, taking precedence over childbearing.[125] After the Reformation, the Council of Trent had no choice, and had to show greater consideration for the daily concerns of lay people, including their sex life. The solutions proposed by the church could no longer rely on an authoritarian view of the church, but had to call, in a greater fashion than before, for personal autonomy and freedom of conscience. A new style began to pervade the field of moral theology, probabilism. This approach promoted practical reasoning in the study of individual cases. In a given situation, the individual conscience is most of the time confronted by opposing views. One, then, needs to follow an inner voice, and not infer the conduct to be adopted from universal principles.[126] In matters of sexual morality, this new view urged for a greater emphasis on erotic pleasure in a relationship. Tomás Sánchez (1550–1610) and Alphonsus de Liguori (1696–1787) did not impute any wrong to sex preliminaries, and they authorized female postcoital masturbation, given the fact that men reached orgasm faster than women. In his *De Sancto Sacramento Matrimonii*, Sanchez reversed the traditional view on the gravity of the vice against nature by emphasizing that anal intercourse and coitus interruptus were preferable to vaginal penetration in extramarital relations, because they safeguarded the sanctity of marriage and the well-being of women in avoiding the birth of an illegitimate child.[127] Spouses could also keep their sexual fantasies alive without guilt in order to facilitate copulation.[128] In short, post-Tridentine moral theology allowed for a greater affirmation of the legitimacy of sexuality in marriage and a greater expression of emotions between spouses. It, thus, signaled the introduction of the modern family in the private sphere and greater freedom for the spouses in the expression of their sexuality.[129]

Male masturbation generally still was severely judged by most post-Tridentine moralists because it was regarded as an act deliberately opposed to generation. Yet, the moralists' focus moved from the act itself and its outcome—discharge of semen—to the sexual actor struggling with his instincts. These moralists turned their attention to the masturbator's mental predispositions—desire (*desiderium*) and fantasies (*delectatio morosa*)—which could trigger the act or accompany it. Thus, the Carmelite School of Salamanca, known as *Salmanticenses*, required from the penitent that he described in confession impure thoughts or fantasies experienced during masturbation, because fantasy was a sin, in addition to the sin of a disordered emission of seed.[130] Unlike the concerns expressed by the desert fathers, the discourse then changes. We are no longer confronted solely with the danger of morning erections or involuntary waste of semen (*periculum pollutionis*) that may result from sexual fantasies in dreams. The combination of peevish delight or *delectatio morosa* and masturbation refers to a libidinal economy that runs without external stimuli, since it is the nature of this kind of pleasure to imagine a sexual act, and delight in it, knowing full well that it cannot be consummated in reality.[131] To emphasize the imaginary dimension of masturbation, the Dominican René Charles Billuart (1685–1757) defined the specificity of the sin of masturbation (*mollities*) by the absence of coitus (*extra omnem concubitum*), while other moralists defined an act against nature as "*ad vas indebitum*"—the use of an improper receptacle.[132] What worried ethicists after Trent was that in masturbation, the libido often embraces an intrapsychic object, in which it voluntarily takes great delight to the point of orgasm (*cum commotione spirituum*).[133] Authors such as the sixteenth-century French Franciscan theologian Jean Benedicti noted the risk of narcissism in masturbation.[134] Efforts by various post-Tridentine moralists to promote a degree of marital intimacy were supported by more repressive measures against the excesses of sexuality, especially in men, who could imperil the domestic ideal. The bourgeois ideal of self-control and rationality is somehow reflected in the moralists' attacks against masturbation. They viewed it not only as a disorderly emission of semen, but also as a source of hyperexcitability and lack of control of the individual, who behaved like an animal or a degenerate aristocrat.[135] This lack of control over male sexuality had been the subject for concern in the past but mostly regarding wet dreams experienced by persons who had taken a vow of chastity. With post-Tridentine moralists, the male body now becomes a source of anxiety, the field of involuntary movements that can bamboozle the new male aesthetics of controlled behavior and reveal his servile animal condition.[136]

Accordingly, Flandrin is surely right about the unprecedented attention given to solitary vice in the literature of the moralists, from the seventeenth to the nineteenth century—especially when he sees it as an unprecedented attempt in the West to control the premarital sexuality of young men and not only that of girls.[137] With industrialization and urbanization, increased education and a belated age for marriage, the regulation of sexuality of single males becomes a matter of public hygiene or social reform. Several moralists rely on the medical view of masturbation. Since the publication in 1760 of Dr. Samuel Tissot's famous essay—*L'Onanisme: Dissertation sur les maladies produites par la masturbation*—several campaigns against masturbation illustrated the dangers of masturbation for men's health. The Trappist Jean Pierre Corneille Debreyne (1786–1867), theologian and doctor of medicine, mirrored how the discourse was still in continuity with the post-Tridentine view, even though the language was borrowed from medicine: "It seems that the frequency of masturbation is a direct result of the development of the nervous system."[138] The French Abbé G. Jacquemet wrote this cutting remark: "To begin with, impurity equals emotional squander."[139] The masturbator presents a deteriorated physical appearance, marked by general weakness and pallor, but above all a moral decay in which "the young victims of this unfortunate and shameful passion lose more or less memory, intelligence, become stupid, foolish."[140] The clergy, together with educators and physicians, instill chastity by attacking the "shameful vice" that threatens young males who are often struggling with idleness, particularly in industrialized cities where they come looking for a job.[141]

Several authors have shown that a large portion of the faithful, from the second half of the nineteenth century, stop applying with rigor the religious teachings on sexuality and fertility. Urban industrial capitalism imposes new economic requirements that are putting new pressures on domesticity and the traditional family unit. Many traditional large family units have a hard time making both ends meet, and popular logic and common sense take precedence over natalistic, religious discourse.[142] Several social reform movements appeared in Europe and America, promoting and protecting traditional family values by fighting against what they called public debauchery or prostitution, pornographic material and obscene shows, as well as homosexuality.[143] These social purity campaigns primarily targeted male sexuality because men enjoyed ample freedom, due to the separation of family and work space—a consequence of industrialized urbanization.[144] These crusades were largely the result of the Anglo-Protestant bourgeoisie in the United States, the United Kingdom, and Canada, but it often rallied the Catholic Church, as in the case of Quebec, in the hope to gain reform legislation that would fight against the scourge of immorality in all its forms.[145]

In the turmoil, the Catholic Church wished to preserve the indissolubility of a monogamous marriage against the growing threats of divorce or common-law unions, which, in its view, threatened the social contract based on the traditional sacrament of marriage. Pope Leo XIII wrote in his Encyclical *Arcanum Divinae* of 1880:

When the Christian religion is reflected and repudiated, marriage sinks of necessity into the slavery of man's vicious nature and vile passions, and finds but little protection in the help of natural goodness. A very torrent of evil has flowed from this source, not only into private families, but also into States. For, the salutary fear of God being removed, and there being no longer that refreshment in toil which is nowhere more abounding than in the Christian religion, it very often happens, as indeed is natural, that the mutual services and duties of marriage seem almost unbearable.[146]

Influenced by neo-Malthusian ideas, some theologians opted for disregarding coitus interruptus, as did Father Jean-Baptiste Bouvier. In 1843, he obtained from the Apostolic Penitentiary in the Vatican guidelines authorizing confessors to avoid systematically interrogating spouses in confession on their sexual practices. Without endorsing onanism as a contraceptive method, this policy of silence corresponded to tacit agreement. Tolerance would, however, not last long. A few years later, the Holy Office required confessors to inquire about this practice during confessions.[147] The Vatican's position became even more demanding, as is reflected by Pope Pius XI in his Encyclical of 1930, *Casti connubii*:

And now, Venerable Brethren, we shall explain in detail the evils opposed to each of the benefits of matrimony. First consideration is due to the offspring, which many have the boldness to call the disagreeable burden of matrimony and which they say is to be carefully avoided by married people not through virtuous continence (which Christian law permits in matrimony when both parties consent) but by frustrating the marriage act. Some justify this criminal abuse on the ground that they are weary of children and wish to gratify their desires without their consequent burden. Others say that they cannot, on the one hand, remain continent nor on the other can they have children because of the difficulties whether on the part of the mother or family circumstances.

But no reason, however grave, may be put forward by which anything intrinsically against nature may become conformable to nature and morally good. Since, therefore, the conjugal act is destined primarily by nature for the begetting of children, those who in exercising it deliberately frustrate its natural power and purpose sin against nature and commit a deed which is shameful and intrinsically vicious.

Small wonder, therefore, if Holy Writ bears witness that the Divine Majesty regards with greatest detestation this horrible crime and at times has punished it with death. As St. Augustine notes, "Intercourse even with one's legitimate wife is unlawful and wicked where the conception of the offspring is prevented. Onan, the son of Juda, did this and the Lord killed him for it."[148]

Pope Paul VI's Encyclical *Humanae vitae* followed the same path, stating that spouses could not act freely with respect to birth control.[149] Their behavior is dictated by the intentionality of the sexual act intended by God, fertility. The concept of "responsible parenthood," brought forward by the encyclical, limits its application to natural contraceptive methods, which concur with women's fertility cycle.[150] It also hardens the tone vis-à-vis neo-Malthusian ethics and family planning:

Neither is it valid to argue, as a justification for sexual intercourse which is deliberately contraceptive, that a lesser evil is to be preferred to a greater one, or that such intercourse would merge with procreative acts of past and future to form a single entity, and so be qualified by exactly the same moral goodness as these. Though it is true that sometimes it is lawful to tolerate a lesser moral evil in order to avoid a greater evil or in order to promote a greater good, "it is never lawful, even for the gravest reasons, to do evil that good may come of it"—in other words, to intend directly something which of its very nature contradicts the moral order, and which must, therefore, be judged unworthy of man, even though the intention is to protect or promote the welfare of an individual, of a family or of society in general. Consequently, it is a serious error to think that a whole married life of otherwise normal relations can justify sexual intercourse which is deliberately contraceptive and so intrinsically wrong.[151]

While reiterating the church's traditional doctrine on birth control, John Paul II's Apostolic Exhortation *Familiaris Consortio* offers a personalist approach to sexuality, highlighting marriage as a close loving communion, based on family and society.[152] According to John Paul II, the family is threatened by a new understanding of freedom as self-assertion: the family is now threatened by "corruption of the idea and the experience of freedom, conceived not as a capacity for realizing the truth of God's plan for marriage and family, but as an autonomous power of self-affirmation, often against others, for one's own selfish well-being."[153] Some speak of a refreshing positive vision of sexuality in what is called John Paul II's "theology of the body," set out in his Wednesday Audiences, from 1979 to 1984. There, the pope indeed developed a complex theological anthropology that focused on the "nuptial meaning of the body," which expresses the pure and untainted communion existing between Adam and Eve in the Garden of Eden. The lack of shame they felt at the sight of their naked bodies illustrates the sheer natural capacity of the sexual body, male and female, to express love, the complete gift of oneself to the other. The unity found in this love between man and woman is a reflection of the love of God within the Trinity. However, this perfect communion of persons was broken with the Fall, which obscures the spirit and allows the body to be faced with carnal desire and lust:

> Lust in general—and the lust of the body in particular—attacks this "sincere giving." It deprives man of the dignity of giving, which is expressed by his body through femininity and masculinity. In a way it depersonalizes man, making him an object "for the other." Instead of being "together with the other"—a subject in unity, in the sacramental unity of the body—man becomes an object for man, the female for the male and vice versa.[154]

For John Paul II, the teachings of *Humane Vitae* with respect to the procreative act fit in well with his own theological anthropology of sexuality as an expression of the gift of love. Conjugal chastity and continence combined with natural contraceptive methods fall within the need to discipline the carnal desire aimed at sexual gratification.[155] Unfortunately, John Paul II's position, while recognizing a certain value to the sexual body, remains tinted with the Augustinian dire consequences he attributes to the original sin. His views on lust are designed in such a way that it becomes difficult to acknowledge sexual pleasure positively.[156] Nowhere is sexual gratification per se hailed as a form of personal fulfillment, which may contribute to enrichment of the communion between two persons. However, a dysfunctional sexual life within marriage may engender division and problems that threaten the stability of a union. It should also be mentioned that the way John Paul II ties sexuality and gender into some kind of natural ontic order also prevents him from contemplating any expression of sex other than heterosexual.

In its document on sexual ethics titled *Persona Humana*, the Congregation for the Doctrine of the Faith recognizes the divine plan for marriage and family in the immutable natural law inscribed in the human heart by God.[157] This same document also believes that homosexuality and masturbation are serious violations of this objective natural order.

In the twentieth century, Reformed churches have instead succumbed to pressure from neo-Malthusians, and have validated contraception, which was originally also judged in a negative way by Luther and Calvin. In his *Commentary on the Book of Genesis*, Luther attacked those who acted against nature and committed the sin of Onan (coitus interruptus), a "sodomitical vice" worse than incest or adultery. After having condemned contraception in a strong way in 1908, the Lambeth Conference of Bishops of 1930, which brought together Anglican Bishops from around the world, moved in favor of the use of various contraceptive methods other than abstinence. Pope Pius XI reacted against this position in *Casti Connubii*.[158] Most Reformed churches quickly followed the position adopted at Lambeth, even among the more conservative evangelical churches in the United States. The issue of abortion, however, brought some Evangelical churches to revert to the traditional anticontraceptive position expressed by Luther, Calvin, and even *Humane Vitae*.

The history of Christianity has portrayed woman as being subordinate to man, from the creation story in Genesis, where she derives her existence from Adam's rib, up to the New Testament. The apostle Paul writes: "A man ought not to cover his head, since he is the image and glory of God; but woman is the glory of man. For man did not come from woman, but woman from man; neither was man created for woman, but woman for man."[159] The story of the original sin depicts Eve as the seductress who will take with her in death Adam and his descendants. As a result of this sin, she will give birth in pain and will be under the domination of her husband: "I will make your pains in childbearing very severe; with painful labor you will give birth to children. Your desire will be for your husband, and he will rule over you."[160]

The subordination of women was also strongly voiced by the church fathers. Augustine commented on the creation story:

> The natural order is also that women in society obey husbands, and children parents: the reason for this is that, in fact, the weakest brain submits to the strongest. In matters of command and obedience, the obvious justice is that those who excel in reason, prevail also in power: and when that order is disturbed in this world, either by the iniquity of man, or by the different species of animals, the just must endure this disorder over time, knowing they will enjoy in eternity true happiness, in full compliance with this order.[161]

Other statements may also be interpreted in support of gender equality. For example, Paul said in Galatians: "For all of you who were baptized into Christ have clothed yourselves with Christ. There is neither Jew nor Gentile, neither slave nor free, nor is there male and female, for you are all one in Christ Jesus."[162] Jesus himself did condemn adultery, male and female.[163] Rodney Stark provides ample evidence for women's attraction and conversion to Christianity because of its opposition to female infanticide and abortion.[164] However, the fact remains that the majority discourse within Christianity fails to challenge the hierarchical arrangement of gender roles. The model of the *Paterfamilias* has triumphed—at least until very recently—with full authority over women and children. In this vision, not only could a woman not hold public or government office, but she was clearly considered as legally incapacitated, under her husband's guardianship. There are of course women who have managed to emancipate within Christianity and have had some influence—Mary mother of Jesus, Teresa of Avila, Hildegard of Bingen,

Catherine of Siena, and so on. Their personal spiritual achievement, however, has failed to cause a reversal of the dominant patriarchal discourse.

Luther's acceptance of the universal priesthood of believers might have indicated a greater openness to gender equality, but women remained excluded from the pastorate until the mid-nineteenth century, if not until the twentieth century in the majority of Reformed churches. Even the ideas of the French Revolution did not change this misogynist scheme. The *Napoleonic Code* of 1804 considered the wife to be under the guardianship of her husband. Jean-Jacques Rousseau, one of the fathers of the Revolution, wrote in *Emile*, "Formed to obey a creature so imperfect as man, a creature often vicious and always faulty, she should early learn to submit to injustice and to suffer the wrongs inflicted on her by her husband without complaint."[165] Industrial capitalism brought disruption to the traditional family, especially with women's work outside the home. Women were no longer confined to their role as mothers and educators in the home. Toward the end of the nineteenth century, the churches, Catholic and Protestant, adopted a defensive strategy to protect the family. It aimed primarily at preserving the traditional roles of men and women within the family. Both parties attempted to strengthen the role of wives and mothers to curb women's work outside the home, which was considered a serious transgression of gender roles.[166] In Quebec, the episcopate and the clergy, including the Jesuits and their magazine *Relations*, waged a relentless campaign against women's emancipation through labor. Not only is the working woman accused of abandoning her young in a nursery, but she is accused of altering her feminine nature by wearing overalls, smoking cigarettes, and carrying a lunch box, like male workers.[167] Even nowadays, Cardinal Ratzinger, the previous Pope Benedict XVI, has stated that gender differentiation is imposed by nature, engraved in biology, a kind of fundamentalist view of gender differentiation, so to speak.[168] Complementarity between the sexes is not conducive of real equality but remains marked by the subordination of women whose existential meaning depends on another person, as is clearly shown by motherhood, which essentially characterizes her personality.

The majority of Christian churches today have a more positive view of the role of women in society and the church. Not only do they recognize the right of women to work and hold public office but, today, several denominations allow the entry of women in the ministry. Despite pronouncements in favor of women's work, the Catholic Church always seems to cling to its views on the traditional family unit and the maternal role of women.[169] Such is the case with the Exhortation *Familiaris Consortio*:

> There is no doubt that the equal dignity and responsibility of men and women fully justifies women's access to public functions. On the other hand, the true advancement of women requires that clear recognition be given to the value of their maternal and family role, by comparison with all other public roles and all other professions. Furthermore, these roles and professions should be harmoniously combined, if we wish the evolution of society and culture to be truly and fully human.[170]

While trying to uphold the equal dignity of women, the Vatican objects to the ordination of women, invoking a secular tradition within the church that goes back to Jesus himself who did not appoint female apostles.[171]

Homosexuality

The founder of Christianity did not speak on the issue of homosexual relations. The *Epistle to the Romans* is the first Christian document with a clear reference to homosexuality.

The Apostle Paul addressed those who, having recognized God's existence through his creation, got subsequently caught up in anthropomorphic or zoomorphic representations of the divine. This wrongdoing caused these people to engage in sexual disorders:

> Because of this, God gave them over to shameful lusts. Even their women exchanged natural sexual relations for unnatural ones (μετήλλαξαν τὴν φυσικὴν χρῆσιν εἰς τὴν παρὰ φύσιν). In the same way the men also abandoned natural relations with women and were inflamed with lust for one another. Men committed shameful acts with other men, and received in themselves the due penalty for their error.[172]

The words "natural" and "unnatural" and the theme of homosexual acts associated with idolatry situate Paul's commitment in the wake of texts from Hellenistic Judaism on the same subject: those of Philo of Alexandria, or the *Wisdom of Solomon* and *Testament of Naphtali*. Paul does not specify the nature of these sexual improprieties, except that the acts are between persons of the same sex. He does not intend to make homosexuality the main focus of his remarks; it is a metaphor for the alienation of the creature against its Creator. Moreover, the apostle further specifies that this estrangement leads to other forms of sin: envy, murder, deceit, and so on.[173] But what is this estrangement? The influence of Stoicism on Hellenistic Judaism was mentioned in the previous chapter, so there is no need to discuss it here. Paul uses in this passage from *Romans* an expression dear to the Stoics, the "natural use" (τὴν φυσικὴν χρῆσιν) of sexual pleasure, that is to say, experiencing pleasure without excessive passion. For the Stoics, the danger lies in desire, when craving becomes the cause for excess.[174] Philo of Alexandria attributed the origin of homosexual passion to a lifestyle dominated by hedonism and luxury. This lifestyle leads man to excessive use (μεγίστη δ'ἀρχὴ κακῶν) of pleasures, as it happened to the inhabitants of Sodom who enjoyed a life of luxury and material wealth without any sharing.[175] Lack of control of the sexual urge (ἐπιθυμίας) leads men to defy what nature dictates (τὸν τῆς φύσεως νόμον), and they then engage in all forms of vices: gluttony, drunkenness, and adultery. Philo adds to this list of orgies homosexual acts that show gender inversion, because those who engage in them behave effeminately, and let their bodies endorse feminine grace (τὰ σώματα μαλακότητι καὶ θρύψει γυναικοῦντες). This behavior is not addressed as such by Paul in Romans, but he does not seem to be totally unfamiliar with it, since he rates effeminate males (μαλακοί) and homosexuals (ἀρσενοκοῖται) alongside thieves, drunkards, and adulterers, among those who will not inherit the Kingdom.[176]

Clement of Alexandria took the same arguments against pederastic homosexuality as Philo, particularly when he focused on the so-called Alexandrian rule, which admitted as legitimate sexual relations only those intended to procreate within a monogamous marriage.[177] Clement thinks that an insatiable sexual appetite drives men to use boys sexually, as if they were girls. He develops his argument by employing the image of the hypersexuality of the hare, which he believed had many anuses, and the hyena, which displayed a third opening under the tail, other than the anus and the vagina, thereby facilitating sexual relations at all times, as well as homosexual relations.[178] John Chrysostom (347–407) read in the Sodom narrative against pederasty divine retribution,[179] and added that homosexuality was wrong because it had its origin in excess:

> And reflect too how significantly he uses his words. For he does not say that they were enamoured of, and lusted after one another, but, "they burned in their lust one toward another." You see that the whole of desire comes of an exorbitancy which endureth not to abide within its proper limits. For everything which transgresseth the laws by

God appointed, lusteth after monstrous things and not those which be customary. For as many oftentimes having left the desire of food get to feed upon earth and small stones, and others being possessed by excessive thirst often long even for mire, thus these also ran into this ebullition of lawless love. But if you say, and whence came this intensity of lust? It was from the desertion of God: and whence is the desertion of God? From the lawlessness of them that left Him; "men with men working that which is unseemly."[180]

He also echoed the Judaic objection to anal sex relations, based on the transgression of gender roles. Homosexuality generates a true battle of the sexes:

It was meet, that the twain should be one, I mean the woman and the man. For "the twain," it says, "shall be one flesh" (Gen. 2: 24). But the desire of intercourse effected, and united the sexes to one another. This desire the devil having taken away, and having turned the course thereof into another fashion, he thus sundered the sexes from one another, and made the one to become two parts in opposition to the law of God. For it says, "the two shall be one flesh;" but he divided the one flesh into two: here then is one war. Again, these same two parts he provoked to war both against themselves and against one another.[181]

From Paul to Clement of Alexandria or John Chrysostom, the "natural use" of pleasure never refers to a specific configuration of sexual desire, which indicates a preference of the subject for a partner of the same sex. The expression rather means the use of sexual pleasures with moderation, that is to say, sex in the conjugal bed for procreation.

The authors of medieval Penitentials did not clearly define what they meant by sodomy. The context is not always homosexual, except for St. Columba and Burchard, bishop of Worms.[182] Among nonprocreative practices, heterosexual or homosexual oral sex was frowned upon, according to Theodore of Canterbury.[183] The *Liber Gomorrhianus* of Peter Damian described sodomy as a vice against nature (*contra naturam vitium*), primarily homosexual, but he did not limit it to anal penetration. Sodomy, he said, included four different vices: masturbation (*propriis minibus*), mutual masturbation (*inter se*), interfemoral (*inter femora*) sex, and anal penetration (*in terga*).[184]

Ambiguity and confusion hence marked the penitential literature on the subject of sex, sometimes with unexpected insistence on masturbation and homogenital contacts. One has to consider that this genre is often the creation of monks in search of discipline in the monastic life, which would account for a greater emphasis on such practices, more so than adultery.[185] The author of the *Liber Gomorrhianus* wanted to convince Pope Leo IX to act swiftly to curb the vice of sodomy because it plagued the clergy. Peter Damian proposed the removal of sodomites from monastic orders, including adepts of the solitary vice and all those who engaged in homogenital contacts, such as mutual masturbation, fellatio, or anal intercourse. For him, the categorization of punishments based on the frequency and nature of the act, as advocated by the authors of Penitentials, was useless. He denounced the bishops' silence regarding the growth of the vice, and he reported the difficulty of eradicating the scourge because sodomites confessed among themselves. Chapter 17 of the *Liber* provides an explanation for the ferocious attack conducted by its author: sodomites threaten the medieval social and cultural order because they destroy the frontiers between the masculine and the feminine, between active and passive roles in sexual relations.[186] Many of Peter Damian's attacks targeted the bishops themselves, who did not fear a life of debauchery with women and men, even among the clergy.[187] The pope, while describing these actions as despicable, did not welcome the severity of

Peter Damian's arguments. Bishops had clerics and boys (*laici puri*) at their personal service in their bedrooms, which was an occasion for sexual improprieties that led Pope Gregory the Great to ask bishops to hire mature clerics for these tasks, individuals with irreproachable conduct.[188] In the second chapter, it was mentioned that companionship of a boy helper or a novice was widespread in Buddhist monasteries, in Japan and China. Many of the stories recounted did mention or allude to sexual misconduct happening in an all-male environment. A similar scenario unfolded in Christian eremitic enclosures during the late Antiquity or the Middle Ages.[189]

As in medieval Hebrew and Arabic poetry, although less extensive, a Christian poetry in praise of love affairs with boys did exist. It was mainly the work of Latin poets belonging to the Loire School. Interestingly, all these poets were bishops: Marbod of Rennes (1035–1123), Baldric of Bourgueil (1046–1130), and Hildebert of Lavandin (1056–1133). Even if they speak in the first person, it remains unclear whether their works are autobiographic or literary fiction, just like the works of ancient poets Ovid and Martial. These authors let their literary imagination wander into erotic descriptions of male love and, then, end paradoxically their fantasies with religious disapproval.[190] Were some of them among those sodomites—bishops and clergy—that Peter Damian reported? It is impossible to affirm decidedly. In any case, their complacent recourse to homoerotic fancies remains difficult to justify by purely aesthetic motives, when the ultimate goal they pursue seems its reprobation. Religious discourse often uses sexual metaphors—heterosexual, homosexual, or even transsexual—to express mystical union with the divine, not human depravation. Yet the confession of homosexual attractions, described with emphasis, seems to be part of a cleansing process that ultimately leads to their rejection. Boy love becomes the prism through which the poet expresses the redemption of a natural order that has been subverted. However, Bishop Wulfstan of Worcester seemed more open and guiltless, as it is recorded by the historian monk William of Malmesbury (c. 1095/96–c. 1143):

> Boys of elegant appearance he marked out by fondling them with his holy hands and kissing them [*sane pueros elegantis formae dignanter sacrarum manuum tactu et osculis demulcens*], for he embraced in them the grace of God's handiwork. He drew a moral from the beauty of their features, often exclaiming: "How beautiful must be the Creator who makes such beautiful creatures!"[191]

John Boswell probably should have shown more caution when applying the expression "gay subculture" to this kind of homoerotic literature, which disappeared with the decline of Rome and resurfaced between 1050 and 1150.[192] Peter Damian's attacks, and those of many others like him, who were scandalized to see sodomy so widespread among the clergy, should be read in the broader context of the corruption of sexual morals in the clergy, who feared neither adultery, nor having concubines, nor homosexuality.[193] Some monastic rules, including that of St. Pachomius, St. Basil, and St. Benedict, had tried to prevent physical contact between monks, specifically to eliminate promiscuity with young aspirants and avoid all forms of sexual intimacy.[194] The Third Lateran Council, in 1179, aimed precisely at reforming the morals of the clergy: it punished the priests who would not renounce their cohabitation with their concubine by revoking the benefit of clergy. It also punished incontinence against nature (*illa incontinentia qua contra naturam*). In the latter case, the clergy had to quit their office and retire to a monastery, while lay persons were excommunicated. For the first time, an Ecumenical Council directly punished the culprits, and the Fourth Lateran Council went even further by enabling criminal sanctions.

The first goal of Penitential literature was to quell wrongful acts through confession without paying attention to any theological foundation for an ethics of sex. This was later achieved by scholastic theology. To attain this end, scholastic theologians referred to animal behavior in particular and the idea of nature. The metaphor of nature and its teachings played a pivotal role in the development and definition of Roman natural law. The *Justinian Code* expounds natural law in the light of what nature teaches us about marriage, procreation, and child rearing, through animal behavior.[195] The medieval literary genre of the Bestiary used animal behavior to incite human moral behavior. These works were often inspired by ancient texts such as the anonymous *Physiologus*, or the *Epistle of Barnabas*, which connected the prohibition found in Mosaic Law regarding the consumption of the flesh of certain animals to their aberrant sexual behavior. Thence, the hyena would change sex every year, the hare would develop a new anus yearly, and the weasel practiced fellatio.[196] Peter Damian also made use of animal metaphors, saying that two stallions grazed peacefully together in a meadow, and that only the presence of a mare managed to elicit their sexual appetite.[197]

In *The Complaint of Nature* (*De Planctu Naturae*), the theologian Alain de Lille (c. 1128–1202) insisted upon the allegorical virtues of nature as a teacher (*natura doctor*). The work was intended as an argument in favor of heterosexual fertility, featuring the Goddess Nature; disparaging homosexual acts without ever naming them, or designating them as sodomy. He was probably the first to exploit systematically the unspeakable character (*monstra nefanda*) of this infamous vice, which defied the grammar of Nature—like a hammer (penis) pounding a sterile anvil (anus):

> The sex of active nature trembles shamefully at the way in which it declines into passive nature. Man is made woman, he blackens the honor of his sex, the craft of magic Venus makes him of double gender. He is both predicate and subject, he becomes likewise of two declensions, he pushes the laws of grammar too far. He, though made by Nature's skill, barbarously denies that he is a man. Art does not please him, but rather artifice; even that artificiality cannot be called metaphor; rather it sinks into viciousness. He is too fond of logic, with whom a simple conversion causes the rights of Nature to perish. He strikes on an anvil which emits no sparks. The very hammer deforms its own anvil. The spirit of the womb imprints no seal on matter, but rather the plowshare plows along a sterile beach.[198]

Albert the Great, who studied animal behavior, warned against the dangers of an overactive sex life: hemorrhage, nervousness, and tremors. He did acknowledge sexuality as a natural phenomenon and, as such, he did not see it as resulting from the original sin.[199] Sodomy did offend him because it contradicted human reason and violated nature.[200] The learned Dominican identified as lust (*luxuria*) any form of sexual pleasure that went against what nature intended for the reproduction of the species. Procreation had its source in the complementarity of unalike genitalia, that is, male and female.[201]

From the eleventh century, poets, philosophers, and theologians sought to ground moral action more systematically on the universal laws derived from nature. Some authors even believed that sexuality expressed a law of nature, and did not derive from sin.[202] An anonymous poem of the twelfth century, *Quam Pravus est Mos* (*A Perverse Custom*), discussed the perversity of boy love. The practice was deemed against nature because it was absent from the animal kingdom.[203] However, the use of the animal realm had no empirical basis. Modern animal science has documented the existence of homogenital contacts among animal species.[204] The Augustinian idea of a disorder arising from the sexual appetite, nonetheless, continued to prevail among the great masters of Scholasticism. Referring explicitly to Augustine, Aquinas maintained that beasts are without reason. In this way, man becomes, as it were, like them in coition, because he cannot moderate concupiscence. In the state of innocence, nothing of this kind would have happened that was not regulated by reason, not because delight of sense was less, as some say (rather indeed would sensible delight have been the greater in proportion to the greater purity of nature and the greater sensibility of the body), but because the force of concupiscence would not have so inordinately thrown itself into such pleasure, being curbed by reason, whose place it is not to lessen sensual pleasure, but to prevent the force of concupiscence from cleaving to it immoderately.[205]

The *Summa Theologica* ascertained four sexual acts against nature: masturbation, bestiality, sodomy, and improper modes of copulation. Usually, the *vitium sodomiticum* denounced these four practices indiscriminately. Yet, Thomas specifically circumscribed homogenital contacts, male or female, to "copulation with an undue sex (*ad non debitum sexum*), male with male, or female with female, as the Apostle states (Romans, 1:27): and this is called the 'vice of sodomy.'"[206] The vice against nature is particularly serious because it directly violates the order of nature intended by God for the conservation of the species, which is not the case, for example, in rape, adultery, or incest committed by a father on his daughter.[207] Adulterers or rapists lack charity but do not violate the natural order. Acts against nature fall under the category of the most serious sins of lust and, among them, *vitium sodomiticum* lodges second only to bestiality. By restricting the definition of sodomy to acts *ad non debitum sexum*, not only is the issue of the disordered emission of seed condemned, but the aberration is now assigned to the choice of the sexual object, which defies the natural complementarity of the two sexes. The meaning of sodomy found in the *Liber Gomorrhianus* or the works of decretalists such as Ivo of Chartres and Gratian was narrowed down.

Parallel to the theological charge just observed, the thirteenth century provided an opportunity for a more efficient repression against homosexual acts by ecclesiastical authorities. In 1233, Pope Gregory IX wanted to end the Cathar heresy (Albigensians) in Occitania, and he implemented the Tribunal of the Inquisition, staffed by Dominicans and Franciscans. The Cathar doctrine was influenced by Gnosticism and Manichaeism, and it resembled that of the Bogomils of Bulgaria and Bosnia Herzegovina, with whom they had forged ties. Despite the triumph of the Crusade against the Albigensians and the surrender of their patron, Count Raymond VI of Toulouse, Gregory IX failed to obtain the count's assistance in denouncing the Cathars. Like many early Gnostic-inspired sects of the early Christian centuries, the Albigensians rejected marriage and procreation, which only projected the imprisonment of the soul in a physical body. Very quickly in the popular imagination, Cathars and Bogomils became identified with nonprocreative sexual acts, including homosexuality. The French word "*bougre*" and the English "bugger" are derived from the Latin word "Bulgarus," and they designate the heretic and the sodomite indifferently.[208] In a context of persecution, it is not uncommon to propagate about one's enemy rumors depicting him in a state of perpetrating the worst abominations. Philippe IV, the Fair, fully used this technique of defamation against the Templars, and delivered them in the hands of the Inquisition. The Inquisitors meticulously obtained the confessions of the accused who, under torture, admitted crimes of sodomy and participation in secret ceremonies of apostasy, during which they performed profaning gestures and acts with a homosexual connotation.[209] Often the charge of sodomy, called *nefando pecado* (the unspeakable sin), was brought out when evidence for heresy became elusive. Hence, the Aragonese Inquisition, who wished to convict a converted Jew, Don Sancho Caballeria, obtained from Pope Clement VII permission to punish the sodomites in 1524. Several hundred men were put on trial by the Inquisitors in Valencia, Zaragoza, and Barcelona and about 12 percent were condemned (*auto da fé*) to be burned in the public square.[210] Many suffered imprisonment, forced labor, or banishment. The Portuguese Inquisition also persecuted homosexuals, but it made fewer deaths.[211]

The twentieth-century Lutheran theologian Helmut Thielicke thinks Luther and German Lutheran theology have not made much case of homosexuality.[212] He is wrong. In his *Lectures on Genesis*, Luther sees the sin of Sodom as a vice against nature, man seeking a man instead of women. For him, God implanted in man a natural desire for the opposite sex and homosexual desire is the work of Satan. He clearly contrasted rightful sex within marriage and the hypocrisy of failed celibacy in monasteries, where monks engage in "Italian weddings."[213] Even if he rejects the sacramental nature of marriage and turns it into an institution under civil authority, he firmly believes that heterosexual marriage is part of the order of creation willed by God.[214] It seems very difficult to interpret the rejection of the sacramental nature of marriage and clerical celibacy as an openness to recognize homosexual unions as part of the creational order, as some much later Lutheran theologians try to encourage.[215] In any case, Luther's position on the civil nature of marriage allows the most liberals to accommodate homosexual civil unions without endorsing religious gay marriage. John Calvin in his *Commentary on Genesis* interprets the sin of Sodom as a vice against nature resulting from a general state of iniquity, leading its inhabitants to believe they can do anything, including the most abominable crimes. Louis Crompton notes that the theocratic system imposed by Calvin in Geneva proved a lot tougher on homosexual practices than in the rest of the Protestant world, particularly under the auspices of Calvin's successor, Theodore Beza.[216] The doctrine of predestination whereby God has chosen the fate of humanity, electing some to salvation and condemning others, contributes to Calvinist austerity.[217] This doctrine, however, remains problematic. Even if it has God as the sole initiator of salvation, it, however, leaves no room for mercy.[218]

Among Catholics, the vast majority of moralists after Thomas Aquinas applied a stricter definition of sodomy, confining it to homogenital relations exclusively. Anal heterosexual intercourse was defined as *sodomia imperfecta* because the evil of sodomy resided precisely in the misguided choice of a sexual object, a same-sex partner.[219] Some authors limited sodomy to anal penetration, as the Carmelite School of Salamanca for whom "emission of sperm is not required for sodomy to apply, anal penetration is sufficient."[220]

Alphonsus Liguori (1696–1787) and other authors include in their understanding of sodomy a number of homosexual practices: "Sexual intercourse between two women and between two men is true sodomy, in whatever parts of the body it takes place. For usually there is always a desire for the improper sex."[221] Here, I want to stress the desire for a same-sex object (*affectus ad indebitum sexum*) has gained prominence. Tommaso Tamburini (1591–1695) wrote:

> But the question is this: When is it that mutual masturbation among males or females should be called masturbation and when sodomy? When sexual intercourse is motivated by the desire for the person, if it is with the improper sex, that is, between two men or two women, such is sodomy; when mutual masturbation is only intended to extend one's sexual pleasure without being drawn to the person, then it is masturbation. Thus, if two men embrace each other and move their bodies so as to masturbate, or touch one another immodestly driven by the desire for the improper sex, it is certainly sodomy if there follows emission of sperm in the receptacle (anus) and is also proven to be sodomy even when emission of sperm occurs outside, without copulation, because the intercourse was motivated by sexual desire for the improper sex, which specifically defines sodomy.[222]

Moralists did not always pay attention to active or passive roles in anal homosexual penetration. Some authors believed, however, that the confessor should inquire about it from the penitent. The importance of this detail may be explained by the possibility for the passive partner not to experience ejaculation, which would then result in a less serious sin for him.[223] Gender inversion associated with passivity is never mentioned, neither as dangerous nor as a specific sin. It did not happen until later in the nineteenth century when moralists imported this type of discourse from medical theories on sexual perversions. Several moralists unequivocally employed the medical vocabulary in their writings— words such as *uranistae, sexualitas contraria, homosexualitas, perversio sexualis,* and so on.[224] The meaning of the expression "against nature" was quietly transformed in their works. Gender inversion slowly became the determiner of a new category—the intermediate sex. What then determines the significance of the expression has to be found in the sexual actor's personality, rather than in the nature of a sexual act that frustrates the finality of reproduction. Giuseppe Antonelli, in his treatise on pastoral medicine used the word *urning* to describe as homosexual, a word borrowed from Karl Ulrichs who had coined it to describe a female soul trapped in a male body: "The most obvious sign is that they all behave like women; they indeed dress as women and wear jewelry, their walk and gesture are feminine; they imitate the female voice."[225] The use of medical perversion led moralists into unfamiliar terrain. They could not conclude regarding moral agency in the way of their medical muses who excused the agent due to congenital pathological inclinations. For most moralists, homosexuality, even if imputed to disease, had to be fought, and they objected to view it as an innate condition. Dominikus Prümmer requested confessors not to acquiesce to the idea promoted by some psychiatrists that homosexual tendencies could be so compelling in an individual that it was impossible for him to resist.[226]

Purity crusades in the nineteenth century led many educators, both among Protestants and Catholics in Europe and America, to denounce "les amitiés particulières" (particular friendships, love affairs between schoolboys). Some authors often linked this phenomenon to solitary vice, a real plague in colleges and boarding schools, older boys dragging the younger into it.[227] A French priest named Canon Caulle wrote:

> There is a particularly perverse mode of debasement which operates through the guise of friendship. Old as the world, it plagued with infamy the shores of the Dead Sea, before the rain of sulphur had engulfed Sodom; it brought God's curse on the people of Canaan; it was not unknown among the Hebrews since Leviticus calls it an abomination and punishes it with utter severity... Christian teachers now are deploying more careful supervision. Nevertheless, they still will not prevent these horrible affections to reach their boarding schools, as in others, which are designated as particular friendships. Their students are not of a nature apart from other students. Alongside excellent students, restless evil doers make their way. (...) Their natural instinct is to corrupt. They truly conspire against decency. (...) Shame on the schoolhouses where these monsters have introduced themselves; children cannot easily avoid their stratagems! Because of them, an epidemic of sodomy has arisen. Young teenagers, who in college become spoiled, then spoil their friends during holidays, when there is less adult supervision and more freedom. Corruption spreads;... it eats away the fiber of the youth, it even attacks people in their middle age. It is not uncommon to encounter, without going to Prussia, in all wakes of life, men enslaved in vile habits against nature.[228]

Starting from the nineteenth century, masturbation and particular friendships became a prime concern for Christian educators. What used to be regarded as a fancy among young persons had become a sort of contagious disease that could affect adult life and individual sexual development.[229] The Anglican priest and educator Edward Lyttelton wrote: "The secret sin which has been learned in a private school, imported to the public school, and there taught to the youngest boys, will inevitably produce the more fashionable vices of the larger society."[230] Educators conceived particular friendships with the help of the medical stereotype of the pervert, or the effeminate invert, and feared that homosexual experiences could affect the teenager trying to cope with his sexual identity and make him a homosexual later.[231] The description of these friendships by the Jesuit G. Hoornaert leaves no doubt on the stereotyping of the homosexual that was going on: "The special affection discussed here, which is basically love for a woman but at the wrong address, imagines in the loved one charms reminiscent of the other sex, not so much male beauty but a rather 'effeminate' beauty. One falls in love with the handsome beardless young male adolescent"[232] The social purity campaigns reflect the growing anxiety of a capitalist industrial society in mutation, to which Christian educators and clergy merely added their voice. Governments moved in the same direction toward the late nineteenth century by adopting a series of legislative measures to counter public immorality. The amendment to the Criminal Code presented by MP Henry Labouchere, and adopted by the British Parliament in 1885, illustrates this new mindset. Acts of sodomy that involved anal penetration were condemned by English law long before, but the amendment introduced the concept of gross indecency, which now allowed punishment for all forms of homosexual activity.[233] With this amendment passed, it became possible to indict the famous writer Oscar Wilde in 1895. The Parliament of Canada imitated the United Kingdom, and adopted a similar bill in 1890: "Every male person is guilty of an indictable offence and liable to five years' imprisonment and to be whipped who, in public or private, commits, or is a party to the commission of, or procures or attempts to procure the commission by any male person of, any act of gross indecency with another male person."[234] This measure, with a series of others on the seduction of a minor girl or on prostitution, turned out to be a strategy to protect marriage and family, both deemed to be threatened by uncontrolled male libido.[235]

During the twentieth century, several countries decriminalized homosexual acts between consenting adults. In France, the Constituent Assembly of 1789 abolished sodomy laws in its criminal code. As a result of the Napoleonic conquests, sodomy was also abolished in Belgium, Holland, and Italy. In England, Parliament approved its decriminalization in 1967, following the recommendations of the Wolfenden Report (*Report of the Departmental Committee on Homosexual Offences and Prostitution*) of 1957. In 1969, the Canadian Parliament passed the *Omnibus Bill C-150*, which abolished any sanction against homosexual acts between consenting adults. Prime Minister Pierre Elliot Trudeau believed that the nation had no place in the bedroom of citizens. Both in England and in Canada, the separation of public and private spheres became the backbone of legislative reform. These amendments to the Criminal Code led to bitter debates in parliaments where both sides fiercely clashed. Traditionalists, often inspired by religious motives, objected to these changes, fearing the promotion of homosexuality—the symbol of a decadent society. The other faction did not observe any negative impact of homosexuality on family or society, and, instead, adopted the medical model, which considered homosexuality as innate and irreversible.[236] Many churches supported the proposal to decriminalize homosexuality, and accepted the principle that the state should not interfere with the sexual lives of consenting adults, and what was considered sin was not necessarily a crime. In England, the Anglican and Methodist Church, and an ad hoc Catholic committee, approved the Wolfenden recommendation.[237] The Presbyterian

Church of Scotland remained opposed to such liberalization. In Canada, the Lutheran Church, the Baptist Church, and the United Church of Canada were in favor of *Bill Omnibus*, while the Catholic Church chose to remain silent.

The discourse on the decriminalization of homosexuality led to a change of the paradigm of homosexuality, from perversion to the notion of sexual orientation, and provided a space for freedom of expression for all those who claimed the right to a homosexual identity in the public sphere. Taking advantage of the wind of liberation brought by the sexual revolution of the 1960s, gay advocacy movements appeared simultaneously in the United States, Australia, Canada, and Europe. The highlight of the gay liberation movement is the Stonewall riot in New York, which occurred in June 1969, outside a bar frequented by a gay clientele, the Stonewall Inn in Greenwich Village. The police came to raid the bar but had to face the anger of the crowd as they were greeted by rocks thrown by demonstrators who chanted "Gay Power!" Since Stonewall, the gay movement has succeeded in promoting the rights of homosexuals, and has forced significant changes in favor of the protection of homosexual civil rights in various countries. Quebec was one of the first states in the world to include in its *Charter of Rights and Freedoms* sexual orientation as grounds for discrimination.

Acceptance of the concept of sexual orientation in the scientific community and in the general population, as well as the recognition and protection of the rights of homosexuals, and recently the legalization of homosexual unions or gay marriage have forced the Christian churches to debate homosexuality and the ordination of openly gay priests or pastors. In 1986, the Roman Catholic Church, for the first time, in a document entitled *Letter to the Bishops of the Catholic Church on the Pastoral Care of Homosexual Persons*, reluctantly concedes that the dignity of homosexual persons is somewhat severely tainted, and that such violations cannot be tolerated. The author, Cardinal Ratzinger, the pope who resigned recently, confines his intention of respecting human dignity to negative expressions—no insults and no violence against homosexuals. He does not venture into the realm of positive affirmation of the rights of homosexuals in society. Yet the Pastoral Constitution *Gaudium et Spes* of Vatican II offers a foundation that would have allowed him to be more insistent:

> At the same time, however, there is a growing awareness of the exalted dignity proper to the human person, since he stands above all things, and his rights and duties are universal and inviolable. Therefore, there must be made available to all men everything necessary for leading a life truly human, such as food, clothing, and shelter; the right to choose a state of life freely and to found a family, the right to education, to employment, to a good reputation, to respect, to appropriate information, to activity in accord with the upright norm of one's own conscience, to protection of privacy and rightful freedom even in matters religious.[238]

Nonetheless, the Vatican's agenda seems to be moving toward a rather candid opposition to any form of support to civil legislation intended to protect the constitutional rights of homosexuals:

> There is an effort in some countries to manipulate the Church by gaining the often well-intentioned support of her pastors with a view to changing civil-statutes and laws.
> But the proper reaction to crimes committed against homosexual persons should not be to argue that the homosexual condition is not disordered. When such a claim is made and when homosexual activity is consequently condoned, or when civil legislation is introduced to protect behavior to which no one has any conceivable right, neither

the Church nor society at large should be surprised when other distorted notions and practices gain ground, and irrational and violent reactions increase.[239]

The Vatican whitewashes the entire issue of violence made against homosexuals. Yet it did officially denounce the violence. Why this inconsistency? In 1976 the Vatican set the tone of its doctrinal approach with regard to homosexuality in the Declaration *Persona Humana*:

> At the present time, there are those who, basing themselves on observations in the psychological order, have begun to judge indulgently, and even to excuse completely, homosexual relations between certain people. This they do in opposition to the constant teaching of the Magisterium and to the moral sense of the Christian people.
> A distinction is drawn, and it seems with some reason, between homosexuals whose tendency comes from a false education, from a lack of normal sexual development, from habit,..., and is transitory or at least not incurable; and homosexuals who are definitively such because of some kind of innate instinct or a pathological constitution judged to be incurable.
> In regard to this second category of subjects, some people conclude that their tendency is so natural that it justifies in their case homosexual relations within a sincere communion of life...
> In the pastoral field, these homosexuals must certainly be treated with understanding and sustained in the hope of overcoming their personal difficulties and their inability to fit into society. Their culpability will be judged with prudence. But no pastoral method can be employed which would give moral justification to these acts on the grounds that they would be consonant with the condition of such people. For according to the objective moral order, homosexual relations are acts which lack an essential and indispensable finality.[240]

> The Catholic Church acknowledges that homosexuality is an innate tendency for some people. It perceives it, however, as an incurable disease, a social maladjustment, which requires from pastors a compassionate approach, without ever condoning homosexual acts. Homosexuality is an "objective disorder," and the homosexual person is urged to remain chaste. The Catholic Church and its moral theology have not moved one notch; sexuality manifests itself as the natural order—a law inscribed by God in the human heart—dictating its finality, procreation within marriage.[241]

Joseph Ratzinger repeats the same doctrine, in 2003, in *Considerations Regarding Proposals to Give Legal Recognition to Unions between Homosexual Persons*:

> There are absolutely no grounds for considering homosexual unions to be in any way similar or even remotely analogous to God's plan for marriage and family. Marriage is holy, while homosexual acts go against the natural moral law. Homosexual acts close the sexual act to the gift of life. They do not proceed from a genuine affective and sexual complementarity. Under no circumstances can they be approved.[242]

This document clearly reacts to the legalization of homosexual unions, whether gay marriage in some countries, or civil unions in others, including Denmark, Holland, Belgium, and France (social solidarity pact or PACS). The Vatican considers that these societies jeopardize what they owe their survival to, the family. The Vatican goes as far as dictating to Catholic politicians their duty to oppose the adoption of such legislation publicly and vote against it.[243]

Several pedophilia scandals in various countries including the United States, Canada, Belgium, Austria, Holland, and Ireland have denounced the wrongdoings of Catholics priests and brothers with male minors. In addition, the Catholic Church sees itself challenged by the debates in other Christian denominations about the ordination of openly gay pastors. The Congregation for Catholic Education published, in November 2005, a disciplinary text entitled *Instruction Concerning the Criteria for the Discernment of Vocations with regard to Persons with Homosexual Tendencies in view of their Admission to the Seminary and to Holy Orders*. This document reaffirms the doctrinal position determined in *Persona Humana* and reaffirmed in the *Letter to the Bishops of the Catholic Church on the Pastoral Care of Homosexual Persons*: homosexual acts and homosexual tendency or inclination are intrinsically disordered. The *Instruction* goes on to say:

> In the light of such teaching, this Dicastery, in accord with the Congregation for Divine Worship and the Discipline of the Sacraments, believes it necessary to state clearly that the Church, while profoundly respecting the persons in question, cannot admit to the seminary or to holy orders those who practise homosexuality, present deep-seated homosexual tendencies or support the so-called "gay culture."
>
> Such persons, in fact, find themselves in a situation that gravely hinders them from relating correctly to men and women. One must in no way overlook the negative consequences that can derive from the ordination of persons with deep-seated homosexual tendencies.
>
> Different, however, would be the case in which one were dealing with homosexual tendencies that were only the expression of a transitory problem—for example, that of an adolescent not yet superseded. Nevertheless, such tendencies must be clearly overcome at least three years before ordination to the diaconate.[244]

One cannot help but notice a hardening of the Vatican's position. At first, it shows some openness to the person with a homosexual inclination, without approving homosexual acts. Then, the *Letter to the Bishops of the Catholic Church on the Pastoral Care of Homosexual Persons* finally considers the inclination itself as an objective disorder. Despite its declarations in favor of respecting the dignity of homosexuals, the Vatican is fighting against any unequivocally positive affirmation of homosexuality, even within the church.[245] Roman texts deliberately avoid the term "sexual orientation," and prefer to talk about "deep-seated homosexual tendencies." This voluntary omission reflects a sexual anthropology still heavily steeped in Augustinian theology, wherein lust born out of the original sin obscures the true meaning of sexuality. In this perspective, sexual orientation is not part of what defines a person and leads the individual to personal and social development.[246] Rather, it becomes a "disordered sexual inclination, fundamentally characterized by self-complacency."[247] The *Guidelines for the Use of Psychology in the Admission and Formation of Candidates for the Priesthood* uses the expression "sexual orientation," but it associates it with some psychopathic disturbance or grave psychological immaturity.[248] Furthermore, deceitfully refusing to take sides in favor of recognizing the civil rights of homosexuals, the Catholic Church tries to reconnect with an old theology that wished civil authorities would uphold its moral views on sexual behavior.

In 1991, the House of Bishops of the Church of England issued a statement declaring that heterosexual marriage remained the appropriate embodiment of human sexuality.[249] As in the Catholic documents, somehow, homosexual orientation cannot be an alternative to the creational order, which God planned to be heterosexual. Nevertheless, the declaration differs from the Vatican's opinion insofar as it states very clearly that the church must respect the decision of persons who have decided to live in a homosexual relationship seen as their calling. In such cases, the church must accept them fully. Reception, however, does not lead to acceptance of sexually active gay couples in the clergy.[250] This approach was not unanimous, and in February 1997, Anglican bishops representing the South met in Kuala Lumpur, and they decided by a large majority that homosexuality was a sin. They expressed their concern over the welcoming attitude toward homosexuals in the North, particularly regarding the blessing of homosexual unions and ordination of gays. The following year, at the Lambeth Conference of 1998, the two views clashed. Ultimately, the conservative wing made up of traditionalists from Africa, Asia, and elsewhere won. They adopted Resolution 1.10 declaring the practice of homosexuality to be contrary to the Scriptures, by a vote of 526 in favor, 70 against, and 45 abstentions. The Anglican Church of Canada and the American Episcopal Church, however, posed gestures that led the Anglican Communion to the edge of schism. In May 2002, the Anglican Diocese of New Westminster, in British Columbia, decided to authorize a rite of blessing for homosexual unions. The General Assembly of the American Episcopal Church, in 2003, endorsed the election of an openly gay priest, Gene Robinson, as bishop of New Hampshire. These positions resulted in serious dissent. Nine parishes from the Diocese of New Westminster decided to break off and join the Episcopal Church of Rwanda. Several American Episcopalian churches sought affiliations with more conservative dioceses in Africa, or Latin America, threatening to leave the bosom of the Episcopal Church. Finally in 2009, dissenters from Asia, Africa (Nigeria, Uganda, and Kenya), and North America joined in the formation of the Anglican Church in North America.[251] The Anglican Church of South Africa showed a more open-minded attitude, thanks to the support of the former archbishop of Cape Town Desmond Tutu. He denounced the homophobic attitudes of his African colleagues, especially concerning the election of Bishop Gene Robinson, and asserted that homosexual love was as valid before God as heterosexual love.[252] Archbishop of Tutu's successor, Archbishop Njongonkulu Ndungane, declared that the Anglican Church of South Africa was pleased to welcome into its ranks gay bishops, but they had to remain sexually abstinent.[253] In 2005, the Church of England reacted to the legal recognition of gay civil unions in the *Civil Partnership Act* of 2004. It reaffirmed its position, and continued to believe that the only legitimate sexual activity was that within the marriage of a man to a woman. It showed itself more open than the Catholic Church because it recognized the legitimacy of civil unions, provided they remained chaste.[254] The Church of England even admitted that the clergy could sign a contract of civil union, provided they respected the teachings of the church and abstained from sex. This position seems incongruous and hypocritical when viewed from the outside. In order to understand it, one must, first, go back in history to the positions of the church about homosexuality and, second, understand the way authority is exercised within the Anglican Communion. On this last point, the archbishop of Canterbury has a form of moral authority within the communion. The general orientations for the communion are adopted democratically by the majority in the Lambeth Conferences held every ten years. The real decisions affecting the concrete life of the church are taken by general and diocesan synods. This explains the range of positions that exist between various churches on a national or international level. The democratic exercise of power by consensus implies a climate of continuous dialogue between the parties and a readiness to compromise. The Anglican position is perhaps not entirely clear and consistent, but it tries to reconcile contrasting views, while, at the same time, it reflects the involvement of the church from the 1950s to promote respect for the dignity of homosexual persons. This translates into a larger reception of the concept of sexual orientation in the church, contrary to the Vatican's position. The issue of homosexuality in the Anglican Communion is democratically debated, and positions will probably change again. The necessity for a continuing dialogue on same-gender relations was reaffirmed at the last Lambeth Conference in 2008. The current position is no more bizarre than its position on divorce, where the practice of religious remarriage is accepted while the official doctrine continues to defend the principle of indissolubility.[255] The real challenge for the Anglican Communion is to find ways to leap from an ongoing "mutual listening process" to common purpose, something the communion is trying to achieve with the Indaba project.[256]

The General Council of the United Church of Canada adopted a resolution in 1988 that allowed candidates with a homosexual orientation to be recognized full members of the church and, as such, eligible for the pastorate. The resolution passed by a majority of 3 against 1, but the discussions were very passionate. Opponents regrouped into new religious communities. Despite this, the United Church continued to treat homosexuals inclusively and, in 1992, the General Council authorized blessing ceremonies for same-sex unions. The United Church also spoke publicly in favor of equal rights for homosexual couples in obtaining social benefits (S. C. 2000, c. 12 [Bill C-23]) and also in favor of recognizing homosexual civil unions. For this church, marriage is not a sacrament, and procreation is not what defines it, with the result that since 1988 the United Church does no longer make any distinction between heterosexual and homosexual unions, and the church believes that all partners, regardless of the type of union, have the same obligations before God:

> The United Church of Canada has made various statements regarding marriage. Prior to 1980, marriage was named as a union between a woman and a man. Subsequently, it was reported at the 30th General Council that the life and ministry of Jesus demonstrated what it means to be a full human being made in the image of God. The primary characteristic is complete self-giving love to the other. In 1988, the General Council affirmed that all enduring relationships—and note the omission of the word marriage— need to be faithful, responsible, loving, just, health-giving, healing, and sustaining of community and self. The implication is that these standards apply both to heterosexual and to homosexual couples, as the United Church has come to recognize that gay and lesbian members need to make the same lifelong commitments heterosexual members make and to make their solemn vows with communities of faith who will support them in their commitments.
>
> As a Protestant denomination, the United Church is part of the Christian tradition that does not consider marriage as a sacrament, and procreation is not a defining feature of marriage in the United Church. Nor does the church condemn people who choose to divorce. Divorced people receive the communion of the church and may remarry. Nevertheless, the United Church places an extremely high value on the seriousness of vows taken before God and in the presence of witnesses. The church urges congregations to help couples prepare for a life together and offers counselling and enrichment courses.[257]

Lutheran churches are also divided on the issue of homosexuality. Scandinavia and Germany have adopted a liberal stance. In 1996, the Council of the German Evangelical Church recognized that homosexual unions can be a valid lifestyle for Christians, just as heterosexual marriage or celibacy, all equally acceptable.[258] The General Synod of the Lutheran Church of Norway, in 1997, after having denied access to homosexuals living in a civil union to the pastorate, decided, in 2007, to leave to bishops the prerogative of ordaining gay pastors who live in a civil union. This turn followed the report of the Doctrinal Commission of the Church of Norway on homosexuality in 2006. It also signaled a split within the church on the subject of marriage—an almost equal number of members of the commission declared that homosexual civil unions promoted values consistent with the Gospel, while others saw homosexual acts as condemned by the Scriptures. Marriage between same-sex partners is perfectly legal in Norway since January 1, 2009, but the Synod still does not allow its national pastors to celebrate such unions. Denmark was the first country to legalize same-sex civil unions in 1989. In 1997, an Episcopal committee of the Lutheran Church recommended that civil unions benefit from a blessing ceremony in the church during a regular worship service—a proposal that was not unanimous, leaving to pastors the free initiative of conducting such blessings. In 2005, a majority of Danish bishops proposed a guide for the celebration of same-sex unions in church, stressing that there was no theological reason for the ritual surrounding this ceremony to be different from traditional religious marriage. Since 2005, the Lutheran Church of Sweden agrees to celebrate homosexual unions with a special ritual, but distinct from marriage. In March 2007, the General Assembly of the Lutheran Church of Sweden said it was in agreement with a bill recognizing the legal equality between marriage and civil unions, which would allow pastors to celebrate on a voluntary basis same-sex unions in church, with the same legal consequences as heterosexual marriage. Since May 1, 2009, homosexual marriage has legal force in Sweden but the Lutheran Church still wants to celebrate homosexual unions with a separate ritual.

In 1991, the Evangelical Lutheran Church of America expressed its commitment to the full inclusion of gays and lesbians in the ecclesial community. However, in 1993, the Episcopal Conference, representing 65 synods, refused to approve a ritual blessing of homosexual unions.[259] The church did not permit the ordination of nonabstinent homosexual candidates.[260] In 2001, the Church Worldwide Assembly believed there was a need for the study of sexuality, and homosexuality in particular, and mandated a task force to produce documents for guidance and discussion in the church. The mandate was to produce statements to be submitted for approval at the 2007 World Assembly. In 2003, the working group produced an orientation document on the church and homosexuality with objective, contrasted views on the matter.[261] The 2007 target was postponed to 2009, and in August of that year, the General Assembly adopted a text that reflected the different viewpoints.[262] This document does not waive the Lutheran doctrine of *sola scriptura* in its search for truth, but it said that the Scriptures are constantly reinterpreted and received by the community, guided by the Holy Spirit, through time and space. Although the Christian tradition has traditionally judged homosexual conduct a sin, the community, through the concept of freedom of conscience, can still walk with faith in God's grace (*sola fide*), which releases humanity from the shackles of the law and opens new horizons. The document notes historical changes in the attitude of the Lutheran communion concerning slavery, women's role in the church, as well as divorce and remarriage. In August 2009, the World Assembly of the Evangelical Lutheran Church of America agreed, divisively, upon the blessing of homosexual unions and ordaining sexually active gay candidates. This new position brought a lot of frustration in the more conservative wing of the church, grouped in a coalition known as the Lutheran Core. Will this church experience a schism, like others, due to liberal positions on gay ordination or gay marriage? Another family of American Lutherans, the Lutheran Church-Missouri Synod, displays a more conservative attitude toward homosexuality. For them, the Bible condemns any sexual act between same-sex persons, and teaches that all homosexual desire is the result of the sin inherited from Adam and Eve.[263] Homosexual attraction is a perversion of the natural order created by God, who wants man to find his complement in woman; and sexual intimacy is the favored moment to experience its fullness. This church spread to Canada and formed an independent entity. It shares the same negative judgment on homosexuality with her American counterpart. The homosexual is asked to confess his condition as a sinner, repent, and seek to abstain from any sexual relation with a same-sex partner. The Evangelical Lutheran Church of Canada has quite the same policy as its American sister: no blessings of homosexual unions, and no ordaining of gay candidates with an active sex life. Like other Lutheran churches, the Lutherans of Canada have taken up, since 1999, the path of dialogue with homosexuals, gays, and lesbians, but have not arrived at a settled or conclusive opinion.[264] At the biennial convention in July 2005, in Winnipeg, delegates from the Evangelical Lutheran Church in Canada rejected divisively (55 against, 45 in favor) a suggestion of the National Council that sought to enable pastors to celebrate homosexual unions. In 2007 at the biannual convention, the delegates rejected again (200 against, 181 in favor) the same proposal. While its American cousin has come out in favor of the ordination of gay pastors and gay marriage, the Evangelical Lutheran Church in Canada has a policy of frank, open, and democratic dialogue on these subjects.[265] At its latest National Council in 2011, this church decided to pursue the policy adopted in 2009, leaving it to local communities to decide if they are prepared to bless homosexual unions and ordain gay pastors.[266] The real question is raised by the church: is it not hypocritical to welcome homosexuals into the ecclesial community and ask them to remain sexually abstinent to become pastor, while the sexual intimacy enjoyed by heterosexual married pastors does not seem to compromise their pastoral functions?

In France, the Reformed Church of France and the Evangelical Lutheran Church initiated cooperative thinking on homosexuality, through the Lutheran-Reformed Permanent Council.[267] They affirm the principle of an unconditional acceptance of homosexuals in the community, but they reject the ordination of homosexuals and the blessing of same-sex unions, arguing that local communities are not yet ready to host a gay pastor. They also think that a liturgy of blessing would maintain confusion between heterosexual and homosexual couples.[268] The Evangelical Churches grouped in the Evangelical Federation of France display an even more conservative point of view, saying homosexuality is a sin, and condemning the celebration of homosexual unions and the ordination of homosexuals.[269] In Switzerland, the Evangelical Reformed Churches are divided on the issue of homosexuality. German-speaking churches promote the blessing of homosexual unions, while French-speaking ones object to it. For example, the Synod of the Canton of Vaud in 2008, and those of Geneva and Neuchatel, rejected the blessing of such unions. That synod, however, appeared liberal on the issue of ordaining gay pastors by declaring that no one can be forced to reveal his sexual orientation to become a pastor, but it asked the ministers not to make use of their office as a place for activism and protests.[270]

Baptists are usually conservative and literalist in their interpretation of the Bible. They believe that the Bible condemns homosexuality as a perversion, an abomination in the eyes of God, for which the offender must ask forgiveness.[271] Unlike many Protestant denominations that recognize the civil rights of gays and lesbians, the Southern Baptist Convention, the largest Baptist group in the United States, opposed any form of civil acceptance or endorsement of equal rights for gays and lesbians.[272] This church even suggested that homosexuals were punished in their bodies—a barely veiled reference to HIV, seen as divine retribution against the abomination.[273] Baptist groups have obviously expressed their strong opposition to any form of acceptance of homosexual relationships, either civil unions or marriage, saying there cannot be a union between a man and a man.[274] The Southern Baptist denomination, Baptist Faith and Message, amended its proclamation of faith in 1963 to include a comprehensive section on the definition of marriage between a man and a woman, the only valid form of sexual expression according to the will of God. It was again amended in 2000 to condemn homosexuality, adultery, and pornography.[275] Since the 1960s, conservative and fundamentalist ideas have taken over, including the promulgation of biblical inerrancy, the predominant role of men in the exercise of authority within the family, and male exclusivity in the office of pastor in the community. Some Baptist congregations have not followed the conservative leadership of the Southern Baptist Convention, and, in 1987, created together the Alliance of Baptists. In 2004, they sided with gay marriage on the controversy surrounding this issue, in the American presidential election.[276] A dialogue has been initiated within the Alliance of Baptists with a clear openness to a new reading of the Bible, which listens to the stories of gay and lesbian people.[277] The Alliance of Baptists figures among several religious denominations, including Jewish and Sikh groups, which addressed a letter to support the repeal of the "Don't Ask Don't Tell" (DADT) American policy banning openly gay persons from the military.[278] The Southern Baptist Convention fought against the repeal, along with the Catholic Church and the Orthodox Church in America. In Quebec, the Association of Evangelical Baptist Churches declares homosexuality as a sin that must be confessed, and homosexuals must defeat their inclination, and become heterosexual.[279] The group, therefore, opposed the new, inclusive definition of marriage adopted by the Canadian Parliament.[280] In Canada, the Evangelical Fellowship of Canada decided against a redefinition of heterosexual marriage, as well as the Canadian Baptist Ministries.[281]

Orthodox churches are in direct continuity with the view of the church fathers on sexuality, which only has legitimacy within heterosexual marriage. Their position on homosexuality is similar to that of Catholicism, with perhaps the feature that national Orthodox churches often seek to influence legislation in order to deny equal rights for gays and lesbians, especially in Romania, Greece, and Russia.[282] The Orthodox Church of Greece objected fiercely to the concept of civil unions proposed by a leftist parliamentary coalition in 2008. The Orthodox do not feel very comfortable with the issue of homosexuality within the World Council of Churches, given the liberal attitude of many Reformed churches.[283]

Instead of suffering from the ostracism and indifference of their communities, many Christian gays and lesbians chose instead to gather for worship and pastoral counseling in churches receptive to their lifestyle. One of the first experiments of this kind began in California, in 1968, with Rev. Troy Perry, a pastor of the Pentecostal Church, defrocked because of his homosexuality. He established the Metropolitan Church of Christ, which now operates in 22 countries, including Canada, Great Britain, Denmark, Mexico, South Africa, Brazil, Argentina, and Australia. This Protestant Church has long been celebrating gay marriages and has also developed a support group for people with HIV. In 1966, a group of gays in the Church of Jesus Christ of Latter-Day Saints decided to create its own Mormon Church, The United Order Family of Christ.[284] Gay Mormons of the Church of Latter-Day Saints, who could not bear the rejection within their church, also formed a group in 1978, in Salt Lake City, Utah, called Affirmation. The group, which is active in some American states and in some countries including Canada, helps gays and lesbians of the Mormon community by providing advice on Mormon spirituality and on how to respond to disciplinary action taken by their church against homosexuals, which can vary from aversion therapy developed by Brigham Young University to excommunication.[285] Another schismatic church appeared in 1985 in California, the Restoration Church of Jesus Christ, which brings together excommunicated gay Mormons. But it is really in the Catholic Church that the first gay schismatic church appeared, as early as 1946 in Atlanta, Georgia, under the name of the Eucharistic Catholic Church. A former seminarian, George Hyde, and a Greek Orthodox bishop who migrated to the United States—defrocked after revealing his sexual orientation during a synod—decided to help gays and lesbians of the Sacred-Heart Catholic Parish in Atlanta to whom priests refused to give communion. The Eucharistic Catholic Church became active in Montreal in the

1970s under the leadership of a priest ordained in the Old Catholic Church, Lionel Hervé Quessy. The church now seems more involved in Toronto under the name "Church of the Beloved Disciple" established by Brother La Rade, founder of the Franciscan Order of the Annunciation. This order, in the Old Catholic tradition, also looks after the Mission St. Serge and St. Bacchus, in Massachusetts. The first Old Catholic Church to bear the name Church of the Beloved Disciple was opened in Manhattan in 1968 by a priest ordained in the Old Catholic tradition, Bishop Robert Mary Clement, a native of Pennsylvania. He continued the work of Hyde's Eucharistic Catholic Church. He was the first clergyman to attend, dressed as clergy, the first gay pride parade in New York, after the Stonewall riots. There are a few other schismatic churches in the Old Catholic tradition, whose primary mission is to serve as pastors in the gay community, such as the Benedictine Order of St. John the Beloved Apostle, in Pennsylvania. It might seem odd that these churches appear so liberal in terms of sexual morality and support the continuation of the old Latin rites. Two factors may explain this. On the one hand, they are autocephalous churches that do not accept papal infallibility and, on the other hand, they were created in most cases by priests who openly declared themselves gay. Other Catholics have decided to stay within the Roman Catholic Church but are grouped in militant organization, such as the movement Dignity USA or Dignity Canada.

Conclusion

From its early beginnings, the Christian religion has displayed ascetic tendencies, which were already at work in some streams of Hellenistic Judaism and philosophical currents, in particular, Stoicism. But what distinguishes this new religion from asceticism based on the moderate use of pleasures is its negative perception of pleasure and sexual desire, especially from Augustine onward. Sexual appetence, or lust, can never be beneficial since it results from sin. The sexual body, especially the male body, is perceived as an obstacle to one's spiritual vocation. The dominant discourse settled for the most complete denial and contempt for pleasure, which can only be tolerated in the marital bed and for the sole purpose of procreation. Any sexual activity that is intended solely for enjoyment is considered to be against nature. The Reformation revalorized sexuality as a compelling natural function, and rehabilitated the joys and importance of sexual intimacy within marriage. But for the main Reformers, such intimacy can only occur in a marriage between a man and a woman.

Obviously, Christianity has modulated its position on homosexuality according to the times by borrowing from different schools of thought. The New Testament alone cannot, in fact, support the argument for the condemnation of homosexuality as formulated later by Clement of Alexandria and Thomas Aquinas. Christian thought on homosexuality moved toward a tightening position, clearly discernible from the twelfth century with the Lateran Council III, but most importantly after the publication of Aquinas's *Summa Theologica*. His theology of the vice against nature played a vital role in the West in creating the social stigma of the homosexual as a pervert or invert, up into the second half of the twentieth century. Many Reformed Churches sincerely attempt to break with the past, and some of them have made giant strides in the last 30 years, but not without rift. The recognition by these churches of a new understanding of sexuality, gender, and homosexuality, through the concept of sexual orientation, has called for a reinterpretation of the Scriptures that has led to greater inclusion, beyond the categories imposed by culture and history. The Catholic Church and the Orthodox Churches are still trapped in an outdated essentialist sexual anthropology, a major obstacle to changing their views on homosexuality.

Finally, I think that the emergence of the Western concept of sexual orientation is intimately tied to the history of personal autonomy and self-identity, which emerged with the development of Christian thought. Jesus himself taught freedom of conscience as the foundation of a true relation to God:

> One Sabbath Jesus was going through the grain fields, and as his disciples walked along, they began to pick some heads of grain. The Pharisees said to him, "Look, why are they doing what is unlawful on the Sabbath?" He answered, "Have you never read what David did when he and his companions were hungry and in need? In the days of Abiathar the high priest, he entered the house of God and ate the consecrated bread, which is lawful only for priests to eat. And he also gave some to his companions." Then he said to them, "The Sabbath was made for man, not man for the Sabbath. So the Son of Man is Lord even of the Sabbath."[286]

However, Christianity had to wait for Luther and the Reformation to see the principle of the autonomy of individual conscience come to its full implementation. Luther's insistence on the priesthood of all believers and Calvin's doctrine of predestination progressively led to the central idea of individualism in the West. These ideas were quickly incorporated into the secular sphere, which promoted the democratic ideal of the equality of all citizens and respect for the dignity of the person. As Charles Taylor argued, during the eighteenth century, the concept of individualism becomes more and more associated with self-exploration, inwardness, and authenticity.[287] From these notions stems the modern view that each human being has his own personal way of determining for himself the good life. It is through the development of these unique ideas that the concept of sexual orientation has been possible in the West.

5

ISLAM

RELIGION

Islam has over 1 billion followers worldwide.[1] Indonesia has the highest number, 182.2 million, followed by Pakistan, Bangladesh, and India, all having over 100 million. In the Middle East, Iraq leads with 21.4 million and Islam's birthplace, Saudi Arabia, holds 16 million. In fact, the Arab world represents only about 15 percent of the entire Muslim population. Asia, including the Middle East, alone represents 69 percent and Africa 29 percent of all Muslims. Egypt leads with 52.6 million, Nigeria 40.2 million, Algeria and Morocco each with 29.1 million. Islam is growing rapidly in Europe due to immigration, mainly in France between 5 and 6 million, and Germany, 3 million. Turkey, which is now part of Europe, has 68 million, of which 2.2 million live in Albania, and 1.5 million in Bosnia-Herzegovina. In Canada, the 2001 census mentions almost 600,000 Muslims. Its Muslim population doubled between 1991 and 2001, and the 2011 National Home Survey estimates it as over 1 million.[2] Montreal had over 100,000 Muslims in 2001.[3] In the near future, Islam will probably be the fastest growing religion in Canada and it is estimated that among Canadian non-Christians they will account for 1 person out of 2.[4] In the United States, there are approximately 2 million Muslims, most of them foreign born and among the native born, half are African Americans.[5] Only 15 percent of all Muslims are Shi'ites, mainly found in Iran (95 percent), Iraq (60 percent), Bahrain (70 percent), Azerbaijan (67 percent), and Lebanon (38 percent).

Islam in Arabic means voluntary "submission" to Allah (God). The one who submits is called a "Muslim" in Arabic, which became the English word Muslim. God communicated his will—the divine law imposed by the Creator of all things—to the first man, Adam, the first prophet (*nabi*). Soon his descendants deviated from the right path and began to worship idols. So Allah used prophets (*al-Anbiya*) to bring humanity into submission to God. In succession came Noah and Ibrahim (Abraham), Musa (Moses) with the *Torah*, Isa (Jesus of Nazareth), and finally Allah's great messenger (*Rasul*), Muhammad who revealed the Qur'an:

> To Moses and Aaron We granted the criteria of discerning right from wrong, and We gave them the light and a reminder to the pious ones who fear their unseen Lord and are anxious about the Day of Judgment.
>
> This (Qur'an) which We have revealed is a blessed reminder. Will you then deny it?
>
> To Abraham We gave the right guidance and We knew him very well.
>
> Abraham asked his father and his people, "What are these statues which you worship?"
>
> They replied, "We found our fathers worshipping them."
>
> He said, "Both you and your fathers have certainly been in error."[6]

The Qur'an describes Abraham as being neither Jewish nor Christian, but a true believer (*hanif*) because he turned away from the polytheists (*mushrikin*) and fully submitted to God.[7] I mention, in passing, the notion of *fitra* or natural religion, which remains in every man as the survival of the Adamic and prophetic covenants, a kind of natural inclination to believe in a single god.[8] Here, we enter the heart of this religion—rejection of any form of polytheism (*shirk*) and faith in the uniqueness and absoluteness of God are the core of this religion. Allah's uniqueness excludes any form of "terrestrialness of the Absolute," as expressed by Frithjof Schuon.[9] Profession of faith (*shahada*) in Allah's oneness (*tawhid*) is the central teaching of the Qur'an and the first of the five pillars or religious duties of Islam—the other four being the five daily prayers toward Mecca (*salat*), giving to the poor (*zakat*), fasting from sunrise to sunset during Ramadan (*sawm*), and the pilgrimage to Makkah (Mecca) once in a lifetime (*hadjj*).

Every Muslim must demonstrate his faith by proclaiming that there is no other true god but Allah and that Muhammad is his messenger. This pithy sentence is not found verbatim in the Qur'an, which, however, contains several paraphrases:

> (Muhammad), tell them, "People, I have come to you all as the Messengers of God, to whom the Kingdom of the heavens and the earth belongs. There is no God but He. In His hands are life and death. Have faith in God and His Messengers, the unlettered Prophet who believes in God and His words. Follow him so that you will perhaps have guidance."[10]

Idol worship or polytheism (*shirk*) is the worst sin that a person can commit. This refers to the formative period of Islam in the Arabian Peninsula. The main documentary sources for the pre-Islamic period show a variety of beliefs and rites in honor of various deities. The Iraqi historian and geographer of the tenth century, al-Mas'udi, describes it thus:

> The Arabs, in ages of ignorance [*Jahiliyya*], were divided in their religious views. Some proclaimed the unity of God, affirmed the existence of a Creator, believed in the resurrection, and held for certain that one day the Supreme Judge would reward the faithful and punish transgressors. Already in this work and in our other writings, we talked about those who, during the Interval, called men to know the Lord Almighty and aroused their attention on his miraculous signs. Among these were Koss ben Saidah, Riat as-Shanni and Buhaira the monk, of the tribe of Abd al-Qays. Others, among Arabs, confessed the Creator, and supported the establishment claimed that on the day of resurrection men would be returned to another life, but they denied the mission of prophets and showed themselves committed to the worship of idols. (...). Still others believed the Creator, but denied the mission of the prophets and the resurrection; they indulged in the aberrations of their fellow men. God alluded to their ungodliness, and reported on their infidelity, when He said: "The only life is this worldly life and here we shall live and die. It is only time which will destroy us" (Qur'an XLV, 24). (...). Others leaned towards Judaism or Christianity. There were some who, following no other way than pride, indulged in all their passions. There was among the Arabs, a category of people who worshiped the angels who they claimed to be daughters of God, and adored them for their intercession with the Supreme Judge. They are those whom God speaks in verse: "They ascribe daughters to God, God is too Exalted to have daughters, but they can have whatever they want" (Qur'an, XVI, 57). And secondly, he said, "Have you seen al-Lat, al-Uzza and al-Manat, the third deity?"[11]

Muslim historiography qualifies that period by the Arabic word "*jahiliya*," meaning ignorance. It is a ploy to emphasize the freshness and grandeur of the Prophet's message.[12] At the time of Muhammad, the religious beliefs of the Qurayshi tribe to which he belonged demonstrated a rich diversity. Christians and Jews lived in Mecca but according to the ninth-century Iraqi historian ibn Hisham al-Kalbi, most Meccans worshiped tribal deities and domestic idols.[13] Mecca became a vital commercial hub, a crossroad between Yemen and Palestine, and between the Persian Gulf and Ethiopia. The Qurayshis were, since the fifth century, the guardians of a sanctuary called the Ka'aba, near the Zamzam well. Bedouin tribes fled there to seek the protection of the gods, the god Hubal and the three goddesses, al-Lat, al-Uzza, and al-Manat.[14] Several idols took the shape of a natural stone or sometimes were carved in human form. The pilgrims circumambulated around them in prayer.[15] It seems well established today that the religion of the Bedouins of the Arabian Peninsula worshipped a protective deity, supreme creator of all things, *al-Illah*, or Allah in its contracted form. Ibn Kalbi described pre-Islamic henotheism:

> Thus, whenever the Nizar raised their voice the *tahlil*, they were wont to say: "Here we are O Lord! Here we are! Here we are! Thou hast no associate save one who is thine Thou hast dominion over him and over what he possesseth." They would thus declare His unity through the *talbiyah* and at the same tune associate their gods with Him placing their affairs in His hands. Consequently, God said to His Prophet, "And most of them believe not in associating other deities with Him."[16]

Several clues in the Qur'an suggest that Muhammad's religion, at least in its infancy, did not deny the existence of other deities. Several Islamic scholars see in the "Satanic Verses" a probable allusion to a less rigid form of monotheism than the Prophet's, capable of meeting the Qurayshis' beliefs.[17] The Persian historian Tabari (839–923) reported that Muhammad recognized the validity of the intercession of secondary divinities only to ease the discontent of Meccans resenting his message.[18] Here is what Tabari said:

> Then God revealed: By the Star when it sets, your comrade does not err, nor is he deceived; nor does he speak out of (his own) desire. And when he came to the words: Have you thought upon al-Lat and al-Uzza and Manat, the third, the other? Satan cast on his tongue, because of his inner debates and what he desired to bring to his people, the words: These are the high-flying cranes; verily their intercession is accepted with approval. When Quraysh heard this, they rejoiced and were happy and delighted at the way in which he spoke of their gods, and they listened to him, while the Muslims, having complete trust in their Prophet in respect of the messages which he brought from God, did not suspect him of error, illusion, or mistake. (...) The Quraysh left delighted by the mention of their gods which they had heard, saying, "Muhammad has mentioned our gods in the most favorable way possible, stating in his recitation that they are the high-flying cranes and that their intercession is received with approval."
>
> The news of this prostration reached those of the Messenger of God's Companions who were in Abyssinia and people said, "The Quraysh have accepted Islam." Some rose up to return, while others remained behind. Then Gabriel came to the Messenger of God and said, "Muhammad, what have you done? You have recited to the people that which I did not bring to you from God and you have said that which was not said to you." Then the Messenger of God was much grieved and feared God greatly, but God sent down a revelation to him, for He was merciful to him, consoling him and making the matter light for him, informing him that there had never been a prophet or a messenger before him who desired as he desired and wished as he wished but that Satan had cast words into his recitation, as he had cast words on Muhammad's tongue. Then God cancelled what Satan had thus cast, and established his verses by telling him that he was like other prophets and messengers, and revealed: Never did we send a messenger

or a prophet before you but that when he recited (the Message) Satan cast words into his recitation (*umniyyah*). God abrogates what Satan casts. Then God established his verses.[19]

The story presents the invocation of local deities as a mistake, probably unintentional on the part of Muhammad, since Satan suggested the alteration of the controversial verses, hence the epithet "Satanic Verses." This interpretation of verses 19–23 of Surah 53, *The Star*, probably aimed at erasing any vestige of a departure from strict monotheism. Quranic texts have traditionally purged these verses of any reference to any plea in favor of polytheistic beliefs on Muhammad's part. Another interpretation sees the Prophet drawn somehow into some form of accommodation with the Qurayshis to try and rally them to his ideas, as suggested by Tabari in his commentary on the Qur'an.[20]

What exactly is Muhammad's message or preaching? Like Moses on Mount Horeb in the Sinai desert, Muhammad has a mystical experience. Most likely, pious Qurayshis had the habit of retreating into mountains in the desert a few days a year, according to the testimony of Tabari and ibn Hisham, an Iraqi grammarian of the ninth century.[21] Ibn Battuta, the famous fourteenth-century Moroccan explorer, related that:

> Mount Hira, north of Mecca, stands at a distance of about one parasang from this city (Mekka). It dominates Mina, rises towards the sky, and its top reaches a considerable height. The Messenger of God often made his devotions there before initiating his prophetic mission; it is here that the truth was brought to him by his Lord and the revelation began. The mountain became restless and the Prophet said: "Rest in peace, as there is on you a prophet, a man of truth and a true martyr."[22]

Tradition ascribes to Surah 96, *The Clot (al-Alaq)*, the Prophet's first revelation, through the intervention of Archangel Jibril (Gabriel)[23]:

> (Muhammad), read in the name of your Lord who created (all things).
> He created man from a clot of blood.
> Recite! Your Lord is the most Honorable One,
> Who, by the pen, taught the human being:
> He taught the human being what he did not know.
> Despite this, the human being still tends to rebel
> Because he thinks that he is independent.[24]

The Prophet is said to have been severely traumatized by this spiritual experience, to the point where he wanted to die, but he ran to his wife, Khadija, to seek solace.[25] The Qur'an poses the preaching of Muhammad as an authentic transmission of the Archangel's divine instruction.[26] Far from being focused on Allah's oneness (*tawhid*), its initial emphasis is on preaching the greatness of the creator and the arrogance of man who does not acknowledge Him as such, and thinks he is self-sufficient: "Everyone on earth is destined to die. Only the Supreme Essence of your Glorious and Gracious Lord will remain forever."[27] Several surahs allude to the power of Allah, the Creator of all that exists, but Surah 87, *The Most High*, magnifies the author of harmony in the universe, the very one who leads man in the right path:

> (Muhammad), glorify the Name of your lord, the Most High,
> Who has created (all things) proportionately,
> Decreed their destinies, and provided them with guidance.

It is He who has caused the grass to grow,
Then caused it to wither away.
We shall teach you (the Quran) and you will not forget it
Unless God wills it to be otherwise. He knows all that is made public and
    all that remains hidden.
We shall make all your tasks easy.
Therefore, keep on preaching as long as it is of benefit.
Those who have fear of God will benefit
But the reprobates will turn away
And suffer the heat of the great fire
Wherein they will neither live nor die.[28]

Allah's benevolence therefore provides for all the needs in his creation, and that goodness will even resurrect he who confesses his power.[29] Recognition of his generosity is not sufficient for the man who wants to earn a better life in the hereafter. He must purify himself by gestures of generosity and turn to the poorest:

We shall facilitate the path to bliss
For those who spend for the cause of God,
Observe piety, and believe in receiving rewards from God.
But for those who are niggardly, horde their wealth,
And have no faith in receiving any reward (from God)
We shall facilitate the path to affliction
And their wealth will be of no benefit to them when they face destruction.
Surely, in Our hands is guidance,
And to Us belong the hereafter and the worldly life.
I have warned you about the fierce blazing fire
In which no one will suffer forever
Except the wicked ones who have rejected the (Truth) and have turned
    away from it.
The pious ones who spend for the cause of God
And purify themselves will be safe from this fire.
They do not expect any reward
Except the pleasure of their Lord, the Most High
And the reward (of their Lord) will certainly make them happy.[30]

The first sermon is intended as a serious disapproval of the lifestyle of his fellow Meccans and their lack of generosity. In Surah *al-Fajr* (The Dawn), the Prophet reminds them of the evils of the rich cities of Iram and Tamud in Southern Arabia—destroyed because of their leaders' greed and avarice.[31] Muhammad appeals to eschatology, the Day of Judgment, to persuade his countrymen to engage in the path that will lead them toward a better life in paradise. Precisely for this reason, Allah reveals his will through the preaching (Qur'an) of his Messenger: "We have revealed the Qur'an to you in the Arabic language so that you could warn the people of the Mother Town (Mecca) and those around it of the inevitable Day of Resurrection when some will go to Paradise and others to hell."[32]

At first, he seems to limit his preaching to intimate circles. According to tradition, his first wife, Khadija, and his cousin and son-in-law, Ali, will become the first converts to the new religion—followed by his faithful companions Abu Bakr, Zayd his Christian slave, and Umar ibn Khattab.[33] According to Tabari, the Prophet undertook under Allah's command his prophetic mission when he was 40 or 43.[34] Muhammad began to preach publicly three years after having received his mission.[35] The Prophet's message angered the wealthy Meccans who refused to join his new creed, and wanted to remain faithful to their traditional beliefs.[36] But was it truly the Prophet's admonitions against the hedonistic and selfish attitude of the wealthy Qurayshis that earned him such a strong opposition? Tradition likes to trace the source of their anger to his fierce rejection of polytheism. As reported by ibn Isham, the Qurayshis blamed the Messenger for insulting their religion and their customs, and causing division in the community.[37]

The ninth-century scholar ibn Sad al-Baghdadi attributed the phenomenon to the increasing number of conversions and the open practice of this new religion, which put the Qurayshis on the defensive, and pushed them to respond vehemently.[38] Tabari describes the violence shown by some Qurayshi leaders against Muslims: "I said to Abdallah b. Amr, 'Tell the worst thing which you saw the polytheists do to the Messenger of God.' He said, 'Uqbah b. Abi Mu'ayt came up while the Messenger of God was by the Ka'bah, twisted his robe round his neck, and throttled him violently.'"[39] Historians reported several incidents in which the Prophet and his companions were lambasted and ridiculed. Abu Jahl went as far as throwing a stone at Muhammad.[40]

The offensive on Mecca, with Abu Jahl in command, wanted to make a difference in 617 AD, when several opponents to the Prophet tried to isolate the Hashemite clan with a blockade.[41] The two most popular collections of hadith, the *Sahih Muslim* and the *Sahih Bukhari*, relate how incredulous Qurayshis abased the Messenger, covering him with the guts of a dead she-camel.[42] Despite various attempts at reconciliation undertaken primarily by Abu Talib, no successful agreement was achieved between the Prophet's followers and the Qurayshis. When his companion died, Muhammad considered retreating to a less hostile place. After having converted pilgrims from Medina in Mecca, at their invitation, in 622, he went with his companions to Yathrib, the city or al-Medina.[43] The inhabitants of Medina, in fact, thought that the messenger could restore harmony within the city, which was divided by clan rivalries. This migration (*hijra*), called the *Hegira* in Latin, marks the starting point of the Muslim calendar.[44] Muhammad became the leader of a much wider community (*umma*) than the natural ethnic borders of the clan. The various social groups that composed Medina's population, on one side the new Muslim followers, Jews, and pagans on the other, all entered into a kind of pact or social contract that established everyone's rights and duties.[45] Ibn Hisham attributed the drafting of an alliance treaty to Muhammad. It is traditionally known as the Constitution of Medina.[46] Was it revenge or the needs of migrants that had Muhammad launch troops to raid Meccan caravans?[47] The caravanners returning from Syria decided to protect their convoy with armed men, and with Abu Sufyan in charge, but the people of Medina succeeded in defeating them at Badr decisively, despite their small numbers. This victory epitomized the Prophet's first triumph over the Meccans, allowing him to consolidate his authority over Medina and assert the superiority of Allah.[48] With his victory, he decided to dismiss those, among the people of Medina, who opposed his view of monotheism.[49] Many Jews in Medina refused, indeed, to accept Muhammad as the Messenger of God, and joined easily with the "hypocrites"—those among the Arabs who converted out of convenience while still maintaining idol worship in their hearts.[50] Those who did not respect the commitments of the treaty, polytheists and Jews, had to be defeated in Allah's name:

> This does not apply to the pagans with whom you have a valid peace treaty and who have not broken it from their side or helped others against you. You (believers) must fulfill the terms of the peace treaty with them. God loves the pious ones.

When the sacred months are over, slay the pagans wherever you find them. Capture, besiege, and ambush them. If they repent, perform prayers and pay the religious tax, set them free. God is All-forgiving and All-merciful.

If any of the pagans ask you to give them refuge, give them asylum so that they may hear the words of God. Then, return them to their towns for they are an ignorant people.[51]

Ibn al-Taimiyya Harrani (1263–1328), the famous Turkish Hanbali theologian, defines the objectives of the fight for Allah, jihad:

Allah said when ordering jihad: Fight them until there is no more schism and the only religion is for Allah. The Prophet was asked: O Prophet of Allah, men can fight by valour, by rage or hypocrisy, who is the one ready to fight for the cause of Allah? The man who fights for the triumph of Allah's words, said the Prophet, is the one who fights for the cause of Allah. This tradition is reported by the two sahih.[52]

The subject of holy war is too complex to be treated fairly here. It probably evolved from a strategy to ensure the survival of the new religion in an often hostile environment and to embrace a more expansionary ideal.[53] The Qur'an states two objectives for jihad: self-defense against all forms of oppression, persecution, or social upheaval (*fitna*); and testimony to the triumph of Allah's truth (*shahada*) by paying the price with one's life.[54] Thus, Muhammad was not exclusively picking on his Meccan opponents. After the battle of Badr, he alleged that Jews did not respect the treaty of alliance, and tried to expel the Jewish tribes out of Medina, as well as Christians, to affirm Allah's supremacy over the entire Arabian Peninsula.[55] Having expelled the Jewish tribe of Banu Qaynuqa, the victory of Meccan forces over Muhammad's troops in Uhud, in 625, raised doubt among the other Jewish tribes about the true power of the leader of Medina.[56] Then the Prophet extirpated from Medina the Banu Nadir by sending them in exile in Khaybar. As for the Banu Qurayza, Muhammad decided to kill all the male subjects because this tribe had collaborated with ibn Sufyan in order to facilitate the entry of Qurayshi attackers in Medina.[57]

The military meaning of "jihad" cannot be escaped or underestimated.[58] However, the word "jihad" may have several meanings, and such meanings have been debated among Islamic scholars and jurists throughout history. Already in the Qur'an it refers to a form of struggle for the sake of Allah, but this fight can just as easily be internal (jihad of the heart where the individual struggles against what estranges him from the Creator) or external (the jihad of the sword against the enemies of Islam). Contextualization is necessary in order to interpret jihad correctly and avoid a caricature of Islam as intrinsically violent.[59]

Historically, the Christian West sustained similar expansionist views with the conversion of Constantine and the Crusades, and the sending of missionaries during the colonial conquest. What remains largely dubious about jihad today is its current use by Muslim fundamentalists, who do not hesitate to use suicide attacks without any real substantial threat to Islam from outside. Ghamini Javed, a progressive Islamic scholar, believes that the jihad against those who rejected Allah's supremacy, immediately after Muhammad's preaching, were perhaps justified to establish Allah's victory over Arabia. However, those days are gone, so jihad for the sole purpose of submitting the infidels cannot be justified.

It was during the Medina period that Islamic law, the Sharia, gradually took shape. A new sociopolitical order appeared—the *Umma* or community—which brought together

Muslim believers and those with whom agreements had been signed for unified governance. The Qur'an served as the primary source for the faithful to understand what Allah expected of them: "We have established for you a code of conduct (*Sharia*) and a religion. Follow it and do not follow the desires of the ignorant people."[60] It contains, indeed, a few principles for rules of conduct in matters of domestic life, family, sexuality, and so on. A sacred text, whether it is the Torah or the New Testament, rarely addresses every aspect of the religious and social life of a community. The Qur'an is no exception to the rule, and that is why an additional source of law is added, the prophetic tradition or the Sunna. The added source includes Muhammad's sayings and deeds, and opinions delivered in a given situation. The prophetic tradition was first formed orally, but the Prophet's death precipitated the need for the development of collections of statements made during his lifetime—the hadiths.[61] These are the object of a science designed to assess their degree of authority based on the reliability of its transmission chain, right to the written form. Muslim jurists, therefore, used the Qur'an and the Sunna to establish jurisprudence or *fiqh*. Other sources of law may also complement the Sunna, such as consensus among lawyers (*ijma*) and analogical reasoning (*qiyas*). Like rabbinical law, *fiqh* seeks to adapt the Sharia to specific situations, which are often unique. So there are several schools of Islamic law, each with their own characteristics. When the law is unclear, a law expert who has authority to issue a fatwa, or legal opinion, is recruited. The Sunnis call this expert mufti and the Shi'ites call this mullah. Among Sunnis, the first school (*madhhad*) is called *Hanafi*, named after its founder, Abu Hanifa, in the eighth century. This school is especially prevalent in Turkey, Pakistan, and India. More flexible in its interpretation, it makes extensive use of analogical reasoning. Introduced by Ahmad ibn Hanbal, the *Hanbali* School, generally more conservative and an enemy of reasoning, is mostly found in the Arabian Peninsula, especially in Saudi Arabia, where it inspired wahhabism.[62] The *Maliki* School founded by Malik ibn Anas remains the first law school of North and West Africa, and it places special emphasis on reasoning. Unlike previous schools, it nevertheless admits as a possible source of law customs held by early generations of the faithful in Medina. Imam Muhammad ibn Idris ash-Shafi'i wrote the first treatise on Islamic law in the ninth century by exposing the sources of law (*usul al-fiqh*), *al-Risala* (The Letter). The *Shafi'i* School restricts the Sunna to the Prophet's actions only, and rejects any interpretation that allows recourse to custom, such as the custom of Medina in the *Maliki* tradition or that of Kuka in the *Hanafi* School. Only the hadiths going back to Muhammad himself can help shed light on the Qur'an, and reasoning becomes complementary.[63] The *Shafi'i* School became the official school during the Abbasids and today it is widespread in East Africa, the Philippines, and Indonesia.

The Sharia wishes to create an ideal city by stating the ritual obligations but also all the rules of human interaction in society (*al muamalat*), which are mainly rules of inheritance or donation, marriage, trade, and crime. When dealing with the Sharia, one also has to bear in mind that it cannot be considered as positive law, as in the West, because Allah alone can determine true Islamic values. Coulson wrote: "In the Islamic concept, law precedes and moulds society; to its eternally valid dictates the structure of State and society must, ideally, conform."[64] The Sharia classifies human actions into five categories: what is prescribed (*wajib*), what is recommended (*mandub*), what is permissible (*halal*) or is reprehensible (*makruh*), and finally what is forbidden (*haraam*). Conformity or its opposite calls for reward or punishment, or no consequence at all, depending on the category in which the action falls. Thus, nonconformity to what is required and the execution of a prohibited act are both punished. Defiance of the recommended will not lead to sanctions, and observance of rules related to this class of action is not prone to reward. The Sharia also provides various penalties for criminal offenses. There are fixed penalties (*hadd, hudud* plural) prescribed by the Qur'an or the Sunna, for which a judge has no discretion. Illicit sex (*zina*) belongs to this group.[65] The punishments for these crimes are mainly physical in nature: death by stoning or beheading, limb amputation for theft, or the whip for drinking alcohol. The law of retaliation (*qisas*) applies in cases of homicide or injury and at the request of the victim's family, who may request instead of corporal punishment monetary compensation, also called blood money (*diyya*).[66] Finally, some acts deserve admonition (*tazir*) from public authorities, although sanctions are left to the discretion of judges because neither the Qur'an nor the Sunna consider these situations, or because certain conditions are lacking to rate an act as punishable by fixed penalty (*hadd*) or by the retaliation (*qisas*).[67] Application of the Sharia somewhat varies in the contemporary Muslim world, ranging from a stricter enforcement in Saudi Arabia or Iran, to situations of hybridized systems of criminal justice, especially in former British colonies, where Common Law and Sharia coexist. Many progressive Islamic thinkers make use of the critical-historical method to rethink Islam, its theology, and legal system. Without revoking the religious nature of revelation, thinkers such as the Algerian Muhammad Arkoun and the Sudanese Abdullahi Ahmed An-Naim stressed the need to emphasize the humanly constructed nature of the Qur'an, the Sunna, and Sharia. These authors, usually exiled because of their ideas, try to restore Islamic reason, the role of reflection (*ijtihad*) in the apprehension of religious truth.[68] In the postcolonial context, some Muslim fundamentalist movements promoted the observance of the Sharia as an instrument of Allah's will to build an ideal society, based on Islamic moral principles. Moreover, the observance of the Sharia became emblematic of their opposition to the said corruption found in the West, where behavior is dictated by the law of the majority and not divine law. Many liberal thinkers insist on a reinterpretation of the Sharia, which should lead to greater respect for human rights, particularly in matters of corporal chastisement and the role of women. Nonetheless, Islamists continue to stress the moral superiority of the Sharia. In a context of globalization, there is no doubt that the strict application of the Sharia has become difficult, and the states whose laws it inspires cannot ignore this new context asking for change.[69]

To complete this section, it is necessary to speak of Muhammad's revenge over Mecca, when on January 1, in the year of 630, he took the city by force. It was an opportunity for the Prophet to destroy the idols in order to assert Allah's sovereignty: "Narrated by Abdullah (ibn Masud): When the Prophet entered Mecca on the day of the Conquest, there were 360 idols around the Ka'aba. The Prophet started striking them with a stick he had in his hand and was saying, 'Truth has come and Falsehood will neither start nor will it reappear.'"[70] As reported by the historian Tabari, Muhammad sacked the idols of the *Ka'aba*, especially the largest, Hubal, but he treated the *Ka'aba* itself—the stone enclosure—with great respect, going in circles around it, as the custom in pre-Islamic religion dictated, then went inside to pray.[71] This stage of the Prophet's life was also marked by allegiance to Allah of eminent Qurayshis, and their leader Abu Sufyan. While the Medina period was characterized by the triumph of the *Umma* on tribal organization, the conquest of Mecca seemed the perfect opportunity to regulate the believer's entire life with a code of life: marriage rules, food taboos, and rituals for personal hygiene.[72] Tradition traces back to this period food taboos on consumption and sale of pork, meat from animals already dead, and wine drinking.[73] The conquest of Mecca and submission of its elite gave the signal for a new starting point for the new religion, seeking to impose itself on all the peoples of the Arabian Peninsula, Syria, and Yemen.[74] He began by submitting the Arab Bedouins, especially the Hawazin and the Thaqif of Ta'if, during the Battle of Hunayn in 630.[75] After the Prophet's death in Medina in 632, his successors (*khalifa*), the first caliphs Abu Bakr (632–634) and Omar ibn al-Khattab

(634–644), successfully launched the conquest of the Byzantine and Sassanid Empires, and the conquest of Egypt.[76] The expansion continued rapidly under the Umayyad caliphs (661–750) and reached Central Asia, India, Spain, France, and the Maghreb. The Umayyads moved the capital of the caliphate to Damascus, and implemented a system of government that attempted to introduce legislation to the various local Muslim customs. This called for a greater diversity in the application of the Sharia. Coulson attributed it to the authority of the *qadis* or judges. Appointed by the government administration, they were responsible for the assessment according to their personal opinion (*ra'y*) of local laws and customs, in light of the Qur'an.[77] The Abbasids (750–1258) sought to standardize the law. Under this dynasty, the foundations of the classical theory of Islamic law were established. Abbasid legal theorists strove to substitute personal opinions and local traditions with a system that relies on the Prophet's authority. This was done by resorting, sometimes artificially, to what He would have done in similar circumstances, to the hadiths transmitted from generation to generation through an unbroken chain (*isnad*).[78] The Sharia is then presented as the divine law as it was transmitted by the Qur'an and the Sunna. Leaving less room for reasoning (*ijtihad*), this approach rather looked for validation from the consensus (*ijma*) of expert learned men. Coulson puts it this way: "The right of *ijtihad* was replaced by the duty of *taqlid* or 'imitation.' Henceforth every jurist was an 'imitator' (*muqallid*), bound to accept and follow the doctrine established by his predecessors."[79]

A few words about Shi'a Islam, the second most important branch of Islam, are in order. It is common to link the emergence of the Sh'ites to the problem of Muhammad's succession as leader of the *Umma*. The Sh'ites did not actually recognize the authority of the first three caliphs, pleading that these caliphs did not belong to the Prophet's family. For them, Muhammad's natural successor had to be his son-in-law, Ali ibn Abi Talib, who had married his daughter Fatima. Ali became the fourth caliph, but he was militarily usurped by Muawiyah, who became the first Umayyad caliph. Ali was assassinated in Kufa, Iraq, and buried in Najaf. These two cities came to be the holy cities of Shi'a Islam, along with Karbala, where Muawiya's son, Yazid, killed Hussein, who was Muhammad's grandson and third imam in Ali's succession.[80] Shi'a clearly reflects the diversity of opinion when it comes to the Prophet's successor as a spiritual and political leader of the community, but the differences go beyond partisanship. It is rooted in Medina's social and cultural diversity, which could explain the two different ways of conceiving the Prophet's succession. According to the Pakistani islamologist Jafri, Abu Bakr's supporters insisted very much on the political role of a caliph, chosen for his exploits, as in the tradition of the nomadic tribes of Northern Arabia. Also according to Jafri, sedentary tribes of Southern Arabia greatly valued the spiritual qualities of their leaders. For the latter, belonging to the clan of the Banu Hashim, the guardians of the *Ka'aba*, had considerable prestige, and family ties (Ahl al-Bayt) linking Ali to the Prophet should have taken precedence over everything else.[81] The Imamate did not have the same resonance for Ali's supporters. They see the imam as a spiritual guide, as expressed very well in a hadith compiled in the ninth century by at-Tirmidhi: "I am the city of knowledge and Ali is its Gate."[82] In Sh'ite theology, Allah sent down (*tanzil*) the exoteric (*zahir*) meaning of his Law through the Prophet but the believer is introduced (*tawil*) to the deep esoteric (*batin*) meaning of this revelation by the imam, who may also bear the name of *ayatollah* or *mullah*.[83] Twelve imams, Ali and eleven others, have a distinct charisma because of their closeness (*walaya*) with Allah. Because of that *walaya*, the imam becomes a spiritual and temporal guide able to lead believers to the light (*nur*) by revealing the hidden meaning of Muhammad's prophetic message.[84] Thus, Muhammad ibn al-Masud al-Ayashi, a Sh'ite commentator of the tenth century, wrote: "There is someone among you, said the Prophet, who fights for the spiritual interpretation (*tawil*) of the Qur'an, as I myself fought for its revealed letter (*tanzil*), and that person is Ali ibn Abi Talib."[85] The imam has a cosmic dimension, being a historical manifestation of divine love that eternally exists, and every age in history has its own spiritual guide. Hence, for the Twelver Sh'ites, the twelfth and last imam, Muhammad al-Mahdi has gone into occultation since the year 940, and will return at the end of time, guided by Allah (meaning of the Arabic word *mahdi*) to defeat Dajjal, the imposter and false prophet.[86] Without imams, theophany of the divine light, which represents the revealed truth, could not be completed. There are other smaller Sh'ite branches that cannot be surveyed here. Among them, the Ismailis accept only seven imams, interrupting the succession with the occultation of Muhammad ibn Ismail, grandson of the sixth Imam Jafar as-Sadiq.[87] Given the imam's central role, Twelver Shi'ism developed a particular conception of Islamic law. The authority of the imam is closer to infallibility and, unlike Sunni Islam, it leaves no room for reasoning (*ijtihad*) or consensus (*ijma*).[88] The Sh'ites recognize as legitimate hadiths only those transmitted by the imams, rejecting the hadiths collected by the Sunnis, because these traditions were transmitted by the Prophet's companions who were not his relatives.[89]

Twelver Shi'ites have their own school of law, the *Jafari*, founded by Jafar as-Sadiq in the eighth century. It relies heavily on the reflection (*ijtihad*) of the person who is responsible to bring out the rule of law, the jurist called the *mujtahid*. This skill is no longer recognized by the Sunnis since the tenth century. The role of the law expert (*mujtahid*) is related to the imamate theory. The imam, like the caliph, had a legislative role, but because of occultation, adepts must now rely on the expert. The imam somehow delegated to the *mujtahid* his responsibility to determine the law from the Qur'an and the *Sunna*, which includes among the Twelver only those traditions related to the Twelve Imams. Thus, the grand ayatollahs in Iran are figures of authority on Islamic law. They are called *Marja e-Taqlid* because their followers follow their fatwas without requiring authentication or evidence of their validity.[90]

The life of the Prophet contains episodes with mystical flavor. It is, therefore, not surprising to encounter an early Islamic movement of mysticism, Sufism. Here is how ibn Khaldun describes the religion of the Sufi adept:

> This science belongs to the sciences of the religious law that originated in Islam. Sufism is based on the assumption that the method of its adherents had always been considered by the important early Muslims, the men around Muhammad and the men of the second generation, as well as those who came after them, as the path of truth and right guidance. The Sufi approach is based upon constant application to divine worship, complete devotion to God, aversion to the false splendour of the world, abstinence from the pleasure, property, and position to which the great mass aspires, and retirement from the world into solitude for divine worship. These things were general among the men around Muhammad and the early Muslims.
>
> Then, worldly aspirations increased in the second [eighth] century and after. People now inclined toward worldly affairs. At that time, the special name of Sufis (*Sufiyah* and *Mutasawwifah*) was given to those who aspired to divine worship.[91]

According to this historian, the Arabic word for wool, *sufi*, would explain the etymology of the word Sufi, as followers wore a gray wool clothing to differentiate them, and show their poverty.[92] This movement gained momentum especially after the tenth and eleventh centuries with the Persians al-Hallaj and al-Ghazali, and then in the thirteenth century with the Andalusian ibn Arabi and the Turk by adoption, Jalal al-Din Rumi, founder of the Mevlevi brotherhood of whirling dervishes. Asceticism also marked the

Sufis, who often lived as solitary hermits before the brotherhoods appeared in the thirteenth century, when many followers who were drawn by a spiritual leader (*Sheik*) started to live a celibate life in convents (*ribat*).⁹³ Islamic theology has not developed the habit of describing the relationship of man to God in terms of love. It prefers to speak of the submission of the creature before God's greatness. The Sufi mystic, however, engages on a path that will lead him by successive steps to express his love for God through renunciation and total abandonment. Besides reciting the Qur'an, the Sufi uses techniques of repetition (*dhikr*) of God's name to induce ecstasy and annihilation (*fana*) in God. Sufism was probably meant to react to the formalism of a religion that gave prominence to the observance of the law at the expense of the purity of heart and sincerity of intentions in compliance with the law. However, although some Sufis believe that mystical union allows direct access to God's will, without recourse to the Sharia, the vast majority of Sufis maintains the obligation to follow the Sharia.⁹⁴

Sexuality

The *Tales of the Thousand and One Nights* have captured the imagination of Westerners for its open eroticism and sexual license. Voluptuous descriptions of harem life during the Caliphates of Baghdad, Cairo, or the Ottoman Empire certainly fed sexual fantasies, in both the East and West. Contemporary Islamic moral reform, more than often, offers a puritanical view of sex, particularly when it comes to female sexuality.⁹⁵ Addressing the issue of sexuality in Islam thus requires a double effort: first to recover an ancient discourse on sex that conservative ideas have occulted and, second, to reach beyond strict gender codes of conduct and into the daily sex lives of people. The inescapable presence of erotology in premodern Arab-Muslim literature should not bring us to contrast two views about sex and pleasure without any explanation: a more open and libertine one, the other conservative and austere. These opposing views were found right from the nineteenth century, whether in Gallant Burton describing the forbidden pleasures of the East or in Voltaire and Renan who saw in Islam backwardness and intolerance. The contrast suggested by Foucault between an Oriental *ars erotica* and a Western *scientia sexualis* remains a shortcut that the history of both cultures simply rejects. Strict religious codes regarding sex have always rubbed shoulders with more permissive cultural expressions. As Lagrange reminds us, these perceptions still exist side by side, and both are in a way an attempt to rehabilitate an essential Islam that does not exist in practice: a premodern Islam praising all sorts of sexual pleasures and a fundamentalist approach that wants to retrieve from the Scriptures and the early tradition a pure teaching, to their own eyes free from corrupted views, such as homoeroticism and homosexuality.⁹⁶ This type of view is not totally absent from the Arab world. For instance, the Syrian scholar Salah al-Din al-Munajjid wrote in 1958 a history of the sexual life of the Arabs, in which he projects an exuberant and liberated sexuality in the past (*jahiliyyah* and Umayyad periods), contrasting it with conservative views that clustered in reaction to the debauchery and the obscenities of the Abbasid caliphates.⁹⁷ Only a believer can contemplate truth or a true essence; the historian is left with shifting discourses and practices that depend on time and space.⁹⁸ Divergent interpretations of the Qur'an and the hadiths on sexual matters coexist, and nonreligious literature often carries us on the ground of transgression, away from the ethical standards set by theology and *fiqh*.

Malek Chebel, an Algerian-born anthropologist, has devoted most of his writings to demonstrating the importance of the aesthetics of love and sensual delight in the development of the Arab-Muslim culture. He quotes the words of ibn Hazm, an Andalusian poet and theologian of the eleventh century:

It is sufficient for a good Moslem to abstain from those things which Allah has forbidden, and which, if he chooses to do, he will find charged to his account on the Day of Resurrection. But to admire beauty, and to be mastered by love that is a natural thing, and comes not within the range of Divine commandment and prohibition; all hearts are in God's hands, to dispose them what way He will, and all that is required of them is that they should know and consider the difference between right and wrong, and believe firmly what is true. Love itself is an inborn disposition; man can only control those motions of his members, which he has acquired by deliberate effort.[99]

The Qur'an and Sunna describe sexuality as highly positive. While Yaweh created man and woman out of the dust of the ground, creation in the Qur'an involves sexual fertilization. Surah 22 refers to it clearly:

People, if you have doubts about the Resurrection, you must know that We created you from clay that was turned into a living germ. This was developed into a clot of blood, which was made into a well formed and partly shapeless lump of flesh. This is how We show you that resurrection is not more difficult for Us than your creation. We cause whatever We want to stay in the womb for an appointed time, We then take you out of the womb as a baby, so that you may grow up and receive strength.[100]

There is no place in the Qur'an for any type of sexual asceticism resulting in celibacy. Instead, it is written: "Marry the single people among you and the righteous slaves and slave-girls."[101] The following verse provides some restraint to the believer's sexual behavior. Sexuality is rightfully expressed within marriage (*nikah*) only, a contract that binds a man to a woman: "Let those who cannot find someone to marry maintain chastity until God makes them rich through His favours." Even the Syrian Hanbali scholar ibn Taimiyya (thirteenth century), who never married, refused to identify celibacy as a valid path to spiritual perfection. Nevertheless, he confessed his personal inadequacy to achieve the prophetic model combining marriage and spiritual quest.[102] For him, passionate love (*ishq*) disturbs the psyche, agitates the body, and brings along pain and weakness, even in marriage. His position has a lot of similarity with Pauline pragmatism observed among Christians—wedlock is presented as an effective remedy in most cases against lust and female seduction. Even for the famed Sufi theologian al-Ghazali, mystical union requires some renunciation (food, shelter, and clothing), but not sexual abstinence:

Another necessary thing—Marriage. Many persons say that if one person gets married or takes several wives, he goes out of the limit of renunciation. The Prophet was the greatest of saints and yet he loved wives. Shall we then go without marriage? The saint Aynah supported this. He said: that Hazrat Ali was the greatest among the companions but he had four wives and twelve slave girls. To us, what the saint Abu Solaiman Darani said is the correct opinion. He said: Whatever thing keeps your mind turned away from God-properties and children, is the sign of your misfortune. When women keep your mind away from God. It is better then to remain unmarried. Not to marry then is included within renunciation. But when passion runs high, to marry is compulsory. If you do not then marry, it will not be renunciation. If one knows that his wife not keep his mind turned away from the remembrance of God, it does not go out of renunciation, as the object of marriage is the birth of children and preservation of human species. By this, merits are acquired for increasing also the followers of the Prophet. A bachelor is like one who gives up food and drink fearing them. That is not renunciation, as to give up food and drink means destruction of body. Similarly, to give up marriage is not renunciation as it will not preserve his dynasty. So to give up marriage for forsaking conjugal joy is not renunciation.[103]

Sexual pleasure enjoyed within its legal framework is natural, and every believer should feel guiltless or shameless about it. The Syrian imam, an-Nawawi (thirteenth century), recounts a hadith where the Prophet answers his companions who ask questions about an alleged spiritual advantage of the rich who can afford giving alms. The Messenger responds that Allah considers that whenever a believer is doing good or avoiding evil, it is a charity, even in the works of the flesh. Astonished by the answer, the companions asked him if performing the sexual act had to be rewarded, and he replied: "To enjoin a good action is charity, to forbid an evil action is charity, and in the sexual act of each of you there is charity."[104] Even in Paradise, carnal pleasure is not left out, with its garden of many rivers and lush vegetation that invite the blessed, lying on beds adorned with precious stones, for relaxation and pleasure: "They will have maidens (*huris*) with large, lovely black and white eyes, like pearls preserved in their shells, as reward for their deeds."[105] In addition to the *huris*, male youths (*ghulman*) are also available in heaven, but they will be discussed in the next section.[106] Erotology textbooks unsurprisingly flourished within the Islamic world. Sheikh Nafzawi, a Tunisian writer of the fifteenth century, prefaced his work *The Perfumed Garden*:

> Praise be given to God, who has placed man's greatest pleasure in the natural parts of the woman, and has destined the natural parts of man to afford the greatest enjoyment to woman. He has not endowed the parts of woman with any pleasurable or satisfactory feeling until the same have been penetrated by the instrument of the male; and likewise the sexual organs of man know rest nor quietness until they have entered those of the female. Hence the mutual operation. There takes place between the two actors wrestling, intertwinings, a kind of animated conflict. Owing to the contact of the lower parts of the two bellies, the enjoyment soon comes to pass. The man is at work as with a pestle, while the woman seconds him by lascivious movements; finally comes the ejaculation.[107]

Imam Qaradawi (1926–) mentions that the Qur'an lays down the universal law of male-female sexual duality and that sexual complementarity is essential to everyone to fully accomplish oneself, male and female.[108] Companionship and mutual love are the primary purpose of marriage, from which naturally flow procreation, family, and ultimately society. The complementarity of both sexes serves to naturalize heterosexuality as the only valid sexual identity.[109] Ibn Hanbal narrated a tradition dating back to the Prophet, who reportedly criticized Uthman, after his wife had complained to the Prophet's wife, Aisha, about her husband who stood the night in prayer and fasted all day. Muhammad then made him understand that intercourse with one's wife belonged to the wisdom of his Sunna, which should always respect the limitations of the human condition. Sleeping, eating, and copulating are an integral part of the prophetic Sunna, as pointed out by the traditionist ad-Darimi (ninth century).[110] Temporary marriage (*zawaj muta*), licensed for a fixed period during trips and wars, or coitus interruptus (*azl*) are all licit practices that place pleasure at the center of sex life, before the duty of reproduction.[111] The Qur'an allows men to have up to four wives, provided specifically that they be fair to each.[112] After Khadija's death, the Messenger lives with eleven wives in Medina and tradition does not spare the comments on his private life, especially with Aisha and Zaynab.[113] When the Prophet wanted to sleep with a spouse whose turn it was not, because of his sense of fairness and his perfect manhood, he did not hesitate to visit them all the same night.[114]

The philosopher al-Ghazali even allowed himself to describe the Prophet's orgasm, who made a point of having sex with his wife and ejaculating without emitting a sound.[115]

The Qur'an imposes relatively few limits on marital sexuality, as stated in this verse: "Your wives are as fields for you. You may enter your fields from any place you want."[116] Most commentators see in this immense sexual freedom, and it does not necessarily need to be interpreted as the denial of female sexual pleasure. The Hanbali Imam, ibn Qudama (twelfth century) said:

> It is expedient for the husband to stimulate and fondle his wife before vaginal penetration, to increase her desire, and to make sure she gets during intercourse as much pleasure as he does. As reported by Umar ibn Abdel Aziz, the Prophet said: "Do not penetrate her until she has as much desire as you, so you do not come before her. Kiss her, give her a wink, hug her, and when you see she has reached the same level of desire as yours, then do it."[117]

Is the verse "enter your field from any place you want" opening the door to fellatio, cunnilingus, sodomy, and heterosexual masturbation? Imam ibn Qudama emphasized the need for foreplay between partners, and encouraged reciprocity in pleasure.[118] Most major jurists agree to consider fellatio or cunnilingus as *halal* (legal), since no verse in the Qur'an or hadith mentions it. Imam as-Shafi'i decreed that all parts of the body, with the exception of the anus, could be solicited during extravaginal intercourse.[119]

The Shafi'i an-Nawawi implicitly condemned cunnilingus because the husband who stared at his wife's sex committed a despicable act.[120] According to Abu Abdullah ibn Ahmad al-Bija'i, Hanafi and Maliki *fiqh* believe that fellatio and cunnilingus are *halal* because neither the Qur'an nor the hadiths disallow it specifically.[121] Some prominent contemporary jurists accept fellatio and cunnilingus as *halal* practices in marital sex.[122] Others, more conservative, issue notices to ban a practice estimated detestable, making man like unto the beast.[123]

According to traditionist at-Tirmidhi, ibn Abbas and Khuzaymah ibn Thabit have transmitted hadiths prohibiting sexual intercourse of a man into the anus of a woman.[124] The *Tafsir ibn Abbas* interprets verse 223 of Surah "The Cow" to indicate one of two ways of licitly penetrating the vagina, either by the front or from behind. In this exegesis, the "field" (*harts*) can only refer to the vagina, where fertilization occurs.[125] The Afghani traditionist, Abu Dawud (ninth century), relates that the Prophet gave a favorable opinion concerning this sexual position, following a complaint from a Medinan woman, whose Meccan husband penetrated her from behind. This hadith mentioned that the sex position was appreciated by Meccans but unknown in Medina, whose inhabitants followed Jewish customs, with the woman lying on her back.[126] According to this tradition, vaginal penetration from behind is quite legitimate, not anal penetration.[127] The Shafi'i jurist, ibn Kathir (fourteenth century) cited several hadiths to confirm that the "field" is nothing else but the vagina, and the Messenger in this verse authorized vaginal penetration from behind and not anal penetration.[128] Contemporary jurists, such as Sheikh al-Albani and al-Qaradawi, take up this viewpoint.[129] The latter adds an argument rarely found in the commentaries and hadith collections: anal penetration of one's wife is akin to "minor pederasty," which would make it a horrible sin (*haram*).[130] Hocine Benkheira argues that *hadith* literature interprets verse 223 as being strongly against heterosexual anal sex, while the verse could simply suggest that any possible position is licit.[131] He argues that jurists and theologians had different opinions on the subject.[132] The stricter interpretation triumphed, adopting a more moralizing attitude from the ninth century, under the influence of Judaism and Christianity.

About masturbation, al-Ghazali was consistent with the remarks of ibn Abbas, who advised a young bachelor with strong sexual urges to masturbate rather than risking fornication.[133] Al-Ghazali did not totally condemn masturbation, though he did not consider it harmless. It was a sin that one should afford in order to avoid a greater fault such as adultery (*zina*). Hanafi and Hanbali Schools typically argue that in such circumstances masturbation becomes more or less prescribed (*majid*). The Maliki and Shafi'i Schools condemn it unreservedly.[134] Imam Shafi'i bases his opinion, like many other jurists, on the Surah "The Believers" (23:6–7) to lambast masturbators. In fact, the surah accuses of wrongdoing precisely those who are sexually active outside marriage, but for Shafi'i any use of the penis outside the vagina remains prohibited.[135] The Maliki jurist of Cordoba, ibn Qurtubi, follows the same reasoning.[136] The Yemeni traditionist, Abdr ar-Raqqaz (ninth century), in his hadith collection *al-Mussannaf*, mentions ancient traditions that allow warriors to masturbate to relieve sexual tension, in the absence of women.[137] Ibn Taimiyya summarizes the experts' various opinions:

> Question about a man who has to deal with an unyielding sexual urge. So he masturbates with his hand, and at times closes thighs against his penis. He knows that fasting can put an end to this behaviour; although fasting is difficult.
>
> Response. There is no sin when the emission of pre-ejaculatory fluid is involuntary. However, he must practice a major ablution (*gnus*) after having ejaculated. Voluntarily procuring ejaculation by masturbation is forbidden (*haram*) according to most scholars, and it is one of the two views expressed by Ahmad (ibn Hanbal)—rather the most obviate of both—and in his other opinion, it is condemned (*makru*).
>
> But if it is induced by uncontrollable circumstances—for instance if a man is afraid of committing adultery or becoming sick if he does not masturbate–the ulemas say two well-known things about this matter. Various groups of elders (*salafs*) and those who followed (*khalafs*) have authorized it in such situations, while others have banned it. And God knows best![138]

Ibn Taimiyya's mention of masturbation as a possible remedy for disease is probably an implicit reference to the theory of humors, found in Galenic or Aristotelian medicine. In both of these medical theories, metabolic balance requires a periodic excretion of bodily fluids, including semen.[139] The eminent physician ibn Sina recommends youth to have sex regularly rather than masturbate, for health reasons.[140] Ottoman medicine recommends masturbation in the absence of sex with a partner, without excess because it is a source of anxiety, debilitating the mind and weakening the penis.[141] The contemporary Imam, al-Albani, stigmatizes the practice of masturbation as a prohibited act (*haram*), because the Qur'an implicitly prohibits it when it restricts the exercise of sexuality within marriage (23:7–8), and requires abstinence from unmarried individuals (24:33).[142] Sheikh al-Albani also points out that repeated masturbation may cause adverse health consequences. With some Shi'ites, the ban appears to be complete and can carry heavier consequences than among Sunnis. Shi'ite imam Sayed Mohammad Rizvi reports that Imam Jafar as-Sadiq ranked masturbation with extramarital sex, and the masturbator could be brought to trial before an Islamic court.[143] The Sunni Egyptian jurist, as-Sayed Sabiq, seems more realistic when he views masturbation akin to sexual touching or fondling, which excludes vaginal penetration. A judge could theoretically punish such behavior by a discretionary sentence, but it would be extremely difficult, in practice, to prove because of the absence of witnesses. Instead, they are acts of an individual conscience facing the Creator.[144] Despite a normative discourse sometimes hard on masturbation, the multiplicity of terms used to designate it suggests that its practice is far from being curbed.[145] There is also the recognition by all that it cannot easily or effectively be punished. Thus, in rural Morocco, masturbation, sometimes in groups, is part of a learning process about sex among adolescents.[146] As such, it is tolerated while it is considered shameful if practiced by an adult. A survey of students in Turkey showed the popularity of this practice even if young people do not seem very comfortable with it for religious reasons.[147]

The emission of semen outside the vagina is not a problem for theologians or lawyers. Coitus interruptus is permitted, and a menstruating spouse may also masturbate her husband.[148] The Qur'an strictly forbids sexual intercourse during menstruation, until the woman is purified by a major ablution (*ghusl*). Menstrual blood is not the only body fluid to require a washing of the whole body considered to be polluted (*junub*). In the same class are: the emission of semen in masturbation, or as a result of a thought or a gaze with a sexual intent, the emission of sperm or vaginal secretion during intercourse. The intromission of the penis into the vagina or anus, be it the length of the glans, entails an obligation (*fardh*) of major ablution.[149] Bouhdiba draws attention to the fact that pollution is the result of the physiological functions of elimination and excretion, and not because of the commission of a fault or sin. This is proven by the fact that perfectly lawful intercourse also may cause pollution.[150] Purification (*tahara*) by water means that the faithful must always pray in a state of spiritual and physical purity. Book II of the *Muwatta* by Malik ibn Anas is devoted to ritual purity, and Chapter 16 includes several *hadiths* that require minor ablutions (*wudu*) after touching one's penis.[151] This position seems to be accepted by most schools, but its application may vary because of the interpretation given to certain situations. There is even a ritual that guides the practitioner in the art of urinating, the *istibra*.[152] In an interesting article, Brannon Wheeler explained that the reason why someone has to do minor ablutions is not because of any sexual intent or as a result of masturbation.[153] The probable cause for impurity lies in the fact that the penis excretes body fluids—urine, semen, and prostatic fluid. Touching the penis, the organ of reproduction and excretion, reminds the faithful of his finite condition and imperfection, in contrast to Edenic perfection, where these physiological functions are absent. *Wudu* temporarily restores purity that existed before the original sin and symbolically creates the sacred space within which the believer is in intimate contact with the deity.

Because sexuality is legitimate only in the context of marriage, religion displays a strong intolerance toward fornication, that is to say, sex between unmarried persons or adultery for married people. In both cases, the illegal act is called *zina*. The Qur'an does punish both: "Flog the fornicatress and the fornicator with a hundred lashes each. Let there be no reluctance in enforcing the laws of God, if you have faith in God and the Day of Judgment. Let it take place in the presence of a group of believers."[154] Tradition has stoning for punishment in cases of adultery.[155] All Sunni schools of jurisprudence agree that *zina* concerns penetration only, and excludes any other form of sexual caress.[156] For the penalty to apply, admission of guilt is required, or the intervention of four male witnesses who observed, simultaneously, first hand, the act of penetration. Corporal punishment is also imposed by the Sharia in the case of false accusation. The need for proof beyond a reasonable doubt, corroborated by four witnesses, also makes the use of penalties relatively rare, although Islamic courts in Nigeria (north), Pakistan, and Iran still have recourse to the procedure.[157] The degree of proof required suggests that the real offense is public outrage done to the institution of marriage, not to mention the dishonor of the cuckold's family. Nothing in *zina* associates the offender to a fault intrinsically linked to turmoil of the senses.

Islam, more often than not, projects an image of women that hurts the egalitarian consciousness of the West in some respects. The Qur'an promises to men and women equally their entry into Paradise. It does however seem to have much more to say about the bliss that awaits men in the garden of delights than what awaits women.[158] During their lifetime, women are relegated to an inferior status, since men have authority (*qawama*) on them, and they must obey their husbands.[159] Inequality is particularly reflected in inheritance law where a husband's share is twice that of a wife, and in matters of evidence where a man's testimony has to be matched by that of two women to be of equal value. This patriarchal approach is based on traditional stereotypes, such as women's lack of rationality.[160] The same bias has been used to justify the trusteeship of a male adult (*wali*) for the marriage of a virgin, even in adulthood.[161] Inequality between the sexes is clearly reflected in the body parts that must remain hidden in public for modesty (*awra*). A man must not offer his genitals to the gaze of others, but a woman must hide almost her whole body.[162] The Qur'an has this to say:

> (Muhammad), tell the believing men to cast down their eyes and guard their carnal desires; this will make them more pure. God is certainly aware of what they do.
> Tell the believing woman to cast down their eyes, guard their chastity, and not to show off their beauty except what is permitted by the law. Let them cover their breasts with their veils. They must not show off their beauty to anyone other than their husbands, father, father-in-laws, sons, step-sons, brothers, sons of brothers and sisters, women of their kind, their slaves, immature male servants, or immature boys. They must not stamp their feet to show off their hidden ornaments. All of you believers, turn to God in repentance so that perhaps you will have everlasting happiness.[163]

As noted by Malek Chebel, enclosure and use of the veil have the same etymological root.[164] The Qur'an requires women to stay behind the walls of their home, hidden from view: "Do not display yourselves after the manner of the (pre-Islamic) age of darkness. Be steadfast in the prayer, pay the religious tax, and obey God and His Messenger. People of the house, God wants to remove all kinds of uncleanliness from you and to purify you thoroughly."[165] If several codes of law now recognize the right of a woman to leave home to work, most of the time she cannot do so without the consent of her husband or her guardian.[166]

Homosexuality

The Qur'an's positive vision of heterosexuality and the importance given by the Prophet to marriage as an instrument of personal achievement, both physically, emotionally, and spiritually, leave little room for marginal forms of sexual expression. A keen observer of the Arab-Muslim civilization, ibn Khaldun stated the following:

> Among the things that corrupt sedentary culture, there is the disposition toward pleasures and indulgence in them, because of the great luxury (that prevails). It leads to diversification of the desires of the belly for pleasurable food and drink. This is followed by diversification of the pleasures of sex through various ways of sexual intercourse, such as adultery and homosexuality. This leads to destruction of the (human) species. It may come about indirectly, through the confusion concerning one's descent caused by adultery. Nobody knows his own son, since he is illegitimate and since the sperm (of different men) got mixed up in the womb. The natural compassion a man feels for his children and his feeling of responsibility for them is lost. Thus, they perish, and this leads to the end of the (human) species. Or, the destruction of the (human) species may come about directly, as is the case with homosexuality, which leads directly to

the nonexistence of offspring. It contributes more to the destruction of the (human) species (than adultery), since it leads to (the result) that no human beings are brought into existence, while adultery only leads to the (social) nonexistence of those who are in existence.[167]

What was ibn Khaldun referring to when he spoke of homosexuality or *liwat*? Is it precisely the love of boys as in Greece, or any form of homosexuality? A Shi'ite traditionist from the seventeenth century, Muhammad al-Hurr al-Alimi reported a hadith with a very narrow definition of the word. The companion Ali reportedly said that the sin of *liwat* applied to anal penetration of a handsome youth (*al-ghulam*), and the reason for the ban was because the act interfered with reproduction.[168] The word *liwat* is a derivative of *lata* or *latawa*, a denominative of Lut—the Arabic name of the biblical Patriarch Lot, who witnessed the burning of his hometown, Sodom.[169] The Qur'an recalls the incident:

> Lot told his people, "Why do you commit such indecent acts (*fahisha*) that have never been committed by anyone before?
> You engage in lustful activities with people instead of women. You have become transgressing people (*musrifun*)."
> His people had no answer to his remarks but to tell one another, "Expel him from our town; he and his people want to purify (*tahir*) themselves."
> We saved (Lot) and his family except his wife who remained with the rest.
> We sent a torrential rain unto the (unbelievers). Consider how disastrous the end of the criminals (*mujrimin*) was![170]

The scandalous behavior is clearly homosexual.[171] Lot accuses the people of Sodom to be transgressors (*mutadun*) blocking the road (*qata as-sabil*) and being ignorant (*jahil*).[172] The Qur'an does not qualify *liwat* morally in any specific way by using *fahisha* and other words to highlight specifically the seriousness of the sin compared to other forms of sexual or nonsexual behavior.[173] Quranic texts condemn the actions of the people of Lot, but do not specify what punishment awaits those who would indulge in such acts. In fact, to understand the nature of the alleged act and to know the penalties attached to them, one must turn to hadiths. Ibn Malik reported that ibn Shihab al-Zuhri had told him that the perpetrator of *liwat* had to be stoned.[174] The traditionist Abu Dawud identified another story, reportedly dating back to the Prophet, and transmitted by his cousin Abdullah ibn Abbas. According to this hadith, anyone caught in the act of sodomy shall be put to death, both the active and the passive actors.[175] By mentioning the active/passive role, this hadith implies that *liwat* is defined by anal penetration and no other forms of homogenital contact. The four main law schools agree that *liwat* means *senso strictu* anal penetration between a man and a woman, or between two men.[176]

Fiqh schools do not all agree on the severity of the punishment attached to sodomy, and this disparity appears to be based on the fact that at least two schools, the Shafi'i and the Hanbali, associate anal penetration with fornication through analogical reasoning, contrary to the Hanafi School. The Maliki School rates sodomy a sin in a class of its own, which deserves stoning for both partners, whether married or not.[177] Perhaps, Al-Shafi'i expresses in the clearest possible way the idea that sodomy is akin to fornication, stating that the unmarried inserter was punishable by a hundred lashes, and stoning if married. The insertee deserved a hundred lashes and exile, married or single.[178] However, among Shafi'i jurists, some advocate the death penalty without discriminating between the passive and the active.[179] Ibn Hazm of Cordoba, who adopted the Zahiri view of the literal letter of the law, rejected the death penalty by stoning or fire, simply because it was not supported by any quranic evidence, or any reliable tradition with a strong chain of transmission.[180] According to ibn Hazm, men who have sex with men should be subject to a correction of 10 lashes and prison.[181] The Hanbali School follows roughly the same trajectory as the Shafi'i, but today's Salafists promote the strictest interpretation, namely, the death penalty without any distinction. The Hanafi School acknowledges that the Qur'an does not prescribe any punishment (*hadd*) against sodomites and that no hadith with unquestionable authority exists. From a Hanafi point of view, since the alleged act is not sanctioned explicitly by the Sharia, it can only be disciplined (*tazir*) by the civil authority.[182] Generally, the civil penalty is softer, for example, fewer whip lashes, but ultimately leading to the death penalty in cases of a subsequent offense. There is also a minority opinion within the Hanafi School that adopts a similar position to the Shafi'i or Hanbali majority opinion. Shi'ites jurists tend to have a wide definition of *liwat*, which includes all forms of homogenital contacts (excluding fellatio) being considered as major sins.[183]

A quick review of legal opinions shows that opinions vary considerably from one school to another or even between jurists of the same tradition, even if the condemnation of sodomy seems general, be it heterosexual or homosexual in nature. Legal models that exclude death penalty in whole or in part claim that sodomy does not pose a threat to society, while adultery or fornication threatens the family.[184] In a society where single men do not have easy access to women and where the virginity of future spouses is associated with the honor of the father, tutor, and future husband, homogenital practices in private, including sodomy, are more easily tolerated socially.[185] This context may explain the observation of the Shi'ite theologian al-Wahhab Abdel Sharani (sixteenth century, Egypt) about the lack of desire to avenge the sodomized male, in contrast to the frenzy that grips the feuding family where a daughter was involved in an act of fornication.[186] Moreover, the application of the Sharia somehow suggests greater aversion toward anal sex. A discussion related by Muhammad Amin ibn Abidin (nineteenth century) shows a mutazilite scientist claiming that sodomy is legitimized in Paradise. What forbade sodomy on earth—the nonreproductive character and impurity (*adha*) of the anus—disappears altogether in heaven.[187]

The four major schools refuse to include in their definition of sodomy (*liwat*) any other type of homogenital practice, other than the penetration of a penis into the anus of a partner.[188] However, Twelver Shi'ites cracked down hard not only on sodomy by imposing the death penalty on both partners, but also against other homogenital practices by inflicting one hundred lashes for the guilty.[189] This echoes the severity of Ali's reply to his companion Abu Bakr in saying that the man who has sex with a male partner has to be burned.[190] This story shows that it is for Companions united in council to make decisions upon such case, because obviously the Prophet had not issued a clear position on the issue during his lifetime. It does cast doubt on the authenticity of the chain of transmission of the hadith going right back to the Prophet himself.[191]

Countries that are predominantly Hanafi in tradition, such as Turkey, Syria, Iraq, and the Balkans, do not normally adopt antisodomy laws, nor laws prohibiting homosexual relations in general. The Ottoman Empire showed some originality in the development of its legal tradition by codifying *fiqh*. Civil and criminal laws, the *Qanun*, was then applied by civil courts, whose judges were appointed by the state. Upholding the Hanafi tradition, the *Qanun* prescribed a correction (*tazir*) for sodomites in the nature of a fine, which varied according to the marital status of the accused inserter, while lashes were added to the fine for the insertee.[192] From the second half of the nineteenth century on, the Ottoman government discarded *fiqh* in criminal matters, and looked to the Napoleonic penal code for inspiration.[193] The *Ottoman Penal Code*, first enacted in 1858, contained no mention of sodomy, and just as the *Penal Code of 1810* in France, it only punished those who attempted to violently assault persons of both sexes, or made indecent assaults on children.[194] The *Criminal Code of the Republic of Turkey*, adopted in 2004, repeats the substance of the *Ottoman Penal Code*, and homosexual acts between consenting adults are not subject to any sanction.[195] The absence of specific provisions against homosexual acts between consenting adults does not imply the general approval of this type of sexual conduct by Turkish society.[196] Like many other countries, the Western medical model of the pervert emerged at the turn of the twentieth century, and overruled a tradition of social tolerance vis-à-vis homosexual practices in Ottoman society.[197] Despite the apparent legality of homosexual acts between consenting adults, several authors and groups defending the rights of gays and lesbians, including KAOS GL, founded in Ankara in 1994, underline the discrimination, violence, and police repression suffered by some men who have sex with men.[198] Negotiations concerning Turkey's inclusion process into the European Union created a window of opportunity for advocacy groups to assert their rights and demand changes in Turkish law.[199] Even if Turkey appears today as a country where debate on gay rights seems more advanced than any other Muslim culture country, the battle is far from won. In April 2008, police raided the offices of Lambda Istanbul, an advocacy group that has fought for LGBT rights since 1995. The police claimed that the organization promoted prostitution. The governor of Istanbul succeeded in obtaining a court decision ordering the closure of Lambda; the court of first instance motivated its decision on the fact that the goals of Lambda are contrary to morality and family. The Court of Appeal, however, rejected the trial judge's decision in January 2009.

Egypt has been influenced by the Ottoman legal tradition but also by European traditions. In particular France gained a lot of influence after Napoleon Bonaparte's Egyptian campaign in 1798, and under the leadership of Mehmet Ali Pasha, governor (*wali*) of the Ottoman Province of Egypt from 1805 to 1848. The *Egyptian Penal Code* entirely disregards homosexual acts between consenting adults, but in fact the government and police crackdown on men who have sex with men. The witch hunt has had a global impact in the press, when in 2001 some 50 men were arrested in Cairo, on a floating bar on the Nile, the *Queen Boat*. The state argued that the men indulged in debauchery in public, and that their actions were to be interpreted as contempt of religion under section 98f) of the *Penal Code*.[200]

Iraq followed a path similar to that of Egypt, but in 2001 Saddam Hussein's regime decreed the death penalty applicable to persons convicted of prostitution, homosexuality, incest, and rape. The *Coalition Provisional Authority*, established following the American invasion of Iraq, suspended the application of the death penalty in cases of rape or sexual assault, and re-enforced the *Iraqi Penal Code* of 1969 with some amendments.[201] Since the inception of the interim Iraqi government, some more conservative trends launched attacks on homosexuality, as shown by Ayatollah as-Sistani, who issued a fatwa in 2006, calling on believers to kill homosexuals. After that, militiamen belonging to the Badr group, linked to the *Supreme Council for Islamic Revolution* in Iraq, killed several men because of their sexual orientation.[202]

Iran has chosen to implement the Sharia in cases of sodomy, which means the death penalty as provided by the *Islamic Penal Code*, adopted by the Iranian National Assembly in 1991. In addition to sodomy, which requires evidence of anal penetration, the code prescribes the whip for all other forms of homogenital contact, up to one hundred lashes.[203] If the acts are repeated more than three times, the judge may order the death penalty. Recently, severe application of the Sharia resulted in casualties, including two juveniles accused of sodomy and hanged in the public square of Mashad, in July 2005.[204] In this context, the situation of homosexuals is extremely perilous, and many of them resort to sex change surgery in resignation and hope of escaping from oppression. They take advantage of the fact that Ayatollah Khomeini issued a fatwa in 1978, in Paris, authorizing this type of surgery for a man who believes his true identity belongs to the opposite sex.[205] While other societies acknowledge some ambiguity in the expression of sexuality, here there is only one possible way to go—be a man and woman and get married. Tanaz Eshaghian, a New York filmmaker of Iranian origin, produced in 2008, *Be Like Others*, a widely acclaimed documentary on the conditions of gay men willing to change sex to live safely as a couple, according to the morality of the country.

The Hanafi tradition is widespread in India, Pakistan, and Bangladesh, but the British legal system has left its imprint on criminal law. The provisions of section 377 of the Penal Code applicable in India and Pakistan in 1860 still remain in force for Pakistan and Bangladesh, but they were recently overturned by higher courts in India. This section provides a penalty of up to life imprisonment for sodomy. It is not impossible for stoning to be applied in Northwest Pakistan, where extremist groups, inspired by Afghani Talibans, seek to impose the Sharia upon those men who have sex with men.[206]

Saudi Arabia strictly applies the Sharia, based on jurisprudence and principles of interpretation of the Hanbali tradition. Saudi Islamic courts can sentence to death those who are convicted of sodomy under the rules of evidence established by the Sharia, estimating that sodomy should be equated with adultery or fornication (*zina*).[207] Sudan, Yemen, Mauritania, the UAE, and Northern Nigeria also apply the Sharia to persons convicted of sodomy.[208] The fact that the death penalty is not always applicable because of the required rule of evidence (four witnesses to penetration, or confession) or the fact that homosexual acts are not always acts of anal sex may explain why the death penalty still remains rare. Pressures of international organizations, Amnesty International, the UN, Human Rights Watch, and the International Lesbian and Gay Association, are also responsible for this rarity. However, Islamic courts in countries applying the Sharia do not hesitate to sentence to physical punishment, or imprisonment, those who they believe have engaged in homosexual conduct.[209] In some cases, accusations of homosexuality have been used to eliminate opponents to Islamist radical ideas, associating homosexuality with a variety of Western perversion.[210]

Homosexuality in Southeast Asian countries with large Muslim populations, Indonesia and Malaysia, for instance, present distinctive features in comparison to the rest of the Muslim world. In many of these traditional societies, gender categories are not dualistic and transgressive gender behavior or gender pluralism has many centuries of history with often pre-Islamic origins related to shamanistic practices. Perhaps the most documented instances are the *bissu* among the Bugis of South Sulawesi, and the *sida-sida* of Malaysia. Although the discourse of Islamic rulers tried to discourage these practices, it seems that until recently sanctions have not been applied with consistency.[211]

Normative religious discourse about homosexual practices often contrasts with the homoeroticism that is apparent in Arab-Muslim literature, poetry, and civilization. Several European explorers and travelers contributed to the description of a tolerant Oriental sensuality, licentious and marked by greater fluidity between heterosexuality and homosexuality. Not only was the West fascinated by the East, in many cases meeting the Other (stranger) became, consciously or not, an encounter with the exotic and the barbaric. Sexuality often became synonymous with an unrepressed civilization, not under the control of reason, and where homosexuality became the symbol of weakness or political impotence of the colonized nation.[212] The translation of *Arabian Nights*, Persian tales of the eighth century, first in French by Antoine Galland in the early eighteenth and then in English at the end of the nineteenth by Sir Richard Francis Burton, enlightened European imagination with its descriptions of sexual libertinage in the harem or of the love of handsome male youths.[213] Burton's fascination even drove him to construct a theory of geographical and climatic pederasty that spread in an area encompassing the Mediterranean, the Middle East, India, Japan and China, Pacific Islands, and parts of America, or for all intents and purposes, the entire world.[214] Gustave Flaubert's travel narratives in Egypt in 1849–1850 illustrate this uncensored and ambivalent passion, which he observed with fascination. In a letter to his friend Louis Bouilhet, he admits with some amusement to have finally consummated "that business at the baths. Yes, and on a pockmarked young rascal wearing a white turban."[215] On the other hand, Muslim travelers to the West, such as Egyptian al-Tahtawi Rifa'ah, wondered why when in Paris he could not encounter love poetry dedicated to beautiful boys (*ghulams*).[216] He was puzzled by the fact that men did not flirt with handsome boys, a comment totally agreed upon later by the Moroccan scholar Muhammad al-Saffar.[217] Yet marginal sex observed and experienced by Flaubert in the hammam seems neither pure fantasy nor exaggeration. Bouhdiba actually describes it as a "highly eroticized place" in the Arab world, to the point where "going to the hammam" in different countries is synonymous with "making love."[218] Abu Nuwas alludes to the flirtatious atmosphere of the hammam:

> And in the hamman, it is revealed to you, the secrets of pants
> Come and see clearly-look with two eyes without restraint:
> You see an ass outshining a back of the slenderest elegance,
> They murmur to one another *takbir* [God is Great] and *tahlil* [there is no God but God]
> O you beloved hammam, of places delightful
> Even when the companions of the towel spoil the pleasure a little.[219]

A document from Ottoman archives describes the beauty of young boys hired to wash and massage clients (*tellak*) and lists prices charged for their services, including those of a sexual nature.[220] Shadow plays allude to the reputation of the Ottoman hammam as a place for pederasty. In the *Great Marriage* (*Büyük Evlenme*), Kagaröz, a leading character of this kind of theater, learned along the way home that a group of women were going to his house to celebrate a marriage, of which he was the groom to be. Under the cover of anonymity, they reported that the man was a homosexual, who spent most of his time in the hammam.[221] The prince of Gurgan (northern Iran) Kaykavus ibn Iskandar ibn Qabus (eleventh century) wanted to educate his son and gave him this advice:

> UNDERSTAND, MY SON, that when you go to the warm baths it should not be at a time when you are sated with food, that being a dangerous course. Further, do not indulge in sexual congress at the baths, especially in the hot chamber. Muhammad son of Zakarīyā of Rayy [Rhazes] somewhere says: "I marvel when any man, having eaten his fill and then had sexual intercourse at the baths, does not immediately die."[222]

The public bath is certainly charged, to say the least, with an atmosphere of "homosensuality," in the words of Malek Chebel.[223] Rifa'a al-Tahtawi, a nineteenth-century Egyptian intellectual who spent five years in Paris, was amazed by the fact that Parisian public baths did not have one big general tub, so that nobody could look at another person's genitals. He deemed the Parisian baths cleaner, but he held the Egyptian hamman in higher esteem.[224] The film by Egyptian director Salah Abuseif titled *The Bathhouse of Malatily* (1973) introduces the viewer to the ambiguous universe of the hammam where young men from the countryside, who often sell their charms to provide for their families, meet and interact with men whose preferences are clearly homosexual.[225]

With the religious injunctions, the severity of which varied from school to school but all seeming to point the finger at male anal penetration, there coexisted, especially from the Abbasid period, a world where homoeroticism became fashionable. Based on various sources, including the *Kitab al-Aghani* (Book of Songs) by Abu al-Faraj (tenth century), Rowson revealed the existence of male transvestite singers and musicians in Medina and Mecca.[226] Forming an organized group under the Umayyads, the *mukhannathun*, these troubadours, effeminate in their gestures and garments, were reprimanded by the Prophet. He is said to have denounced their regular appearance in female quarters, either because they were sexually interested in the women—contrary to what one might think—or because they were acting as paid go-betweens for men who had no access to the harem.[227] The taste and experience of the *mukhannathun* in sexual matters is not exactly known, but some of them were attracted by handsome young men. For example, a certain ad-Dalal required two young male slaves as payment for his services as singer and matchmaker for an officer of Caliph al-Hassan.[228] At another point in time, ad-Dalal, who accompanied a group of young people on an excursion to the countryside, was attracted by the youngest of them. But suddenly law enforcement officers came, and ended the festive picnic, washed down with plenty of wine. The others managed to flee the scene, and only ad-Dalal and the youngest boy were arrested, and brought before the governor. When the governor ordered the whip, ad-Dalal replied with a fine example of obscene language (*mujun*) found in Arabic literature by responding that he usually gets whipped all day by the penis of devoted Muslims![229] Ad-Dalal had the reputation of being a *mabun*—the passive actor in anal penetration. The same ad-Dalal possibly instigated the castration of *mukhannathun*, ordered by Caliph Suleiman in 717. The *Kitab al-Aghani* reported different versions of this event, focusing on two. In the first, Suleiman appears, in the desert, in the pleasant company of a young female slave, distracted by the serenade sung by a *mukhannath*. Enraged and jealous, the caliph has him castrated and commands the governor to do the same with all alike.[230] The second depicts ad-Dalal as a go-between, who first has intercourse with the bride and then with the groom, to appease the sexual ardor of the future husband. Filled with anger, Suleiman enacts the castration of all the *mukhannathun* in Medina. Ad-Dalal, with another named al-Mukhannath Gharid, particularly attracted to beautiful young men, are the only two troubadours from pre-Abbasid times known for homosexual practices. Under the Abbasids, the musical career of the *mukhannath* became that of a public entertainer or jester, a master of *mujun*. During this period, many poets spoke of male love, especially love of the *ghilman* (pl. of *ghulam*), beardless youth, which could explain the origin of a new public awareness of the *mukhannath* as *baghgha'* or passive homosexual.[231] Abu Sa'id al-Husayn ibn Mansur al-'Abi (eleventh century) in his book *Nathr al-Durr* relates the words of a *mukhannath*, who shouted: "We are the best of people, when we speak, you laugh; when we sing, you are ravished with delight; when we lie down, you mount!"[232] Abbada, the most popular *mukhannath* of the Abbasid period, answered affirmatively to Caliph al-Mutawakkil (847–861), who had asked him if all *mukhannathun* were passive homosexuals, saying: "it is like a judge without a judge's hat."[233] The two go hand in hand. While the *mukhannath* of early Islam may have been an effeminate entertainer without any reference to some kind of sexual preference, it seems well established that as of ninth century the effeminate and the passive sodomite were often perceived as a single person.[234] The *mukhannath* is not always depicted as the inserter, as shown in this verse about Abbada taken from the *Kitab al-Aghani*: "Abbada went one day to the Hammam and saw a youth with a huge instrument, which he immediately seized. 'But what are you doing? Asked the other, may God heal you.' And Abbada answered: 'don't you know the poet's verses: If you see the banner of glory raised/With his right hand Araba seizes it.'"[235] According to the Persian philosopher of the tenth century Muhammad ibn Ahmad ibn Miskawayh, the *mukhannath* condition is inherited biologically, but reversible.[236] Without reducing it to a basic physiological cause, Muhammad ibn ar-Razi Zakaryia (865–932) and ibn Sina, both physicians, also see in the passive homosexual, *al-ubna*, a kind of behavior that, if it becomes routine for an effeminate male, may develop into some illness (*aegritudo* in the Latin translation by Gerard of Cremona).[237] Instead of physiological etiologies, ibn Sina seems to favor a psychological cause, that is to say, an overwhelming desire to be penetrated. Ibn Sina thinks this affliction to be incurable, unlike his predecessor ar-Razi, who proposes various treatments.[238] As in the ancient world, literary works comparing the benefits of the love of women over the love of boys appeared in the Arab-Andalusian world.[239] In the *Book of Qabus* (*Qabus Nama*), the prince of Gurgan (Northern Iran) found it quite natural to teach his son about the merits of the love of women but also of boys, stating that the best boys were recruited among Turkish slaves.[240] Ibn Qabus sets bisexuality as a normal sexual behavior: "As between women and youths, do not confine your inclinations to either sex; thus you may find enjoyment from both kinds without either of the two becoming inimical to you."[241] The prince also warned his son against the dangers of passionate love (*ishq*), which must be contained by reason. He illustrates his point through an anecdote about his grandfather who purchased a slave at a high cost. The grandfather finally freed the slave because he was seduced by his beauty. Surprised by this decision, the vizier asks him for an explanation. The grandfather's reply left no doubt about the passion that inspired him:

> Today such-and-such an incident occurred. It would be a hideous offence if a prince over seventy years of age should become the victim of passion. I should at that age be fully occupied in the protection of God's servants and seeking the welfare of my people, my army and my possessions. Were I now to engage in dalliance, I should find forgiveness neither in the eyes of God nor of man.[242]

The Ottoman court regaled in the love of boys. The Turkish armies brought back some young boys as war booty. For instance, Sultan Mehmet II, conqueror of Constantinople in 1453, kept a harem of over 200 boys from ages eight to sixteen, dressed in feminine garments and hairless. They danced before the court, and they were taken to his bedroom.[243] The Ottoman sultan Selim I (sixteenth century) wrote a poem titled "He" in which he said: "While lions were trembling in my crushing paw fate made me fall prey to a doe-eyed darling."[244] An eighth-century poet of Persian origin, who immigrated to Baghdad, Abus Nuwas, did not hide his preference for boys and handsome young cupbearers:

> *Song of a Gazelle's Gift*
> Now, wine is a thing which I guzzle well
> And my usual mount is a slender gazelle.
> I'm kin to all men who hunt treasure
> In thickets, and in taverns of pleasure.
> Then drink to the boy! So lanky, so sleek!
> The grape is ripening, now, in his cheek.
> His gaze seems to take in far-distant lands,
> For his eyes have sorcery, just like his hands.

His fingertips touch the chalice—so fine
That Beauty himself tumbles into the wine!
And when the shy robe of nightfall slips down,
When the song of the lute no longer resounds,
Then I go to him, and proceed to take
The gift he's been preparing to make.[245]

Male beauty is often the theme of love poems (*ghazal*), especially handsome, smooth male youths. This literary form has its origins in pre-Islamic courtly poetry, with clearly heterosexual patterns—mourning the absence of the beloved, celebrating the lover's passion, and consumed by suffering at a distance.[246] Under the Abbasids, male beauty is celebrated, and the female beloved, once celebrated as the *ghazal* (masculine in Arabic), is now replaced by the male favorite. Sometimes, one may be mistaken about the anatomical sex of the person desired.[247] However, several texts describing the beauty of teens have for a leitmotif the appearance of down (*idar*) signaling the end of the relationship, a clear evidence of a homoerotic context.[248] The Iranian satirist Ubaid Zakani (fourteenth century) wrote a book about the power of seduction of handsome young men, as opposed to those who have beards.[249] The great poet of the Abbasid court Abu Nuwas describes a beautiful young man named Hamdan:

First Fuzz
He saw, from his cheeks sprouting, the first down,
And said, "No more kissing!" with a frown.
"Today I become a full-grown man,
And a grown man doesn't kiss another grown man.
What we did in my youth is all over now."
And he went on complaining, and how!
I said: "You're so proud of that beard, today!
But you've just grown old enough now to play
The Real Game! You still have saffron and musk
Which wafts from your hair; your eyes at dusk
Are still magically fair, and I'm up for it—
Biting your cheeks, and drinking your honey spit!"
"This cannot be! This is WRONG!" was his cry
As I bent and embraced him, so sly,
So quick! I struggled with his embarrassed age
And turned all to trembling his red-faced rage,
Until we were hugging hard, and at last
My prick was plunged up right in his ass![250]

He was the undisputed master of Bacchic poetry, the *khamriyya*.[251] This style combined the pleasures of wine drinking with the love of courtesans (*qain*), as well as boys—the *saqi* who served wine during receptions at the court or in cafes. *Khamriyya* has pre-Islamic origins in the poetry and songs of Arab Bedouins, but Abu Nuwas transformed the licentious philosophy of carpe diem into a clearly transgressive and blasphemous genre. Drunkenness and homosexuality are seen as actualizing the promises of paradise, where wine flows without the danger of one becoming intoxicated, and where *huris* and *ghulman* abound.[252] The actual occurrence of the transgression does not matter.[253] What deserves attention is the naturalness with which homoeroticism is used as an expression of love and as an epiphany of the suavity of eternal life. Love rhymes (*ghazal*) with homoerotic themes did not die with Abu Nuwas but extended beyond Baghdad into Persia, Egypt, Andalusia, and later to Mughal India from the thirteenth century in Urdu, and in Turkish in the Ottoman Empire.[254] Muhammad an-Nawaji (fifteenth century) wrote an entire book devoted to the taste of male youth. Here is what he had to say about the young Hamza: "With diligence, I took pains to please him, / But I have not reached my goal: to touch this male gazelle / Who spent the night frolicking in the meadow of my heart."[255] The aesthetic appreciation of a handsome young man portends nothing perverse in Arabic poetry, and it was never denounced by religious authorities as abnormal, at least as long as the suitor remained chaste. Through anecdotes and poems in his *Ring of the Dove*, ibn Hazm of Cordoba celebrated his passions toward slave girls and handsome male teenagers in a balanced and relaxed manner, both felt to be as perfectly natural impulses of soul. The author, near the end, reassured his readers by professing that he never committed any unlawful sexual act, and told about the trials and tribulations of Muslim scholars who, in full view of everyone, had affairs with boys:

> Abu 'l-Husain Ahmad ibn Yahya ibn Ishaq al-Rawandi in his book entitled "*Pronunciation and Correction*" mentions that Ibrahim ibn Saiyar al-Nazzam, the head of the Mu'tazili sect, for all his reputation in scholastic theology and his ultimate mastery of the higher knowledge, in order to enjoy forbidden relations with a certain Christian boy whom he loved to madness went so far as to compose a treatise extolling the merits of the Trinity over Monotheism. Good Lord, preserve us from the machinations of Satan, and suffer us not to be abandoned by Thy loving protection! Sometimes it happens that the trial becomes so great, and the lusts are so voracious, that abomination seems a mere trifle, and religion proves a poor and feeble thing; in order to achieve his desires a man will then: consent to the filthiest and most outrageous acts. Such was the catastrophe which overwhelmed 'Ubaid All ibn Yahya al-Azdi, better known as ibn al-Jaziri.[256]

The Cairo-based medical encyclopedist Dawud al-Antaki (sixteenth century) mentioned a number of jurists and theologians well-known for their appreciation of male youths.[257] Discretion, sometimes even hiding one's true feelings toward the beloved, often put the young prey at ease, preventing him from fleeing or fearing the consequences of such a relationship. However, indiscretion and obsessive pursuits and attachments to the beloved may bring about gossip, negative publicity, causing humiliation and marginalization.[258] The enjoyment of beauty and appreciation of the attractive silhouette of male youth are licit, as long as the intent is not direct sexual satisfaction. Al-Ghazali, probably influenced by Plato, made a clear distinction between the love of beauty for its sake and sexual desire that seeks only to be relieved.[259] The Hanbali jurist and distinguished traditionist ibn al-Jawzi (twelfth century, Baghdad) said that anyone who claimed not to be attracted by the beauty of youth was a liar![260] The famed Persian master of *ghazal* Hafez i-Shirazi (fourteenth century) dared to claim that sexual licentiousness, including the love of boys, like drunkenness, was a greater gateway to wisdom than Sufi asceticism.[261] Ruzbihan Baqli Shirazi (twelfth century), an influential Persian Sufi master, in his presentation on the ecstasy of love as a licit path to God, cited a hadith attributed to the Prophet: "He, who loves and remains chaste and conceals his secret and dies, dies a martyr (true witness)."[262] Was this love (*ishq*) assuredly sublimated at all times? One is certainly well advised to question the moral strength of many of those boy lovers, as did several witnesses. Thus, the poet Hakim Sana'i of Ghazni (twelfth century) ridiculed a Sufi scholar of Herat who could no longer contain his passion for a young boy. The scholar found refuge with his conquered youth in a mosque, but they were caught in the act by a pious man, who severely blamed the scholar's wrongdoing, making it responsible for the drought affecting the region.[263] Sheikh Sa'adi Shirazi (thirteenth century) took a violent dislike for the hypocrisy of ascetics. In one of his stories, a recluse finally yielded to the charms of a handsome teenager, after having resisted the advances of a young girl.[264] Several of Sa'adi's stories and poems describe the delights of the love of boys, sometimes chaste, sometimes transgressive. Indeed, the poet directed some warnings against the shallowness, ingratitude, and even the cruelty of these beloved youths, leaving deep wounds in the suitor's heart and destroying him. All of these sharp attacks suggest that this passion was probably not so sublimated.[265] The love of handsome boys paves the way for the moral transformation taking place within the lover. His appreciation of their physical beauty improves his ability to discern ethical qualities in others. Sa'adi expressed this opinion when speaking of a teacher dazzled by the beauty of his young protégé:

> A schoolboy was so perfectly beautiful and sweet-voiced that the teacher, in accordance with human nature, conceived such affection towards him that he often recited the following verses:
>
> > I am not so little occupied with thee, O heavenly face,
> > That remembrance of myself occurs to my mind.
> > From thy sight I am unable to withdraw my eyes
> > Although when I am opposite I may see that an arrow comes.
>
> Once the boy said to him: "As thou strivest to direct my studies, direct also my behaviour. If thou perceivest anything reprovable in my conduct, although it may seem approvable to me, inform me thereof that I may endeavour to change it." He replied: "O boy, make that request to someone else because the eyes with which I look upon thee behold nothing but virtues."
>
> > The ill-wishing eye, be it torn out Sees only defects in his virtue.
> > But if thou possessest one virtue and seventy faults
> > A friend sees nothing except that virtue.[266]

The Persian poet Omar Khayyam (twelfth century) reported contemplating God's grace in the face of beardless boys—a practice known as the "witness game" (in Persian, *shahed-bazi*), which produces noble feelings of compassion and generosity.[267] Among the methods of meditation (*muraqaba*) to achieve mystical union with the divine, Sufis employed *shahed-bazi* or *nazar ill'al-murd*—the chaste contemplation of the beautiful face of an Adonis.[268] The witness' (*shahed*) beauty blossoms as a living sign (*ayat*) of the truth, which will lead the meditator to God.[269] Another Persian poet, close to Sufi circles, Farid ad-Din Attar (twelfth century, Nishapur), wrote several pages on the love of boys as a method of elevating the soul to God. However, this pedagogical tool can become an obstacle to spiritual growth and must be abandoned en route. In Attar's *Book of God* (*Elahi-Nama*), a caliph teaches the spiritual path to his six sons lured by sensual pleasures and power. This path requires renunciation, and the caliph shows his third son the limits of human love by telling him an anecdote about a young slave, Ayaz, a favorite of Sultan Mahmud of Ghazni. The sultan asked his beloved if he knew a sovereign more powerful than he. Ayaz's reply startled him:

> Mahmud one day asks Ayaz: "Do you know any king who's greater and more powerful than I am?" The slave answers: "Yes. I'm a greater king than you." Mahmud asks: "What reason do you have for saying this?" Ayaz answers: "Why do you ask? You know it yourself. You're king alright, but your king is your heart. And I'm king over your

heart. The sky itself must envy me for my high rank. Because I'm forever king over the king."[270]

This pair of lovers is often depicted in Persian literature extolling the virtues of platonic love. In *Bustan*, Sa'adi evoked the purity of feelings; when Mahmud met someone who blamed him for being attracted to a person who was not particularly attractive: "My love, O Sir, is for virtue, not for form or stature."[271] Jaffar Ahmed ibn as-Sarraj (eleventh century) wrote several stories, defending the chaste nature of *shahed-bazi*. In one story, Sheikh Abul Qasim Junayd al-Baghdadi (ninth century) went to a school in Baghdad, where he was fascinated by the beautiful appearance of the teacher, and of the boys. One by one, the boys recited their lessons until the very last, the best and brightest. Then the teacher hit him with a stick. The pupil began weeping, and the master with him. Unable to apprehend the reason why the scene kept being repeated day after day, the boy asked for an explanation from the master. The teacher resolved it by saying he had to beat the boy because he was too close to his heart, which should be exclusively dedicated to Allah. The boy asked him to ease his passion, but the teacher refused and expelled him from school. The boy's candid offer would, in fact, extinguish his languor for the boy.[272] Suffering as a martyr through renunciation of carnal pleasure brings one closer to Allah! The sexual tension present in these unconsummated love affairs is often the hallmark of the emotional ties that bind the Sufi master and his disciple; it is also characteristic of the premodern Islamic rhetoric of love.[273]

The revered Sufi poet Jallal ad-Din Rumi, of Afghani origin but established in Turkey in the thirteenth century, founded the order of the Whirling Dervishes (*Mawlawi*). He, like others, used the homoerotic *ghazal* style in his mystical poetry. Everywhere his work bears the imprint of his love for an eccentric wandering dervish, Shams i-Tabrizi, to whom he specifically dedicated a collection of poetry, the *Divan-i Shams-i Tabrizi*. Shams looked nothing like a beautiful young man, when he encountered Rumi in Konya in 1244, but Rumi fell under his spell. The two lived together until Shams disappearance in 1247, abducted by Rumi's jealous disciples, who allegedly murdered him.[274] The poet describes Shams's beauty, a true fountain of eternal truth, but mourns his absence, longing through mystical union to be reunited with the Beloved in a paradisaic decor, filled with flowers and beautiful, young cupbearers:

> Each moment I catch from my bosom the scent of the Beloved;
> How should I not take my self every night into his bosom?
> Last night I was in Love's garden; that desire ran into my head;
> His sun peeped out of my eye, so that the river began to flow.[275]

Was such passionate love always sublimated? No real clues can shed light on this aspect. The Sufi master Shah Qasim al-Anwar was much criticized because of the sexual licentiousness of his followers, who were fond of beardless boys.[276] Al-Ghazali denounced the imposture of antinomian (*ibahis*) Sufis who engaged in all sorts of carnal pleasures including sex and alcohol.[277] Although some of the hagiographers' critics are the product of rivalry between schools, sexual and homosexual libertinism cannot be simply dismissed, according to Karamustafa who says that:

> Rejection of marriage, or even of the female sex, does not entail complete abstinence from sexual activity. Celibacy, in this context, meant primarily the refusal to participate in the sexual reproduction of society and did not exclude unproductive forms of sexual activity. It is likely, therefore, that antisocial ways of sexual gratification came to be

included in the deliberately rejectionist repertoire of some dervishes. The existence of a distinct group of youths known as *köçeks* (from Persian *küchak*, "youngster") among the Abdāls is certainly suggestive in this regard.[278]

Rumi and Shams were opposed to the ephebophiliac practice of *shahed-bazi*, notably to one of its ardent defenders, Awhad ud-Din Hamid Kirmani. Shams asked al-Kirmani to clarify the techniques of *shahed-bazi*. Al-Kirmani compared it to contemplating the beauty of the Creator through its creature, like watching the moon reflected on the wave. Shams's response was scorching: why don't you look directly at the moon in the sky? Rumi, meanwhile, showed little faith in the purity of al-Kirmani's intentions and thought that the old man's age accounted for his chastity.[279] The continuous quest for an unconsummated love and the lover's suffering due to the absence of the beloved did serve as true metaphors for the genuine nature of the soul in search for its divine component. The Sufi idea of creation as a bridge to God may constitute a direct assault on the idea of God's absolute transcendence and oneness. The Hanbali ibn Taimiyya did not hesitate to equate *shahed-bazi* to a form of immanence akin to idolatry. Ibn Qayyim al-Jawziyya (fourteenth century) reported that ibn Taimiyya addressed reproaches one day to a Sufi who was gazing at a male youth. The Sufi replied he saw God through the youth's beauty. The sceptical ibn Taimiyya retorted that he surely had a sexual contact with the teenager, and then seeing that the Sufi exonerated himself he had this quip: "God curse a community which sleeps with the one they honour as God!"[280] Several jurists condemn *nazar* or *shahed-bazi* in the same manner they condemn gazing at a woman who is not one's spouse. Temptation comes from both—beautiful male teenagers and beautiful women. The Shafi'i Sheikh Sayed al-Alwan Hamawi objected to some lawyers' views, who considered the ban applicable only if the teenager is beautiful. In this case, then gazing should be avoided, though it is permitted to look at him for teaching or training purposes.[281] The Hanafi Sufi, Abdel al-Ghani an-Nabulusi (Syria, eighteenth century), refuted this kind of extreme position. In his opinion, the general prohibition could not be applied, except when a lascivious intent is obvious, because a teenager, even beardless, belongs to the male gender, and there exists no natural sexual attraction between persons of the same sex.[282] He seems to follow the opinion of the Shafi'i, Abu al-Qasim Abd al-Karim ar-Rafi'i (thirteenth century) who sees no harm in it, whenever there is an absence of sexual desire.[283] According to Khaled el-Rouayheb, the majority of Ottoman lawyers espoused a position similar to that of an-Nabulusi, among them sixteenth-century Egyptian Shafi'i, al-Khatib Shirbini, and Shams ud-Din Muhammad ar-Ramli. The latter considered to be a sinner he who gazed with pleasure and delight at a teenager without expressly desiring intercourse.[284] Jurists all seem to agree on condemning any form of touching or promiscuity with beautiful young males.[285] The condemnation of homogenital acts, as it is in legal or theological literature, does not preclude certain forms of homoeroticism. However, if the ephebe is considered a natural object of desire for the normal man in premodern Muslim societies, the relation between the two is socially perceived in a way that differs from egalitarian same-sex in the West. The inserter is never infamous; the desire for passive penetration in an adult male is considered as evil or pathological, even when laughed at. Satire (*hija'*), obscenity (*sukhf*), insult, and denunciation in some respects may even be the only legitimate form of expressing a same-sex sexual preference that is gender-based and makes fun of religious or legal disapproval. François Lagrange has shown how Abu Hayyan al-Tawidhi in his work *Kitab Akhlaq al-Wazirayn* (The Blame of the Two Viziers), makes use of the literary genre of the *adab* (cultured literature) to describe through insult the vizier Ibn 'Abbad al-Sahib as a "homosexual character," calling him in turns, regardless of the role played in intercourse, an effeminate, a passive sodomite, an old queen (*mukkhanath ashmat*), and at the same time an active sodomite or *luti*.[286] This type of literature may help to identify the gap that probably existed between the religious discourse denouncing forbidden acts and the literary discourse describing persons with anomic tastes or preferences in sexual matters.

Before leaving this section, a few words on the neotraditionalist discourse about homosexuality are required. I am referring here to Muslims who, since the 1970s, criticize postcolonial regimes as too complacent toward Western values and are advocating the defense of Islamic values against assaults by external forces that bring social problems and personal distress. For many neotraditionalist thinkers, homosexuality is a Western import that traditional values of Islam must fight. We earlier discussed Imam Yusuf al-Qaradawi's vision of heterosexuality as the natural condition of human sexuality, marked by gender differences or sexual dimorphism. Surprisingly, al-Qaradawi superimposes on his view of sexuality the theological concept of *fitra*. In this way, he "equates an innate disposition to believe in God with an innate heterosexual orientation, making homosexuality a form of *kufr* or infidelity."[287] Al-Qaradawi, following some hard-line legal experts, reaffirms the need to punish by death those who commit homosexual acts, and totally rejects the idea of a homosexual orientation. However, this type of theological reasoning needs to be reconsidered, because the natural disposition referred to in the concept of *fitra* does not apply to what connects us to the animal kingdom—sexual instinct and reproduction of the species.[288] *Fitra* is a natural disposition, found in human beings alone, an innate knowledge that guides them to the knowledge of God. Al-Qaradawi makes no distinction between homosexual acts, sodomy, and homosexuality, leaving no room for the emotional and psychological dimensions of same-sex attraction, yet an aspect strongly asserted in Muslim civilization, as I have shown. Neotraditionalists, such as al-Qaradawi, Taha Jabir al-Alwani, and Muzammil Siddiqi, see any Western protection of gay rights as an assault on Islamic values but are incapable of viewing their heteronormative concept of sexuality as a cultural thing that maintains masculine domination over women.[289]

Conclusion

Until the twentieth century, Arab-Persian culture adopted a fairly optimistic attitude vis-à-vis same-sex sexual attraction, provided it was aimed at a teenager. If intercourse occurred, the teenager had to play the passive role, and the adult male the active role. In this way, the adult was not compromising his masculinity. Religion severely sanctioned anal penetration, but to the same extent and with the same intensity as fornication and adultery. The religious ban did not rest upon the idea of a disorder of nature, a perversion of sexual desire, as long as the subject is an adult playing the active role. Same-sex relations do not espouse the Western paradigm of sexual orientation. Inequality in homosexual relations, built around two poles, activity or passivity and the age difference, marks both the normative discourse and popular imagination. However, individual practices sometimes exceed these prescribed limits. The Tunisian at-Tifashi refers to versatile boys who do not hesitate to reverse roles.[290] Al Raghbi al-Asfahani (eleventh century) confirms that male slaves were seens on their masters' back.[291] The Persian satirist Zakani, parodying the *Shahnameh*, a national epic written by Ferdowsi (late tenth century), shows the legendary hero Rustam in full action with Human, both nude in combat after having laid aside their armor: "Hamun also exhibited a monstrous and legendary shaft, and according to what his ancestors had taught him, he trushed it in, etc. After, came Hamun's turn to act as bottom."[292]

Homoeroticism, in Sufi poetry in particular, serves to convey the spiritual aspirations of the follower, which only shows once again some positive attitude toward homosexual feelings. The attitude of some hardline Salafi fundamentalists from the twentieth century contrasts with traditional Islamic culture to the extent that it makes homosexual sexual misconduct more serious than any other sexual act, by putting the blame on some kind of perversion within the sexual actor, paradoxically under the influence of Western modern medical discourse. Many fundamentalists accuse homosexuality of being a Western imported evil. Muslim feminists have nevertheless opened the way for a reinterpretation of the Qur'an, which further militates in favor of gender equality, as opposed to male superiority promoted by the Sharia. Using a new interpretation (*ijtihad*) could also create a new legal interpretation of homosexuality, a task that remains to be accomplished by the promoters of a new enlightened Islam.

6

AFRO-CARIBBEAN AND
AFRO-BRAZILIAN RELIGIONS

RELIGION

The slave trade brought Africans by force to work in the United States, the Caribbean, Brazil, and also in Venezuela and Colombia. It marked the history of the Americas in a distinctive way. The slaves were captured from different parts of Africa, and came to the New World with their languages, cultures, and religious systems. For various reasons, which it would be out of place to develop here, slaves that came directly from Africa—called *bozales* in Cuba, *bossales* or *nèg Guinen* in Haiti—and, subsequently, their descendants managed to maintain a piece of their religious culture of origin while adapting it to a new socioeconomic context. Thus, three major African American systems of religious syncretism gradually emerged: Santería in Cuba, Candomblé in Brazil, and Voodoo in Haiti. Other African-inspired religions developed in the Americas, but they were never as influential as these three.[1] All three systems have an undeniable kinship because all are tied to neighboring African civilizations, the Yoruba of Nigeria and Benin (former Dahomey) in the case of Candomblé and Santería, and the Fon from the ancient Kingdom of Dahomey for Voodoo. This does not preclude other influences, as it will soon be demonstrated.

No official statistics exist on these religions because the states that host them do not include them in their census. Historically, these beliefs were banned by the colonial authorities and the clergy, both Catholics and Protestants. To be honest, they were demonized, associated with black magic, witchcraft, cannibalism, and human sacrifice, or sexual orgies. Colonial authorities did not hesitate to classify these religious practices as crimes of magic and mutiny. Such was the view in the notorious *Black Code*—enacted in 1685 by Louis XIV to regulate the life of slaves in the Antilles and Guyana.[2] The code prohibited any religious practice other than Roman Catholicism and punished any form of gathering or meeting of slaves. Above all, the ban clearly demonstrated the colonizers' fear of runaways. Their suspicions were not entirely unfounded, since the slaves' protest drew strength from their ancestral brought from Africa, enabling them to oppose their European masters' political and cultural domination. For example, Boukman, a Voodoo priest, an *oungan* in Creole, presided over the ceremony of Bois Caïman on August 14, 1791. During the ceremony, an animal was sacrificed to the ancestors, which led to the massacre of white settlers. This ceremony is considered the founding moment of the Haitian Revolution and independence, which was finally proclaimed on January 1, 1804, by Jean-Jacques Dessalines.[3] Leaders of the indigenous movement—a kind of cultural resistance to the American occupation from the 1920s—such as Jean Price-Mars and Justin-Chrysostome Dorsainvil saw Boukman's experience as a paradigm for the liberating energy contained in ancestral religion.[4]

In Cuba, African traditions were perpetuated in the daily lives of maroons (*cimarrones*) in the *palenque* (meaning a stockade, free zone, a walled enclosure), particularly in Santiago (East of the island). There, in the mountain range of El Cobre, in the Oriente Region, was created the *Palenque El Portillon*, where many fugitives flocked to the copper mine in the town of Cobre. They erected a shrine to the *Virgen de la Caridad*, patron saint of Cuba, representing the Santería *oricha* (spirit) Ochún.[5] Spanish colonization allowed slaves greater civil liberties than the French or English systems, including the right to property and marriage, which favored the emergence of a large class of emancipated slaves. The Spanish Church required that slaves convert to Catholicism, but unlike what happened in the French Antilles with the *Black Code*, it wished to promote the integration of newly arrived slaves and emancipated slaves (*de color libres*) to Cuban life. Thus, the church allowed them to form, along the lines of their ethnicity, cultural associations, the *cabildos*.[6] These groups secured the survival of African cults, especially in Havana and Matanzas.

In Brazil, during the seventeenth century, many maroons congregated in Pernambuco, in the Serra da Barriga, in small enclaves of freedom—the *quilombos*. These havens of freedom were formed under the leadership of a king or master—Ganga Zumba or Zumbi—and were known as the Republic of *Os Palmares*.[7] The *quilombos* perpetuated cults to African deities (*orixás*), fused with elements of Catholicism and perhaps cults from Indians of the Amazon rainforest. King Ganga Zumba was probably chosen because of the religious functions he held during the celebration of these African cults.[8] Today, a statue still honors the memory of Zumbi in the city of Salvador. In this same city, many sculptures of *orixás* are found in public parks and gardens, particularly in the districts of Pituba, Rio Vermelho, and in Dique do Tororó Park.

Santería, Candomblé, and Voodoo no doubt contributed to the survival of African cultures in America, and they inspired the slaves' political struggle against the colonizer. Even today, many people, often among the poorest, find in these religions the courage needed to face daily misery, and they run up to them as a "place of invulnerability against their exploiters."[9] In Haiti, intellectuals, such as Francois Duvalier, used Voodoo to promote Haitian nationalism, but official endorsement of Voodoo only happened in 2003, when the state formalized the validity of birth certificates, weddings, and funerals issued by an *oungan*. Since the colonial years, a number of obstacles have stood in the way of formal recognition. Opposition came not only from the Catholic clergy, but also from intellectuals and the Haitian political class who tried to distance themselves from practices often charged as witchcraft or plain superstition. The *Penal Code*, promulgated in 1835 under President Jean-Pierre Boyer, severely punished the practice of "zombification" and magic spells, coming from "all makers of *ouangas, caprelatas, vaudoux, donpèdres, Macandal.*"[10] Louis-Joseph Janvier and Hannibal Price strove after the creation of a kind of black Enlightenment, which would make of Haiti a black France, free from the defects of barbarism carried by African Voodoo.[11] This "African barbarism," it must be added, was the image held by nineteenth-century Europeans! Later, several writers disparaged the cultural alienation resulting from the persecution by Roman Catholicism of Voodoo, but without necessarily acknowledging its role as an instrument of national liberation. For many of them, Voodoo would simply disappear of its own, as the country developed and the people became more educated.[12] The socialist novelist Jacques Stephen Alexis wrote in *The Musician Threes*: "The loas grow from our soil because our land is miserable, but they will die one day, thanks to electricity and agricultural machinery."[13]

In Brazil, even after the destruction of the Republic of Palmares in 1694, the authorities continued to identify Candomblé with the emancipatory image of the *quilombo*, and they punished followers, slaves, and emancipated slaves found in places of worship (*terreiros*).[14] The Catholic Church in Brazil, especially in Salvador da Bahia, condemned African religions, as it happened elsewhere in the Americas. At the same time, the Portuguese missionaries furthered their growth through the creation of *irmandades*, lay associations for mutual assistance, most notably in regard to funeral rites. The *irmandades* consisted mostly of people from the same ethnic group (*nações*). From the nineteenth century, they brought together many slaves of different ethnic origins, *crioulos* (slaves born in Brazil) and *mulatos*. The church believed it would, in this way, win their support by allowing them to speak African languages, through their native songs and dances on Sundays after the Sunday mass in church.[15] From the second half of the nineteenth century, the church began to lose some of its influence on the slave population because of its ban on burials inside churches or in private places of burial for reasons of public hygiene. Slaves became less fond of their *irmandades*, and gradually abandoned them.[16] Other factors may explain this drop: in the second half of the nineteenth century, abolitionist and republican ideas made their way in the slave population, and new forms of associations fighting for the emancipation and equality attracted blacks.[17]

The *quilombo* and *irmandade* remain, even today, powerful metaphors in the construction of what Joao Jose Reis calls "*a consciência negra*."[18] Cachoeira, a small city in the state of Bahia, still houses the *Irmandade da Nossa Senhora da Boa Morte* (*Our Lady of the Good Death*), and each year it still solemnly celebrates the Assumption of the Virgin in August with a blending of Catholic celebrations and African rituals. The Brazilian Constitution of 1988, for the first time, acknowledged the land claims of *quilombo* descendants. Intellectuals and the clergy, Catholic or Protestant, often continue to identify Candomblé with magic or witchcraft. In the early twentieth century, Raimundo Nina Rodrigues, a mulatto and forensic doctor, became the first to insist on describing in detail the Candomblé of Bahia and its Afro-Brazilian traditions. For him, the *quilombo* only brought Brazilians of African descent back to "African barbarism" or "tribal regression," adding that the black presence was a disadvantage for Brazil.[19] The positive contribution of Africans to the Brazilian national identity became truly recognized only with Gilberto Freyre and his book *Casa Grande e Senzala, Masters and Slaves*, released in 1933. From the 1950s, Roger Bastide and Pierre Verger highlighted the ingenuity and rich complexity of Candomblé, and they somehow acclaimed this Afro-Brazilian cult alongside other world religious systems. Prejudices, however, failed to disappear as it was well illustrated by author Alfredo Dias Gomes in his play of 1960, *O Pagador de Promessas, Keeper of Promises*, which was made into a movie two years later by Anselmo Duarte. Zé do Burro, a Bahian peasant who had carried a cross on a long distance, went to hoist it in the church, hence keeping a promise he had made to Santa Barbara if she cured his donkey. The priest did not allow him to enter the church, accusing Zé of having invoked Yasã, the *orixá* of storm, who is venerated by means of the Christian representation of Saint Barbara.

The word "Voodoo" derives its origin from the word *vodun*, a word meaning spirit in the Fon language, spoken in the ancient Kingdom of Dahomey. In the seventeenth century, the kingdom extended to the present borders of Togo and Benin, and well into present-day southwestern Nigeria. Abomey was the capital; it became heavily involved in the slave trade, especially through the ports of Whydah and Allada after their recapture from the Portuguese. Many slaves—Fon, Ewe, and Aja—were taken by force from this region to the Caribbean, particularly to the French Antilles. Other ethnic groups joined them. The Yoruba kingdom of Oyo gradually subjugated its neighbor, the Kingdom of Dahomey, in the early eighteenth century. Oyo got involved in the slave trade, as did the Yoruba Kingdom of Ketu, in northern Benin. All these ethnic groups (*nazyon*) contributed to the establishment of Voodoo in Haiti. *Rada* refers mainly to religious beliefs and practices of the Ewe, Fon, Aja, and Mahi. Nagô (a Fon word meaning Yoruba) refers to Yoruba beliefs, and Congo to beliefs derived from slaves taken from the Kongo Empire. This empire included the northwestern part of Angola, Cabinda, and the Western part of the Democratic Republic of Congo and Congo-Brazza. Congo rituals are usually called *Petro*. They were popularized in the second half of the eighteenth century by various slaves from the Kingdom of Kongo.[20]

Voodoo ceremonies (*sèvis-loa, cérémoni*) held in each ritual seek the protection of spirits, the *loas*, against disease, famine, infertility, failure in love affairs, and so on. By means of offerings and sacrifices followers make sure they are protected against the *loas'* anger. In *Rada* ceremonies, *loas* are sometimes called *mistè* (mystery) or *z'ange*, and are usually of Dahomean origin. Every ceremony usually starts with an invocation to the Creator of the universe, *Bondye Papa* or *Bondye Mama*, and the following plea: "*pa pèmysion Gran-Met là*" (with the will of God Almighty).[21] God the Creator does not interfere in the lives of men and of the cosmos, nor in relations between men and nature; the *loas* provide for that.[22] A Creole proverb illustrates the neutrality of *Bondye*: "*sa nèg fè nèg, Bondye ri sa*" (God does not care what a man does to another).[23] This *Deus otiosus* (idle god) is also found in the Lukumi pantheon of Cuba under the name of Olofin, father of heaven and earth, and Olodumare, mother of heaven and earth. These two created the *orichas*. Olofin and Olodumare cannot "ride" a *santero* (follower) or a *babalawo* (priest). Laennec Hurbon has shown that God must remain for the voodooist outside of any transaction with the human realm to remain the "Other." Man's spiritual journey is achieved through the symbolic act of *loa* worship and personal quest for harmony in the universe.[24]

In the *Rada* pantheon to which we confine our analysis, each *loa* has its corresponding Catholic saint. As already said, the slaves' African cults were first banned by the European settlers, but later black political and religious elites followed in their footsteps. Voodooists made use of the Catholic statuary to conceal their true object of worship, the *loas*. Each *Rada loa* has a tree where it lodges, an emblem, a color, specific food, function, and dance. Damballa remains the most popular *loa*, together with his wife Ayida Wedo. With his symbols the serpent and the rainbow, he is honored as a benevolent spirit, genius of fertility and rain, inhabiting mainly springs and streams. He also takes refuge in trees, but prefers cotton; he also adores eggs, a symbol of fertility, and chickens.[25] Those who want to honor him, or offer him a sacrifice, must be clad in white. Damballa and his wife bring marital success and happiness, especially with the sacrifice of a cock and a white hen.[26] The Catholic St. Patrick corresponds to Damballa, while Ayida Wedo is represented by St. Elizabeth of Hungary. Legba or Papa Legba, depicted as an old man smoking pipe with a bag slung across his shoulder, facilitates entry into the world of the *loas*. Every ritual must begin with an invocation such as "*Papa Legba louvri baryè a pou mwen pase*" (Papa Legba, open the door for me to pass).[27] A rural spirit, he lives at crossroads, and people pay tribute to him by putting tobacco, rice, and green bananas in a bag and hanging it from his favorite tree, the hog plum tree (*spondias purpurea*). A true trickster, he knows how to use deceit to manipulate the *loas*, but depending on his mood, things often turn against the disciple. He is depicted as St. Peter holding the keys of paradise, and sometimes as St. Anthony (invoked to recover lost things).[28] Erzulie Freda, the sexy mulatto goddess of love, appears in the form of the Virgin Mary (Our Lady of Sorrows), and has a pierced heart as symbol.[29] She is particularly fond of blue or pink dresses, jewelry and perfume, and has many lovers—Damballa, Ogou-Feray, and Agoué. In the *Petro* rite, Erzulie Dantò is shown in the guise of an old amazon, protector of children, also called Erzulie *yé-ruj* (red eyes), a fierce warrior equipped with a dagger.[30] She figures as Our Lady of Mount Carmel or the Black Madonna of Czestochowa. The blacksmith

Ogou Feray is the spirit of war, and lives in a calabash tree. He handles fire and iron with ease and is symbolized by a sword planted in the ground. With red as his color, he is pleased by the sacrifice of a red rooster or red kidney beans. In the Catholic tradition, he is St. James (the Greater). Baron Samdi rules, with his wife Maman Brigit, over the domain of the spirits of ancestors, the *guédé* or guides to the underworld. He inhabits the cross at the entrance to cemeteries, but also takes refuge with the *guédé* in a kapok tree (*mapou*).[31] Dressed in old clothes and a black top hat, Baron Samdi and the *guédé* disrupt the ceremonies with sexual innuendos, drinking *clairin* (strong cane spirit, less refined than rum) supplemented with *piman bouk* (habanero) to show their invincibility. There are several other secondary *loas* in the *Rada* pantheon, such as Kouzen Zaka, the guardian of agriculture, or Loko-Atisou, the spirit of vegetation, also in charge of healing the sick, the father of phytotherapy, and protector of herbalists, named in Creole *doktè fèy*.[32] Other popular spirits come from *Petro* rites, and are associated with magic and sorcery, including *Petro yé-ruj* (red eyes) and his wife Marinette (*Marinet bra-chech*), Kita, and the Simbis—Simbi dlo (Water Simbi), Simbi Makaya, Simbi Andezo (Simbi of two waters), and Grand Simba, all water gods in Kongo rituals. Alongside these *loas* exist other spirits: the tutelary spirits of the lineage, the spirits of ancestors or family *loa-rasin* (root-*loa*). For some time now, ancestor worship has tended to disappear, making way for the Voodoo pantheon. The breaking up of the traditional social structure of the extended family around a patriarch, the *lakou* (courtyard), may help explain its disappearance, as the religion turned itself into a private experience rather than a lineage ritual.[33] Probably originating from ancestor worship, but now integrated in the Voodoo pantheon, the *loa Marassa* represent twins, living or dead. Every year on January 6, families honor twins as exceptional beings with food offerings, the *Manjé-Marassa*.

Because Mother Africa was so distant, the difficulties of the slaves' daily lives meant that religious life directly addressed basic problems, survival, and resistance to oppression. This probably explains, in part, why Dahomean mythology did not survive in a narrative form, but was and still is perpetuated in rituals and dance.[34] Lilas Desquiron notes this aspect of Voodoo: slave society killed the myths, but it could not stop the body from remembering the ritual. Therefore, we can argue that Haitian Voodoo is in its essence a "danced religion" in the broadest sense, because all that survived was memorized by the body.[35]

Let us now turn to the ceremonies or the *sèvis-loa*. Voodoo rituals take place in a temple called *ounfò* (*houmfort*). Akin to an ordinary home, it must include, besides the *oungan*'s (priest) or *manbo*'s (priestess) quarters, an open shed where the public ceremony is held, the *péristil*. In the middle of the *péristil* stands an erected pillar, the *poto-mitan*, a pathway for the *loas* to descend into the human world.[36] Around the *poto-mitan*, the ground is marked with symbolic figures made out of corn flour or ashes—the *vèvè* representing the attributes of a *loa*. The *ounfò* houses the *bagui*, also called *kay mistè* (house of mysteries). This room displays on its walls the symbols of the *loas* and altars (*pé*) with crucifix, necklaces, stones, statues of saints, the *oungan*'s *asson* (sacred rattle), *govis* or jugs containing the spirits of the ancestors and *potèts* or jugs containing hair and nails belonging to *ounsis* (initiates meaning in Fon language "wives of *loas*").[37]

In Voodoo, the core of the liturgy highlights the offering or sacrifice to the *loas*, the *Manjé-Loa*. It is preceded by a preparatory rite whereby drums and songs invite the various *loas*, after the invocation to *Gran Mèt*. Drums are sacred objects symbolizing the resonant voice of the spirits. *Pè savann* (bush priest) intervenes during the liturgy to honor *Gran Mèt* and the Catholic saints, and recite the Lord's Prayer, Hail Marys, and the Apostles Creed.[38] The *Manjé-Loa* consists in purifying the sacrificial victim, usually a chicken or a goat. After that comes the address to Papa Legba, "*Louvri baryè pou mwen lò ma tuni ma remèsie ou*" (Open the gate for me, when I come back I will thank you).[39] The *loas* reveal their presence within the perimeter of the *péristil* through dances of different styles. The main *Rada* rhythms are called *yanvalou* (Fon: come to me) executed in a kneeling position, *zepol* (shoulders), and *mayi* (the Mahi of Dahomey).[40] Dancing to the beating of drums often leads to spirit possession, also known as *kriz-loa* (*loa*-crisis). During this epiphany of spirits, the *loa* "rides" the devotee, who becomes the *loa*'s mount (*loa monte chwal li*: the *loa* rides his horse). Possession, which has nothing to do with any manifestation of hysteria or mental disorder, takes the form of a liturgical drama with its own syntax.[41] The audience identifies the *loa* through gestures, words, and colors of the mount's clothing.[42] In *Manjé-Loa*, spiritual energy is sustained by the offerings of food and sacrifice to the *loa* and then communicated to the follower, who suddenly becomes capable of extraordinary things, like walking on embers.[43] To understand the importance of possession, one must understand Voodoo anthropology. The individual personality is composed of a material principle, the body or *kadav-kò*, and two supernatural principles: *gwo-bonanj* (chief guardian angel), the principle of life attached to the body, and *ti-bonanj* (little guardian angel), a more subtle and vulnerable principle, corresponding to individual consciousness and intellect, in charge of personal protection.[44] During a possession crisis, *ti-bonanj* vanishes, giving way to the *loa* dancing in the *ounsi*'s head. During an initiation, for example, the *loa mèt-tet* (master of the head) takes over the *ti-bonanj*.[45] The *Manjé-Loa* ceremony ends with the sacrifice of an animal, which is then cooked and eaten by the participants. At the end, the *guédé* often come out nowhere and spread fear.[46]

Initiation or *kanzo* has as its primary purpose the anchoring of the *loa* in the head so that the person falls under its personal protection. According to Alfred Métraux, initiation "acts as a guarantee against the tricks of fate, bad luck and above all, illness."[47] It starts with a preparatory phase during which the future initiate visits the *ounfò* regularly for a few weeks to become familiar with the rites and receive ritual baths. The second step in the ceremony is the "sleeping of the *oungnò*" (novices), during which the *oungan* or *manbo* confines the novice to the seclusion room (*djèvo*) for a week. There will be held the *potèt* ritual in which hair, nails, and body hair taken from the novice are placed.[48] The same room is also the setting for the ceremony of *lave-tèt* (washing the head) during which the disciple's hair and head are washed with an infusion of medicinal herbs and also the blood of sacrificed animals and other food offered to the *loa*. The *oungan* then proceeds to attach the *loa-tèt* firmly to the novice's head by a series of gestures and incantations. The initiation comes to completion with the ceremony of *boule-zen* with burning pots (*zen*) coated with oil. The hands and feet of new initiates are thrust into the flames as a means of purification.[49] Like many other initiation rites, the *kanzo* uses the symbolic transition from death, experienced by the initiate in the form of reclusion from the world, to rebirth into a new life, under the guardianship of a personal *loa*, purified by water and fire. A *boule-zen* ritual, similar to this one, is also practiced to mark another significant passage, death. The corpse is ritually bathed, and the *govi* containing the person's *ti-bonanj* is burned to allow him to rejoin the ancestral spirits, after having dwelled for a year on the ocean floor.[50] Funeral rites include the *Manjé-Lèmò* (eating the dead), which takes place on the anniversary of a follower's death. Food offerings are placed in a closed room to feed the spirits of the dead, something that is of paramount importance for the survival of the community, because "the cult of the dead is always a sending back of the dead, by which, paradoxically, they are recalled and reintegrated into the human community as protectors."[51] The initiate may also marry mystically with his patron *loa* during a special ceremony presided over by a *Pè savann*; this marriage may have consequences for his own sex life. Thus, if the recruit is not married and has for guardian

Erzulie, she could request that he remain single. If he is already married, he cannot have sex on Tuesdays and Thursdays.[52]

This brief discussion of Voodoo ends with some reflections on the place of magic and witchcraft in this religious system. Voodoo has often had a bad name because it is regularly associated with magic. Some do not hesitate to reject it, including Catholics and Protestants, who portray it as a satanic cult.[53] Others, like Roger Bastide, tend to oppose, on one hand, the worship of spirits in the *Rada* rite—considered as a legitimate form of religion—and, on the other hand, magical practices of Bantu origin found in the *Petro* rite.[54] In reality, the genuine nature of Voodoo probably rests somewhere between these two extremes. I agree with what Alfred Métraux says, despite the somewhat derogatory tone:

> We must take—and have taken—magic to include any manipulation of occult forces, any use made of the virtues or properties immanent in things, and in human beings and any technique through which the supernatural world becomes submissive to domination and exploitation for personal ends.
>
> Taken in this sense magic is inextricably mixed up with what people are pleased to call "the Voodoo religion."[55]

Some magical practices, called *pwen* or *paket-Congo*, seek to protect the person with charms and amulets against individual misfortunes or against evil spells—*ouanga* cast by a *bòkò* (magician) or an *oungan*. Healers, or *doktè fey*, have the ability to cure diseases with herbs and barks. Among the most powerful *ouanga* aimed at harming a person, the best known certainly is casting spells using dolls or objects belonging to the victim, a lock of hair or a piece of clothing. According to popular belief, evil spirits (*baka*) assist the *bòkò* in cursing people with disease and death. Zombification is an evil technique by which a *bòkò* captures a person's *ti-bonanj* and turns it into a *zombie* at his command. Magic and witchcraft are part of the symbolic Voodoo worldview, in which personality cannot be constructed without the necessary, although dangerous, irruption of the *loas* for protection, an impossible task for the *ti-bonanj* alone.[56]

Santería, also known as *Regla de Lucumí*, mostly stemmed from Yoruba religion brought by the slaves from Nigeria and Benin. Besides the Yoruba, slaves from diverse ethnic groups were brought to the island of Cuba from the Kongo Kingdom, the region of Calabar (Ibo and Efi), and West Africa (Bambara, Ashanti, Fulani, Hausa). In the end, historical factors may account for the predominance of Yoruba influence, including the influx of members of this ethnic group on the slave market after the collapse of their kingdom in Oyo in the early nineteenth century. The majority of slaves brought to Cuba by force between 1820 and 1840 were Yoruba. The demand for slaves grew because of the boom in sugarcane plantations, with the British occupation of 1797.[57] In Cuba, the *cabildos de nación* played a significant role in the development of Santería, as suggested by Bastide, as well as in the survival and growth of various Bantu cults from the Congo or Angola—the *Palo Monte*, sometimes called *Palo Mayombe* or *Reglas de Congo*. The Spanish colonial policy of *coartación* enabled slaves to buy their freedom after seven years and to gradually repay their master a price determined in advance. The abolition of slavery in 1880 no longer provided newcomers for the ranks of the *cabildo de nación*. In addition, rebellions and Independence Wars from the second half of the nineteenth century, and the fear of seeing the case of Haiti repeated, led to the disappearance of the *cabildo de nacion*, seen by the Europeans as a hotbed for African insurgency.[58] Thus, at the turn of the twentieth century, the *cabildos*, often created by freedmen in cities, included within their ranks a majority of *criollos* from various ethnic groups. For example, the *Cabildo Africano Lucumí* of Havana, also called *Sociedad de Santa Barbara*, despite its name welcomed some non-Yoruba followers. This new type of *cabildo*, then bearing the name *casa de ocha*[59] (*orichas'* house) or *casa de santo*, attached more importance to the priestly lineage of two orders: the *babalawos* from the *Regla de Ifá* and the *babalochas* from the *Regla de Ocha*.[60] The *babalawos* form an exclusively male brotherhood, distinguished from others by their ability to practice the Ifá method of divination. The *babalochas* (fathers of the spirits or spiritual fathers) are initiated men who can in turn train other people. This function may also be performed by women called *iyalochas* (mothers or wives of spirits).

The Lucumí pantheon and its hierarchy are not a mere replica of the Yoruba pantheon transplanted to America. Some degree of hybridization was brought into play by theorists of Afro-Cuban religion in the early twentieth century, with Catholicism or with the Greco-Roman and Egyptian mythology.[61] Olodumare is the creator of all things—gods, humans, animals and plants, and so on. In reality, to shape the universe Olodumare uses his son Obatalá, the master of all *orichas*.

Represented by an old man, he is the grand *oricha* of purity and wisdom, able to respond favorably to other *orichas*. Obatalá can take many forms (*caminos*): as women, mostly portrayed in the shape of the *Virgen de la Merced*, or as men, in the shape of Chalofon or San Manuel. Eleggua or Elegba plays the same role as Papa Legba in Voodoo.[62] A playful trickster, whose colors are red and black, he is the Infant Jesus of Atocha. He may also become a much less amicable spirit known as Echú. Next, Changó, probably an ancient Yoruba king of Oyo, embodies the god of thunder and virility, with the colors red and white. A passionate lover, he has had several women—Oya and the sexy Ochún—besides his lawful wife Oba. His symbol is the double ax, and he is associated with St. Barbara. Myth narratives (*pataki*) describe Changó's sexual prowess, even his sodomizing of his adoptive mother, Yemayá.[63] Ochún, goddess of rivers, embodies the sensual, feminine beauty and charm. She had several affairs with Ogun and Changó, while married to Orunmila. She has as distinctive emblem the yellow fan, and is often depicted as *Nuestra Senora de la Caridad del Cobre*, patron saint of the island of Cuba, known affectionately as "*la mulata*." Mistress of the sea, wearing blue, Yemayá takes the form of the *Virgen de la Regla*. Like the sea, she is considered the mother of all living beings and the goddess of fertility. She once reprimanded Changó for his uncontrolled sex drive—chasing him into the sea until he nearly drowned in the waves. He was rescued by her, after he promised to show more respect for women in the future.[64] Yemayá may also appear in a male form as Olokun, god of the deep sea, which holds the dead. Ogun, a violent warrior god, molds metal into weapons. His emblem is a machete, and his colors are green and black. He is also represented as St. Peter. Ochosi, god of the hunt, joins the warrior *orichas*, Elegba and Ogun, with the bow and arrow as his emblems. Those encountering problems with law enforcement officers invoke him. Orunmila, titular *oricha* of the Ifá divination system is the patron of *babalawos* who practice it by casting palm nuts (*ikin*) on a wooden tray—the *opón Ifá*. The tray serves as the emblem of Orunmila, whose colors are green and yellow. He is identified with St. Francis of Assisi. Babaluayé, St. Lazare, is the patron of the poor and the sick, particularly invoked to cure skin diseases. According to a myth, Babaluayé is an inveterate womanizer. He got covered with skin wounds after disobeying Orunmila, who had advised him not to make love on Thursdays so as not to offend Olodumare.[65] The champion of healers with herbs is Osain, the spirit of vegetation identified with St. Sylvester.

Though myth narratives are more salient in Santería than in Voodoo, liturgy is also central to Cuban religion. Four major festivals mark the liturgical calendar: September 8 in honor of the *Virgen de la Caridad* or Ochún, September 24 dedicated to *Nuestra*

Señora de las Mercedes or Obatalá, December 4 in honor of St. Barb or of Changó, and St. Lazare on December 17 or the Feast of Babaluayé.[66] Apart from these festivals, a special service may be required by the practitioner to acquire the distinct favor of an *oricha*, or for initiation. Santería worship displays substantially the same structure as the one described for Voodoo, with the calling of the *orichas* led by Elegba the door opener, with songs and dances unique to each *oricha* invoked, and possession (*asiento*) during which the *oricha* enters the head of the recruit (*iyawó*) and transmits its energy (*aché*), with sacrificial offerings to the *orichas*, and with a communal meal. Initiation (*kariocha*) also has a similar structure to Voodoo initiation: washing of the body, especially the head with herbs, and possession (*asiento*) during which the porcelain pot (*sopera*[67]) painted in the color of the guardian *oricha* (*oricha de cabeza, cabecera, dueño de la cabeza, angel de la guardia*) is seated on the novice's head. After a week of seclusion in la *casa de santo*, the *iyawó* is introduced to the public—often dressed in white, with neck collars (*collares de mazo*) coded to the colors of the *orichas* that descended upon him. The second day of initiation, *el dia del medio*, has distinct features not found in Voodoo liturgy. Crowned as king or queen on the ritual stool (*pilón*), a small throne located inside the house, the initiate is shown to the initiated members of the house of worship on a dais (*trono*), draped with fabric in the color of his guardian *oricha* and other *orichas* manifested during the *asiento*.[68] In Santería, confinement continues, loosely, beyond the initiation week until up to three months, during which the initiate is somewhat grounded and must remain sexually abstinent.[69] After three months, the initiate may keep the *soperas* in his house, in a special cabinet called a *canastillero*.[70]

Scholarly studies on Afro-Brazilian cults generally oppose Candomblé Nagô, derived from the Yoruba religion, to other cults grouped under the name of Umbanda, a set of practices that have more in common with witchcraft, Bantu magic—*macumba*—and Western spiritualism. Even more, ethnologists and anthropologists have often focused their research on three principal Bahian *terreiros* as the ideal expression of religious practices brought by African slaves: *Engenho Velho, Axis Opô Afonja*, and *Gantois*.[71] This view of the Afro-Brazilian religious domain, put forth notably by Roger Bastide, no longer garners consensus among researchers who increasingly point toward the interpenetration of practices from different origins.[72] Thus, many Candomblé priests interpret the *exu-egun* and *pombagiras* or the spirits of the dead in spiritualism by Africanizing them in the role of servants of the *orixás*.[73] The Umbanda got organized as a religious system only in the early twentieth century, borrowing from Western spiritualism and integrating *caboclos* (spirits of the native Indians) and *orixás* from Candomblé, as well as Catholic saints.[74]

The place where *orixás* are worshipped is called *terreiro* or Candomblé. As in Santería and Voodoo, the ethnic diversity of African slaves gave rise to different *terreiros*: Nagô, Angola/Congo also known as Batuque, Jéjé with Vodun from the Fon and Ewe people. This chapter deals primarily with Nagô. There are many similarities between the Lucumí pantheon of Cuba and the Nagô of Brazil. Olorum, the creator of heaven and earth, petitions Obatalá or Oxalá to create life on earth. The grand *orixá* of purity and light, whose color is white, he is also known as *Nosso Senhor do Bonfim*, patron of the city of Salvador. Exu, the Fon Legba, plays the mediator in human transactions and encounters and between men and *orixás*. He is, therefore, found at crossroads, in market places and on the doorstep of houses and *terreiros*.[75] His favorite instrument of negotiation remains the Ifá method of divination traditionally done with palm nuts (*opelé*), but now done with cowries (*dilogún*).[76] The *despacho* or *padê* is the ritual whereby Exu is dispatched to *orixás* to coax them with songs and offerings of water and cassava flour.[77] Exu also has a feminine shape, Pomba Gira, who represents a cynical and dangerous aspect, associated with unquenchable female sexual appetite and sexual sorcery.[78] On February 2, thousands of

Bahian celebrate in style Yemanjá, grand *orixá* of the sea and protector of sailors, *Nossa Senhora dos Navigantes*. They joyfully gather on the beach of Rio Vermelho, singing, drinking beer and *caipirinha*, and dancing to the drums. Flowers and other offerings are carried out to sea by boat and then left for the queen of waves, Yemanjá. As Oxalá's wife, she is considered the mother of all *orixás* and all living beings. Her color is blue and her *axé* (energy) resides in stones and sea shells. Oxum, Xangô's wife and goddess of fresh waters, embodies sensual love, feminine beauty, and prosperity. She is *Nossa Senhora da Candelária*. All the *terreiros* of Bahia celebrate the feast of Oxossi, praying for the healing power and protection by this warrior *orixá* living in the forest.[79] There is no need to further describe Nagô *orixás* because of their resemblance with the deities of the Cuban Lucumí pantheon, with some differences in their relationship with Catholic saints. This is especially true for Yansã, *orixá* of the wind (Oyá in Cuba) associated in Brazil with St. Barb and the cult of the dead, personified by Changó in Cuba, while the Brazilian Xangô is St. Jerome. A *babalorixá* (*pai de santo*) or a *yalorixá* (*mãe de santo*) conducts ceremonies (*obrigações*) dedicated to *orixás* and initiations (*feituras de santo*) follow much the same pattern as that observed in Santería.[80] The initiate may finally, after seven years, bring home his *orixá*'s stone (*otã*). He may then create his own *terreiro*, while remaining faithful to that of his initiation.

Sexuality and Homosexuality

Unlike the approach taken in previous chapters, sexuality and homosexuality will be dealt together in this section. Unlike other religions contemplated in this book, Afro-Caribbean and Afro-Brazilian religions did not develop texts or moral codes establishing standards for human behavior. Afro-Caribbean and Afro-Brazilizan religions believe that every individual has a personal destiny and a guardian angel watching, protecting and guiding the person in achieving a balanced life.[81] A child is born with a body, a heart, and a guiding inner principle—a guardian angel known as the head (*ori* in Yoruba religion). Problems, life hazards, and diseases are all seen as disturbances of the spiritual principle. Rituals are used to restore the pristine energy of this principle, by sacrificing to the gods. Normativity is sought through the individual's quest for equilibrium, by means of sacrifices, trances, and divination practices to discover the follower's destiny. Thus, same-sex attraction is commonly understood in terms of personal destiny, as underscored by several participants in the documentary *Des dieux et des hommes* by Haitian filmmakers Anne Lescot and Laurence Magloire (2002).[82]

The slave mode of production resulted in the separation of sexuality, conjugality, and family. Family dismemberment caused by the slave trade, which dragged individuals away from their families, lived on across the Atlantic. Slave masters provided little support for marriage and traditional family because they feared slaves would develop networks of solidarity. Male slaves outnumbered female slaves, especially in the beginning. Nonetheless, the masters' willingness to increase the number of Creole slaves shaped Afro-Caribbean and Afro-Brazilian sexuality in a definite way. A land tenure system composed of large plantations imposed mobility on rural male labor, which caused paternal absence leading to matrifocal family dynamics.[83] Urban poverty perpetuated the system, insofar as women continued to be the family cornerstone while the father relocated afar to work. Cohabitation without legal marriage, called *plasaj* in Haiti, especially in its polygynous form, has long been prevalent in the countryside: a man with some concubines (*fanm jaden*—garden spouses) living on his land, consuming and selling what they collect—he visiting them each in turn. In this system, the woman essentially assumes the role of parent, and the man's role is more or less reduced to being a provider. During the colonial period in Cuba, racism resulted in the marginalization of black women who had sex with a white man.[84] They had to raise their offspring alone. Similarly, matrifocal dynamics has certainly shaped Bahian society in a distinctive way, since Afro-Brazilian women still control small business and religion.[85] Matrifocal families coexist today with westernized nuclear families, promoted by the church or the state, but the traditional model, inherited from colonization and slavery, still has its imprint on families of African descent. I cannot further expand on this form of parenting. But awareness of its existence is indispensable for understanding the context in which religion regulates sexuality. In her reading of the cult to Erzulie Freda and Erzulie Dantò, Elizabeth McAlister skillfully synthesizes the socioeconomic conditions of matrifocality with gender, sexuality, and Haitian Voodoo.[86] According to McAlister, Erzulie Freda, often called *Metrès* (mistress), the mulatto goddess of love, evokes the Creole women of the past who fanned the passions of their white masters, and whose erotic experience was somewhat tainted by sexual servitude to the planter. Possession by Erzulie Freda is often accompanied by gestures of violence, which may be regarded as a historical reminder of these Creole women, well-dressed and perfumed, who served as prostitutes for the planters. Beautiful sexy mistresses, they never reached the level of sharing domestic life with the planter. These distant mistresses embodied frustration and revenge against the master.[87] Erzulie Freda symbolizes romantic escape from everyday life and harsh economic reality.[88]

Erzulie Dantò represents fertility, the average poor, independent Haitian woman, the struggling mother protecting her offspring. To illustrate the importance of maternal bonding, McAlister mentions this prayer to Erzulie Dantò:

> Erzulie, if your mother was dying, you would cry.
> If your husband was dying, you would find another one.
> *Ezili, si maman'w mouri, w'ap kriye.*
> *Si mari'w mouri, w'a jwenn yon lòt, O.*

Eroticism, love and seduction, fertility and motherhood are shared by the two Erzulies, a metaphor for a social reality where Haitian sexuality, eroticism, and conjugal life do not always blend in harmony. The strongest male figure in Voodoo, the warrior and blacksmith Ogou Feray identified with Sen Jak Majè (St. James the Greater), rides a rearing horse, and holds a sword in his hand.[89] As a military figure, he is associated with the struggles for liberation from slavery and protection of the people. Ogou communicates to his followers the energy of anger to encourage them in their fight against all forms of injustice: "*Jou-en kolè enryè pasa fè mwen*" (the day I am angry, nothing will happen to me); includes police exactions or abuses by civil authorities.[90]

In Cuba and Brazil, the *orichas/orixás* embrace well-defined gender roles. Ochún/Oxum represents feminine beauty and charm, while Yemayá/Yemanjá is the icon for motherhood. Changó/Xangô and Ogun/Ogum embody manhood and military power. From a liturgical point of view, however, it soon becomes apparent that male or female attributes do not always correspond to the expected anatomical sex. First, whatever their anatomical sex, all followers of Santería, Candomblé, and Voodoo are called wives (*iyawó/iyaô* and *ounsi*). During ceremonies, their minds are linked to their deities by means of mystical eroticism and sacred marriage—the highlight being expressed by the riding of the *loas* or *orichas/orixás*, which symbolically penetrate inside the initiate, as in the act of copulation. Second, the follower, regardless of his own anatomical sex, wears the insignia of the spirit riding the person. The liturgy introduces the worshipper into a world qualitatively different from the secular world, and for which a new gender configuration is required. Concerning this gender twist in possession ceremonies, McAlister had this to say:

> Through possession, the body becomes a carnivalesque body, a body witnessing an ongoing subversion of identity, marital status, and binary gender codes. Trance immediately implies "transsexuality" because the loas mount ounsis regardless of their gender. Ridden by Ogun (warrior god), the frailest of girls brandishes a machete in the air for a sword, affecting a drunkard's language, asking loud and clear for rum and flirting with the ladies present. Possessed by Erzulie Freda (equivalent of Aphrodite), the most masculine of men will apply makeup, remove his pants in favor of a dress, and with a hip swing, look languidly at the men, as he wanders among them in search of a kiss or caress.[91]

In Cuba, the *iyawó* will eagerly adopt feminine body language during an *asiento* by Ochún or Yemayá, sometimes wearing women's jewelry, but will not go as far as wearing a skirt.[92] The presence in Cuba of male-only secret societies like the Abakuá, or the persistence of the rule of Ifá prohibiting women the priesthood—both denying the presence among them of homosexuals—have possibly devaluated the feminine and inspired contempt for gender ambiguity. *Palo Monte* also shows signs of homophobia in refusing to accept homosexuals in their ceremonies.[93] In contrast, in Bahian Candomblé, which has maintained regular contact with Africa, the social and religious role of women has gained more esteem than in Cuba, and the rule of Ifá never settled down. As in Yorubaland, the follower will adopt the gender of the *orixá* riding him in the liturgy. If an *orixá* is female, the follower is clothed in dresses, and wears jewelry and perfume.[94]

Transvestism and passive homosexuality in these three Afro-based religions may derive from a tradition that existed in Yoruba religion, especially in the Kingdom of Oyo.[95] For the African American anthropologist James Lorand Matory, cross-dressing priests in Oyo, ridden by Shango, should not be decoded in sexual language. In Yoruba culture, it must be understood as a symbol for submission to the gods, the word *yiawó* (wife) referring first and foremost to a hierarchical deference to one's husband.[96] For this author, gender reversal goes beyond cross-dressing, as priests in Oyo sometimes carry water jugs on their heads, become basket weavers, or operate a small bar—all tasks normally reserved for women.[97] If Matory admits that the mounting ceremony refers to penetration in a symbolic way, possession in Yoruba culture is not understood as imitating homosexual body language, and does not mean sex between men.[98] For Matory, Yoruba gender grammar, which sometimes allows men to be known as wives to demonstrate their subordination to the king or a god, was used in the Afro-Brazilian *terreiros* in the northeast as a template to include passive homosexuals, *bichas* or *adés*, in the role of priests or *pais-de-santo* (godfathers).[99] If the presence of the *adé* today is greater in Angola or Caboclo *terreiros* than in the Nagô or Jéjé ruled by *mães-de-santo* (godmothers), men—*pais-de-santo* or *adés*—used to be present in large numbers early in the twentieth century in Nagô and Jéjé *terreiros*.[100] The *terreiro* can however be seen as a sacred site where, based on the liturgy of possession, a new gender is created, opening the way for a variety of homoerotic experiences or feelings. It is a production site for nonheternormative sexuality that can range, in the context of globalization, from the self-asserted *bicha* or *adé* to the secretive active homosexual, and to the openly gay person.[101]

The issue of African homosexuality is beyond the context of our discussion, but manifestations of denial should be noted in both the popular culture and intellectual or political elite circles. This attitude views homosexuality as a vice imported into Africa by European settlers, which was totally alien to indigenous traditions.[102] The Brazilian historian and anthropologist Luiz Mott has found evidence about African slaves condemned by the Portuguese Inquisition for sodomy—*o pecado nefando da sodomia*.[103] During a visit by the Portuguese Inquisitor in 1591, in Salvador da Bahia, a black slave, named Francisco Manicongo, was condemned for being a witch dressed in women's clothing, as well as other slaves, such as Mateus Lopes and later on Moleque.[104] The runaway slave, Esteban Montejo, reported that male slaves in Cuba, whose number exceeded that of women, lived in *barracones*, and had sex with one another. Some seem to have lived quite freely as a couple, some preparing meals for their "husbands" (*maridos*).[105] Montejo notes the absence of social stigma by observing that the "*afeminado*" emerged after the abolition of slavery. The existence of homosexual relations in slave barracks cannot constitute conclusive evidence of male same-sex relations in their societies of origin. In ancient tales written by travelers and missionaries, two perceptions of the reality of men who have sex with men may be found. Some see it as a perversion brought by the settlers, as shown in the official report of the Portuguese inquisitor in charge of investigating the numerous acts of sodomy by the governor of Cape Verde in the seventeenth century, Cristóvão Cabral.[106] Mott is probably right when he attributes the origin of the myth of the absence of homosexual relations in precolonial Africa to the colonial perspective of the primitive Negro endowed with such a bestial sexuality that he dares not go against what nature dictates—understood here as heterosexuality. Others, like the Capuchin friar Giovanni Antonio Cavazzi of Montecuccolo (1621–1678), who wrote a history of the Kingdom of Kongo and Angola, reported that transvestite sorcerers practiced sodomy.[107]

Moreover, several studies show the existence of homosexual relations in some traditional African societies, especially among the Fon and the Hausa.[108] The case of the Hausa in northern Nigeria is particularly interesting because of the existence of a possession cult, called *bori*, and because the Hausa are probably the originators of the equestrian symbolism of riding (mounting) in the Yoruba religion.[109] The *bori* cult is practiced by the Muslim Hausa and the Maguzawa, people of Northern Nigeria, over which the Hausa have historically exercised political and cultural domination. This pre-Islamic cult originated among the Maguzawa—a liturgy mainly focused on the possession of women and "men who talk like women" (*yan daudu*)—the mares of the gods.[110] Several authors state that the *yan daudu* have sex with men, but a careful analysis of the role they play in Hausa society does not work in favor of an interpretation that would make their sexual preferences the main reason for their adhesion to this lifestyle.[111] Within the male dominant Hausa culture, the *bori* cult provides for marginal expression of greater freedom for Maguzawa women. On the other hand, divorced Hausa women live together on the outskirts of the walled city (*birni*) with non-Muslim foreigners, under the guidance of an older woman (*maigijiya*), and earn their living by selling sexual services to men, following an ancestral tradition of "courtisanerie" called *karuwanci*.[112] The *yan daudu* live with prostitutes or courtesans, the *kurawai*, in an environment where Islamic moral pressure is weaker. They often take on women's jobs such as running small snack bars, but their main economic activity is to serve as go-betweens for the *kurawai* and their male clients. The *yan daudu* are perceived in the community as men, but their effeminate behavior and their reputation as men having sex with men make of them ideal go-betweens. Since they act like women, they do indeed interact with women without difficulty but at the same time, they bring to the margins of mainstream society male control over these women, without being perceived as rivals by men. Gender ambiguity and the fact that they live with women facilitate sexual contact between them and the men (*maza*) who do their business with other men (*masu harka*), that is to say, men who sexually prefer men.[113]

It remains difficult to determine with absolute certainty the origin of the presence of men who transgress gender dimorphism and claim a cultural space outside the moral code of the dominant society, whether Islamic, as in the case of the *yan daudu*, or Christian, as in the case of the *masisi* of Haiti, the Cuban *afeminado*, and the Brazilian *bicha*. However, I certainly rule out a model of analysis of Afro-Caribbean and Afro-Brazilian cults like the one proposed by I. M. Lewis, who suggests that possession cults of African or other origin were created to attract victims of discrimination—women and other marginalized individuals—viewing them as mediums able to express their grievances about social structures validated by a dominant religious system.[114] People taken or driven by their desire to express sexual feelings that deviate from heterosexual norms or gender dimorphism may feel at home within these cultic groups. As tempting as it may seem, this interpretation cannot, at any rate, apply to African American possession cults, as their symbolic structure aims at making sense of everyday life for the whole society, and not just specifically for marginalized groups.[115]

In all cases, either due to symbolic mounting, or due to the gender reversal required in the hierophany of female *orichas* (*orixás*), Ochún/Oxum or Yemayá/Yemanjá, for example, women or effeminate homosexuals (*afeminados, adés, masisis*) prove to be an ideal channel or medium.[116] Cameroonian sociologist Charles Gueboguo defines this type of homosexuality as "defined through gender."[117] In this particular context, homosexuals are not readily seeking to identify themselves as persons consciously attracted to the same sex, as opposed to heterosexuals, or as having a homosexual orientation. The symbolic structure of possession rituals and myths rather serves as an index of a social organization that developed in parallel, or in opposition to the dominant model of strict Christian monogamous and patriarchal values. Thus, several stories and dances do celebrate heterosexuality but certainly not in its Christian form. Ogou was ruined by his numerous mistresses.[118] Xangô had three wives, Yansã, Oxum, and Oba. Oxum did not hesitate to repudiate Oba, his lawful wife, when he learned that, mad with jealousy, she consulted with Oxum to find out how she drew Xangô in bed so easily.[119] The *oricha* of lightning and war, Changó concentrates his strength in his genitals, and this flowing energy is expressed by movements lowering the arms raised to heaven and pointing them to his genitals.[120] The dances and songs in honor of the most popular *loa*, Erzulie Freda, queen of feminine beauty and seduction, plainly imitate the sexual act itself, as is expressed in the song: "*Ezuli map dodoyé-zo.*"[121] A song addressed to Kouzen Zaka shows this spirit of agriculture being blamed for losing his mind when he abandons a respectable woman to live with tramps "*ou vlé kité fam dé bien pou al viv ak al vagabon Cousen Zaka ou enrajé.*"[122] Here, even the *loa* seems incapable of living up to higher ethical standards because he embraces the reality of Haitian peasant social structure, marked by *lakou*, and for historical or economic reasons he may have, in addition to his *fanm kay* (housewife), a *fanm jaden*. Rita Laura Segato wrote about irony in Candomblé, used as a tool to subvert the patriarchal model. In my opinion, this strategy can be extended to Santería and Voodoo without any problem. Like Kouzen Zaka or Ogou, Yemanjá, the great symbol of motherhood, also abandoned her children, who were brought up by Oxum, the childless goddess of fertility![123] The cult of Pomba Gira, whose sexual appetite seems insatiable, symbolizes the search for sexual pleasure outside the reproductive monogamous model. Here, obviously it is the woman who controls male sexuality. Pomba Gira left her husband and killed her offspring.[124] Gender ambiguity also inoculated a healthy dose of irony and criticism into the dominant social model. This ambiguity is manifested by cross-dressing during the mounting ceremony but also by the androgyny of certain spirits. The *orixá* Logunedé, son of Oxum and Oxossi, spends six months of the year as a hunter in the forest and lives six months in the body of a beautiful river nymph.[125] La Siren, a *loa* of the sea and Agoué's wife, forms an androgynous pair with La Balen, an avatar of Olokun, a male *loa* of the ocean depths paired with Yemayá.[126] Lachateñeré understands Changó, Obatalá, and Yemayá as hermaphrodite *orichas* because they appear in both forms, male and female. In fact, they are paired consorts who, on the one hand, express as a couple the fullness of the divine and who, on the other hand, may possess any follower of both genders by adapting to the follower's gender. The *afeminados* can sometimes identify with a male such as Changó. Chased by Ogun, he disguised himself to escape from her by wearing his wife's (Oya) clothes. Obatalá has female avatars, Oshanlá (Orishanla) and Obanlá.[127] Guédé Nibo, son of Baron Samdi and Maman Brigit Samdi, is perhaps hermaphrodite[128] and takes pleasure in anal penetration.[129] These phallic spirits are especially fond of *la betiz* (coarse language of a sexual nature) and, during ceremonies, simulate intercourse, homosexual or heterosexual, often with a *zozo* (penis) made of wood. Gender subversion and plasticity do not appear to be directly related to the believer's sexual preference; at most, they allow in a protected cultic environment for greater tolerance vis-à-vis this behavior where gender is not compatible with anatomical sex.

The sacred metamorphosis of gender found in Voodoo and Yoruba-inspired cults provided an opportunity for people with same-sex attraction to express themselves, and even rule over houses of worship. However, the only identity model available remains confined to the passive and effeminate homosexual male. Such a display of tolerance for sexual ambiguity does not translate into general social acceptance of homosexuality. Ketu *terreiros* remain on the whole less open-minded about allowing visibility to gay followers, afraid of losing adepts. Luis Felipe Rios comes to that conclusion after observing *veados* (*viados*[130]) taking over the streets of Rio de Janeiro, during the festival dedicated to Yemanjá on February 2.[131]

Brazil probably has a more liberal approach to homosexuality than Cuba or Haiti. Emperor Dom Pedro I sanctioned the Penal Code in 1830, which decriminalized homosexual acts. In reality, several other provisions in this legislation relating to public decency and vagrancy allowed the arrest of men having sex with men.[132] The medicalization of homosexuality, which first appeared in Europe, soon made its appearance in Brazil, during the last quarter of the nineteenth century. The thesis presented at the University of Rio, in 1872, by the physician Francisco Ferraz de Macedo is a striking example of this new trend. The jurist, Francisco José Viveiros de Castro, and the physician, José Ricardo Pires de Almeida, took up the medical approach. Sometimes adopting the etiological model of congenital sexual inversion, or at times emphasizing the social causes of male prostitution, their descriptions pinpoint the proliferation of homosexual encounters in Rio, either in brothels, boarding houses, or in public places—Praça Tiradentes or the Theatro São Pedro de Alacântara.[133] Praça Tiradentes was a popular park well frequented with what Viveiros de Castro named *frescos*—effeminate dandies seeking sexual partners or prostitutes. Afro-Brazilian journalist and essayist João Rio (João Paulo Cristóvão dos Santos Coelho Emilio Barreto, died in 1921) cleverly described the world of these nightwalkers.[134] It also became an easy target for mockery in the satirical magazine *O Malho* (The Sledgehammer). In its series of *Contos Rapidos*, the *Rio Nu* journal published in 1914 a homoerotic tale, *O Menino do Gouveia* (Gouveia's Boy), the story of the young Bembem meeting Gouveia, an older man—a *fanchono*—who initiated him to sex in the Largo do Rossio.[135] Bembem was portrayed as a passive homosexual, as suggested by the author's description of the boy experiencing orgasm without erection, when Gouveia fondled his breasts. Afro-Brazilian novelist Adolfo Caminha published *Bom Crioulo* in 1895, in which a runaway slave, Amaro, enlisted in the navy and became acquainted with a young apprentice, Aleixo, with blue eyes. Amaro is described as a handsome, muscular *fanchono*, whose passion for Aleixo leads him to murder. The two have sex at sea, but things eventually go wrong in their love nest in Rua da Misecordia. Aleixo falls in love with their landlady, Carolina, causing Amaro's raging jealousy, which ultimately drags him to kill his young lover. In the 1930s, influenced by Doctor Leonido Ribeiro's work, which attributed homosexuality to hormonal causes, Brazilian society considered homosexuals as perverts and criminals. They either had to be imprisoned, or treated in mental health institutions.[136] Despite the social stigma, an entire subculture continued to grow around Praça Tiradentes, but also settled in Copacabana where some gay bars opened in the 1950s.[137] Rio de Janeiro's carnival has become an opportunity for *bichas* to come out, in balls and parades, extravagantly dressed as women.

In November 1995, Bill N. 1151 on the recognition of civil unions between same-sex partners was submitted to the Federal Chamber of Deputies of Brazil, but it has never been adopted. However, various legislative measures to protect the rights of homosexuals against discrimination and homophobia were adopted by state authorities (Bahia, Federal District, Minas Gerais, Paraíba, Rio de Janeiro, Rio Grande do Sul, Santa Catarina, and São Paulo).[138] In May 2004, the Brazilian government, in collaboration with the Brazilian gay movement, launched a program to fight against homophobia, implemented by the National Council against Discrimination, *Programa Brasil Sem Homofobia*. However, this relatively high-leveled legal protection does not always prevent actual discrimination against homosexuals, and some observers, including Amnesty International, or the *Grupo Gay da Bahia*, condemn the violence against gays. More than 100 homicides in 2007 and 190 in 2008 were committed against homosexuals.[139] President Luiz Inácio Lula da Silva launched the First National Conference of GLBT (gay, bisexual, lesbian, and transgendered) by presidential decree, and promised at the opening in June 2008 that he would criminalize homophobia. He lashed out directly at the Catholic discourse on homosexuality. In May 2011, Dom Maurício José Araújo de Andrade, primate of the Episcopal Anglican Church of Brazil, supported the recent decision by the Brazilian Federal Supreme Court to approve same-sex civil unions.[140] However, the court's judgment was strongly criticized by Robinson Cavalcanti, bishop of the Anglican diocese of Recife, which severed from the Episcopal Anglican communion on the issue of same-sex relationships and became affiliated with the Anglican Church of the Southern Cone. The Catholic Church also protested against the judgment, but the greatest opposition will probably come from Pentecostal Churches, such as the Assemblies of God (*Assembleias de Deus*) and the Universal Church of the Kingdom of God (UCKG, from *Igreja Universal do Reino de Deus*), known for their antigay preachings.

In Cuba, repression of homosexual acts dates back to colonial times during which offenders were referred to the Spanish Inquisition. Slaves sometimes used denunciation of the *pecando nefando* to buy their freedom.[141] In the seventeenth century, a capitán general burned some 20 effeminate men, but more often the men accused of this vice were exiled to a small island in the Bay of Havana, known as Cayo Puto (masculine form of whore).[142] The struggle for independence, marked by the Ten Years' War (1868–1878) and the War of Independence (1895–1898), shaped the character and national identity, including the social perception of masculinity. Making war is manly business, meant for genuine, virile heterosexual men, and not for effeminate men—*maricones*.[143] There are exceptions to the rule. Capitán Manuel Rodríguez, nicknamed la *brujita* (little witch) in Espiritu Santo, was known as a crazy and effeminate character, who could also turn into a fierce lion on the revolutionary battlefield.[144] The general ambience of the time is given by poet and national hero José Martí, especially in his reply to an article in the March 6, 1889, Philadelphia newspaper *The Manufacturer*, in which Republican politicians questioned the relevance of Cuba's annexation to the United States, given the lack of courage and manliness of Cubans. Martí's answer ascribed to Spanish rule a certain degree of feminization of men in Cuban cities.[145] Nation and heroic masculinity create a distinctive combination, which must not tolerate any kind of gender ambiguity and deviation from heterosexual normativity. While defending the merits of revolutionary men, the poet remains on the defensive. He is aware, for sure, of an existing group of *maricones* with its own venues and code of conduct. Historian Abel Sierra Madero described this Havana subculture populated by strange creatures: "Women from the belt up, men from the waist down; but neither men nor women from head to feet."[146] Cuban medicine, influenced by its European counterpart, also contributed to the stereotyping of the *afeminado*, especially with the work of physician Benjamin Céspedes, published in 1889 under the title *La prostitución en La Habana*.[147] The book alludes to a boarding house lodging Spanish foreign workers—*los dependientes*—where they indulged in homosexual acts.[148] It is probable that the good doctor was a proud nationalist who was trying to suggest that homosexuality came from abroad and was not indigenous to the island, but his testimony cannot be set aside on behalf of a mere rhetorical device. Moreover, Pedro Giralt y Aleman's reply confirmed the presence of homosexual encounters in Havana, at the turn of the twentieth century. Giralt also denounced the hypocrisy present in Céspedes's views by showing that the *maricones*' customers were from the Creole bourgeoisie of the island![149] Early-twentieth-century Cuban literature did not hesitate to address homosexual themes, often heavily influenced by medicine. This is especially true of Alfonso Hernández Catá's novel *El Ángel de Sodoma*, published in 1928. The novel tells the tragic story of José María, struggling with his homosexual desires, hoping to defeat them by being exceedingly macho. When he finally decides to follow his feelings, he leaves his small town to lead a new life in Paris. There, he receives a letter from his family, informing him of his Brother Jaime's death, who also had left home for a better future. He feels immediately and inescapably caught up by his past, and tragically takes his own life under the wheels of a subway train before ever having his first homosexual experience.[150] In the first half of the twentieth century, despite social stigma and the marginalization of *maricones*, partly because of a law on public decency in 1938, which banned all homoerotic expression in public,[151] a homosexual underground, often linked to prostitution, certainly existed. It even made of Cuba a Mecca for gay tourism during President Fulgencio Batista's era.[152]

The postrevolutionary period was marked by a nationalist and Marxist discourse that sought to eliminate society of all forms of social deviance. Homosexuals were seen as the product of capitalism, or agents of imperialism. In the 1960s and 1970s, the state engaged in a real hunt for homosexuals, and many sought exile to avoid internment in reeducation camps, located in the region of Camaguey—the *Unidades Militares Ayuda a la Producción*.[153] The witch hunt was based on profiling (*para-métraje*), and chucked out anything that deviated from the communist social model.[154] Many intellectuals and artists whose homosexuality was known lost their jobs in education and culture. They were sometimes imprisoned, such as writer Rainaldo Arenas, author of the autobiographical novel *Antes que anochezca* (Before Night Falls), written during his incarceration from 1974 to 1976. Other notable authors, such as Virgilio Piñera and José Lezama Lima, were also persecuted and imprisoned. What seemed to hurt the government further was not homosexuality as such but the claims made for homosexuality as a locus for dissent and freedom. This seems even more apparent in *Paradiso* by Lezama Lima, published in 1966. Here, homosexuality and poetry symbolize freedom, while socialist revolutionary values are totally absent.[155] Any literary work with a homosexual theme was subject to state censorship, especially after 1971, at the First National Congress of Culture and Education. It enacted the pathological nature of homosexuality and the consequent refusal to provide financial assistance for homosexual artists, so they would not be in a position to represent Cuban values for the Cuban public, on the island or overseas.

Several factors help explain a greater openness of the Castro regime from the 1980s: economic difficulties leading to further development of international tourism, the need to fight effectively against HIV, given the failure of quarantine policies and reports from abroad of human rights violations, reports coming from exiled gays primarily. From the 1980s, police repression in public places visited by homosexuals became infrequent, sign of a new government position.[156] In 1979, the Cuban government decriminalized same-sex acts by consenting persons, aged 16 and over. In 1988, it revoked the penal provisions relating to public displays of homosexuality. Released in 1993 in Cuba, the popular film *Fresa y chocolate* by Cuban director Tomás Guiterrez Alea became a landmark in this new policy of openness. Free from any frontal attack on the Castro regime and its abuses vis-à-vis homosexuals, the film portrays Diego, an open homosexual who loves his island. He enters into conversation with young David, a hard-nosed member of the Communist Youths, who is startled by Diego's effeminate manners. Diego introduces David to a whole body of Island literature banned by censorship, which leads the young man to adopt a more critical perspective, and eventually leave Cuba, during the exodus of 1980. During that year, 125,000 Cubans left for Florida from the port of Mariel. Economic difficulties of the day had brought 10,000 islanders to take refuge at the Embassy of Peru, and the government adopted the policy of letting those homosexuals who wanted to leave to do so. Writer Reinaldo Arenas left the Island, along with many other homosexuals. Nowadays, homosexuals meet in bars, cafes, and restaurants without necessarily the risk of being harassed or arrested by police.[157] The *Centro Nacional d'Educación Sexual* (CENESEX), headed by Fidel's niece Mariela Castro Espín, daughter of President Raúl Castro, includes sexual diversity in its program on national sex education.[158] CENESEX demands constitutional changes to establish legal protection against discrimination based on sexual orientation.[159] Since 2008, it organizes, with state support, the World Day against Homophobia, held annually on May 17. A bill recognizing same-sex marriage is under review at the National Assembly since 2007. In 2008, the Catholic archbishop of Havana Cardinal Jaime Ortega Alamino denounced the government's intention to recognize same-sex unions and its liberal approach to sex education.[160]

To my knowledge, no systematic research on homosexuality in Haiti has ever been done. Besides the documentary film by Lescot and Magloire, *Des dieux et des hommes*, the only available and reliable source remains a study conducted by the *Panos Caribbean Institute*, with headquarters in Port-au-Prince.[161] Panos' work demonstrates that there are many ways in Haiti for homosexuality to exist. As elsewhere, married men occasionally have sex with men, including prostitutes. They do not identify as homosexual, unlike the *masisi* or the effeminate homosexual. The *masisi* does not conceal his sexual preferences, and often plays a social role traditionally assigned to women, such as vendor in the markets controlled by women. Many youths engage in prostitution with men for economic reasons, with both native islanders and tourists. Some theories attributed the spread of AIDS in the USA to gay tourism, flourishing in Haiti in the 70s and 80s.[162]

Lescot's film well illustrated the social stigma suffered by the *masisi*. Nicknames are often attached to them that speak volumes about the rejection they experience: *makomè, de sis cole, bouzen, lougawou, lapli sou kay*.[163] A *Rara* song evokes in *la betiz* (coarse language) the paradox of homophobia in Haitian society, in which rejection and recognition of sexual pleasures of men having sex with men is combined: "*Chawonj! Masisi pi dous* [Rubbish! Masisi is softer] / *Chawonj! Masisi pi dous.*"[164] Popular opinion often attributes homosexuality, especially in the *masisi*'s case, to the workings of a *loa*, mainly Erzulie Dantò, who chooses for herself a young male boy for a mystical marriage.[165]

In Voodoo, supernatural fate imposes a form of passive acceptance of homosexuality, despite the presence of homophobia in society. Christians, especially Evangelicals, work hard at dislodging popular beliefs. Gregory Toussaint, a Haitian American pastor of the Tabernacle of Glory Church based in Miami, travels regularly to Haiti to exorcise the spirit of Erzulie Dantò, whom he declares to be the cause for debauchery and fornication on the island! Despite pervasive homophobia, in 2008, a group of young HIV-positive homosexuals marched and demonstrated in the streets of St. Marc, located one hundred kilometers from the capital. They all wore t-shirts on which was inscribed "*mwem se masisi*" (I'm gay). However, the January 2010 earthquake has had a significant impact on the *masisis* of Port-au-Prince. Many of them have been victims of sexual abuse or rape in the camps for displaced persons, and many have suffered verbal abuse or have been denied food for being homosexual. *Masisis* have also been blamed for incurring the wrath of God and causing the earthquake because of their sins.[166]

Conclusion

I wanted to include this chapter because currently most African governments adopt open homophobic policies and support repressive laws in respect of homosexuality. Most of the time their leaders justify their methods of operation by the fact that homosexuality is an evil imported by colonization, without any roots in African traditions. While not entirely African, Afro-based religions in Cuba, Haiti, and Brazil draw their ancient origins from Africa. The study of these religious systems demonstrates that sexual relations between persons of the same sex are symbolically legitimized in the liturgy of possession. The worship place becomes a venue for the expression of sexual variance through dance and dress codes. Although the gender fluidity expressed in some rituals and in the rare myths allows a certain reception of same-sex attraction in the community, it also tends to reinforce sexual stereotyping, which incites social stigma. The tension may well be felt by gay rights supporters in the countries concerned, a topic to be discussed in the final conclusion.

General Conclusion

I hope the word "diversity" will remain in the minds of the readers; diversity, not only in sexual fantasies and practices but first and foremost in the different ways cultural and religious systems picture sexuality and gender. The multiplicity of codes offers a rich mosaic that is part of the living heritage of humanity. It should help us understand how societies have shaped human sexuality through the ages and across space, but also allow us to put in context the position of each tradition in relation to the other. Unfortunately, many historical events have caused religion to be associated with intolerance as far as homosexuality is concerned. However, homosexuality concerns human behavior after all and has nothing to do with the nature of the divine, so why dig one's heels in absolute viewpoints. Why not try to understand instead of condemning and why not borrow from the valuable lessons of others?

We are in an era of globalization, which often appears as one dimensional, that is to say, the same model tends to impose itself everywhere. However, a closer look at what is truly happening in some emerging economies (China and India, for example) shows new structures being superimposed on old ones without necessarily destroying them and new social economic models emerge with local flavor. Global circulation of information through television, music, movies but also increasingly in the Internet has profoundly changed people's attitudes toward sexuality everywhere in the world. Through globalization, greater permissiveness and hedonism are promoted. Who would have predicted not long ago that countries, with traditionally macho cultural values like Uruguay, Brazil, and Argentina, would finally recognize same-sex marriage? Without any doubt, legal recognition of civil unions, or even in some cases of same-sex marriages, as in Canada and various European countries, as well as the protection of the rights of homosexuals against discrimination in these countries have had a ripple effect on other societies. Nothing, however, suggests that the Western model of sexual orientation based on the sex of the individual's sexual desire will prevail throughout the world. Other forms of homosexual experience, which do not necessarily seek to identify the sexual actor with his homosexual impulses, will continue to exist, as the *panthi* of India, or all those men who have sex with male prostitutes, for example, the *kathoey* in Thailand, the *masisi* in Haiti, or the *bicha* in Brazil. Many men will continue to relate to a model that blends homosexuality with gender identity and assign them to a "third sex," such as the *hijra*, the *masisi*, *bicha*, or *kathoey*. The Western reductionist model could modify this rich diversity of nonheterosexual experiences or what might be called queer sexuality, that is, any form of sexuality or gender that is resistant to normative patterns. Thus, a queer theory of Indian sexuality would still leave room for traditional notions such as *hijra* or *tritiya prakriti*, which encompasses concepts related to transsexuality, bisexuality, homosexuality, hermaphroditism, or transgender. Several sexual experiences described in the previous chapters shatter the dimorphic and the hetero/homo binomial concepts to which, at least in the West, sexuality and gender are usually confined. The study of different religious traditions invites us to go beyond these borders and cross into unfamiliar territory.

The sacred space tends to exclude sexuality often considered as an obstacle to spiritual self-achievement. This trend occurs primarily in world-renouncing religions to facilitate union with the divine or enlightenment, which will eventually end suffering and the cycle of rebirths. In this context, sexual abstinence becomes the emblem for the individual's quest for spiritual perfection. This approach to spirituality strongly marked Theravada Buddhism and Christianity, especially in its Roman Catholic form, for whom religious or monastic life signals a higher level of spiritual perfection. Other religious systems have found a way not to eliminate but to relax the tension between sex impulses and the ideal of perfection. Hinduism has devised its view of the four stages of life, thus leaving some time for a person to experience sexuality. The Protestant Reformation opposed monastic asceticism. It valued marriage and offered a new approach to Christian perfection, which consisted in obeying God's commands in everyday, ordinary life and ignoring the exacting demands of celibacy.[1] Mahayana Buddhism also offers a model of perfection accessible to laymen with a much less ascetic view of sexuality.

Islam does not rate sexuality among the barriers to spiritual life and even includes it in its vision of the afterlife. Judaism conceives of sexuality within the covenant with God, ensuring the survival of God's people. Human love is used as a metaphor for the covenant. However, the love of God toward his people is described as a jealous passion that excludes any other form of worship. This probably explains the ferocity with which the prophets attacked cultic expressions of neighboring peoples who deified various expressions of sensuality, including same-sex practices. In fact, both Orthodox Judaism and Islam severely condemn homosexual anal penetration, because according to them, it undermines masculinity. A suspected violation of gender boundaries certainly seems to be the source of all their concern because it leaves an area where the relationship between gender and anatomical sex gets blurred. Homosexuality somehow clouds the issue of strict gender boundaries in a society where the segregation of men and women is essential. Gender segregation might explain why gay Iranians willingly agree to a solution as drastic as reconstructive surgery. In such a society, you are either man or woman, there is no in-between, and a sex change opens the door to having sex with a partner without the danger of persecution by the state. In Orthodox Judaism, the only valid expression of sexuality remains marriage between a man and a woman, a rigid approach that leaves homosexuals in the Orthodox Jewish communities, especially among the Hasidim, to suffering and abandonment. In societies or cultures marked by strict gender codes, the other side of the coin is that homosocialization often favors open homoerotic expressions. I found this situation to be present in the Jewish world, especially among the Sephardim of Andalusia or the Hasidim of Eastern Europe, but still more in the Muslim world. Paradoxically, social segregation of the sexes in Islamic environment, especially in Persia and during the Ottoman Empire, opened the door to gender ambiguity in ephebophilia, where androgyny becomes the canon of beauty. This passion for the beauty of young male bodies has found its spiritual expression in gazing at the beauty of a young, beardless Adonis transformed into a spiritual technique that is deemed capable of elevating the soul to God. Usually, when they came in contact with Western civilization and were colonized, these cultures attempted to establish a new canon of beauty, the feminine, and tried to get rid of more ambiguous expressions of gender by establishing a binary model of gender and marginalizing any behavior that clashed with it, which came to be known as perversion.[2]

The love of boys in the Arab-Persian Muslim culture is not the only example of the intervention of homosexual desires and practices in the sacred space through gender ambiguity. In India, where the sacred is everywhere, we must never lose sight of the fact that the *Kama Sutra* figures as a holy book, which has nothing to do with titillating pornography. However, its mapping of sexuality and gender crosses the boundaries of the typical male and female pair engaged in heterosexual intercourse. Gender fluidity often found in Hindu mythology was also transposed in the expression of certain devotees, such as Ramakrishna or with some Krishna sects. The concept of a third sex or gender confirms sexual ambiguity or nonconformity and legitimates public demonstration of sexual variance, especially during religious festivals.

Without developing a theory of the third sex, Afro-Caribbean and Afro-Brazilian religions create a sacred space where sexual difference can be expressed freely in dance and music through the event of "mounting" by the spirits and the mystical union of the believer with his guardian angel spirit. As in the case of Hinduism, these religious experiences should not be referenced as ritualized homosexuality, such as practiced, for example, by the Sambias of Papua-New Guinea or other peoples of Melanesia.[3] Both in Haiti and Cuba or Brazil, homosexual relations, like heterosexual relations, are not part of any religious rite. However, the symbolism of possession and spiritual marriage in Santería, Candomblé, and Voodoo is perfectly permeable to gender transgression in the worship space. The syncretic character of these religions is again operating in their capacity to include men who have sex with men and who would otherwise be socially rejected. Not all Brazilian men have access to the westernized global gay community, but it is possible for those who cannot to celebrate their difference openly in their temples or even on the streets.[4]

It should be clear by now that religious systems do not treat every same-sex experience in the same way. Hinduism and Afro-Caribbean and Afro-Brazilian religions, in their own way, embed same-sex relations in their religious world and the men who practice it are given some sort of legitimacy, one that civil society often continues to deny. Many Christian churches in North America and Europe, as well as some Liberal and Conservative Jewish groups, have developed a new hermeneutics of homosexuality, after acknowledging the acceptance of civil rights for homosexuals. In some cases, this new vision goes beyond mere acceptance and extends to homosexual unions and celebration of same-sex marriages. The Catholic Church objects to it and continues to define homosexuality as a disorder of nature. The compassion it would sometimes like to express toward homosexuals does not seem to be imbued with genuine sincerity. Besides, its alleged sincerity is seriously challenged by the determination of ecclesiastical authorities to hide or ignore sex scandals involving members of its clergy. Some Muslims also believe that an inclusive hermeneutics of homosexuality is possible, but this remains to be done.[5] The majority of Muslim jurists acknowledge that the Qur'an does not explicitly provide punishment for sodomy, and that the hadiths that do provide for it do not seem genuine. Though many traditionists adhere to the same hadith, unfortunately, they do not dare to use reflection (*ijtihad*), a source of law recognized by the discipline of legal interpretation, to explore new avenues. A younger generation of specialists in Islamic studies does come out and propose new avenues of interpretation. Islamologist Scott Sirajul Haq Kugle, an American convert and openly gay, suggests as research hypothesis that the sayings of the Prophet's Companions on sexual acts between men do not belong to the Sunna of the Prophet. The cultural context often pressured jurists to include sodomy in the Sharia, a culture that considered women and homosexuals to be inferior to the straight man.[6] New Western perceptions of homosexuality and gay rights owe their success, in part, to the feminist struggle against gender inequalities and stereotypes affecting gender. One will probably not happen without the other in the Muslim world and among Orthodox Jews. The feminist Islamic scholar Kecia Ali thinks the fear of marriage between persons of the same sex is related to the fact that it calls into question all existing contractual structure in the current Muslim marriage, which defines the rights in accordance with the sex of the spouses, leaving to the husband control over the union and the exclusive power to unilateral repudiation of the wife.[7]

Finally, we must look ahead to the future bearing in mind that both religious and civil debates about homosexuality are not over, even in Europe or America, where equality rights are better protected. Reflection must continue on an open and undogmatic basis, on both sides. Societies are increasingly becoming ethnically and culturally diverse. Managing diversity and freedom is not easy. There is an urgent need for all religious systems, to distinguish what is rooted in the culture from the core teachings of religion. The recent debate in France over the books and statements made by the well-known Islamic scholar Tariq Ramadan offers a compelling example of the difficulty of discussing these issues. He advocates "living together" in a space where European Islam can grow and access modernity through *ijtihad* without abandoning its fundamental principles. His identity claims seem outrageous to secular Republicans. His vision of things, generous at times, also suffers from ambiguity. Thus, confronted with the issue of homosexuality, he declares his steadfast adherence to Islam and endorses the traditional condemnation of homosexuality while expressing respect for homosexuals. His position is reminiscent of the Catholic Church's position: no judgment about the person but no endorsement of the act.[8] He opposes sanctions against homosexuals and rejects any form of homophobia. How can one say "I accept you as a person, but I reject that which is your innermost self?" The problem may be that Tariq Ramadan has not strictly applied his methodology to the issue of homosexuality because real critical thinking in this regard is clearly missing. Homophobia varies from one tradition to another and may vary according to time periods within any particular religious system. Making use of Gale Rubin's "ideological formations," such as "sex negativity," "hierarchical valuation of sex acts," "domino theory of sexual peril," and "benign sexual variation" may provide a clearer explanation of the degree of homophobia present in a given cultural context.[9] For instance, "sex negativity" is more present in the history of Christianity and its theology. Certainly more than in Islam, Judaism, and Hinduism, for instance, where celibacy is not valued at all or restricted to certain stages of life. The concept of "benign sexual variation" certainly lends itself to Hindu and Buddhist religious life. This is manifest in the phenomenon of *dosti* or friendships between young unmarried Hindu males, which is considered as an excusable sexual outlet before marriage. Moreover, procreation is certainly a priority once the person enters into the second stage of life but it does not govern sexual practices between partners. Buddhism is little concerned about procreation and nonprocreative sexual acts. What directs personal sexual conduct has nothing to do with a purported "naturalness" of sexual acts; the real measure to evaluate the morality of any type of sexual conduct resides in how it prevents one from extinguishing pleasure or committing actions that are detrimental to others, because they break harmony in the family or society, or because they are nonconsensual (rape, violence). Homosexual acts may be judged in this context "benign variations," compared to adultery and violent sexual acts. I would certainly argue, with nuance, that a culture with a high degree of "sex negativity," combined with a "hierarchical valuation of sex acts" that legitimates sex for procreation only, tends to be more homophobic than others, especially those that make room for the concept of "benign sexual variation." The most visible marker of homophobia emerges within the context of "domino theory of sexual peril." According to Rubin, this theory implies that there is bad and good sex entrusted with social respectability. Bad sexuality, such as prostitution, homosexuality, or masturbation, creates social chaos because it threatens the entire society. If the state fails to respond and lets it happen, youth, family, and the nation will be destroyed. This kind of thinking has emerged mainly in the West, following the industrial revolution and urbanization. Few examples can be traced back before this period. Among them, ancient Judaism should be mentioned, with its ban on male cultic prostitution or passive anal homosexual relations understood as imported practices threatening Israel's covenant with God. In seventeenth-century China, the Qing code sought to protect Confucian family values by criminalizing sexual acts between men. Peter Damian's *Liber Gomorrhianus* may be related to the domino theory as it claimed that the vice of sodomy among unworthy priests was the ruin of the people. In many non-Western traditions, the domino effect becomes perceptible in the context of colonialism or international trading posts seeking to impose Western values. A new social respectability had to be traced along new acceptable sexual norms, as in the case of Thailand and Japan of during the Meiji Restoration. Stricter rules concerning nudity in public, gender differentiation, and homosexual practices were then adopted. A similar pattern is observable in the case of India during the colonial period for which Ruth Vanita and Saleem Kidwai detailed evidence, drawn from legal and medical discourses mimicking the social perils of homosexuality contemplated in English Victorian society.[10] However, the colonizer is not solely responsible for the domino theory of sexual peril, which amplified homophobia by the marginalization of androgynous gender traditions such as *tritiya pakriti*. According to Ashis Nandy's analysis, *klibatva* (gender nonconformity or feminity-in-masculinity) became the "intimate enemy" as it threatened from within the Indian national perfection, a defect that would prevent it from becoming a nation as strong and virile as the colonizer and capable of becoming independent one day.[11] Hypermasculinity rhymes with the word "nationalism" and it is still present today in the Hindutva movement. Similar voluntary erasures of gender ambiguity can also be found within the Arab-Muslim world during the colonial and postcolonial periods. Many authors, Jurji Zaydan (1861–1914), Taha Husayn (1889–1973), Abdl al-Latif Shararah, Salamah Musa (1887–1958), and many others, saw in past sexual deviance, especially the love of boys during the Abbasid period and masturbation, an inbuilt threat endangering the construction of modern Arab nations.[12] The views expressed by neotraditionalists, such as the one exposed by Al-Qaradawi, can be explained by the domino effect in the context of postcolonialism.

Religions cannot ignore the new global context and are, therefore, forced to react. Some religious actors keep repeating the same denunciatory discourse while others seem more willing to welcome homosexual persons in their congregations. The Anglican Church, the Lutheran churches, as well as other Reformed churches (including the United Church of Canada) showed that a change of attitude vis-à-vis homosexuality is possible through honest and open debate. It can only be achieved by delegating to local communities the responsibility to adhere to a new perspective without imposing on them a policy in an authoritarian manner. Dialogue has sometimes led to disagreements and repositioning within these churches. Can such a climate of dialogue be sustained for long inside a church or are schisms inevitable? The archbishop of Canterbury offers a more pluralistic approach to the exercise of authority in the Anglican Communion that is more akin to decision-making in state federations.[13] Liberal Jews and even Conservatives have followed a similar path. Both Jewish and Christian liberal reformers were able to find within their own tradition the foundation needed to accommodate homosexuality positively without placing themselves in a state of complete rupture with their core beliefs. It remains to be done for many other traditions. Yet in many of them, stepping stones to greater openness vis-à-vis homosexuality are already in place. Consider for a moment the "third gender" of Hinduism and Afro-Caribbean and Afro-Brazilian religions: both favor gender ambiguity allowing homosexuals some kind of coming out within the community through designated religious roles. The same basis for openness may be found in the homoeroticism present in the Islamic tradition and Zen Buddhism. In the first case, if love for Allah may be expressed in the masculine, why would homoeroticism suddenly be suspect when it becomes flesh? In the second case, if ultimate reality is beyond all mental categories, including those of moral conduct, why then severely judge homosexual conduct?

No month goes by without the media reporting significant legislative changes regarding the rights of homosexuals worldwide. As rejoicing as it may be, we must at the same time be aware that legal solutions have their limits. Indeed, the mandatory character of the law sometimes leads the conservative elements of society to a hardening of their positions and to ghettoization behind the banner of the tradition. Protection of human rights and the right to equality become a threat. This phenomenon is observed in the Orthodox Jewish community and among Salafi fundamentalists. In addition, legal battles fought by different organizations to defend the rights of gays and lesbians have sometimes left a legacy, especially in the West, about gay marriage, a conformist view of homosexuality. Homosexual couples aspire to the same goods in marriage as heterosexual couples, and thus to the same rights. Adoption of children has necessarily become a corollary of this argument. The discourse on equality insists more often on uniformity or similarity rather than difference. The natural tendency of this type of discourse carries with it the danger of excluding those who do not conform to the monogamous model of marriage, whether heterosexual or homosexual.[14] While recognizing marriage as a fundamental institution of civil society, the discourse on equality must not exclude from moral legitimacy those who choose to live in cohabitation, homosexual or heterosexual, and even as singles. Homosexuals are no better citizens or better believers because they are married or live in a civil union. Such a narrow frame of mind recalls attitudes that emerged within the Western gay liberation in the 1970s. That is when, in fact, fashion trends emphasizing a form of hypermasculinity and gay rejection vis-à-vis effeminate homosexuals appeared.

Today, in many societies religion has become a personal thing and religious institutions have lost considerable sway over the individual. People look more and more for wisdom and harmony with their own person and nature, and less and less for a doctrine or a creed. They are less likely to accept that their actions be dictated by the religious apparatus. In many religious traditions, I have suggested that control of sexuality goes far beyond simply banning a particular type of sexual act. Through the prohibition of homosexuality, heteronormativity is accomplished and seeks to preserve a social model strongly determined by gender dimorphism and family oriented—reproduction of the species and upbringing of children. Several societies have initiated sweeping changes in relation to the traditional family model. Traditional gender roles have significantly changed, though in some societies progress is still slow, and more single-parent families are everywhere on the planet. Some men feel that they can have sex with male partners without disclosing a homosexual identity. They will simply not renounce the right or duty to have a family. This is present in several traditions. In Western societies where gay rights are protected, more and more people are now asking for the right to choose, that of being bisexual. This breakdown of values can be intimidating and sometimes lead to an exaggerated attachment to tradition, without perceiving how it can serve as a driving force for change. Several mutations in relation to the perception of homosexuality have only occurred recently, challenging many religious traditions and asking them to take a stand. When we talk about sexuality, religion has traditionally acted as a key determinant of social norms in civil society. This function has often proven to be effective even in the context of the separation of church and state. However, secular values, such as the right to privacy and the right to equality before the law, questioned a number of these traditionally acquired values, and has helped to go beyond the attitude that seeks to oppose the doer and the act, the sinner and the sin. Secularism challenged many religious assumptions in the past and brought many changes to various religious perceptions. Sexuality appears to remain the last bastion to resist change in attitudes. I do hope that this book will contribute to a genuine intercultural and interfaith dialogue on homosexuality.

I cannot conclude without mentioning the many attempts of gay men at reclaiming their religious lives. Although this book puts forward a social-scientific approach to religion and puts in parenthesis the experience of faith as such, I think they merit more attention and consideration in terms of a critical comparative approach. It could indeed be the topic for an entire book, but that I leave to experts in that field. I have mentioned several gay approaches to spiritual life, such as GALVA (Gay and Lesbian Vaishnava Association, Inc.), special Hindu festivals and the *hijra* culture, Friends of the Western Buddhist Order, Andrew Ramer of the Reform Congregation Sha'ar Zahav in San Francisco who uses Midrash and poetry inspired by Jewish poets of al-Andalus to weave homoerotic love and feelings into Jewish spiritual expression, Greenberg's *Wrestling with God and Men*, various Christian gay-oriented churches and movements within the Christian churches to include gays, Scott Sirajul Haq Kugle's positions in the Islamic tradition. For those who would like to read more on the topic, I suggest Donald L. Boisvert, *Out on Holy Ground: Meditations on Gay Men's Spirituality* and *Sanctity and Male Desire: A Gay Reading of Saints*, where, through the rhetoric of experience, the author invests male saints with male same-sex erotic desire; and Robert E. Goss, *Queering Christ: Beyond Jesus Acted Up*. Concerning several traditions, see Kath Browne et al., *Queer Spiritual Spaces: Sexuality and Sacred Places*.

NOTES

INTRODUCTION

1. Mary Douglas, "Judgments on James Frazer," *Deadalus*, Fall 1978, 161.
2. The Austrian psychiatrist Richard von Krafft-Ebing published in 1886 a work titled *Psycopathia Sexualis* in which he describes homosexuality as a neuropsychopathology affecting the sexual drive and causing inversion. The German physician Magnus Hirschfeld developed his theory of the third sex in several writings: *Berlins Drittes Geschlecht* (Berlin: H. Seemann, 1904); *Die Homosexualität des Mannes und des Weibes* (Berlin: Louis Marcus, 1914). He was an ardent activist promoting decriminalization of homosexuality and equality rights for transgender and homosexual persons.
3. Greenberg (1998), 408–409. In 1864 and 1865, Ulrichs, under the pen name of Numa Numantius, came up with his theory of the third sex in a series of essays compiled under the title *Forschungen über das Rätsel der mannmännlichen Liebe*.
4. McIntosh; John Gagnon and William Simon; Plummer (1975), (1981); Jeffrey Weeks (1977), (1981), and (1985).
5. Michel Foucault (1976), 1, 59.
6. Boswell (1980).
7. Boswell (1994). The book had as mixed reception, most notably by the Orthodox churches. Boswell interprets the ritual of ἀδελφοποίησις (*adelphopoiesis*) as a ritual celebration of homosexual unions, even though he admits that the celebration had a spiritual meaning only. For others, the ritual appears to be one by which someone adopts a brother. The latter signification is more in tune with the literal meaning of the Greek word.
8. See Mangeot.
9. Halperin (1990).
10. Kosofsky Sedgwick (1991), the Introduction. See the retort in Halperin (2002).
11. Habib (2007), 64.
12. Trevisan, 8.
13. Ibid., 9. See Foucault, *Foucault Live*, 369–370.
14. Janet R. Jakobsen, *Working Alliances and the Politics of Difference* (Bloomington, IN: Indiana University Press, 1998), 14.
15. Hurteau (1991).
16. Faderman, 17.
17. On gender and male status, see Wood, Eagly.
18. The reader may find some explanation on the various reasons why lesbianism and female homoeroticism in the context of religion are understudied in Habib (2007); Booten; and Zeidman, 24–38.

1 HINDUISM

1. *Census of India 2001, Census Abstract*, T 00–003, *Population by sex and sex ratio*.
2. *Census India 1991*. Does not include data from the states of Jammu and Kashmir because of the ongoing civil war.
3. *Census of India 2001, the first Report on Religion*.

4. Government of Nepal, Ministry of Population and Environment, *National Population Report 2002*, Chapter 5, table 5.4.
5. Sri Lanka, Department of Census and Statistics, *Census of Population and Housing 2001*, Population by Religion according to district and sector (provisional).
6. People's Republic of Bangladesh, Bureau of Statistics, Population Census of 1991.
7. Republic of Mauritius, *Population Census*, July 2000.
8. *Census*, April 2001, Office for National Statistics.
9. Statistics Canada, *2001 Census of Canada, Population by Religion*.
10. Gonda, I, 99. This notion of regularity of natural phenomena revealing a cosmic law is well expressed in a hymn to creation in the *Rig Veda Samhita* X, 190.
11. Thus, the gods Varuna and Mitra draw their strength from *Rta*, *Rig Veda Samhita*, I, 2, 8.
12. The equation of cosmic law (*Rta*) and truth (*satya*) is also found in the *Rig Veda Samhita*, VII, 56, 12, since it was by observing the cosmic law that *rishis* reached the truth.
13. *Chandogya Upanishad*, VI, 8, 7.
14. *Mandukya Upanishad*, verse 2.
15. The phrase "mass migration" is deliberately used as modern archeological discoveries have helped to move away from nineteenth-century theories of a so-called Aryan invasion, mainly imagined by Friedrich Max Müller (1823–1900) from philological knowledge of Sanskrit and European languages, and Vedic texts. See "Indo-Aryan Migration," at http://en.wikipedia.org/wiki/Indo-Aryan_migration.
16. The Indus Valley was the site of flourishing civilizations between 2800 and 1800 BC. The main sites were Harappa and Mohenjo-Daro, in what is now Pakistan. Other sites probably existed on the banks of the Ghaggar (Pakistan) and Hakra (northwest India). Their writing has not yet been deciphered, but some argue in favor of a proto-Dravidian origin. See "Indus Valley Civilization," at http://en.wikipedia.org/wiki/Indus_Valley_Civilization.
17. This site is now in Pakistani Baluchistan. See the article "Mehrgarh," at http://en.wikipedia.org/wiki/Mehrgarh.
18. Kenoyer.
19. Daniélou (1984), 52–53. The author quotes the *Shathapatha Brahmana*, XII, 7, 3, 20, and the *Shiva Purana, Rudra Samhita*, V, 9, 13–21, concerning Shiva as Rudra or Pashupati.
20. Daniélou (1984), 56. The author quotes the *Linga Purana* I, 3, 7, stating that Shiva is the origin of things and must be honored in the shape of a *lingam*.
21. Doniger (1973), 256–257; Daniélou (1984), 63; and Jain and Daljeet.
22. The *Vamana Purana* (Chapter 6) tells the story of Shiva joining ascetics in the forest of Daru and his castration by them, after having seduced their wives. The *Linga Purana* also refers to Shiva in the guise of a beggar, naked, and dancing lasciviously to seduce women. Daniélou (1984), 55, where he also cites the *Shiva Purana, Koti Rudra Samhita*.
23. *Shiva Purana, Vidyeshvara Samhita*, 9, 20.
24. According to Gonda (1979), 214, the Upanishads bring us from a religion centered on earthly happiness to the wisdom of spiritual liberation or salvation.
25. *Katha Upanishad* II, 6, 11; *Maitreyana Brahmana Upanishad*, IV, 4.
26. *Mundaka Upanishad*, III, 1, 1–5. The divine light inhabits the body, but is accessible only through ascetic practices, including sexual abstinence (*brahmacharya*). For more details, see Heinrich Zimmer, 371.
27. *Aitareya Upanishad*, 3, 3.
28. *Ishvara* means the Supreme Being or the Lord of the universe.
29. *Shvetashvatara Upanishad*, IV, 1, 9–11.
30. *Taittirya Upanishad*, II, 6.
31. On the idea of a progressive revelation of the Divine, see Doniger (1980), 68–69.
32. *Bhagavad Gita*, XII, 5.
33. Daniélou (1987), 15–16.
34. *Rig Veda Samhita*, X, 90, 12.
35. I use indifferently the word "caste" to describe the four major groups, or *varnas*, and the numerous castes or *jatis* with its emphasis on inheritance along with function. See in this regard, the study of Louis Dumont, 71ff; T. N. Madan, "Caste," *Encyclopedia Britannica*, www.britannica.com/eb/article-219067.

NOTES

36. *Manu Smriti*, I, 91. Various theories account for the origin of *Shudras*, especially regarding their ethnicity. Proponents of the theory of an Aryan invasion associated them with the Dasas or Dasyus, indigenous peoples, possibly of Dravidian origin. However, this theory is disputed, and some archeologists believe that these people who were enemies of the Aryans, belonged to the Indo-European civilization of the Oxus (modern Amu Darya), who initially rejected the religion of the Aryans as described in the *Rig Veda*. The article "Dasa" at www.wikipedia.org is instructive in this regard.
37. This name originates from the initiation ritual (*upanayana*) during which a male child receives the sacred thread, which brightens his mind and inaugurates his period of *brahmacharya*.
38. *Manu Smriti*, 2, 36–249.
39. Ibid., Chapter 3.
40. Ibid., 6, 1–32.
41. Ibid., 6, 33–85.
42. *Chandogya Upanishad*, V, 10, 7.
43. *Bhagavad Gita*, song I, 28–47.
44. Ibid., song II, 31–33.
45. Ibid., song II, 47–48.
46. Ibid., song XVIII, 41–54.
47. Ibid., song XVIII, 54–57.
48. Smart, 85–87.
49. Ramanuja's thought is nondual, like that of Shankara, the great Vedanta philosopher and theologian of the eighth century, but it also opposes the latter's philosophy of *Advaita Vedanta* (nondualism). Ramanuja acknowledges reality to the attributes of the Absolute, which is why his thought is designated as (*vashishtadvaita*), while Shankara sees only illusion (*maya*) in them. See "Ramanuja" at www.wikikipedia.org.
50. *Bhagavata Purana*, 1, 3, 28, proclaims the supremacy of Krishna. *Bhagavata Purana* 12, 13, 15, indicates the position of this work in comparison to Vedic literature. The work was written in the tenth century.
51. The word "mistress" is used deliberately because the *gopis*, who were married women, were attracted to Krishna without ever marrying (*parakiya*) him. This resulted in the *Vaishnava* tradition in a number of debates on the morality of such a relationship proposed as ideal love. Thus, Kaviraja Goswami Krishnadasa (sixteenth century) asserts, in his *Chaitanya Charitarmrta, Adi Lila* 4, the superiority of the love relationship outside marriage (*parakyia*) as an expression of the relationship to the divine, but justifies this position by the fact that this form of expression must be understood on a spiritual and not material plane. Radha is the feminine expression of the Absolute, while Krishna the masculine expression. On the transcendental plane, Krishna and Radha are one.
52. *Bhagavata Purana*, 10, 30, 1–4.
53. *Chaitanya Chartamrita, Adi Lila*, 4, 107–108.
54. Ibid., 4, 79–81. Krishnadasa explains how the *gopis* and Radha are but manifested forms of *shakti*, the feminine energy that makes possible Krishna's sweet bliss (*rasa*). Radha and Krishna are inseparable to make the Absolute accessible to the devotee.
55. This is the *Charyapada*, a collection of poems composed between the ninth and eleventh centuries. These texts are translated into English on the web by Hasna Jasimuddin Moudud at www.bongoz.com/history.
56. On the possible connections between *Gaudiya Vaishnava* and *Sahajiya* cult, see Demock (1989).
57. To learn more about Kashmiri Shaivism, see Pandit and Silburn.
58. Chalier Visuvalingam.
59. Kripal (1995), especially Chapter 2. According to the author, Ramakrishna preferred playing the role of the child rather than the hero (*vira*), namely, because of his misogyny.
60. In accordance with Puranic cosmology, the world is created and destroyed in cycles, each cycle consisting of four phases or ages lasting one day of Brahma, i.e., one *kalpa* or 4.32 billion solar years. At the end of the cycle, fire and water destroy the universe and Brahma re-creates it to follow the same cycle. We are currently in the last age, or *Kali Yuga*, which began in 3012 BC, and will last 432,000 solar years.

61. *Rig Veda Samhita*, X, 90.
62. Ibid., X, 129.
63. Ibid., X, 121
64. *Manu Smriti*, I, 1–58. In this myth of origins, the Self-Manifested Absolute (*Svayambhu*) lived in darkness, imperceptible and indistinguishable. Desiring to create from itself, it impregnated the primordial waters with its semen and conceived a golden egg.
65. *Shatapatha Brahmana*, VI, 1, 1, 5. On Prajapati's sacrifice, see *Shatapatha Brahmana*, XI, 1, 1, 1; V, 2, 1, 2. See Gonda, 227–237; Hopkins, 32–35.
66. The *rishis* and the ancestors can replicate the heat or cosmic energy, *Rig Veda Samhita*, X, 109, 4; 154, 2.
67. *Shatapatha Brahmana*, X, 4, 2, 2; III, 9, 1, 1.
68. *Shatapatha Brahmana*, VI, 1, 2, 12–13.
69. On the macrocosmic benefits of the Vedic sacrifice, see Gonda, 230–237.
70. *Brihad-aranyaka Upanishad*, I, 4, 1–5.
71. Ibid., I, 1, 2; VI, 4, 3.
72. *Aitareya Brahmana*, 13, 9–10, and *Shatapatha Brahmana*, I, 7, 4, 1–7, portrait Prajapati. Brahma's incestuous conduct has several versions, including *Matsya Purana*, III, 30–44, and *Shiva Purana*, II, 2, 2, 15–42.
73. In *Rig Veda Samhita*, VIII, 31, 8–9, spouses have a long and accomplished life alongside their children, and responding to the call of love, they honor the gods. The *Aitareya Brahmana*, VII, 14, says that the seed of the father enters his wife's womb, becomes an embryo, so that the father is said to experience a rebirth. That is the why his wife is also called his mother.
74. *Aitareya Brahmana*, VII, 13, *Shatapatha Brahmana*, XIV, 4, 3, 24–25; *Manu Smriti*, IX, 106–107; *Vishnu Smriti*, XV, 43–46.
75. *Rig Veda Samhita*, I, 72, 5; I, 131, 3; VIII, 31, 5–7; *Taittirya Brahmana*, II, 2, 2, 6. Buch, 146.
76. *Taittirya Aranyaka*, I, 10, 12.
77. *Chandogya Upanishad*, VIII, 1, 5; VIII, 2, 1–9; VIII, 4, 3; *Brihad-aranyaka Upanishad* III, 4, 5–7; IV, 4, 6–7; *Mundaka Upanishad* III, 2, 2.
78. *Chandogya Upanishad*, VIII, 5, 1–3.
79. Ibid., II, 23, 1.
80. *Brihad-aranyaka Upanishad*, III, 5, 1; IV, 4, 22.
81. *Katha Upanishad*, I, 25–27; II, 21–24; III, 3–8.
82. Doniger (1973), 68.
83. *Mahabharata, Adi Parva*, 220, 5–20.
84. *Rig Veda Samhita*, I, 179, 1–6.
85. *Mahabharata, Aranyaka Parva*, 96.
86. Ibid., 97–98. Agastya is presented in the *Ramayana* (*Aranya Kanda*, 12) as the leader of a shrine south of the Vindhya Mountains separating the Hindustan from the Deccan. There, he met Rama and Sita in exile and he gave him Vishnu's sword, which will help him defeat the demon Ravana.
87. *Mahabharata, Shalya Parva*, 52.
88. *Manu Smriti*, III, 45–50.
89. *Mahabharata, Anusasana Parva*, 162,41–42; *Shanti Parva*, 221, 11. The *Ramayana* expresses the same idea: Meyer, 214–228.
90. Kakar, 19–20.
91. *Shiva Purana, Rudra Samhita*. Book II of the *Linga Purana* includes a version of this story.
92. There are several versions of this story, with some variations: *Matsya Purana*, 158, 27–50; *Padma Purana, Shrishti Khanda* (5, 41: 118–142); *Skanda Purana* V, 1, 34: 60–66; *Shiva Purana, Rudra Samhita*.
93. *Mahabharata, Anusana Parva*, 84.
94. *Vamana Purana*, 34, 2–3.
95. *Manu Smriti*, VIII, 353–387. Adultery committed with a prostitute, a dancer, or singer is not liable to punishment.
96. *Bhagavad Gita* I, 40–43.

Notes

97. *Vishnu Smriti*, XXXIV, 1–2; XXXVI, 4–5. *Vishnu Smriti*, V, 42. Bestiality entails the same punishment as adultery with a woman of a lower caste. Also in *Vishnu Smriti*, XXXVIII, 6, bestiality, and a homosexual act, could result in the loss of caste. In the *Narada Purana*, I, 15, 93–94, bestiality is compared to masturbation.
98. *Vishnu Smriti*, LIII, 4.
99. *Manu Smriti*, XI, 120–121–123.
100. *Vishnu Smriti*, XXVIII, 51.
101. Kakar, 118–122. The author quotes several passages from Gandhi's writings.
102. *Bhagavad Gita*, VII, 9. Swami Sivananda (1887–1963) described up and down the importance of semen retention for spiritual development and the adverse consequences of any loss of semen, especially in *Practice of Brahmacharya*, Chapter I.
103. Kakar, 120.
104. *Mahabharata, Adi Parva*, 130.1ff. Section 131 tells how the great master of arms Drona was born, following an involuntary ejaculation of the ascetic Bhiradvaja, aroused at the sight of the *apsara* Ghritachi. His semen was collected in a vase (*drona*). The reader will find several references to similar stories in Meyer 261–263, and Doniger (1973), 42–54.
105. *Apastamba Dharma Sutra*, I.9.26.7. There is a similar expression in the *Vishnu Smriti* LIII, and the *Narada Purana* I, 15, 93.
106. *Vishnu Smriti*, XXXV, 5.
107. *Vashishta Smriti*, XII, 23.
108. *Kama Sutra*, II, 9, 25, 28–30.
109. Vatsyayana compiled in the fourth century AD various works known as *Kama Shastras*, in existence since the fourth century BC. Daniélou's translation, 4.
110. *Kama Sutra*, II, 9, 26. The twelfth-century commentary, Yashodhara's *Jayamangala*, made similar remarks, adding that the man who gets sucked acts as a prostitute but not the woman who sucks—no doubt to condemn the man's passive attitude. Sharma (1993), 57, seems to think that heterosexual oral sex is not condemned when referring to the *Manu Smriti* (V, 130), which states that a woman's mouth is pure. He fails to see that the main concern is most likely the risk of ingesting semen; purity of the woman's mouth changes little to the argument of the *Kama Sutra*.
111. *Kama Sutra*, II, 9, 34, 43–44. Yashodhara believes that the views found in legal texts (*smriti*) have less authority than revealed texts (*shruti*).
112. Ibid., II, 9, 38. *Jayamangala* II, 9, 38. According to Yashodhara, the fact that the crow does not defile its beak with impurities while eating explains why oral sex carried that name. Again, the concern is impurity and not the nonprocreative nature of such practice.
113. *Gautama Dharma Shastra*, XXIII, 3; *Manu Smriti*, IV, 222.
114. The most famous story is probably that of Agni who swallows Shiva's sperm, and spits it out because it causes heart burns. It, then, forms a huge pond from which Parvati drinks and becomes pregnant: *Matsya Purana* 158, 27–50; *Padma Purana* 5, 41: 118–142. The *Skanda Purana* 5, 1, 34: 60–66, mentions Agni's shame.
115. *Sushruta Samhita*, III.2.38. Doniger (1980), 51–52, also provides references to Tantric literature and various popular beliefs about sperm ingestion. The *Kama Sutra*'s modern commentator, Devadatta Shastri, believes that the ingestion of semen during oral sex offends morality (Daniélou [1994], 188). Vatsyayana recommends oral sex when a man experiences erectile problems: *Kama Sutra*, VII, 2, 3.
116. *Kama Sutra*, II, 6, 49.
117. Ibid., II, 6, 50.
118. Kakar.
119. Orthodox Brahmins defined the code in the *Manu Smriti*.
120. Ibid., II, 67.
121. Ibid., V, 155–158.
122. *Mahabharata, Vana Parva*, 231 (*Draupadi-Satyabhama Samvada*).
123. Catherine Merrien summarizes this as follows: "A woman has no personal identity, no substance of her own. Her religious merit totally depends on her relationship with her husband, which excludes the idea of a personal relationship with a god." The whole text is worth reading.

124. Merrien, 28. The *Mahabharata, Anusana Parva*, 38, shows women as the cause for all evil because of their uncontrollable sexual appetite.
125. Meyer (260–263) reports many of these stories: the sage Vishwamitra seduced by the *apsara* Menaka, who then gives birth to Shukuntala; the celestial nymph Janapadi seduces the sage Gautama, and gives birth to twins—Kripi and Kripa.
126. Pattanaik (111–112) rightly stresses the homoerotic atmosphere emerging from the story. Rishiasringa perceives the courtesan's gender to be male and is seduced. The two cuddle and kiss.
127. *Mahabharata, Vana Parva*, 110–114.
128. *Matsya Purana*, 155–158; *Skanda Purana*, 1: 2: 27: 58–84; 1: 2: 28: 1–14; 1: 2: 29: 1–8; *Padma Purana*, V, 41, 1–118.
129. *Mahabharata, Adi Parva*, 95.
130. *Mahabharata, Anusana Parva*, 104, 150.
131. *Manu Smriti*, V, 148–149.
132. Sil, 63–83. Kripal (1995) speaks of Ramakrishna's disgust for female sexuality rather than misogyny (285–287).
133. These turmoils are described in her autobiography, *Atmanivedana*, or in some of the 350 hymns she composed. See MacGee.
134. Merrien (37–41) illustrates the situation of contemporary female ascetics and gurus defying the traditional roles assigned to women and violating the traditional religious norms of men, who assign to men only the teaching of religion and philosophy. Women are not allowed to practice monasticism.
135. In matters of civil law, the colonizers incorporated the *Dharma Shastras* in the Common Law. The standard was first established by the East India Company, which had them translated to English, and assigned pundits to assist judges in the application of these traditional Hindu laws. See "Hindu Law" at www.wikipedia.org.
136. Edward Said (1978) was the first deconstructionist of colonialism to highlight the feminization of the Other, the colonized Arab, as a domination strategy. Sinha (1995) took up the idea in the context of the Indian subcontinent.
137. On the evolution and role of Indian feminism, see Sen (2000).
138. Government of India, *Act No 45 of 1860*.
139. Vanita and Kidwai, *Same-Sex Love in India*, XVIII; Siddharth Narrain; Bondyopadhyay.
140. 9 George IV c. 31 sec. 15, quoted by E. Deacon, 1236.
141. Vanita and Kidwai, VIII.
142. Sherry, 150–154.
143. Human Rights Watch, Asian Division (2002), "India. Epidemic of Abuse: Police Harassment of HIV/AIDS Outreach Workers in India," July 2002, Vol. 14, N. 5 (C), p. 19.
144. *The Times of India*, "Call Boy Racket Sends Shock Waves in Lucknow," July 9, 2001.
145. Bondyopadhyay.
146. *Naz Foundation* vs *Government of NCT of Delhi*, Delhi High Court at New Delhi, WP(C) No.7455/2001, July 2, 2009.
147. Khan, 2.
148. Ibid., 4.
149. Ibid., 10–11; People's Union for Civil Liberties-Karnataka, 19.
150. People's Union for Civil Liberties-Karnataka, 19–21; Khan, 10. People's Union for Civil Liberties-Karnataka, p. 20.
151. People's Union for Civil Liberties-Karnataka, 20.
152. Khan, 22.
153. People's Union for Civil Liberties-Karnataka, 20, 24; Khan, 33; Rahman, 47–49. *Giriyas* show a lot of violence toward *kothis* when they sustain lasting relationships in the Delhi region.
154. *Kothis* and *hijras* give a moving testimony on the sexual abuse they undergo, in People's Union for Civil Liberties-Karnataka, 25–38.
155. Khan, 26.
156. Ibid., 11.

157. Merchant, XVI. The book contains excerpts from many authors who tell of lasting friendships involving sex.
158. Merchant, XXIII; Rao; Ashok Row Kavi.
159. Rahman, 51.
160. Ibid., 40; Khan, 4.
161. Khan, 11.
162. Vanita and Kidwai, 209.
163. Sharma (1993), 48–49.
164. Ibid., 68–69. The author cites, among others, J. L. Nehru who wrote that homosexual relations were absent from Sanskrit literature, were not approved by Indian society, and were rare, unlike in Iran.
165. Vanita and Kidmai, XXIII–XIV. As recently as 2004, the Delhi High Court judges used such reasoning in the case of Naz.
166. *Manu Smriti*, XI, 175.
167. Sharma (1993), 51.
168. *Manu Smriti*, XI, 213, this penance consists in fasting for 24 hours and ingesting urine, dung, curd, and an herb called *kush* in Sanskrit (scientific name: *desmostachya bipinnata*).
169. Sharma (1993), 52–53.
170. *Manu Smriti*, XI, 68; *Vishnu Smriti*, XXXVIII, 5.
171. *Manu Smriti*, XI, 55–71.
172. Ibid., X, 126, quoted by Sharma (1993), 54.
173. *Vishnu Smriti*, XXXVIII, 7, XLVI, 10, 19.
174. *Manu Smriti*, XI, 125.
175. Sharma (1993), 54.
176. *Vishnu Smriti*, XLVI, 24.
177. *Artha Shastra*, IV, 13, 40.
178. Ibid., IV, 13, 32.
179. Ibid., IV, 12, 3.
180. *Manu Smriti*, VIII, 353.
181. Bullough (1976), 261. Without any textual evidence, he affirms that legislators consider oral sex as a serious offense, comparable to killing a Brahmin. Sharma (1993), 56, refers to Bullough without any additional information. The only passage that could, in my view, be alluded to, is found in the *Vishnu Smriti*, XXXV, 5–6, when it comes to oral sex, without specifying the genders involved. The context seems to favor an interpretation in the sense of heterosexual contact since there also is mention of vaginal intercourse with an untouchable. The *Vashishta Smriti*, XII, 23, also talks about heterosexual oral sex.
182. *Kama Sutra*, II, 9. 3.
183. Ibid., II, 9. 1.
184. *Jayamangala*, commentary on ibid., II, 9.1.
185. *Sataphata Brahmana*, V, 5, 4, 35, quoted in Sweet and Swilling, 601.
186. *Sataphata Brahmana*, XII, 7, 2, 12, quoted in Sweet and Swilling, 601. *Brihad-aranyaka Upanishad* VI, 1, 12 defines the word *kliba* as the inability to produce sperm.
187. *Charaka Samhita*, *Sarirasthana*, 4. 10, 14.
188. *Mahabharata*, *Anusasana Parva*, 145, 52. In Meyer, 242.
189. *Manu Smriti* IX, 201–203.
190. The *Sushruta Samhita* III, 2, 38, proposes as a treatment the ingestion of semen, and the *Kama Sutra* (VI, 1, 10) suggests impotent men (*pandakas*) make use of prostitutes. The Jayamangala uses here *napumsaka*.
191. Among the eight sexual dysfunctions listed in the *Charaka Samhita* (IV, 2, 17–21) are mentioned the *narasandha*, the *narisandha*, and the *vatikasandha*. Sweet and Zwilling translate into effeminate homosexual, lesbian, and sterile man (p. 593). The *Sushruta Samhita*, III, 2, 37–43, lists six dysfunctions named *sandha*. The simplified transliteration for the Sanskrit word षण्ढ meaning impotent is *shandha*, but I have used the Harvard-Kyoto system, which gives *sandha*. The reason for this choice is that *sandha* is more commonly found in the literature.

192. Sweet and Zwilling, 592; Wilhelm, 8. See also Annex 3, where Wilhelm cites the Sanskrit dictionary *Sabda-kalpa-drum*, compiled in the nineteenth century. It gives various lists of sexual anomalies from various sources.
193. According to the *Sushruta Samhita*, a father's poor quality of semen will prompt his offspring to practice fellatio and semen ingestion.
194. According to the *Sushruta Samhita* (III, 2, 37–43) if a man copulates lying under the woman, the male child to be will be effeminate and the daughter to be will show masculine features and behavior.
195. Sweet and Zwilling (1993), 593, draw a complete list of these anomalies from the *Sushruta Samhita* and the *Charaka Samhita*. The *Narada Smriti* (chapter XII) has a similar list.
196. Wilhelm, 7.
197. Ibid., 47–51.
198. Gannon. The ancient legislators exclude "eunuchs" from inheritance, notably Yajnavalkya and Manu. See *Digest of Hindu Law*, II, Book V, Chapter 5.
199. Zahid Chaudhary, "Controlling the Ganymedes," in Srivastava, 82–98.
200. According to the embryology exposed in the *Saritasthana* of both the *Charaka Samhita* and the *Sushruta Samhita*, if the semen (*shukra*) overpowers the ovum (*artava*) a boy will be born, a daughter in the opposite. If they are quantitatively equal, a *napumsaka* or *sandha* will be born, with male or female features.
201. Sweet and Zwilling (600) think that the expression *tritiya pakriti* is used for persons who are still biologically male, but other authors consider that it may also include women with anatomical or physiological disabilities (Penrose, and Gyatso). Ayurvedic medicine considers that these women do not menstruate (*Sushruta Samhita*, 6, 38, 18).
202. *Kama Sutra*, II, 9, 6.
203. Ibid., II, 9, 25, 35. Vatsyayana emphasizes the androgynous appearance of these servants by suggesting they wear earrings and Yashodhara adds that they are beardless.
204. Some authors, including Sweet and Zwilling and Wilhelm, suggest that the masseurs and young servants of the *Kama Sutra* are *napumsaka*. However, this identification is achieved mainly through Yashodhara's use, ten centuries later, of *napumsaka*, completely absent from Vatsyayana's text. This reading gives rise to interpretations that, I think, go beyond the text. At least, that is the case with Wilhelm who wants the masseurs to represent gays of a more masculine type in contrast to effeminate gays described in the preceding verses.
205. Chapter 2 of Book VII of the *Kama Sutra* deals with medicine and pharmacopoeia used in cases of impotence and erectile difficulties.
206. *Kama Sutra*, II, 9, 36.
207. *Mahabharata, Virata Parva*, 2, 21–27. The text uses three idioms—*kliba, sandha*, and *triitya prakriti*—in reference to Arjuna's transformation.
208. *Mahabharata, Virata Parva*, 36–38.
209. Ibid., 10, 7.
210. According to a Tamil version of the *Mahabharata*, the nymph Urvashi castrated Arjuna or rendered him impotent (the term used here is *sandha*) during his exile (*Vana Parva*, 46–47). See Pattanaik, 89–99.
211. Allen (1998). The author shows that Arjuna's journey has a yogic dimension.
212. *Padma Purana, Uttara Khanda*, 74, 60–189. Reported in Vanita and Kidwai, 91–93.
213. *Mahabharata, Sauptika Parva*, 12, 27–28, *Drona Parva*, 79. In Vanita and Kidwai, 5.
214. *Bhagavad Gita*, XI, 41–42.
215. *Srimad Bhagavatam*, I, 15, 4.
216. *Charitamrita, Madhya Lila*, 74–75.
217. *Bhakti Rasamrita Sindhu*, II, 5, 30. Bhaktivedanta Swami Prabhupada (1970), *The Nectar of Devotion*, Chapters 41–42, describes in detail this form of devotion.
218. *Srimad Bhagavatam*, XI, 15, 14–17.
219. Doniger (1980), 298–299.
220. Vanita and Kidwai, 103–105.
221. On all issues and guidelines put forward by GALVA, consult the Internet at www.galva-108.org.

Notes

222. "Ramakrishna's Impulses Spark Row," *The Times of India*, April 10, 1997. Jeffrey Kripal's interpretation at www.ruf.rice.edu/~kalischi/index.html.
223. Kripal (1995), 63–75.
224. Swami Tyagananda. His criticism is mainly directed at Kripal's lack of knowledge of the Bengali language.
225. *Sri Ramakrishna Lilaprasanga*, V, 3, 6, (824).
226. Ibid., V, 3, 6.
227. Ibid., V. 5, 14, (857).
228. Ibid., V, 3, 7, (825).
229. Ibid., V, 3, 7, (825).
230. Sil, 96–97.
231. Ibid., 97.
232. Ibid.
233. Ibid., 92–96.
234. Ibid., 95.
235. *Yogavashsishta Maharamayana, Nirvana Prakarana*, 9–11. This work was abridged by Abhinanda Pandita as the *Laghu Yogavasishta*, and our history is found in Chapter IX. The story is reported by Pattanaik, 35–37, and Doniger (1999), 287–289.
236. *Mahabharata, Adi Parva*, 19.
237. *Brahmanda Purana*, IV, 10, 41–77. According to *Shiva Purana* III, 20, 3–7, from this union is born the ape-like god Hanuman.
238. *Bhagavata Purana*, VIII, 12, 12–38, in particular verse 37.
239. Vanita and Kidwai, 69.
240. Srikant, 38.
241. Pattanaik, 75–77; Vanita and Kidwai, 94–99.
242. Osella.
243. *Shiva Purana*, IV, 2, 9–12, *Skanda Purana*, I, 1, 27. Vanita and Kidwai, 77–80. In the first text, Agni in the shape of a dove, collects Shiva's sperm, and, in the second, he takes the form of an ascetic who swallows Shiva's sperm.
244. Vanita.
245. Vanita and Kidwai, 60.
246. On the *ali* and *aravani*, and perceptions about their sexual identity, see Mahalingam. Santosh Sivan directed the 2005 film *Navarasa (Nine Emotions)* about the *aravanis*, both fiction and documentary, shot during the Kuvakkam festival. It tells the story of a young 13-year-old girl who discovers that her uncle dresses as a woman every night. When she confronts him, he says he wants to meet Aravan during the Kuvakkam festival.
247. Menon, 3. See also Niklas.
248. Ulrike Niklas produced a video on the festival: *Aravan's Brides*, Karuppan Productions, Pondicherry 2003.
249. Pattanaik, 108; Penrose, 9; and Bradford.
250. Hiltebeitel (1995).
251. Nanda (1994), 383.
252. Nanda (1990), 25–26.
253. Nanda (1994), 384.
254. Nanda (1990), 13.
255. Nanda (1994), 386–387.
256. Ibid., 385.
257. Hiltebeitel.
258. The Humsafar Trust, 16.
259. Jaffrey (2003), 25, 43. Delhi holds more than 30,000 *hijras*, according to the *All-India Hijra Kalyan Sabha* (AIHKS). Shveta Bhagat, "Eunuchs Not Always Born but Made," *The Times of India*, Monday, September 5, 2005.
260. Nanda (1994), 403. Lynton and Rajan, 190–206, observe that a period of homosexual activity often precedes the entry of new recruits in the *hijra* family.
261. Reddy (2005).

262. Carstairs; Sinha (1967).
263. Reddy (2003).
264. Sharma (1993), 68.
265. Dumont, 191.
266. See Gayatri Reddy, "Crossing 'Lines' of Subjectivity,'" in Srivastava, 149. She reacts to D. Altman, "Global Gaze/Global Gays," GLQ: A journal of Lesbian and Gay Studies, Vol. 3, n. 4 May 1997: 417–436.

2 BUDDHISM

1. National Statistical Office Thailand, *Population and Housing Census 2000*.
2. Union of Myanmar, Department of Religious Affairs.
3. Sri Lanka, Department of Census and Statistics, *Census of Population and Housing 2001*.
4. A Pali word, "Theravada" means "the way the elders." Pali is essentially a literary and liturgical language that originated from ancient Prakrit dialects of India.
5. Agency for Cultural Affairs, December 2002. The Japanese government does not identify religious affiliation in its census.
6. Korea National Statistical Office, *Participation of Religious Action 2003*.
7. General Statistics Office of Vietnam, *Vietnam Population and Housing Census 1999*. According to the census 80.3 percent of the population have no religion. According www.adherents.com, 55 percent of Vietnam's population is Buddhist.
8. According to the *Taiwan Yearbook 2005*, but www.adherents.com shows nine million.
9. These figures are provided by Baumannn.
10. Ibid.
11. Statistics Canada, Census 2001.
12. Gautama Siddhartha's oldest biography was compiled by Ashvaghosa in the first century AD, and is titled *Buddhacarita*. On his birth, see *Buddhacarita*, I, 20.
13. Deep meditation (*dhyana* in Sanskrit, *jhana* in Pali) may also carry imperfection because of its impermanence. The Buddha understands it as suffering (*dukkha*) in the sense that its passing nature brings about frustration. He exposes this idea in the *Majjhima Nikaya, Mulapannasa, Sihannada Vagga, Mahadukkhakkandha Sutta*.
14. *Samyutta Nikaya, Mahavagga, Sacca Samyutta, Dhammachakkapavattana Sutta*.
15. Rahula, 16–20. For an interesting parallel between the concept of *dukkha* and anxiety in existentialist philosophy (Kierkegaard, Heidegger, and Sartre) and in Freud's thinking, see De Silva (1974), 49–59.
16. *Khuddaka Nikaya, Itivuttaka 58, Tanha Sutta*.
17. *Samyutta Nikaya, Sagatta Vagga, Brahma Samyutta, Ayacanna Sutta*.
18. *Samyutta Nikaya, Khandha Vagga, Khandha Samyutta, Anattalakhana Sutta*.
19. The Buddha uses the concept of aggregate to explain the components that form the basis of false belief in the personality.
20. Rahula, 20.
21. *Visuddhimagga*, XVI, 90, 587.
22. *Anguttara Nikaya, Tika Nipata, Dhamma-niyama Sutta*. The same idea is found in many texts, e.g., *Majjhima Nikaya, Mulapannasa, Opamma Vagga, Alagadupamana Sutta*.
23. *Samyutta Nikaya, Salayatana Vagga, Salayatanna Amyutta, Aniccavaggo*.
24. *Visuddhimagga*, XX, 18, 710.
25. The word "conditional" more clearly indicates the simultaneous appearance of combined factors producing an effect and their inexistence as separate entities. See Trotignon.
26. This law of causality or conditional coproduction is found in several places in the Pali Canon, e.g., in the *Anguttara Nikaya, Dasaka Nipata, Vera Sutta*.
27. *Samyutta Nikaya, Nidana Vagga, Nidana Samyutta, Paticca-samuppada-vibhanga Sutta*.
28. *Samyutta Nikaya, Nidana Vagga, Nidana Samyutta, Paticca-samuppada-vibhanga Sutta*.
29. *Sankhara* here has the meaning of *karma* or karmic formations, whereas in the theory of aggregates *sankhara* means motivation. See Padmasiri De Silva (1973), 15.

30. *Samyutta Nikaya, Nidana Vagga, Nidana Samyutta, Paticca-samuppada-vibhanga Sutta.*
31. *Majjhima Nikaya, Mulapannasa, Opamma Vagga, Maha-hatthipadopama Sutta.*
32. *Majjhima Nikaya, Mulapannasa, Mulapariyaya Vagga, Sammaditthi Sutta.*
33. *Digha Nikaya, Mahavagga, Maha-nidana Sutta*; *Kuddhaka Nikaya, Sutta Nipata, Atthaka Vagga, Kalaha-vivada Sutta.*
34. The most extensive discourse by the Buddha on this technique of meditation is in the *Digha Nikaya, Mahavagga, Mahasattipatthana Sutta.*
35. *Digha Nikaya, Mahavagga, Maha-parinibbana Sutta*; *Anguttara Nikaya, Catukka Nipata, Anubuddha Sutta.*
36. *Anguttara Nikaya, Chakka Nipata, Nibbedhika Sutta.*
37. *Kuddhaka Nikaya, Dhammapada*, 1.
38. *Kuddhaka Nikaya, Dhammapada*, 165.
39. *Anguttara Nikaya, Tika Nipata, Kalama Sutta.*
40. *Vinaya Pitaka, Mahavagga, Maha Khandaka* 7, *Pabajja Katha.*
41. *Vinaya Pitaka, Mahavagga, Maha Khandaka* 14, *Sariputta Mogallana Pabajja Katha.*
42. *Vinaya Pitaka, Mahavagga, Maha Khandaka* 20, *Panamanakhampana.*
43. *Digha Nikaya, Mahavagga, Mahapadana Sutta.*
44. *Vinaya Pitaka, Kullavagga, Bhikkhuni Khandaka* 1–2.
45. *Vinaya Pitaka, Mahavagga, Maha Khandaka.*
46. His real name is Sudatta. He was nicknamed Anathapindaka—the feeder of the helpless—because of his generosity toward the *sangha*. Narada Maha Thera, 164.
47. *Vinaya Pitaka, Kullavagga, Senasana Khandhaka* 4. Anathapindaka gives to the Buddha and his disciples their first monastery, Jevatana.
48. The three other stages to enlightenment are: *sakadakagami* or one that will experience rebirth only once; *anagami* or one will not be reborn in the sensory world (*kama loka*); and the wait for the last stage (*arahant*) in celestial spheres (*suddhavasa*).
49. *Anguttara Nikaya, Ekadasaka Nipata, Mahanamma Sutta*. The five precepts are also found in the *Digha Nikaya, Pathika Vagga, Sigalovada Sutta.* Rahula, 11; Khantapilo.
50. The Buddha explains the eight rules to a lay woman named Visakha, in *Anguttura Nikaya, Atthaka Nipata, Vishakuposatha Sutta.*
51. The three baskets are: *Sutta Pitaka*, a collection of the Buddha's sermons, or sermons attributed to Sariputta, Ananda, or Mogallana; *Vinaya Pitaka*, or rules of monastic discipline; *Abhidhamma Pitaka*, a collection of philosophical writings on Buddhist psychology.
52. Vasubandhu wrote the *Dasabhumika Sutra-Shastra* in the fourth century AD and Bodhiruci translated it in Chinese (*Shidi Jinglun* 十地經論) in the sixth century. It belongs to the *Flower Adornment Sutra* (*Avatamsaka Sutra, Huayan Jing* 華嚴經).
53. The perfections are mostly described in *Prajnaparamita Sutras* and in the *Lotus Sutra* (*Saddharma Pundarika Sutra, Miaofa Lianhua Jing* 妙法蓮花經): generosity (*dana*), moral conduct (*sila*), tolerance (*khanti*), courage (*virya*), meditation (*dhyana*), and wisdom (*prajna*). The *Dasabhumika Sutra* adds four other: skilful means (*upaya*), resolution in keeping the bodhisattva's vow (*pranidhana*), spiritual fortitude (*bala*), and knowledge of the true nature of all phenomena (*jnana*).
54. *Prajnaparamita Hridaya Sutra* (*Boreboluomiduo Xinjing*, 般若波羅蜜多心經), *Taisho*, v. 8, n. 251, 848c.
55. *Vajracchedika-prajñāpāramitā-sūtra, Jin'gang Banruo Boluomi Jing* (金剛般若波羅蜜經), *Taisho*, v. 7, n. 235.
56. *Mahaprajnaparamita Shastra, Le traité de la grande vertu de sagesse*, Étienne Lamotte, III, 1229.
57. The *Diamond Sutra* is fond of reasoning aimed at destabilizing conventional logic. Thus, the Buddha says to Subhuti that his teachings on impermanence and suffering have no reality in themselves.
58. *Mahaprajnaparamita Shastra, Le traité de la grande vertu de sagesse*, Étienne Lamotte, II, 656.
59. May, 126–127.
60. This teaching of an inherent Buddha nature (*dharma dhatu tathagatagarbha*) is found in many sutras, among which is the *Mahaparinirvana Sutra* (*Niepan Jing*, 涅槃經). In the second

chapter of the *Platform Sutra of the Sixth Patriarch* (*Liuzu Tanjing*, 六祖壇經), Huineng said explicitly that the principle of enlightenment lies in everyone, obscured by ignorance.

61. Bodhidharma's method is described in a treatise ascribed to him by tradition, the *Two Entrances and Four Acts Treaty* (*Erhru Sixing Lun*, 二入四行論). Bodhidharma states that there are two possible approaches to enlightenment, the more abstract path of study, and daily life practice. He favors a nonspeculative approach to the nonduality of phenomena and their emptiness. For more details, see McRae, 28–33.
62. *The Blue Cliff Record* (*Biyan Lu* 碧巌錄), case n. 12.
63. This controversy arose from Shenhui's (神會) campaign against gradualism and Shenxiu's sitting in meditation, which he coined as the Northern School, as opposed to Huineng's doctrine of sudden awakening, which he called the Southern School. See McRae (2003), 55, quoting from Shenhui's *Illuminating the Essential Doctrine* (*Xianzong Ji* 顯宗記).
64. Shenxiu detailed his meditation technique in his *Treatise on the Contemplation of the Mind* (*Guanxin Lun* 觀心論).
65. *Linji Lu* (臨濟錄), *The Record of Linji*, trans. Ruth Fuller Sasaki, 185.
66. *Sukhavativyuha Sutra* (*Wuliang Shou Jing* 無量壽經). There is a shorter version, *The Sutra of Visualizing the Buddha of Immeasurable Length of Life* (*Fo Shuo Wuliang Shou Jing* 佛說無量壽經). English translation of both sutras, Luis O. Gómez, *Land of Bliss: The Paradise of the Buddha of Measureless Light: Sanskrit and Chinese versions of the Sukhāvatīvyūha Sutras* (Honolulu: University of Hawaii Press, 1996).
67. Ch'en, 338–350.
68. Technique developed by Daochuo (道綽; 562–645) and Shandao (善道; 613–681), which consists in repeating "Hail to Amida Buddha," *Namu Amituofo* (南無阿彌陀佛). Ch'en, 345–346.
69. Tanluan probably was the first to use the expression "other power" (他力) *tali* (Japanese *tariki*) as opposed to "self- power," *sili* (自力) (Jap. *jiriki*) in reference to the easier path of those who turn to faith in the Buddha, in his *Commentary to the Treaty on Birth in the Pure Land of Vasubandhu*. Nagarjuna had described the easy path in his *Dasabhúmika Vibhasa Shastra*. This saving power of Amida, *tariki*, became a key concept in the hands of the great Japanese master Shinran who made faith (信 *shin*) in Amida the essence of his teaching. See Gira.
70. Chapter 25 of the *Lotus Sutra* introduces the bodhisattva Avalokiteshvara as "He who Observes the Sounds of the World" and who comes to the rescue of those who invoke his name.
71. *Samyutta Nikaya, Mahavagga, Satipatthana Samyutta, Makkata Sutta*.
72. *Samyutta Nikaya, Salayatana Vagga, Salayatana Samyutta, Punna Sutta*. The logic of pleasure and desire is neatly analyzed by De Silva (1973), 95 ff.
73. *Anguttara Nikaya, Catukka Nipata, Anana Sutta*.
74. *Digha Nikaya, Pathika Vagga, Sigalovada Sutta*.
75. *Majjhima Nikaya, Mulapannasa, Culavagga Vagga, Cula-vedalla Sutta*.
76. *Khuddhaka Nikaya, Sutta Nipata 766–771, Kama Sutta*.
77. *Khuddhaka Nikaya, Theraghata 459–465*.
78. *Anguttara Nikaya, Navaka Nipata, Ganda Sutta*.
79. *Digha Nikaya, MahaVagga, Mahasatipatthana Sutta*; *Visuddhimagga* VIII, 42–144, *Kuddhaka Nikaya, Kuddhakapata 3, Dvatimsakara*.
80. *Samyutta Nikaya, Mahavagga, Bojjhanga Samyutta, Ahara Sutta*.
81. *Anguttara Nikaya, Sataka Nipata, Sanna Sutta*.
82. *Khuddhaka Nikaya, Itivuttaka, Tika Nipata, Asubhanupassa Sutta*.
83. *Samyutta Nikaya, Salayanata Vagga, Salayanata Samyutta, Malunkyaputta Sutta*.
84. *Anguttara Nikaya, Atthaka Nipata, Mahavagga, Panhamabandha Sutta* and Dutiya *Sutta*.
85. *Anguttara Nikaya, Ekaka Nipata, Pariyadana Sutta*.
86. Visakha felt sorry after her grandson's death. For the occasion, the Buddha mentions that attachment to dear ones brings about sorrow and suffering. Those who remain free from emotional attachment experience true freedom. *Khuddhaka Nikaya, Udana, Pataligamiya Vagga, Visakha Sutta*.
87. *Khuddhaka Nikaya, Dhammapada 209–220*; *Samyutta Nikaya, Salayatana Vagga, Gamani samyutta, Gandhabhaka Sutta*.

88. *Digha Nikaya, Silakkhandha Vagga, Samannaphala Sutta.*
89. *Khuddhaka Nikaya, Sutta Nipata* 35–75, *Khaggavisana Sutta.*
90. Dhirasekera, 38–39. The author employs many references to the *Sutta Pitaka*, among which are the *Majjhima Nikaya, Mulapannasa, Sihanada Vagga, Culadukkakhandha Sutta.*
91. Stevens, 1–21.
92. Faure (2003), 267. The author cites the medieval Japanese tale *Joruri Junidan Soshi* (The Tales of Joruri into Twelve Chapters). This piece of Japanese puppet theater (*Bunraku*) depicts the meeting of Joruri, a beautiful girl born to a prostitute, and lord Yoshitsune who falls for her. He manages to conquer her pure heart, mentioning that Shakyamuni himself married Yashodhara.
93. Nayanatiloka, 89.
94. Saddhatissa, 106.
95. Nanamoli. According to the Buddha, there are three ways by which the body can be involved in nonmeritorious acts, harmful to the spiritual progress of an individual: killing, stealing, and having sex with a minor female or already involved with someone, *Anguttara Nikaya, Dasaka Nipata, Cunda kamaraputta Sutta.*
96. *Anguttara Nikaya, Catukka Nipata, Samajivina Sutta.* A man having sex with a woman other than his wife is compared to an outcast. *Khuddaka Nikaya, Sutta Nipata* 123, *Vasala Sutta*; *Khuddaka Nikaya, Dhammapada* 246.
97. *Bhuddhacarita*, Chapters 2 and 4.
98. Dhammananda.
99. *Samyutta Nikaya, Sagatha Vagga, Bhikkhuni Samyutta, Cala Sutta.*
100. Ling for Sri Lanka; and for Thailand, Knodel, Chamratritirong, and Debavalya.
101. Dalai Lama XIV (1996), 46. He expressed the same view in June 1997 during a meeting with leaders of the gay Buddhist community in San Francisco. On this subject, see Dennis Conkin, "Dalai Lama Urges 'Full Human Rights for All,' Including Gays," *Bay Area Reporter*, June 19, 1997; Steve Peskind, "According to Buddhist Tradition: Gays, Lesbians and the Definition of Sexual Misconduct," *Shambala Sun*, March 1998. The Dalai Lama expressed the same view in an interview he gave to the magazine *Le Point*, March 22, 2001, 116.
102. Dennis Conkin.
103. This statement is found in an updated version on the Internet by Steve Peskind of his 1999 article "According to Buddhist Tradition." Gampopa in his book *The Precious Ornament of Liberation* in Chapter 5 defines what is meant by bad behavior in violation of the third precept. He includes all forms of sexual activity practiced in the orifices of the mouth or anus, with a woman, even one's wife, or a man.
104. Faure (1998), 67.
105. Jackson (1998), 60–61.
106. *Vinaya Pitaka, Suttavibhanga* 1. 7, *The Book of Discipline*, Vol. 1, I. B. Horner, Pali Text Society, 1970, 39.
107. The Burmese monk Damma Sami maintains, since 2003, a very good website at the following address: www.dhammadana.org, click "*sangha*" to find fairly detailed rules of monastic discipline, degrees in penalties and reparation.
108. The *Suttavibhanga* explains the origin of the rule of *parajika* 1 with two stories; the monk Sudinna who slept with his ex-wife for the sole purpose of having an offspring and that of a monk who had sexual relations with a female monkey.
109. Horner's translation is not so clear about this. It is without doubt the mouth, anus, and vagina after reading the following commentary on the *Vinaya Pitaka*: *The Samantapasadika* of Buddhaghosa, (*Shanjianlü Piposha* 善善見律毘婆沙), VII. 31–58, trans. V. Bapat, 195–206.
110. *Vinaya Pitaka, Suttavibhanga*, I. 8. 5, 48.
111. *Vinaya Pitaka, Suttavibhanga*, I. 10. 8, 55.
112. *Vinaya Pitaka, Suttavibhanga*, I. 10. 9, 55.
113. *Vinaya Pitaka, Suttavibhanga*, I. 10. 10, 55.
114. Thanassiro (1994).
115. Disciplinary measures and probation relating to breaches of monastic discipline are codified in the first three *Khandaka* in the *Kullavagga* of the *Vinaya Pitaka*. Thanissaro (2002),

Buddhist Monastic Code II, Chapter 19, gives an excellent account, as well as Dhamma Sami (2003).
116. *Vinaya Pitaka, Suttavibhanga, Sanghadisesa* 2. 1, 196.
117. *Vinaya Pitaka, Suttavibhanga, Sanghadisesa* 1.1, 192.
118. Horner deliberately omits the analysis of ejaculation related to various sexual pleasures because the subject may offend the reader. Dhamma Sami displays the contents of this list under the heading "Development of *sanghadisesa* 1."
119. For a detailed view on this aspect, see Harvey (1999).
120. *Vinaya Pitaka, Suttavibhanga, Parajika* 1. 8. 9, 51.
121. *Vinaya Pitaka, Suttavibhanga, Parajika* 1. 10. 19, 59. If the monk awakens and consents to the act, the offense then entails exclusion, 1. 10. 18, 58.
122. *Vinaya Pitaka, Suttavibhanga, Sanghadisesa* 1. 2. 4, 197.
123. The first case is enunciated in the *Shanjian Piposha*, XII. 73, 361. It states that if the monk is masturbating at the sight of this woman, he is committing a wrongful act in the category of *sanghadisesa* 1. The second case assumes that the monk should, directly or indirectly, refer to the vagina, anus of the woman, or to having intercourse with her.
124. The word *pandaka* will be defined in the next heading more accurately.
125. Bernard Faure (1998), 43–44.
126. Stevens, 52. *Srimaladevi-simha-nada-sutra, Shengman Shizi Hu Yisheng Da Fangbian Fangguang Jing* (勝鬘師子吼一乘大方便方廣經).
127. Stevens, 54–55. Original text in *Taisho* v. 17, n. 818, 825.
128. Stevens (1990), 56.
129. Faure (1998), 120.
130. *Chigo* means a young boy, aged between 7 and 14, and living in a monastery. A *chigo* usually does housework and is schooled by the monks. Childs (1980), 127.
131. For the narrative in English, Childs (1980).
132. Zen monk Ikkyu (1394-1481) popularized this legend in Japan. Monju (Jap. for Manjusri) set the example and Kukai, also known as Kobo Daishi, imported the legend from China. Schalow (1992), 216.
133. *Song of Understanding the Source*, *Taisho* v. 51 n. 2076, 461b, *Tengteng Heshang Liaoyuan Ge*, 騰騰和尚了元歌.
134. Nagarjuna, *Traité de la grande vertu de sagesse*, v. 1, 398-402.
135. The trickster is a god, demiurge or legendary hero, cunning, funny, found in most cultures. He is a cultural hero who likes to break the rules of gods or nature, often showing gender bending.
136. Among the critics, physiognomists adopted "pure criticism" *qingyi* 清議, and "pure conversations" *qingtan* 清議. The more philosophical current of the arcane or *xuanxue* 玄學, including Wang Bi 王弼, favored natural spontaneity through "effortless action" (*wuwei* 無為) instead of the formalism of Confucian rites. On this subject, see Hurteau (1983).
137. Xiang Warner.
138. Shan Tao (山濤), wife of one of the seven sages observed, with her husband's consent, his sexual exploits with Ruan Ji and Xi Kang. See Hinsch (1990), 68-71.
139. Faure (1998). 105-108. Shahar, 61, 70.
140. Kieschnick, 53.
141. On this new approach to discipline and morality in Chinese Mahayana, see Chu; Faure (1998), 89ff.
142. Faure (1998), 92.
143. Sponberg, 3–36; Levering, 136-156.
144. Sponberg links this tendency to Indian ascetic traditions of the time.
145. The eight additional rules are described in the *Vinaya Pitaka, Kullavagga*, X, 1.
146. Faure (2003), 63. On women's "three dependences" in China, read Chapter X of the *Book of Rites* (*Liji* 禮記) and Rosenlee, 47.
147. According to the *Abhidhamma Pitaka, Dhammasangani, Rupa Kandha*, and its commentary by Buddhaghosa, the *Atthasalini*, gender is classified as a physical phenomenon (*rupa*).

Itthindriya or femininity causes feminine appearance and behavior, and *purishindriya* or masculinity produces male appearance and behavior. Gender is not completely cultural.
148. Barnes, 116–118.
149. Bloom.
150. *Udayanavatsaraja-parivartah, You Tian Wang Jing* 優填王經 (*Taisho* v. 12, n. 332). English translation by Paul, 27-50.
151. *Zokuzokyo* (*Xuzang Jing*, 續藏經), v. 87, 921.
152. English translation by Cole, 202–207. Faure (2003), 73–78, is informative on the role played by the sutra in Chinese and Japanese popular imagination.
153. Faure (2005), 124.
154. In the *Sukhavativyuha Sutra*, the bodhisattva's thirty-fifth vow makes it a requirement to women's entrance into Pure Land.
155. *The Vimalakirti Sutra*, McRae, 130ff.
156. Bloom.
157. Cabezón, 181–199; Faure (2005), 131. Based on Tsong Khapa's writings (1357–1419).
158. Faure (1998), 138–139.
159. Levering.
160. Ordinance N. 2 of 1883, *An Ordinance to Provide a General Penal Code for Ceylon*, section 365; Union of Burma, *Penal Code, India Act XLV*, 1860 (May 1, 1861), section 377.
161. On Thai legislation, see Jackson (2003).
162. Nguyen Ngoc Huy, Ta Van Tai, and Tran Van Liem.
163. *Vinaya Pitaka, Mahavagga, Khandhaka* 1, 61.
164. *Vinaya Pitaka, Mahavagga, Khandhaka* 1, 68–69. Gyatso, 93–94; Zwilling (1992), 206.
165. Zwilling (1992), 204; Sweet and Zwilling (1993), 598–599, explain the list and its connexion with Ayurvedic medicine.
166. *Vinaya Pitaka, Mahavagga, Khandhaka*, 61. Gyatso, 93, note 9.
167. Blackstone, 298. Different physical handicaps may justify a refusal to ordain a monk.
168. Zwilling (1992), 205; Gyatso, 111–113.
169. On public opinion and its role, see Zwilling (1998), 47–48.
170. Zwilling (1998), 48.
171. Harvey (2000), 417–418. The author refers to the *Abidharmakosa, Visuddhimagga* IV, 41, and Nagasena's *Questions of King Milinda*, 310.
172. Harvey (2000), 421–422.
173. Zwilling (1992), 205. The idea could have been imported from the *Mahabharata*, which announced an increase of homosexual practices during the age of decline, the *Kali Yuga*.
174. Zwilling (1998), 53. The *Saddharma Smrityupasthana Sutra*.
175. According to Buddhist cosmology, the universe consists of three realms: the realm of desire (*kama loka* or *kama dathu*) inhabited by human beings, animals, and certain kinds of spirits and various hells, the realm of form (*rupa loka*) inhabited by gods, and the realm of the formless (*arupa loka*), the pure abode of the *anagamis*, the partially enlightened nonreturners.
176. Richard Hakluyt mentions these observations made by Fitch in his series *The Principal Navigations, Voyages, Traffiques and Discoveries of the English Nation*, published in London in 1599. The fragment may be found in the *SOAS Bulletin of Burma Research*, v. 2, n. 2, Autumn 2004, www.soas.ac.uk/burma/bulletin.htm.
177. Jackson (2003).
178. Huxley.
179. Neither the *Vientiane Code* nor the Mon *Dhammasats* contain any prohibition against homosexual acts. These documents limit sexual misconduct to adultery. See Raquez, 403ff, and Hla. The penalties sometimes take the form of physical correction, fine, or chores.
180. These details were personally communicated to me by Andrew Huxley. Cambodian codes refer to *Vinaya* rules concerning sodomy between monks and bestiality performed by a monk. *Kram Sanghkrey* seems to punish homosexuality and bestiality by lay people with a small fine. See Leclère, v. 1, 301, 318, 322. For some unexplained reason, section 22 of the Code (301) considers bestiality as more severe, and sometimes entailing confiscation of the culprit's assets

and the pillory for seven days. The Thai *Mangraisat* makes no mention of homosexual acts, although it does not endorse adultery, sexual immorality such as touching the breasts of a woman, or bestiality. See Wichienkeeo and Wijeyewardene.
181. Jackson (1998), 60, notes that, in Thailand, the third precept concerns adultery.
182. Jackson (1998), 65–69.
183. Peltier.
184. Guillon.
185. Peletz.
186. Matzner.
187. Jackson (1998), 79. On the question of karmic responsibility and its source, see Harvey (2000), 419.
188. *Therigatha*, 400–447, in particular verse 442. The *Therigatha* is part of the *Khuddaka Nikaya*, one of the Three Baskets.
189. Taywaditep, Coleman, and Dumronggittigule, 1040.
190. Jackson (1995).
191. Methangkun Bunmi (1986), *Khon pen kathoey dai yang rai* (*How Can People Be Kathoeys?*) referred to by Jackson (1998), 82.
192. Taywaditep, Coleman, and Dumronggittigule, 1039.
193. Jackson (1989), 23–44.
194. Ibid., 52–62. The author mentions a letter from young 28-year-old Roeng, who had sexual experiences with men and enjoyed them more than heterosexual relations. He sincerely believed that homosexual desires were related to karmic retribution. He also expressed his fears about stigma and said he was tired of leading a double life. The columnist, nicknamed Uncle Go, encouraged him to keep his secret.
195. Jackson (2004), "The Performative State," 181–218; Jackson (2004), "The Thai Regime of Images." See Loos who analyzes sexual life in the Inner City where minor wives continue to exist, female homosexuality, as well as male homosexuality. King Vajiravudh (early twentieth century) had a clear preference for men.
196. Jackson (2003).
197. French colonizers also found equally hard to differentiate genders in Indochina and perceived the masculine as being androgynous. Gender isomorphism was sometimes used to excuse the homosexual adventures of certain settlers with natives. See Proschan.
198. Jackson (1997). In 1956 the prestigious Thai encyclopedia *Saranukrom Thai* takes on a definition influenced by the Western biomedical model and saves the word to mean hermaphroditism.
199. Allyn. The use of the word "gay" has spread only over the last ten years, slightly less in the masses.
200. Ibid.
201. Ibid.
202. Ibid.
203. *The Nation*, "Editorial: Healthy Attitudes toward Homosexuals," December 27, 2002.
204. Jackson (1995).
205. Hinsch (1990), 20–21, quotes the *Hanfeizi* (韩非子), Chapter 12, *Shuonan* (說難). See Haggerty (2000), v. II, 185; Crompton, 214–215. The historian Sima Qian (司馬遷; 145–90 av. AD) in *Historical Records* (*Shiji* 史記) devotes Chapter 125 to the favorites at the Han court, the *Ningxing liezuan* 佞幸列傳 (*Biographies of Flatterers*), translation Watson (1993), 462–468. The word *ningxing* means one who manipulates words to flatter, and does not have any sexual connotation. However, Sima Qian mentions that the flatterers enjoyed the favors of the emperor not only because of their eloquence, but also because of their physical beauty, which brought them to share the imperial bed. See Kang, 27.
206. Crompton, 215–216.
207. Ibid., 217. This story is taken from a Song work, the *Taiping Guangji* (太平廣記, Extensive Records of the Taiping Era), roll 389. Archeology and the study of mortuary epigraphy revealed that the practice of common burial of spouses was frequent in Ancient China and Imperial China; see Yao.

208. Crompton, 218.
209. Kang, 23–24.
210. Hinsch (1990), 52–53. He cites this story from a book of the Northern Wei period, the *Weishu* (魏書) by Wei Shou (魏收), but the *Hanshu* (漢書), *Dong Xian Zhuan* (董賢傳) also has it.
211. Reported by the *Records of the Three Kingdoms*, Chapter 3, *Book of Wei*, *Sanguo Zhi*, *Wei Shu* (三國志卷三・魏書三). The same chronicle also mentions the love of Cao Cao's grandson, the king of Wei (明帝) Ming, for his cousin Cao Zhao (曹肇) and a Qin Lang (秦朗) he made captain of cavalry.
212. The *Book of Chen* (Chenshu, 陳書), biography 14. Van Gulik also mentions several male love affairs at the imperial court.
213. This poem is part of the anthology by Xu Ling (徐陵; 507–583) entitled *New Songs from the Jade Terrace*, *Yutai Xinyong* (玉臺新詠). See Hinsch (1990), 70–71; Crompton, 223.
214. Crompton, 228–230. See Mowry, 140–141.
215. Crompton, 231. For a detailed analysis, see Huang.
216. The story is found in volume IV of the fiction *Pleasant Spring and Fragrant Character* (*Yichun Xiangzhi*, 宜春香質).
217. Ruan (1997), 59–60.
218. Huang (2001), 177ff.
219. Crompton, 234–235. The two stories are analyzed by Vitiello (2000).
220. Vitiello (2000).
221. Vitiello (2011), 53–55.
222. Hinsch (1990), 135; Crompton, 231–233. The *Rou Putuan* is translated in English by Hanan (1990).
223. Partially narrated by Crompton, 231–233.
224. Partial summaries of this work to be found in Hinsch (1990), 156–161; Crompton, 242–244. Starr and McMahon discuss the novel.
225. See McMahon.
226. Louie and Low, 33–34; Wu (2004), 17ff.
227. Volp.
228. Sommer (1997), 144.
229. Ruskola.
230. Literally, the phrase translates into "naked branch," meaning a childless male, but *gun* also has a phallic meaning in the vernacular, so that it also has the meaning of "thug." See Sommer (2002), 67–88; and Ownby, 226–250.
231. Sommer (2002).
232. Ruskola, 2540, 2561. Section 160 of the *Criminal Code of the People's Republic of China* (*Zhonghua Renmin Gongheguo Xingfa* 中华人民共和国 刑法) presents this catchall aspect. The author notes that the laws on prostitution do not worry about male prostitution, 2559.
233. *Tongxinglian* was coined by Chinese sexologists and psychiatrists during the Kuomintang years (1912–1949) to translate the word "homosexuality," meaning word for word "attraction or affection for the same sex." The word "*tongxing'ai*" (同性爱) is also used, *ai* designating love. For a brief history of these terms, see Zhongxin, Farrer, and Choi.
234. Cristini, 4–5.
235. Li Yinhe, Wang Xiaobo (1992), *Tamende Shijie, Zhongguo Nan Tongxinglian Qunluo Toushi* (Their World, A Look inside the Male Homosexual Community, 他们的世界・中国男同性恋群落透视). Professor Li Yinhe has published a second book on the subject in 1998, *Tongxinglian Ya Wenhua* (The Homosexual Subculture, 同性恋亚文化), in which she demonstrates unavoidable changes in Chinese society, which must now take on the reality of homosexual unions and accept some form of legal recognition. Liu Dalin (2005), *Zhongguo Tongxinglian Yanjiu* (Study on Chinese Gays, 中国同性恋研究), Beijing Shi: *Zhongguo Shehui Chubanshe* (China Social Press, 北京市・中国社会出版社).
236. Liu Dalin (达临; 1992), *Zhongguo dang dai xing wen hua : Zhongguo liang wan li "xing wen ming" diao cha bao gao Zhongguo Dandai Xingwenhua* (Sexual Behaviour in Modern China:

A Report of the Nation-wide "Sex Civilisation" Survey on 20 000 Subjects in China, 中国当代性文化·中国两万例"性文明"调查报告, Xinhua shudian Shanghai). See Cristini, 72.
237. Zhongxin; Chou.
238. Beichuan and Kaufman.
239. Ibid.
240. *Mengzi*, IV, 6, translation by Lau, 169.
241. Hinsch (2005). The author makes a review of the literature published in Chinese.
242. Huang (2006), 148–154.
243. Edwards, 73–75.
244. Huang (2006), 78–80. The author illustrates his point of view from the sarcastic comments of Yan Yuan (颜元) and Wang Yuan (王源), who ridicule the quietism of neo-Confucian Song scholars, which he holds responsible for their lack of virility.
245. On the role of *yin/yang* theory in the perception of masculinity in imperial China, see Song.
246. Spence, 210ff; Vitiello.
247. Offermanns; Gernet, 290–299.
248. Ricci, *China in the Sixteenth Century: The Journals of Matthew Ricci, 1583–1610*, trans. Louis J. Gallagher, Random House, New York, 1953, 402. Gernet, 290.
249. Matteo Ricci wrote in 1595 *Jiaoyou Lun* (On Friendship, 交友論) and in 1647 another Jesuit Martino Martini wrote, *Qiuyou Pian* (The Search for Friends, 逑友篇). Timothy James Billings translated *On Friendship* (Columbia University Press, 2009).
250. Faure (1998), 207ff; Offermanns, 28–29.
251. He wrote *Tiandi Yinyang Jiaohuan Dale Fu* (Poetical Essay on the Supreme Joy of the Sexual Union of Yin and Yang and Heaven, 天地陰陽交歡大樂賦). See details in Van Gulik, 202–208. The work is part of the *Dunhuang Yiyao Wenxian Jijiao* (The Dunhuang medical texts edited and collated, 敦煌醫藥文獻輯校).
252. Faure (1998), 237.
253. *The Carnal Prayer Mat*, 304.
254. *Taisho* v. 22, n. 1428, 568–580.
255. Pachow, 39.
256. *Sifenlü*, *Taisho* v. 22, n. 1428, 812c; also the *Sarvastivada Vinaya*, *Shisonglü* 十诵律, *Taisho* v. 23, n. 1435, 153c. The *Lotus Sutra*, translated into Chinese by Kumarajiva, says that the bodhisattva should avoid familiarity with these five categories of men lacking virility, *Miaofa Lianfa Jing* (妙法蓮華經), *Taisho* v. 9, n. 262, 37b7.Vasubandhu (*Abhidharma Kosa*) *Jushe Lun* (俱舍論), Taisho v. 41, n. 1821, 56c.
257. Ch'ü and Dull, 374. Faure (1998) mentions the Japanese translation of *huang men* into *komon* by Zen master Dogen, 215 n. 30.
258. *Sifenlü*, *Taisho* v. 22 n. 1428, 812c.
259. Black, 166–195.
260. Kieschnick (2008), "Celibacy in East Asian Buddhism," in Olson, 228.
261. This book belongs to supernatural fiction known as "accounts of anomalies" (*Zhiguai Xiaoshuo*, 志怪 小說)—stories about supernatural beings unknown to Confucianism, which seeks to order the world according to reason (*li* 理) and eradicate superstition.
262. Pflugfelder, 158–162.
263. Furukawa.
264. McLelland. The author shows the historical development of the use of the word *hentai* in magazines, comics, or *manga*, and animation after the war. These books include all sorts of sexual practices: homosexuality, fetishism, sadomasochism, suicide lovers, etc.
265. The genre is composed of eight books: *Aki no yo no nagamonogatari*, *Genmu Monogatari*, *Ashibiki*, *Hanamitsu*, *Matsuho ura Monogatari*, *Toribeyama Monogatari*, *Monogatari Saga*, and *Ben No Soshi*. Faure (1998), 241.
266. The two temples belong to the Tendai sect founded by Saicho on Mount Hiei in the late sixth century. The Onjo-ji was built in the late seventh century. Both temples fraternized, but they quickly became enemies from the ninth century as a result of disputes over the appointment of an abbot from Miireda, to lead the Enryaku-ji. The struggle turned violent and brought about their partial destruction, both monasteries recruiting fighter monks (*sohei*).

267. Childs (1980).
268. The story is found in Childs (1991), 31–52.
269. Faure (1998), 245.
270. Watanabe and Iwata, 41.
271. *Tsurezuregusa*, 54; English translation by Keene, 47–48.
272. English text in Schalow (1992), 216–220.
273. Faure (1998), 211.
274. The word *ukiyo* (憂き世) translates the Buddhist concept of samsara. In the Tokugawa era, the homonym with a different graph (浮世) meant the floating, an expression used to describe the red-light districts of Kyoto, Tokyo, and Osaka. It surely alluded to the Buddhist doctrine of ignorance, attachment to the pleasures as the source of human suffering.
275. Ihara Saikaku, *Five Women Who Loved Love*, Book V, *Gengobei the Mountain of Love*, trans. de Bary, 195ff.
276. Ihara Saikaku, *The Life of an Amorous Man*, trans. Masakazu Kuwata, 36–39, for his first sexual experience with a prostitute from the Kabuki. As for his continuing enjoyment of male actors, see 147ff.
277. Traditional epic theater, initiated in the seventeenth century by a woman and played by women until the Shogun forbade performances by women, who were first replaced by youths, themselves replaced by mature men because they aroused the passions of their male audience, and, like women actresses, got involved in prostitution.
278. Ihara Saikaku, *The Great Mirror of Male Love*, trans. Paul Gordon Schalow (1990).
279. Schalow (1990), 219ff.
280. See section 2:5 "Nightingale in the Snow," Schalow (1990), 118ff. Two adolescent pages are sent to a Samurai to obtain nightingale feathers, which would help their master's son heal from smallpox. They were sent after a first attempt to obtain the feathers was made by girls who were sent back home by the woman-hater. He gave them the feathers and after having resolved that matter with their master they came back to the Samurai Shimamura Tonai, and asked him to teach them the way of boy love. He happily greeted the two acolytes who were prepared to die for him and vowed an eternal love to the two youths, Dannosuke and Naiki.
281. Schalow (1992), 4.
282. Schalow (1990), 181ff.
283. Ibid., section 7:4.
284. *Tales of Moonlight and Rain*, trans. Leon M. Zolbrod, 185ff.
285. Translation in Schalow (1998), 107–124.
286. Founded in 1967, in London, by an English monk, who took the name of Sangharakshita when he was ordained in 1950.
287. Harvey (2000), 428–430.
288. Wu, 26.
289. *Samyutta Nikaya, Sagatha Vagga, Bhikkhuni Samyutta, Soma Sutta*.

3 JUDAISM

1. *American Jewish Year Book 2002*.
2. *National Jewish Population Survey (NJPS) 2000–01*, 7. The observance of the *Seder* is at 67 percent, *Hanukkah* at 72 percent, and *Yom Kippur* at 59 percent.
3. *Bereshit* (Genesis), 11.
4. Ibid., 17.
5. *Shemot* (Exodus), 20:1–21, contains the Ten Commandments as such, while *Shemot*, 20:19–23, 33 contains the Code of the Covenant. The latter is probably a later addition, since the more elaborate rules reflect elaborate social conditions, related to the settlement and not simply roaming through the wilderness; e.g., *Shemot*, 22:5, 29 refers to cultivation of fields and vineyards.
6. Ibid., 32.

7. Ibid., 34.
8. *Torah* means law or teaching.
9. These books are: *Bereshit* (Genesis), *Shemot* (Exodus), *Vayikra* (Leviticus), *Bamidbar* (Numbers), *Devarim* (Deuteronomy).
10. The *Tanakh* does not mention 613 rules but tradition assigns their origin to Rabbi Simlai (third century AD). The philosopher Maimonides (1135–1204) lists the 613 *mitzvoth* with examples in his *Sefer ha-Mitzvoth* (Book of Commandments).
11. *Shemot*, 25:10–21.
12. *Nevi'im*, *Yehoshua* (Book of Joshua), 6.
13. *Shemot*, 36:8–38.
14. 2 *Shmuel* (Samuel), 6.
15. 2 *Melachim* (Kings), 8:1–13.
16. 1 *Melachim*, 12.
17. 2 *Melachim*, 17:5–6.
18. Ibid., 24:10–25.
19. For the causes that led the Northern Kingdom to fall in the hands of the Assyrians, see ibid., 17:7–23; on the fall of Judah to the Babylonians, see ibid., 21:10–17.
20. *Sefer Yshayah* (Isaiah), 1:2, the first 12 chapters in a general fashion.
21. This story is found in the *Kebra Nagast* (The Book of the Glory of Kings), a book of the fourteenth century. The text is translated from Ge'ez by Budge. See Chapters 46 and 48 for sure.
22. This legend is based on a mention in 2 *Maccabees* 2:1–8 referring to records supplied by the prophet Jeremiah to the exiled in Babylon. Rabbi Rachnael Steinberg and Rabbi Mendel Tropper discovered a text by Rabbi Naftali Hertz Ben Yaakov Elchanan of Frankfurt, the *Emeq ha-Melech* (Valley of the King), dating from 1648.
23. *Yeshayahu*, 11; *Yehezqel*, 40.
24. *Vayikra*, 1–7. Various forms of sacrifice are mentioned: communion, atonement, reparation.
25. During this festival, Jews are required to take their meals in huts (*sukkah*) for seven days to commemorate the passage in the desert of the Jewish people, on the way to the Promised Land. According *Vayikra*, 23, 42 Jews were required to live in these shelters for seven days, and sleep in them. The festival is still observed today by Orthodox Jews who build a *sukkah* outside their house or apartment. In cold climates, sleeping there is not required.
26. *Yirmiyahu* (Jeremiah), 7:21–23.
27. *Yirmiyahu*, 3:16.
28. *Nahemya*, 8; on Ezra and Nehemiah's missions, see *Ezra* 7 and 8.
29. Neusner (1970), 5.
30. Grabbe, 148.
31. Ibid., 131.
32. Ibid., 148–149.
33. The story of the Maccabean revolt and the establishment of the Hasmonean Dynasty is narrated by the Jewish historian Flavius Josephus in *War of the Jews* [Φλαυίου Ἰωσήπου ἱστορία Ἰουδαικοῦ πολέμου πρὸς Ῥωμαίους], Book I.
34. Rituals accompanying animal and grain sacrifices are preserved for posterity in a later work the *Mishnah*, which appeared after the destruction of the Temple in 70 AD. It includes 63 tractates (*masechtot*) divided into six orders (*sedarim*). The sixth order is entitled *Kodahim* or the "sacred objects" needed for the sacrificial rites. The second order of the *Mishnah*, *Moed* (Festival) deals with various rituals to be observed during Jewish holidays.
35. See Wilhelm Bacher (1901–1906), "The Great Synagogue," *The Jewish Encyclopedia*, 640–643. In the *Babylonian Talmud*, 33a, *Seder Zaraim*, *Berakhot*, Rabbi Yohanan attributes the making of prayers to the Great Assembly.
36. In the *Babylonian Talmud*, 26b, *Seder Zaraim*, *Berakhot*, Rabbi Yehoshua ben Levi explicitly said that the three daily prayers (*tefillot*) were introduced to replace the sacrifices.
37. Maimonides, *Mishneh Torah*, *Ahavah* (Love), 1, 1–5.
38. Cohen, 146.
39. Flavius Josephus, *Jewish Antiquities*, XIII. 10. 6. According to this witness, the Pharisees and the Sadducees existed, for the least, in the second century BC. In his *Wars of the Jews*, II. 8. 14,

he still shows them closely tied to the Mosaic Law, but he does not develop this aspect further. Writing in another context, after the destruction of the Temple, Josephus aimed at a wider audience, and preferred to address the conflict between these groups in terms of their philosophy rather than see their opposition at the level of their application of the law.
40. See *Ezra*, 9; and *Nahemya*, 10. For an overview of both groups, see the articles by Kaufman Kohler (1901–1906), "Pharisees," and "Sadducees," *The Jewish Encyclopedia*, v. IX, 661–666, and v. X, 630–633.
41. All males aged more than 13 years are required to wear the *tefillin*—two wooden boxes covered with leather, one on the left arm and the other on the head—at the time of the morning prayer, which begins with the words "*Shema Yisrael*," "Hear O Israel" (*Devarim* [Deuteronomy], 6:4–9). The *tefillin* contain these texts, also contained in the *mezuzah*—the parchment inserted into a decorative box on the right doorpost of houses and synagogues. This shows that the place of worship is not the temple, and, therefore, there is no need for the intercession of a priest. The *tefillin* and *mezuzah* are symbols of democratization, the *tefillin* replacing the turban and the breastplate worn by the High Priest, and the *mezuzah* transforming the house into a temple or sacred place. See Kaufmann Kohler (1901–1906), "Pharisees," *The Jewish Encyclopedia*, v. IX, 662.
42. Neusner (1970), 161.
43. Wilhelm Bacher and Jacob Zallel Lauterbach (1901–1906), "Sanhedrin," *The Jewish Encyclopedia*, v. XI, 41–44.
44. *Mishnah, Pirke Avot*, 1–2.
45. These sages are first called *Zugot* (pairs) to denote five pairs of rabbis, the president and vice president of the Sanhedrin, and they represent the highest authority in the interpretation of Mosaic Law. The best known are probably Hillel and Shammai. After them come the *Tannaim*, and the last is Yehuda ha-Nasi, the compiler.
46. Neusner (1999), 79–80.
47. For an overview of the *Talmud*, see Wilhelm Bacher (1901–1906), "Talmud," *The Jewish Encyclopedia*, v. XII, 1–28.
48. The *Bavli* was compiled primarily in the Sura Yeshiva, by two Amoraim, Rav Ashi and Ravina II, in the last quarter of the fifth century. It often highlights discussions between two Amoraim of the third century, Rabbi Arika in charge of the Sura Yeshiva, and Rabbi Shmuel, president of the Nehardea Yeshiva.
49. *Bavli*, 60b, *Seder Nashim*.
50. Wilhelm Bacher and Jacob Zallel Lauterbach (1901–1906), "She'elot u-teshuvot," *The Jewish Encyclopedia*, v. XI, 240–250.
51. The epithets "Sephardic" and "Ashkenaz" have a rather ethnic and cultural flavor than religious. There are some differences in the liturgy and in the application of *kashrut*. The Sephardic community is certainly the oldest, but the smallest today. The presence of Ashkenazim goes back to Germany, probably in the eleventh century, or shortly before, first in Rhineland cities such as Worms, Speyer, and Mainz. Among the chief rabbis of that time, whose comments are still authoritative, are Rabbi Shlomo ben Yitzhak of Troyes, in Champagne, known as Rashi (1040–1105), and Gershom ben Judah of Mainz (960–1028).
52. The medieval rabbinic era is known as *Rishonim* and extends to the fifteenth century.
53. Herman Rosenthal and Peter Wiernik (1901–1906), "Haskalah," *The Jewish Encyclopedia*, v. VI, 256–258.
54. Spinoza considered Mosaic Law as not revealed by God to Moses, but rather a later invention to promote a particular sociopolitical vision copied from Ancient Israel. Judaism, therefore, cannot claim to present a universal truth.
55. On Mendelssohn's position vis-à-vis Mosaic Law, see Arkush, 167–239.
56. In 1793, Saul Berlin, son of the Grand Rabbi of Berlin, and himself a master of Talmudic literature, published *Besamim Rosh* (Incense and Spices), a collection of 392 *responsa* he fictitiously attributed to a rabbi of the fourteenth century and in which he relativizes the authority of the *Talmud*, advocating more flexibility in the observance of the Sabbath and certain dietary laws.
57. This policy statement is known as the Pittsburgh Platform and makes use of the principles of the reform initiated in Germany. The text is available on the website of the *Central Conference of American Rabbis*: www.ccarnet.org/documentsandpositions/platforms/.

58. Frankel uses the historical-critical method in his study of the *Mishnah, Darke ha-Mishnah*, to demonstrate the evolving nature of *Halacha* in rabbinical literature.
59. Bolesław Pobożny ratified on September 8, 1264, a charter of rights for the Jews, the *Statut Kaliski*.
60. In 1495, the Jews were accused of setting fire to buildings and expelled from the city of Kraków to the nearby town of Kazimierz. They were granted the privilege of building a wall around the city to protect themselves.
61. Hundert, 15.
62. In 1569, the *Union of Lublin* created the Polish-Lithuanian Commonwealth until 1791.
63. Hundert, 33.
64. For further readings, see Baumgarten.
65. The *Litvish* also include Jews from Latvia, Belarus, and the region of Suwałki in Northeastern Poland.
66. *Likoutei Amarim*, Part I, Chapter 8.
67. *Bereshit*, 1:27–28.
68. *Hosea*, 2:4–5. The prophet Ezekiel, in Chapter 16, compares Israel to a prostitute because it turned away from the Lord to worship the surrounding gods of Egypt, Assyria, Chaldea, and Canaan. The *Song of Songs (Shir ha-Shirim)* is probably the *locus classicus* for the celebration of human love seen as a blessing or an allegory for God's love for his people.
69. Biale, 11–13.
70. *Vayikra*, Chapters 18–22.
71. Ibid.,18:23.
72. Ibid., 18:1–4.
73. *Bereshit*, 2:24.
74. This prohibition is found in *Devarim*, 7:1–3. In *Ezra*, 9–10, Jews returning from exile and who had taken a foreign wife, pledge to repudiate her.
75. *Devarim*, 7:3–4. On this question, see Hayes, 25–28. The author points out that the uncleanness mentioned by Ezra is not merely moral, but becomes hereditary because only the seed of Israel is holy. In addition, the *Torah*'s prohibition is but partial, since it is not directed at all foreigners, and only high priests are required to marry a virgin belonging to their tribe. In postexilic times, the prohibition is universal, since the entire nation is regarded as the holy Temple.
76. This principle is clearly expressed in the *Mishnah, Qiddushin*, 3, 12 quoted by Cohen. It seems well established that Jewish society was first patrilineal, and then gradually moved toward the matrilineal—probably a consequence related to prohibition of mixed marriages in postexilic times—which automatically transferred the mother's nationality to the child born of a mixed union. Cohen links the origin of mishnaic matriliny to the influence of Roman law and the Judaic laws on mixtures (*kilayim*). See Susan Sorek. The author offers a feminist reading of this change by showing women were more likely to transmit the values of charity (*hesed*) needed for the progress of Jewish religion, after the destruction of the Temple.
77. Marriage in Hebrew is *Qiddushin* from *Qadosh*, which means holy.
78. *Bavli*, 20a, *Seder Nashim, Nedarim, Gemara*.
79. *Mishneh Torah, Sefer Kedusha, Issurei Biah* 21:9.
80. Eleazar of Worms, *Sefer ha-Rokeah* (The Perfumer), *Hilkhot Teshuvah*, n. 14, 27, in Biale, 78.
81. *Sefer Hasidim*, n. 1084, 275, in Biale, 78.
82. Boyarin (1993), 52. The author cites the *Bavli*, 5b, *Seder Nezikin, Avodah Zara*, which explains the interpretation of the Babylonian rabbis. For them, sexuality is related to the command to multiply received by Adam in Eden, but also the order given by Yahweh to his people in the Sinai to return to the joys of privacy in their tents (*Devarim*, 5:30)—a thinly veiled reference to the full legitimacy of the joy of sex.
83. Maimonides, *Mishneh Torah, Issurei Biah*, 21:9.
84. Maimonides, *Moreh Nevuchim (Guide for the Perplexed)*, Book 3, Chapter 49, Friedländer, v. III, 267, 270.
85. Philo of Alexandria, *De Specialibus Legibus*, 1. 8–9.
86. Diamond, 129.

Notes

87. Satlow (1996), 22-24.
88. The Essenes of Qumran, as well as the *Therapeutae* in the region of Alexandria, practiced celibacy. On this question, see Eliezer Diamond, 34. Among Christians, the Montanists and the Encratrites advocated celibacy.
89. Clement of Alexandria, *Stromata*, Book III, Chapter 11, n. 71: "'You have heard that the law commanded, Thou shalt not commit adultery. But I say, Thou shalt not lust.' That the law intended husbands to cohabit with their wives with self-control and only for the purpose of begetting children is evident from the prohibition which forbids the unmarried man from having immediate sexual relations with a captive woman. If the man has conceived a desire for her, he is directed to mourn for thirty days while she is to have her hair cut; if after this the desire has not passed off, then they may proceed to beget children, because the appointed period enables the overwhelming impulse to be tested and to become a rational act of will."
90. Origen, *Commentarius in Epistolam ad Romanos*, Book I, Chapter 12, Scheck, 80-81.
91. John Chrysostom, *De Virginitate*. Augustine expressed the same idea in *De Sancta Virginitate*, 15, and St. Jerome, *Adversus Iovinianum* 1, 12 (*Patrologia Latina*, 23, 237-38).
92. *De Bono Conjugali*, 24.
93. The Gospel of Thomas reported the need to break with earthly things to reach the spiritual being within, similar to the androgynous primordial being of Genesis, I:27. Tertullian, in his *Liber de Monogamia*, Chapter 3, promotes the superiority of abstinence over marriage—the abstinence practiced by eunuchs (Latin *spado*) for the Kingdom, imitating the emblematic eunuch, Christ himself: "Seeing that the Lord Himself opens 'the kingdoms of the heavens' to 'eunuchs,' as being Himself, withal, a virgin; to whom looking, the apostle also–himself too for this reason abstinent–gives the preference to continence."
94. Eusebius, (*Historia Ecclesiastica*), *Church History*, Book VI, Chapter 8, 1-5.
95. Biale, 40, mentions a passage from the *Mishnah* alluding to a eunuch named Ben Megosath (*Bavli*, 79b, *Seder Nashim*, *Yevamoth*). The rabbis seem to follow the disapproval of castration found in *Devarim*, 23:2. Voluntary castration goes directly against the divine order to multiply (*Bavli*, 111a, *Seder Moed*, *Shabbat*).
96. *Bavli*, 63b, *Yevamot*.
97. Boyarin (1993), 135.
98. Biale, 98, describes this type of criticism found in a thirteenth-century apologetic treatise, the *Sefer Nizzahon Yashan* (The Book of Polemic), which discusses the differences between Judaism and Christianity.
99. *De Virginitate*, 1, 1.
100. Boyarin (1992), 1. In reference to Augustine's *Tractatus adversus Judaeos*, VII, 9.
101. *Bavli*, 69b, *Seder Moed*, *Yoma*. Boyarin (1992), 61.
102. *Bavli*, 20b, *Seder Nashim*, *Nedarim*, *Gemara*.See also *Bavli*, 86a, *Seder Moed*, *Shabbat*, and 17a, *Seder TohorothMelachim*, *Niddah*.
103. *Bavli*, 20b, *Seder Nashim*, *Nedarim*, *Gemara*.
104. *Bavli*, 20b, *Seder Nashim*, *Nedarim*, *Gemara*.
105. *De Nuptiis et Concupiscentia*, 2. 5. 14.
106. According to the midrashic commentary of Genesis, *Bereshit Rabbah*, 18:6, the snake goes mad with desire for Eve, and, seeing her having sex with Adam, it sexually assaults her. There is no sexual sin between Adam and Eve. See Boyarin (1993), 83; and Biale, 45.
107. *Vayikra*, 15.
108. Boyarin (1993), 91-92.
109. *Bavli*, 64b, *Seder Nashim*, *Ketubot*, Biale, 52.
110. *Bavli*, 64b, *Seder Nashim*, *Ketubot*. See Sarah Rosenthal. To illustrate the power of male desire, she quotes a passage from *Bavli* 75a, *Seder Nezikin*, *Sanhedrin*, in which a man's arousal at the sight of a woman threatens his health. The doctors consulted recommend that he satisfies his desire with the woman, to which the rabbis objected.
111. *Bavli*, 5a, *Seder Zaraim*, *Berakhot*. Satlow (1996), 32.
112. On these two positions, see Boyarin (1993), 142-144. In *Bavli*, 29b, *Seder Nashim*, *Qiddushin*, both positions are presented—that of Babylon by the Rabbi Shmuel and that of Palestine by

Rabbi Yohanan, for whom the duties of marriage would be for the student a millstone around the neck.
113. Biale, 130.
114. Ibid., 130–137.
115. Ibid., 104–105. Reference made to an anonymous work from the thirteenth century, *Iggeret ha-Kodesh* (Holy Epistle).
116. *Bavli*, 13a, *Seder Tohorot, Niddah, Gemara*. Some rabbis urge followers to urinate without touching the penis.
117. *Bavli*, 13a, *Seder Tohorot, Niddah, Gemara*. In this tractate, Rabbi Yohanan refers to the story of Onan, but the intent moves far beyond the prohibition of coitus interruptus to include all forms of wasting sperm.
118. Biale, 73.
119. Hundert, 132. *Shulhan Aruch, Even ha-Ezer*, 23.
120. Hundert, 131–137. The author associates the new rigor with increasing the age of marriage, which leaves many young single men struggling with their libido.
121. *Likoutei Amarim*, Chapter 7.
122. Central Conference of American Rabbis (1979), *Responsa No 153 Masturbation*; see also Stein.
123. *Bavli*, 47b, *Seder Nashim, Ketubot*. Biale, 53–57.
124. Satlow (1995), 27–29. The author gives several references to Talmudic and Midrashic literature, such as *Bavli*, 19a, *Seder Nezikin, Avodah Zara*, which welcomes the fact that men, unlike women, can by prayer and study of the *Torah* control their sexual impulses (*yetzer ha-ra*). See Rosenthal.
125. Satlow (1995), 29. Biale, 19–20.
126. *Bavli*, 22b, *Seder Nezikin, Sanhedrin*.
127. *Bavli*, 50a, *Seder Nashim, Nedarim*. For more information on women and domesticity, see Baskin.
128. *Bavli*, 84a, *Seder Nezikin, Baba Mezia*; Boyarin (1997), 127–150.
129. Boyarin (1997), 136, aptly notes that the Talmudic story excludes Rabbi Yohanan from its wishlist of the most beautiful men precisely because he is beardless.
130. Boyarin (1997), 66–67; Hundert, 52–53.
131. Boyarin (1995), 69. The author discusses circumcision perceived negatively by the dominant culture as feminization.
132. Boyarin (1997) quotes Glückel's autobiography, a seventeenth-century Jewish shopkeeper from Hameln. The qualities she boasts to find in her husband are ones that the German bourgeois society of the time rather applied to women (53–55). The author also demonstrates his point by using the Yiddish folklore of Eastern Europe (68–70).
133. Hyman, 41. The author makes the necessary nuances between the German situation and the situation of Jewish women of Eastern Europe, where the economic situation was more precarious and women often less educated, especially in areas where the Jews settled. However, progressive ideas (*Haskalah*) were not completely absent; i.e., demands for greater gender equality, among other things.
134. Adler.
135. On the right of women to the Rabbinate and its history, see Nadell.
136. *Mishneh Torah, Sefer Nashim, Hilkhot Ishut*, Chapter 15:20. Orthodox women also claim their rights to participate as equals in leadership and religious worship, such as the American Blu Greenberg of the Jewish Orthodox Feminist Alliance.
137. *Vayikra*, 18.
138. Ibid., 18: 22.
139. Ibid., 20: 13.
140. *Bavli*, 82a, *Seder Nashim, Qiddushin*. See Solomon, 76.
141. Bavli, 56, *Seder Nezikin, Sanhedrin* lists the Seven Laws of Noah: no blasphemy, illicit sexual unions, idolatry, murder, theft, eating the flesh of a live animal, and the obligation to set up courts of justice. See Greenberg (2004), 70. The author refers to *Midrash Sekhel Tov* of Menachem ben Solomon ben Isaac (twelfth century) and the *Midrash Yalkut Shimoni*,

Ezekiel 373 (anonymous twelfth century), which incorporate homosexual anal relations in the Noachide Code. The idea was already expressed by the Amoraim Talmudist Ulla in *Bavli, Sefer Qodashim, Hullin*, 92b. According to Ulla, other nations practiced male sodomy (*mishkav zachur*) but did not allow prenuptial contracts (*ketubah*) between males.

142. Maimonides, *Mishneh Torah, Issurei Biah* 1:14; 22: 2. In the second passage, Maimonides sees no problem if two men are together in a confined space but *Shulhan Aruch, Even ha-Ezer*, 24, will change the rule in the sixteenth century, justifying it by the salacious mores of the period.
143. The word "abomination" (*toevah*), which means "mistake," is associated with idolatrous worship of other nations in the Deuteronomic Code (*Devarim*, 23:18–19) and by Yhezqel, 6:9–11. Nissinen, 39, and Olyan (1994), 180, 199.
144. On this hypothesis, see Olyan (1994), 198–199.
145. *Devarim*, 23:18–19. The Deuteronomic Code consists of Chapters 12–26.
146. In the cuneiform, *assinnu* means "dog/man-woman" (ambiguous gender), an allusion to the androgynous nature of this character. See Nissinen (1998), 28. The word "dog" is used negatively to describe the kind of person, and it is worth noting that this same word is also applied by the Deuteronomic Code to a *qadesh*.
147. Nissinen, 28–33; Leick, 158–161.
148. Nissinen, 40. The author cites several passages from *Melachim* I and II, some of them suggesting a link between the presence, in the Temple dedicated to Yahweh, of *qedeshim* associated with the worship of Canaanite deities—the gods of rain and fertility, Baal and Asherah or Athtart, the mother goddess of Ugarit.
149. Olyan (1994), 180–188. Nissinen, 44. The analysis of the words used leads to one conclusion– comparing the position of the insertee to the woman's position during vaginal penetration can only describe homosexual penetration.
150. Greenberg (2004), 82.
151. Olyan (1994), 188–189. According to the author, the second release of the ban was posterior.
152. *Devarim*, 23:2, proscribes castration; cross-dressing is prohibited in 22:5. See Nissinen, 42–43.
153. Guinan.
154. Olyan (1994), 191–194; Nissinen, 26–28.
155. Olyan (1994), 202–203. Biale, 29–30, offers such an interpretation by setting the ban on anal intercourse in the overall context of *Vayikra* 18 where the majority of sexual prohibitions are intended to prevent the waste of male seed, as in bestiality or sex with a menstruating woman.
156. *De Specialibus Legibus*, 3.39; *De Abrahamo*, 135. Satlow (1994), 8, and Nissinen, 95.
157. *War of the Jews*, Book IV, Chapter 9:10.
158. Nissinen, 93–95, 99. In *Bavli*, 17a, *Sefer Moed, Shabbat*, the sages warn boys against attempts by heathen males to seduce and corrupt them.
159. Satlow (1994), 9–10.
160. Boyarin (1995a), 340–344. *Vayikra*, 19:19 forbids sowing seeds of two species in the same field; breeding two animals of different species; or weaving a garment with two different fibers.
161. Few people question the sexual nature of the gesture that is attempted by the men of Sodom, even if the verb used (*yada*) means "knowing." It is often used elsewhere in the Hebrew Bible to mean sexual intercourse.
162. *Yshayahu*, 1:10–17; *Yehezqel*, 16: 48–49. Loader, 43, 59–65.
163. *Matthew*, 10:15, 11:20–24; *Luke*, 10:10–12, 17:22–37. Loader, 118–127. The only explicit reference to the sexual nature of the fault is in 2 Peter 2: 6.
164. Nissinen, 89–93; Loader, 80–85.
165. *Bereshit*, 6:1–4. The sexual union of heavenly beings with earthly women is an example of the evil that caused the flood. Hellenistic Judaism interpreted the union as a perversion of the created order, like the intention of the men of Sodom. See Nissinen, 91; Loader, 81–82.
166. *Testament of Naphtali*, 3: 2–5.
167. Philo of Alexandria, *De Abrahamo*, 136–166. Flavius Josephus, *Jewish Antiquities*, 1: 194–206; *Against Apion*, 2: 273–275. See Loader, 86–103.

168. Loader develops this view particularly well. For example, the allegorical interpretation of Sodom is used by Philo to illustrate how hedonistic passions can blind individuals and destroy an entire nation (37, 91–92, 112).
169. *Bavli*, 109, *Sanhedrin, Seder Nezikin*; *Bereshit Rabbah*, 42–43.
170. I *Shmuel*, 18–23.
171. Ibid., 20:41.
172. II *Shmuel*, 1:26.
173. See Horner (1978), 26–39. The author provides a homosexual reading of the existing friendship between the two men, but his argument does not rely on solid textual evidence. To learn more about the two readings of this story, see Römer and Bonjour, 61–80; Nissinen, 55–56.
174. Römer analyzes some of the words of both heroes expressing love and affection, and finds them used elsewhere in the Hebrew Bible in an erotic or downright sexual context. Also Nissinen, 56.
175. Walls, 17–76.
176. *The Epic of Gilgamesh*, Tablet I, Maureen Gallery Kovacs translator, 12.
177. Roth (1989), 91–118; Schirmann.
178. Medieval *responsa* on homosexuality are nonexistent, except for Rabbi Joseph Ibn Abitur who gave his opinion on the promiscuous conduct of a dissolute *hazzan* (cantor) with women and a teenager. Rarity does not substantiate the absence of pederasty among Andalusian Sephardic Jews, since few *responsa* written at the time of the Andalusian poets have survived. Mentions exist elsewhere. For example, Saadia Gaon is accused of committing homosexual acts with male teenagers during his stay in Iraq as *gaon* (director) of the Pumbenita Talmudic Academy. See Roth (1982), 23.
179. Eron, 114–115; Solomon, 77.
180. Biale, 157–158.
181. *Pesikta Zutrata*, Solomon 76.
182. Epstein, *Torah Teminah, Vayikra*, 18: 22. Solomon 76.
183. Lamm, 198.
184. Feinsein, *Iggerot Moshe, Orach Chayyim*, quoted in Magonet, 81.
185. Greenberg (2004), 136–137.
186. Freundel.
187. *Le Figaro*, July 2, 1996 (my translation). His positions are more detailed in a book written in collaboration with a psychoanalyst; Joseph Sitruk and Daniel Sibony, 24–25. He objects to homosexuality and the recognition of homosexual unions, civil or religious.
188. *Lyon Capitale*, February 13, 2007.
189. Gugenheim.
190. Canada, 38th Legislature, 1st session, Legislative Committee on Bill C-38, *Evidence*, June 8, 2005.
191. Greenberg (2004), 182–183.
192. Ibid., 178.
193. Ibid., 192–213.
194. Read Saul M. Olyan's (2005) critique.
195. Greenberg (2004), 147.
196. Ibid., 154. The author quotes *Bavli*, 13b, *Sefer Tohoroth, Niddah*, to show that the sin of Onan (*Bereshit*, 38) does not consist in ejaculating outside the vagina but failing the duty of levirate to Tamar, his brother Er's widow, by taking advantage of her sexual favors without trying to procure a male offspring.
197. Greenberg (2004), 156.
198. On this aspect, Greenberg refers to the authority of the great twelfth-century French tosafist, Rabbi Yaakov Ben Meir Tam.
199. Ibid., 162.
200. Solomon B. Freehof (1973), Central Conference of American Rabbis, *American Reform Responsa, Responsum No 13*, "Judaism and Homosexuality," v. LXXIII, 1973, 115–119.
201. *Resolution Adopted by the CCAR, Report of the Ad Hoc Committee on Homosexuality and the Rabbinate*, 1990.

Notes

202. *CCAR Responsa, On Homosexual Marriage, 5756.8*, 1996: www.ccarnet.org/.
203. *Resolution Adopted by the CCAR, Resolution on Same Gender Officiation*, March 2000.
204. *Resolution Adopted by the CCAR, Proposed Federal Marriage Amendment to the United States Constitution*, June 2004.
205. *Reference re Same-Sex Marriage*, SCC 79.
206. Ramer, *Queering the Text*.
207. *Responsa of the CJLS 1991–2000, Consensus Statement on Homosexuality*, EH24.1992a, 612. Available at: ww.rabbinicalassembly.org / law / teshuvot_public.html.
208. Artson.
209. Roth, *Responsa of the CJLS 1991–2000, Homosexuality*, EH24.1992b, 613–675.
210. Roth, *Responsa of the 1991-CJLS 2000, Homosexuality* EH24.1992b, 621. The author refers to Rashi's comment in *Bavli, Sefer Qodashim, Hullin* 92b, which states that even in societies where homosexual liaisons are durable; they have no legal recognition in the form of a legal contract. *Bereshit Rabbah*, 26.5 has Rabbi Huna declare that the generation of the flood was not erased from the earth until the appearance of nuptial songs, celebrating sex between males. The *Sifra, Aharei Mot*, 8:8–9 speaks of same-sex unions in the surrounding cultures of Israel.
211. Dorff, Nevins, and Reisner, 5. This *responsum* is approved divisively: 13 rabbis in favor, 12 against.
212. Dorff, Nevins, and Reisner, 6–7.
213. *Mishneh Torah, Issurei Biah*, 21:1; *Sefer ha-Mitsvoth* n. 352–353.
214. *Shulhan Aruch, Even ha-Ezer*, 20:1.
215. *Vayikra*, 18: 6 "None of you will approach its close relative, to find out the nudity," the phrase "to find out the nudity" means having sex.
216. Dorff, Nevins, and Reisner, 6–8.
217. Roth (2006), "Homosexuality Revisited," 9–13, Committee on Jewish Law and Standards (CJLS EH 24.2006a), http://www.rabbinical assembly.org/teshuvot/docs/20052010/roth_revisited.pdf. Based on Talmudic principles of exegesis, the author believes that oral sex and homosexual intercrural relations are among illicit relations, while Rabbi Simcha Roth's *responsum* (2003) includes mutual masturbation: "Dear David: Homosexual Relationships—A Halakhic Investigation," http://www.bmv.org.il/ab/dd.as.
218. Dorff, Nevins, and Reisner, 22–25.
219. Rabbi Joseph H. Prouser.
220. Rick Kardonne, "Split between US-Canadian Conservative Jews Possible: Canadian Rabbis Assert," *Jewish Tribune*, December 14, 2006, 1.
221. Yiddish word meaning "little bird," and used to describe a homosexual.
222. God is spelled G-d to mark the traditional idea that God's name should not be written.
223. This is well explained by Boyarin (1997), 17–18.
224. www.massresistance.org/docs/issues/bullybill/Levin_press_release_010511.pdf.

4 Christianity

1. Statistics Canada, *Census 2001*.
2. Ibid.
3. Statistics Canada, *Home National Survey 2011*, http://www.statcan.gc.ca/daily-quotidien/130508/dq130508b-eng.htm?HPA.
4. The Pew Forum on Religious and Public Life, *U.S. Religious Landscape Survey*, 10–14.
5. Luke 1:26–28. The Angel Gabriel announces to Mary that she will bear a son who will become famous; he will reign without end over the house of Jacob (Israel). Mark (2:1–12) tells the story of the Magi who traveled from the Orient to pay homage to the newborn King of the Jews.
6. Matt. 1:1–17; Luke 3:23–38.
7. John 1:31–34.
8. John 1:40–51. "Son of Man" is used as a synonym for Messiah, as in Dan. 7.
9. Matt. 16:16; Mark 8:29; Luke 9:20.

10. Matt. 16:20.
11. See Matt. 26:31–46. In this passage, Jesus refers to the Last Judgment, when the Son of Man will welcome to his right all those who have assisted the sick, prisoners, foreigners, those who were hungry, and so on.
12. Matt. 5:21–22.
13. Mark. 2:27–28.
14. Matt. 26:1–5.
15. Matt. 26:37–64.
16. John 12:23–24.
17. Isa. 53:8.
18. Schüssler Fiorenza, 22.
19. Acts 2:29–33.
20. Phil. 3:20–21. See also Eph. 1:20–21.
21. Eph. 1:22. Paul uses the word *Pantocrator* once (2 Cor. 6:18) to refer to Jesus, but it is used several times in the Apocalypse.
22. Acts 2:37–47; 4:32–37.
23. Acts 15.
24. Gal. 2:16.
25. Text found in *The Nag Hamadi Scriptures*, 473–486. According to the Gospel of Peter, Jesus did not die on the cross but was "taken up" by the Father.
26. In 1907, Pope Pius X condemns modernism in a detailed fashion in the Encyclical *Pascendi Gregis Domenici*. In 1864, Pope Pius IX had already made a list of "modern errors" in his *Syllabus*.
27. *Pastor Aeternus* (1870), Chapter 4.
28. Matt. 8:18–22.
29. Matt. 12:46–50.
30. Matt. 5:31–32.
31. 1 Cor. 7; see Elizabeth A. Clark (1995), 359.
32. Despland, 31. My translation.
33. Michel Foucault well emphasized this new subjectivity that came with the Roman Empire, and which he used as subtitle in Volume 3 of his *History of Sexuality, Care of the Self*. On the pathologized view of sexuality in the Empire, Bernos, 39–42.
34. Luke 5:29–32. See Garrett, 71–96; Smith, "Full of Spirit and Wisdom: Luke's Portrait of Stephen (*Acts* 6: 1–8: 1a) as a Man of Self-Mastery," in Vaage and Wimbush, 115.
35. 1 Thess. 4:3–5.
36. Elizabeth A. Castelli, "Disciplines of Difference: Asceticism and History in Paul," in Vaage and Wimbush, 179–181.
37. 1 Cor. 10:8, 11–12; Rom. 2:22.
38. Gaca, 138–145.
39. Ibid., 150–151.
40. Brown (1988), 55.
41. 1 Cor. 7:29, 39–40.
42. 1 Cor. 10:1–15; Gaca, 154–156.
43. Rom. 7:14–25.
44. Clark (1999), 27–33.
45. Ibid., 32; Abbott, 75–76; Gaca, 227.
46. Tatian's extravagant views are reported by Clement of Alexandria in *Stromata*, III. 81. 1–2, *Ante-Nicene Fathers*, Vol. 2; and by Jerome in *Adversus Jovinianum*, *Nicene and Post-Nicene Fathers*, Series II, Vol. 3. See Gaca, 225.
47. Tertullian, *De carne Christi*, IV. 1, *Ante-Nicene Fathers*, Vol. 3.
48. Tertullian, *Adversus Marcionem*, I. 29, *Ante-Nicene Fathers*, Vol. 3. Tertullian, while asserting the superiority of celibacy, is opposed to a negative view of sexuality. Sexuality is there to remain because God is responsible for the survival of humanity.
49. St. Athanasius, *Vita Antoni* (*Life of Antony*), *Nicene and Post-Nicene Fathers*, Series II, Vol. 4, 188ff.

50. Bernos et al., 64–66.
51. Palladius, *Historia lausica*, XXIII, *Translations of Christian Literature*, Series 1, Greek Texts, 101.
52. Rousselle, 197; Abbott, 104–105.
53. John Cassian, *Conferences*, Conference 12. *The Second Conference of Abbott Chaeremon. On Chastity*. An English translation of this chapter is usually absent from the Conferences, as, e.g., in Gibson's translation of 1894, in *A Select Library of Nicene and Post-Nicene Fathers of the Christian Church*. The translation here is mine from the French version by Cartier. An excellent rendering of these excerpts is by Kardong, *Cassian on Chastity, with an instructive introduction*.
54. John Cassian, *Conferences*, XII, 7.
55. John Cassian, *The Twelve Books of John Cassian on the Institutes of the Cœnobia, and the Remedies for the Eight Principal Faults*, VI, 20. My translation from the French version by Cartier. See VI, 10–11.
56. John Cassian, *The Institutes of the Cœnobia*, V, 11 in *Nicene and Post-Nicene Fathers*, Series II, Volume 11.
57. John Cassian, *Conferences*, XXII, 3. *The Institutes*, VI, 9–11. John Cassian ventures into physiological explanations for nocturnal erections and emissions; they are the product of gluttony, which causes and stores humors in the marrow or of a full bladder causing the swelling of the penis. The connexion made between food and sex probably goes back to Constantinus Africanus, *De Coitu*; see Sauer, 114.
58. Evagrius Ponticus, *The Praktikos: Chapters on Prayer*, trans. John Eudes Bamberger. Cistercian Studies 4 (Spencer, MA: Cistercian Publications), 1972, Book 8.
59. Ibid., 54–56. See Charles Stewart's article.
60. John Cassian, *Conferences*, XXII, 5.
61. The author quotes Deut. 23:9–11: "When you are encamped against your enemies, keep away from everything impure. If one of your men is unclean because of a nocturnal emission, he is to go outside the camp and stay there. But as evening approaches he is to wash himself, and at sunset he may return to the camp."
62. Palladius, *Historia lausica*, LXVIII. *Tranlations of Christian Literature*, Series 1, Greek Texts, 174.
63. Abbott, 108–110.
64. *The Testament of Truth*, trans. Birger A. Pearson, *The Nag Hamadi Scriptures*, 613–.
65. Ascetic movement from Syria that rejected marriage, meat, and wine consumption.
66. Clement of Alexandria, *Paedagogus* (The Instructor), II, 10, *Ante-Nicene Fathers*, Vol. 2.
67. Philo, *De specialibus legibus* (The Special Laws), IV, 85, 92–94. Gaca (2003), 194–196.
68. Philo, *De specialibus legibus*, IV, 100–118.
69. Philo, *De specialibus legibus*, IV, 84; *De Decalogo*, 142–143, 173–174. Gaca, 200–202.
70. Philo, *De Iosepho* (On Joseph), 43.
71. Philo, *De specialibus legibus*, III, 32–33: "(32) And there are particular periods affecting the health of the woman when a man may not touch her, but during that time he must abstain from all connection with her, respecting the laws of nature. And, at the same time, he must learn not to waste his vigour in the pursuit of an unseemly and barbarous pleasure; for such conduct would be like that of a husbandman, who, out of drunkenness or sudden insanity, should sow wheat or barley in lakes or flooded torrents, instead of over the fertile plains; for it is proper to cast seed upon fields when they are dry, in order that it may bear abundant fruit. (33) But nature each month cleanses the womb, as if it were some field of marvellous fertility, the proper season for fertilising which must be watched for by the husband as if he were a skilful husbandman, in order to withhold his seed and abstain from sowing it at a time when it is inundated; for, if he do not do so, the seed, without his perceiving it, will be swept away by the moisture, not only having all its spiritual energies relaxed, but having them, in fact, utterly dissolved. These are the persons who form animals in that workshop of nature, the womb, and who perfect with the most consummate skill each separate one of the parts of the body and soul. But when the periods of illness which I have spoken of are interrupted, then he may with confidence shower his seed into the ground ready to receive it, no longer fearing that there will be any loss of the seed thus sown."

72. Philo, *De specialibus legibus*, III, 37–39: "(37) Moreover, another evil, much greater than that which we have already mentioned, has made its way among and been let loose upon cities, namely, the love of boys, which formerly was accounted a great infamy even to be spoken of, but which sin is a subject of boasting not only to those who practise it, but even to those who suffer it, and who, being accustomed to bearing the affliction of being treated like women, waste away as to both their souls and bodies, not bearing about them a single spark of a manly character to be kindled into a flame, but having even the hair of their heads conspicuously curled and adorned, and having their faces smeared with vermilion, and paint, and things of that kind, and having their eyes pencilled beneath, and having their skins anointed with fragrant perfumes (for in such persons as these a sweet smell is a most seductive quality), and being well appointed in everything that tends to beauty or elegance, are not ashamed to devote their constant study and endeavours to the task of changing their manly character into an effeminate one. (38) And it is natural for those who obey the law to consider such persons worthy of death, since the law commands that the man-woman who adulterates the precious coinage of his nature shall die without redemption, not allowing him to live a single day, or even a single hour, as he is a disgrace to himself, and to his family, and to his country, and to the whole race of mankind. (39) And let the man who is devoted to the love of boys submit to the same punishment, since he pursues that pleasure which is contrary to nature, and since, as far as depends upon him, he would make the cities desolate, and void, and empty of all inhabitants, wasting his power of propagating his species, and moreover, being a guide and teacher of those greatest of all evils, unmanliness and effeminate lust, stripping young men of the flower of their beauty, and wasting their prime of life in effeminacy, which he ought rather on the other hand to train to vigour and acts of courage; and last of all, because, like a worthless husbandman, he allows fertile and productive lands to lie fallow, contriving that they shall continue barren, and labours night and day at cultivating that soil from which he never expects any produce at all."

73. Clement of Alexandria, *Stromata*, II. 23. 137.1, *Ante-Nicene Fathers*, Vol. 2.

74. Clement of Alexandria, *Stromata*, II. 23. 142–143, *Ante-Nicene Fathers*, Vol. 2: "But they who approve of marriage say, Nature has adapted us for marriage, as is evident from the structure of our bodies, which are male and female. And they constantly proclaim that command, 'Increase and replenish.' And though this is the case, yet it seems to them shameful that man, created by God, should be more licentious than the irrational creatures, which do not mix with many licentiously, but with one of the same species, such as pigeons and ringdoves, and creatures like them. Furthermore, they say, 'The childless man fails in the perfection which is according to nature, not having substituted his proper successor in his place. For he is perfect that has produced from himself his like, or rather, when he sees that he has produced the same; that is, when that which is begotten attains to the same nature with him who begat.'"

75. Clement of Alexandria, *Stromata*, III. 7. 57–58, *Ante-Nicene Fathers*, Vol. 2: "57. The human ideal of continence, I mean that which is set forth by Greek philosophers, teaches that one should fight desire and not be subservient to it so as to bring it to practical effect. But our ideal is not to experience desire at all. Our aim is not that while a man feels desire he should get the better of it, but that he should be continent even respecting desire itself. This chastity cannot be attained in any other way except by God's grace. That was why he said 'Ask and it shall be given you.' This grace was received even by Moses, though clothed in his needy body, so that for forty days he felt neither thirst nor hunger. Just as it is better to be in good health than for a sick man to talk about health, so to be light is better than to discuss light, and true chastity is better than that taught by the philosophers. Where there is light there is no darkness. But where there is inward desire, even if it goes no further than desire and is quiescent so far as bodily action is concerned, union takes place in thought with the object of desire, although that object is not present. 58. Our general argument concerning marriage, food, and other matters, may proceed to show that we should do nothing—from desire. Our will is to be directed only toward that which is necessary. For we are children not of desire but of will. A man who marries for the sake of begetting children must practise continence so that it is not desire he feels for his wife, whom he ought to love, and that he may beget children with a chaste and controlled will. For we have learnt not to 'have thought for the flesh to fulfil its desires.' We are to 'walk honourably as in

the way', that is in Christ and in the enlightened conduct of the Lord's way, 'not in revelling and drunkenness, not in debauchery and lasciviousness, not in strife and envy.'"
76. Clement of Alexandria, *Stromata*, III.12. 83–84, *Ante-Nicene Fathers*, Vol. 2.
77. Clement of Alexandria, *Paedagogus*, II. 100.1, *Ante-Nicene Fathers*, Vol. 2.
78. Clement of Alexandria, *Stromata*, III. 11.71.4, *Ante-Nicene Fathers*, Vol. 2: "'Thou shalt not lust.' That the law intended husbands to cohabit with their wives with self-control and only for the purpose of begetting children is evident from the prohibition which forbids the unmarried man from having immediate sexual relations with a captive woman. If the man has conceived a desire for her, he is directed to mourn for thirty days while she is to have her hair cut; if after this the desire has not passed off, then they may proceed to beget children, because the appointed period enables the overwhelming impulse to be tested and to become a rational act of will." See Gaca, 265–266.
79. Flandrin, 101.
80. Clement of Alexandria, *Stromata*, III. 12. 82, 85, *Ante-Nicene Fathers*, Vol. 2.
81. Tertullian, *De exhortatione castitatis* (On Exhortation to Chastity), Chapter 1; *Ad uxorem* (*To his Wife*), I. 3, *Ante-Nicene Fathers*, Vol. 3.
82. Origen, *Commentaria in Evangelium secundum Mattheum*, XIV. 25. *The Ante-Nicene Fathers*, Vol. X : "Now after these things, having considered how many possible accidents may arise in marriages, which it was necessary for the man to endure and in this way suffer very great hardships, or if he did not endure, to transgress the word of Christ, the disciples say to him, taking refuge in celibacy as easier, and more expedient than marriage, though the latter appears to be expedient, 'If the case of the man is so with his wife, it is not expedient to marry.' And to this the Saviour said, teaching us that absolute chastity is a gift given by God, and not merely the fruit of training, but given by God with prayer, 'All men cannot receive the saying, but they to whom it is given.' Then seeing that some make a sophistical attack on the saying 'To whom it is given,' as if those who wished to remain pure in celibacy, but were mastered by their desires, had an excuse, we must say that, if we believe the Scriptures, why at all do we lay hold of the saying, 'But they to whom it is given,' but no longer attend to this, 'Ask and it shall be given you,' and to that which is added to it, 'For every one that asketh receiveth'? For if they 'to whom it is given' can receive this saying about absolute purity, let him who wills ask, obeying and believing Him who said, 'Ask and it shall be given you,' and not doubting about the saying, 'Every one that asketh receiveth.'"
83. Jerome, *Adversus Jovianum* (*Against Jovianus*), I. 12. *Nicene and Post-Nicene Fathers*, Series II, Vol. 6. Read I. 3 to have a glimpse of his views on marriage.
84. Gregory of Nyssa, *De virginitate* (On Virginity), III. *Nicene and Post-Nicene Fathers*, Series II, Vol. 5.
85. Clark (1995). John Chrysostom, XIX, 6. *Homelies on First Corinthians*, *Nicene and Post-Nicene Fathers*, Series II, Vol. XII; Ambrose of Milan, *De viduis* (Concerning Widows), 81. *Nicene and Post-Nicene Fathers*, Series II, Vol. 10.
86. Augustine, *De nuptiis et concupiscentia* (On Marriage and Concupiscence), I, 5, *Nicene and Post-Nicene Fathers*, Series I, Vol. 5.
87. *De nuptiis et concupiscentia*, I, 19.
88. *De bono conjugali* (On the Good of Marriage), III, *Nicene and Post-Nicene Fathers*, Series I, Vol. 3: "Marriages have this good also, that carnal or youthful incontinence, although it be faulty, is brought unto an honest use in the begetting of children, in order that out of the evil of lust (*ex malo libidinis*) the marriage union may bring to pass some good."
89. *De nuptiis et concupiscentia*, I, 19.
90. Ibid., I, 27.
91. Ibid., I, 16. In the same chapter: "For thus says the Scripture: 'Let the husband render unto the wife her due: and likewise also the wife unto the husband. The wife hath not power of her own body, but the husband: and likewise also the husband hath not power of his own body, but the wife. Defraud ye not one the other; except it be with consent for a time, that ye may have leisure for prayer; and then come together again, that Satan tempt you not for your incontinency. But I speak this by permission (*venia*), and not commandment.' Now in a case where must be given, it cannot by any means be contended that there is not some amount of sin. Since, however, the

cohabitation for the purpose of procreating children, which must be admitted to be the proper end of marriage, is not sinful, what is it which the apostle allows to be permissible, but that married persons, when they have not the gift of continence, may require one from the other the due of the flesh—and that not from a wish for procreation, but for the pleasure of concupiscence? This gratification incurs not the imputation of guilt on account of marriage, but receives permission on account of marriage."

Mary and Joseph did not have sex because sex is accompanied by lust, which is the consequence of sin. Christ could not be born of such an act (ibid., I, 13).

92. Ibid., I, 17: "It is, however, one thing for married persons to have intercourse only for the wish to beget children, which is not sinful: it is another thing for them to desire carnal pleasure in cohabitation, but with the spouse only, which involves venial sin. For although propagation of offspring is not the motive of the intercourse, there is still no attempt to prevent such propagation, either by wrong desire or evil appliance. They who resort to these, although called by the name of spouses, are really not such; they retain no vestige of true matrimony, but pretend the honourable designation as a cloak for criminal conduct."
93. Ibid., I, 7.
94. *Adversus Julianum* (Against Julian), III, 57.
95. Sawyer; Despland, 43–44.
96. Augustine, *Confessions*, VIII. 5. 2, *Nicene and Post-Nicene Fathers*, Series I, Vol. 1.
97. *Confessions*, VIII. 7. 17.
98. Ibid., VIII. 12. 30.
99. *De nuptiis et concupiscentia*, I, 15.
100. Ibid., I, 16.
101. Bernos et al., 101; Brundage, 156–158.
102. Ivo of Chartres, *Decretum, Patrologia Latina*, 161, 048–1022, IX, 110. According to Ivo, to act against nature implies the unnatural use of the reproductive organs. An unnatural intercourse between legitimate spouses constitutes a greater sin than natural intercourse in adultery or fornication. See Brundage (1994), 61.
103. Gratian, *Decretum*, pars secunda, causa XXXII, questio vii, c. 11 : "*Sed omnium horum pessimum est quod contra naturam fit, ut si vir membro mulieris non ad hoc concesso voluerit uti.*" This is the same formulation used by Ivo and defines any improper use of the penis with a woman as against nature.
104. Gratian, *Decretum*, pars secunda, causa XXXII, questio vii, c. 11–12. He asserts the severity of sins against nature in the following way: "*Minus est secundum naturam coire, quam contra naturam delinquere.*" [The person who sins by having sexual intercourse in a natural way commits a less serious offense than the person who has sexual intercourse against nature.]
105. *Poenitentiale Cummeani*, II. English translation in McNeill and Gamer, 102–104. A layman who engages in fornication with a woman will do penance by food deprivation for three years; on bread and water during the first year, and during three periods of 40 days for the other two years. Bestiality deserves a one-year penance; masturbation is punishable by three periods of 40 days for the layman, one year for a cleric, and 40 days for a 15-year-old.
106. Hincmar of Reims, *De divortio Lotharii regis et Theutebergae reginae*, interrogatio XII: "*Nemo igitur dicat, non perpetrare eum peccatum sodomitanum, qui contra naturam in masculum vel in feminam turpitudinem, et attritu, vel attractu, seu motu impudico, ex deliberatione et studio imundus efficetur.*" English translation in Boswell, 1980), 203: "Therefore, let no one claim he has not committed sodomy if he has acted contrary to nature with either man or woman or has deliberately and consciously defiled himself by rubbing, touching, or other improper actions."
107. Burchard of Worms, *Decretum*, XIX, *Patrologia Latina* (*PL*), 140, col. 537–1058. Book XIX was a widely used penitential in the Middle Ages, entitled *Corrector et Medicus*. The author assigns a penance of 10 days on bread and water for masturbation, 30 days for mutual masturbation, 80 days for the husband who commits adultery with a woman followed by 14 years of penance.
108. *Poenitentiale Columbani*. For the English translation: McNeill and Gamer, 250–257. For comments, see Bullough, (1976), 359. Greater severity toward sodomy is also observable in

the Penitential of Theodore of Tarsus (668–690), archbishop of Canterbury, the *Poenitentiale Theodori* I. II (English translation in McNeill and Gamer, 184–185), where homogenital relations are classified in the category of *fornicatio* and accompanied by a ten-year penance, without specifying the nature of the alleged acts. Burchard of Worms imposes a penance of ten years to a married man who practices sodomy once or twice, but twelve years for those who enjoy it assiduously.
109. *Prefatio Gildae de penitentia*, 1. English translation: McNeill and Gamer, 174.
110. Regino Prumensis, *De synodalibus causis et disciplinis ecclesiasticis*, II. 255; *Patrologia Latina*, 132, col. 186–370.
111. A phrase borrowed from Michel Foucault, *The History of Sexuality*, Volume 1, Chapter 3. According to the author, introspection and confession gave rise to a proliferation of discourses on sexuality in the West, first religious then medical, while the East developed an *ars erotica*, which focused on the joy of sex.
112. *Summa Theologica*, Ia-IIae. Q. 33. A. 3: "On the other hand bodily pleasures hinder the use of reason in three ways. First, by distracting the reason. Because, as we have just observed, we attend much to that which pleases us. Now when the attention is firmly fixed on one thing, it is either weakened in respect of other things, or it is entirely withdrawn from them; and thus if the bodily pleasure be great, either it entirely hinders the use of reason, by concentrating the mind's attention on itself; or else it hinders it considerably. Secondly, by being contrary to reason. Because some pleasures, especially those that are in excess, are contrary to the order of reason: and in this sense the Philosopher says that 'bodily pleasures destroy the estimate of prudence, but not the speculative estimate,' to which they are not opposed, 'for instance that the three angles of a triangle are together equal to two right angles.' In the first sense, however, they hinder both estimates. Thirdly, by fettering the reason: in so far as bodily pleasure is followed by a certain alteration in the body, greater even than in the other passions, in proportion as the appetite is more vehemently affected toward a present than toward an absent thing. Now such bodily disturbances hinder the use of reason; as may be seen in the case of drunkards, in whom the use of reason is fettered or hindered."
113. Ibid., I-IIae. Q. 34. A. 1.
114. Ibid., I-IIae. Q. 31. A. 7. For Aquinas, sexual pleasure remains natural (*delectabilia naturaliter*) insofar as the sexual act (*venereorum usus*) is performed for the conservation of the species.
115. Ibid., IIa-IIae. Q. 154. A. 1.
116. Ibid., I. Q. 98. A. 2.
117. *Scriptum super Sententiis* (Commentary on the Sentences of Peter Lombard), IV. D. 33. Q. 1, A. 3. Qc. 1: "*Finis autem quem natura ex concubitu intendit, est proles procreanda et educanda; et ut hoc bonum quaereretur, posuit delectationem in coitu; ut Augustinus dicit. Quicumque ergo concubitu utitur propter delectationem quae in ipso est, non referendo ad finem a natura intentum, contra naturam facit.*" [But procreation and the education of offspring is what nature intends for intercourse, and it [nature] has put pleasure in the union in order that this good becomes accomplished, as Augustine says. Whoever engages in sexual intercourse for pleasure, without intending what nature ordained, acts against nature]. My translation.
118. *Quaestiones disputatae, De malo*, Q. 15. A. 2 : "*Aliquando vero inordinatio concupiscentiae non tollit ordinem ultimi finis, quando scilicet aliquis etsi superabundet in concupiscentia delectationis venereae, tamen potius ab ea abstineret quam contra Dei praeceptum ageret: nec istam mulierem aut aliam cognosceret, si sua uxor non esset, quod tunc concupiscentia sistit infra limites matrimonii, et est peccatum veniale.*" [And the disorder of the desire sometimes does not eliminate the ordination of the ultimate end, namely, when a man, although excessively desiring sexual pleasure, would abstain from it before he would act contrary to God's precept, and he would not have intercourse with any woman unless she were his wife. And then the desire stays within the bounds of marriage and is a venial sin.] The disruption that comes along with pleasure does not annihilate the finality of marriage.
119. *Quaestiones disputatae, De malo*, Q. 15. A. 1: "*Et quod omnis talis actus sit inordinatus secundum seipsum, apparet ex hoc quod omnis actus humanus dicitur esse inordinatus qui non est proportionatus debito fini; sicut comestio est inordinata, si non proportionetur corporis salubritati,*

ad quam ordinatur sicut ad finem Finis autem usus genitalium membrorum est generatio et educatio prolis; et ideo omnis usus praedictorum membrorum qui non est proportionatus generationi prolis et debitae eius educationi, est secundum se inordinatus. Quicumque autem actus praedictorum membrorum praeter commixtionem maris et feminae, manifestum est quod non est accommodus generationi prolis."

120. *Quaestiones disputatae, De malo,* Q. 15. A. 2: *"Propinquius autem ordinatur ad vitam hominis semen humanum, in quo est homo in potentia, quam quaecumque res exteriores; unde et philosophus in sua politica dicit in semine hominis esse quiddam divinum, in quantum scilicet est homo in potentia. Et ideo inordinatio circa emissionem seminis est circa vitam hominis in potentia propinqua. Unde manifestum est quod omnis talis actus luxuriae est peccatum mortale ex suo genere."* [And human semen, in which there is a potential human being, is more closely ordained for human life than any external things. And so also the Philosopher says in the Politics that there is something divine in human semen, namely, inasmuch as there is a potential human being. And so the disorder regarding the emission of semen concerns human life in proximate potentiality. And so it is clear that every such act of sexual lust is a mortal sin by reason of its kind.]

121. *Summa Theologica,* II-II. Q. 153. A. 2: "A sin, in human acts, is that which is against the order of reason. Now the order of reason consists in its ordering everything to its end in a fitting manner. Wherefore it is no sin if one, by the dictate of reason, makes use of certain things in a fitting manner and order for the end to which they are adapted, provided this end be something truly good. Now just as the preservation of the bodily nature of one individual is a true good, so, too, is the preservation of the nature of the human species a very great good."

122. Ibid., II-II. Q. 154. A. 11.

123. Ibid., II-II. Q. 154. A. 12: "Wherefore just as in speculative matters the most grievous and shameful error is that which is about things the knowledge of which is naturally bestowed on man, so in matters of action it is most grave and shameful to act against things as determined by nature. Therefore, since by the unnatural vices man transgresses that which has been determined by nature with regard to the use of venereal actions, it follows that in this matter this sin is gravest of all. After it comes incest, which, as stated above (Article [9]), is contrary to the natural respect which we owe persons related to us." [*Et ideo, sicut in speculativis error circa ea quorum cognitio est homini naturaliter indita, est gravissimus et turpissimus; ita in agendis agere contra ea quae sunt secundum naturam determinata, est gravissimum et turpissimum. Quia ergo in vitiis quae sunt contra naturam transgreditur homo id quod est secundum naturam determinatum circa usum venereum, inde est quod in tali materia hoc peccatum est gravissimum. Post quod est incestus, qui, sicut dictum est, est contra naturalem reverentiam quam personis coniunctis debemus.*]

124. Brundage, 552.

125. Hurteau, "Catholic Moral Discourse," 7.

126. On the probabilist method of moral reasoning, see ibid.

127. Sanchez, *De sancto matrimonii sacramento,* IX. 9. Q. 7.

128. Alphonsus Liguori, *Homo apostolicus instructus in sua vocatione ad audiendas confessiones sive praxis et instructio confessariorum* (hereafter cited as *Instructio*), Chapter XVIII. 42: "*Quaeres hic, an tactus et delectationes morosae conjugibus permittantur. Resp. i° Tactus etiam impudici, si ad copulam ordinantur, sine dubio conjugibus permittuntur.*" [You ask if fondling or impure thoughts are allowed between spouses. I answer that, fondling is permissible between spouses, without a doubt if it is intended for copulation.] My translation.

129. Daumas.

130. 69 Collegii Salmanticensis (hereafter cited as *Salmanticenses*), *Cursus theologiae moralis,* 6. 26. 7. 2. n. 12, 45: "*Notandum tamen hic est, quod si, dum quis se polluit, habet delectationem morosam, aut desiderium alicujus personae sacrae, conjugatae, vel solutae, aut ex vi hujus delectationis desiderii, aut turpis cogitationis in pollutionem volontarie labitur, debet has circumstantias in confessione explicare. Et ratio est, quia tunc ultra malitiam pollutionis est novum peccatum desiderii, aut delectationis coitus cum illis personis: ergo explicanda est dicta circumstantia.*" [It should indeed be noted that if while masturbating one delights in sexual fantasies, whether in the form of desire for another person, consecrated, married, or single, or in the form of simply

enjoying the power of that desire, or whether one voluntarily slips toward it through indecent thoughts, these circumstances must be explained in confession. The reason is that because there is on top of the evil of pollution an added sin of desire or fantasizing intercourse with these persons, the circumstance must be detailed.] My translation from Hurteau, "Catholic Moral Discourse," 20.

131. Liguori, *Theologia moralis*, 2: 723 : "Delectatio morosa denique respicit tempus praesens ; et est quando per imaginationem phantasiae quis reddit sibi praesens opus peccati, nempe actum fornicationis, et de illa deliberato consensu delectatur, tamquam actualiter fornicaretur, sine tamen desiderio exsequendi." [*Delectatio morosa* is only concerned with the present; it occurs when one brings to his mind through fantasies a sinful act, for instance, an act of fornication, and takes pleasure in it with a deliberate consent, as if he was really fornicating, without however any desire to carry it out in reality.] My translation from Hurteau, "Catholic Moral Discourse," 21.
132. Billuart, *Summa Sancti Thomae*, 15.6.10, 361. This work was written between 1746 and 1751.
133. The phrase is used by Liguori in his *Instructio*, Chapter IX. 3.
134. Benedicti, *La somme des pechez et le remède d'iceux*, 2.7.
135. Hurteau, "Catholic Moral Discourse," 23–24.
136. See Murray (1997). The author shows how the subject of wet dreams in penitential literature and confessors' handbooks shifts from ritual impurity preventing a priest from celebrating the Eucharist to an approach wherein impurity is related to intrapsychic phenomena. For instance, Thomas of Chobham thinks involuntary nocturnal emissions can be a sin if the person can trace the cause of these emissions to impure thoughts. The French theologian, Jean de Gerson (1363–1429), seems to be the first to extend this concept to the laity.
137. Flandrin, 280, 296–298; Hurteau, "Catholic Moral Discourse," 19.
138. Debreyne, 78. My translation.
139. Jacquemet, 46. My translation.
140. Debreyne, 87.
141. Hurteau, « L'homosexualité masculine et les discours sur le sexe en contexte montréalais de la fin du XIXe siècle à la fin de la Révolution tranquille », 54–55.
142. Noonan, 461–470; Philippe Lécrivain, "Une traversée difficile," in Bernos (1985).
143. Hurteau, « L'homosexualité masculine et les discours sur le sexe en contexte montréalais de la fin du XIXe siècle à la fin de la Révolution tranquille », 42–46.
144. Hurteau (1991), 140–142.
145. Hurteau, 44.
146. Leo XIII, *Arcanum divinae*, n. 27, February 10, 1880.
147. Langlois, 219, 413, 445.
148. Pius XI, *Casti connubii*, n. 53–55, December 31, 1930, n. 53–55.
149. Paul VI, *Humanae vitae*, n. 10, July 25, 1968.
150. Paul VI, *Humanae vitae*, n. 14–15.
151. Paul VI, *Humanae vitae*, n. 14.
152. John Paul II, *Familiaris consortio*, n. 11; 14; 18; 29, November 22, 1981.
153. John Paul II, *Familiaris consortio*, n. 6.
154. "General Audience of 23 July 1980," *L'Osservatore Romano*, weekly edition in English, July 28, 1980, 1; see also "General Audience of 17 September 1980," *L'Osservatore Romano*, September 22, 1980, 11.
155. "General Audience of 7 November 1984," *L'Osservatore Romano*, weekly edition in English, November 12, 1984, 1.
156. Charles E. Curran, "Pope John Paul II's Teaching on Sexuality and Marriage: An Appraisal,"
157. Sacred Congregation for the Doctrine of the Faith, *Persona Humana, Declaration on Certain Questions Concerning Sexual Ethics*, n. 3, December 29, 1975.
158. See Carlson. John Calvin wrote: "When a woman in some way drives away the seed out the womb, through aids, then this is rightly seen as an unforgivable crime. Onan was guilty of a similar crime, by defiling the earth with his seed, so that Tamar would not receive a future inheritor" (*Commentary on Genesis*, Vol. II, part 16). Martin Luther wrote: "But the

exceedingly foul deed of Onan, the basest of wretches, follows [here Luther quotes Gen. 38;9–10]. Onan must have been a malicious and incorrigible scoundrel. This is a most disgraceful sin. It is far more atrocious than incest and adultery. We call it unchastity, yes a Sodomitic sin. For Onan goes in to her; that is, he lies with her and copulates, and when it comes to the point of insemination, spills the semen, lest the woman conceive. Surely at such a time the order of nature established by God in procreation should be followed. Accordingly, it was a most disgraceful crime to produce semen and excite the woman, and to frustrate her at that very moment. He was inflamed with the basest spite and hatred. Therefore he did not allow himself to be compelled to bear that intolerable slavery. Consequently, he deserved to be killed by God. He committed an evil deed. Therefore God punished him...That worthless fellow...preferred polluting himself with a most disgraceful sin to raising up offspring for his brother" (*Commentary on Genesis*, *Luther's Works*, Vol. 7, 20–21).

159. 1 Cor. 11:8–9.
160. Gen. 3:16.
161. Augustine, *Quaestiones in Heptateuchum*, 153, *Patrologia Latina*, 34: "*Est etiam ordo naturalis in hominibus, ut serviant feminae viris, et filii parentibus, quia et illic haec iustitia est infirmior ratio serviat fortiori. Haec igitur in dominationibus et servitutibus clara iustitia est, ut qui excellunt ratione, excellant dominatione; quod cum in hoc saeculo per iniquitatem hominum perturbatur, vel per naturarum carnalium diversitatem, ferunt iusti temporalem perversitatem, in fine habituri ordinatissimam et sempiternam felicitatem.*" My translation.
162. Gal. 3:28.
163. Matt. 5:28.
164. Stark, Chapters 4 and 5.
165. Jean-Jacques Rousseau, *Emile*, trans. Barbara Foxley (Middlesex: Echo Library, 2007), 313.
166. Hurteau (1991), 142–152.
167. Jeanne Grisé-Allard, "Vides creusés par la guerre," *Relations* n. 37 (February 1944): 39–40.
168. Sacred Congregation for the Doctrine of the Faith, *Letter to the Bishops of the Catholic Church on the Collaboration of Men and Women in the Church and in the World*, May 31, 2004. See Denise Couture.
169. Sacred Congregation for the Doctrine of the Faith, *Letter to the Bishops of the Catholic Church on the Collaboration of Men and Women in the Church and in the World*, n. 13.
170. John Paul II, *Familiaris Consortio*, 23.
171. Paul VI, "Response to the Letter of His Grace the Most Reverend Dr. F. D. Coggan, Archbishop of Canterbury, concerning the Ordination of Women to the Priesthood," November 30, 1975: AAS 68 (1976), 59; Sacred Congregation for the Doctrine of the Faith, *Inter Insigniores, Declaration on the Question of Admission of Women to the Ministerial Priesthood*, October 15, 1976; John Paul II, *Ordinatio Sacerdotalis, Apostolic Letter on Reserving Priestly Ordination to Men Alone*, May 22, 1994.
172. Rom. 1:26–27.
173. Rom. 1:28–30. Nissinen, 106, wisely points out that same-sex relations fit to perfection the metaphor for the reversal of the order of creation willed by God, much better than say murder and deceit.
174. Epictetus compares the man who feverishly clings to wealth, public office, or a wife, to the man who cannot quench his thirst; while the healthy man, that is to say, the one who is moderate in the use of pleasure, is not struggling with jealousy, greed, and passions (*The Discourses*, Book III. 3). Concerning the influence of Stoic ideas on Paul's thoughts, see Fredrickson, 197–222.
175. Philo of Alexandria, *De Abrahamo* (On Abraham), 133–136, *Ante-Nicene Fathers*, Vol. 2.
176. 1 Cor. 6: 9–10: "Or do you not know that wrongdoers will not inherit the kingdom of God? Do not be deceived: Neither the sexually immoral nor idolaters nor adulterers nor men who have sex with men nor thieves nor the greedy nor drunkards nor slanderers nor swindlers will inherit the kingdom of God." A note says: "The words men who have sex with men translate two Greek words that refer to the passive and active participants in homosexual acts." The New King James Version uses the word "homosexuals" to translate the Greek μαλακοὶ and "sodomites" for the Greek ἀρσενοκοῖται. A note on "homosexuals" has catamites for

NOTES

synonym, pointing to softness or effeminacy. The use of both words could refer to the active and passive role during intercourse. See Nissinen, 113–118. A lot has been written on these two words; either to condemn homosexual acts or limit their meaning to nonconsensual acts or pederasty. See David F. Wright, "Homosexuals or Prostitutes: The Meaning of arsenokoitai (I Cor. 6:9; I Tim. 1:10)," *Vigiliae Christianae* 38 (June 1984): 125–153; "Translating arsenokoitai I Cor. 6:9; I Tim. 1:10)," *Vigiliae Christianae* 41 (December 1987): 398. Wright's response to the article by W. L. Petersen, "Can Arsenokoitai be Translated by 'Homosexuals'? (I Cor. 6.9; I Tim. 1:10)," *Vigiliae Christianae* 40 (June 1986): 187–191. I personally find Dale Martin's approach more balanced than the aforementioned ones because it opens up the strict linguistic approach to historical context. He shows how the word ἀρσενοκοῖται cannot be reduced to its linguistic meaning—to sleep with men. It was often used in the context of rape or prostitution (economic gain). The word μαλακοὶ simply refers to effeminate behavior and could also apply in a heterosexual context. Dale B. Martin, "Arsenokoitês and Malakos: Meanings and Consequences," in Brawley, 117–136.

177. Clement of Alexandria, *Paedagogus*, II. 10. 90, *Ante-Nicene Fathers*, Vol. 2. An English translation of Book II, Chapter 10, may be found in Boswell (1980), 355.
178. Clement of Alexandria, *Paedagogus*, II. 10. 83–84, *Ante-Nicene Fathers*, Vol. 2.
179. John Chrysostom, *Homily on First Thessalonians*, VIII, 3. *Nicene and Post-Nicene Fathers*, Series 1, Vol. XIII. In his *Homilies against the Jews*, I. II. 7, he pictures the Jews as "effeminates" (μαλακοὶ). He also writes in I. III. 1: "But the synagogue is not only a brothel and a theater; it also is a den of robbers and a lodging for wild beasts. Jeremiah said: 'Your house has become for me the den of a hyena.' He does not simply say 'of wild beast,' but 'of a filthy wild beast,' and again: 'I have abandoned my house, I have cast off my inheritance.' But when God forsakes a people, what hope of salvation is left? When God forsakes a place, that place becomes the dwelling of demons." *Discourses against Judaizing Christians, Fathers of the Church*, Volume 68, trans. Paul W. Harkins (Washington DC: Catholic University of America Press, reprint 2002). Clearly, John Chrysostom's intention is to stigmatize the Jews by comparing the synagogue to a hyena's den. He seems fully aware of the association of the hyenas with homosexual relations.
180. John Chrysostom, *Homilies on the Epistle of St. Paul to the Romans*, Homily IV, *Nicene and Post-Nicene Fathers*, Series 1, Vol. XI.
181. Ibid.
182. *Poenitentiale Columbani*, B. 15, which refers to the layman who fornicates like the sodomites, that is to say, fornicating with a male as if with a woman, "*id est cum masculo coitu femineo peccaverit*" and Burchard, *Decretum*, XIX, *Patrologia Latina* 140, col. 967D, talks about fornicating like the sodomites for anyone who puts his penis in the fundament of a man; "*fecisti fornicationem, sicut Sodomitae, ita ut in mascula terga et in posteriorem virgam immiteres.*" I personally think that Boswell (1980), 289–290, tends to minimize the homosexual content of certain views held by Yvo of Chartres (*Decretum* IX. 105, 106, 109 to 115) or Gratian (*Decretum* II, causa 32, quaestio 7, c. 14).
183. *Poenitentiale Theodori*, I. II. 15: "*qui semen in os miserit, VII annos peniteat: hoc pessimum malum*" [He who discharges semen in the mouth will do penance for seven years, it is the worst possible evil]. His position is not clear since he refers to others who consider a heavier penance of 12 years. He states that is the most horrible sin but he mentions a penance of 10 years for a male who has intercourse with a male (I. II. 5). Latin text in Haddan and Stubbs, III, 177.
184. *Liber Gomorrhianus*, *Patrologia Latina*, 145, col. 159–190D, *Caput Primum*. See Jordan, 46.
185. Bullough (1976), 360–361; Brundage, 165–166. St. Columba proposes two years of fasting for the lay masturbator and three years for the cleric.
186. *Liber Gomorrhianus*, *Patrologia Latina*, 145, col. 178: "*Dic, vir evirate; responde, homo effeminate, quid in viro quaeris, quod in temetipso invenire non possis? Quam diversitatem sexuum? Quae varia lineamenta membrorum? Quam mollitiem? Quam carnalis illecebrae teneritudinem? Quam lubrici vultus jucunditatem? Terreat te, quaeso, vigor masculini aspectus, abhorreat mens tua viriles artus? Naturalis quippe appetitus officium est, ut hoc unusquisque*

extrinsecus quaerat quod intra suae facultatis claustra reperire non valet. Si ergo te contrectatio masculinae carnis oblectat, verte manus in te: et scito, quia quidquid apud te non invenis, in alieno corpore in vacuum quaeris." [Unmanned man, speak! Respond, effeminate man! What do you seek in a male which you cannot find in yourself? What sexual difference? What different physical lineaments? What softness? What tender, carnal attraction? What pleasant smooth face? Let the vigour of the male appearance terrify you, I beseech you; your mind should abhor virile strength. In fact, it is the rule of natural appetite that each seek beyond himself what he cannot find within the cloister of his own faculty. Therefore, if contact with male flesh delights you, turn your hand to yourself. Know that whatever you do not find in yourself, you seek vainly in another male body.] *Book of Gomorrah*, trans. Payer, 68.
187. McLaughlin, 18–21.
188. *Decretales Pseudo-Isidorianae (Pseudo-Isidorean Decretals)*, *Decreta S. Gregorii Papae*, II, in Hinsch, 746. McLaughlin, 24.
189. For the Middle Age period, see Sauer; and for the Late Antiquity, Krueger.
190. Pugh. For the homoerotic tone in these odes, see Stehling, 153ff.
191. William of Malmesbury, *Saints' Lives*, ed. and trans. Winterbottom and Thomson (New York: Oxford University Press, 2002), 118.
192. Boswell entitled Chapter 9 of his *Christianity, Social Tolerance, and Homosexuality* "The Triumph of Ganymede." In addition to the poets of the Loire Shool, Boswell lays great emphasis on the figure of the English Cistercian monk Aelred of Rivaulx (1110–1167), who favored tangible expressions of affection between monks in his *De amicitia spirituale (On Spiritual Friendship)*, 221–226.
193. Greenberg (1988), 286–288; Bullough (1976), 393.
194. Greenberg (1988), 284–285; Bullough (1976), 276. *The Rule of St. Benedict* (n. XXII) shows some concern about the chastity of the monks by imposing single beds and maintaining a lit candle all night in the dormitory. According to Kardong (1996), 228, St. Benedict's Rule seems more relaxed than its anonymous source of inspiration, *The Rule of the Master*.
195. Justinian, *Corpus juris civilis, Institutes*, I. I. II: "*Jus naturale est, quod natura omnia animalia docuit : nam jus istud non humani generis proprium, sed omnium animalium, quae in terra, quae in mari nascuntur, avium quoque commune est. Hinc descendit maris atque feminae coniunctio, quam nos matrimonium appellamus, hinc liberorum procreatio, hinc educatio : videmus etenim cetera quoque animalia, feras etiam istius juris peritia censeri.*" [The law of nature is that law which nature teaches to all animals. For this law does not belong exclusively to the human race, but belongs to all animals, whether of the earth, the air, or the water. Hence comes the union of the male and female, which we term matrimony; hence the procreation and bringing up of children. We see, indeed, that all the other animals besides men are considered as having knowledge of this law.] Fordham University, Internet Medieval Sourcebook, http://www.fordham.edu/Halsall/basis/535institutes.asp#I.Justice.
196. Boswell (1980), 137–145; 304–305.
197. *Liber Gomorrhianus*, *Patrologia Latina*, 145, col. 178c. Peter Damian also states that a male goat would not satisfy its sexual appetite with a male goat, neither a ram with another ram, nor a bull with a bull. See Payer trans. 68. Peter Damian believes that people learn from animal behavior what to imitate and what to avoid, *De bono religiosi status et variarum animantium tropologia*, *Patrologia Latina*, 145, col. 767, quoted in Boswell (1980), 304.
198. Alain of Lille, *De planctu Naturae*, I, *The Complaint of Nature*, trans. Moffat.
199. See Brundage, 287, 421.
200. Bullough (1976), 379.
201. Jordan, 130–133.
202. Brundage, 423 mentions the *Roman de la Rose* by Jean de Meung, the *Breviari d'amor* by the Franciscan theologian Matfré Ermengaud, who did not hesitate to incorporate love poems by Occitan troubadours in his theology of creation. See also Bullough (1994), 55–58.
203. Boswell (1980), 389.
204. Crompton, 188.
205. *Summa Theologica*, I. Q. 98. A. 2. Aquinas admits that pleasure in marital sex is not a sin, *Summa Theologica*, Ia-IIae, Q. 34. A. 1–2.

206. *Summa Theologica*, IIa-IIae, Q. 154. A. 11.
207. Ibid., IIa-IIae, Q. 154. A. 12.
208. Crompton, 190.
209. Ibid., 192–196.
210. Fernandez.
211. Crompton, 308–313.
212. Thielecke, 269.
213. Puff, 136–137. The phrase "Italian wedding" or "Italian custom"—synonyms for homosexual anal relations—is often used by Luther to attack the Church of Rome. In a way, the tone is polemical and nationalist as it also underlines the foreign origin of the vice.
214. See his work *On the Estate of Marriage*, Part I, in *Luther's Works*, Vol. 45.
215. Pless. The author describes the opposing views of theologian Edward Schroeder from the Missouri Synod, who believes that homosexual orientation is part of God's plan, and Gerhard Forde, a theologian of the Evangelical Lutheran Church in America.
216. Crompton, 324–325.
217. Calvin, *Institutes of the Christian Religion*, III. 21. 5.
218. Greenberg (1988), 314.
219. *Salmanticenses*, 6. 26. 7. 5 n. 82, 158: "*Talem coitum non esse veram sodomiam, sed peccatum contra naturam, essentialiter et specifice ab illa diversum, quod ob defectum proprii nominis dicitur innaturalis modus concumbendi.*" (Such intercourse is not sodomy proper but a sin against nature and different from it in essence and form, called improper modes of intercourse, through a lack of a better term). The same opinion is expressed by Charles-René Billuart, *Summa Sancti Thomae hodiernis academiarum moribus accomodata, sive cursus theologiae*, 15.6.10, 361.
220. *Salmanticenses*, 6. 26 .7.5 n. 87, 159: "*Ad rationem sodomiae non requiritur seminum emissio, sed sat est vasis penetratio : ergo semel, quod quis penetret vas indebitum, aut penetrari patiatur, sodomia incurritur, et seminis emissio est solum complementum.*"
221. Alphonsus Liguori, *Instructio*, I. 9. 3. n. 24: "*Quod coitus feminae cure femina, et masculi cum masculo, perfecta est sodomia, in quacumque parte corporis fiat congressus, quia ordinarie semper adest tunc affectus ad indebitum sexum.*" [And sexual intercourse between two women and between two men is true sodomy, in whatever parts of the body it takes place. For usually there is always a desire for the improper sex.] For more details, see Hurteau, "Catholic Moral Discourse," 8–16.
222. Tommaso Tamburini, *Theologia moralis*, 1. 7. 7, 191: "*Sed hic est quaestio, quandonam mutua procuratio pollutionis inter mares, vel inter feminas, debeat dici mollities, quando sodomia? Resp. quando ex affectu ad personam adest concubitus, si sit inter indebitum sexum, hoc est inter virum, et virum, feminam, et feminam, tunc est sodomia, quando vero est mutua pollutio, absque concubitu, sed solum explandam libidinum, est mollities. Hinc si duo mares commisceant corpora, moveantur ad procurandam pollutionem, vel quomodocumque se tangant impudice ex affectu indebiti sexus, ita ut effusio séminis vel sit intra vas est certum, si vero sit extra, probatur, quia quamvis non sit copula, tamen per ilium concubitum est affectus venereus ad indebitum sexum, qui proprie constituit sodomiam.*"
223. Alphonsus Liguori, *Instructio*, I. 9. 3. n. 24; Lacroix, *Theologia moralis*, Book II, 199, n. 1080; Patuzzi, *Ethica Christiana sive theologia moralis*, 6. 12. 3, 249; Billuart, *Summa Sancti Thomae*, 15 .6. 10, 362. Hurteau (1993), 14.
224. Hurteau (1991), 110–113; « L'homosexualité masculine et les discours sur le sexe en contexte montréalais de la fin du XIXe siècle à la fin de la Révolution tranquille », 63–64.
225. Antonelli, 249.
226. Prümmer, 531. Marc and Gestermann, I, 512.
227. Hurteau, « L'homosexualité masculine et les discours sur le sexe en contexte montréalais de la fin du XIXe siècle à la fin de la Révolution tranquille », 55–58; Hudon et Bienvenue.
228. Caulle, 147–149. My translation.
229. Flandrin, 296–298. The author traces this concern back to the eighteenth century, although I personally think that it started in the nineteenth, as surveillance and repression against masturbation and particular friendships intensified in colleges.

230. Lyttelton, 29.
231. Hall, 374. This author believes that the fear of homosexuality as an outcome of masturbation is not a concern of educators and teachers. I find it quite present in several works dedicated to the moral edification of the youth during that period.
232. Hoornaert, 135.
233. England, *Criminal Law Amendment Act*, Vict. 48–49 [1885] c. 69, s. 11. In 1553, Henry VIII introduced for the first time a civilian law against sodomy: *The Buggery Act*, 25 Henry VIII c. 26.
234. Canada, *Statutes of Canada*, 53 Vict. c. 37, s. 5. This section of the *Canadian Criminal Code* at the time was more severe than the British legislation, which provided for a maximum penalty of two years with or without hard labor, and without whip.
235. Hurteau, « L'homosexualité masculine et les discours sur le sexe en contexte montréalais de la fin du XIXe siècle à la fin de la Révolution tranquille », 44–48.
236. For a detailed analysis, see Hurteau (1991), 208–219.
237. Machin, 157–158.
238. Vatican II, *Gaudium et Spes*, 26: 2.
239. Sacred Congregation for the Doctrine of the Faith, *Letter to the Bishops of the Catholic Church on the Pastoral Care of Homosexual Persons*, n. 9–10, October 1, 1986.
240. Sacred Congregation for the Doctrine of the Faith, *Persona Humana, Declaration on Certain Questions Concerning Sexual Ethics*, n. 8, December 29, 1975.
241. Ibid., n. 3–5.
242. Sacred Congregation for the Doctrine of the Faith, *Considerations Regarding Proposals to Give Legal Recognition to Unions between Homosexual Persons*, June 3, 2003. The last sentence of the quotation refers to the *Catechism of the Catholic Church* (1993), sections 2357 and 2358: "2357. Homosexuality refers to relations between men or between women who experience an exclusive or predominant sexual attraction toward persons of the same sex. It has taken a great variety of forms through the centuries and in different cultures. Its psychological genesis remains largely unexplained. Basing itself on Sacred Scripture, which presents homosexual acts as acts of grave depravity, tradition has always declared that 'homosexual acts are intrinsically disordered.' They are contrary to the natural law. They close the sexual act to the gift of life. They do not proceed from a genuine affective and sexual complementarity. Under no circumstances can they be approved.

2358. The number of men and women who have deep-seated homosexual tendencies is not negligible. They do not choose their homosexual condition; for most of them it is a trial. They must be accepted with respect, compassion, and sensitivity. Every sign of unjust discrimination in their regard should be avoided. These persons are called to fulfill God's will in their lives and, if they are Christians, to unite to the sacrifice of the Lord's Cross the difficulties they may encounter from their condition."
243. Sacred Congregation for the Doctrine of the Faith, *Considerations Regarding Proposals to Give Legal Recognition to Unions between Homosexual Persons*, n. 10, June 3, 2003.
244. Congregation for Catholic Education, *Instruction Concerning the Criteria for the Discernment of Vocations with regard to Persons with Homosexual Tendencies in view of their Admission to the Seminary and to Holy Orders*, n. 2, November 4, 2005.
245. Sacred Congregation for the Doctrine of the Faith, *Letter to the Bishops of the Catholic Church on the Pastoral Care of Homosexual Persons*, n. 9–10, October 1, 1986. Without naming them explicitly, the Vatican is undoubtedly targeting homosexuals who are out, identify as gay, and claim their place in the church through advocacy groups. In the United States and Canada, these groups have existed since the 1970s, including *Dignity* and *New Ways Ministry*.
246. Ibid, n. 6.
247. Ibid.
248. Congregation for Catholic Education, *Guidelines for the Use of Psychology in the Admission and Formation of Candidates for the Priesthood*, n. 9–10, June 29, 2008.
249. Church of England, House of Bishops (1991), *Issues in Human Sexuality*.
250. This is probably the reason why this document does not mention sexual orientation or homosexual relationships, but uses the term "homophile relationships" or "homophile orientation" in order to mark the exclusion of sexual activity within these relationships.

251. Anglican Church in North America, *Our Genesis*, http://www.anglicanchurch.net/media/genesisJuly2010.pdf.
252. See the authorized biography of Desmond Tutu by Allen (2006), 372–374.
253. Sharon Lafraniere, "Inviting Africa's Anglicans to Gather under a Bigger Tent," *The New York Times*, February 10, 2007.
254. *Civil Partnerships—A pastoral statement from the House of Bishops of the Church of England*, July 25, 2005.
255. House of Bishops (2003), *Some Issues in Human Sexuality*, 1. 2. 48.
256. For more information on the Indaba Project, seehttp://www.anglicancommunion.org/listening/continuing_indaba/description.cfm.
257. Parliament of Canada, 37th Parliament, 2nd Session, Standing Committee on Justice and Human Rights, *Evidence*, Thursday, February 13, 2003, Ms. Alison Huntley (Researcher, United Church of Canada).
258. The Council made its position known in a document entitled *Mit Spannungen Leben. Eine Orientierungshilfe des Rates der Evangelischen Kirche in Deutschland zum Thema "Homosexualität und Kirche,"* 1996. (Living with Tensions. A position paper of the Council of the Evangelical Church in Germany on the issue of "Homosexuality and the Church).
259. Evangelical Lutheran Church in America, Conference of Bishops, "Blessing of Homosexual Relationships," CB 93.10. 25, October 5–8, 1993, http://www.elca.org/faithfuljourney/pdf/study02.pdf.
260. The Church Council of the Evangelical Lutheran Church in America, "Vision and Expectations: Ordained Ministers in the Evangelical Lutheran Church in America," October 1990.
261. Task Force for Evangelical Lutheran Church in America, Studies on Sexuality (2003), *Journey Together Faithfully, Part Two: The Church and Homosexuality*, www.elca.org/faithfuljourney.
262. Evangelical Lutheran Church in America, Church wide Assembly, "Human Sexuality: Gift and Trust," A Social Statement of the Evangelical Lutheran Church adopted August 19, 2009.
263. Lutheran Church—Missouri Synod, Task Force on Ministry to Homosexuals and their Families (1999), *A Plan for Ministry to Homosexuals and their Families*, www.lcms.org/president/minhom fam.html.
264. In 1999, the National Convention adopted a policy of grassroot dialogue in the church on homosexuality, called *Caring Conversations*.
265. See the orientation document produced by Buck (2001). This document was produced at the request of the National Council of the Church by the author, a professor of New Testament at the Lutheran Theological Seminary in Saskatoon. The document is available on the web:http://elcic.ca/Study-On-Sexuality-And-The-Church/Table-of-Contents/default.cfm. At the convention in June 2009, the Evangelical Lutheran Church in Canada maintained its commitment to dialogue with the publication of the paper *Study of Human Sexuality, Session 6: Orientation*.
266. Twelfth Biennial Convention, Evangelical Lutheran Church in Canada, Vancouver BC, June 25–28, 2009, Session Seven: Saturday, June 27, 2009, 1:30 PM. *Resolutions NC-09-42, NC-09-43*.

    Evangelical Lutheran Church in Canada, *Social Statement on Human Sexuality*, approved at the 2011 National Convention, July 15, 2011: "Our church is conflicted on how to acknowledge covenants of fidelity made by same-sex couples. While acknowledging same-sex couples is troubling to some members of this church, failure to acknowledge these covenants of fidelity is troubling to others. At this moment in time, this church is being called in the spirit of St. Paul (Galatians 2) to respect and to allow space for varied understanding and practices."

    Http://elcic.ca/Human-Sexuality/documents/APPROVEDELCICSocialStatement onHumanSexuality.pdf
267. An orientation document was discussed in the parishes of the four member churches: the Church of the Augsburg Confession of Alsace and Lorraine, the Evangelical Lutheran Church of France, the Reformed Church of Alsace, and Lorraine the Reformed Church of France.
268. Conseil Permanent Luthéro-Réformé, « Église et personnes homosexuelles. Avis du CPLR », February 1, 2004.

269. Fédération Évangélique de France, « Positions sur l'homosexualité de différentes instances évangéliques françaises », Press statement, June 4, 2004.www.lafef.com/UserFiles/File/Bibliotheque/Ethique/BNF_Reflexions_sur_homosexualite.pdf.
270. Église évangélique réformée du Canton de Vaud, "Résolutions du Synode extraordinaire des 25 et 26 janvier 2008," Lausanne, www.protestant-vaud.ch.
271. Southern Baptist Convention, "Resolution on Homosexuality," San Antonio, Texas, June 1988.
272. Southern Baptist Convention, "Resolution on Homosexuality," June 1985, Dallas, Texas: "Be it therefore RESOLVED, that we, the messengers of the Southern Baptist Convention meeting in Dallas, June 11–13, 1985, deplore the proliferation of all homosexual practices, and reaffirm the biblical position of Southern Baptists that all such practices are sin and are condemned by the Bible; and Be it further RESOLVED, that we, oppose the identification of homosexuality as a minority with attendant benefits or advantages; And Be it finally RESOLVED, That we affirm that while the Bible condemns such practice as sin, it also teaches forgiveness and transformation, upon repentance, through Jesus Christ our Lord."
273. Southern Baptist Convention, Ethics and Religious Liberty Commission, "Nashville Declaration on Same-Sex Marriage," March 2005.
274. Southern Baptist Convention, "Resolution on Same-Sex Marriage," June 2003, Phoenix AZ. The statement deplored the recognition by many countries of gay civil union or marriage and called on politicians to fight it.
275. A reading of the texts of the confessions of 1925 (the first), 1963, and 2000 reveals a resurgence of conservative orthodoxy, gaining impetus in the 1960s. www.sbc.net/bfm/bfmcomparison.asp.
276. Alliance of Baptists, "Statement on Same Sex Marriage," Dayton OH, April 17, 2004.
277. In 2005, the Alliance published a document to promote dialogue on the issues surrounding of same-sex relations and sexual orientation in local congregations: *A Clear Voice. Task Force onHuman Sexuality. A Document for Dialogue and Study*, www.allianceofbaptists.org.
278. S. 4023 [111th], *Don't Ask, Don't Tell Repeal Act of 2010*. The Act became effective as of September 20, 2011. *Faith-Based Organizations Letter in Support of the Military Readiness Enhancement Act of 2009* (H.R. 1283 & S. 3065), April 28, 2010.
279. Association d'Églises Baptistes Évangéliques au Québec, « Sorti de l'homosexualité », *En Action*, Vol. 3, N. 1, 2003.
280. Association d'Églises Baptistes Évangéliques au Québec, « La définition du mariage », *En Action*, Vol. 3, N. 1, 2003.
281. Parliament of Canada, House of Commons, Standing Committee on Justice, 37th Legislature, 2nd Session, *Evidence*, February 13 and April 9, 2003.
282. Lienemann; Alfeyev.
283. Hammar.
284. O'Donavan. The essay is very well researched and tells the story of gay presence in the Mormon Church and its repression.
285. Private university belonging to the Church of Latter-Day Saints based in Provo, Utah. Founded in 1875, it now hosts nearly 35,000 students.
286. Mark 2: 23–28.
287. Taylor.

5 Islam

1. *Britannica Yearbook 1997*.
2. Statistics Canada, *2011 National Household Survey*, http://www.statcan.gc.ca/daily-quotidien/130508/dq130508b-eng.htm?HPA.
3. Statistics Canada, *2001 Census: Analysis Series, Religions in Canada*, Catalogue no. 96F0030 XIF2001015, May 13, 2003.
4. Statistics Canada, *Projections of the Diversity of the Canadian Population 2006–2031*, Catalogue no. 91–551-X, March 9, 2010.

Notes

5. Pew Research Center, *Muslim Americans, Middle Class and Mostly Mainstream*, May 22, 2007.
6. Qur'an, Surah 21:48–54.
7. Qur'an, Surah 3:67. The term "*al mushrikun*" means "the polytheists," but is often translated as "the idolaters" or "the pagans." Qur'an, Surah 2:135 contrasts "*hanifa*," Abraham's faith in one God, to "*al-mushrikun.*"
8. Gardet, 301. There is a debate among theologians and jurists as to the meaning of *fitra*. Is it a natural disposition toward the good, an inner light that guides humans to the knowledge of god, or the religion of Islam? See Camilla Adang (2000), Atonella Straface, and Gobillot.
9. Schuon, 13.
10. Qur'an, Surah 7:158.
11. Al Mas'udi (*Muruj adh-dhahab, Meadows of Gold*). My translation from *Les Prairies d'Or*, Book 3, Chapter XLVII, 256–257. Only partial English translations of the work exist.
12. There are several examples of this inclination to paint the cultures of the Arabian Peninsula as taken by barbarism and obscurantism before the introduction of Islam. Sayyid Abul A'la Maududi, 38–40. For ancient exaggerated descriptions of *jahiliya*, see *Documents sur les origines de l'Islam*, n. 28, www.islam-documents.org.
13. Al Kalbi, *The Book of Idols* (Kitab al-Asnam), 13–15. Al Waqidi, a historian of the eighth-century Medina, describes the fabrication of Qurayshi household gods that Muslims attempted to destroy after the preaching of the Prophet (*Kitab al-Tariq wa al-Maghazi* [Book of Expeditions] 64).
14. Rodinson, 38–39.
15. Al Kalbi, *The Book of Idols*, 28–29.
16. Ibid., 5. The *talbiyah* is as follows: "Here I am at Thy service O Lord, here I am. Here I am at Thy service and Thou hast no partners. Thine alone is All Praise and All Bounty, and Thine alone is The Sovereignty. Thou hast no partners."
17. Rodinson, 113–115; Watt, 61–62.
18. Rodinson, 107–108.
19. At-Tabari, *The History of at-Tabari* (*Ta'rikh al-rusul wa'l-muluk*), Vol. VI: *Muhammad at Mecca*, 107–108.
20. At-Tabari, *Tafsir*, 17:119, *Documents sur les origines de l'Islam*, no. 108, www.islam-documents.org.
21. At-Tabari, *The History of at-Tabari*, Vol. VI, 70; ibn Hisham, *The Life of Muhammad: A Translation of Isḥāq's Sīrat rasūl Allāh* (*Sira rasul Allah Muhammad ben Abd Allah*), 105.
22. Ibn Battuta, *The Travels of ibn Battuta* (*Kitab rihlat ibn Batutah*). My translation from the French, *Voyages* I, 257, http://dx.doi.org/doi:10.1522/030078802.
23. At-Tabari, *The History of at-Tabari*, Vol. VI, 67. According to Al-Bukhari, a ninth-century Uzbek Imam, the tradition regarding the origin of the initial message to Muhammad must be attributed to Aisha. Al-Bukhari, *Sahih Boukhari*, I. 1. 1–3, Khan, 50.
24. Qur'an, Surah 96:1–7.
25. Al-Bukhari, *Sahih* Bukhari, I. 1. 1–3, Khan, 50; at-Tabari, *The History of at-Tabari*, Vol. VI, 72.
26. Qur'an, Surah 53:1–7: "By the declining star, your companion is not in error nor has he gone astray; He does not speak out of his own desires. It is a revelation which has been revealed to him and taught to him by the great mighty one (Gabriel), the strong one who appeared on the uppermost horizon."
27. Qur'an, Surah 55:26–27.
28. Ibid., 87:1–13.
29. Ibid., 86:5–8.
30. Ibid., 92:5–21.
31. Ibid., 89. See also Surah 90, entitled "The City" (*Al-Balad*) in which Muhammad criticizes the rich merchants of Mecca.
32. Qur'an, Surah 42:7.
33. At-Tabari, *The History of at-Tabari*, Vol. VI, 76, 80.
34. Ibid., Vol. VI, 60–61.

35. Ibid., Vol. VI, 88.
36. Qur'an, Surah 43:23–24: "In the same way, whenever We had sent a Messenger before you to warn a town, the rich ones therein said, 'We found our fathers following a certain belief and we follow in their footsteps.' The Messengers would say, 'Would you still follow in the footsteps of your fathers even if I was to bring you better guidance?' They would say, 'We have no faith in your message.'"
37. Ibn Hisham *The Life of Muhammad*, 130; at-Tabari depicts Abu Talib as the negotiator between the Messenger and angry Qurayshis, after Muhammad had reviled theirs gods during a public prayer (*The History of at-Tabari*, Vol. VI, 94–98).
38. Ibn Sad al-Baghdadi, *Kitab Tabaqat Al-Kubra*, I: 230. Quoted in *Documents sur les origines de l'Islam*, no. 263, www.islam-documents.org.
39. At-Tabari, *The History of at-Tabari*, Vol. VI, 102. Abu Talib is the leader of the Hashemite clan of the Qurayshi tribe. He is Muhammad's uncle and the father of Ali, the Prophet's cousin. Abu Talib supports and does his best to protect the Prophet who is also of Hashemite descent (*The History of at-Tabari*, Vol. VI, 92–96).
40. Ibn Hisham, *The Life of Muhammad*, 135.
41. Ibid., 144–145.
42. Muslim ibn al-Hajjaj (Persian, ninth century), *Sahih Muslim*, Book 19, Chapter 38, hadith 4421.
43. Rodinson, 139–144. Before the flight to Medina, some of Muhammad's supporters had already emigrated to Ethiopia. See Rodinson, 113–115, and at-Tabari, *The History of at-Tabari*, Vol. VI, 98–101. Before moving to Medina, the Prophet also tried in vain to settle in Ta'if, a cool mountain resort known to wealthy Meccans (at-Tabari, *The History of at-Tabari*, Vol. VI, 115–117).
44. Rodinson, 146.
45. Ibid., 152–153.
46. Ibn Hisham, *The Life of Muhammad*, 231–234.
47. At-Tabari, *The History of at-Tabari*, Vol. VII, 10ff.
48. Qur'an, Surah 3:123–124: "God gave you victory in the battle of Badr where your forces were much weaker than those of the enemy. Have fear of God so that you may give Him thanks. Also, remember when you said to the believers, 'Is it not enough that your Lord is helping you with a force of three thousand angels sent (from the heavens)?'"
49. Ibn Battuta depicts Badr as Allah's victory over the polytheists, *Travels in Asia and Africa, 1325–1354*, Book I, Chapter 1, 75.
50. Qur'an, Surah 3:57–72. According to at-Tabari, the Jews have deliberately removed from the *Torah* passages that proclaimed the coming of the Prophet Muhammad. (The Chronicle III, 103.)
51. Qur'an, Surah 9:4–6.
52. *Kitab al-Siaysah al-Sha'iyah*. My translation from the French translation by Henri Laoust. There is an English translation, which is not readily available: Omar Farrukh, *Ibn Taimiya on Public and Private Law in Islam* (Beirut: Khayats, 1966).
53. Qur'an, Surah 22:39–40; Surah 2:181–191. These two texts clearly show the defensive nature of jihad originally. Surah 9:29–39 advocates a more aggressive posture against infidels. The fourteenth-century Syrian jurist, Ibn Kathir, seems to favor a conquering jihad: "This is a promise from Allah to His Messenger that He would cause his Ummah to become successors on earth, i.e., they would become the leaders and rulers of mankind, through whom He would reform the world and to whom people would submit, so that they would have in exchange a safe security after their fear. (...). After the Prophets, the world never saw anyone like 'Umar in excellence of conduct and perfect justice. During his time, the rest of Syria and Egypt, and most of Persia, was conquered. Kisra was defeated and utterly humiliated, and he retreated to the furthest point of his kingdom. Mighty Caesar was brought low, his rule over Syria was overthrown, and he retreated to Constantinople. Their wealth was spent for the sake of Allah, as the Messenger of Allah had foretold and promised. May Allah's perfect peace and purest blessing be upon him. During the rule of 'Uthman, the Islamic domains spread to the furthest points of the earth, east and west. The lands of the west were conquered as far as Cyprus and Andalusia,

NOTES

Kairouan and Sebta which adjoins the Atlantic Ocean." (*Tafsir ibn Kathir*, Surah 24:55, Vol. 18, 126.)
54. Qur'an, Surah 8:39. See Ghamdi' article.
55. Rodinson, 171–173.
56. Ibid., 182–184.
57. Ghamdi. The time during which the Prophet made his message known to foreigners is called *al-itmam ujjah*.
58. Bernard Lewis, *The Political Language of Islam* (Chicago: University of Chicago Press, 1988), 72; and Marie-Thérèse Urvoy, « Guerre et Paix » in M. A. Amir-Moezzi, *Dictionnaire du Coran* (Paris: Robert Laffont, 2007), 374–375.
59. Bonner, 22.
60. Qur'an, Surah 45:18.
61. Sunnis recognize the existence of six collections, but the two most used are the *Sahih Bukhari* and the *Sahih Muslim*.
62. Wahhabism consists of a rigorous and puritanical interpretation of Islam, introduced in the eighteenth century by Muhammad ibn Abd al-Wahhab in Saudi Arabia.
63. Coulson, 60: "*Qiyas* or analogical reasoning, then, is a particular form of *ijtihad*, the method by which the principles established by the Qur'an, *sunna*, and consensus are to be extended and applied to the solution of problems not expressly regulated therein."
64. Ibid., 85.
65. Ibid., 120. Along with homicide, other crimes are: illicit sex, slander about illicit sex, wine-drinking, theft, armed robbery, and apostasy.
66. Qur'an, Surah 2:178–179; 17:33.
67. Mohamed.
68. Arkoun; An-Naim (2008), 321–341. For a general outlook on the new Islamic thinkers, see Benzine.
69. An-Naim (2003), 25–48.
70. *Sahih Muslim*, Book 059, hadith no. 583.
71. At-Tabari, *The History of Al-Tabari*, Vol. VI, 58, 72, 101. Rodinson, 284–285.
72. Blachère, « Coran » in *Dictionnaire de l'Islam*, 219–220.
73. *Sahih Muslim*, Book 10, hadith 3840, 3842.
74. *Sahih Muslim*, Book 1, hadith 33: "The Prophet said: 'I have been commanded to fight against people till they testify there is no god but Allah, that Muhammad is the Messenger of Allah, and they establish prostration prayer, and pay Zakat. If they do it, their blood and property are protected.'" *Sahih Bukhari*, Book 53, hadith n. 79: "Narrated By ibn 'Abbas: The Prophet said, on the day of the Conquest of Mecca, 'There is no migration (after the Conquest), but Jihad and good intentions, and when you are called for Jihad, you should immediately respond to the call.'"
75. At-Tabari, *The History of Al-Tabari*, Vol. IX, 1–39.
76. In 630, Muhammad launched an unsuccessful assault on the Byzantine forces in Tabuk (*The History of Al-Tabari*, Vol. IX, 47ff). For an outlook on the expansion of Islam ouside of Arabia, see Albert Hourani, *A History of the Arab Peoples* (London: Faber and Faber, 2nd Revised Edition 2002).
77. Coulson, 30.
78. Ibid., 43.
79. Ibid., 80.
80. Hasan, Ali and Fatima's eldest son, is considered to be the second imam in line.
81. Jafri, Chapter 1.
82. At-Tirmidhi, *Sunan at-Tirmidhi*, hadith no. 3723.
83. Esposito, 292–293; Corbin, « Shiisme » in *Dictionnaire de l'Islam*, 775–782.
84. Amir-Moezzi.
85. Al-Ayashi, *Tafsir*, 1:15–16. My translation of a passage quoted by Amir-Moezzi.
86. They account for 80 percent of all Shi'ites, mainly in Iran and Iraq.
87. Davis, 11. The Twelver Shi'ites acknowledge as the seventh imam, Musa al-Kazim, Jafar as-Sadiq's eldest son.
88. Coulson, 107.

89. The major Shi'ite collections of hadith are *Kitab al-Kafi* (The Book of that which is Sufficient) compiled by al-Kulayni, *Kitab Man la al-Yadhuhuru al-Faqih* (The Book of One Who Has no Doctor Next to Him) of ibn-al-Babawaih al-Qummi, *al Tahdhib al-Ahkam* (Review of Principles) of Shaykh al-Tusi.
90. *Taqlid*: Arabic word for imitate or follow someone; *marja* means benchmark.
91. Ibn Khaldun, *Muqaddimah*, VI: 16, trans. Rosenthal, 356 (abridged).
92. Ibn Khaldun, *Muqaddimah*, V: 16, trans. Rosenthal, Vol. III, 77 (unabridged): "I say: The most obvious etymology, if one uses one, is that which connects the word with *as-suf*, because Sufis as a rule were characterized by the fact that they wore woolen garments. They were opposed to people wearing gorgeous garments, and, therefore, chose to wear wool."
93. Esposito, 302ff.
94. Shafiq ur-Rahman, "Sharia and Tasawwuf," http://www.masud.co.uk/ISLAM/misc/shafiqur.htm. The author quotes Sheik Ahmed Zarruq, a fifteenth-century Moroccan Sufi master, for whom works without the sincerity of the heart provided by the Sufi schools are worthless. However, he does not reject the Sharia, which is the true vehicle of expression for God's will. Al-Ghazali expressed similar ideas.
95. Modern fundamentalists or salafists offer an ascetic vision of the body and sexuality. See Lamchichi. The French journalist Martine Gozlan proposed to explain how the Islamists turned the eroticism of the *Arabian Nights* into *thanatos*.
96. Lagrange (2007), 3–6.
97. Masad, 101–103. Salah al-Din al-Munajjid wrote *al-Hayah al Jinsiyyah 'ind al-'Arab* (History of the Sexual Life of the Arabs).
98. Lagrange (2007), 4. Here, I paraphrase the author.
99. Ibn Hazm, *The Ring of the Dove*, Chapter 11, "Of Concealing the Secret."
100. Qur'an, Surah 22:5.
101. Ibid., 24: 32.
102. Michot.
103. Al-Ghazali, *Ihya Ulum-id-Din* (Revival of Religious Learnings), Vol. IV, Part I, Chapter 4, "Poverty and Renunciation," 228.
104. An-Nawawi, hadith 25.
105. Qur'an, Surah 56:22–24. *Hur* is a term used to describe the large black eyes of the addax antelope of the desert. The Qur'an uses it as a metaphor to picture these eternally youthful virgin girls, who inhabit the paradise for the pleasure of the righteous. See Chebel (2003), Volume I, 411–414.
106. Qur'an, Surah 52:24.
107. *The Perfumed Garden*, 7.
108. Imam Qaradawi, at http://pendidikanislam.net/index.php/learn-english/51-readings-on-islam/470-the-philosophy-of-marriage-in-islam.
109. Siraj, 51.
110. Ibn Hanbal, *Musnad*, and al-Darimi, *Sunan*, quoted by Michot.
111. Sunnis prohibited temporary marriage in the first century of Islam but the practice continued to exist among the Twelver Shi'ites. The majority of Hanafi and Shi'ites jurists allow coitus interruptus, which was used by several contemporary jurists, Sunni and Shi'a, as a basis for legislation in favor of contemporary methods of contraception. Medieval Arab medicine dealt with the subject of contraception without moral judgments. However, the traditionalists are reporting conflicting traditions. In *Sahih* al-*Bukhari*, the Prophet, according to Jabir, would have allowed it (7. 62 136), while according to Abu Said al-Khudri it should be prohibited (9. 93. 506). Al-Ghazali deems it permissible or forbidden when a virtue is abandoned (*The Etiquette of Marriage*, section *Coitus interruptus*). Some interpret it as follows: the Prophet allowed contraception in the case of sex with a slave, but not with a free woman. See Rispler-Chaim (1993), 10–11, and Musallam.
112. Qur'an, Surah 4:3.
113. Goslan, Chapter 1, deals with the Messenger's sex life and the sensuality present in his relationship with Aisha. At-Tabari alluded to Zaynab's exceptional beauty (*The History of al-Tabari*,

NOTES

Vol. VIII, 2–3). Al-Qurtubi mentioned that her fine body attracted Muhammad's sexual interest (*Tafsir* 14/190).
114. Al-Ghazali, *The Book on the Etiquette of Marriage*, Section *Equality among Wifes*.
115. Ibid., Section *Etiquette of Intimate Relations*.
116. Qur'an, Surah 2:223.
117. Ibn Qudama, *al-Mughni*, X, 232. My translation from the French found under the tab "Relations intimes" at salafs.com.
118. Chebel (2003), II, 217.
119. As-Shafi'i, *Kitab al-Umm, Nikah*.
120. Kotb, 162. Physician and sexologist, she animated the first TV program on sex, in Egypt. She quoted an-Nawawi's *Kitab ur-Raudah*. According to a sixteenth-century jurist, Muhammad Khatib as-Shirbini, fellatio is reprehensible for similar reasons.
121. Kotb, 163–164. Al-Qurtubi, Andalusian scholar of the thirteenth century, states in his *Tafsir* 24: 31, that the requirements of modesty forbidding one not to look at the genitals only relates to good manners, but in reality both spouses can make use of any body part during sex, except the anus.
122. Sheikh Mohammad Said al-Buti from the University of Damascus, *Ma'a an-Nas* (With People), 84, quoted by Kotb, 163. Qatari Imam, Yussef al-Qaradawi, adopted a similar position, adding, however, that oral sex is considered objectionable by some lawyers when it results in the emission of seminal fluid (*madyi*); Kotb, 166.
123. According to Shaikh Salih ibn Ghanim as-Sadlan in his book *Fiqh Az-Zawaj* (Marriage Case Law), Shaikh Abdallah ibn Muni and the Saudi integrist Shaikh Salih al-Luhaydan reject fellatio. Syrian Shaikh Wahbah Az-Zuhayli in his book *Al-Fiqh al-Islami wa Adill atuhu* (Islamic Jurisprudence and its Arguments), Book 4, 2641, reported by Anas Ahmad Lala, on the website www.maison-islam.com under the tab "intimate questions."
124. At-Tirmidhi, hadith 3192, 3195.
125. *Tanwir al-Miqbas min Tafsir ibn Abbas*, Surah 2:223: "Your women are a tilth for you (to cultivate). He says: the vulvas of your wives are plantations for your offspring (so go to your tilth) your plantations (as ye will) as you please, from behind or front as long as the penetration is in the pudendum, (and send [good deeds] before you for your souls) righteous children, (and fear Allah) regarding penetrating your wives in their anus or having sex with them during menstruation, (and know that ye will (one day) meet Him) that you will see Him after you die and He will reward you according to your deeds. (Give glad tidings to believers (O Muhammad)) Allah says: give glad tidings, O Muhammad, to the believers, who ward off penetrating their wives in their anus and further abstain from having sex with them when they are menstruating, that Paradise will be theirs."
126. *Sunnan Abu Dawud, Kitab an-Nikah*, hadith 2157; *Kitab al-Kahanah wa at-Tatayyur*, hadith 3895.
127. *Sunnan Abu Dawud, Kitab an-Nikah*, hadith 2159.
128. *Tafsir ibn Kathir*, Surah 2:223.
129. Al-Qaradawi, *The Lawful and Prohibited in Islam*, "The Relationship between Husband and Wife," at http://www.witness-pioneer.org/vil/Books/Q_LP/. Sheikh al-Albani, *The Etiquette of Marriage and Weddings*, n. 6–7.
130. A similar view is expressed by Muhammad Said Abdul Rahman, 215–219. According to Rahman, ibn Taymyiah said in *al-Fatwa al-Kubra* (3:104–105) that heterosexual anal sex is *haram* because it is still sodomy, even though it may be considered as imperfect compared to homosexual sodomy.
131. Benkheira, 151–162.
132. *Sahih Bukhari*, Volume 6, Book 60, Number 50, 51.
133. Al-Ghazali, *The Book on the Etiquette of Marriage*, Section "Satisfying Sexual Desire."
134. See Sheikh Muhammad bin Amin; Chebel (2003), II, 85.
135. As-Shafi'i, *ul-Umm*, 5/94.
136. Al-Qurtubi, *Tafsir, Surah am-Muminun*.
137. Amin.
138. *Majmu al-Fatawa*, and *Fatawa al-Kubra*; my translation from Michot.

139. In his theory of generation, Aristotle takes into account semen only, while Galen thinks that assistance of male and female (ovum) body fluids are to be considered.
140. Ibn Sina, *Poem on Medicine* (*Al-Arjuzat fi at-Tibb*), 25.
141. Ze'evi (2006), 31–34.
142. Al-Albani, *Fataawa of Shaikh Al-Albaanee*, translated by Isma'eel Alarcon, Islamic Society of Calgary, www.iisc.ca.
143. Rizvi. The author refers to the collection of hadiths *Wasail al-Shi'a*, compiled in the seventeenth century by a Persian, Sheikh Muhammad al-Amili. It is reported that Imam Ali beat the hands of a masturbator, until they turned red.
144. Sayid as-Sabiq, « Qu'est-ce que la fornication? » www.islamophile.org, under the tab "fatwa."
145. Chebel (2003), II, 85; Bullough (1976), 220.
146. Nadia Kadiri, M. D., and Abderrazak Moussaïd, Abdelkrim Tirraf, Abdallah Jadid, "Morocco" in Francoeur.
147. Hamdullah Aydin, Zeynep Gülçat, "Turkey" in Francoeur.
148. Al-Ghazali, *The Book on the Etiquette of Marriage*, Chapter III, Sections "*Coitus Interruptus*" and "Intimate Relations."
149. On pollution and rites of purification, see Bouhdiba, Chapter 5 "Purity Lost, Purity Regained."
150. Bouhdiba, 44.
151. Malik ibn Anas, *al-Muwatta*, Book II, hadith 60–65. *Wudu* is an orderly ritual ablution consisting of washing hands, rinsing the mouth, teeth brushing, cleaning sinuses, and finally the face, ears, and feet. This ablution is usually performed individually before personal prayer, unless the causes of impurities require a complete wash (*ghusl*).
152. Bouhdiba, 46. In the *Sahih Muslim*, hadith 453, one reads: "Abdullah b. Zaid b. 'Asim al-Ansari, who was a Companion (of the Holy Prophet), reported: It was said to him (by people): Perform for us the ablution (as it was performed) by the Messenger of Allah (may peace be upon him). He ('Abdullah b. Zaid) called for a vessel (of water), and poured water from it on his hands and washed them three times. Then he inserted his hand (in the vessel) and brought it (water) out, rinsed his mouth and snuffed up water from the palm of one hand doing that three times, He again inserted his hand and brought it out and washed his face three times, then inserted his hand and brought it out and washed each arm up to the elbow twice, then inserted his hand and brought it out and wiped his head both front and back with his hands. He then washed his feet up to the ankles, and then said: This is how God's Messenger (peace be upon him) performed the ablution."
153. Wheeler.
154. Qur'an, Surah 24:2.
155. *Sahih Muslim*, hadith 4194: "'Abdullah b. 'Abbas reported that 'Umar b. Khattab sat on the pulpit of Allah's Messenger (may peace be upon him) and said: Verily Allah sent Muhammad (may peace be upon him) with truth and He sent down the Book upon him, and the verse of stoning was included in what was sent down to him. We recited it, retained it in our memory and understood it. Allah's Messenger (may peace be upon him) awarded the punishment of stoning to death (to the married adulterer and adulteress) and, after him, we also awarded the punishment of stoning, I am afraid that with the lapse of time, the people (may forget it) and may say: We do not find the punishment of stoning in the Book of Allah, and thus go astray by abandoning this duty prescribed by Allah. Stoning is a duty laid down in Allah's Book for married men and women who commit adultery when proof is established, or if there is pregnancy, or a confession."
156. Abu Dawud relates how the Prophet condemned to stoning a man who had confessed to have committed adultery four times, only after Muhammad was satisfied that the man had inserted his penis into the vagina of a woman, *Sunan*, hadith 4414. See in this regard, Karamah.
157. The case of Amina Lawal traveled around the world. In 2002, she was sentenced to stoning by an Islamic court in Katsina (Nigeria), after having confessed to giving birth to a daughter more than nine months after her divorce. She was eventually exonerated by a civil court of appeal on procedural grounds. Media pressure probably played in her favor, as in other cases.

158. Qur'an, Surah 4:124.
159. Ibid., 4:34: "Men are the protectors of women because of the greater preference that God has given to some of them and because they financially support them. Among virtuous women are those who are steadfast in prayer and dependable in keeping the secrets that God has protected. Admonish women who disobey (God's laws), do not sleep with them and beat them. If they obey (the laws of God), do not try to find fault in them. God is High and Supreme."
160. The *Sahih Bukhari* refers to a lack of intelligence in women: "Narrated Abu Said Al-Khudri: Once Allah's Apostle went out to the Musalla (to offer the prayer) of 'Id-al-Adha or Al-Fitr prayer. Then he passed by the women and said, 'O women! Give alms, as I have seen that the majority of the dwellers of Hell-fire were you (women).' They asked, 'Why is it so, O Allah's Apostle ?' He replied, 'You curse frequently and are ungrateful to your husbands. I have not seen anyone more deficient in intelligence and religion than you. A cautious sensible man could be led astray by some of you.' The women asked, 'O Allah's Apostle! What is deficient in our intelligence and religion?' He said, 'Is not the evidence of two women equal to the witness of one man?' They replied in the affirmative. He said, 'This is the deficiency in her intelligence. Isn't it true that a woman can neither pray nor fast during her menses?' The women replied in the affirmative. He said, 'This is the deficiency in her religion'" (Book 6: Menstrual Periods, Volume 1, Book 6, Number 301). See Lagrange (2007), 23; Ghassan Ascha, « Femme ,» *in Dictionnaire de l'Islam*, 308–311.
161. Al-Hibri, 10–11.
162. The male *awra* may vary in time and places. The Egyptian Yusuf al-Shirbini (seventeenth century) castigates the young peasants of the Nile, who till the soil with "their penis erected as a pointed hat." Lagrange (2007), 47.
163. Qur'an, Surah 24:30–31.
164. Chebel (1995), 144.
165. Qur'an, Surah 33:33.
166. Al-Hibri, 20.
167. Ibn Khaldun, *Muqaddimah*, Book I, Chapter 4, Section 18 (abridged) 288. The term "homosexuality" is used to translate the Arabic *liwat*. See Chebel (1995), 25.
168. Al-Amili, *Wasail al-Shi'a*, Vol. 14, hadith 12. Quoted by el-Rouayheb, 16. The term designates the active partner, the inserter.
169. Pellat.
170. Qur'an, Surah 7:80–84.
171. Literally, the verse says "you lust (*shahwatan*) for men instead of women."
172. Ibid., 26:165–166; 29:28–35. In verse 29, Lot accuses the sodomites of blocking the road and robbing travelers. The context could favor an interpretation that sees Lot's charge directed against those who impede procreation by not using the natural receptacle. Jamel, 25, note 30. On the ignorance of sodomites, see Qur'an, Surah 27:55–59. Jamel, 25, note 30.
173. Jamel. The word *fahisha* is also used to condemn adultery or fornication (*zina*).
174. Ibn Malik, *Al-Muwatta*, 41. 1. 11: "Malik related to me that he asked ibn Shihab about someone who committed sodomy. Ibn Shihab said, 'He is to be stoned, whether or not he is *muhsan*.'" *Mushan* refers to a man who has contracted a valid marriage.
175. Abu Dawud, *Sunan*, hadith 4447: "Narrated Abdullah ibn Abbas: The Prophet (peace-be-upon-him) said: If you find anyone doing as Lot's people did, kill the one who does it, and the one to whom it is done."
176. El-Ruayheb, 136. For example, the twelfth-century Maliki jurist al-Dardir defined as *liwat* the introduction of the glans in a man's anus.
177. Shalakany.
178. El-Ruayheb, 119–120; Shafaat.
179. El-Ruayheb, 121.
180. See Camilla Adang (2003a).
181. Ibid., 22.
182. El-Ruayheb, 118.
183. See Lagrange (2007), 137.

184. El-Ruayheb, 128. The author mentions the Shafi'i jurist, Ali as-Shabramallisi (seventeenth century, Egypt) and the Hanbali, Muhammad as-Saffarani (eighteenth century, Palestine). For these jurists, sodomy causes less damage to families because there is no possible reproduction.
185. Chebel (1995a), 91–140.
186. Al-Sharani, *Al Mizan al-Kubra* (*Balance in Islamic Law*), 2: 136. Quoted by el-Ruayheb, 128.
187. Ibn Abidin, *Radd al-Muhtar* (*The Selected Answer*), 3: 156. Quoted by al-Ruayheb, 131–132.
188. El-Ruayheb, 137–138. The author cites various sources and among them a Maliki jurist, al-Dardir, and the Egyptian Shafi'i, ibn Hajar al-Haytami (sixteenth century), Yusuf as-Shirbini (seventeenth century), and Suleiman al-Bujayrimi (eighteenth century)—all of whom consider interfemoral intercourse (*mufakhadhah*) as a minor sin that can be disciplined (*tazir*), but certainly not sanctioned by the *Sharia*.
189. El-Ruayheb, 121–122.
190. Al-Bayhaqi (eleventh century), *Shuab al-Imam* (The Ramifications of Faith), quoted by Shafaat.
191. Kugle, 150–153. Adang (2003a), 21.
192. El-Ruayheb, 119.
193. Miller, 291.
194. Sections 197 and 198 of the first *Ottoman Penal Code* proscribe a minimum prison sentence of six months if the outrage is perpetrated against a child under 11 and a discretionary sentence of imprisonment in other cases, together with hard labor if the offence is accompanied by violence. Sections 330 to 332 of the Penal Code of 1810 show some differences, particularly with regard to the age of consent set at 15 years, and the severity of sentences of imprisonment is 5 to 10 or 20 years for crimes committed on a child. *The Imperial Ottoman Penal Code.* J. Bucknill and H. Utidjian trans. (London: Oxford University Press, 1913).
195. *Türk Ceza Kanunu* (Turkish Penal Code), Law n. 5237, September 26, 2004.
196. Gelbal and Duyan.
197. Ibid., 573. The authors did not specify whether the victims were passive or active subjects, but probably many cases involved passive subjects since it is they who are victims of social stigma in a society that equates passivity with femininity or a lack of masculinity. See Huseyn Tapinc, "Masculinity, Femininity, and Turkish Male Homosexuality," in Plummer (1992), 39–49. Tapinc shows how several men, who define themselves as heterosexual or as homosexual, have sex with men as active partners without feeling that they risk their masculine identity. Lambevski used Tapinc's analytical framework to apply it to the gay scene in Skopje, where Muslim citizens of Albanian origin are active subjects, while the Macedonian Orthodox traditionally play the passive role in the relationship.
198. KAOS GL, "Discrimination of Sexual Orientation and Law Report," October 2008,news.kaosgl.com/item/2008/10/12/turkey-discrimination-of-sexual-orientation-and-law-report.See Yuzgun.
199. KAOS GL, "LGBT Turkey Report to the European Social Charter," March 2008,news.kaosgl.com/item/186.
200. The UN Human Rights Council decried the misuse of this vague provision of the *Egyptian Penal Code*, not only to persecute religious minorities but also all forms of literary expression, political, artistic, or otherwise, which is contrary to the moral code of Islam. UN Human Rights Council, Ninth Session, A/HRC/9/NGO/33, August 29, 2008.
201. Coalition Provisional Authority, "Modifications of Penal Code and Criminal Proceedings Law," CPA/ORD/September 10, 2003/31, Section 3.
202. Amnesty International, document: MDE 14/030/2006 (Public), Bulletin n. 211, August 10, 2006. The Ayatollah had to withdraw the fatwa from his website because of pressures from the Iraqi LGBT group, in exile in London; www.si-lgbt.org/article.php3?id_article=89. This document explains how homosexuals become victims of entrapment by the militia.
203. Sections 108–126 of Iran's *Islamic Criminal Law* deals with sodomy and other forms of homosexual contact. This code is available in English on the Internet athttp://www.iran-law.com/IMG/pdf/Iran_Criminal_Code_in_English.pdf.

204. *The Times* (London), Dominic Kennedy, "Gays Should Be Hanged, Says Iranian Minister," 13 November, 2007. Iran Student News Agency released around the world stunning photos of the public hanging.
205. Caroline Mangez, « Iran pas de fatwa pour les transsexuels ," *Paris Match* no. 2936, August 25, 2005.
206. This information is released by the UN High Commissioner for Refugees, and is broadcasted by the Immigration and Refugee Board of Canada. Document PAK102660.EF of November 29, 2007, at www.unhcr.org/refworld/docid/47d651b71e.html.
207. Jeheoda Sofer, "Sodomy in the Law of Muslim States," in Schmitt and Sofer eds., 141.
208. To understand the legal situation in each country, see Ottosson and Amnesty International, *Love, Hate and the Law. Decriminalizing Homosexuality, Appendix 1: The Application of the Death Penalty for Consensual Same-sex Sexual Relations*, 2008, document no. POL 30/003/2008.
209. In 2005, nearly a hundred men attending a party were arrested by police in Jeddah, and sentenced to flogging and imprisonment, ranging from six months to two years, because they danced and behaved like women. Brian Whitaker, "Saudis' tough line on gays," *Guardian*, Saturday, April 9, 2005 www.guardian.co.uk/world/2005/apr/09/saudiarabia.brianwhitaker.
210. Khalid Duran, "Homosexuality and Islam," in Swidler, 194.
211. Peletz.
212. The phenomenon has already been noted in the chapters on Hinduism, Buddhism, and Judaism.
213. Gallant voluntarily omitted obscene passages, especially those referring to pederastic love, while Burton translated them for a restricted audience in a special edition. His translation intended for the general public omitted them. Joseph-Charles Mardrus, a Cairo-born French physician, will also publish an unadulterated version.
214. Burton developed this unsubstantiated theory in his "Terminal Essay," annexed to the English translation of *Arabian Nights*, in 1885. He named the region "the sotadic zone," recalling the Greek poet Sotades (third century BC) and his poems on male love.
215. *The Letters of Gustave Flaubert: 1830–1857*, trans. Francis Steegmüller (Cambridge, MA: Harvard University Press, 1980), 121.
216. El-Ruayheb, 2.
217. Massad, 34. Al-Saffar, *al-Rihlah al-Titwaniyyahila al-Diyar al-Firansiyyah 1845–1846*, translated into English by Susan Gilson Miller as *Disorienting Encounters: Travels of a Moroccan Traveler in France in 1845–1846* (Berkeley: University of California Press, 1992).
218. Bouhdiba, 165.
219. Abu Nuwas, *Diwan* 708, in *Carousing the Gazelles*, 24.
220. *Dellakname-i Dilküşa*: www.glbtq.com/social-sciences/turkey,2.html, *GLBTQ, An Encyclopedia of Gay, Lesbian, Transgender and Queer Culture*.
221. Ze'evi, 41.
222. *A Mirror for Princes: The Qabus Nama*, 78.
223. Chebel (2003), I, 377–380.
224. Massad, 33. Al-Tahtawi, *Takhlis al-Ibriz fi Talkhis Bariz*, translated into Eglish as *An Imam in Paris* by Daniel L. Newman (London: Saqi Books, 2011).
225. See Habib (2007), 120–125.
226. Rowson (1991) and Rowson (2003), 45–72.
227. Narrated by Aisha in the *Sunan* of Abu Dawud, hadith 4095. It shows that all male transvestites are not devoid of desire for women.
228. *Kitab al-Aghani*, 4: 67, in Rowson (1991), 684.
229. Rowson (1991), 685.
230. *Kitab al-*Aghani, 4: 59–60. Rowson (1991), 690–691. According to Rowson, castration included the removal of the penis and the testicles.
231. Rowson (2003), 59. Rowson also quotes al-Jahiz, a black poet of the ninth century in Baghdad, who tries to explain the sudden rise in popularity of homosexual practices. He says the Abbasid soldiers got into the habit during military campaigns in Iran, and then brought it home.

232. *Nathr ad-Durr* (Scattered Pearls), 5: 277. Quoted in Rowson (2003), 59.
233. Rowson (2003), 59. The author mentions this reply by Abu Ali as-Shabushti in his *Kitab al-Diyarat* (Book of Monasteries).
234. See Lagrange (2007), 86.
235. Quoted by ibid., 86.
236. Ibn Miskawayh, *Hawamil was-Shawamil* (Rambling and Comprehensive Questions), in Rowson (2003), 64.
237. Murray and Roscoe, 29. Ibn Sina (*Canon medicinae*, III. XX. 1. 42) appears to be aware of Aristotle's theory in his *Problemata*. Aristotle linked the homosexual desire to be penetrated anally with congenital malformations of the vas deferens causing an accumulation of sperm in the anal area, which required evacuation by the friction of the penis into the anus. See Jordan, 115–123.
238. Rosenthal (1978).
239. Al-Jahiz, *Kitab mufaharati al-jawari wal-ghilman* (The Book of Dithyramb of Concubines and Ephebes). No English translation available.
240. *A Mirror for Princes: The Qabus Nama*, 99ff. The author gives several tips on buying male slaves: physical beauty of the slave, softness of the skin, roundness of the buttocks, and so on. He warns the prospective buyer against being led by sensuality only.
241. *A Mirror for Princes: The Qabus Nama*, 77.
242. Ibid., 74. Also mentioned in the same chapter is the story of Sultan Masud I of Ghazni (eleventh century), Capital of the Ghaznavi Empire, located in Eastern Afghanistan. The sultan had ten slaves in charge of his wardrobe, all of whom he treated equally. After taking one too many a drink, the sultan expressed a preference for one of them, and ordered goods and benefits bequeathed to his favorite slave.
243. Drake.
244. Halman, xii.
245. Abu Nuwas, *Carousing with Gazelles: Homoerotic Songs of Old Baghdad*, 3.
246. Chebel (2006), 77–119.
247. The metaphor of the gazelle can be misleading because of the masculine gender of the word in Arabic; see al-Rouyaheb, 61–62. The homoerotic motifs were sometimes used in a satirical way to ridicule the effeminate manners of a new urban lifestyle in contrast to the rough life of the Bedouins, and to ridicule the religious hypocrisy of the elite; see J. W. Wright Jr, "Masculine Allusion and the Structure of Satire in Early 'Abbasid Poetry," in Wright Jr. and Rowson, 1–23.
248. El-Rouyaheb, 62–63; James T. Monroe, "Abu Bakr's Naughty Son," in Wright Jr and Rowson, 121.
249. *Rishnameh* (Book of the Beard), Alessandro Bausani, *Il Libro della barba di 'Obeid Zakani* (Roma: G. Bardi), 1964.
250. Abu Nuwas, *Carousing with Gazelles: Homoerotic Songs of Old Baghdad*, 4.
251. Abd-el-Jalil, 97–98.
252. Wright Jr. and Rowson, 11–13. Bencheikh, « Khamriyya," *Encyclopedie de l'Islam*, IV, 1030B–1041a. Kennedy.
253. The *Tafsir al-Baydawi* (Surah 2:25) notes that sex in Paradise is metaphorical. The quranic text does not mention intercourse with adolescent boys while it does in the case of the *huris*; only gazing, flirting, and having a good time, admiring the beauty of these eternally male youths (*wildan mukhalladun*) seem permissible (Qur'an, 56:17; 76:19). Al-Ghazali echoed this distinction in *Ihya'*. See Lagrange (2007), 38.
254. The Urdu poetry of Mir Taqi (eighteenth century, Delhi), Saleem Kidwai, "Mir Taqi 'Mir': Autobiography (Persian) and Poems (Urdu)," in Vanita and Kidwai, 188–190.
255. An-Nawaji, *The Meadow of Gazelles*, my translation from *La prairie des gazelles, Éloge des beaux adolescents*, 28.
256. Ibn Hazm, *The Ring of the Dove*, Chapter 28.
257. Al-Antaki, *Tazyin al-aswaq bi-tasfsil ashwaq al-ushshaq* (Decorating Markets with the News of Lovers), Book 6, *Ishq al-ghilman wal-hayawan wan-nabat* (The Love of Ephebes, Animals, and Plants), quoted by Chebel (2006), 240.

258. Camilla Adang (2003b). For instance, the author mentions the case of Ahmad ibn Fath, a member of the upper class of Cordoba, whose career as a scholar was destroyed because of his passion for a lower-class youth named Ibrahim ibn Ahmad (*The Ring of the Dove*, Chapter 12). Another story involves a man with a high social standing, Muqaddam ibn al-Asfar, who got punched in the face by a youth named Ajib, because of his obsessive staring at the youth in the mosques of Cordoba (*The Ring of the Dove*, Chapter 13). A punch in the face is probably a gesture by Ajib to assert his masculinity, coping with the possible social stigma attached to the male passive partner.
259. El-Rouayheb, 54.
260. Wright Jr. and Rowson (1997), 117. James T. Monroe mentions case law discussions on the dangers of unintentional ejaculation at the sight of the buttocks of beautiful youths prostrated during the prayer at the mosque.
261. The article "Homosexuality," in *Encyclopædia Iranica*, ed. Yarshater Ehsan, http://www.iranicaonline.org/articles/homosexuality-iii, quotes Hafez's homoerotic poems and provides relevant explanations on the social context of ephebophilia in Persia.
262. Ruzbihan Baqli Shirazi, *Kitab-e 'Abhar al-ashiqin* (*The Jasmine of Lovers*), 72.
263. *Hadiqat al-haqiqa wa-Shariat al-tariqa* (Garden of Truth and Path to Enlightenment), in Sprachman, "Le beau garçon sans merci," in Wright Jr. and Rowson, 199–200.
264. *Gulistan* (*The Rose Garden*), Chapter 2, Story 34. Sprachman highlights the sarcastic sense of humor often directed against Sufi ascetics ("Le beau garçon sans merci" in Wright Jr and Rowson, 201).
265. Southgate, 434.
266. *Gulistan*, Chapter V, Story 5. Sa'adi's *Bustan* (*The Orchard*) also contains many homoerotic stories in Chapter 2. See Southgate.
267. Omar Khayyam, *Naruznameh* (The Book of the New Year Festival), in Southgate, 429.
268. In 2002, Sirus Shamisa, a professor of Persian literature, published a book entitled *Shahedbazi dar adabiyat e-farsi* (Male Love in Persian Literature), in which he explains the ubiquity of the love of boys in Persian literature, which earned him censorship from the Iranian government and the removal of his book from bookstore shelves.
269. Omar Khayyam, *Naruznameh*, in Southgate, 430.
270. Ritter, 379.
271. Sa'adi, *Bustan*, Chapter 3.
272. Ritter, 476. The author cites *al-Masari Ushshaq* (Falling in Love), a Hanbali anthology of love. Ritter refers to many other stories about the efforts of the Sufi order not to give into temptation.
273. Bashir, 111–113.
274. Reported by Shams ud-Din Ahmad Aflaki (death 1356), *The Feats of the Knowers of God: Manaqeb al-'Arefīn*, 484–485.
275. Rumi, *Divan* 1077; trans. Arberry, poem 136, 153.
276. Bashir, 145–146.
277. Karamustafa (2007), 160.
278. Karamustafa (1994), 20–21.
279. Jim Wafer, "Vision and Passion: The Symbolism of Male Love in Islamic Mystical Literature," in Murray and Roscoe, 118–119; Ritter, 488, 490–491. Ahmad Aflaki mentions a similar story with the use of the mirror metaphor applied to *shahed-bazi*, *The Feats of the Knowers of God: Manaqeb al-'Arefīn*, 434.
280. Ibn Qayyim al-Jawziyya, *Rawdat al-muhibbin wa nuzhat al-mushtaqin* (The Garden of Lovers and Their Frantic Stroll), in Ritter, 474.
281. El-Ruayheb, 112. Al-Hamawi, as well as ibn Hajar al-Haytami (sixteenth century, Egypt) try to support their position on unreliable hadith material, as well as on the opinions of Abu Hanifah and ibn Hanbal, who both have highlighted the dangers of being in the company of male youths and enjoying their beauty.
282. El-Ruayheb, 114–115.
283. According to el-Ruayheb (114), proponents of the hard line sees in the ephebe a being more akin to the female, and, as a consequence, they apply the same restrictive rules concerning a

man looking at a woman foreign to his household. Less restrictive interpretations consider a male youth as male gendered (116).
284. *Nihayat al-Muhtaj*, quoted in ibid., 117.
285. Ibid.
286. Lagrange (2006). Abu al-Abbas Ahmad ibn Muhammad al-Jurjani (eleventh century) portrays a Qadi of Baghdad, Yahya ben Aktam, as having a marked preference for men, in *al-Muntakhab min kinayat al-udaba' wa isharat al-bulagha'* (Anthology of Metonymic Devices Used by the Literati and Allusions in Eloquent Speech), in Habib (2007).
287. Kugle and Hunt, 269, 271.
288. See See Camilla Adang (2000), Atonella Straface, and Gobillot.
289. Barbara Zollner.
290. Stephen O. Murray (1995).
291. Al-Raghib al-Asfahani, *Muhadarat al-udaba wa-muhawarat al-shuara wa-al-bulagha* (The Ready Replies of Cultured Men and Poets' and Orators' Conversation) in Habib (2007), 49.
292. Quoted by Surieu, 130. My translation.

6 AFRO-CARIBBEAN AND AFRO-BRAZILIAN RELIGIONS

1. Bastide (1972). Some groups of black slaves have intermarried with the Carib Indians, in the islands of St. Vincent and St. Lucia, as well as on the east coast of Honduras, with a religious system borrowing from African and Indians cultures. The Maroons established small republics in Guyana, Suriname, and Jamaica, with religious systems inspired by the Ashanti civilization of Ghana.
2. Hurbon (1988), 111.
3. In 1757, a slave from Guinea, Makandal, tried with other runaway slaves to escape by poisoning the European settlers, but he was arrested and burned.
4. Dimitri Béchacq, « La construction d'un vodou haïtien savant », in Hainard, 31.
5. Brandon, 67.
6. Murphy (1993), 25–28; Lachatañeré, 241–260; 288–291.
7. Unicef, *Manual de los Afrodescientes de las Américas y del Caribe*, Ciudad de Panamá, 2006, 29.
8. María Laura Bergel, "Quilombos and Their Influence on Afro-Brazilian Cultural Interpretation," April 2006, www.choike.org/nuevo_eng/informes/4423.html. It is possible that Ganga Zumba was a title rather than a person's name. The origin of the word *quilombo* dates back to the encounter of the Imbangala people of Angola with the Portuguese. They consisted of various ethnic groups assembled in fortified military camps called "*kilombo*" in the Kimbundu language. For them, the phrase "*nzumbi nganga*" meant a religious leader in charge of ancestor worship. See Robert Nelson Anderson III, "The Slave King," *Brazzil*, October 1995, www.brazzil.com/cvroct95.htm.
9. Hurbon (2002), 87. The author, a former Catholic priest, does not hesitate to see in the opposition of the Church to Voodoo practices the trademark of a cultural alienation of the masses. The population finds comfort in their ancestral deities, while the Catholic discourse is rather on the side of those in power and the ruling class.
10. Hurbon (1988), 112–114. A zombie is a person living in a lethargic condition because a sorcerer has captured its soul. The word *ouanga* means any king of magic used in order to harm someone. The *caprelata* or *pwen* (point) is the magical power that can be used against *ouanga*. It refers either to the magician or an amulet. *Donpèdre* means nothing other than the *Petro* rite. *Macandal* refers to herbal healers who use the power of plants to hurt people. Macandal was a slave who had a great knowledge of medicinal herbs, and who attempted, in 1757, with the help of maroons to poison the French settlers of St. Domingue.
11. In 1883, Louis-Joseph Janvier published: *Un peuple noir devant les peuples blancs. Étude de politique et de sociologie comparée : la République d'Haïti et ses visiteurs, 1840–1882*. In 1891, Hannibal Price wrote: *De la réhabilitation de la race noire par la République d'Haïti*. See Hurbon (1988), 55–75.

NOTES 239

12. Hurbon (2002), 38–45. The author writes a brief analysis of the novel *Gouverneur de la rosée*, by Jacques Roumain (1907–1944) and of *L'arbre des musiciens* by Jacques Stephen Alexis (1922–1961).
13. Quoted in Hurbon (2002), 41. My translation.
14. João José Reis, "Afro-Brazilian Religion in 19th Century Bahia: Slave Resistance or Resistance to Slavery?" March 2007. Presented at a research seminar in Salvador da Bahia.http://www.socialsciences.manchester.ac.uk/disciplines/socialanthropology/postgraduate/clacs/documents/SlaveResistance_Reis.pdf.
15. Harding, 122–146.
16. Ibid., 125–126.
17. Bergad, 11–12. In 1850, the last emperor of Brazil, Dom Pedro II, was abolitionist and made sure that the importation of African slaves ceased in Brazil, although slavery was not officially abolished in Brazil until 1888.
18. Reis (1996), 18.
19. Bertrand and Marin, 131–150.
20. de Heusch, 103–120; Desquiron, 193.
21. Joint, 83.
22. Hurbon (2002), 185.
23. Joint, 136. God is not concerned with human activities.
24. Hurbon (2002), 183–191.
25. Ibid., 104; Joint, 66. According to the latter, the bougainvillea would be Damballa's favorite tree.
26. Joint, 67.
27. Ibid., 68.
28. Hurbon (2002), 104.
29. Ibid.
30. Joint, 81.
31. Hurbon (2002), 157.
32. Joint, 76–77.
33. Desquiron, 156–159.
34. Métraux, 92–93.
35. Desquiron, 162.
36. The *axis mundi*, which connects heaven and earth is well-known in the history of religions and takes various forms, including the mountains or the tree. They became sacred spaces because they were perceived as a pathway that allowed travels from higher to lower cosmic regions. See Eliade, 53.
37. Joint, 86, 91.
38. Ibid., 49. The author explains that the origin of this informal priest goes back to the time when Dessalines subordinated the church to Haitian civil authority and appointed the priests.
39. Hurbon (2002), 96.
40. For more details on these paces and rhythms, see Fleurant, 24–29; Métraux, 190–191.
41. Hurbon (2002), 138–141.
42. Joint, 94.
43. Hurbon (2002), 142.
44. Ibid., 231–234.
45. Hurbon (1988), 236.
46. Hurbon (2002), 96–97.
47. Métraux, 192.
48. Hurbon, (2002), 145–146.
49. Joint, 97–98, 104; Métraux, 204.
50. See Joint, 99, on the meaning of the funeral ceremony of *wete mò nan dlo* (remove the body from the water). Hurbon (1988) explains that the bather washes the deceased with certain plants to prevent any danger of bad spells or attempted zombification (235).
51. Hurbon (2002), 156; my translation.
52. Joint, 50, 215, 261; Hurbon (2002), 104.
53. For a fine example of this campaign against Voodoo, see the work of Father Carl Edward Peters, *La Croix contre l'Asson*, (Port-au-Prince: La Phalange, 1960).

54. Bastide (1972), 145. The French Catholic priest Jean Kerboull adopts a similar approach in his work *Le vodou : magie ou religion?*, (Paris: Robert Laffont, 1973). See Hurbon (1988), 223.
55. Métraux, 266. Long before Métraux, the German sociologist Max Weber clearly demonstrated that magic is not opposed to religion. Instead, it represents some degree of abstraction in the symbolic world of religious representations. For Weber, theologians eventually located the finality of religion—redemption or salvation—outside this world, outside the daily concerns of lay persons who will not cease to use the symbolism of magic in order to solve their problems. According to Weber, there is no evolutionary scheme, simply because primitive thought does not exist. See Max Weber, *The Sociology of Religion*, trans. Ephraim Fischoff (Boston: Beacon Press, 1993).
56. Hurbon (1988), 272.
57. Murphy, 21–25.
58. Brandon, 82–83. According to Brown (2003), 68, *bozales* accounted for only 1 percent of the total population of the island in 1899, and only 10 percent of *criollos* had personally experienced slavery.
59. *Ocha* is a contraction used in Cuba for the word *oricha*. See Capone, 14.
60. Brown (2003), 62, 74.
61. Ibid., 124–130.
62. Lachatañeré, 123.
63. De La Torre, 73.
64. Lachatañeré, 62.
65. Isabel Castellanos, "A River of Many Turns, The Polysemy of Ochun in Afro-Cuban Tradition," in Murphy and Sanford, 38.
66. Lachatañeré, 323.
67. The *sopera* contains colored stones symbolizing the *orichas*. These stones are the physical carrier (*fundamento*) for their *ache* (power). Brown (2003), 166.
68. Ibid., 193. See Clark (2007), 127–128. The *pilon* plays the same role as the *vèvè* in Voodoo; it is the *axis mundi*, a medium between spirits and man.
69. Lachatañeré, 322.
70. Brown (2003), 168.
71. Capone, 20–21.
72. Ibid., 22.
73. Ibid., 26.
74. Giobellina Brumana and Martinez, 36.
75. Capone, 60.
76. Ibid., 63.
77. Ibid., 76.
78. Ibid., 109–115. Pomba Gira could be connected to Maria Padilla, the gypsy mistress of Don Pedro I, king of Castile in the fourteenth century and a witch practicing black magic. Gypsies, expelled by the Inquisition from Portugal, probably brought this character to Brazil, where she was identified with Exun's wife found in the Yoruba tradition.
79. Murphy (1993), 66.
80. A description of the initiation ritual is found in ibid., 66–68.
81. Clark (2007), 67–70. The author deals with Santería, but his observations may equally apply to Candomblé and Voodoo.
82. A similar analysis is presented by Clark (2005), 62–63.
83. Bastide (1972), 33.
84. On matrifocality in Cuba, view Martinez-Alier, 126–128.
85. American anthropologist Ruth Landes describes the phenomenon in a book on the women of Salvador da Bahia, published in 1947 as *The City of Women*.
86. McAlister (2004).
87. Dayan, 54–65.
88. McAlister (2004): "The way Ezili Freda embodies both romance and frustration can be understood as a kind of criticism of everyday life of poor Haitians, men and women. Indeed,

the poor women of Haiti have little chance of one day experiencing romantic love."; My translation.
89. Ibid.
90. Brown (1997), 74, 86.
91. McAlister (2004); my translation.
92. Brown (2003), 206–207; Clark (2007), 100–101.
93. Clark (2007), 63.
94. Dos Santos, 4–5.
95. Matory (2004), 157–190; Sweet (1996).
96. Matory (2005), Chapter 5.
97. Matory (2008), 521.
98. Matory (2005), 212; (2008), 522, 526–528. The author mentions, however, the testimony of a Yoruba priest, who says he witnessed homosexual anal sex practiced by priests dedicated to the worship of Shango in a sanctuary in Oyo. Matory (2004), 178.
99. Matory (1988), 215–231.
100. Matory (2005), 189–196. The author attributes the drop of *adés* in Nagô and Jêjé *terreiros* to Ruth Landes's incidental homophobia. She puts forth a theory of a primitive cultic matriarchy that was recently replaced by the presence of *adés* (198). This veiled homophobia has also won the Brazilian national spirit, which would preferably let the leadership of Candomblé in the hands of the black mammy (*mãe preta*)—an important figure in the heart of every Brazilian, white or black, according to Freyre—rather than in the hands of effeminate men.
101. Mesquita.
102. Oyewumi, 117. A sociologist of Yoruba origin, she teaches at the University of Stony Brook, New York. This book made her famous because she argued against the use in Yoruba cultural context of the Western notion of gender, which is correlated with anatomical sex.
103. Mott.
104. Grupo Gay Negro da Bahia, *Boletim do Quimbanda-Dudu*, "Afro-brasileiros homoeróticos de maior destaque no Brasil," N. 6, 2005.
105. Lumsden, 50. Montejo's testimony was reported by Miguel Barnet, *Biografía de un Cimarron*. Lumsden also mentions the testimony of an eighteenth-century Cuban theologian José Agustín Caballero.
106. Mott, 10–11. The inquisitors accuse the governor for having introduced the vice in the colony.
107. Ibid., 15–16. The friar's testimony is corroborated by Captain Antônio de Oliveira de Cadornega, the author of a history book on the Angolan war in the seventeenth century.
108. Murray and Roscoe (2001), 91–105; Murray (2002), 337–342.
109. Matory (1994).
110. This phrase was first used by Jacqueline Monfouga-Nicolas (1967). She has also published: *Ambivalence et culte de possession. Contribution à l'étude du bori hausa* (Paris: Anthropos, 1972). Monfouga-Nicolas thinks the *bori* cult was a reaction of Maguzawa women against Hausa domination in the nineteenth century—a view challenged by Besmer (1983).
111. See the different views expressed by Sinikangas. She mainly blames Rudolf Gaudio for his haste in identifying the *yan daudu* with a homosexual person, without carefully taking into account the role they play in Hausa society, socially and economically.
112. Pittin, Chapter 7.
113. Gaudio, 9.
114. Ioan Myrddin Lewis.
115. This is precisely the angle used by Lambek (1981).
116. In Cuba, effeminate homosexuals who agree to passive anal relations are called *afeminados* versus *bugarones* who are men who refuse to identify themselves as homosexuals. The latter, often married, have sex with men but they always act as inserters. Dianteill, 6, 22. The same phenomenon is observed in Brazil, where effeminate gay men are called *viados*, and the more virile are called *fanchonos* or *malandros*. See Green, 34, 88–91.
117. Gueboguo.
118. Castor, 109–110.

119. Bastide (2000), 221.
120. Daniel, 262.
121. Fleurant, 98–99. According to the author, these words denote lascivious dancing.
122. Ibid., 64.
123. Segato, 8.
124. Capone, 100.
125. Conner, 79.
126. Ibid., 59.
127. Dianteill, 23–24.
128. Marcelin, 181.
129. Conner, 63.
130. Both words are used to describe homosexuals, although there still remains some confusion as to the origin of their use. Milton Ribeiro believes that *veado* (a buck) refers to bucks grouping together after being defeated by dominant males during the mating season. He rejects the etymology of *viado* as being a corrupted form of *desviado* (deviate). *A origem da utilização da palavra "Veado" para designar homossexuais no Brasil*, http://miltonribeiro.opsblog.org/2010/01/19/a-origem-da-utilizacao-da-palavra-"veado"-para-designar-homossexuais-no-brasil/.
131. Rios, 39.
132. Green, 21–22.
133. Ibid., 17–62.
134. Ibid., 52.
135. El Far. See Green, 32. Largo do Rossio was the name of Praça Tirandentes during the empire.
136. Green, 107–146.
137. Ibid., 150–159.
138. Yanagui. The author reviews case law in favor of the protection of equality rights and protection against discrimination based on sexual orientation in Brazil.
139. Immigration and Refugee Board of Canada, *Brazil: The situation of homosexuals; availability of support groups and state protection*, Research Directorate, Ottawa, September 3, 2008; Fabiana Frayssinet, "Rights-Brazil: Gay-Bashing Murders Up 55 Percent," International Press Service (IPS), Rio de Janeiro, April 22, 2008, www.ipsnews.net/news.asp?idnews=46596.
140. The Primate's statement can be read at: http://ns.ieab.org.br/wp-content/uploads/2011/05/Committed-to-Human-Dignity.pdf.
141. De la Fuente, Note 62. The author mentions the case of a slave attempting to secure his release from the city council of Havana, in 1597.
142. Sierra Madero (2003).
143. Sierra Madero (2004).
144. Sierra Madero (2003). He draws this information from Serafín Sánchez, *Héroes humildes y los poetas de la guerra*, published in Havana in 1911.
145. Bejel, 13–15.
146. Sierra Madero (2003). My translation of an excerpt quoted by the author from an article entitled "Los maricones," published in 1889 in the journal *La Cebolla*.
147. Montero, 92–114. In a chapter on male prostitution, Dr. Cespedes alludes to homosexuals and sex perverts, who swarm the streets of Havana. Sierra Madero (2003).
148. Montero, 101–102.
149. Ibid., 105.
150. For a short description of this novel see Bejel, 66–77. The novel contains a foreword by Dr. Gregorio Marañón and a postscript by the criminal lawyer Jiménez de Asúa, which advocates the decriminalization of homosexuality. Dr. Marañón was a Spanish endocrinologist known in Spain for his theories on intersexuality in the early twentieth century. See also "Reframing Sodom: Sexuality, Nation and Difference in Hernández Catá's El Ángel de Sodoma," *Ciberletras* n. 16 (January 2007),http://www.lehman.cuny.edu/ciberletras/v16/mejiaslopez.html.
151. Section 490 of the *Código de defensa social, 17de Abril de 1936 [1938]*. Lumsden, 82.

152. Green, 442.
153. The film directed by Néstor Almendros and Orlando Jiménez Leal, *Conducta impropia* (The Misconduct) (1984), tells the story of homosexual prisoners held in these camps.
154. Rainaldo Arenas alluded to this policy in his novel *Antes que anochezca*. See Sevillano, 83.
155. See Bejel's analysis (114–125) on homosexuality as a metaphor for poetic creativity, which, according to José Lezama, would benefit the new Cuban society.
156. Lumsden, 91.
157. The website globalgayz.com releases precious information on the current situation of homosexuals in Cuba.
158. CENESEX has a website with a strong focus on the issues of sexual diversity, homosexuality, transsexuality, and homophobia, www.cenesex.sld.cu/webs/diversidad/diversidad.htm.
159. Pereira Ramírez. The journal is produced by the CENESEX.
160. "Consideraciones acerca de los proyectos de reconocimiento legal de las uniones entre personas homosexuales," *Palabra Nueva, Revísta de la Arquidiócesa de La Havana*, Junio 2008, N. 175. http://www.palabranueva.net/contens/0806/000105.htm.
161. Panos Caraïbes, « Homosexualité masculine et VIH/Sida », Press kit n. 16, Port-au-Prince, Janvier 2008.
162. American journalist Randy Shilts was one of the propagators of these theories in his book *And the Band Played On* (1987).
163. *Makomè* means gossiper, *de sis cole* refers to the popular image of 66 for sodomy, *bouzen* means prostitute, *lougawou* indicates an evil spirit, while *lapli sou kay* literally means the rain that falls on the house and probably is a metaphor for the boisterous, uninhibited *masisi* easily recognized by his speech and manners, like the noise made by the rain on a tin roof.
164. McAlister (2002), 75. The word *chawonj* (putrefying flesh, garbage) designates the person who sleeps with the firstcomer. *Rara* is a kind of street music deployed especially during the Holy Week, inspired by Voodoo, and often flavored with political and social criticism.
165. The idea is expressed by some characters in the documentary film by Lescot and Magloire, but it is also found in the press kit of Panos Caribbean.
166. International Gay and Lesbian Human Rights Commission and SEROVIE, "The Impact of the Earthquake, and Relief and Recovery Programs on Haitian LGBT People," http://www.iglhrc.org/binary-data/ATTACHMENT/file/000/000/504-1.pdf.

7 General Conclusion

1. Luther opposed monastic asceticism and salvation by works in the sections, 20, 23, 27 of the Augsburg Confession. Sociologist of religion Max Weber distinguished two kinds of asceticism or religious discipline, which consists of abstaining from worldly matters, *ausserwltliche Aksese*, and a discipline aimed at transforming the world through action, *innerweltliche Aksese*.
2. See Dahklia (2007). The Iranian case is unique. The modernization undertaken by the Qajar rulers focused more on the modernization of social space including the fact that disappearance of the veil should keep men away from the love of boys, which would disappear by itself. Homosexuality would then become a mere passing fancy before marriage. Asfaneh Najmabadi, "Types, Acts, or What? Regulation of Sexuality in Nineteenth Century Iran" in Babayan and Najmabadi, 275–296.
3. See the works of Herdt (1981) and (1984); and Godelier. In many Melanesian cultures, insemination by fellatio or sodomy is part of initiation rites for boys, to transfer masculine strength and power.
4. Van de Port, 22.
5. Habib (2008). In late 2009, this author published *Islam and Homosexuality* at Praeger.
6. Kugle, 152–153.
7. Ali, 95.
8. Zemouri, 179–180.
9. Rubin, 267–319.

10. For a general outlook on these issues, see Arvind Narrain, 40ff.
11. Nandy, 2, 8.
12. See Massad. This issue is a central theme of his book.
13. Rowan Williams, *Reflections on the Episcopal Church's 2009 General Convention from the Archbishop of Canterbury for the Bishops, Clergy and Faithful of the Anglican Communion*, July 27, 2009, www.archbishopofcanterbury.org/2502.
14. Nedelsky, Hutchinson, 52–53.

BIBLIOGRAPHY

SCRIPTURES, COMMENTARIES, SPIRITUAL WRITINGS, AND RELIGIOUS HISTORIOGRAPHY

Abu Dawud, *Sunan Abu Dawud*, 3 Vols., English translation with explanatory notes and introduction by Ahmad Hasan (New Delhi: Kitab Bhavan, 2007).
Aflaki Shams ud-Din Ahmad, *The Feats of the Knowers of God: Manaqeb al-'arefin*, trans. John O'Kane (Leiden: Brill, 2002).
Aitareya Brahmana, the Aitareya and Kausitaki Brahmanas of the Rigveda, trans. Arthur Berrieddale Keith (New Delhi: Motilal Banarsidass, 1998).
Alain of Lille, The Complaint of Nature, trans. Douglas Maxwell Moffat, Yale Studies in English, Vol. 36 (New York: H. Holt and Co, 1908).
Andilly, Arnauld d', *Les Vies des saints Pères des déserts et de quelques saintes, écrites par des Pères de l'Église*, 3 Vols. (Paris: Louis Josse, 1733).
Ante-Nicene Fathers, Alexander Roberts and James Donaldson, eds. (Edinburgh: T. and T. Clark, 1867-1873).
Antonelli Giuseppe, *Medecina pastoralis in usum confessiorum, professorum theologiae moralis et curiarum ecclesiaticorum*, Vol. 1 (Romae: F. Pustet, 1932).
Augustine of Hippo, *Against Julian*, trans. Matthew A. Schumacher, *The Fathers of the Church*, Vol. 35 (New York: Fathers of the Church Inc., 1957).
Benedicti, Jean, *La somme des pechez et le remède d'iceux* (Lyon: Charles Pesnot, 1584).
Bhagavad Gita, trans. Sri Swami Sivananda (Rishikesh, UP: The Divine Life Society), http://www.SivanandaDlshq.org.
Bibliothèque de Qumrán (La), Édition bilingue des manuscrits à l'initiative d'André Paul, dirigée par Katell Berthelot, Thierry Legrand et André Paul (Paris: du Cerf, 2008).
Billuart, Charles René, *Summa Sancti Thomae bodiernis acade-miarum motibus accomodata, sive cursus theologiae* (Paris: Méquignon, 1828).
Biyan lu, The Blue Cliff Record, trans. Thomas Cleary and J. C. Cleary (Boston: Shambala Publications, 1977).
Brahmanda Purana, trans. G. V. Tagare, 5 Vols. (New Delhi: Motilal Banarsidass, 1999).
Buddhacarita, E. H. Johnston, *The Buddhacarita or Acts of the Buddha*, 2 Vols. (Calcutta: Baptist Mission Press, 1835-1836).
Buddhaghosa, Athasalini, trans. Pe Maung Tin (London: Pali Text Society, 1979).
———, *Samantapasadika, Shanjianlü piposha* (善見律毘婆沙), trans. P. V. Bapat and A. Hirakawa (Poona: Bhandarkar Oriental Research Institute, 1970).
Bukhari, Muhammad Al-, *Summarized Sahih Al-Bukhari*, trans. Muhammad Mushin Khan (Riyadh: Maktaba Dar-us-Salam, 1994).
Calvin, John, *Commentary on Genesis*, trans. John King, 2 Vols. (Edinburgh: The Banner of Truth Trust, 1975).
———, *Institutes of the Christian Religion*, trans. Henry Beveridge (Peabody, MA: Hendrickson Publishers, 2008).
Caraka samhita, English translation by P.V. Sharma, 4 Vols. (Varanasi, Delhi: Chaukhambha Orientalia, 1981-1994).
———, *Traité fondamental de la médecine ayurvédique : Tome 1, les principes*, translation Jean Papin (Paris: Almora, 2006).

246 BIBLIOGRAPHY

Calvin, John, *Traité fondamental de la médecine ayurvédique* : Tome 2 : *Les thérapeutiques*, Jean Papin (Paris: Almora, 2009).

Cassian, John, *Conférences de Cassien sur la perfection religieuse*, traduites par E. Cartier, Paris, Poulsielgue frères, 1868, édition numérisée sur le site de la bibliothèque virtuelle de l'Abbaye St-Benoît de Port-Valais, www.abbaye-saint-benoit.ch/saints/augustin/index.htm.

———, *Institute 6, Conference 12, Conference 22. Cassian on Chastity*, trans. Terrence G. Kardong (Richardton, ND: Assumption Abbey Press, 1993).

———, *Institutions de Cassien*, traduites par E. Cartier, Paris, Mame, 1872. www.abbaye-saint-benoit.ch/frame.html.

Caulle, E., *La morale catholique et la pureté* (Paris: Bloud et Gay, 1912).

Central Conference of American Rabbis, *American Reform Responsa: collected response of the Central Conference of American Rabbis, 1889–1983*, Walter Jacob ed. (New York: CCAR Press, 1983).

Damian, Peter (*Liber Gomorrhianus*) *Book of Gomorrah: An Eleventh Century Treatise against Clerical Homosexual Practices*, trans. Pierre J. Payer (Waterloo, ON: Wilfrid Laurier University Press, 1982).

Debreyne, Pierre Jean Corneille, *Essai sur la théologie morale, considérée dans ses rapports avec la physiologie et la médecine* (Paris: Poussielgue-Rusand, 1843).

Dharma Sutras, Dharmasutras. The Law Codes of Ancient India, A new translation by Patrick Olivelle (Oxford: Oxford University Press, 1999).

Dictionnaire de L'islam, Religion et civilisation (Paris: Encyclopaedia Universalis, Albin Michel, 1997).

Dorff, Elliot N., Daniel S. Nevins, and Avram I. Reisner, "Homosexuality, Human dignity and Halakha: A Combined Responsum for the Committee on Jewish Law and Standards" (New York: The Rabbinical Assembly, December 2006).

Epic of Gilgamesh (The), trans. Maureen Gallery Kovacs (Stanford, CA: Stanford University Press, 1989).

Evagrius Ponticus, *The Praktikos: Chapters on Prayer*, trans. John Eudes Bamberger, *Cistercian Studies* 4 (Spencer, MA: Cistercian Publications, 1972).

Flavius Josephus, *Works of Josephus*, trans. William Whiston (Peabody, MA: Hendrickson Publishers, 2009).

Gampopa, Seunam Rinchen, *The Jewel Ornament of Liberation*, trans. Herbert V. Guenther (Boston, MA: Shambala, 2001).

Ghazali, *Ihya Ulum id-Din* (Revival of Religious Learnings), trans. Fazlul-Karim, 4 Vols. (Lahore: Sind Sagar Academy, 1978).

———, *Marriage and Sexuality in Islam: A Translation of Al-Ghazali's Book on the Etiquette of Marriage from the Ihya*, trans. Madelain Farah (Salt Lake City: University of Utah Press, 1984).

Goswami, Krishnadasa Kaviraja, *Caritamrta, Adi lila, The Pastimes of Lord Chaitanya* Mahaprabhu, trans. Swami Bhaktivedanta Prabhupada (Los Angeles, CA: Bhaktivedanta Book Trust, 1975), www.bvml.org/books/CC/index.html.

Gratian, *Decretum Magistri Gratiani*, in Emil Albert and Aemilius Ludwig Richter, *Corpus Iuris Canonici*, editio Lipsiensis Secunda, Vol. I (Leipzig: Tauchnitz, 1879).

Hanfeizi, Translations from the Asian classics, trans. Burton Watson (NewYork: Columbia University Press, 2003).

Holy Bible (The), New International Version, http://www.biblica.com/bibles/.

Holy Qur'an (The), Arabic Text and English Translation, trans. Muhammad Sarwar, online edition (New York: The Islamic Seminary Inc., 2001), http://www.theislamicseminary.org/quraN.html.

Hoornaert, G., *Le combat de la pureté* (Paris: Desclée de Brouwer, 1931).

House of Bishops, *Issues in Human Sexuality* (London: Church House Publishing, 1991).

———, *Some Issues in Human Sexuality, A Guide to the Debate* (London: Church House Publishing, 2003).

Ibn Abbas, *Tanwir al-Miqbas min Tafsir Ibn Abbas*, trans. Mokrane Guezzou, Royal Aal al-Bayt Institute for Islamic Thought (Amman: Royal Aal al-Bayt Institute for Islamic Thought), www.altafsir.com.

BIBLIOGRAPHY

Ibn Battuta, *Travels in Asia and Africa, 1325-1354*, trans. H. A. R. Gibb (Abingdon: Routledge and Courzon, [1929] 2005).

———, *Voyages I, de l'Afrique du nord à La Mecque*, translation from Arabic by C. Defremery et B. R. Sanguinetti (1858), Paris, Maspero, 1982, bibliothèque numérique Les classiques des sciences sociales de l'Université du Québec à Chicoutimi, http://dx.doi.org/doi:10.1522/030078802.

Ibn Hazm, *The Ring of the Dove*, trans. A. J. Arberry (London: Luzac and Co, 1997).

Ibn Hisham (Ibn Ishaq), (*Sira Rasul Allah Muhammad ben Abd Allah*), The Life of Muhammad, trans. Alfred Guillaume (Karachi: University of Oxford Press, 2011).

Ibn Kathir, *Tafsir Ibn Kathir*, trans. Muhammad Saed Abdul-Rahman, 30 Vols. (London: MSA Publications, 2nd edition, 2009).

Ibn Khaldun, *The Muqadimmah, An Intoduction to History*, 3 Vols. (unabridged), trans. Franz Rosenthal, Bollingen Series XLIII (New York: Princeton University Press, [1958], 2nd edition, 1967), abridged version published in 1967.

Ibn Sina, (*Al'-Arjuzat fi al-tibb*) *The Poem on Medicine*, trans. Haven G. Krueger, M. D. (Springfield IL: Charles C. Thomas, 1963).

Ibn Taimiya, (*Kitab as-Siyasah as-shar'iah*), *Le Traité de droit public d'ibn Taimiya*, trans. Henri Laoust (Beyrouth: Institut Français de Damas, 1948).

Jewish Encyclopedia (The), Isidore Singer and Cyrus Adler et al. eds. (New York: Funk and Wagnalls, 1901–1906), www.jewishencyclopedia.com.

Kaykavus Ibn Iskandar Ibn Qabus, *A Mirror for Princes: The Qabus Nama*, trans. Reuben Levy (London: Cresset Press, 1951).

Kebra Nagast, The Queen of Sheba and Her Only Son Menyelek I, E. A. Wallis Budge (London: Oxford University Press, 1932).

Kumarajiva, *Scripture of the Lotus Blossom of the Fine Dharma: The Lotus Sutra* (*Saddharma Pundarika Sutra, Miaofa Lianhua Jing* 妙法蓮花經), trans. Leon Hurvitz (New York: Columbia University Press, 1976).

Lacroix, Claude, *Theologia moralis* (Venetiis: N. Pezzana, 1734).

Liguori, Alphonse-Marie de, *Instruction pratique pour les confesseurs*, *Œuvres Complètes*, trad. française sous la direction des abbés Vidal, Delalle et Bousquet, (Paris: Parent-Desbarres, tomes XXIII–XXVI, 1834-1838).

———, *Theologia moralis*, 4 Vols., Léonard Gaudé ed. (Rome: Typographia Vaticana, 1905).

Liji, The Sacred Books of China. The Sacred Books of the East 3, trans. James Legge (Oxford: Clarendon Press, 1879).

Likutei Amarim, Rabbi Schneur Zalman of Liadi, trans. Nissan Mindel, Nissan Mangel, Zalman Posner, and Jacob Immanuel Schochet (Brooklyn, NY: Kehhot Publication Society, 1984).

Linga Purana, 2 Vols., trans. J. L. Shastri (New Delhi: Motilal Banarsidass, 2007).

Linji Lu 臨濟錄, *Entretiens de Lin-tsi*, traduit du chinois par Paul Demiéville (Paris: Fayard, 1972).

Luther, Martin, *Luther's Works*, American Edition, 55 Vols., ed. Jaroslav Pelikan and Helmut T. Lehmann (Philadelphia: Fortress, 1965).

Mahabharata of Krishna-Dwaipayana Vyasa, trans. Kisari Mohan Ganguli (New Delhi: Munshiram Manoharlal, 2004).

Mahaprajnaparamita shastra, Le traité de la grande vertu de sagesse, trad. Étienne Lamotte, (Louvain: Bureaux du Muséon, 5 Vols., 1944–1980).

Maimonides, *Mishneh Torah*, edited by Rabbi Eliyahu Touger, vowelized Hebrew text with modern English translation and a commentary, 29 Vols. (New York: Moznaim, 2000).

———, (*Moreh Nevuchim*) *The Guide for the Perplexed*, trans. Michael Friedländer (New York: Cosimo Books, 2007 [1904]).

Malik, Abu Abdallah ibn Anas, *Al-muwatta*, trans. A'isha Abdarahman at-Tarjumana and Ya'qub Johnson (Norwich: Diwan Press, 1982).

Manusmriti, The Law Code of Manu, trans. Patrick Olivelle (New York: Oxford University Press, 2004).

Marc, Clément, Gestermann François-Xavier, *Institutiones morales alphonsianae* I, (Paris: Emmanuel Vitte, 1933 (19th edition).

Markandeya Purana, Sanskrit text with English translation by F. Eden Pargiter, edited and revised by K. L. Joshi (Delhi: Parimal Publications, 2004).
Matsya Mahapurana, Sanskrit text and English translation by K. L. Joshi, 2 Vols. (Delhi: Parimal Publications, 2007).
McNeill John T., and Helena M. Gamer, *Medieval Handbooks of Penance: A Translation of the Principal Libri Poenitentiales and Selections from Related Documents* (New York: Columbia University Press, [1938] 1990).
Midrash Rabbah, trans. H. Freedman and Maurice Simon, 2 Vols. (London: Soncino Press, 1939).
Migne, Jacques-Paul, éd., *Patrologiae cursus completus, Series graeca* (PG), 161 Vols., (Paris: 1857–1866).
———, *Patrologiae cursus completus, Series latina* (PL), 217 Vols., (Paris: 1844–1864).
Muslim, ibn al-Hajjaj, *Sahih Muslim*, trans. Abdul Hamid Siddiqi, 4 Vols. (Lahore: Sh. Muhammad Ashraf, 2004).
———, *Sahih Muslim*, Hamid Siddiqi, msa-usc Compendium of Muslim Texts (Muslim Students Association-University of South California), www.msawest.net/islam/fundamentals/hadithsunnah/muslim/smtintro.html.
Nag Hamadi Scriptures (The), Marvin Mayer ed. (New York: Harper Collins, 2007).
Narada Purana, trans. G. V. Tagare, 5 Vols. (New Delhi: Motilal Banarsidass, 1998).
Nayanatiloka, Mahathera, *Buddhist Dictionary, Manual of Buddhist Terms and Doctrines* (Kandy: Buddhist Publication Society, 1970).
Nicene and Post-Nicene Fathers, Philip Schaff ed. (Edinburgh: T. and T. Clark, 1886–1900).
Padma Purana, trans. N. A. Deshpande, 10 Vols. (New Delhi: Motilal Banarsidass, 1992).
Palladius, *The Lausiac History of Palladiusus, Historia lausica, Tranlations of Christian Literature*, Series 1, Greek Texts, trans. W. K. Lowther Clarke (London: McMillan, 1918).
Pathamamulamuli: Tamnan Khao phi LannA, Pathamamulamuli ou l'origine du monde selon la tradition du Lan Na. The Origin of the world in the Lan Na Tradition, translation by Anatole-Roger Peltier (Chiang Mai: Surivong Book Centre, 1991).
Patuzzi, Giovanni, *Ethica Christiana sive theologia moralis*, Vols. 3–4, *Tractatus de decalogi praeceptis* (Bassani: Remondini, 1790).
philo Judaeus (of Alexandria), translated from the Greek by Charles Duke Yonge (London: H. G. Bohn, 1854–1890) 234 *RKEI AVOT, Sayings of the Jewish Fathers*, trans. Charles Taylor (London: Cambridge University Press, 1897).
Prümmer, Dominikus, *Manuale theologiae moralis secundum Sanctae Thomae Aquinatis*, II, (Friburgi Brisgoviae: Herder, 1923).
Rig-Veda Samhita, The Hyms of the Rigveda, trans. R. T. H. Griffith (Kotagiri, 1896).
Rumi, Mawlana Djalal od-Din, *(Divan-e Chams-e Tabrizi), Mystical Poems of Rumi*, trans. A. J. Arberry and Ehsan Yarshater (Chicago: The University of Chicago Press, 2009).
Sánchez, Tomás, *De sancto matrimonii sacramento disputationum*, 3 Vols. (Venetiis: Pezzana, 1726).
Sarananda, Swami, *Sri Ramakrishna the Great Master*, Vol., II, trans. Swami Jagadananda (Chennai: Sri Ramakrishna Math, 2004).
Satapatha Brahmana, Sanskrit text with English translation, edited by M. Deshpande, 4 Vols. (Delhi: New Bharatiya Book Corporation, 2008).
Shiji, Records of the grand historian: Han dynasty II by Sima Qian, trans. Burton Watson (New York: Columbia University Press, revised edn, [1961] 1993).
Shiva Purana, J. L. Shastri ed., 4 Vols. (New Delhi: Motilal Banarsidass, 2005).
Shivananda, Sri Swami, *The Practice of Brahmacarya* (New Delhi: The Divine Life Society, [1934] 2006).
Skanda Purana, trans. G. V. Tagare, 20 Vols. (New Delhi: Motilal Banarsidass, 2003).
Śrīmad Bhāgavatam, A. C. Bhaktivedanta Swami Prabhubada, http://srimadbhagavatam.com/eN.
Srimaladevi simha nada sutra, Shengman shizi hu yisheng da fangbian fangguang jing (勝鬘師子吼一乘大方便方廣經), *The Lion's Roar of Queen Srimala*, trans. Alex and Hydeko Wayman (New York: University of Columbia Press, 1974).
Susruta Samhita, P. V. Sharma ed., with English translation of text and Dalhana's commentary along with critical notes, 3 Vols. (Varanasi: Chaukhambha Visvabharati, 1999–2001).

Sutta Nipata, translation from the Pali Canon by H. Saddhatissa (London: Curzon Press, 1994).
At-Tabari, *The History of at-Tabari* (*Ta'rikh al-rusul wa'l-muluk*), 40 Vols., trans. W. M. Watt and M. V. McDonald (Albany, NY: State University of New York Press, 1988).
———, *Tafsir, Commentaire du Coran de Tabari*, traduit par Pierre Gode, (Paris: Les Heures Claires, 5 Vols., 1983–1989).
Taisho Shinshu Daizokyo (大正新脩大藏經), Takakusu Junjiro et Watanabe Kaikyoku eds., 100 Vols. (Tokyo: Taisho issaikyo kankokai, 1924–1935).
Taittirya Brahmana, The Taittirya Brahmana of the Black Yajur Veda, trans. Rajandra Lala Mitra (Calcutta: Bibliotheca Indica, 1865).
Talmud Bavli, The Babylonian Talmud, Rabbi I. Epstein, ed. (London: Soncino Press, 1935–1945).
Talmud Yerouchalmi, The Jerusalem Talmud, trans. Jacob Neusner and Tzvee Zahavy (Peabody, MA: Hendrickson Publishers, CD-ROM.
Tamburini, Tommaso, *Theologia moralis, tomus primus, De prae-ceptis Decalogi*, (Venetiis: N. Pezzana, 1755).
Tanakh, trans. A. J. Rosenberg, online translation of the *Tanakh* and Rashi's entire commentary http://www.chabad.org/library/archive/LibraryArchive.asp?AID=63255.
Thanassiro, Bhikkhu, *Buddhist Monastic Code II*, www.accesstoinsight.org/lib/authors/thanissaro/bmc2/bmc2.intro.html, 2007.
———, *Introduction to the Patimokkha Rules*, online version, www.accesstoinsight.org/tipitaka/vin/sv/bhikkhu-pati-intro.html, 1994.
Thomas Aquinas, *Commentaire des Sentences de Pierre Lombard* IV (*Scriptum super Sentenciis*) trad. Jacques Ménard, édition numérique 2007, http://docteurangelique.free.fr.
———, *De malo*, trans. Richard J. Regan (New York: Oxford University Press, 2001).
———, *Summa Theologica*, trans. Fathers of the English Dominican Province (Notre Dame, IN: Christian Classics, 1981).
Tipitaka, The Pali Canon, by John T. Bullitt, *Access to Insight*, June 7, 2009, http://www.accesstoinsight.org/tipitaka/index.html.
At-Tirmidhi, Abu Isa Muhammad ben Isa, *Al-Jami'* (*Sahih at-Tirmidhi*), trans. Rafique Abdur Rehman, 2 Vols. (Karachi: Darul Ishaat, 2007).
Upanishads, The Golden Book of Upanishads, trans. Mahendra Kulasrestha (Twin Lakes, WI: Lotus Press, 2007).
Valmiki, *Ramayana*, trans. Romesh C. Dutt (Whitefish, MT: Kessinger Publishing, 2004).
Vamana Purana, Sanskrit text, English translation, O. N. Bimali and K. L. Joshi, eds. (Delhi: Parimal Publications, 2005).
Vasubandhu, *L'Abhidharmakosa*, traduit et annoté par Louis de la Vallée Poussin, (Paris: Guenther, 5 Vols. 1923).
Vatsyayana, *The Complete Kama Sutra*, including the *Jayamangala* commentary by Yashodhara and extracts from the Hindi commentary by Devadatta Shastra, translated by Alain Danielou (Rochester, VT: Park Street Press, 1994).
———, *Les Káma-sútra*, texte intégral traduit du sanskrit par Jean Papin (Paris: Zulma, 2003).
Vimalakirtinidesa, The Vimalakirti Sutra, trans. John McCrae (Berkeley, CA: Numata Center for Buddhist Translation and Research, 2004).
Vinaya Pitaka, Suttavibhanga, The Book of Discipline, trans. I. B. Horner (London: Pali Text Society, 1938).
Visnu (Vishnu) Purana: trans. H. H. Wilson (Delhi: Parimal Publications, 2005).
Xu zang jing (續藏經), Supplement to the Chinese Buddhist Canon, 150 Vols. (Hong Kong: Yingyin Xuzanjing Weiyuanhui (影印續藏經委員會), 1967–1977).
Yajnavalkyasmrti, Sanskrit text, English translation by Nath Dutt (Delhi: Parimal Publications, 2005).

General References

Abbott, Elizabeth, *A History of Celibacy* (Cambridge, MA: Da Capo Press, [1999] 2001).
Abd-El-Jalil, J. M., *Brève histoire de la littérature arabe* (Paris: G.P. Maisonneuve, 1947).

BIBLIOGRAPHY

Abdul Rahman, Muhammad Saed, *Jurisprudence and Islamic Rulings, Transactions—Part 7, Islam Questions and Answers*, Vol. 26 (London: MSA Publications, 2004).

Abu Nuwas, *Carousing with Gazelles: Homoerotic Songs of Old Baghdad*, trans. Jaafar Abu Tarab (Lincoln NE: iUniverse Books, 2005).

Adang, Camilla, "Ibn Hazm on Homosexuality. A Case-Study of Zahiri Legal Methodology," *Al-Qantara* 24, 1(2003): 5–31.

———, "Islam as the Inborn Religion of Mankind: The Concept of *Fitra* in the Works of Ibn Hazm," *Al-Qantara* 21(2000): 391–410.

———, "Love between Men in Tawq al-Hamama," in *Identidades Marginales*, ed. Cristina de la Puente (Madrid: Consejo Superior de Investigaciones Cientificas, 2003)

adler, Rachel, *Engendering Judaism: An Inclusive Theology and Ethics* (Philadelphia, PA: Jewish Publication Society, 1998).

Al Jahiz, (*Kitab mufaharati al-jawari wal-ghilman*) *Éphèbes et courtisanes*, trad. Maati Kabbal, préface et notes de Malek Chebel (Paris: Rivages Poche, 1997).

Al Mas'udi, (*Muruj adh-dhahab*) *Les Prairies d'Or*, translation to French by C.-A.-C. Barbier de Meynard et A. Pavet de Courteille (Paris: Société Asiatique, 9 tomes, 1861–1877).

Al Waqidi, Mohammad ibn Omar, *Kitab al-Maghazi* (*Muhammad in Medina*), German translation by Julius Wellhausen (Berlin: G. Reimer, 1882).

Alfeyev, Hilarion, "Christian Witness to Uniting Europe: A View from a Representative of the Russian Orthodox Church," *The Ecumenical Review* 55.1 (2003): 76–86.

Ali, Kecia, *Sexual Ethics And Islam: Feminist Reflections on Qur'an, Hadith And Jurisprudence* Oxford: Oneworld Publications, 2010).

Allen, John, *Desmond Tutu. Rabble-Rouser for Peace* (New York: Free Press, 2006).

Allen, Nicholas J., "The Indo-European Prehistory of Yoga," *International Journal of Hindu Studies* 2 (1998): 1–20.

Allyn, Eric G., "Trees in the Same Forest: The Thai Gay World," 2002, www.floatinglotus.com/tmot/gaythai.html.

Amin, Sheikh Muhammad bin, "The Islamic Ruling on Masturbation," www.ibnamiN.com/masturbation_en htm.

Amir-Moezzi, Mohammad Ali, «Notes à propos de la *walaya* imamite (aspects de l'imamologie duodécimaine, X),» *Journal of the American Oriental Society* 122.4 (2002): 722–741.

An-Naim, Abdullahi Ahmed, "Neither the 'End of History' nor a 'Clash of Civilizations,'" in Gerrie Ter Haar and James J. Busuttil eds., *The Freedom to Do God's Will: Religious Fundamentalism and Social Change* (London: Routledge, 2003).

———, "Sharia in the Secular State. A Paradox of Separation and Conflation," in Peri Bearman, Wolfhart Heinrich, and Bernard G. Weiss eds., *The Law Applied. Contextualizing the Islamic Shari'a* (London: I. B. Tauris, 2008).

Arenas, Reinaldo, *Before Night Falls*, trans. Dolores Koch (New York: Penguin Books, 1994).

Arkush, Allan, *Moses Mendelssohn and the Enlightenment* (Albany, NY: State University of New York Press, 1994).

Artson, Bradley, "Gay and Lesbian Jews: An Innovative Jewish Legal Position," *Jewish Spectator* (Winter 1990–1991): 6–14.

Babayan, Kathryn, and Afsaneh Najmabadi, eds., *Islamicate Sexualities: Translations across Temporal Geographies of Desire*, Volume 39, Harvard Middle Eastern Monographs (Cambridge, MA: Center for Middle Eastern Studies, Harvard University, 2008).

Barnes, Nancy Shuster, "Buddhism" in Arvind Sharma (1987).

Barnet, Miguel, *Biografía de un cimarrón*, (La Habana: Instituto de Etnología y Folklore, 1966), traduit en français par C. Couffon, *Esclave à Cuba* (Paris: Gallimard, 1967).

Bashir, Shazad, *Sufi Bodies, Religion and Society in Medieval Islam* (New York: Columbia University Press, 2011).

Baskin, Judith Reesa, "Bolsters to Their Husbands: Women as Wives in Rabbinic Literature," *European Judaism* 37.2 (2004): 88–102.

Bastide, Roger, *African Civilization in the New World*, trans. Peter Green (New York: Harper and Row, 1972).

———, *Le candomblé de Bahia* (Paris: Plon, collection Terre humaine poche, [1958] 2000).

Baumannn, Martin, "The Dharma Has Come West: A Survey of Recent Studies and Sources," *Journal of Buddhist Ethics* 4 (1997): 194–211.
Baumgarten, Jean, *La naissance du hassidisme : mystique, rituel et société (XVIIIᵉ-XIXᵉ siècle)* (Paris: Albin Michel, 2006).
Beichuan, Zhang, and Joan Kaufman, "Men with Same Sex Sexual Behavior in China: Recent Progress and Continuing Challenges," Paper Prepared for the Conference on Sexuality, Gender, and Rights: Exploring Theory and Practice in South and East Asia, Bellagio Italy, September 22–26, 2003.
Bejel, Emilio, *Gay Cuban Nation* (Chicago: The University of Chicago Press, 2001).
Bencheikh, Jamel Eddine, «Thèmes bachiques et personnages dans le dîwân d'Abû Nuwâs,» *Bulletin d'Études Orientales* XVIII (1963–1964): 7–84.
Benkheira, Hocine, «Moralisation et politique du sexe dans l'Islam médiéval,» in Jacques Maître, Guy Michelat éds., *Religion et Sexualité* (Paris: L'Harmattan, 2003).
Benzine, Rachid, *Les nouveaux penseurs de l'islam* (Paris: Albin Michel, 2004).
Bergad, Laird W., *The Comparative History of Slavery in Brazil, Cuba and the United States* (New York: Cambridge University Press, 2007).
Bernos, Marcel, Jean Guyon, Charles de la Roncière, and Philippe Lécrivain, *Le fruit défendu. Les Chrétiens et la sexualité de l'Antiquité à nos jours* (Paris: Le Centurion, 1985).
Bertrand, Michel, and Richard Marin, *Écrire l'histoire de l'Amérique latine. XIXᵉ–XXᵉ siècles* (Paris: CNRS, 2001).
Besmer, Fremont E., *Horses, Musicians and Gods: The Hausa Cult of Possession-Trance* (South Hadley, MA: Bergin and Garvey Publishers, 1983).
Biale, David, *Eros and the Jews. From Biblical Israel to Conptemporary America* (New York: Basic Books, 1992).
Bian er chai 弁而釵, *Épingle de femme sous le bonnet viril. Chronique d'un loyal amour*, André Lévi (Paris: Mercure de France, 1997).
Black, Alison H., "Gender and Cosmology in Chinese Correlative Thinking," in Carolyn W. Bynum, ed., *Gender and Religion: On the Complexity of Symbols* (Boston: Beacon, 1986).
Blackstone, Kate, "Damming the Dhamma: Problems with Bhikkhunis in the Pali Vinaya," *Journal of Buddhist Ethics* 6 (1999): 292–312.
Bloom, Alfred, "Rennyo's View of the Salvation of Women: Overcoming the Five Obstacles and Three Subordinations," in *The Rennyo Shonin Reader* (Kyoto: Institute of Jodo Shinshu Studies, 1998): 5–33, www.shindharmanet.com/writings/womeN.htm.
Boisvert, Donald L., *Out on Holy Ground: Meditations on Gay Men's Spirituality* (Cleveland: The Pilgrim Press, 2000)
———, *Sanctity and Male Desire: A Gay Reading of Saints* (Cleveland: The Pilgrim Press, 2000).
Bondyopadhyay, Aditya, «Rompre avec la camisole de force culturelle : pourquoi l'orientation sexuelle et l'identité de genre sont des litiges dans l'ordre du jour des Pays du Sud,» Allocution au Palais des Nations, Genève, April 13, 2004.
Bonner, Michael, *Jihad in Islamic History: Doctrines and Practice* (Princeton, NJ: Princeton University Press, 2006).
Boone, Joseph, "Vacation Cruises; or, the Homoerotics of Orientalism" in John C Hawley, ed., *Post-Colonial Queer: Theoretical Intersections* (New York: State University of New York Press, 2001).
Booten, Bernadette J., *Love between Women: Early Christian Responses to Female Homoeroticism* (Chicago: The University of Chicago Press, 1996).Boswell, John, *Christianity, Social Tolerance, and Homosexuality* (Chicago: University of Chicago Press, 1980).
———, *Same-Sex Unions in Premodern Europe* (New York: Villard Books, 1994).
Bouhdiba, Abdelwahab, *Sexuality in Islam*, trans. Alan Sheridan (London: Saqi Books, 2004).
Boyarin, Daniel, "Are there any Jews in the History of Sexuality," *Journal of the History of Sexuality* 5.3 (1995): 333–355.
———, *Carnal Israel: Reading Sex in Talmudic Culture* (Berkeley, CA: University of California Press, 1993).
———, "Homotopia: The Feminized Jewish Man and the Lives of Women in Late Antiquity," *Differences* 7.2 (1995): 41–81.

Boyarin, Daniel, *Unheroic Conduct. The Rise of Heterosexuality and the Invention of the Jewish Man* (Berkeley, CA: University of California Press, 1997).
Bradford, Nicholas, "Transgenderism and the Cult of Yellama: Heat, Sex and Sickness in South Indian Ritual," *Journal of Anthropological Research* 39.3 (Fall 1983): 307–322.
Brandon, George, *Santería from Africa to the New World* (Bloomington, IN: Indiana University Press, 1997).
Brawley, Robert Lawson, *Biblical Ethics and Homosexuality: Listening to Scripture* (Louisville, KY: Westminster John Knox Press, 1996).
Brito Yanagui, Viviane, *União homossexual—Necessidade de reconhe cimento legal das relações afetivas entre pessoas do mesmo sexo no Brasil* (Brasília: Universidade do legislativo Brasileiro, 2005), www.senado.gov.br/sf/senado/unilegis/pdf/UL_TF_DL_2005_Viviane_Brito.pdf.
Brown, David H., *Santería Enthroned* (Chicago: The University of Chicago Press, 2003).
Brown, Karen McCarthy, "Systematic Remembering, Systematic Forgetting: Ogou in Haiti," in Sandra T. Barnes, ed., *Africa's Ogun: Old World and New* (Bloomington, IN: Indiana University Press, 2nd edition, 1997).
Brown, Peter R., *The Body and Society: Men, Women, and Sexual Renunciation in Early Christianity* (New York: Columbia University Press, 1988).
Browne, Kath, Sally Munt, and Andrew K. T. Yip, *Queer Spiritual Spaces: Sexuality and Sacred Places* (Burlington, VT: Ashgate Publishing Company, 2010).
Brownell, Susan, and Jeffrey Wasserstrom, eds., *Chinese Feminities/Chinese Masculinities* (Berkeley, CA: University of California Press, 2002).
Brundage, James A., *Law, Sex and Christian Society in Medieval Europe* (Chicago: The University of Chicago Press, 1987).
Brundage, James A., and Vern L. Bullough, *Sexual Practice and the Medieval Church* (Amherst, NY: Prometheus Books, [1982] 1994).
Buch, Maganlal A., *Principles of Hindu Ethics* (Delhi: Bharatiya Kala Prakashan, [1921] 2003).
Buck, Erwin, *Studies on Homosexuality and the Church* (Winnipeg: Evangelical Lutheran Church in Canada, 2001).
Bullough, Vern L., *Sexual Variance in Society and History* (Chicago: The University of Chicago Press, 1976).
Cabezón, José Ignacio, ed., *Buddhism, Sexuality and Gender* (Albany, NY: State University of New York Press, 1992).
Caminha, Adolfo, *Bom Crioulo: The Black Man and the Cabin Boy*, trans. E. A. Lacey (San Francisco: Gay Sunshine Press, 1982).
Capone, Stefania, *Les Yoruba du Nouveau Monde : religion, ethnicité et nationalisme noir aux États-Unis* (Paris: Karthala, 2005).
Carlson, Allan, "Children of the Reformation. A Short and Surprising History of Protestantism and Contraception," *Touchstone*, May, 2007.
Carstairs, George Morrison, "Hinjra and Jiryan: Two Derivatives of Hindu Attitudes to Sexuality," *British Journal of Medical Psychology* 28.5 (1956): 128–138.
Castor, Kesner, *Éthique vaudou* (Paris: L'Harmattan, 1998).
Chalier-Visuvalingam, Elizabeth, *Union and Unity in Hindu Tantrism*, www.svabhinava.org, 2007.
Chebel, Malek, *Encyclopédie de l'amour en Islam*, 2 Vols. (Paris: Petite Bibliothèque Payot, [1995] 2003).
———, *L'Esprit de sérail. Mythes et pratiques sexuels au Maghreb* (Paris: Petite Bibliothèque Payot, 1995).
———, *Le Kama-Sutra arabe* (Paris: Pauvert, 2006).
Ch'en, Kenneth, *Buddhism in China. A Historical Survey* (Princeton, NJ: Princeton University Press, 1964).
Childs, Margaret, "*Chigo Monogatari*: Love stories or Buddhist sermons?" *Monumenta Nipponica* 35.2 (1980): 127–151.
———, *Rethinking Sorrow: Revelatory Tales of Late Medieval Japan*, Michigan Monograph Series in Japanese Studies 6 (Ann Arbor, MI: Center for Japanese Studies, 1991).
Chou Wa-Shan (Zhou Huashan), "Homosexuality and the Cultural Politics of Tongzhi in Chinese Societies," *Journal of Homosexuality* 40.3–4 (2001): 27–46.

BIBLIOGRAPHY

Chu, William, "Bodhisattva Precepts in the Ming Society: Factors behind their Success and Propagation," *Journal of Buddhist Ethics* 13 (2006), http://jbe.gold.ac.uk/.

Ch'ü T'ung-Tsu, and Jack L. Dull, eds., *Han Social Structure* (Seattle: University of Washington Press, 1972).

Clark, Elizabeth A., "Antifamilial Tendencies in Ancient Christianity," *Journal of the History of Sexuality* 5.3 (1995): 356–380.

———, *Reading Renunciation: Asceticism and Scripture in Early Christianity* (Princeton, NJ: Princeton University Press, 1999).

Clark, Mary Ann, *Santería: Correcting the Myths and Uncovering the Realities of a Growing Religion* (Santa Barbara, CA: Greenwood Publishing, 2007).

———, *Where Men are Wives and Mothers Rule, Santería Ritual Practices and Their Gender Implications* (Gainsville, FL: University of Florida Press, 2005).

Clarke, Shayne, "Monks Who Have Sex: Parajika Penance in Indian Buddhist Monasticisms," *Journal of Indian Philosophy* 37.1 (2009): 1–43.

Cohen, Shaye J. D., *From the Maccabees to the Misnah* (Louisville, KY: John Knox Press, 1989).

Cole, Alan, *Mothers and Sons in Chinese Buddhism* (Stanford, CA: Stanford University Press, 1998).

Conner, Randy P., *Queering Creole Spiritual Traditions* (Binghamton, NY: Harrington Park Press, 2004).

Coulson, Noël J., *A History of Islamic Law* (Edinburgh: Edinburgh University Press, [1964] 1994).

Couture, Denise, «La subordination de la femme à l'homme selon le Saint-Siège,» *Revista de Estudos da Religião* 3 (2005): 14–39.

Cristini, Remy, *The Rise of Comrade Literature, Development and Significance of a New Chinese Genre*, MA thesis, University of Leiden, 2005.

Crompton, Louis, *Homosexuality and Civilization* (Cambridge, MA: The Belknap Press of Harvard University Press, 2003).

Curran, Charles E., "Pope John Paul II's Teaching on Sexuality and Marriage: An Appraisal," *University of St. Thomas Law Journal*, Vol. 1: Iss. 1, Article 27. Available at: http://ir.stthomas.edu/ustlj/vol1/iss1/27.

Dakhlia, Jocelyne, «Homoérotismes et trames historiographiques du monde islamique,» *Annales. Histoire, Sciences Sociales*, Paris, éditions de l'École des Hautes Études en Sciences Sociales, 62, 5, 2007.

Dalaï-Lama XIV, *Beyond Dogma: Dialogues and Discourses* (Berkeley, CA: North Atlantic Books, 1996).

Daniel, Yvonne, *Dancing Wisdom, Embodied Knowledge in Haitian Vodou, Cuban Yoruba, and Bahian Candomblé* (Urbana and Chicago: University of Illinois Press, 2005).

Daniélou, Alain, *Gods of Love and Ecstasy. The Traditions of Shiva and Dionysus* (New York: Inner Traditions International, 1992).

———, *While the Gods Play: Shaiva Oracles and Predictions on the Cycles of History and the Destiny of Mankind* (Rochester, VT: Inner Traditions International, 1987).

Daumas, Maurice, «Sexualité et mariage. La sexualité dans les traités sur le mariage en France, aux XVIe et XVII siècles,» *Revue d'histoire moderne et contemporaine* 51.1 (January–March 2004): 8–33.

Davis, Jimmy R., *The Shia Imami Ismaili Muslims: A Short Introduction* (Raleigh, NC: Lulu, 2007).

Dayan, Colin Joan, *Haiti, History, and the Gods* (Berkeley, CA: University of California Press, 1998).

De la Torre, Miguel A., *Santería: The Beliefs and Rituals of a Growing Religion in America* (Grand Rapids, MI: Wm. B. Eerdmans Publishing, 2004).

De Silva, Padmasiri, *Buddhist and Freudian Psychology* (Colombo: Lake House, 1973).

———, *Tangles and Web* (Colombo: Lake House, 1974).

Deacon, Edward Erastus, *A Digest of the Criminal Law of England*, Vol. 2 (London: Saunders and Benning, 1831).

Demock, JR Edward C., *The Place of the Hidden Moon. Erotic Mysticism in the Vaishnava-Sahajiya Cult of Bengal* (Chicago: The University of Chicago Press, 1989).

Despland, Michel, *Christianisme, dossier corps* (Paris: du Cerf, 1987).
Desquiron, Lilas, *Racines du Vaudou* (Port-au-Prince: Henri Deschamps, 1990).
Dhammananda, K. Sri, *A Happy Married Life, a Buddhist perspective* (Kuala Lumpur: The Buddhist Missionary Society, 1987).
Dhirasekera, Jotiya, *Buddhist Monastic Discipline* (Sri Lanka: Ministry of Higher Education Research Publication Series, 1982).
Diamond, Eliezer, *Holy Men and Hunger Artists: Fasting and Asceticism in Rabinnic Culture* (New York: Oxford University Press, 2003).
Dianteill, Erwan, «Les Trois visages de l'Oricha. La relation entre homme et dieu dans la Santería cubaine,» *Archives des sciences sociales des religions* 100.100 (1997): 5–29.
Digest of Hindu Law on Contracts and Successions: With a Commentary by Jagannatha Tercapanchanana, trans. H. T. Cloebrooke, 2 Vols (Madras: Higginbotham, 4th edition, 1874).
Doniger, Wendy, *Śiva the Erotic Ascetic* (New York: Oxford University Press, 1973).
———, *Splitting the Difference, Gender and Myth in Ancient Greece and India* (Chicago: The University of Chicago Press, 1999).
———, *Women, Androgynes, and Other Mythical Beasts* (Chicago: The University of Chicago Press, 1980).
Drake, Jonathan, "'Le Vice' in Turkey," *International Journal of Greek Love* 1.2 (1966): 13–27.
Dumont, Louis, *Homo Hierarchicus, the Caste System and Its Implications*, trans. George Weidenfeld (Chicago: The University of Chicago Press, [1970] 1980).
Edwards, Louise, «Gender Imperatives in *Honglou meng*: Baoyu's Bisexuality,» *Chinese Literature: Essays, Articles, Reviews (CLEAR)* 1.12 (December 1990): 69–81.
El Far, Alessandra, "Crítica social e idéias médicas nos excessos do desejo: uma análise dos 'romances para homens' de finais do século XIX e início do XX," *Cadernos Pagu* 28 (2007): 285–312.
Eliade, Mircea, *The Sacred and The Profane*, trans. Willard Tranck (Orlando, FL: Harcourt, 1987).
Eron, Lewis John, "Homosexuality and Judaism," in Swidler (1993).
Esposito, John L., *Oxford Dictionary of Islam* (New York: Oxford University Press, 2003).
Faderman, Lilian, *Surpassing the Love of Men, Romantic Friendship and Love Between Women from the Renaissance to the Present* (New York: Quill/William Morrow, 1981).
Faure, Bernard, *Le bouddhisme* (Paris: Flammarion, 1997).
———, *The Power of Denial. Buddhism, Purity and Gender* (Princeton, NJ: Princeton University Press, 2003).
———, *The Red Thread: Buddhist Approaches to Sexuality* (Princeton, NJ: Princeton University Press, 1998).
———, *Sexualités bouddhiques. Entre désirs et réalités* (Paris: Flammarion, 2005). Paru la première fois en 1994, éditions Le Mail.
Fernandez, André, "The Repression of Sexual Behavior by the Aragonese Inquisition between 1560 and 1700," *Journal of the History of Sexuality* 7.4 (1997): 469–502.
Flandrin, Jean-Louis, *Le sexe et l'Occident : Évolution des attitudes et des comportements* (Paris: Seuil, 1981).
Fleurant, Guerdès, *Dancing Spirits: Rythms and Rituals of Haitian Vodou, the Rada Rite* (Westport, CT: Greenwood Publishing, 1996).
Foucault, Michel, *Foucault Live: Collected Interviews 1961–1984*, ed. Sylvère Lotringer (New York: Semiotext(e), 2nd edition, January 1, 1996).
———, *The History of Sexuality, Volume 1: An Introduction* (New York: Vintage Books, 1990).
———, *The History of Sexuality, Volume 3: The Care of the Self* (New York: Vintage Books, 1988).
Francoeur, Robert T., ed., *The International Encyclopaedia of Sexuality*, Volume I–IV, 1997–2001, www2.hu-berliN.de/sexology/IES/index.html.
Frankel, Jonathan, ed., *Jews and Gender: The Challenge to Hierarchy* (New York: Oxford University Press, 2000).
Fredrickson, David, "Natural and Unnatural Use in Romans 1: 24–27: Paul and the Philosophic Critique of Eros," in David L. Balch, ed., *Homosexuality, Science and the "Plain Sense" of Scripture* (Grand Rapids, MI: William B. Eerdmans, 2000).
Freundel, Barry, "Homosexuality and Judaism," *Journal of Halacha and Contemporary Society* XI (1986): 60–97.

Freyre, Gilberto, *The Masters and The Slaves. A Study in the Development of Brazilian Civilization,* trans. Samuel Putnam (Berkeley: University of California Press, 1986).
De la Fuente, Alejandro, "Slave Law and Claims-Making in Cuba: The Tannenbaum Debate Revisited," *Law and History Review* 22.2 (Summer 2004): 339–369.
Furukawa, Makoto, and Angus Lockyer, trans., "The Changing Nature of Sexuality: The Three Codes Framing Homosexuality in Modern Japan," *U.S.-Japan Women's Journal, English Supplement* 7 (December 1994): 98–127.
Gaca, Kathy L., *The Making of Fornication: Eros, Ethics, and Political Reform in Greek Philosophy and Early Christianity* (Berkeley, CA: University of California Press, 2003).
Gagnon, John and William Simon, *Sexual Conduct. The Social Sources of Sexual Meaning* (Chicago: Aldine, 1973).
Gannon, Shane, "Exclusion as Language and the Language of Exclusion: Tracing Regimes of Gender through Linguistic Representations of the 'Eunuch,'" *Journal of the History of Sexuality* 20.1 (January 2011): 1–27.
Gardet, Louis, *Dieu et la destinée de l'homme*: les (Les grands problèmes de la théologie musulmane: essai de théologie comparée (Paris: Librairie Philosophique J. Vrin, Études musulmanes, IX, 1967).
Garrett, Susan R., "Beloved Physician of the Soul? Luke as Advocate for Ascetic Practice," in Vaage and Wimbush, eds. (1999).
Gaudio, Rudolf, *Allah Made Us: Sexual Outlaws in an Islamic African City* (Hoboken, NJ: John Wiley and Sons, 2009).
Gelbal, Selahattin, and Vel Duyan, "Attitudes of University Students towards Lesbians and Gay Men in Turkey," *Sex Roles: A Journal of Research* 55.7/8 (October 2006): 573–579.
Gernet, Jacques, *Chine et christianisme* (Paris: Gallimard, 1982).
Ghamdi, Javed Ahmad, "The Islamic Law of Jihad," trans. Shehzad Saleem, *Renaissance, A Monthly Islamic Journal* 12.6 (June 2002).
Giobellina Brumana, Fernando, and Elda Gonzales Martinez, *Spirits from the Margin, Umbanda in São Paulo, a Study in Popular Religion and Social Experience* (Stockholm: Uppsala Studies in Cultural Anthropology 12, 1989).
Gira, Dennis, «Une mystique bouddhique des pauvres,» *Chemins de dialogue* 6 (October 1995): 109–127.
Gobillot, Geneviève, *La fitra. La conception originelle, ses interprétations et fonctions chez les penseurs musulmans,* (Le Caire:Institut Français d'Archéologie Orientale, 2000 «Cahiers des Annales Islamologiques,» 18).
Godelier, Maurice, *La production des grands hommes. Pouvoir et domination masculine chez les Baruya de Nouvelle-Guinée* (Paris: Fayard, 1982).
Gonda, Jan, *Les religions de l'Inde 1–Védisme et hindouisme ancien* (Paris: Payot, [1962] 1979).
Goslan, Martine, *Le Sexe d'Allah* (Paris: Grasset, Le Livre de Poche, 2004).
Goss, Robert E., *Queering Christ: Beyond Jesus Acted Up* (Cleveland: The Pilgrim Press, 2002).
Grabbe, Lester L., *Judaic Religion in the Second Temple Period: Belief and Practice from the Exile to Yavneh* (New York: Routledge, 2000).
Green, James N., *Beyond Carnival, Male Homosexuality in Twentieth-Century Brazil* (Chicago: The University of Chicago Press, 1999).
Greenberg, David F., *The Construction of Homosexuality* (Chicago: The University of Chicago Press, 1988).
Greenberg, Steven, *Wrestling with God and Men: Homosexuality in the Jewish Tradition* (Madison, WI: University of Wisconsin Press, 2004).
Gueboguo, Charles, «L'homosexualité en Afrique. Variations et sens d'hier à nos jours,» *Socio-Logos, revue électronique de l'Association Française de Sociologie,* October 2008, www.socio-logos. revues.org.
Gugenheim, Grand Rabbin Michel, *Et tu marcheras dans Ses voies, Les multiples facettes de l'éthique juive* (Paris: éditions Association S. et O. Levy, 2006).
Guillon, Emmanuel, "The Ultimate Origin of the World, or the Mula Muh, and other Mon Beliefs," *Journal of the Siam Society* 79.1 (1991): 22–29.
Guinan, Ann Kessler, "Auguries of Hegemony: The Sex Omens of Mesopotamia," *Gender and History* 9.3 (1997): 462–473.

Gyatso, Janet, "One Plus One Makes Three: Buddhist Gender, Monasticism and the Law of the Non-Excluded Middle," *History of Religions* 43.2 (November 2003): 89–115.

Habib, Samar, *Female Homosexualities in the Middle East. Histories and Representations* (New York: Routledge, 2007).

———, "Queer-Friendly Islamic Hermeneutics," *ISIM Review*, Leiden International Institute for the Study of Islam in the Modern World, no. 21 (Spring 2008): 32–33.

Hafez E-shirazi, *Divan-i-Hafiz*, trans. H. Wilberforce Clarke (Bethesda, MD: Ibex Publishers, 1997).

Haggerty, George G., John Beynon, and Douglas Eisner, eds., *Encyclopedia of Lesbian and Gay Histories and Cultures* 2 Vols. (New York: Garland Publishing Inc., 2000).

Hainard, Jacques, Philippe Mathez, and Olivier Schinz, éds., *Vodou* (Genève: Musée d'ethnographie de Genève, 2008).

Hall, Lesley A. (1992), "Forbidden by God, Despised by Men: Masturbation, Medical Warnings, Moral Panic, and Manhood in Great Britain, 1850–1950," *Journal of the History of Sexuality* 2.3 (1992): 365–387.

Halman, Talat Sait, trans., Warner Jane L., *Nightingales and Pleasure Gardens: Turkish Love Poems* (Syracuse, NY: Syracuse University Press, 2005).

Halperin, David, *How to Do the History of Homosexuality* (Chicago: The University of Chicago Press, 2002).

———, *One Hundred Years of Homosexuality and Other Essays on Greek Love* (New York: Routledge, 1990).

Hammar, Anna Karin, "Staying Together? On Ecumenism, Homosexuality and Love," *The Ecumenical Review* 56.4 (2004): 448–458.

Harding, Rachel E., *A Refuge in Thunder, Candomblé and Alternative Spaces of Blackness* (Bloomington, IN: Indiana University Press, 2000).

Harvey, Peter, *An Introduction to Buddhist Ethics: Foundations, Values, and Issues* (Cambridge: Cambridge University Press, 2000).

———, "Vinaya Principles for Assigning Degrees of Culpability," *Journal of Buddhist Ethics* 6 (1999): 271–291.

Hayes, Christine E., *Gentile Impurities and Jewish Identities: Intermarriage and Conversion from the Bible to the Talmud* (New York: Oxford University Press, 2002).

Herdt, Gilbert, ed., *Guardians of the Flutes: Idioms of Masculinity* (New York: McGraw-Hill, 1981).

———, *Homosexuality Ritualized in Melanesia* (Berkeley: University of California Press, 1984).

Heusch, Luc de, "Kongo in Haiti: A New Approach to Religious Syncretism," in Darién J. Davis, ed., *Slavery and Beyond, the African Impact on Latin America and the Caribbean* (Lanham, MD: SR Books, 1995).

Hibri, Azizah al-, "Islam, Law and Custom: Redefining Muslim Women's Rights," *American University Journal of International Law and Policy* 12.1 (1997): 1–44.

Hiltebeitel, Alf, "Dying Before the Mahabharata War: Martial and Transsexual Body-Building for Aravan," *The Journal of Asian Studies* 54.2 (May 1995): 447–473.

———, "Siva, the Goddess, and the Disguises of the Pandavas and Draupadi," *History of Religions* 20.1–2 (1980): 147–174.

Hinsch, Bret, *Passions of the Cut Sleeves. Male Homosexual Tradition in China* (Berkeley, CA: University of California Press, 1990).

———, "Van Gulik's *Sexual Life in Ancient China* and the Matter of Homosexuality," *Nan Nü* 7.1 (2005): 79–91.

Hla, Nai Pan, and Ryuji Okudaira, *Eleven Mon Dhammasat Texts* (Tokyo: The Centre for East Asian Cultural Studies for UNESCO, 1992).

Horner, Thomas M., *Jonathan Loved David: Homosexuality in Biblical Times* (Philadelphia: The Westminster Press, 1978).

Huang, Martin W., *Desire and Fictional Narrative in Late Imperial China* (Cambridge, MA: Harvard University Asia Center, Harvard University Press, 2001).

———, *Negotiating Masculinities in Late Imperial China* (Honolulu: University of Hawaii Press, 2006).

———, "Sentiments of Desire: Thoughts on the Cult of Qing in Ming-Qing Literature," *Chinese Literature: Essays, Articles, Reviews (CLEAR)* 20 (December 1998): 153–184.
Hudon, Christine, and Louise Bienvenue, «Entre franche camaraderie et les amours socratiques. L'espace trouble et ténu des amitiés masculines dans les collèges classiques (1870–1960),» *Revue d'histoire de l'Amérique française* 57.4 (2004): 481–507.
Hundert, Gershon David, *Jews in Poland-Lithuania in the Eighteenth Century: A Genealogy of Modernity* (Berkeley, CA: University of California Press, 2004).
Humsafar Trust and Population Services International, "Knowledge, Attitudes and Practices of Male Sex Workers based at Truckstops," 2007, http://www.humsafar.org/rc/Truckers%20Baseline.pdf
Hurbon, Laënnec, *Dieu dans le Voudou haïtien* (Paris: Maisonneuve et Larose, nouvelle édition 2002).
———, *Le barbare imaginaire* (Paris: du Cerf, 1988).
Hurteau, Pierre, "Catholic Moral Discourse on Male Sodomy and Masturbation in the Seventeenth and Eighteenth Centuries," *Journal of the History of Sexuality* 4.1 (1993): 1–26.
———, *Homosexualité, religion et droit au Québec. Une approche historique*, thèse de doctorat, (Montréal: Université Concordia, 1991).
———, *Les penseurs xuanxue et le bouddhisme de la période Wei-Jin*, mémoire de maîtrise, (Montréal: Université Concordia, 1983).
———, «L'homosexualité masculine et les discours sur le sexe en contexte montréalais de la fin du XIXᵉ siècle à la fin de la Révolution tranquille,» *Histoire sociale—Social History* XXVI.51 (May 1993): 41–66.
Huxley, Andrew, ed., *Thai Law: Buddhist Law: Essays on the Legal History of Thailand, Laos and Burma* (Bangkok: White Orchid Press, 1996).
Hyman, Paula E., "Two Models of Modernization: Jewish Women in the German and the Russian Empires," in Frankel (2000).
Ibn Al Kalbi, Hisham, (*Kitab al-asnam*) *The Book of Idols*, trans. Nabih Amin Faris (Princeton, NJ: Princeton University Press, 1952).
Ihara Saikaku, *The Great Mirror of Male Love*, trans. Paul Schalow (Stanford, CA: Stanford University Press, 1990).
———, (*Koshoku gonin onna*) *Five Women Who Loved Love*, trans. William Theodore de Bary (Rutland, VT: Tuttle Publishing, 1958).
———, (*Koshoku ichidai otoko*), *The Life of an Amorous Man*, trans. Masakazu Kuwata (Rutland, VT: Charles E. Tuttle, 1964).
Jackson, Peter A., "Male Homosexuality and Transgenderism in the Thai Buddhist Tradition," in Winston Leyland ed. (1998).
———, *Male Homosexuality in Thailand: An Interpretation of Contemporary Thai Sources* (Elmhurst, NY: Global Academic Publishers, 1989).
———, "Performative Genders, Perverse Desires: A Bio-History of Thailand's Same-Sex and Transgender Cultures," *Intersections: Gender, History and Culture in the Asian Context* 9 (August 2003), www.intersections.anu.edu.au/issue9/jackson.html.
———, "The Performative State: Semi-coloniality and the Tyranny of Images in Modern Thailand," *SOJOURN: Journal of Social Issues in Southeast Asia* 19.2 (October 2004): 219–253.
———, "Thai Buddhist Accounts of Male Homosexuality and AIDS in the 1980s," *The Australian Journal of Anthropology* 6.3 (1995): 140–153.
———, "The Thai Regime of Images," *SOJOURN: Journal of Social Issues in Southeast Asia* 19.2 (October 2004): 181–218.
———, "Thai Research on Male Homosexuality and Transgenderism and the Cultural Limits of Foucaultian Analysis," *Journal of the History of Sexuality* 8.1 (1997): 52–86.
Jacquemet, Abbé G., *Tu resteras Chaste!* (Paris: Bloud and Gay, 1931).
Jaffrey, Zia, *The Invisibles: A Tale of the Eunuchs of India* (New York: Vintage Books, 1996).
Jafri, Syed Husain Mohammad, *The Origins and Early Development of Shi'a Islam* (London and New York: Longman, 1979).
Jain, P. C., and Dr. Dajjeet, "Ardhanarishvara in Art and Philosophy," www.exoticindia.com/article/ardhanarishvara, 2005.

Jamel, Amreen, "The Story of Lot and the Qu'ran's Perception of the Morality of Same-Sex Sexuality," *Journal of Homosexuality* 41.1 (2001): 1–88.
Joint, Gasner, *Libération du vaudou dans la dynamique d'inculturation en Haïti* (Rome: Pontificia Università Gregoriana, 1999).
Jordan, Mark D., *The Invention of Sodomy in Christian Theology* (Chicago: The University of Chicago Press, 1997).
Justinian, *Corpus juris civilis, Institutiones*, Fordham University, Internet Medieval Sourcebook, http://www.fordham.edu/Halsall/basis/535institutes.asp#I.Justice.
Kakar, Sudhir, *Intimate Relations, Exploring Indian Sexuality* (Chicago: The University of Chicago Press, 1989).
Kang, Wenqing, *Obsession: Male Same-Sex Relations in China, 1900-1950* (Hong Kong: Hong Kong University Press, 2009).
Karamah: Muslim Women Lawyers for Human Rights, "Zina, Rape and Islamic Law: An Islamic Legal Analysis of the Rape Laws in Pakistan" (Richmond, VA: University of Richmond Law School), www.karamah.org/articles.htm, 2005.
Karamustafa, Ahmet T., *God's Unruly Friends: Dervish Groups in the Islamic Later Middle Period, 1200–1550* (Salt Lake City, UT: University of Utah Press, 1994).
———, *Sufism: The Formative Period* (Berkeley: University of California Press, 2007).
Kavi, Ashok Row, "The Changing Image of the Hero in Hindi Films," *Journal of Homosexuality* 39.3/4 (2000): 307–312.
Kennedy, Philip F., *The Wine Song in Classical Arabic Poetry, Abū Nuwās and the Literary Tradition* (Oxford: Clarendon Press, 1997).
Kenoyer, Jonathan Mark, "Early Developments of Art, Symbol and Technology in the Indus Valley Tradition," www.harappa.com/hindus3/e1.html.
Khan, Shivananda, *Perspectives on Males Who Have Sex with Males in Bangladesh and India* (London: Naz Foundation, 1997).
Khantapilo, Bhikkhu, *Lay Buddhist Practice*, The Wheel Publication N. 206/207 (Kandy: Buddhist Publication Society, 1982).
Kieschnick, John, *The Eminent Monk: Buddhist Ideals in Medieval Chinese Hagiography*, Kuroda Institute Studies in East Asian Buddhism, no. 10 (Honolulu: University of Hawaii Press, 1997).
Knodel, John, Aphichat Chamratritirong, and Nibhon Debavalya, "The Cultural Context of Thailand's Fertility Decline," *Asia-Pacific Population Journal* 1.1 (March 1986): 23–48.
Kotb, Heba G., *Sexuality in Islam*, PhD thesis, North Miami, Florida, Maimonides University, 2004.
Kripal, Jeffrey, *Kali's Child, The Mystical and the Erotic in the Life and Teachings of Ramakrishna* (Chicago: The University of Chicago Press, 1995).
Krueger, Derek, "Between Monks: Tales of Monastic Companionship in Early Byzantium," *Journal of the History of Sexuality* 20.1 (January 2011): 28–61.
Kugle, Scott Sirajul Haqq, "Sexual Diversity in Islam," in Omid Safi, ed., *Voices of Islam*, Vol. 5, (Westport, CT: Praeger, 2007).
Kugle, Scott Sirajul Haqq, and Stephen Hunt, "Masculinity, Homosexuality and the Defence of Islam: A Case Study of Yusuf al-Qaradawi's Media Fatwa," *Religion and Gender* 2.2 (2012): 254–279.
Lachatañeré, Rómulo, *El systema religioso de los Afrocubanos* (La Habana: Editorial de Ciencias Sociales, [1992] 2007).
Lagrange, Frédéric, *Islam d'interdits, Islam de jouissances, La recherche face aux représentations courantes de la sexualité dans les cultures musulmanes*, Recherche inédite en vue de l'Habilitation à Diriger la Recherche (HDR), Université Paris Sorbonne IV, 2007–2008, http://mapage.noos.fr/fredlag/Habilitation-recherche.pdf.
———, «L'obscénité du vizir,» *Arabica*, Tome LIII, N. 1, 2006: 54-107. An abridged English version in Babayan and Najmabadi.
Lambek, Michael, *Human Spirits. A Cultural Account of Trance in Mayotte* (Cambridge: Cambridge University Press, 1981).
Lambevski, Sasho, "Suck My Nation—Masculinity, Ethnicity and the Politics of (Homo) Sex," *Sexualities* 2.4 (1999): 397–419.

BIBLIOGRAPHY

Lamchichi, Abderrahim, «Éros et sacré. Sociétés, religion et éthique sexuelle,» *Confluences Méditerranée* 41 (printemps 2002): 9–21.
Lamm, Norman, "Judaism and the Modern Attitude to Homosexuality," *Encycopaedia Judaica Year book 1974* (Jerusalem: Keter, 1974).
Langlois, Claude, *Le crime d'Onan. Le discours catholique sur la limitation des naissances (1816–1930)* (Paris: Les Belles Lettres, 2005).
Lazar, Moshe, and Norris J. Lacy, eds., *Poetics of Love in the Middle Ages* (Fairfax, VA: George Mason University Press, 1989).
Leclère, Adhémard, *Les codes cambodgiens*, tome 1 (Paris: Ernest Leroux, 1898).
Leick, Gwendolyn, *Sex and Eroticism in Mesopotamian Literature* (New York: Routledge, 1994).
Levering, Miriam, "Lin-chi (Rinzai) Ch'an and Gender: The Rhetoric of Equality and the Rhetoric of Heroism," in Cabezon (1992).
Lewis, Ioan Myrddin, *Ecstatic Religion: A Study of Shamanism and Spirit Possession* (New York: Routledge, [1971] 2003).
Leyland, Winston, ed., *Queer Dharma* (San Francisco, CA: Gay Sunshine Press, 1998).
Li Yu, *The Carnal Prayer Mat (Rou Putuan)*, trans. Patrick Hanan (New York: Ballantine Books, 1990).
———, *Silent Operas (Wusheng Xi)*, trans. Patrick Hanan (Hong Kong: Research Centre for Translation, Chinese University of Hong Kong, 1990).
Lienemann, Wolfgang, "Churches and Homosexuality: An Overview of Recent Official Church Statements on Sexual Orientation," *The Ecumenical Review* 50.1 (1998): 1–27.
Ling, Trevor, "Buddhist Factors in Population Growth and Control," *Population Studies* 23 (1969): 53–60.
Loader, James A., *A Tale of Two Cities, Sodom and Gomorrah in the Old Testament, Early Jewish and Early Christian Traditions* (Kampen, the Netherlands: J.H. Kok, 1990).
Loos, Tamara, "Sex in the Inner City: The Fidelity between Sex and Politics in Siam," *The Journal of Asian Studies* 64.4 (November 2005): 881–909.
Louie, Kam, and Morris LOw, eds., *Asian Masculinities: The Meaning and Practice of Manhood in China and Japan* (London: Routledge Curzon, 2003).
Lumsden, Ian, *Machos, Maricones, and Gays: Cuba and Homosexuality* (Philadelphia, PA: Temple University Press, 1996).
Lynton, Harriet Ronken, and Mohini Rajan, *The Days of the Beloved* (New Delhi: Orient Longman, [1974] 1987).
Lyttelton, Edward, *The Causes and Prevention of Immorality in Schools* (London: The Social Purity Alliance, 1887).
MacGee, Mary, "Bahinabai: The Ordinary Life of an Exceptional Woman, or, the Exceptional Life of an Ordinary Woman" in Steven J. Rosen, ed., *Vaisnavi: Women and the Worship of Krishna* (Delhi: Motilal Banarsidass, 1996).
Machin, George Ian Thomas, *Churches and Social Issues in Twentieth-Century Britain* (Oxford: Oxford University Press, 1998).
Martín Sevillano, Ana Belén, "De Virgilio Piñera a Reinaldo Arenas: homosexualidad o disidencia," *Revista Hispano Cubana* no. 4 (Madrid, 1999): 77–86.
McAlister, Elizabeth, «Amour, sexe et genre incarnés: les esprits du vaudou haïtien,» 2004, wwww. africultures.
———, *Rara! Vodou, Power, and Performance in Haiti and Its Diaspora* (Berkeley, CA: University of California Press, 2002).
McIntosh, Mary, "The Homosexual Role," *Social Problems* 16.2 (1968): 182–192.
McLelland (2006), "A Short History of *Hentai*," *Intersections: Gender, History and Culture in the Asian Context*, Issue 12, January 2006, http://intersections.anu.edu.au/.
McLaughlin, Megan, "The Bishop in the Bedroom: Witnessing Episcopal Sexuality in an Age of Reform," *Journal of the History of Sexuality* 19.1 (January 2010): 17–34.
McMahon, Keith, "Sublime Love and the Ethics of Equality in a Homoerotic Novel of the Nineteenth Century: *Precious Mirror of Boy Actresses*," *Nan Nü* 4.1 (April 2002): 70–109.
McRae, John R., *Seing through ZeN. Encounter, Transformation, and Genealogy in Chinese Chan Buddhism* (Berkeley, CA: University of California Press, 2003).

Maududi, Sayyid Abul A'la, *Towards understanding Islam* (New York: Islamic Circle of North America, 1986).
Magonet, Jonathan, ed., *Jewish Explorations of Sexuality* (Providence, RI: Berghahn Books, 1995).
Mahalingam, Ramaswami, "Essentialism, Culture, and Beliefs about gender among the Aravanis of Tamil Nadu, India," *Sex Roles, A Journal of Research* 49.9–10 (November 2003): 489–496.
Mangeot, Philippe, «De l'autre côté du placard. Entretien avec George Chauncey, auteur de *Gay New York*,» *Vacarme*, 26 hiver 2004, www.vacarme.org.
Marcelin, Milo, *Mythologie vodou*, t. 1 (Port-au-Prince: Éditions haïtiennes, 1949).
Martinez-Alier, Verena, *Marriage, Class, and Colour in Nineteenth-Century Cuba: A Study of Racial Attitudes and Sexual Values in a Slave Society* (Ann Harbor, MI: University of Michigan Press, 1989).
Massad, Joseph Andoni, *Desiring Arabs* (Chicago: The University of Chicago Press, 2007).
Matory, J. Lorand, "Homens montados: homossexualidade e simbolismo da possessão nas religiões afro-brasileras," in João José Reis, ed., *Escravidão e invenção da liberdade : estudos sobre o negro no Brasil*, Editora Brasiliense em co-edição com o Conselho Nacional de Desenvolvimento Científico e Tecnológico, 1988.
———, "Rival Empires: Islam and the Religion of Spirit Possession among the Oyo-Yoruba," *American Ethnologist* 21.3 (1994): 495–515.
———, "Sexual Secrets. Candomblé, Brazil, and the Multiple Intimacies of the African Diaspora," in Andrew Shryock, ed., *Off Stage/on Display: Intimacy and Ethnography in the Age of public Culture* (Palo Alto, CA: Stanford University Press, 2004).
———, *Black Atlantic Religion: Tradition, Transnationalism, and Matriarchy in the Afro-Brazilian Candomblé* (Princeton, NJ: Princeton University Press, 2005).
———, "Is There Gender in Yoruba Culture?" in Jacob Kehinde Olupona and Terry Rey, eds., *Òrìṣà Devotion as World Religion, The Globalization of Yorùbá Culture* (Madison, WI: University of Wisconsin Press, 2008).
Matzner, Andrew, "On the Questions of Origins: *Kathoey* and Thai Culture," 2002, web.hku.hk/~sjwinter/TransgenderASIA/paper_on_the_question_of_origins.htm.
May, Jacques, «La philosophie bouddhique de la vacuité,» *Studia Philosophica* XVII. 9 (1958): 123–137.
Mei Yüan, (*Zi Buyu* 子不語), *Censored by Confucius: Ghost Stories by Yuan Mei*, trans. Kam Louie and Louise P. Edwards (Armonk, NY: M.E. Sharpe, 1996).
Menon, Sunil, "Koothandavar festival at Koovakkam," *Pukaar, The Naz Foundation Newsletter*, no. 31, October 2000.
Merchant, Hoshang, *Yaraana* (New Delhi: Penguin Books, 1999).
Merrien, Catherine, «L'hindouisme,» in *Droits humains et religion. Les femmes*. Amnesty International, Section française, February 2006, www.amnesty.asso.fr/02_agir/24_campagnes/vcf/pfs_vcf.htm.
Mesquita, Ralph Ribeiro, "Entre Homens e Deuses: Identidade, gênero e (homo)sexualidade no contexto religioso afro-brasileiro," *Gênero* 4.2 (2004): 95–117.
Métraux, Alfred, *Voodoo in Haiti*, trans. Hugo Charteris (New York: Schocken Books, 1972).
Meyer, Johann Jakob, *Sexual Life in Ancient India* (New York: Dorset Press, [1930] 1995).
Michot, Yahya, «Un célibataire endurci et sa maman : ibn Taymmyia (m. 728/1328) et les femmes,» *Acta Orientalia Belgica XV, La femme dans les civilisations orientales*, Bruxelles (2001): 165–190.
Miller, Ruth, "The Legal History of the Ottoman Empire," *History Compass* 6.1 (2008): 286–296.
Mohamed, Mahfodz bin, "The Concept of Ta'zeer in the Islamic Criminal Law," *Hamdard Islamicus* 16 (winter 1994): 5–12.
Monfouga-Nicolas, Jacqueline, «Les juments des dieux: Rites de possession et condition féminine en pays Hausa,» *Études Nigériennes* no. 21, Niamey: IFAN-CNRS, 1967.
Montero, Oscar, "Julián del Casal and the Queers of Havana," in Emilie L. Bergmann and Paul Julian Smith eds, *¿Entiendes? Queer Readings/Hispanic Writings* (Durham, NC: Duke University Press, 1995).
Mory, Li Hua-yuan, *Chinese Love Stories from "Ch'ing-shih"* (Hamden, CT: Archon Books, 1983).

Mott, Luiz, "Raízes históricas da homossexualidade no Atlântico lusófono negro," Centro de Estudos Afro-Orientais da Universidade Federal da Bahia, *Afro-Asia*, no. 33 (2005): 9–33, www.afroasia.ufba.br.
Murphy, Joseph M., *Santería, African Spirits in America* (Boston: Beacon Press, second edition 1993).
Murphy, Joseph M. and Mei-Mei Sanford, eds., *Ọṣun Across the Waters: A Yoruba Goddess in Africa and the Americas* (Bloomington, IN: Indiana University Press, 2001).
Murray, Jacqueline, "Men's Bodies, Men's Minds: Seminal Emissions and Sexual Anxiety in the Middle Ages," *Annual Review of Sex Research* 8 (1997): 1–26.
Murray, Stephen O. and Will Roscoe, *Islamic Homosexualities* (New York: New York University Press, 1997).
———, *Boy-Wives and Female Husbands: Studies in African Homosexualities* (New York: Palgrave, [1998] 2001).
Murray, Stephen O., "Southwest Asian and North African Terms for Homosexual Roles," *Archives of Sexual Behavior* 24.6 (1995): 623–629.
———, *Homosexualities* (Chicago: The University of Chicago Press, 2002).
Musallam, Basim F., "Why Islam Permitted Birth Control," *Arab Studies Quarterly* no. 2 (Spring 1981): 181–197.
Nadell, Pamela, *Women Who Would Be Rabbis: A History of Women's Ordination 1889–1985* (Boston: Beacon Press, 1998).
an-Nafzawi, Muhammad, *The Perfumed Garden*, trans. R. F. Burton (Whitefish, MT: Kessinger, 2003).
Nanamoli, Bhikkhu, *The Discourse on Right View, The Sammaditthi Sutta and its Commentary*, The Wheel Publication N. 377/379 (Kandy: Buddhist Publication Society, 1991).
Nanda, Serena, "Hijras: An Alternative Sex and Gender Roles in India," in Gilbert Herdt, ed., *Third Sex, Third Gender, Beyond Sexual Dimorphism in Culture and History* (New York: Zone Books, 1994).
———, *Neither Man nor Woman: The Hijras of India* (Belmont, CA: Wadsworth, 1990).
Nandy, Ashis, *The Intimate Enemy* (Delhi: Oxford University Press, 1992).
Narada, Maha Thera, *The Buddha and His Teachings* (Kuala Lumpur: The Buddhist Missionary Society, 1977).
Narrain, Arvind, *Queer: "Despised Sexuality," Law, and Social Change* (Bangalore: Books for Change, 2004).
Narrain, Siddharth, "Sexuality and the Law," *Frontline, India's National Magazine* 20.26 (December 20, 2003–January 2, 2004).
an-Nawadji, Mohammad, *La prairie des gazelles, Éloge des beaux adolescents*, traduit de l'arabe par René R. Khawam (Paris: Phébus, 1989).
Nedelsky, Jennifer, and Roger Hutchinson, "Clashes of Principle and the Possibility of Dialogue: A Case Study of Same-Sex Marriage in the United Church of Canada," in Richard Moon, ed., *Law and Religious Pluralism in Canada* (Vancouver-Toronto: UBC Press, 2008).
Neusner, Jacob, *The Four Stages of Rabbinic Judaism* (New York: Routledge, 1999).
———, *The Way of the Torah. An Introduction to Judaism* (Encino, CA: Dickenson Publishing Co, 1970).
Nguyen Ngoc Huy, Tai Ta Van, and Van Liem Tran, *The Le Code: Law in Traditional Vietnam. A Comparative Sino-Vietnamese Legal Study with Historical Juridical Annalysis and Annotations*, 3 Vol. (Athens, OH: Ohio University Press, 1987).
Niklas, Ulrike, "The Mystery of the Threshold 'Ali' of Southern India," A Documentary Project in Collaboration with Pondicherry University (Indo-German Project of Cultural Anthropology), *Kolam*, Vol. 1, January 1998.
Nissinen. Martti, *Homoeroticism in the Biblical World: A Historical Perspective*, trans. Kirsi Stjerna (Minneapolis, MN: Augsburg Fortress Press, 1998).
Noonan. John T. Jr., *Contraception. A History of its Treatment by the Catholic Theologians and Canonists* (New York: Mentor-Omega Books, 1967).
O'Donavan. Connell, *"The Abominable and Detestable Crime Against Nature": A Revised History of Homosexuality and Mormonism, 1840–1980*, 2004, www.connellodonovaN.com/lgbtmormons.html.

Offermanns. Jürgen, "Debates on Atheism, Quietism, and Sodomy: the Initial Reception of Buddhism in Europe," *Journal of Global Buddhism* 6 (2005): 16–35.

Olson. Carl, ed., *Celibacy and Religious Traditions* (New York: Oxford University Press, 2008).

Olyan. Saul M., "And with a Male You Shall Not Lie the Lying Down of a Woman," *Journal of the History of Sexuality* 5.2 (1994): 179–206.

———, "Wrestling with God and Men: Homosexuality in the Jewish Tradition," *Shohar, an Interdisciplinary Journal of Jewish Studies* 23.4 (2005): 195–196.

Osella, Filippo, and Caroline Osella, "Ayappam Saranam: Masculinity and the Sabiramala Pilgrimage in Kerala," *Journal of the Royal Anthropological Institute* 9.4 (December 2003): 729–753.

Ottosson. Daniel, *Homophobie d'État. Une enquête mondiale sur les lois qui interdisent la sexualité entre adultes consentants de même sexe*, Rapport de l'ILGA (International Gay and Lesbian Association), avril 2007, www.ilga.org/statehomophobia/Homophobie_d_Etat_ILGA_2007.pdf.

Ownby, David, "Approximations of Chinese Bandits: Perverse Rebels, Romantic Heroes, or Frustrated Bachelors," in Brownell (2002).

Oyewumi, Oyeronke, *The Invention of WomeN. Making an African Sense of Western Gender Discourses* (Minneapolis, MN: University of Minnesota Press, 1997).

Pachow, Wang, *A Comparative Study of the Pratimoksa on the Basis of its Chinese, Tibetan, Sanskrit and Pali Versions* (Delhi: Motilal Banarsidass, [1955] 2000).

Pandit, Moti Lal, *The Trika Saivism of Kashmir* (New Delhi: Munshiram Manoharlal, 2003).

Pattanaik, Devdutt, *The Man Who Was a Woman and Other Queer Tales from Hindu Lore* (Binghampton, NY: Harrington Park Press, 2002).

Paul, Diana, *Women in Buddhism: Images of the Feminine in Mahayana Tradition* (Berkeley, CA: Asian Humanities Press, [1979] 1985).

Peletz, Michael G., "Transgenderism and Gender Pluralism in Southeast Asia since Early Modern Times," *Current Anthropology* 47.2 (April 2006): 309–340.

Pellat, Charles, «*Liwat,*» in *Encyclopédie de l'Islam*, tome V (Paris: Brill, 1983).

Penrose, Walter, "Hidden in History: Female Homoeroticism and Women of a Third Nature' in the South Asian Past," *Journal of the History of Sexuality* 10.1 (January 2001): 3–39.

People's Union for Civil Liberties—Karnataka, *Human Rights Violations against the Transgender Community, a Study of Kothi and Hijra Sex Workers in Bangalore, India*, 2003, www.ai.eecs.umich.edu/people/conway/TS/PUCL/PUCLReport.html.

Pereira Ramírez, Rita M., "El derecho a la libre orientación sexual : un derecho sexual sin protección legal en Cuba," *Sexología y Sociedad* no. 36 (Abril de 2008), www.cenesex.sld.cu/webs/revista.htm.

Pew Forum on Religion and Public Life (The), *U.S. Religious Landscape Survey Religious Affiliation: Diverse and Dynamic* (Washington, DC: Pew Research Center, February 2008), http://religions.pewforum.org/pdf/report-religious-landscape-study-full.pdf.

Pflugfelder, Gregory M., *Cartographies of Desire: Male-Male Sexuality in Japanese Discourse, 1600–1950* (Berkeley, CA: University of California Press, 2000).

Pittin, Renée Ilene, *Women and Work in Northern Nigeria: Transcending Boundaries* (New York: Palgrave, 2002).

Pless, John T., "The Use and Misuse of Luther in Contemporary Debates on Homosexuality: A Look at Two Theologians," Aquinas-Luther Conference/Center for Theology, Lenoir-Rhyne College, Hickory NC, October 23, 2004.

Plummer, Kenneth, *Sexual Stigma: An Interactionist Account* (Boston: Routledge, 1975).

———, ed., *The Making of the Modern Homosexual* (London: Hutchinson, 1981).

———, ed., *Modern Homosexualities. Fragments of Lesbian and Gay Experience* (London: Routledge, 1992).

Proschan, Frank, "Eunuch Mandarins, Soldats Mamzelles, Effeminate Boys, and Graceless Women: French Colonial Constructions of Vietnamese Genders," *GLQ: A Journal of Lesbian and Gay Studies* 8.4 (2002): 435–467.

Prouser, Rabbi Joseph H., "The Conservative Movement and Homosexuality: Settled Law in Unsettling Times," *United Synagogue Review* 55.1 (Fall/Winter 2006).

Pugh, Tison, "Personae, Same-Sex Desire, and Salvation in the Poetry of Marbod of Rennes, Baudri of Bourgueil, and Hildebert of Lavardin," *Comitatus: A Journal of Medieval and Renaissance Studies* 31 (2000): 57–86.
Rahman, P. K. Abdul, "Masculinity and Violence in the Domestic Domain: An Exploratory Study among the MSM Community," in *Men, Masculinity and Domestic Violence in India* (Washington, DC: International Center for Research on Women, 2002).
Rahula, Walpola, *What the Buddha Thaught* (New York: Grove Press, 1974).
Ramer, Andrew, *Queering the Text* (Maple Shade, NJ: White Crane Books, 2010).
Rao, R. Raj, "Memories Pierce the Heart: Homoeroticism, Bollywood-Style," *Journal of Homosexuality* 39.3/4 (2000): 299–306.
Raquez, Alfred, *Pages laotiennes : le haut-Laos, le moyen-Laos, le bas-Laos* (Hanoi: F. H. Schneider, 1902).
Reddy, Gayatri, "'Men' Who Would Be Kings: Celibacy, Emasculation, and the Re-Production of Hijras in Contemporary Indian Politics," *Social Research* 70.1 (Spring 2003): 163–200.
———, *With Respect to Sex, Negotiating Hijra Identity in South India* (Chicago: The University of Chicago Press, 2005).
Reis, João José, "Identidade e Diversidade Étnicas nas Irmandades Negras no Tempo da Escravidão," *Tempo*, Rio de Janeiro 2.3 (1996): 7–33.
Ricci, Matteo, *On Friendship*, trans. Timothy Billings (New York: Columbia University Press, 2009).
Rios, Luis Felipe, "Performando a traditionalidade : geração, gênero e erotismo no candomblé do Rio de Janeiro," in Anna Paula Uziel, Luis Felipe Rios, and Richard Guy Parker, *Construções da sexualidade : gênero, identidade e comportamento em tempos de aids* (Rio de Janeiro: Pallas Editora, 2004).
Rispler-Chaim, Vardit, *Islamic Medical Ethics in the Twentieth Century* (Leiden: Brill, 1993).
Ritter, Helmut, *The Ocean of the Soul: Men, the World and God in the Stories of Farid al-Din 'Attar*, trans. John O'Kane (Leiden: Brill, 2003).
Rizvi, Sayyid Mohammad, *Marriage and Morals in Islam* (Scarborough, ON: Islamic Education and Information Centre, 2nd edition, 1994), www.al-islam.org/m_morals/index.htm.
Rodinson, Maxime, *Muhammad: Prophet of Islam* (London: Tauris Parke Paperbacks, 2002).
Römer, Thomas, and Bonjour Loyse, *L'homosexualité dans le Proche-Orient ancien et la Bible* (Genève: Labor et Fides, 2000).
Rosenlee, Li-Hsiang Lisa. *Confucianism and Women: A Philosophical Interpretation* (Albany, NY: State University of New York Press, 2006).
Rosenthal, Franz, "Ar-Râzi on the Hidden Illness," *Bulletin of the History of Medicine* 52 (1978): 45–60.
Rosenthal, Rachel Sara, "Of Pearls and Fish: An Analysis of Jewish Legal Texts on Sexuality and Their Significance for Contemporary American Jewish Movements," *Columbia Journal of Gender and Law* 15.2 (2006): 524–538.
Roth, Norman, "The Care and Feeding of Gazelles: Medieval Arabic and Hebrew Love Poetry," in Lazar (1989).
———, "'Deal Gently with the Young Man': Love of Boys in Medieval Hebrew Poetry of Spain," *Speculum* 57 (1982): 20–51.
el-Rouayheb, Khaled, *Before Homosexuality in the Arabic-Islamic World, 1500–1800* (Chicago: The University of Chicago Press, 2005).
Rousselle, Aline, *Porneia. De la maîtrise du corps à la privation sensorielle, IIe–IVe siècles de l'ère chrétienne* (Paris: Presses Universitaires de France, 1983).
Rowson, Everett K., "The Effeminates of Early Medina," *Journal of the American Oriental Society* 111.4 (October–December 1991): 671–693.
———, "Gender Irregularity as Entertainment: Institutionalized Transvestism at the Caliphate Court in Medieval Bagdhad," in Sharon Farmer and Carol Braun Pasternack, eds., *Gender and Difference in the Middle Ages* (Minneapolis, MN: University of Minnesota Press, 2003).
Ruan Fang-Fu, "China. Male Homosexuality," in Donald J. West and Richard Green, eds., *Sociological Control of Homosexuality. A Multi-Nation Comparison* (New York: Plenum Press, 1997).

Rubin, Gayle, "Thinking Sex. Notes for a Radical Theory of the Politics of Sexuality," in Carole Vance, ed., *Pleasure and Danger. Exploring Female Sexuality* (Routledge & Paul Kegan, 1984): 267-319.

Ruskola, Teemu, "Law, Sexual Morality, and Gender Inequality in Qing and Communist China," *The Yale Law Journal* 103.8 (June 1994): 2547-2548.

Ruzbehan i-Baqli, *Le Jasmin des fidèles d'amour*, translation by Henry Corbin (Paris: Verdier, 1991).

Sa'adi Shirazi, *The Bustan of Sadi*, A. Hart Edwards (London: John Murray, 1911).

———, *Gulistan; or, Flower-garden*, trans., with an essay, by James Ross: and a note on the translator by Charles Sayle (London: W. Scott, 1890).

Saddhatissa, Hammelewa, *Buddhist Ethics* (London: Allen and Unwin, 1970).

Said, Edward, *Orientalism* (New York: Pantheon Books, 1978).

Santos, Milton Silva dos, "Mito, possessão e sexualidade no candomblé," *Revista Nures*, Publicação Eletrônicado Núcleo de Estudos Religião e Sociedade, Programa de Estudos Pós-Graduados em Ciências Sociais da Pontifícia Universidade Católica de São Paulo, Janeiro/Abril 2007: 1-9, http://www.pucsp.br/revistanures/revista8/nures8_milton_02.pdf.

Satlow, Michael L., *Tasting the Dish: Rabbinic Rhetorics of Sexuality* (Atlanta, GA: Scholars Press, 1995).

———, "'They Abused Him Like a Woman': Homoeroticism, Gender Blurring, and the Rabbis in Late Antiquity," *Journal of the History of Sexuality* 5.1 (1994): 1-25.

———, "Try to be a Man: The Rabbinic Construction of Masculinity," *Harvard Theological Review* 89.1 (1996): 19-40.

Sauer, Michelle M., "Uncovering Difference Encoded Homoerotic Anxiety within the Christian Eremitic Tradition in Medieval England," *Journal of the History of Sexuality* 19.1 (January 2010): 133-152.

Sawyer, Erin, "Celibate Pleasures: Masculinity, Desire, and Asceticism in Augustine," *Journal of the History of Sexuality* 6.1 (1995): 1-29.

Scanlon, Larry, "Unspeakable Pleasures: Alain de Lille, Sexual Regulation and the Priesthood of Genius," *The Romanic Review* 86.2 (1995): 213-242.

Schalow, Paul G., "Kukai and the Tradition of Male Love in Japanese Buddhism," in Cabezon (1992).

———, "Spiritual Dimensions of Male Beauty in Japanese Buddhism," in Leyland (1998).

Schirmann, Jefim, "The Ephebe in Medieval Hebrew Poetry," *Sefarad* 15 (1955): 55-68.

Schmitt, Arno, and Jeheoda Sofer, eds., *Sexuality and Eroticism among Males in Moslem Societies* (New York: Harrington Park Press, 1992).

Schuon, Frithjof, *Understanding Islam*, trans. D. M. Matheson (London: George Allen and Unwin, 1963).

Schüssler Fiorenza, Francis, *Foundational Theology: Jesus and the Church* (New York: Crossroad, 1984).

Sedgwick, Eve Kosofsky, *Epistemology of the Closet* (Berkeley, CA: University of California Press, 1990).

Segato, Rita Laura, "The Factor of Gender in the Yoruba Transnational Religious World," Instituto de Ciências Sociais, Universidade de Brasília, *Série Antropologia* no. 289, 2001, www.unb.br/ics/dan/Serie289empdf.pdf.

Sen, Samita, *Toward a Feminist Politics. The Indian Women's Movement in Historical Perspective*, World Bank, Policy Research Report on Gender and Development, Working Paper Series no. 9, April 2000.

Shafaat, Ahmad, *Punishment for Adultery in Islam*, Part II, Chapter V, "Death Penalty for Homosexuality, Incest, and Bestiality," 2005, www.islamicperspectives.com/Stoning5.htm.

Shahar, Meir, *Crazy Ji: Chinese Religion and Popular Literature* (Cambridge, MA: Harvard University Asia Center, 1998).

Shalakany, Amar, "Comparative Law as Archeology, Deviant Sexuality, Human Rights and Islamic Law," Conference at the Bernard and Audre Rapoport Center for Human Rights and Justice, University of Texas at Austin, School of Law, October 2006, http://www.utexas.edu/law/academics/centers/humanrights/events/Shalakany.pdf.

Sharma, Arvind, ed., "Homosexuality and Hinduism," in Swidler (1993).
———, *Women in World Religions* (Albany, NY: State University of New York Press, 1987).
Sherry, Joseph, "The Law and Homosexuality in India," Center for Enquiry Into Health and Allied Themes Research Centre of Anusandhan Trust (CEHAT), International Conference on Preventing Violence, Caring for Survivors: Role of Health Professionals and Services in Violence, YMCA, Mumbai, November 28–30, 1998.
Sierra Madero, Abel, "La policía del sexo, la homofobia durante el siglo XIX en Cuba," *Revista Sexología y Sociedad*, La Habana, CENESEX, Vol. 9, No. 21, Abril de 2003: 21–44.
———, "Sexualidades disidentes en el siglo XIX en Cuba," *Catauro. Revista cubana de antropología*, La Habana, Fundación Fernando Ortiz, año 5, N. 9, 2004: 39–63.
Sil, Narasingha P., *Ramakrishna Revisited. A New Biography* (Lanham, MD: University Press of America, 1998).
Silburn, Lilian, *La Kundalini ou l'énergie des profondeurs* (Paris: Les Deux Océans, 1983).
Sinha, A. P., "Procreation among the Eunuchs," *Eastern Anthropologist* 20.2 (1967): 168–176.
Sinha, Mrinalini, *Colonial Masculinity: The "Manly Englishman" and the "Effeminate Bengali" in the Late 19th Century* (Manchester: Manchester University Press, 1995).
Sinikangas, Maarit, "Yan Daudu. A Study of trangendering Men in Hausaland West Africa," Master's Thesis in Cultural Anthropology, Uppsala University, Department of Cultural Anthropology and Ethnology, 2004.
Siraj, Asifa, "The Construction of the Homosexual 'Other' by British Muslim Heterosexuals," *Contemporary Islam* 3.1 (2009): 41–57.
Sitruk, Joseph, and Daniel Sibony, *Judaïsme et sexualité* (Le Bouscat: L'Esprit du temps, 2001).
Smart, Ninian, *The World's Religions* (Englewood Cliffs, NJ: Prentice-Hall, 1989).
Solomon, Mark, "Strange Conjunction," in Magonet (1995).
Sommer, Matthew, "Dangerous Males, Vulnerable Males, and Polluted Males: The Regulation of Masculinity in Qing Dynasty Law," in Brownell (2002).
———, "The Penetrated Male in Late Imperial China; Judicial Constructions and Social Stigma," *Modern China* 23.2 (April 1997): 140–180.
Song Geng, *The Fragile Scholar: Power and Masculinity in Chinese Culture* (Hong Kong: Hong Kong University Press, 2004).
Sorek, Susan, "Mothers of Israel: Why the Rabbis Adopted a Matrilineal Principle," *Women in Judaism: A Multidisciplinary Journal* 3.1 (2002): 35–40.
Southgate, Minoo S., "Men, Women, Boys: Love and Sex in the Works of Sa'di," *Iranian Studies* 17 (Autumn 1984): 413–452.
Spence, Jonathan, *The Memory Palace of Matteo Ricci* (New York: Penguin Books, 1985).
Sponberg, Alan, "Attitudes toward Women and the Feminine in Early Buddhism," in Cabezon (1992).
Srikant, Vijay, and C. V. Manoj, *Sabarimala, Its Timeless Message* (Payyanur: Integral Books, 1998).
Srivastava, Sanjay, *Sexual Sites, Seminal Attitudes, Sexualities, Masculinities and Culture in South Asia* (New Delhi: Sage Publications, 2004).
Stark, Rodney, *The Rise of Christianity: A Sociologist Reconsiders History* (Princeton, NJ: Princeton University Press, 1996).
Starr, Chloe, "Shifting Boundaries: Gender in *Pinhua Baojian*," *Nan Nü. Men Women and Gender in Early and Imperial China* 1.2 (October 1999): 268–302.
Stehling, Thomas "To Love a Medieval Boy," in Stuart Kellogg, ed., *Literary Visions of Homosexuality* (New York: Haworth Press, 1983).
Stein, Jonathan A., "Toward a Taxonomy for Reform Jews to Evaluate Sexual Behaviour," *Central Conference of American Rabbis Journal* (Fall 2001).
Stevens, John, *Lust for Enlightenment. Buddhism and Sex* (Boston: Shambala, 1990).
Stewart, Charles, "Erotic Dreams and Nightmares from Antiquity to the Present," *Journal of the Royal Anthropological Institute* 8.2 (June 2002): 279–309.
Straface, Antonella, "La Fitrah come espressione di iman," *Oriente Moderno*, Nuova serie, Anno 11 (72), Nr. 7/12 (Luglio–Dicembre 1992): 69–86.
Surieu, Robert, *L'art et l'amour—Perse : Essai sur les représentations érotiques et l'amour dans l'Iran d'autrefois* (Genève: Nagel, 1975).

Sweet, James H., "Male Homosexuality and Spiritism in the African Diaspora: The Legacies of a Link," *Journal of the History of Sexuality* 7.2 (1996): 184–202.

Sweet, Michael, and Leonard Swilling J., "The First Medicalization: The Taxonomy and Etiology of Queerness in Classical Indian Medicine," *Journal of the History of Sexuality* 3.4 (April 1993): 590–697.

Swidler, Arlene, ed., *Homosexuality and World Religions* (Harrisburg, PA: Trinity Press International, 1993).

Taylor, Charles, *Sources of the Self: The Making of the Modern Identity* (Cambridge: Cambridge University Press, 1989).

Taywaditep, Kittiwut Jod, Eli Coleman, and Pacharin Dumrong-Gittigule, "Thailand," The Kinsey Institute, *The Continuum Complete International Encyclopedia of Sexuality*, 2004, www.kinsey-institute.org/ccies/pdf/ccies-thailand.pdf.

Thielicke, Helmut, *The Ethics of Sex*, trans. John W. Doberstein (New York: Harper and Row, 1964).

Toussaint, Frantz, *Chants d'amour et de guerre de l'Islam* (Paris: Robert Laffont, 1942).

Trevisan, Silvério João, *Perverts in Paradise (Devassos no Paraíso)*, trans. Martin Foreman (London: GMP Publishers, 1986).

Trotignon, Dominique, «La coproduction conditionnée. Selon le bouddhisme ancien,» *Les Cahiers bouddhiques* no. 2 (décembre 2005): 9–46.

Tyagananda, Swami, *Kali's Child Revisited or didn't Anyone Check the Documentation?*, 2000, http://home.earthlink.net/~tyag/Home.htm.

Ueda, Akinari, *Ugetsu monogatari: Tales of Moonlight and Rain*, trans. Leon M. Zolbrod (Sydney: Allen and Unwin, 1974).

Vaage, Leif, and Vincent Wimbush, eds., *Asceticism and the New Testament* (New York: Routledge, 1999).

Van de Port, Mattijs, "Candomblé in Pink, Green and Black. Re-scripting the Afro-Brazilian Religious Heritage in the Public Sphere of Salvador, Bahia," *Social Anthropology*, 13.1 (2005): 3–26.

Van Gulik, Robert, *Sexual Life in Ancient China* (Leiden: Brill Academic Pub., 1961).

Vanita, Ruth, "Born to Two Mothers, the Hero Bhagiratha, Female-Female Love and Miraculous Birth in Hindu Texts," *Manushi, A Journal about Women and Society* no. 146 (March–April 2005): 22–33.

Vanita, Ruth, and Saleem Kidwai, eds., *Same-Sex Love in India* (New York: Palgrave, 2001).

Vitiello, Giovanni, "Exemplary Sodomites: Chivalry and Love in Late Ming Culture," *Nan Nü, Men, Women and Gender in Early and Imperial China* 2.2 (April 2000): 207–257.

———, *The Libertine's Friend: Homosexuality and Masculinity in Late Imperial China* (Chicago: University of Chicago Press, 2011).

Volpp, Sophie, "The Literary Circulation of Actors in Seventeenth-Century China," *The Journal of Asian Studies* 61.3 (August 2002): 949–984.

Walls, Neal, *Desire, Discord and Death* (Boston: American School of Oriental Research Books Vol. 8, 2001).

Ward, Benedicta, trans., *The Desert Fathers: Sayings of the Early Christian Monks* (London: Penguin Books, 2003).

Watanabe Tsuneo, and Jun'ichi Iwata, *The Love of the Samurai: A Thousand Years of Japanese Homosexuality* (London: Gay Men Press, 1989).

Watt, Montgomery, *Muhammad: Prophet and Statesman* (London: Oxford University Press, 1961).

Weeks, Jeffrey, *Coming Out. Homosexual Politics in Britain, from the Nineteenth Century to the Present* (London: Quartet, 1977).

———, *Sex, Politics and Society. The Regulation of Sexuality since 1800* (London: Longman, 1981).

———, *Sexuality and Its Discontents* (London: Routledge, 1985).

Wheeler, Brannon, "Touching the Penis in Islamic Law," *History of Religions* 44.2 (2004): 89–119.

Wichienkeeo, Aroonrut, and Gehan Wijeyewardene, trans., *The Laws of King Mangrai (Mangrayathammasar)* (Canberra: R. Davis Fund, 1986).

Wilhelm, Amara Das, *Tritya-Prakriti: People of the Third Sex* (Bloomington, IN: Xlibris, 2003).
Wood, Wendy, and Alice H. Eagly, "A Cross-Cultural Analysis of the Behaviour of Women and Men: Implications for the Origins of Sex Differences," *Psychological Bulletin* 128.5 (2002): 699–727.
Wright, Jr J. W., and Everett K. Rowson, *Homoeroticism in Classical Arabic Literature* (New York: Columbia University Press, 1997).
Wu Cuncun, *Homoerotic Sensibilities in Late Imperial China* (New York: Routledge, 2004).
Wu Jingzi, *The Scholars (Rulin Waishi* 儒林外史), trans. Yang Xianyi and Yang Gladys (New York: Columbia University Press, 1992).
Xiang Warner Ding, "Mr. Five Dippers of Drunkenville: The Representation of Enlightenment in Wang Ji's Drinking Poems," *Journal of the American Oriental Society* 118.3 (1998): 347–356.
Yao Ping, "Until Death Do Us Unite: Afterlife Marriages in Tang China 618-906," *Journal of Family History* 27.3 (July 2002): 207–226.
Yokobue no soshi, Histoire de Yokobue, Jacqueline Pigeot traductrice, *Bulletin de la Maison Franco-Japonaise, Nouvelle Série,* tome IX, n° 2 (Paris: Presses Universitaires de France, 1972).
Yoshida Kenko, *Tsurezuregusa, The Miscellany of a Japanese Priest,* trans. William N. Porter (London: Humphrey Milford, 1914).
Yutai xinyong 玉臺新詠, *Chinese Love Poetry, New Songs from a Jade Terrace: A Medieval Anthology,* trans. Anne Birrell (New York: Penguin, 1995).
Yuzgun, Arslan, "Homosexuality and Police Terror in Turkey," *Journal of Homosexuality* 24.3–4 (1993): 159–169.
Ze'evi, Dror, *Changing Sexual Discourse in the Ottoman Middle East, 1500–1900* (Berkeley, CA: University of California Press, 2006).
———, "Hiding Sexuality. The Disappearance of Sexual Discourse in the Late Ottoman Middle East," *Social Analysis* 49.2 (Summer 2005): 34–53.
Zeidman, Reena, "Marginal Discourse: Lesbianism in Jewish Law," *Women in Judaism: A Multidisciplinary Journal* 1.1 (Fall 1997): 24–38.
Zemouri, Aziz, *Faut-il faire taire Tariq Ramadan?* (Paris : L'Archipel, 2005).
Zhongxin Sun, James Farrer, Kung-He Choi, «L'identité des hommes aux pratiques homosexuelles à Shanghai,» *Perspectives chinoises* no. 93 (January–February 2006): 2–13.
Zimmer, Heinrich, *Philosophies of India* (Princeton, NJ: Princeton University Press, 1974).
Zollner, Barbara, "*Mithlliyyun* or *Lutyiyyun*? Neo-Orthodoxy and the Debate on the Unlawfulness of Same-Sex Relations in Islam," in Samir Habib, ed., *Islam and Homosexuality* (Santa Barbara: ABC-Clio, 2010): 193–222.
Zwilling, Leonard, "Avoidance and Exclusion: Same-Sex Sexuality in Indian Buddhism," in Leyland (1998).
———, "Homosexuality as Seen in Indian Buddhist Texts," in Cabezón (1992).

Printed in the United States of America